ASSESSING YOUNG CHILDREN

Gayle Mindes
DePaul University

Boston Columbus Indianapolis New York San Francisco Upper Saddle River
Amsterdam Cape Town Dubai London Madrid Milan Munich Paris Montreal Toronto
Delhi Mexico City Sao Paulo Sydney Hong Kong Seoul Singapore Taipei Tokyo

To friends near and far who show up and listen

Vice President and Editor in Chief: Jeffery W. Johnston
Senior Acquisitions Editor: Julie Peters
Editorial Assistant: Tiffany Bitzel
Vice President, Director of Marketing: Quinn Perkson
Marketing Manager: Erica DeLuca
Senior Managing Editor: Pamela D. Bennett
Production Editor: Kerry Rubadue
Project Manager: Susan Hannahs
Senior Art Director: Jayne Conte
Cover Designer: Suzanne Behnke
Photo Coordinator: Carol Sykes
Cover Art: Ariel Skelley, Getty Images
Full-Service Project Management: Mohinder Singh/ Aptara®, Inc.
Composition: Aptara®, Inc.
Printer/Binder: Hamilton Printing Co.
Cover Printer: Lehigh/Phoenix
Text Font: Times

Credits and acknowledgments borrowed from other sources and reproduced, with permission, in this textbook appear on appropriate page within text

Every effort has been made to provide accurate and current Internet information in this book. However, the Internet and information posted on it are constantly changing, so it is inevitable that some of the Internet addresses listed in this textbook will change.

Child study details are based on experiences of the writer and on teacher candidate work in assessment courses. Details are altered and situations combined so that no real persons are featured.

Photo Credits: Anne Vega/Merrill, pp. 3, 25, 48, 68, 88, 92, 192, 193, 288, 375; Nancy Sheehan Photography, pp. 16, 34; David Mager/Pearson Learning Photo Studio, pp. 27, 148; Ken Karp/PH College, p. 50; KS Studios/Merrill, p. 73; Barbara Schwartz/Merrill, p. 75; Courtesy of Christopher House, Chicago, Illinois, p. 76; Scott Cunningham/ Merrill, pp. 99, 118, 141, 200, 363; Kathy Kirtland/Merrill, p. 105; George Dodson/PH College, p. 109; istockphoto.com, pp. 111, 336, 362; Anthony Magnacca/Merrill, pp. 113, 143, 293, 313, 356; Lori Whitley/Merrill, p. 137; Laima Druskis/PH Collge, pp. 138, 297; Tom Watson/Merrill, p. 170; Maria B. Vonada/Merrill, p. 187; Dan Floss/Merrill, p. 196; Teri Leigh Stratford/PH College, p. 334; BananaStock, p. 386

Library of Congress Cataloging-in-Publication Data
Mindes, Gayle.
Assessing young children/Gayle Mindes.—4th ed.
p. cm.
ISBN-13: 978-0-13-700227-6
ISBN-10: 0-13-700227-0
1. Child development—United States—Testing. 2. Early childhood education—United States—Evaluation. 3. Educational tests and measurements—United States. I. Title.
LB1131.M6146 2011
372.126—dc22
2010001271

10 9 8 7 6 5 4 3 2 1

www.pearsonhighered.com

ISBN 10: 0-13-700227-0
ISBN 13: 978-0-13-700227-6

PREFACE

We live in a challenging time for American education. Some of the important issues facing educators today include accountability (No Child Left Behind, Head Start Outcomes), high-stakes tests, management of scarce resources, and shortage of highly qualified early childhood teachers, multicultural curriculum, and inclusion. For early childhood educators, the first formal teachers in the lives of young children, the challenges are enormous. Family collaboration, respect for cultural diversity, appropriate early intervention assessment, and linking curriculum and assessment practices appropriately are just a few of the demands.

ASSESSMENT IS A REQUIRED COMPETENCY FOR EARLY CHILDHOOD TEACHERS

Crafting an assessment system is one of the most important tasks and challenges for early childhood educators. Early childhood teachers must, therefore, be mindful of the responsibilities they assume as they assess and participate in teaching, evaluating, and placing the young children and families they serve. Thorough knowledge of child development, formal and informal assessment measures, data collection, statistics, as well as characteristics of standardized measures, variables in consultation with families, and portfolio and performance assessment are required competencies for the professional early childhood educator. Early childhood assessment decisions affect infants, young children, and their families for life.

ABOUT THIS TEXT

This book is written for the teacher who wants to understand and deliver an effective educational program for all young children from birth through age 8. Accordingly, it reflects the knowledge base of early childhood and early childhood special education. It provides illustrations of appropriate practice for prospective teachers and discusses current trends for experienced teachers. It approaches assessment as an integral part of the teaching and learning process. Key components of the assessment system include cultural sensitivity, family collaboration, and a vision of inclusionary practice in all early childhood environments—child care and school. Relevant professional standards are addressed throughout. The text is written in nontechnical language with support from the most current research. All "hot topics" are included as well—standards-based and outcomes-based teaching, high-stakes testing, Response to Intervention (RTI), coping with legislative demands, as well as relevant technology in the assessment process.

ORGANIZATION OF THIS TEXT

The book is organized holistically. Chapter 1 begins with an orientation to assessment through the age span of early childhood: birth through age 8. Family collaboration and involvement is introduced in Chapter 2 as an important element in assessment. Chapter 3 discusses observation as the heart of all assessment. Chapters 4 and 5 describe the basic concepts of measurement and where and how an educator can put them into practice. Chapter 6 addresses the use of alternative assessment strategies to facilitate individualization of instruction and behavioral management; attention is directed toward the classroom teacher's role in Response to Intervention (RTI). Chapter 7 shows how to record and report assessment results to others, with an emphasis on learner empowerment and family involvement. Chapter 8 consists of real-life examples and 32 child studies showing how child studies aid in understanding child progress, by providing formative assessment data. The chapter guides the student in building a child study. Chapters 9 through 11 focus on the special assessment issues for infants and toddlers, preschoolers, and children in the primary grades.

KEY FEATURES OF THE TEXT

- Throughout the text, there is a spotlight on inclusion of children with disabilities.
- Issues related to English language learners are woven into the discussion.
- Collaboration with families is emphasized.
- Learner empowerment and self-assessment is illustrated.
- The No Child Left Behind legislation is discussed thoroughly throughout the text with emphasis on issues regarding reauthorization.
- Each chapter includes terms to know, focus questions, reflection questions, technology links, out-of-class activities, case vignettes, activities for classroom discussion, and suggested further readings.
- The book includes a child development milestone guide, a test review guideline, reviews of commonly used tests, a glossary, a pretest of assessment terminology for readers, guidelines for choosing technology and software, and practical examples throughout. Additional features include a portfolio template, additional example checklists and rating sheets, and blank templates that can be reproduced for teacher use.
- New in this edition: increased attention to English language learners, and the process of Response to Intervention (RTI); increased discussion within the chapters of selected assessment instruments including—the classroom observation system—Classroom Assessment Scoring System CLASS™, The Ounce Scale™, and Work Sampling System™ and technology applied to assessment; added figures and charts; examples of school district practice; additional forms for teachers to use; and an annotated list of websites that address assessment for teachers of young children. All chapters have updated research, websites, and recommended readings. Also new to this edition is a feature called Voices from the Field, which are summaries of conversations between educators in schools/centers and the author.

NEW TO THIS EDITION

Chapter 2: Shift from parent involvement to reciprocal, collaborative family involvement. A discussion of universal preschool with updated statistics on children/families using child care. Attention to the role of learning standards in early childhood education. Detailed attention to the role that culture plays in family, child, and school life. Attention to data-based decision-making in finding young children with special needs. Accountability issues post-NCLB with a discussion of the role that achievement tests will continue to play. An examination of the achievement gap and the role that formative assessment might play in mitigation of the problem. Expanding on the emphasis on families as experts, attention is drawn to communicating with families who are English language learners and those whose children face developmental and learning challenges. Featured is an example of a school district in transition as it strives toward best child and family practice in an accountability atmosphere, plus family vignettes.

Chapter 3: Observation at the heart of assessment includes attention to the variables of classroom setting and life as well as a focus on individual children. Featured is discussion of Classroom Assessment Scoring System (CLASS™). Added attention to the Reggio Emilia Documentation Panel as formative and summative evaluation process. Expansion of published checklists, an example of a reading running record, and attention to child involvement in the portfolio process.

Chapter 4: Updates in this chapter feature a streamlined and updated discussion of the concept of validity. Assessment as inquiry is highlighted, with links to statistics of testing and an elaborated discussion of choosing tests for population, specifically issues of culture and disability. A new example of criterion-referenced instrument, as well as links to tests and the self-empowered learner. Focus is on teachers building a working understanding of measurement.

Chapter 5: Enhanced discussion of appropriate rule of tests with links to documenting child progress on learning standards and the 21st Century Skills. Testing and data gathering as part of RTI. Illustrations of published instruments as used in the classroom for screening, planning, and intervention. Linking tests to data management, planning and reporting systems is featured. Formative assessment as a critical component of data-gathering and individualization of instruction is emphasized.

Chapter 6: RTI is linked to individualization of instruction, data-gathering, and inclusion. Additional examples of questions as the hallmark of inquiry-based teaching. Attention to the practical development of behavioral intervention plans and peer-mediated intervention. Expanded discussion of multiple intelligences and the classroom setting in assessment and more examples of graphic organizers as assessment tools.

Chapter 7: Added feature of electronic systems used for data management and reporting. Focus on data gathering as part of RTI. Families represented as integral to the RTI process with illustrations such as active listening for improved reciprocal communication. Additional attention to culture as a variable in family partnerships. Tools for conference pre-planning are added as are ways to manage conflict. Additional focus on student-led conferences. Planning tools for grading in the primary years and standards-based grading. Renewed attention to writing comments on report cards. Increased attention to communicating when families are clients. Use of dialog journal for special communication circumstances. Teacher's role in RTI conferences and expanded attention to pre-referral conferences.

Chapter 8: Revised description for the preparation of child study. Child study in the RTI process. Twenty-eight new child study examples showing informal and formal assessment and stakeholder reports—demonstrating the gamut of ways such studies offer teaching starting points as well as child progress documentation.

Chapter 9: Emphasis on reciprocal family partnership and the changing status of the infant/toddler care field. Featured discussion of infant/toddler instruments with an exhibit of the Ounce Scale. Updated discussion of IDEA and best practice with families. Expanded practical discussion of IFSP. Emphasis on assessment of typical infants for planning as well as those perceived to be at risk. Discussion of documentation of learning and development in typical child-care setting and communication form as illustration on the importance of communication with family.

Chapter 10: Link to universal preschool conversation and need and funding for Head Start. RTI in preschool settings with emphasis on screening and the role of culture/language in the process. Use of published checklists linked to curriculum and enhanced emphasis on inquiry-based questioning strategies. Additional examples and forms for record-keeping. Expanded coverage of child-involvement in portfolio process.

Chapter 11: Accountability legacy of NCLB and discussion of achievement testing as continued accountability feature. Expanded discussion of transition from preschool to kindergarten. Formative assessment at the center of inquiry-based curriculum and accountability planning. Performance assessment with technology. Increased attention to child questions in the portfolio conference. Eight new forms to illustrate child-progress documentation. Featured discussion of the Work Sampling System. Discussion of accommodations necessary for children with disabilities when they are involved in achievement testing. Expanded discussion of test prep with illustration of a third-grade prep guide.

ACKNOWLEDGMENTS

Thanks to the thousands of children, parents, undergraduate and graduate students, and colleagues who have influenced my thinking and practices over the years. In particular, I appreciate the contributions of Carol Mardell-Czudnowski and Harold Ireton, who collaborated with me on the first edition of this book. I value the care and hard work of Rebecca Manuel, DePaul University, who compiled and updated the reviews of early childhood tests and the websites on assessment for young children. Thanks to my colleagues at DePaul University and early childhood educators elsewhere for their assistance and support in discussing the revisions for this edition. In particular, I appreciate the suggestions of Mojdeh Bayat, Marie Donovan, and Alice Moss, who critiqued the third edition as they used it in teaching. Bridget Amory, DePaul alumna and the principal of Lake Forest South Elementary School in Harrington, Delaware, always keep me grounded in the real world with her enthusiasm and stories from the field. The Voices from the Field teachers and instructional leaders were very generous with their time during the busy school year; I am grateful for their help. The voices are Joseph Accardi, Ashley Devonshire, Holly Hermsted, Melinda Jackson, Sonia Lascelles, Morgan Linton, Janet Olson, Anna Pollack, Carolyn Price, Debbie Ridgeley, and Shannon Vier. Special thanks to my colleague and friend Barbara Radner, who works tirelessly to improve the educational lives of Chicago children and adolescents with creativity, innovation, and best practices, as she also makes time for supporting doctoral students and colleagues. Finally, I am especially indebted to my son, Jonathan, for his never-ending support and contribution of his professional, editorial opinions throughout the writing process.

I appreciate the support, encouragement, and vision from Julie Peters, Tiffany Bitzel, Kerry Rubadue, and others behind the scenes at Pearson.

My appreciation is extended to the reviewers for their constructive criticism and helpful suggestions: Johanna Darragh, Heartland Community College; Fatema Zarghami, St. Cloud State University; Joohi Lee, University of Texas, Arlington; L. Kathryn Sharp, University of Memphis; Colleen Klein-Ezell, Southeastern Louisiana University.

BRIEF CONTENTS

CONTENTS

CHAPTER 1

A Comprehensive Assessment System for Birth Through Age 8

TERMS TO KNOW

- stakeholders
- assessment
- techniques
- accountability
- formative assessment
- high-stakes decisions
- authentic assessments

CHAPTER OVERVIEW

Assessment is an integral part of the total picture of child care and education. Information gathered through informed observation and other methods guides the countless decisions at the heart of solid and appropriate instruction and intervention. Some of these decisions can be made easily and as a matter of course: Should the program move on to the next theme in the curriculum? Are children growing in their abilities to follow directions and to share cooperatively? Other decisions, by their nature, require more systematic and intensive assessment information collection due to the life consequences that may result. Does the baby need early intervention? What specialized support might enhance a child's participation in a typical preschool situation? Does this child need to be enrolled in a special program? What opportunities will result? What, if any, stigma may be attached to such placement?

By definition, best practice dictates that all decisions be based upon assessment information gleaned from multiple sources. In addition, everyone involved in the care and education of the child—family, teachers, and other related service personnel—must be included in the process. Because the techniques for gathering information and the steps involved in intervention and educational decision making are varied, the task of assessing young children is a tremendous responsibility. The aim of this book is to help you to learn the rudiments of assessment: the why, the how, and what to do with assessment information gathered. Toward this end, this initial chapter focuses on exploring the early childhood assessment system and related current events.

ASSESS AS YOU READ

- What is assessment? How is assessment the same or different than a test?
- What assessment methods are most suitable for infants and toddlers? Preschoolers? School-age children?
- How do you use your knowledge of child development in assessment?
- How do you use assessment data to plan and individualize program goals?
- What do parents, principals, and others want to know about assessment results?

THE AGE SPAN OF EARLY CHILDHOOD

Birth through age 8 . . . wow . . . think of the differences: Cute and helpless babies depending on the adults in their lives for care, nurturance, and development; energetic and determined toddlers moving away from the adults to stake out and explore their world through play while helping themselves to feed and dress; fanciful and creative preschoolers launching into friendships and dramatic play; earnest and curious young school-agers attacking the challenges of reading, writing, mathematics, and technology. In these eight intervening years, children change more than during any other life period.

Beginning with the reflexes of the newborn, through the first smile, word, and step, the infancy years fly by quickly. Toddlers establish autonomy, self-help skills, and sophistication in their language and movement. Preschoolers cooperate with each other, develop themes in their play, and learn elaborate cognitive and gross- and fine-motor skills. At school age, young children engage their curiosity for the purpose of learning, become even more self-sufficient in their own care, and play games with rules in their leisure, as well as learn to read, to write, and to problem-solve. These developmental changes and milestones, and others, occur in a social/cultural context that influences the acquisition and elaboration of this growth and intellectual achievement (cf. Berk, 2008).

Parents, caregivers, teachers, and others who influence the lives of young children must not only be familiar with the broad aspects of development in this period—the usual and typical growth patterns—but must also be sensitive to variations within typical development that affect temperament, learning style, fine- and gross-motor skills, and language acquisition. These significant adults must remember that developmental processes in young children occur in a social context shaped by diverse familial, cultural, geographic, social, and economic factors influencing developmental progress. In a major way, the age span of early childhood contributes to the complexity of developing a comprehensive assessment system. Intricately intertwined with the issue of the age span is the difference in types of settings where infants, toddlers, and young children are served. Along with diverse purposes for the implementation of care, education, and intervention, the complexity of the assessment task is staggering. Before looking at types of assessment, you must consider the places where the care and education of young children occurs.

MATCHING ASSESSMENT METHODS TO EARLY CHILDHOOD SETTINGS

The care and education of infants and toddlers occurs at home, in home child care, and in group child-care settings. Often, those with special needs are found in typical early care centers as well as in early intervention settings. Among other things, caregivers in these settings need to know:

- What the crying baby wants
- When to feed, diaper, and soothe babies
- When to talk with and stimulate with toys
- When to allow "me do it"
- When something is "off" with the baby and whether the problem is serious

In each of these situations, caregivers assess the needs of the baby by observation. They compare their knowledge of the individual baby to past experience with the baby, to their experiences with babies in general, and to their knowledge of infant/toddler development. After reflecting on their observations, caregivers change the intervention, routine, or educational plan. When caregivers believe that their capacity to care appropriately and responsively for a particular infant/toddler is limited, the next assessment step is family involvement. This conversation evolves from the regular and routine conversations that have set the tone for family partnerships and collaboration. Thus, the discussion of concern can proceed more naturally when a basic rapport is already established between the caregiver and family. So, by comparing caregiver knowledge with family knowledge regarding a troubling problem, the difficulty can be resolved or referred for specialist evaluation.

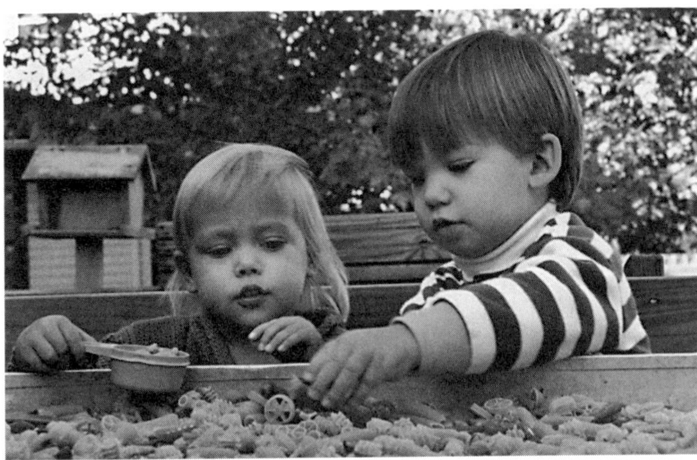

Preschoolers can be found in all of the locations previously described (home, home-based child care, and child-care centers). Some states offer "universal" preschool for all four-year-olds and in some cases, for all three-year-olds, as well. The offerings and regulations vary by state (cf. Bushouse, 2009). In addition, in many states, young children are located in compensatory educational programs for the "at risk"; special programs for those with disabilities; and increasingly, in inclusive environments. Among other things, caregivers and teachers in these settings need to know:

- When to move the story time to closure
- When to change the curricular theme
- When to intervene in conflicts between children
- When to provide enrichment activities for a precocious reader
- When to ask the speech therapist or other related service person to observe and/or assess a particular child

Many of the decisions of preschool caregivers and teachers in these and other situations involve a consideration of the group of children and the group's best interests. These are teaching decisions that teachers and caregivers make based on the overall plan for the center or program and the pacing decisions that teachers make based on the needs of the group for the particular day. Assessment methods for these situations can be accomplished through the use of observation. Informed observation consists of knowledge of child development, curricular goals, and expected learning outcomes, as well as state or national leaning standards. An integral part of the use of informed observation is the choice of a record-keeping system.

For those decisions that involve a question or concern about developmental progress or process, the first step is conversation and collaboration with the child's family. If family and caregivers or teachers have serious concerns, a referral for specialists' assessment may be in order. The use of tests for these occasions is discussed. Special issues of preschool-age children and the current events influencing philosophy and program practice are considered.

Young school-age children receive care in locations similar to those of infants and toddlers (at home, in home child care, and in center-based child care), and in public and private settings where they begin "school" and are introduced to the privileges and responsibilities associated with formal education. Teachers of primary-age children and their caregivers need to know:

- When to use cooperative group activities for the curricular goal
- How to incorporate phonics or character education in the teaching theme
- How to meet standards AND employ an inquiry approach to learning
- How to prepare children for the accountability tests in their school
- What kind of "homework" will meet the needs of the children, the after-school setting, and the parents

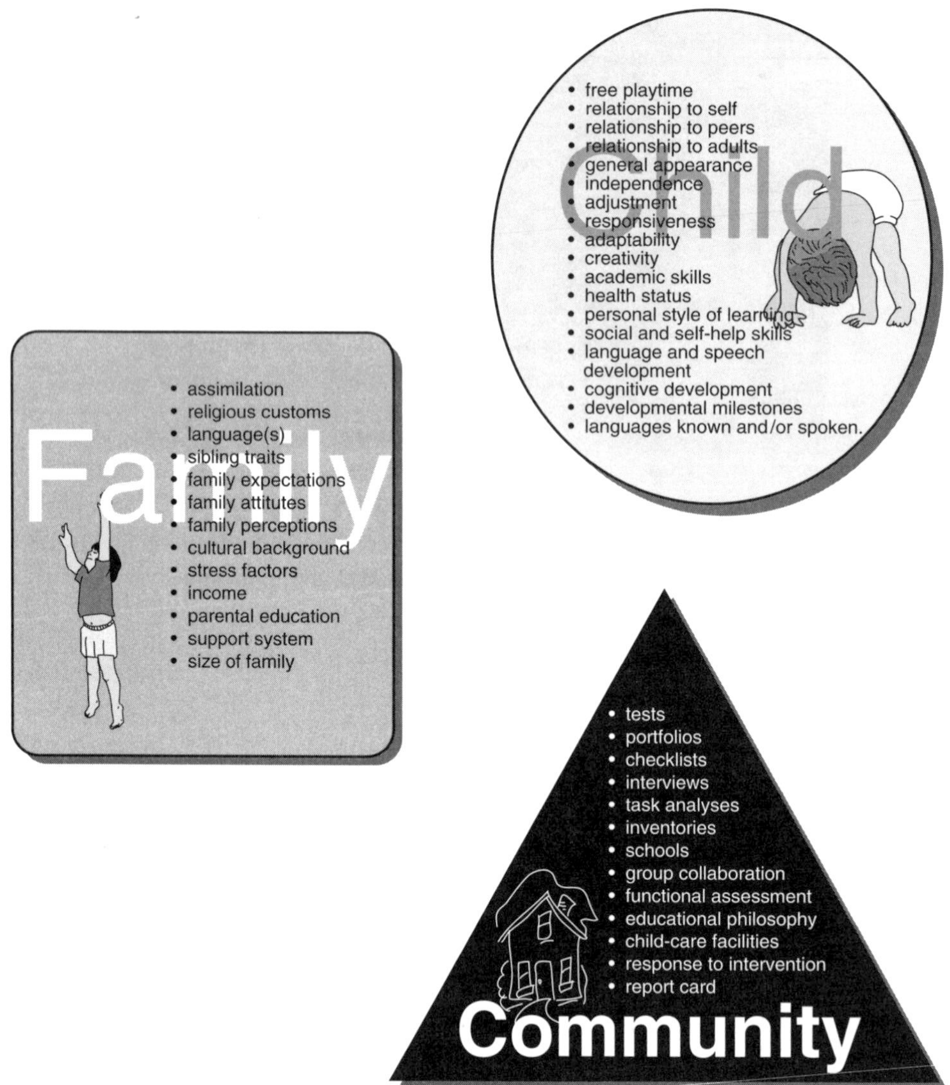

FIGURE 1.1 Essential components for total assessment.

- How to include the young child with special needs in the group
- How to prepare young children for standardized accountability tests

Assessment decisions in these situations appropriately rely primarily on teacher observation. Tests appear as a feature of the primary years—classroom tests, standardized achievement tests, and diagnostic assessments. Special assessment techniques for including and referring children with special needs are important features of the teacher's knowledge base. The special issues of the primary years, including accountability in its current form, are a feature. Each of these assessment situations rely on the components illustrated in Figure 1.1.

STAKEHOLDERS IN THE PROCESS

In each early childhood setting, the need for information about infant/toddler/child progress varies. Collecting information, choosing appropriate methods, thinking about the information gathered, and planning the next step based on the assessment are all approached and handled in

TABLE 1.1 Method of Assessment of Frequency of Use

Stakeholder	Observation	Special Alternative Method	Test and Performance Assessment
Family	daily and routinely	rarely	never
Paraprofessional caregiver	daily and routinely	rarely	under supervision
Infant teacher	daily and routinely	rarely	screening, regularly
Infant specialist	daily and routinely	often	diagnostic
Paraprofessional preschool caregiver	daily and routinely	rarely	under supervision
Preschool teacher	daily and routinely	sometimes	screening and performance tasks
Preschool specialist	daily and routinely	often	diagnostic
Primary paraprofessional caregiver	daily and routinely	never	under supervision
Primary teacher	daily and routinely	sometimes	screening, diagnostic, performance tasks, accountability
Primary specialist	daily and routinely	often	diagnostic
Administrators	rarely	never	review results for accountability
Policy boards	rarely	never	review results for accountability
Legislators	rarely	never	review results for accountability

different ways by each of the young child's "important people." The primary "important people," or **stakeholders**, in the "need to know" loop or assessment system are each child's family and caregivers/teachers. These, however, are not the only stakeholders in the process; others include related service personnel, program funders and administrators, legislators, and the public at large. Each of these stakeholders seeks different pieces of information.

stakeholders people important in the lives of children, especially regarding the assessment of children.

Families want to know how their children are developing and learning. They are interested not only in their own opinions, but also in those informed opinions shared by caregivers and teachers in informal and formal conversations, conferences, and reports. Because paraprofessionals want to meet the needs of the child in the particular setting, they will want to be able to make decisions about particular children and groups based on the guidelines developed by the teachers they collaborate with. Teachers and specialists need information to keep programs running well for the groups of children and for particular children with special needs. Administrators, policy boards, and legislators are accountable for the progress of groups of children. They need to know that programs are working.

Each stakeholder comes with varying degrees of knowledge about the unfolding of development during the early childhood age span. Families, paraprofessionals, policy boards, and legislators have practical knowledge, diverse experiential knowledge, and various pieces of contextual information. Most do not have professional information. The professionals—caregivers/teachers, administrators, and related service personnel—have diverse training experiences that shape their notions of the best ways to gather assessment information. All stakeholders have the best interests of young children in mind. The definition and criteria for the demonstration of the progress of development and education vary with the stakeholders (see Table 1.1). Thus, defining a comprehensive assessment system for young children is extremely complicated. It requires teachers and others to keep assessment firmly in mind when thinking about: What to teach? How? To whom? And when?

DEFINING AND CREATING A COMPREHENSIVE ASSESSMENT SYSTEM

In view of the myriad and differing needs of stakeholders previously outlined, creating and implementing a truly comprehensive assessment system is an enormous task. It is not an insurmountable one, however, as you will learn by reading this book. Keep in mind that as a teacher, you will be one of the important stakeholders in the lives of young children. It is your relationship with each young child and your teaching and learning approach that will shape young children's view of teachers, school, and learning. You are in the position to model that learning involves self-reflection and empowers learners to make decisions about approaches to gaining additional knowledge and skills. You will plan to gather information to assist you in guiding learning for the children you serve. In addition, you will need to document child progress and communicate regularly with the other stakeholders—the child, family members, administrators, boards, and ultimately, legislative bodies. The procedures for gathering information discussed in this book are drawn from the following beliefs:

- Learning for children is best when their physical needs are met.
- Learning happens when children feel psychologically safe and secure.
- Learning of knowledge, skills, and dispositions requires opportunities for children to construct their experiences—to learn through inquiry.
- Learning occurs through social interaction with adults and other children.
- Learning requires opportunities for children to reflect upon initial awareness, then moving to exploration, to inquiry, and finally to utilization.
- Learning happens through play and question-based activities.
- Learning is motivated by child curiosity, interests, and "need to know".
- Human development and learning are characterized by individual variation. (Copple & Bredekamp, 2009)

With these beliefs in mind, you will choose assessment techniques suited to the needs of your program from those discussed in the text. Your decisions will be based on knowledge of the needs of the particular age span you serve and the setting for your program. The assessment process and its components are described and illustrated next. Each component is multidimensional and interactive with the other components.

Definition of Assessment

Before considering the design of an assessment system, it is important to define what is meant by "assessment." The definitions are many. Common elements of the definitions include the ideas that assessment:

- is a process
- is a decision-making tool
- can apply to an individual or a group
- generates products

assessment process for gathering information to make decisions.

In this book, **assessment** *is a process for gathering information to make decisions about young children. The process is appropriate when it is systematic, multidisciplinary, and based on the everyday tasks of childhood. The best assessment system is comprehensive in nature. That is, the assessment yields information about all the developmental areas: motoric, temperament, linguistic, cognitive, and social/emotional.*

A comprehensive assessment system must consider the following factors:

- The child as an individual and as a group member
- The other stakeholders—families, teachers, administrators, policy board members, and legislators—as participants in the process as well as consumers of the products
- The program philosophy and the curriculum or intervention strategy of the program
- The purpose for evaluating, measuring, or documenting progress
- Available methods and the accuracy, usability, and meaning of the results

The settings for the age span contribute to the immense task of developing a comprehensive assessment system, because the meaning of assessment varies with each of the factors just listed.

Assessment information may be gathered in a variety of formal and informal ways. **Techniques** employed for gathering information must be nondiscriminatory and continuous, and must result in meaningful documentation of child progress. The technique also must yield information that can be used easily and accurately by stakeholders.

techniques methods, whether formal or informal, for gathering assessment information.

Techniques for assessment decisions must be matched to purpose: Why is the information needed? What will happen when the information is gathered? Will changes in care or education follow? Will stakeholders document existing knowledge? The answers to each of these questions will influence the choice of technique for information gathering. An analogy to consider is as follows. Suppose you are cooking a dinner. If the dinner is a picnic, you may choose to fry a chicken at home or buy a bucket on the way to the park. You make this choice based on the weather (hot), food safety (no refrigeration), ease of serving, your skill as a cook, and so on. If the dinner is a celebration for a friend who is retiring after 40 years of teaching, you will use your best recipe for chicken that may take several hours to prepare (or cater from the best). You make this choice based on the occasion (celebration), your skill as a cook, and the time you have available for preparation. If the dinner is for 200 at the local community center, you grab a friend or two and choose a baked chicken recipe that can be made easily by several cooks. You make the decision based on the equipment available, the food interests of the group, and the ease of preparation and serving.

In each of these situations, you considered the purpose of the dinner, the social context, the expectations of the participants, the techniques available in your repertoire, and the skill that you have in using them. No matter how casually you gathered information for this dinner decision, you matched the purpose of the dinner to the techniques employed. It is the same with assessment; you must choose the techniques to suit the purpose. If you choose a test to gather information, you must know the important technical qualities of the test. You must consider factors of efficiency, accuracy, usability, appropriateness for the children you wish to examine, limits of the test, and others. All of these factors are discussed.

All assessment activities must be conducted for a particular purpose at a particular point in the lives of young children.

Decisions

Why are you gathering information on the children in your program? Reasons may include that it is time to decide what to teach or how to modify your instruction or intervention; it is time to report progress to parents; there is a concern about developmental progress of an individual or group on the part of parents or others; it is required to determine eligibility for service for special needs; or it is time to be accountable to the program or legislative body. *All of these occasions should be ongoing and routine in the lives of teachers and children.* These are important assessment situations in the lives of young children. It is important that their caregivers and teachers understand the stakes as they choose the technique to answer the questions. At best, an assessment not matched to purpose may just yield no important information related to purpose. At worst, assessment decisions based on incomplete, inaccurate, or otherwise technically flawed information may damage the life of a child.

Methods

The most basic technique that sustains most early childhood assessment is informed observation of the infant/toddler or child in action. To be an effective and accurate observer, the watcher must have the capacity to separate judgment from watching. For example: You look out your window and see several buildings of various ages. You describe the three brick buildings: one with concrete pillars and balconies, one with neo-classic Greek ornamentation, and one with a chain-link fence on top of it. You judge the one with the fence on top as "ugly," according to your (previously defined) criteria for "ugly" city skyscrapers. Contrast this with saying simply: "There are three brick buildings outside my window. One of them is ugly!"

Notice the missing information in the two descriptions. If the observation report were on a child, much information would be lost and decisions would be made based on fragmentary information. Another important consideration for the teacher or professional observer is knowledge of child development and all the other variables that affect development.

In addition to observation, techniques of assessment include interview and presentation of task to an individual or group. These may be structured or open-ended. There may be criteria for judging the information gathered or the assessor may be expected to bring clinical and contextual knowledge to bear when interpreting the way in which the child completes the interview or task. Some assessment procedures are specialized teaching techniques that give you an opportunity to gather information to solve an individualization of instruction problem. These techniques are called *task analysis,* a procedure for gathering detailed information about the learning activity of a particular child, and *functional analysis,* a procedure for reviewing behavior that may be inhibiting learning for a particular child in a particular program.

Finally, some techniques require that the child read, interpret, and solve paper-and-pencil activities that relate to definitions of development or curriculum. These measures are usually group achievement tests that are used primarily as accountability information (information gathered to see whether the program is working). These paper-and-pencil measures are least appropriate for the youngest pupils in our age span. When choosing paper and pencil, you will need to be aware of the issues surrounding the limitations, use, and misuse of these measures.

Each of these techniques may be employed in a standardized or performance-based setting. The rules for interpretation and the limits for use of the results will vary accordingly. Each of these methods has strengths and limitations. Issues of accuracy, usability, defined limitations, and bias must be considered when applying any assessment technique. In all cases, the interpretation of an assessment measure must be related to the program and purpose for its use. For example, to be eligible for public services for children with special needs, standardized instruments must be used and applied with the appropriate limitations. This is the case because eligibility for service definitions includes test scores as one of the criteria. Of course, the score must be considered as only one of the pieces of information needed to make a final determination for program placement and participation.

Whenever information is gathered by assessment techniques, the information must then be applied to practice. That is, the information gathered for the purpose of program eligibility in the previous example becomes the baseline information that is used to plan intervention strategies. Interpreting assessment information and decision-making is an ongoing process. Information is continuously compared to standards, theory, and curricula so it can be evaluated. Evaluation occurs through matching information to standards for developmental and educational practice. The stakeholders in the assessment system then draw plans to advance and facilitate development. The assessors must remember that assessment results indicate the child's situation at only that moment in time. Further assessment may yield similar results, but only then is a pattern suggested. Even a pattern of assessment results, however, must be subjected to verification. For, if the assessment measure is biased, or if only some players in the system are in action, then the results may present only part of the story. "Any assessment results are like a photograph of a child: they only give one picture of the many-sided child" (Deno, 1990).

Table 1.2 lists some assessment decisions accompanied by examples of methods to address the questions. Column 1 lists some common assessment decisions. Column 2 lists methods for gathering information to make decisions for the questions. Column 3 raises contextual ambiguities that influence the choice of assessment method.

Assessment decisions are never as easy as they first appear. By keeping an open mind, having an awareness of the complexity of the task, and using your knowledge of child development, appropriate curricular implementation based on these principles will assist you in the development of a repertoire of assessment techniques to apply in the situations where you must determine child progress and report your decisions to parents and others. Throughout this book, you will be shown a range of assessment techniques appropriate for the children who you serve. After

TABLE 1.2 Assessment Decision

Decision	Methods to Consider	Contextual Ambiguities
1. Shall I introduce a new food to baby Shiloh?	observation of adjustment to previous foods; expert consultation	For Shiloh, critical variables include which stakeholder is making the decision and Shiloh's age. The decision is appropriately made by parents. If she is 1 month old, hopefully the parents will consult an expert. If she is 18 months old, previous experience and knowledge of the expert's previous advice may guide the decision.
2. Is baby Nicholas getting a long enough nap?	observation of waking state and comparison to knowledge of his previous patterns	Nicholas and the nap is an assessment decision that may be made by parents or caregiver, based on knowledge of Nicholas. Even then, issues of teething, overstimulation, and other variables may come into play here. Care interventions will vary depending on the available information. An ongoing adjustment to Nicholas's sleeping routine will be made.
3. Is toddler Debbie's speech developing typically?	observation of Debbie in various situations requiring conversation; interview of Debbie's parents; developmental screening	If Debbie is saying only a few words, the assessment decision may seem to point to developmental screening. The decision changes, however, if the context includes a bilingual situation. Intervention and teaching activities will then support both languages and a hasty judgment of deficient will be curtailed.
4. Are the children in my preschool group playing cooperatively?	observation and comparison to definition of cooperative play; performance task	Group process evaluation seems to contain no ambiguity for the assessment decision-maker. However, definition of cooperation and previous experiences of children influence the context of this decision. Teachers must provide descriptors for those tasks that they wish to use as evaluation markers. If the purpose of the assessment is to judge whether more experience is needed, then teachers observe and intervene accordingly.
5. Are the children tired of easel painting?	collection of paintings; frequency checklists	No one is easel painting. What is the reason? Maybe you need to change the paint colors. Maybe you need to see what else is available. Maybe it is not important that no one is painting. You make a teaching decision for yourself based on reflection about these and other hypotheses.
6. Shall the preschool class study "our families"?	review of curricular goals; evaluation of child interest through discussion	Several children in your class report that they will soon have new brothers and sisters. Your program guide calls for the inclusion of a theme on families. You make teaching plans based on this and other information.
7. Is Oswald's conflict with peers as expected developmentally?	observation of Oswald in diverse settings; interview of Oswald's parents; developmental screening; diagnostic assessment by specialist	Oswald is indeed combative. He kicks, screams, bites, spits, and throws toys. This pattern of behavior has been consistent since September. In conversations with his mother you note that she is similarly bothered at home with these outbursts. It is indeed time to seek an expert. If, however, Oswald started this stream of acting out following a major life crisis (new sibling, loss of family member, move, and so on), you may first plan intervention in the program geared toward reassuring Oswald.

(continued)

TABLE 1.2 Assessment Decision (*continued*)

Decision	Methods to Consider	Contextual Ambiguities
8. Do the first graders in my program understand the concept of a story?	review of checklist record according to criteria for the definition; performance task	Concept of a story, as empirically defined by your program, seems to be critical piece of information most first graders will need to know. Your choose an appropriate technique (e.g., story map) to gather the information and plan further teaching for those who have not developed an awareness or mastery of this concept. The contextual variables include definitions of the task, child experience with stories, and language development.
9. Are the third graders mastering the mathematical knowledge required by the state goals?	checklist comparison to the state goals: performance tasks; required achievement tests.	Third-grade teachers are indeed responsible for state learning goals. So you plan to meet the goals through the implementation of a curriculum that is derived from these as well as other goals. You teach, you assess, you reteach. But, what if the goals, are unrealistic? You do not have an assessment question; you have a policy problem that you and other stakeholders, parents, principals, and others must solve in the best interest of the children.
10. Is Louis demonstrating a talent for visual arts?	collection of art products; expert consultation	Louis seems to produce paintings and drawings unlike any that you have seen in second grade. You can enjoy these paintings, assist Louis in developing his talent, or refer to an expert. You must consider the wishes and interests of Louis and his parents before following up, as there may be important sociocultural variables that influence whether Louis should be encouraged in artistic activities.

choosing appropriately from among these techniques, you will consider the issues of reporting to parents and others. Assessing children for teaching, for monitoring individual progress, and for the reports that you make are among your most important duties and responsibilities.

Ethics and Responsibilities

The foundation of ethical behavior is personal recognition of the rights of children and families, the limits of personal knowledge, and the choice of appropriate assessment methods for programmatic decisions. Another key factor is keeping personal biases out of the process. This is particularly important when serving children whose social and cultural experiences may be different from your own. You must keep in mind that your sociocultural lens may affect your objectivity when you interact with children and families from diverse cultures. Some principles to keep in mind about culture are as follows:

- Behavior of families and young children is influenced by their cultural rules; that is, people from specific cultures use their rules so they can understand each other readily.
- Families teach implicitly and explicitly the rules and traditions of their culture.
- Families decide whether to observe cultural rules and traditions completely or partially.
- Culture is dynamic, changing in response to interactions with outsiders as well as exposure to technology and other artifacts of modernity (Day, 2006, pp. 27–28).

Specifically, you may see cultural differences in families and young children in the ways that they perceive and relate to "authority" figures—including teachers, the ways that family members interact with each other, as well as appropriate relationships between and among peers. For example, is it acceptable for young girls and boys to play games together in the traditional culture? What about sitting next to each other in circle? At desks or tables? Traditional cultural views about competition, individualism, and collaboration also vary. As well, there are conventions of politeness and formality that influence interactions with families from diverse cultures. Appreciate the differences and encourage your students to respect and tolerate each other and their diverse beliefs (Brown, 2007, pp. 133–134). You need to get to know the cultures of the families that you serve in all of their nuances.

You must also remember that families do not exist in a static definition of a particular culture. Our society is composed of socioeconomic variables that impact family identification as well as the "traditional" cultural norms. In addition, families choose, on the basis of their experiences, whether or not to identify with "mainstream American values" some or all of the time. Accordingly, it is crucial to take your cues from the family when considering issues of culture, social class, and ethnicity that may affect an assessment plan. You want the family to know that you accept and value the learner, that you have knowledge of the family's cultural and linguistic background, that you recognize and appreciate the differences in school and home culture, and finally that you grasp the cultural transitions and other support needed by the family (Lynch & Hanson, 2004; National Association for the Education of Young Children, 2005; Bowman & Moore, 2006). Failure to consider the complexity of the social and cultural context can result in serious damage, setting up young children for lifelong misery in school.

In particular, all teachers will be involved with families and children who are learning English. "English-language learners (ELLs) are the fastest growing student population in U.S. public schools. . . . In 2004–2005, approximately 5.1 million students, or 10.5 percent of the U.S. population, were ELLs. Approximately 79 percent of ELLs nationally are from Spanish-language backgrounds. . . . California educates one-third of all nation's ELL students—1.6 million students; 85 percent of all ELLs in California speak Spanish" (Payan & Nettles, 2007). "We're no longer talking about dealing with a minority of our population. . . . We are in fact talking about the part of the population that is very quickly becoming the majority part of our K–12 student cohort" (Landgraf, 2008, p. 2; see also Garcia & Jensen, 2009; Garcia, Jensen, & Scribner, 2009).

With the changing demographics of schools and child care centers in mind, it is imperative that you practice culturally responsive care and education. The five core elements of this culturally responsive care are:

1. Understand how racism impacts child self-identity and attitudes toward others.
2. Building on the culture of families and promoting cross-cultural understanding of young children in schools and child-care centers.
3. Work to preserve home languages and encourage learning English.
4. Collaborate with families and maintain a dialog with them.
5. Engage in regular self-reflection about diversity (Gonzalez-Mena, 2009, p. 352).

Culturally responsive teachers are aware of these variables as they consider best practices for teaching, learning, and assessment. In this way, they avoid past bad educational practice, which ignored diversity and created lifelong negative impact on children and families.

The dreadful history of improper decisions for children includes the mismatch of method to purpose, interpretation of results beyond the limits of the technique employed, and failure to consider the role of contextual factors. Currently, early-childhood educators must wrestle with the demands for accountability and whether the measures employed are appropriate for the children and families that they serve. The risk in ignoring this responsibility is lifetime stigmatization of young children and the foreshortening of educational opportunity. As well, teachers should recognize the messages that they send to children about learning achievement through the decisions that they make about the placement of children in workgroups, the materials that they use with individuals and groups, the ways they motivate (or don't) to try various learning experiences, the choices and responsibilities available for young children to engage, and the overall learning climate as well as relationships with the other stakeholders—parents, community, and so on (Weinstein, 2004).

An important responsibility of child-care and teaching personnel is providing information to parents and others about the developmental process and progress of individual children. This information must be held and shared in confidence. In addition, teachers have a central role in "Child Find." This means that teachers must screen and refer children in their care who may need special intervention. Neisworth and Bagnato (2000; see also *Zero to Three*, 2005; Guralnick & Conlon, 2007; Odom, Horner, Snell & Blacher, 2007) outline best practice for this screening that links to program planning. Best practice includes the need to be sure that the assessment methods are acceptable, authentic, collaborative, convergent, equitable, sensitive, and congruent. In short, this means that assessment for identification for special programs is a process with many technical components that require careful planning, implementation, and interpretation. Equal protection under the law requires that teachers must use techniques appropriate for the situation and the child, as well as participate in the multidisciplinary team that develops the Individualized Education Plan (or the Individualized Family Service Plan for children birth to age 3). Federal legislation (i.e., the Individuals with Disabilities Education improvement Act [IDEA] of 2004) delineates the rights of children for entitlement to special intervention and education to meet special needs so that they may have an equal educational opportunity. Increasingly, young children with special educational needs are located in a typical preschool situation. A best practice approach to working with the young child and family in inclusive situations is the infant mental health approach, which has as "a central tenet . . . that positive development requires the presence of secure relationships with significant others in a child's life. . . . (In this) approach (the program) accommodates a child's individual needs while also eliciting the strengths of . . . classmates . . . incorporating parents . . . so interventions are tailored to the child's unique needs . . . efforts of home and school reinforce those of the other" (Marsili & Hughes, 2009, pp. 10–14; see also Greenspan & Wieder, 2006b). In this way, a collaborative, reciprocal partnership with families and teachers on behalf of young children sets the path for lifelong school success. Besides working with families, teachers in early childhood must also be data gatherers on the part of young children—using the data from observation and informal assessments to adjust curriculum.

This data-based decision-making on the part of teachers in partnership with specialists is the newest aspect of IDEA, which is Response to Intervention (RTI, 2006 IDEA regulations). "The RTI process is designed to identify struggling learners early, to provide access to needed interventions, and to help identify children with disabilities. RTI is a process intended to assist in identifying children with disabilities by providing data about how a child responds to scientifically based intervention as part of the comprehensive evaluation required for identification of any disability" (CEC, 2008, p. 74). RTI involves service to young children offered in levels described as tiers—from modifications to the typical curriculum to more intensive and specialized intervention. It all begins with universal screening. As an early childhood teacher, you will need to know how to use screening instruments as well as how to observe for developmental milestone accomplishments and potential learning difficulties. Effective practice in literacy instruction, and presumably other curricular areas, "is intentionally planned to accommodate the individual differences among children, relies heavily on assessment of (child) skills, is responsive to each (child's) changing status is generally more effective than instruction that treats the classroom more globally, less diagnostically, more intuitively, and less dynamically (Connor, Morrison, Fishman, Ponitz, Glasney, Underwood, Piasta, Crowe, & Schatschneider, 2009, p. 95). Observation is at the core of this best practice approach to teaching. For "(l)iteracy is not just a matter of reading/writing skills or cognitive strategies; it is also a matter of will, feelings, and emotions. Emotions are highly involved when children attempt to communicate, respond to literature, publish their stories, or share what they learn from their books" (Uribe & Nathenson-Mejia, 2008, p. 118). So, your observation and data-gathering approaches will serve young children in your classroom, as well as providing the evidence needed for any planned special intervention. Accordingly, special educational decisions will involve you, the classroom teacher, as a member of a team. You will have help in assuming these responsibilities.

VOICES FROM THE FIELD

Literacy Coordinator for School District: A Comprehensive Process and Plan

Our assessment plan is guided by the State Standards—not the textbooks. Textbooks give structure to instruction. Recently, we piloted and chose a new reading series. We reviewed series by Scott Foresman (the incumbent), Houghton Mifflin, and Treasures by Macmillan–McGraw Hill. The process: three teachers at each grade level piloted the new materials. Besides the piloting teachers, all other teachers in the district were involved in selecting Treasures http://activities.macmillanmh.com/reading/treasures/. Lots of materials come with this series, so teachers need to learn to manage the options for the whole class, groups, and individuals. We love the series, as it comes with leveled readers. We weren't as happy in the first year of implementation with the publisher's tests; they were too broad, including grammar, spelling, and more—the result being not enough depth of skill assessment—only one or two questions per skill, so you're not sure that children really have the skill. Besides, we already had a writing assessment: Six Traits of Writing http://youcanwrite.net/home.html. In our second year with Treasures, we got permission from the publisher to use the stories in their books for a cold or fresh read, i.e., material the reader hasn't seen so that we can assess comprehension skills and strategies. Children didn't perform well on these measures, so we did readability checks, using several different formulas and found that the stories did not match the assigned grade level. For year three, we developed our own fresh read materials by rewriting some of the publisher's stories, writing our own stories, and rewriting the questions. We're pleased with the results.

Our teachers are required to use Dynamic Indicators of Basic Early Literacy Skills *(DIBELS) as well as the three times per year comprehension measure. We contribute to the DIBELS database (https://dibels.uoregon.edu), but keep our own spreadsheets so we can drill down for information at the school, class, and child level. We use DIBELS to form instructional groups. In the past, we did not regularly test the children who met the benchmark for the state tests; now we do, so we can be sure the passing score is not masking skill deficiencies. That is, a child may meet the benchmark, but not fully understand cause and effect—may have missed those items on the test, but still pass.*

For children who do not hit the benchmarks, we target their earliest comprehension need. Do these children have a firm grasp of phonics, phonemic awareness? We use our Response to Intervention (RTI) process to bring this support to children needing it.

All of our instruction is data-based. We want teachers to be comfortable with and use data. We're looking at a couple of solutions: Pearson Benchmark, http://www.pearsonbenchmark.com, and Pearson Inform, http://www.pearsonschoolsystems.com/products/inform/, but we haven't made a decision yet.

We have a district-developed test that we give three times per year—it's a mini state test. We disaggregate the data to the school, grade, class, and the individual. Then, we adjust curriculum and instruction accordingly.

For new teachers we have a three-year mentoring program; they meet in groups as support system and as opportunity to share concerns and learn new practices. Also, all new teachers are assigned a grade-level partner. As Coordinator, I model lessons for new teachers, help them with the technical components, work one-on-one to roadmap a week's reading plan—showing how to use the text and other curricular elements and instructional strategies.

Advice to New teachers

- *DIBELS is a good tool to use for instructional planning. Bad practice that I hear about that concerns me (not in my district)—teachers deviating from the directions—so the child will get a "good" score, using DIBELS stories as homework prior to the testing.*
- *Be prepared for a data-oriented teaching approach.*
- *Know how to use informal assessment—observation, checklist, anecdotal notes.*
- *Know how to incorporate technology for differentiation. We use Renaissance Accelerated Reading and Math: http://www.renlearn.com/ar/.*

- *Know the philosophy behind the various instructional methods so that you can be flexible in your approach to children.*
- *Know how to implement IRI or IRL.*
- *Know the vocabulary of assessment—grade-level equivalent.*

In your own program, however, you must assume the responsibility for the *match of* child, curriculum, and assessment technique. You must apply the current knowledge of early childhood education theory and principles in making this match. "Above all, we shall not harm the child. We shall not participate in practices that are disrespectful, degrading, dangerous, exploitative, intimidating, psychologically damaging, or physically harmful to children" (Feeney & Kipnis, 1989; see also NAEYC, 2005; Copple & Bredekamp, 2009).

In the past, good intentions regarding the gathering of assessment information about children have resulted in inappropriate evaluation decisions. This has happened in large part because one or more elements of the comprehensive assessment system have been ignored or unknown to the individual making the judgments. For example, IQ tests, a form of structured interview and tasks presented individually to children, have often been applied as single-technique options for assessment and placement decisions. The factor of English-language facility has sometimes been ignored. Life chances for children have been affected. When these instruments are used as part of an assessment system, usually when attempting to diagnose disabilities so that a child may be entitled to special educational or intervention services, it is imperative that the instruments themselves be reviewed for cultural bias and that the results found be applied fairly to the child assessed with this standardized format (Baca & Cervantes, 2004; Rhodes, Ochoa, & Ortiz, 2005; Javier, 2007). In the present, early childhood educators struggle with some of the same issues, particularly those surrounding the use of achievement tests in the primary years.

CURRENT ISSUES IN THE ASSESSMENT OF YOUNG CHILDREN

An early childhood assessment system has many players. The central figure is the infant/toddler/child who can participate in more informed and self-conscious ways as maturity and experience are acquired. The second crucial players are the child's family. Families have expectations and personal social/cultural knowledge and information to add to the assessment mix. Teachers, child-care providers, and related service personnel enter as important figures in children's lives and contribute to the information pool. Administrators and boards, as those responsible for program excellence and evaluation, participate in the system. Often administrative and board participation is at the policy level—setting standards, prescribing methods, and designating curricula that match the outcomes for learning. Administrators, of course, are responsible for monitoring the policy requirements of boards, local, state, and federal governmental requirements. As the call for universal preschool continues—"high quality . . . developmentally appropriate . . . comprehensive in scope, targeting the cognitive, social-emotional and physical domains of development . . . available to all three- and four-year-old children whose parents want them to attend" (Zigler, Gilliam, & Jones, 2006), as states launch legislation and programs, and as more and more young children enter the care and education system at younger ages, attention to programs, quality of teachers, and assessment/accountability demands will increase. Therefore, as teachers and advocates for young children and their families, you must be prepared to know about assessment techniques, the limitations of each, and the way to link assessment results to curriculum. Finally, a society that cares for the youngest of our citizens—babies, toddlers, and young children—participates as standard setter and judge. Who are our children? What are their skills, knowledge, and attitudes? The players in the assessment system grapple with many current assessment issues, including accountability, high-stakes decisions, authentic and portfolio assessment, and outcomes-based reporting. None of these issues is simple; many overlap in their origins and complexity. In the next section, each is briefly outlined. These issues are further addressed throughout the book in the context of their impact on the assessment system being described.

Accountability

Stakeholders, most concerned with broad social interests in the provision of equal opportunities for all and the problems inherent in such efforts, have concerned themselves with **accountability**. As well, other national interests result in calls for accountability—improvement and educational reform to improve "results." "(P)ersistent criticism of schools began with the onset of the Cold War soon after World War II ended in 1945. The steady stream of negativity probably accounts for much of our openness to negativity. At that time, politicians, generals, defense specialists, and university professors came to see schools for the first time as integral to national defense and, at the same time, as lacking" (Bracey, 2004, p. 1). Educational accountability is not a new idea (Flesch, 1955), and professionals have usually made their best effort to teach "all" the children. Efforts have sometimes fallen short, as highlighted in the 1983 report *A Nation at Risk* (National Commission on Excellence in Education, 1983). This report suggested that large numbers of American youngsters were being miseducated. In response, across the country, states enacted legislation to "check up" on school districts. These checks were shown in the form of state-mandated testing, state-mandated learning goals, and learner outcomes.

accountability being responsible for the proper education of all children.

Then came No Child Left Behind (NCLB; P.L. 107–110, 2002), a reauthorization of the Elementary and Secondary Act of 1965, requiring increased emphasis on adequate yearly progress of all learners in public schools and third-grade achievement testing in reading and math, state plans for assessment, as well as the mandate for highly qualified teachers across the nation. Failure to comply with these federal demands places school districts at risk for loss of federal funds. With the passage of this law, the debate about what to test—mostly reading and math—how to use the results, and whether the imperatives of the law are realistic and obtainable heightened awareness about schools and schooling. With the NCLB legislation, the following trends began:

- ***School District Report Cards:*** NCLB legislation gives parents report district-wide cards so they can see which schools in their district are succeeding and why. With this information, parents, community leaders, teachers, principals, and elected leaders have access to the information they need to improve schools.
- ***Public School Choice:*** NCLB legislation may let parents transfer their child to another public school if the state says that the child's school is "in need of improvement." The school district may pay for transportation for the child. Contact your school district to find out if your school district offers this opportunity.
- ***Extra Help with Learning:*** NCLB may also provide a child with free tutoring and extra help with schoolwork if the state says that child's school has been "in need of improvement" for at least 2 years. This extra help is often referred to as "supplemental educational services." Contact the child's school district to find out whether a child qualifies.
- ***Parental Involvement:*** NCLB requires schools to develop ways to get parents more involved in their child's education and in improving the school. Parents should contact their child's school to find out how they can get involved.
- ***Scientifically Based Research:*** NCLB focuses on teaching methods that have been proven by research to work. "Experimenting" on children by using educational fads is not advocated.
- ***Reading First:*** NCLB provides more than one billion dollars a year to help children learn to read. Reading First is the NCLB segment dedicated to ensuring that all children learn to read on grade level by the third grade. Reading First provides money to states and many school districts to support high-quality reading programs based on the best scientific research. Contact your school district to find out if its reading program is based on research (http://www.nclb.gov).

Each of these federally required components of NCLB legislation that states must observe are geared toward educational reform, appealing to parents and other stakeholders who remain concerned about the achievement gaps across our country between middle-class children, affluent children, and young children living in poverty. Not many disagree with the above components that seek family involvement in children's education and the assurance that schools will provide appropriate and adequate learning experiences—instead, the crux of the debate about NCLB centers around testing, particularly the role that testing plays in making important, life-altering decisions about child education—**high-stakes decisions**. Examples of high-stakes decisions include decisions for placing children in special programs away from peers made on the basis of one test experience and decisions to retain young children in third grade based on performance on a single standardized test. *While state departments of education make and implement plans and school districts implement various ways to demonstrate compliance with the law, as a teacher you will need to keep up to date on this legislation, because the curricular interpretations by states will have a profound impact on your practice as an educator*. Various organizations and journal publications regularly post and publish updates about this law; check the Internet sites provided in this chapter's Technology Links section. In the meantime, remember as you read that *this reform legislation even though reauthorization is still under consideration, this law influences your teaching—every day*. Standardized testing is still part of school practice in the primary years, because states measure and report accountability status of schools with standardized tests and progress toward state-developed benchmarks. There are, however, some difficulties with this approach. For example, "California projects that by the witching year of 2014, when 100 percent of the nation's students are supposed to be 'proficient,' 99 percent of the state's schools will be labeled as 'failing' under NCLB" (Bracey, 2004, p. 67). "If we assume that we will continue to make the same progress on National Assessment of Educational Progress (NAEP, the federal report card, http://www.ed.gov) in the future as in the previous decade, we can get 100 percent of our students to reach proficiency in mathematics in 61 years at the 4th grade, 66 years at the 6th grade, and 166 years at the 12th grade" (Linn, 2003). Also, "to a very great extent, NCLB equates teaching quality and students' learning with high-stakes test scores . . . this equation precludes the use of multiple measures of progress toward goals and multiple assessments of learning . . . which provide a more complex picture of both students' learning and effective teaching" (Cochran-Smith, 2005, p. 101). As policy-makers discuss reauthorization of NCLB, various adjustments are proposed. Achievement testing still holds great sway as an integral component of newly packaged legislation. Some adjustments that may help are:

high-stakes decision any test applied to make life-affecting decisions for the educational futures of young children.

1. Clear learning targets are centered on the best thinking about the most important learnings of the field of study
2. Commitment to standards-based instruction
3. High-quality assessment—matching the measure to the learning target or expected outcome
4. Anticipation and elimination of all relevant sources of bias
5. Effective and understandable communication of results to all stakeholders (Stiggins & DuFour, 2009, p. 643)

These ideas are among those that are promoted to use assessment data to improve instruction rather than assessment data as "judgment"—high stakes, win or lose. This kind of assessment is called **formative assessment**: data is gathered while teaching or program implementation is occurring; changes to instruction and programs are made while they are in process, changing the formation of the instruction/program and improving the learning for the children. These solutions come from those who have conducted the policy studies to evaluate the impact of the law on educational practice. One such study finds that

formative assessment data is gathered while teaching or program implementation is occurring; changes to instruction and programs are made while they are in process.

- Student achievement in reading and math has gone up since 2002, the year NCLB became law.
- Achievement gaps are narrowing between groups of students, but the gaps are still substantial.
- Achievement change results are difficult to attribute solely to NCLB, as many other educational innovations were implemented.
- Often the state data is difficult to find and filled with discrepancies. (Center on Education Policy, 2007, p. 1)

Even with these findings and others that criticize the use of standardized measures as accountability indexes, "test-based accountability is likely to remain the dominant paradigm for the near future" (McDonnell, 2008, p. 64). Hopefully, the tweaks that come in the next iteration of the NCLB, will incorporate "quality assessments that meet the users information needs, arise from clear and appropriate achievement expectations, yield accurate evidence of achievement, effectively communicate assessment results, keep the learner optimistic and striving for success, (Stiggins, 2008, pp. 229–243). Other problems with the policy concepts of accountability testing are based on an "intuitive" understanding of test theory on the part of legislators and other important stakeholders are the following beliefs: "a test measures what it says at the top of the page; a score is a score is a score; any two tests that measure the same thing can be made interchangeable with a little 'equating' magic; . . . score a test by adding up scores for items; an A is 93%, a B is 85%, a C is 78%, 70% is passing; multiple choice questions measure only recall; . . . can tell an item is good by looking at it" (Braun & Mislevy, 2005, pp. 489–497). None of these assertions are particularly true, even though they may make intuitive sense. Thus, "we need to do a much better job of communicating to a variety of audiences the basics of testing and the dangers we court when we ignore the principles and methods of educational measurement" (Braun & Mislevy, p. 497). Beyond the statistical improbability of meeting the law's requirements, there are many practical issues that affect the everyday lives of teachers, children, and families. For example, for English-language learners (ELLs) who must reach high standards in English-language arts and mathematics by 2014, there are special challenges, including:

1. Historically low ELL performance and slow improvement.
   State tests show ELL performance oftentimes 20–30 percentage points below other students and little improvement across many years.
2. Measurement accuracy.
   . . . Language demands of tests negatively influence accurate measurement of ELL performance. For the ELL, tests measure both *achievement and language ability.*
3. Instability of the ELL subgroup, i.e., the population of children in the group varies across time, adding newly arrived ELLs whose language ability and achievement is typically lower.
4. Factors beyond school control.
   Such as the variability of parental educational achievement within the population that seems to influence student performance on standardized tests. (Abedi & Dietel, 2004, p. 1)

It is also important to recognize that the ELL population is diverse. In Colorado, for example, Escamilla, Chavez, and Vigil (2005) show that the Spanish speakers in English-language acquisition/bilingual classrooms are among the highest achieving students in their schools. The bilingual program no doubt supports the achievement gains, so it is not the students who are a problem, but the program that may be needed to promote achievement. The educational issues are indeed complex. "One-size thinking" can't possibly fit everyone.

"In summary, the NCLB mandated a method for designing achievement standards that . . . depended on each state's political and educational authorities to apply the (standards setting) method as they saw fit. This process has resulted in marked differences across states in the content and difficulty level of tests and in the rigor of achievement standards" (Thomas, 2005, p. 65). Thus, there is some "collateral damage"—high incidence of failing schools, excellent schools dubbed failures, one-size-fits-all error, increased retention in grade rates, high school graduation rates reduced, rule changes continue, and inconsistency across states (Thomas, pp. 66–75). Finally, does research-based mean "value"-neutral? Often research begins from a philosophical stance—a case to be made for an approach. As a result, though most of the national curricular organizations promote practices that center on learner development as well as student achievement, the wary teacher will want to be aware of the philosophical underpinnings that shape district assessment requirements, even if they are research-based. For early childhood programs, learning standards should

1. Emphasize significant, developmentally appropriate content and outcomes
2. Be developed and reviewed through informed, inclusive processes
3. Use implementation and assessment strategies that are ethical and appropriate for young children
4. Be accompanied by support for early childhood programs, professionals, and families (NAEYC, 2002)

At the primary level especially, you will need to be prepared for content learning standards—literacy, mathematics, science, and so on—you will need to keep the above NAEYC position statement in mind, as you interpret and plan for engaged learning while meeting standards (cf. Helms, 2008, pp. 14–20).

High-Stakes Decisions

Accountability decisions become high stakes when funding is appropriated based on the results of tests and when the names of schools "not achieving" are published in the newspaper (i.e., school report cards). Such efforts are thought to call attention to educational malpractice. This may well be so in some cases. Often it is a case of not considering the context of the learning environment, not matching the assessment instrument to the curriculum, interpreting tests beyond their limits, or other errors of measurement application. In examining the "achievement gap"—differences across racial/ethnic and income groups, achievement results are frequently analyzed only according to broad definitions of "proficient." Consequently, the finer points of the success of some groups of children are buried in the aggregated data and the teaching implications are lost. As well, there is the possibility that due to the high-stakes nature of accountability testing—including loss of district reputation and funding—districts choose to focus on the middle level, ignoring children who are high-achieving and those who are achieving at the bottom of the curve (Barton & Coley, 2008). So, while some stakeholders are satisfied with the impact of accountability testing, many educators remain concerned that the emphasis on the tests ignore individual instructional needs, resulting in continued achievement gaps across and between children. Therefore, there are renewed calls to use data in day-to-day situations to document learning outcomes and to improve teaching and curricular planning, as well as for finer-grained analysis of large-scale accountability reports, which are at the center of the debate regarding educational reform today. With these proposed improvements to the "new NCLB" or other accountability legislation, there is the prospect that high-stakes decisions of the past will stop.

Past accountability practices that affected young children unfairly include the following most common errors: using screening and readiness tests to deny kindergarten entrance; retention in kindergarten on the basis of test scores; choice of primary curriculum based on test scores; and third-grade retention on the basis of test scores. Historically, tests have placed children in special education programs on the basis of IQ alone. These decisions are not only wrong; they also have lifelong consequences for the individuals involved—affecting the opportunity for education, self-esteem, and chances to change life goals. When it comes to serving the most vulnerable of our young—those with disabilities—appropriate ethical principles include:

- ***Autonomy:*** supporting the family in ethical decision-making.
  This is the opposite of the past paternalistic practice of the family as client with the expert telling them what should be done. Often the plans were made without regard to the family context, resulting in plans that were not suitable for particular families—they were too "cookie-cutter" and not responsive.
- ***Beneficence and nonmalfeasance:*** a balance of benefits and harms.
  This is the "first, do-no-harm" orientation of traditional medical ethics balanced with the accountability orientation—will there be a benefit?
- ***Justice:*** weighing of risks, costs, and benefits.

These principles apply to making services accessible to all young children (Epps & Jackson, 2000; see also Maeroff, 2006).

Such principles should guide actions and decisions with regard to the moral issues involved in assessment. Because assessment goals will continue to evolve from NCLB and other federal initiatives, you will want to be familiar with the tenets of professional use of achievement testing programs as declared in the American Educational Research Association (2000) position statement that outlines good practice for high-stakes tests:

- Validity statements regarding a test must match the purpose for the high-stakes use.
- Avoid one test for decisions that affect an individual student's life chances or education opportunities.
- When achievement testing is part of reform efforts, students should have adequate resources and an opportunity to learn.
- Policy-makers should be informed of any negative consequences of a testing program.
- The test and the curriculum must be aligned.
- Validity of passing scores and achievement level must be obtained before using them as a high-stakes indication.
- Those who fail must have opportunities for meaningful remediation.
- Attention must be given to those with language differences, as well as disabilities.
- Careful attention must be given to the rules for who should be tested and how.
- Sufficient reliability must be established for each intended use.
- Ongoing evaluation of the testing program is necessary.
- Of fundamental importance to all teachers is the knowledge of the statistical aspects of testing.

You will want to be sure that you understand the technical qualities and limitations of all kinds of tests so that you can advocate for children, especially those who are most vulnerable due to economic, personal, or social conditions that affect learning opportunities. "Bell curve thinking is the enemy of millions of children who have unrecognized genius . . . savage inequalities in schools' services are eliminated by giving students equal access to good teachers. The power of good teaching has overwhelming support in the literature. The high-stakes standardized testing movement advocates cannot ignore the connection of such uses to the pessimists who are, in fact, enemies of the poor . . . in the final analysis, what do we really want? Will we keep weighing the elephant to make it grow? . . . We need high-stakes services for our children. Then, any testing will be a matter of small concern" (Hilliard, 2000, pp. 293–304). As an early childhood teacher, you can make a difference in the lives of children by knowing about the limits of high-stakes assessment and by becoming familiar with the authentic assessment techniques that are part of the curricular planning process. **Authentic assessments** are those that are most similar to

authentic assessment determining developmental progress of children through a variety of means, including observations and special problems or situations.

the tasks of the classroom. Thus, they are the ways that teachers judge every day whether children are learning and lessons are working. These are the assessment methods that are described by early childhood educators in position statements.

Authentic Assessment and Portfolios

As advocates for the best interests of young children, scores of early childhood educators are concerned with appropriate practice that includes authentic assessment (Kamii, 1990; Meisels, 2000; Shepard, Hammerness, Darling-Hammond, & Rust, 2005; Popham, 2008a; Copple & Bredekamp, 2009). Many leaders have articulated the link from theory about child learning to the application for appropriate curriculum. In turn, assessment practices must be consistent with this theoretical knowledge. From the field of early childhood and elsewhere have come assessment activities that more closely resemble the activities of the preschool and primary classroom. This is part of the current trend toward authentic assessment, performance-based assessment, formative assessment, and portfolio assessment. Authentic, performance-based assessment is the evaluation that engages children and teachers daily, in many ways in answer to the basic questions: What learning is occurring? How do we know? What shifts in practice should we make? Portfolios are the vehicles used to gather the documents of learning. An integral part of the gathering of this documentation is reflection on the documents themselves as well as the process of learning. Although these performance-based portfolio assessment trends are promising, the measures are not without limits. In sum, though, authentic assessment and the collection of child work samples in portfolios is at the heart of the everyday work of the early childhood educator. Through the use of this formative assessment—the evaluation that adjusts and shapes instruction—teachers prepare young children for learning accomplishment as measured by comparison to standards and outcomes as well as other accountability measures. It is through this work of linked teaching and assessment that children learn to judge their own progress and begin their journeys as learners in an educational system that demands accountability.

SUMMARY

Each of the players (child, parent, caregivers, teachers, administrators, boards, legislators) in the rearing (care and education) of a child comes to the stage with a distinct knowledge base, potentially dissimilar goals, and often diverse notions of how to gather information for the purpose of judging developmental process and progress. Each of the players applies information to the standards/outcomes that relate to their ideas of important questions and issues to be documented, measured, or otherwise assessed and evaluated. Because of the complexity surrounding the interface of these various players, each must be considered separately, and each must be careful to practice responsible/responsive assessment so that the assessment system and the stakeholders treat children fairly and equitably, both individually and collectively.

FIELD ACTIVITIES

1. On your campus, ask students who are not planning to be teachers to define assessment. With your classmates, review the definitions collected. How do these definitions compare to those discussed in this chapter? What kind of public awareness plan should be made to address students on your campus?
2. Review the week's newspapers or television coverage on education. Note any stories that involve assessment. How are these stories treated? What would you do differently if you were the reporter or newscaster?
3. At the college level, portfolio assessment currently is a part of the way that students document progress. Find out who among your friends—those in education and those who major in the arts or business—is required to participate in the process. Look at the syllabi; talk with your friends about the experiences with the directions and the judgments made. What works?
4. Gather two or three news reports about stakeholders' views of testing in your community. Identify community concerns. Share your information with colleagues.
5. Visit one of the websites listed in the Technology Links section of this chapter. Present information to your colleagues about the site and what you learned about assessment and the policy issues you reviewed.

IN-CLASS ACTIVITIES

1. Reflect on your own experiences with assessment. Which have you enjoyed the most? Which do you hope no one will ever have to repeat? How do your experiences influence what you believe should be done for young children?
2. With a partner, list all of the details that you have heard or read about NCLB. Compare your list to that of NCLB at the http://www.nclb.gov site. Did you get all of the details? Then shift to your state department of education website. What else did you learn about the law and its provisions?
3. Examine the Accountability Illusion located on the Thomas B. Fordham website: http://www.edexcellence.net/index.cfm/news_the-accountability-illusion. See where your state stands in comparison to other states. Discuss the various formulas and procedrues that states use.

STUDY QUESTIONS

1. Identify the issues related to the development of a comprehensive assessment system for the early childhood years.
2. Who are the important stakeholders? How are they involved?
3. For which assessment decisions must early childhood teachers assume primary responsibility? How is this assessment process developed?
4. Which techniques do early childhood teachers use in their assessment activities? What techniques do other stakeholders use?
5. Where do teachers fit in the accountability process? What high-stakes decisions must early childhood teachers prepare for?

REFLECT AND RE-READ

- I can define assessment and describe its components.
- I am becoming aware of the diverse views of stakeholders in the assessment process.
- I can explain high-stakes decisions and give examples.
- I have preliminary familiarity with the complexity of assessment issues in early childhood education.

CASE VIGNETTE

Leisel is a 5-year, 11-month-old girl who attends full-day kindergarten in Cincinnati. Leisel has hazel eyes, brown hair, and a fair complexion. She is of average weight and height. Born in Germany, Leisel lived there with her parents until she came to the United States at age 3½. She has no brothers or sisters. Mr. Braun, her father, was transferred to the United States by his employer for a 5-year contract; Mr. Braun is fluent in English. Mrs. Braun is enrolled in English as Second Language courses at Cincinnati State Technical and Community College and works as a nanny in the mornings. Everyone speaks German at home. At the beginning of Leisel's kindergarten year, she spoke no English. Now in the spring, she speaks English and enjoys friendships with peers in school and outside of school. To date, Leisel's school performance is average, according to her teacher, Mrs. Barnes. Is she ready for first grade? How would you find out? What should Mrs. Barnes do to prepare Leisel for first grade?

Source: From L. Spalding, 2003, submitted in partial fulfillment of T&L 411, Assessment in Early Childhood Education: DePaul University. Used by permission.

TECHNOLOGY LINKS

http://apa.org

American Psychological Association. Position papers and books about assessment.

http://www.aera.net

American Educational Research Association. Position papers and books about assessment.

http://www.annenberginstitute.org

Annenberg Institute for School Reform. Position papers on standardized testing.

http://catalyst-chicago.org

School reform journal in Chicago. Articles applicable to urban settings across the country.

http://www.childrensdefense.org

Children's Defense Fund. Statistics and position papers on the lives of children.

http://www.ccsso.org

Council of Chief State School Officers. Position papers and policy statements on best practices in education.

http://www.bc.edu/research/csteep

Center for the Study of Testing, Evaluation, and Educational Policy (CSTEEP). Position papers and policy statements on assessment and evaluation at Boston College.

http://www.ecs.org

Education Commission of the States. Resources for state leaders and others on educational policy issues.

http://www.learningfirst.org

Learning First Alliance. Coalition of associations with projects, resources, and position papers available online.

http://www.cse.ucla.edu

National Center for Research on Evaluation, Standards, and Student Testing (CRESST). Research center that publishes updates and a newsletter, and holds conferences on assessment and standards.

http://www.fairtest.org

National Center for Fair and Open Testing. An advocacy organization with position papers on tests and assessment, a newsletter, and other activities.

http://www.aecf.org/majorinitiatives/kidscount.aspx

Kids Count is a project of the Annie E. Casey Foundation that tracks the status of children.

http://www.naeyc.org

National Association for the Education of Young Children. With particular interest in children from birth to age 8, this site contains links to position papers, best teaching practices, and other items of educational importance to young children and their families.

http://nga.org

National Governors Association. Best practices and position papers of the states, including many resources on NCLB.

http://www.ed.gov

U.S. Department of Education. A source for legislation, government reports, and links to educational issues.

SUGGESTED READINGS

Copple, C. & Bredekamp, S. (2009). *Developmentally appropriate practice in early childhood programs serving children from birth through age eight.* Washington, DC: National Association for the Education of Young Children.

Gonzalez-Mena, J. & Stonehouse, A. (2008) *Making links: A collaborative approach to planning and practice in early childhood programs.* New York: Teachers College.

Gullo, D. F. (2005). *Understanding assessment evaluation in early childhood education* (2nd ed.). New York: Teachers College Press.

Kohn, A. (2004). *What does it mean to be well educated? And other essays on standards, grading and other follies.* Boston: Beacon Press.

Pelo, A. (2008). *Rethinking early childhood education.* Milwaukee, WI: Rethinking Schools, Ltd.

Popham, W. J. (2004). *America's "failing" schools.* New York: Routledge/Falmer.

School readiness: Closing racial and ethnic gaps. (2005). *The Futures of Children,* 15(1).

CHAPTER 2

Developing Family Partnerships in Assessment

TERMS TO KNOW

- parent perspective
- parental reports
- parent questionnaires
- behavior questionnaires
- parent interview
- parents' rights

CHAPTER OVERVIEW

The early childhood assessment process needs parents and family members as key partners. This partnership shapes the nature of future school and child-care communication in the lives of young children. Questionnaires and interviews with parents are part of an early childhood assessment system. The assessment process links families to parent education programs and parent–teacher collaboration efforts. The partnership assessment process lends itself to problem-solving, prereferral activities, and, finally, the formal process for identifying young children who may have disabilities. This chapter rolls out the underpinnings for partnership relations with parents, setting the stage for collaboration in all assessment practices described throughout the book.

ASSESS AS YOU READ

- What do parents know about their children that they can share with teachers?
- What are the best methods for getting information from parents or other significant family members?
- What are the key elements in educating parents about school and schooling?
- Who makes decisions about intervention plans for young children?

FAMILY PARTNERSHIPS IN THE ASSESSMENT SYSTEM

When families enroll their child in a program, the parents—either casually, formally, or informally—will be interviewed by a teacher, director, social worker, or other early childhood education professional. (See Box 2.1 for a sample enrollment interview form.) This interview forms the foundation for the group care and education process for the life of the child; that is, the first experience that families have with intervention programs, child-care centers, or schools forms a lasting impression. It is your responsibility as an early childhood professional to appreciate

BOX 2.1

Parent Interview at Enrollment

Child ___________ Date ___________

Parent/guardian ___________

Tell me about your family. ___________

What kinds of things do you do as a family? ___________

Who works outside the home? Doing what? Hours? ___________

Who should be contacted in emergency? Is this a relative? ___________

What important things do I need to know about ___________ ? ___________

Can you walk me through a typical day in the life of ___________ ? ___________

Could you tell me a little more about playtime, bedtime, family outings? (This is a follow-up question.) ___________

What are your goals for ___________ this year? ___________

parent perspective a parent's perception of a child's development, learning, and education.

the family perspective. In this way, you can care responsively for the young children and families served in your programs. When teachers begin the enrollment process, they need to keep in mind the **parent perspective**, as well as the infant program, child-care center, or school's "need to know."

Teachers Want to Know

Typically, teachers want to know what families think about their child's development, learning, and education. It is also important to know about the cultural and family traditions that shape the family's view on these important parts of child life. Depending on the enrollment situation, teachers and caregivers will need more information and will require special interview skills to acquire this information. Sometimes you will need to use a family-trusted translator to obtain information. You will also need to know who the culturally traditional family gatekeeper is for outsiders to consult about family "business." Finally, you will need to know family and cultural expectations regarding the discussion of potential "problems" with strangers. Often the teacher is a member of a team in the more specialized situations. The information you need depends on your teaching role.

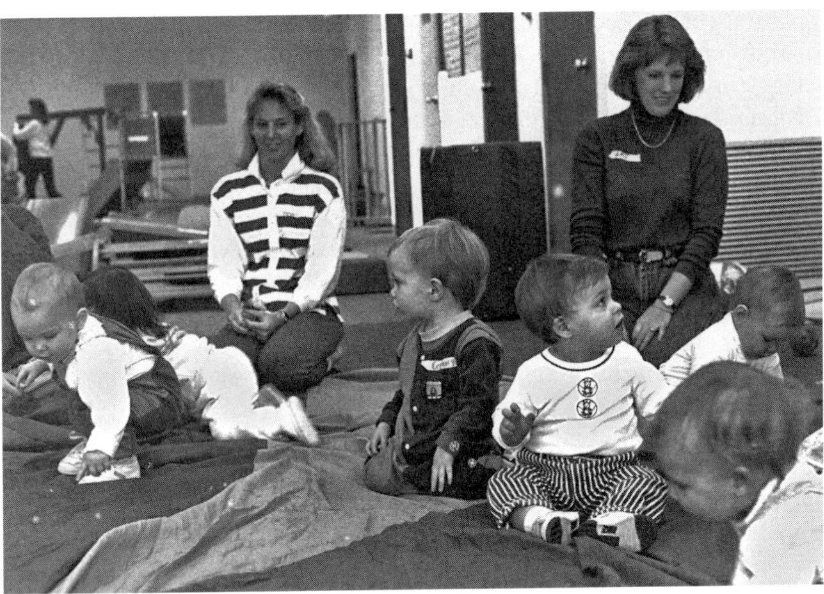

Ms. Vogel, a home-caregiver, requires basic health, safety, and emergency contact information when enrolling baby Leslie. In addition, she needs to know Mr. and Mrs. Jefferson's preferences for naps, feeding, and any special toys that will comfort Leslie. If Ms. Vogel and the Jeffersons are neighbors, the need for additional formal interview may even be less.

As situations become more formal in child-care settings for groups of children, the teacher's "need to know" and the structure for obtaining information becomes more formal. In addition, the issues of cultural group values, language, and social class affect the initial trust for the budding partnership. In situations where young children have special needs and diagnosed disabilities, the teacher needs to know more. In any of these more specialized situations, the teacher relies on consultation or social work intervention that facilitates understanding of the family perspective. The family perspective is the foundation for the development of the Individualized Family Service Plan and an important component of the Individual Educational Plan required by the Individuals with Disabilities Education Act (P.L. 101–476). Sometimes the teacher and the family do not speak the same language. In those cases, teachers will need other personnel who can translate for the family of a young child with a disability. It is critically important that the family's voice be part of the child care or school beginning. Sensitive teachers in any child-care or early education setting are familiar, however, with the many facets that influence the giving and receiving of information to and from families (cf. Berger, 2008; Berns, 2009; Gonzalez-Mena, 2009). As stated in the Division for Early Childhood (DEC) Position Statement on Responsiveness to Family Cultures, Values, and Languages (2002, p. 1), "(R)responsiveness grows from interpersonal relationships that reflect a mutual respect and appreciation for individual's culture, values, and language. . . . Responsive early childhood programs and professionals honor the values and practices within the families." Thus, it is imperative that teachers of young children think about ways to engage families responsively, especially those whose cultures and family systems are different than their own. This includes thinking of information gathering as a conversation rather than a formal "interview." First you must establish rapport with families so that you can collect the vital information that families have to share.

Family Contribution

Families can contribute critical information regarding their children's abilities, strengths, possible problems, and educational needs. Family members have observed their children's behavior in a wide range of situations over a long period. They know whether their child is coordinated enough to play baseball, soccer, or basketball. They know how much sleep their second grader requires to avoid "cranky" behavior. Their descriptions of what their baby or child is doing can provide valuable information about that child's development and personal adjustment. Their questions, concerns, and interpretations regarding their children add an important perspective. As teachers, "we need to examine (diverse and all) families from the standpoint of their own experiences rather than imposing criteria that are not relevant. The 'experts' should be the family members who . . . teach and educate us from the experience of their daily lives" (Erera, 2002, p. 218). As you listen to parents, you find out what they want to know from teachers.

Parents of young children wonder about their child's development: "How is my child doing?" "Is my child doing well enough?" "Will my child learn to read?" "Will my child have friends?" "Will my child learn English at school?" At any given time, the child's parents may be more or less satisfied with what the child is doing, perhaps concerned about the child's development, or may at least have questions regarding the child. Teachers need to know how satisfied the parents are and how and whether they are concerned about something. Often family members are the first people to recognize that their children are not developing well. They may know that their child is "fidgety" or "flighty." Although parents recognize problems and potential problems, they may not be willing to share "everything" they know or "all" of their worries. Skillful and sensitive interviews will permit parents a greater opportunity for sharing their knowledge and concerns.

There is little question that "parents have the most information about the present functioning and past history of the child . . . the parent is the first and often best assessor of his/her child's functioning and problems" (Walker & Wiske, 1981). This important principle is one of those highlighted by the National Education Goals established in 1990. "Parents should be a valued source of assessment information, as well as an audience for assessment results" (U.S. Department of Education, 1991a, p. 6). More than 40 years ago, Gesell and Amatruda (1954) emphasized the importance of involving parents in the identification of developmental problems of their young children. Even then, the point must have seemed self-evident. The Interdisciplinary Council on Developmental and Learning Disorders (ICDL) Clinical Practice Guidelines for Infants, Children, and Families with Special Needs (2000) stress the need for family co-leadership in planning and delivering intervention with their babies and children. This perspective is a shift from mere "family involvement" in which the "expert" determines the intervention or teaching prescription for a child or family. Thus, the foundation for co-leadership is the sharing of information. Through parent conversation at the beginning of programs, teachers meet the fundamental responsibility for "looking at the child as an individual and within the context of family, community culture, linguistic norms, social group, past experience (including learning and behavior), and current circumstances" (Copple & Bredekamp, 2009, p. 10).

Crucial Importance of Family Information

Information from families may cover a wide range of material: medical history and any current symptoms or concerns; the child's current developmental functioning and developmental history; personality and social-emotional adjustment, including behavioral/emotional problems; family information, including relevant stress factors such as loss of a parent through death or divorce; parental loss of employment; and other situational factors that might bear on the child's functioning.

parental reports information from a parent concerning a child.

Although parents possess a wealth of information about their children, one critical question is whether their reports are reliable or accurate. **Parental reports**—information collected by interview or questionnaire about a child, a situation, or problem—are not uniformly dependable; some parents are better observers of children than others. Also, some parents may give biased responses due to their own personal needs. A number of factors influence the accuracy of parental information, including: (a) the parent's willingness to participate, (b) the parent's ability to comprehend the request for information and to provide accurate data about the child, and (c) the professional's ability to create useful parent-involving ways of obtaining information from parents.

However, research demonstrates that parental reports of children's current behavior are usually reliable, especially when teachers obtain these developmental reports through structured interviews or inventories (Liechtenstein & Ireton, 1984). In these situations, parents provide information about their young child's developmental abilities (e.g., "Can your child draw pictures that can be recognized?") in screening and follow-along programs. In some of the first research of this type, Knobloch, Stevens, Malone, Ellison, and Risemberg (1979) used a parent-completed questionnaire including items taken from the Gesell Developmental and Neurological Evaluation to follow high-risk newborns for the first two years of life. In this study, parents' reports were quite similar to the results of professional evaluations. However, parental reports of history or early developmental milestones are not as reliable (Glascoe, MacLean, & Stone, 1991). Parents' concerns about their children's present development and behavioral problems are reliable indicators of problems (American Academy of Pediatrics, 2001; Glascoe, 1998; Tervo, 2009). So, how can families become involved? The best methods flow from the daily or other conversations that teachers have with parents. It is through these contacts that teachers foster "environments in which decision-making with parents is a central tenet of an early childhood program (and) cements the foundation for successful parental involvement in the later years and for positive developmental outcomes for children" (Fields-Smith & Neuharth-Pritchett, 2009, p. 242).

METHODS FOR OBTAINING INFORMATION FROM FAMILIES

Information from families comes to teachers in a variety of ways: informally, in parents' comments about Suzy or Alex; in casual conversations; and in the questions parents ask and the concerns they express. More in-depth information may come in response to your questions at parent–teacher conferences. Sometimes teachers ask families to provide information more systematically through interviews and by completing **parent questionnaires**. Parent questionnaires are sets of questions that collect information from families about the facts and perceptions that families have regarding their child's development and behavior.

parent questionnaires questionnaires given by child-care professionals to parents for obtaining information about a child.

When a child-care center is the first point of entry for a child into the care and education systems, teachers may find an enrollment questionnaire appropriate. Boxes 2.2 and 2.3 show

BOX 2.2

Example of a Program Enrollment Questionnaire

Program Enrollment Questionnaire

Date ___________ Time ___________

Child name ______________________________

Nickname (preferred name) ______________________________

Parent(s) name(s) ______________________________

Address ______________________________

Phone number ______________________________

Parent(s) present ______________________________

With whom does the child live? ______________________________

What do you expect your child to learn and do in preschool? ______________________________

Have you or has your child lived in or visited other places? ______________________________

What types of things do you do together as a family? (vacations, celebrating birthdays and holidays) ______________

Of these, what does your child enjoy most? ______________________________

What does your child do with free time? (favorite activities and interests, likes and dislikes) ______________

Has your child had experience with scissors ______________ paint ______________ play dough ______________?

Does your child listen to stories? ______________________________

Do you spend time reading with your child ___________ coloring ___________ drawing ___________ making things ___________ cutting things out ___________ cooking ___________?

Does your child know colors ___________ numbers ___________ write ___________ emergency procedure ___________ phone number and address ___________?

Does your child have brothers or sisters? ___________

Name(s)	Age/Grade
__________	__________
__________	__________
__________	__________
__________	__________

How does your child get along with siblings? ______________________________

How does your child get along with other children? ______________________________

Has the child been to a babysitter, preschool, or religious school? ______________________________

What is the child's reaction when you leave? ______________________________

How does your child respond to new situations and people? Shy ______________ bold ______________ curious ______________ slow to warm up ______________ initiates conversation ______________

Are there other significant adults in the child's life? (grandparents, aunts, uncles) ______________________________

Does your child pretend in play? Does your child make up friends or places? ______________________________

Is your child attached to a favorite toy, blanket, or stuffed animal? ______

Name of toy? ______

Is your child easily upset? By what kinds of things? Emotional? Fearful? Temper tantrums?

______

______

How do you discipline your child for misbehavior? ______

How does your child respond? ______

Does your child have chores or other responsibilities? ______

Are there any changes in the family—expecting, separation, or divorce—that could affect your child? ______

Are there any physical limitations? (sight, hearing, walking, speech) ______

Is your child frequently ill? (colds, flu, earache, allergies) ______

Does your child take a nap? ______ Sleep patterns: early or late riser? ______

What are your child's eating habits? (meals, snacks, small or large appetite, uses fork and spoon or hands) ______

Does your child have toilet training problems? (accidents, bed wetter) ______

In what ways can we help your child this year? ______

Is there anything else you would like us to know about your child? ______

______

other examples of questionnaires. These questions could form the basis for a systematic interview or the parent could complete the questionnaire alone. An interview conference follows the questionnaire completion.

Parent Questionnaires

Parent questionnaires obtain information similar to that obtained through interviews. Questionnaires completed by families prior to children's enrollment in a program are typically extensive and include questions about the child's health, development, personal habits and preferences, family information, and so on. Usually, such questionnaires include present status and history, such as medical history. These questionnaires serve as an adjunct to the Child Find screening process used by Head Start and other programs that seek to identify young children with disabilities. Typically, the parent questionnaires do not provide any guidelines for interpretation. Sometimes, briefer questionnaires determine more narrowly the child's present development, learning, or adjustment. Often questionnaires are included with published screening instruments that a child-care center or school may use to identify young children at risk for special educational needs or interventions.

Using parent questionnaires routinely prior to parent-teacher conferences often sets an agenda or focus for the meeting. Sometimes parent questionnaires assist teachers in understanding parental perceptions of developmental or educational issues when children present learning or behavioral concerns. Using parent questionnaires can benefit parents and teachers in the following ways:

- Parents have an opportunity to thoughtfully describe their child, answer questions, and express questions and concerns.

BOX 2.3

Child Information Collected at Enrollment by Interview or as Questionnaire

Date ____________________

Child's name is ____________ but likes to be called ____________

Parent/guardian name ____________________

Medical conditions that affect child's activities ____________________

Emergency contact relative? ____________________

Don't ever contact ____________________

Allergies ____________________

Fears ____________________

Favorite toy ____________________

Favorite game ____________________

What does your child do well? ____________________

After-school activities (e.g., What does the child do? Go home? Go to a babysitter? Go to an after-school program?) ______

____

Getting ready for school on a typical day: ____________________

____

Weekend routines: ____________________

____

How do you handle problem behaviors? What are some that you deal with regularly? Occasionally? ____________

____

How would you like to be involved with the school? Is there anything that would make it difficult for you to come to the school?

____

____

- Teachers have advance information, so surprises may be limited.
- Teachers can assess whether the parents and teacher are in accord.
- Questionnaires may inform a later discussion.
- Teachers have an opportunity to educate or communicate program goals to families.
- Families may feel included, respected, and empowered through the responsibility acknowledged for completing the questionnaire.

Questionnaires are of limited value when parent literacy in English is an issue. As well, oftentimes questionnaires do not reflect the nuances of cultural values that may influence the parent's view of development, learning, and behavior. Nevertheless, they may be useful in some situations. One such situation may be when the parent or teacher is concerned about behavioral problems.

Behavior Problem Questionnaires

The design of behavior problem questionnaires gives parents an opportunity to report any behavior problems, usually not to describe the child's overall adjustment. Typically, these questionnaires couch behavior in terms of problems or symptoms and may include a few related questions (Perrin, 1995; Haynes, Hersen, & Heiby, 2003). Usually these brief **behavior questionnaires** do not have norms but may be useful in early childhood settings as part of a screening process for the identification of children who are at risk of disability.

behavior questionnaires questionnaires designed to give parents an opportunity to report any behavior problems of their children.

One limitation with most of these questionnaires is that they address one primary area (e.g., behavior) to the exclusion of other areas. Comprehensive questionnaires that address children's development, learning, adjustment, and health, including both strengths and problems, are more useful for teachers. An example of one such overall instrument is the Child Development Review–Parent Questionnaire (CDR–PQ). The Child Development Review–Parent Questionnaire (CDR–PQ) (Ireton, 1997) is a comprehensive survey of the child's present functioning that covers development, learning, adjustment (including behavior problems), health, vision, and hearing. The CDR–PQ includes six open-ended questions and a 26-item problems list. The CDR–PQ is standardized and there are norms for parents' responses to the six questions and the frequencies of the problem items by age and sex. Validity studies have shown that certain problem items are associated with placement in early childhood special education: These items include difficult-to-understand speech, clumsiness (poor walking and running), poor comprehension, and immaturity (Ireton, 1994). The instrument functions as an adjunct to an enrollment parent conference that follows a month or so after children begin in a program. An example of its use is as follows.

One early childhood teacher used this systematic approach with more than 100 parents of three- to six-year-olds in her preschool program (Ofstedal, 1993, personal communication). She found that parents welcomed the opportunity to complete the questionnaire, that completing it contributed to rapport, and that parents and teachers discussed and dealt with many more issues than in past conferences. Parents' reports helped the teacher prepare for the conference, including bringing along relevant materials for parents. Ms. Ofstedal reports that Bill was 4 when he started at the center. She immediately noticed how bright and curious he was, and was interested to see how his parents filled out the review, wondering what they thought about their son's progress. As she read the report, she saw that Bill's mom addressed many concerns. Ms. Ofstedal soon met with her to sort out her thoughts. She gathered information for the parents concerning disobedience, poor listening skills, and hyperactivity. Bill's mom was excited to have concrete methods for handling situations. Ms. Ofstedal assured her that Bill was busy, but delightful, in school. He just needed structure and guidelines. The parents and Ms. Ofstedal met several times and the parents soon began to see positive changes in their son at home. They spent some "quality time" each day with him and established "rules" for him to follow.

Ms. Ofstedal noted: "Bill is the type of child a teacher loves to have in school. He is excited about everything and anything and flourishes in a structured environment. Our conference could have been 20 minutes of me praising their son without hitting on any of the serious problems they were having at home."

Another popular questionnaire process that is widely used in early childhood programs is the *Ages and Stages Questionnaire,* 3rd ed. (Bricker & Squires, 2009). Parents complete this 30-item illustrated questionnaire at designated intervals. The questionnaire functions as a way to help parents and teachers know about any potential developmental issues in five key developmental areas: communication, gross motor, fine motor, problem-solving, and personal–social. The questionnaires begin at age four months and continue through five years of age. Once completed, teachers convert the parent response to determine a child's progress in each developmental area. In addition to the questionnaires, learning activities are available for both family and teacher use. The activities support early childhood teachers and programs by identifying ways to enhance development related to the five key areas (Twombley & Fink, 2004).

Limitations of the Questionnaire Process

Use of parent questionnaires depends on how comfortable and able parents are to respond to paper-and-pencil forms. One advantage of questionnaires is that they provide advance information that can help focus an interview with the parents. Another advantage is that they may save some professional time, because teachers can read the questionnaires more quickly than they can ask questions and listen for responses. However, questionnaires are a one-way communication device. That is, the teacher cannot observe the parent response. Thus, valuable clues about comfort with the questions and knowledge of their purpose may be lost.

In addition, questionnaires have serious limitations when parents and teachers are communicating in different languages. Paper forms may inhibit the candor with which parents approach the center when parent literacy is a factor, when cultural norms find paper-and-pencil formats "less than friendly," or when parents are enrolling children for less than "choice" reasons.

For example, the public aid caseworker tells Susan Teenager that she must enroll her three-year-old in the local "at risk" program and attend classes to secure her GED. Susan may have many mixed reactions about "the fact" of her child being "at risk," sending her baby to school, attending school herself, and—not the least—"growing up" as another single parent in her peer group. A questionnaire may heighten her feelings of vulnerability or attack her autonomy. After all, she may feel uncertain of her mothering capacities, as well. Susan may choose to answer the questions haphazardly or she may not answer them at all, thus starting the baby's career with "a bad taste" toward teachers in the early childhood setting. A paper cannot answer her questions, comment on what a happy baby she seems to have, and so on.

In addition, many questionnaires lack any kind of standardization. Standardization of formal assessment instruments is an important issue that you must consider when choosing questionnaires. Both the *Child Development Review* and the *Ages and Stages Questionnaires 3* are notable exceptions; both are standardized. In the technical reports available for these questionnaires, you will find ample documentation of research conducted to support both the development and use of these instruments. When choosing or developing your own questionnaire, you must ask yourself: "Why am I asking the questions?" "Will the information help me teach Johan better?" "Am I just being nosy?" If Johan is allergic to chocolate, this is an important piece of information; therefore, asking about allergies is important. Discovering who lives in the home may be an interesting fact to know about, but Johan's parents may find it intrusive. Maybe you will learn this information later in the collaborative partnership. If Arlene's mother is worried about whether her daughter is too "shy" as a three-year-old, this is valuable information that establishes a conversational base for a discussion. You will be able to share your observations from the class and be able to clarify her mother's concern.

Teachers need not know everything immediately. Teachers and parents can communicate regularly and elaborate their partnership. One of the ways that this may happen is through the interview process.

Parent Interviews

parent interview an interview of a child-care professional with a parent for determining how well a child is doing.

Conversations with family members are the most natural situations for teachers to talk with them about their children. There is no substitute for talking with family members about their children. Parents usually enjoy this if they feel comfortable and respected. Sometimes a more systematic **parent interview** that uses set questions or prompts can provide a survey of what the child is doing and tentatively determine how well the child is doing. Particular attention and sensitivity is important when interviewing parents from a culture other than your own. In addition to being respectful, you will want to ask about such things as how long the family has lived in Los Angles? Denver? Or Des Moines? Do they have any relatives in the area? What languages are spoken at home? Does the family use TV to help them learn English? What languages does Cecilia speak at home? Elsewhere? What is a typical day at home like for the family? How does this compare with their experiences in Peru? Interviews work best when the process keys to parental perceptions, concerns, if any, and questions about the child.

For example, Ms. Hawk, a teacher at Corporate Center Child Care, is curious about Tina. Tina entered Corporate Center Child Care about a month ago. She is making some friends and has explored the room and the activities with enthusiasm. Ms. Hawk wants to meet with Tina's mother, Ms. Banker, to check out Ms. Banker's perceptions and to sustain the budding teacher/parent partnership. Ms. Hawk asks the following questions:

- What interests Tina lately?
- How do you see Tina as a person?
- What do you see her strengths to be? How is she special?
- Do you have questions or concerns about her development? Learning? Behavior? Health? Other?
- How are you doing as a parent?
- Is there anything else you can tell me that would help me to understand Tina?

It is usually best to begin by asking parents for their current observations of their child. Asking about their questions and concerns helps to determine how satisfied or concerned they are about their child. When there are concerns or problems, asking families for their ideas about what is wrong, involves them in all aspects of the assessment and educational process. Parents' spontaneous observations of their children may include three kinds of "observations":

1. Descriptions of what the child is doing, including comments about what the child is not doing yet.
2. Questions and concerns regarding whether this is "normal" or not.
3. Attempts to explain "why" this is the case.

For example, a two-year-old child's mother may say, "He is not talking a lot yet, not as much as he should be, but his big sister is always there, handing him things when he makes noises." Please notice that parents engage in the same processes of observation and interpretation that professionals do. An example of another instrument that facilitates the gathering of information to create parent-teacher partnerships is the *Infant-Toddler and Family Instrument* (Provence & Apfel, 2001). The *Infant-Toddler and Family Instrument* (ITFI) "help(s) home visitors and other frontline staff members organize their impressions of family and child well-being. The ITFI includes three components—a parent/caregiver interview, a developmental map, and a checklist of concerns about the child and family" (Apfel, 2001, p. 29). Besides this and other questionnaires found in many early childhood screening kits, some teachers choose to use interviews. As you will see, a variety of formats and issues relate to interviewing.

Interview Formats

Formats differ in the amount of structure prescribed and the amount of latitude allowed the interviewer and the parent. Even a so-called "open-ended" interview has a limited purpose and encompasses a finite amount of territory. Within these boundaries, the interviewer begins with broad questions and continues with focus questions to elicit information from the outlined scope. Teachers tailor the selection, phrasing, and sequence of questions in an open-ended interview by parents' preceding replies. Thus, no two interviews proceed exactly the same way.

Hirshberg (1996) describes the critical importance of listening and withholding judgment as the interview goes along. He also identifies the importance of being clear about the purpose of the interview and ending it with a summary of learned information so that the parent and teacher leave the experience on the same footing. This clinical approach to interview is widely used by social workers, psychologists, and psychiatrists. Teachers and others can employ the principles while sticking to the dimensions of their knowledge (i.e., education and development). Some guidelines to help move the interview along include using transitional phrases, such as *I see, umm;* paraphrasing and restating to be sure that you understood what Mr. Halsted really said; summarizing your understanding based on what you heard to allow Mr. Halsted or Ms. Delta to say, "Oh, no, I meant . . ."; and expressing empathy with what Ms. Delta or Ms. Gazelle said, such as, "Oh, how wonderful that your daughter qualifies for gymnastics," or "My, that will be a challenge to have your husband's family move into your three-room house for a month," and so on. Another interview format used widely in early childhood settings is the structured interview—a format that may be more comfortable for the novice teacher to employ.

In a structured interview, the interviewer asks a predetermined set of questions, usually with the same wording. A branching structure for these interviews introduces some flexibility. For example, if the parent answers "yes" to a question about noticing unusual speech behavior, the interviewer would then ask "What seems to be unusual?" or a related series of questions (e.g., "Is your child's speech intelligible? Does your child speak in sentences?"). The branching questions use some preestablished rule. A structured interview requires less interviewing skill than an open-ended interview, where the professional is simultaneously interpreting data and deciding what to ask next.

Such approaches to interviewing ascertain developmental and curricular concerns of families, as well as serving as information-seeking tools for teachers. This involves answering questions about curriculum and instruction as well as behavioral expectations and home support of the child-care and education program. These conversations help the family–teacher partnership identify goals and topics for educational programs. For example, many parents of preschoolers want to know about "nightmares." What causes them? How do other parents handle them? Do they ever go away? Parents of third graders may wonder whether their children will pass the state-mandated tests. Teachers can delineate both the curricular support for required outcomes and identify ways that parents may support the learning of their children. These concerns and others may come from the conversations, questionnaires, and interviews and can form the basis of the parent-education agenda. Box 2.4 shows evolution of one school district's approach to parent interviews and screening for incoming kindergarteners.

BOX 2.4

Example of Kindergarten Enrollment Process

Every January, in anticipation of the upcoming school year, the Morris Early Childhood Center in the Milford School District announces kindergarten registration and school readiness screening in the local newspaper and greater school community. Families are encouraged to register early to assist the school district in establishing the new kindergarten classes and secure appropriate numbers of teachers. Each family is required to bring the following information in order to register their child for school: the child's original birth certificate; Social Security card; immunization records; insurance card; any pertinent custody information; and proof of residency in the school district, such as a driver's license, lease, mortgage agreement, or utility bill. Once the child has been successfully registered for school, the child's family historically received a kindergarten screening appointment.

As part of this process and in alignment with other school districts in the state, the Milford School District selected the *Developmental Indicator for the Assessment of Learning*, Third Edition (DIAL 3) as their screening instrument. As part of the DIAL 3, each of the children participated in a variety of developmentally appropriate assessment activities, while the families were asked to complete the Parent Questionnaire component of the screening tool. The questionnaire is composed of five parts asking for the parent/family perspective of the child's overall development, including child's health history, background, and self-help and social development (Mardell & Goldenberg, 1998).

After the screening process, the screener, the child, and the family met to review the scores and discuss any questions or concerns regarding the screening and/or general transitioning to school. In the event that the child's performance scores indicated a need for any additional evaluations by the school psychologist, this was also an opportunity to discuss that option. When the children and families completed the screening process, the school administration used the data gained to assist in creating heterogeneous classrooms that represented a variety of school readiness ability ranges. The screening scores were then shared with the assigned classroom teachers to serve as initial student assessment data. The screening information is always kept in the child's cumulative school record and is available for reference to authorized personnel as deemed appropriate throughout the school year.

Beginning in 2009 with the implementation of the recent federal legislation referred to as Response to Intervention (RTI), the Milford School District decided to no longer screen children prior to their entrance to kindergarten. Under the state guidelines for RTI, all children must participate in a school-wide screening three times per year and the district decided that the assessment data obtained through the RTI screening would be helpful data in guiding student instruction and was partially redundant to the school readiness screener. The district, however, was hesitant to lose the parent perspective gained through the traditional screening process and decided to work with a team of school psychologists, speech therapists, kindergarten teachers, and administrators to develop a parent/family questionnaire unique to the Milford School District so the early childhood center would still be able to learn about the children before they start school. The team was sure to include questions about the child's developmental milestones including speech, walking, and/or socialization, which are intended to serve as potential indicators as to whether there might be cause for a follow-up screening for more norm reference screening in addition to the fall RTI screening at the onset of the school year. See the parent questionnaire shown in Figure 2.1.

In the following vignettes, meet some of the kindergarteners, and the pictures created through the interview process.

Meet Thomas

In August, Mr. and Mrs. Smith, parents of Thomas, saw the advertisement for kindergarten registration in the local newspaper. They eagerly waited for the opportunity to register another one of their children for school despite the mixed feelings about their "baby" going off to school. Even though Thomas had been attending child care since infancy and they have older children, the idea of another one of their babies going to school brought about many mixed emotions. Thomas is being raised in a household composed of his biological mother, stepfather, two older brothers, two older sisters, himself, and two younger brothers. The primary language spoken in their home is English and the family reports his strengths to be his soft-heartedness, his helpfulness, and his intense desire to please others. The family also shared that Thomas gets along very well with others and suspects that this is due to his many siblings. They indicated they were looking for a loving, encouraging, and patient teacher, as they fear he may be slow to catch on sometimes, because they feel he is unable to attend to things for an extended time period. They shared that he is eager to go to school and wants to learn like his older siblings.

Meet Evelyn

Evelyn, five years old, lives in a household with her three-year-old sister and one-year-old brother, and is being raised by a single mom. Her mother describes Evelyn as being very independent but good at compromising when necessary. She shared a concern about her ability to get along with others, because the daily medication she takes to treat her diagnosis of Attention Deficit/Hyperactivity Disorder (ADHD) can cause side effects in her behavior. Her mother describes these behaviors as that she does not want to be bothered by others or interact with anyone. When asked how the teacher could best help Evelyn this school year, her mother indicated, "Nothing, really" before adding, "She needs help learning how to write her last name and recognize the alphabet. She can say the alphabet and write her first name but she doesn't know how to spell out loud "Evelyn" if asked." When asked about Evelyn's interests and potential after-school activities, Evelyn's mother shared that she is very involved in her church, as her grandmother has been taking her to church. She explained, "Her teacher might sometimes see Evelyn playing church by praising the Lord and singing church songs." The only concern shared by Evelyn's mother was that she has the tendency to suck her thumb and pull her ponytails and braids. She asked the teacher to stop her if she could but warned, "It's gonna be hard but just bear with her."

Meet Arnold

Arnold is a student getting ready for kindergarten and has participated in the kindergarten registration and screening process, despite the fact that he already as an Individualized Education Plan (IEP) identifying him as an early childhood student with a developmental delay, which has made him eligible to participate in the Milford School District's Special Needs Pre-Kindergarten Program. Although Arnold receives occupational therapy to assist with his fine motor skills through the Pre-Kindergarten Program, his family reported one of his strengths to be that he enjoys being a writer in the Pre-Kindergarten Writing Center, where he often generates detailed stories. The family reported other strengths, including his persistence and caring nature. When asked about which activities Arnold enjoys, they shared that he loves to read books, make up stories, play football, soccer, and swim. Arnold reported, "I really like books, ninja turtles, and power rangers!" The family shared that he loves to learn and is excited about school but can be shy about the unknown. They feel he will easily adjust to kindergarten but expressed that he can get frustrated when things such as handwriting get tough. They also indicated that although Arnold gets along well with others, he has a sensitive side and can have his feelings easily hurt by others. They would like to see him build confidence and reinforce persistence when things get tough. They expressed great interest in learning more about what they can do to help him be successful in the formal school setting. They summarized the family questionnaire by noting that Arnold is a "Great kid with a big heart" and encouraged his teacher to "Enjoy him!"

Meet Jerlyn

The greatest strength of Jerlyn, also known as Jeri, as reported by her mother, is "Talking." Her mother explained that she doesn't mind all the talking, because "She didn't talk much before she got the tubes put in her ears." She lives with her mother, father, grandmother, grandfather, one older brother, and one younger brother. Her mother reported that she does not feel Jeri has any potential learning problems, but feels "Her maturity is a little low." She reports that she gets along exceedingly well with others, particularly her new younger brother, Scott. Mom also reported she is excited about going to school, as she has been exclusively home with a parent or grandparent and does not have any formal school or daycare experience outside their home. She asked her teacher to send home any additional practice work for anything she may have trouble with but indicated that she feels her child is doing well in all major areas of development.

Child's Name: ______________________ Today's Date: ______________

Morris Early Childhood Center
Milford School District

E. I. Morris Early Childhood Center

WELCOME TO THE MORRIS FAMILY!

As your child's parent/guardian, you are their first teachers and we value your input as to the best way to work with your child! To better get to know your child we ask that you complete this questionnaire. We thank you for your time and look forward to learning and growing with your child! Remember, at Morris, we come to learn!

CHILD'S PERSONAL INFORMATION

Child's Full Name: ______________________________

Person completing this form: ____________________ Relationship to student: ______________________

Home Address: ____

Phone Number: ______________ Child's Birthdate: ____________ (month/day/year) Gender: M F

Name/Nickname your child will use at school: ______________________________

Child's Race/Ethnicity:
____ African American ____ Native American ____ Asian/Pacific Islander
____ White/Caucasian ____ Latino/Hispanic ____ Other

Primary Language Spoken in the Home: __________________________________
Does the child speak English? : Y N *Do the adults at home speak English? Y N*

Biological Father's Name: ____________________ Biological Mother's Name: ______________________

Adults who currently live in the home with the child:

Name	*Relationship to Child*
____________________	________________________
____________________	________________________
____________________	________________________

Adults who have legal custody of child: ____
(Please submit any legal custody paperwork)

Please explain if there has been any involvement with the Division of Youth and Family Services? ______________
____

Child's Brothers and Sisters:

Name	*Birthdate*	*Does this child live in the home?*
______________________	____________	Y N
______________________	____________	Y N
______________________	____________	Y N
______________________	____________	Y N
______________________	____________	Y N

Please note any disabilities, delays, emotional concerns or diagnoses of the child's siblings:

FIGURE 2.1 "Welcome to the Morris Family!"

Child's Name: ______________________ Today's Date: ______________

CHILD'S BACKGROUND INFORMATION

Was there anything unusual about pregnancy or birth with this child? Y N Length of pregnancy: ___________

If yes, please describe:____

____

Weight of child at birth: __________ *What was the mothers age at birth?:* ________ *age of father?:* ________

Did the child go home with his/her mother from the hospital? Y N

If no, please describe:____

Was the child in an Intensive Care Unit (ICU) or special care nursery? Y N

If yes, please describe:____

Has your child had any of the following?:

___ Adenoids removed ____ Head injury _____ Seizures

___ Frequent ear infections ____ Vision problems _____ Encephalitis

___ Ear tubes ____ Asthma _____ Tonsils removed

___ Broken Bone (*explain*:: ____)

___ Allergies (*explain:* ____)

___ Food/Diet restrictions (*explain*: ____)

Please describe any major illnesses, surgeries, hospitalizations:____

____

Please list all medications:____

Has your child been diagnosed with any condition (please specify condition, date and doctor)?:____________________

____

Has your child's pediatrician had any concerns about your child's development? Y N

If yes, please describe:____

____

CHILD'S EARLY DEVELOPMENTAL INFORMATION

Please provide approximate age your child achieved the following developmental milestones:

_____ sat alone ____ babbled ____ said one word ____ put two words together

_____ walked ____ became toilet trained ____ learned the alphabet ____ spoke in full sentences

Has your child received any of the following?:

____ Speech Therapy ____ Physical Therapy____ Occupational Therapy _____ Counseling

*If yes, with what agencies:*____

Has your child or family been provided services from the following agencies?:

____ Childfind _____Early Choices ____ Parents as Teachers ____Headstart ____ Other

Please explain: ____

Can grandparents/family/relatives understand when the child speaks? Y N

*If no, please describe:*____

____

Is your child aware of, or frustrated by any speech/language difficulties? Y N

*If yes, please describe:*____

____

FIGURE 2.1 *continued*

Child's Name: ______________________ Today's Date: _______________

Did your child attend daycare, nursery or pre-school? ___Never ___ In the past(not now) ___Yes

*If yes, please provide location(s):*____

____

Has your child's teacher(s)/day care provider(s) expressed any concern regarding your child's progress? Y N

*If yes, please explain:*____

____

Please list any organized and/or extracurricular activities that your child has participated in:

____

Please note whether this N (never), S (sometimes) or O (often) occurs for your child:

Plays cooperatively with other children	N	S	O
Will ask other children to play	N	S	O
Obeys teachers and other adults	N	S	O
Is difficult to calm down	N	S	O
Prefers to play by him/herself	N	S	O
Sleeps with parents	N	S	O
Can pay attention for 5-minutes	N	S	O
Has unusual rituals or behaviors	N	S	O
Separates easily from parents	N	S	O
Makes eye contact	N	S	O
Has temper tantrums	N	S	O
Is hyperactive	N	S	O
Cries excessively	N	S	O
Obeys parents	N	S	O
Aggressive behavior	N	S	O
Stutters	N	S	O
Worries	N	S	O
Lying	N	S	O

Please place an X in the column that best describes your level of worry about each area of your child's development:

Area of Development	My child is doing OK	I'm a little worried	I'm somewhat worried	I'm very worried
General Development				
Health				
Motor Skills				
Understanding and thinking skills				
Speech and Oral Language Skills				
Social skills				
Vision				
Hearing				

Has your child experienced any significant life stressors (i.e. divorce, death of parent, sibling, exposure to trauma/traumatic events, frequent moves, family in the military, etc.)?:_______________________________

____

What are your child's strengths and interests? ____________________________________

____

Is there anything else you feel the school should know about your child?________________

____

What would you like for your child to learn in kindergarten?

____

I would like to speak with the school nurse: Y N I would like to speak to the school counselor: Y N

Thank you for taking the time to complete this survey, we value your opinion and welcome you to the Morris Family!

FIGURE 2.1 *continued*

Child's Name: ______________________ Today's Date: ______________

FIGURE 2.1 *continued*

PARENTS' EDUCATIONAL PROGRAMS

When talking with parents about their children, teachers also learn a lot about how they are doing as parents. Conversations with parents often show how much parents enjoy their child, or identify how frustrated or discouraged they are, and give some idea if there are particular or unusual stressors in their lives. When trying to appreciate how well a parent is doing, it is wise to avoid "diagnosing" them. Instead, try to appreciate their efforts and strengths, as well as recognize their difficulties. This knowledge can form the backdrop to develop parent-education programs. Develop such programs in collaboration with families. This avoids the past tradition of parent education that treats the parent as someone who needs to know rather than someone who brings a set of understandings and curiosities to the process. More appropriately, families assess their own needs, seeking assistance from teachers and others when needed.

The following example shows parents' responses to different parent programs. Inner City Preschool Program A offered "parent education programs" on topics selected by the staff. Topics included "Discipline for 3-Year-Olds," "Nutritious Snacks," and so on. Two parents out of 40 came to each of the sessions. Inner City Preschool Program B scheduled a craft-making meeting. Informally, while making "bleach bottle" baskets for their children, the 20 (out of 40) parents shared experiences and discussed alternatives. Topics ranged from child discipline to managing coupon shopping to new ways to make macaroni. The parents planned to meet again and asked the teacher to schedule a child literacy expert as speaker. The difference between the two scenarios was that parents were in power in Program B. They were assessing their own needs and seeking resources as necessary.

This same parent empowerment can happen at the primary level when teachers find out what parents want rather than try to give parents what they think they need. For example, the teacher may want parents to learn how to teach their children multiplication or may want them to get their kids to bed before 10 P.M. Parents may be more inclined to come to a meeting about science fair projects using household objects or coming to support a special event at the school. Through the informal conversation, teachers have a chance to introduce some of the "parents need to know" items on their agenda. In addition, teachers and parents may increasingly avail themselves of electronic options for informal contact: e-mail, web page chat rooms, or blogs. The point is that whatever the age and stage, parents and teachers can collaborate in the best interests of children. Some out-of-the-box thinking on both sides facilitates a parent education program that accomplishes teacher and parent goals.

There are exceptions to cooperative parent interactions. That is, sometimes teachers must face challenging parents. These include hostile parents, uncooperative parents, perfectionist parents, arrogant parents, dependent parents, overly helpful parents, overprotective parents, and neglectful parents (Seligman, 2000). Using a family systems view, teachers can try to understand the context that leads parents to adopt these roles. Teachers can then appreciate the strengths that parents bring to the care and education session and call on support staff (i.e., social worker or counselor) to assist those who need the extra intervention to support themselves and their children. Before assigning the "difficult" descriptor to parents, teachers need to be sure that they do not stigmatize parents or children, particularly those with disabilities. Parents who have watched adults withdraw from their children may fear this attitude when they have children who drool, speak unclearly, or in other ways seem "different." Teachers need to avoid "blaming the victim," because parents are sensitive about their children who may display symptoms of disability. They may be doing all they can with Sally, who is constantly in motion. Try to remember that teachers and parents are usually on the same side—wanting the best interests of young children to be at the forefront.

Sensitivity to family interests and understandings is particularly important in settings with a diverse population. A special challenge is often the monolingual English-speaking teacher and parents who speak different languages. Conversations through a translator are often stilted and strained. As well, the choice of translator and understanding of parental perceptions of trust related to the translator influence the validity of the conversation. Keep in mind, as well, that families may choose to listen rather than offer their own perceptions due to their view of status differences between teachers and parents (Ramsey, 2004). Additional important considerations that affect teacher–parent communication and collaboration are teacher assumptions that parents share the same belief structure and values. Both may assume that the "home" culture is superior. Prejudice and stereotypes may influence trust in relationship building. Finally, each may be more or less comfortable with the communication styles and procedures of the "other" (Taylor, 1998). As teachers are in the "power" or "expert" position, respect for each child's home culture must be clear and valued (NAEYC, 1996; Copple & Bredekamp, 2009). As part of the assessment process, culture influences all aspects of parent collaboration and communication. A particularly delicate time for honor and respect of diversity is when the family is the client.

Even in these situations, the family must be empowered to prioritize the family intervention plan in collaboration with the relevant professionals. In these cases, a family specialist is the point person in developing rapport and helping parents to establish priorities. Teachers in these situations participate as team members who will follow the directions developed by the family specialist and parent.

In all situations, teachers must establish relationships with parents. These serve to facilitate the young child's adjustment and success in child-care and education settings.

FAMILY–TEACHER COLLABORATION

Knowing the families and their priorities, as well as their child, contributes to effective collaboration. Working with families is a basic tenet of "best practice" in early childhood instruction and assessment. The challenge of finding ways of involving families in the assessment of their children's developmental and educational strengths and problems continues. Although useful methods for obtaining developmental information from parents do exist, professionals' skepticism regarding parental ability to be objective about their children limits the use of this information source. It does appear that teachers and others often give less credit to parents than they deserve for providing valuable information regarding their children's development. In fact, parents may be quite useful in rating the everyday cognitive abilities of their children. Using the *Parent Ratings of Everyday Cognitive and Academic Abilities* (Dewey, Crawford, Creignton, & Sauve, 2000), a recent study showed that parent ratings may be a useful aid to the clinical determination of reading disabilities and attention-deficit/hyperactive disorder (Dewey, Crawford & Kaplan, 2003). Doctoroff and Arnold (2004) report similar findings using parent structured interviews, teacher observation, and parent rating scales.

Collaboration at the assessment level sets the stage for collaboration at other levels. Family involvement begins by providing the parent with an opportunity to report on the child's development and to raise concerns or questions, if any. Assessment data collected and based upon both parent information and on teacher observation, as well as any testing of the child, provides a sound basis for appreciating the child's abilities and educational needs. A positive, informative relationship with parents will be helpful to the parents as well as the child. A school program with these elements optimizes the prospects for making appropriate decisions and lays the groundwork for effective parent–school relationships. In fact, Dunst and Trivette (2009) report that following parent leads in intervention leads to improved child outcomes.

When teachers know the family priorities, as well as observe and record carefully, they can share meaningful examples of child learning with families. Hannon (2000) shares first-hand experience of her growth as a teacher when applying this technique. Besides observing and recording specific behavioral examples for kindergartners, Hannon interviewed the children about their progress, choosing what to say to parents in collaboration with the kindergartners. Thus, Hannon modeled the partnership of teacher, learner, and parent from the earliest days of education. This partnership forms the foundation for prereferral collaboration of parents and the school or child-care setting. "Best practice" includes parents in the assessment process from program beginning through the year and into the transition for the next program. Particularly, when parents and teachers use a problem-solving approach (Kroth & Edge, 1997; NCPIE,

2009), they display a spirit of cooperation that focuses on "the issue" rather than assigning responsibility. For example:

Parents' Thoughts

- If you were a better teacher, this wouldn't be happening.
- Don't bother me with this school stuff.

Teacher's Thoughts

- You're not a good parent; you don't care.
- Didn't you teach your child manners?

Before these tentative perceptions are hardened into beliefs and distrust, teachers and parents need to meet to discuss problems, perceptions, and differences. Then, child, parent, and teacher can feel comfortable about the resolution.

You also need to be familiar with the cultural values for each of the children and their individual families. This includes knowing how the family defines deviancy or difference, as well as their behavioral norms or expectations, which can influence the family's opinions and actions, in addition to acceptable places for the family to seek guidance (Takushi & Uomoto, 2001; Banks, Santos & Roof, 2009). This knowledge is particularly important when considering whether to suggest a formal referral for specialized assessment when you suspect that a young child may have disabilities. In addition, you must be thoroughly familiar with the legal and ethical rights of the parents whose child you may refer for evaluation.

VOICES FROM THE FIELD

Kindergarten Teacher; Holistic Assessment for All Stakeholders

Most of the assessment that I conduct is authentic. Work samples collected over time are very helpful to show parents a child's progress or lack of progress. In addition to work samples, I observe a lot and write anecdotal notes and running records.

I do use workbooks and Benchmarks from our reading series, Storytown (http://www.harcourtschool.com/storytown/) and will use the assessment materials included in our new math series, enVision Math (http://www.pearsonschool.com). We also use Reading A–Z (http://www.readinga-z.com) for language arts skills assessment. In addition, we administer DIBELS three times per year. But I assess each child individually with the workbook and worksheet materials, so that it is low-stress and more like an interview.

Although the school does not have a formal kindergarten screening program, I have a set of checklists that I use to assess children informally for teaching purposes, e.g., letter knowledge. Mostly, I observe and start collecting materials for the working portfolio on each child.

Through the Writers Workshop, children learn to assess their own learning progress and to be peer editors. Once a month, I meet with each child and they select the story they are most proud of. Then, we publish it.

> *Our report cards are checklists for each of the content areas and social skills. In the past, these were distributed four times per year; next year, we will distribute three times per year, so that the last two quarters are not so squashed. We meet with parents in individual conferences in November and April. The turnout for these conferences is 100 percent; if not on the designated day, parents request make-up times.*

PARENTS' RIGHTS

Referral of a child for evaluation by a specialist—psychologist, speech therapist, social worker—is a formal step in the life of the child and family. Federal, state, and local legislation govern the process. At the federal level and since the first legislation requiring that all children

parents' rights as specified in state and federal law, parents are assured that schools and agencies will fully involve and inform parents in the care and education of their children.

with disabilities would have a free appropriate public education (P.L. 94-142, 1975), the law assures parents of the following best practices and **parents' rights**:

- Notice that you intend to refer their child will be given.
- Written permission will be obtained from parents for any formal evaluation.
- All evaluation information will be kept in strict confidence.
- Assessment must be conducted with instruments that are nonbiased.
- Assessment must be multidimensional.
- Assessment must be conducted in the child's native language.
- No single test score may be used to place a child in a program.
- Assessment results will be shared with parents.
- When parents disagree with the school's assessment, they have the right to an independent assessment at public expense.
- Permission will be obtained for any specialized educational services.
- Parent involvement in the development and annual review of Individualized Family Service Plans (IFSPs) or Individualized Educational Plans (IEPs) is manded.
- Parents have the right to appeal plans and decisions made by the educational agency or school.

In addition, the 1997 amendments to the Individuals with Disabilities Education Act (IDEA) assure parents that schools and teachers:

- Will secure *informed* parental consent prior to evaluation or reevaluation. This means that teachers and schools must explain the rationale and process for assessment to parents in ways that they understand. Thus, signing on the dotted line of a generic form—"test my kid"—is no longer possible.
- Will provide notice to parents that they may seek an external evaluation.
- Must collaborate with parents in the development of the IEP. This provision is strengthened with the latest reauthorization of the legislation (U.S. Department of Education, IDEA, 2004). Now collaboration is similar to the process that already exists in the birth-to-three-years range, where the plans take the lead from parents.

Ethical practice grounds all of these legal requirements regarding cooperating and planning with families. Parents have a vested interest in their child's learning, know aspects about their child's strengths and interests that may be helpful in planning educational interventions, and can rehearse or in other ways assist their child with becoming an effective student. However, parents of children with disabilities have special challenges as parents. Often, extra care and teaching at home is required so that their child can keep up. They must help the other children in the family understand the limitations as well as the strengths of their sibling. Sometimes they must cope with the special challenges of child behavior in public that may seem unusual to passersby.

All of these stresses and particular issues may be present even before you consider referring a child for assessment. So, sometimes parents are not ready to hear what you have to say even though they may share some of your impressions about the developmental progress of their child. When such is the case, you must support the parent's decision to wait and see before embarking on a formal assessment. You can encourage parents to think about assessment and from time to time bring data forward about their child. With permission from other parents, you can link them to others who may have faced similar challenges. In many cases, parents will be ready for the assessment step. Therefore, ethical practice principles will be a natural outgrowth of your work with families when you are discussing any special need regarding their child. Some behaviors on your part that will contribute to a breakdown in the process include treating parents as vulnerable clients, being aloof in your conversations about their child, treating all parents as if they need counseling, blaming parents for the behaviors of their child, treating parents as if they were not intelligent, and treating parents as adversaries and labeling them as "difficult," "resistant," or "denying" (Heward, 2009, pp. 104–106). Thus, you must be prepared to meet the parents where they want to start and responsively engage in problem-solving in the best interest of their children.

SUMMARY

When embarking on the road to family partnerships, teachers must remember that partnership implies *partner.* Respect and appreciation for the complex roles of families will ensure the beginning of a smooth and productive relationship in the best interests of children. Parents must be involved in providing information about their children so that teachers may effectively care for and educate them. Child-care and school personnel must understand the values and conventions that shape parent practices and perceptions. Together, families and teachers nurture children so that they may grow to be self-confident, happy, and capable young students. Teachers of young children bear the responsibility for setting the stage for all future school relationships. Many parents of young children have learned to be advocates for their children through the partnership relationships established and utilized in the best interests of young children.

FIELD ACTIVITIES

1. Visit a child-care facility in your community. Ask for a description of enrollment policies and procedures. How are families involved in the process? Do you think the procedures match the potential population?
2. Choose a questionnaire or structured interview. Try it out on a volunteer parent. Summarize the results of your experience. What conclusions can you draw about the parent and about the process? Compare your experiences to those of your classmates.
3. With permission, review the entrance forms or other parent-interview material in the files of two children. Observe the children. Make a tentative judgment about the progress of the children from the time of entrance into the program. Discuss your assessment with the classroom teacher.
4. With permission of the teachers and parents involved, observe several interviews. Write up your understandings, protecting the confidentiality of the parents. Share your experience with your colleagues.

IN-CLASS ACTIVITIES

1. Identify family child-rearing customs—feeding, sleeping, toileting, chores, and so on—and child management techniques—time out, withholding privileges, reasoned discussion, and so on—that members of the class use with their children or that they remember from their experiences as children. Develop an interview protocol to capture this knowledge and experience. Describe how the results fit into an assessment partnership.
2. Think about a child in your program (or a program that you observe) that presents problems. Describe the problem behaviorally. For example: Florence often interrupts children in the story circle when they are responding to questions or making comments. Decide whether she interrupts in other parts of the day. Identify any other behavioral issues that Florence presents. Plan a parent conference to discuss the matter with Florence's parent(s). Pair up with another student in your class to critique and revise your plans.
3. You are teaching in a preschool that recently began accepting young children from immigrant families. Outline a plan for learning more about the new culture. Develop strategies to communicate with families that will honor their perspective of family and school communication.

STUDY QUESTIONS

1. What biases might a teacher carry that may influence family participation? How can teachers overcome biases they may have?
2. How important are parent reports? What information gleaned from parent reports will be most useful to teachers?
3. How are parent questionnaires most effective? What are their limits?
4. What may influence a teacher's decision in using a behavioral or developmental questionnaire? What are some strategies to implement in requesting parental input on such questionnaires?
5. How can the teacher use parent-teacher interviews most effectively? What approaches are most effective in encouraging participation in family education programs?

REFLECT AND RE-READ

- I know some ways to gather information from families.
- I have some ideas about establishing rapport with families.
- I could develop an outline for a parent education program.
- I can identify preliminary questions to problem-solve with parents about educational or developmental issues.

CASE VIGNETTE

Jasmine, your new third grader, lives with her parents—Mr. and Mrs. Burling—and an older brother, Jarrett, who is 12. Anecdotal notes in Jasmine's file depict Jarrett as very protective of Jasmine on the playground and around school; they seem to enjoy a very close relationship. Until this September, Mrs. Burling stayed home with the children and volunteered at an Arts Club after school where Jasmine spent many happy hours. According to records, Jasmine is a bright, motivated, and capable learner. Mr. Burling learned in late August that his job as a computer programmer is in danger; he may be laid off. Mrs. Burling is thinking of looking for work, as the family worries about medical insurance coverage that may be jeopardized with Mr. Burling's unemployment. What classroom plans will you make to support Jasmine through the family crisis? How might you see the effect of the crisis in the classroom? What referral support may you need to offer Mr. and Mrs. Burling?

Source: From Y. Jeong, 2002, submitted in partial fulfillment of T&L 411, Assessment in Early Childhood Education: DePaul University. Used by permission.

TECHNOLOGY LINKS

http://clas.uiuc.edu

Culturally and Linguistically Appropriate Services Research Institute. This site "identifies, evaluates, and promotes effective and appropriate early intervention practices and preschool practices that are sensitive and respectful to children and families from culturally and linguistically diverse backgrounds."

http://www.eparent.com

Exceptional Parent. Covers all aspects of parenting children with disabilities.

http://www.famlit.org

National Center for Family Literacy. Contains program suggestions, statistics, and links to research about the relationships of family literacy, parent involvement, and child success.

http://www.familiesandwork.org/index.html

Families and Work Institute. Research institute on families, work, and communities; focus is on contemporary issues.

http://www.pta.org

National Parent Teacher Association. Hints for parents to promote school success, resource guide on diversity, and other current issues. Some resources available in Spanish.

http://www11.georgetown.edu/research/gucchd/nccc/

National Center for Cultural Competence. Organized "to increase the capacity of health care and mental health care programs to design, implement, and evaluate culturally and linguistically competent service delivery systems to address growing diversity, persistent disparities, and to promote health and mental health equity."

http://www.nhsa.org

The National Head Start Association. This is the advocacy organization for families and children in Head Start. There are links to family-friendly information.

http://www.puckett.org

Orelena Hawks Puckett Institute. This not-for-profit organization seeks to "foster adoption of evidence-based practices that build on the capacities and strengths of children, parents, and families, communities, and public and private organizations."

SUGGESTED READINGS

Barton, P. E. & Coley, R. J. (2007). *The family: America's smallest school.* Princeton, NJ: Educational Testing Services.

Brooks, J. B. (2008). *Process of parenting* (7th ed.). New York: McGraw-Hill.

Gaitan, C. D. (2004). *Involving Latino families in schools: Raising student achievement through home-school partnerships.* Thousand Oaks, CA: Corwin.

Gonzalez-Mena, J. (2009). *The child in the family and the community* (5th ed.). Upper Saddle River, NJ: Merrill/Prentice Hall.

Hale, J. E. (2001). *Learning while Black: creating educational excellence for African American children.* Baltimore: Johns Hopkins University Press.

Lynch, E. W. (2004). *Developing cross-cultural competence: A guide for working with children and their families* (3rd ed.). Baltimore: Paul H. Brookes.

Polakow, V. (2004). *Shut out: Low income mothers and higher education in post-welfare America.* Albany: State University of New York.

Seligman, M. & Darling, R. B. (2007). *Ordinary families, special children: A systems approach to childhood disability* (3rd ed.). New York: Guilford.

Turnbull, A. & Turnbull, R. (2006). *Families, professionals, and exceptionality: Collaborating for empowerment* (5th ed.). Upper Saddle River, NJ: Merrill/Prentice Hall.

CHAPTER 3

Observation as the Key Method in the System

TERMS TO KNOW

- observations
- observation records
- anecdotal notes
- running records
- class journals
- checklists
- frequency records
- event sampling
- time sampling
- rating scales
- portfolios
- documentation panel
- formative evaluation
- summative evaluation

CHAPTER OVERVIEW

The cornerstone of an assessment system is child observation. This chapter describes the observation process, methods for recording information, and procedures for interpreting and using the results of observation. Emphasized in the discussion are the important procedural and ethical responsibilities and variables that lie beneath this seemingly straightforward activity that is anything but casual. Incorporated in the discussion is the role of observation in the development of portfolios and documentation panels.

ASSESS AS YOU READ

- What is the difference between watching children play or work and observing them?
- How do you choose a recording method?
- What goes in the portfolio? How is it different from a "laundry basket of stuff"?
- Why do we need tests if we observe the children regularly?
- Why must time be budgeted for observation?
- What are the limitations of observation? How do you avoid bias in the process?

OBSERVATION IN THE ASSESSMENT SYSTEM—PLANNING, DECIDING, AND RECORDING

Teachers make many important decisions that affect the lives of children. Observation is the basis for many child-care and educational decisions, both informal and formal. Teachers decide what to teach on a day-to-day basis for a group of children and how to individualize activities for particular children. Teachers decide what kinds of materials and equipment to use to carry out the curriculum. Teachers decide whether to use themselves in the teaching process as models, as guides, or as directors of the learning task. Finally, teachers set up rules and expectations about how the children will interact with each other.

Teachers Are Decision-Makers

observations systematic means of gathering information about children by watching them.

Observations of the children in the program inform the decisions of teachers. Observations are the most important assessment tool, more so than any book or set of packaged tests. Teachers spend several hours a day with the children they teach. Teachers who regularly and systematically observe young children use the soundest informational basis for curricular and instructional planning. By knowing what to look for and how to observe children, teachers make accurate inferences regarding the needs of children.

Both preschool and primary teachers learn more about young children by using the observation process. Also, family intervention specialists observe babies as part of their work. By keeping their eyes open, teachers and interventionists gather the information needed to assess developmental progress. They find out how well the children in the program are learning and how they get along with other children, teachers, and other adults. Teachers decide whether to begin, continue, or change an activity. They decide which children to group in various activities based on what they see.

The records of these observations allow teachers to reflect and to inform decision-making. The records also document progress, which is useful for filing reports and report cards and for discussion in family conferences. Thus, early childhood education programs must include all of the following forms of **observation records**:

observation records written records of the observations of a child, including anecdotes, daily logs, and in-depth running records.

- Brief, casual anecdotal observations of various children throughout the day, perhaps recorded on sticky notes
- Daily logs written at the end of each day
- In-depth running record observations, about 10 minutes long, of particular children or situations
- Samples of children's artwork or other graphic depictions
- Documentation of the curriculum with display panels, large charts, or other visuals
- Teacher- or program-developed prepared forms that include focus points for notes
- Reflective journals focusing on group issues regarding curriculum or behavior
- Concept map that shows how children are processing information (e.g., what do they know about fractions?)
- Graphic organizers that show the curricular topics explored by individuals or the class

Regular, data-based decision-making is important to the early childhood program. Teachers want to avoid "hit or miss" decisions so that they do not misjudge children and their progress. All teachers want to help children learn and adjust. No one wants to be judged on the performance of

an "off day." Nor do teachers want to base all curricular decisions simply on a child's "peak performance." Spotty observation notes may not catch the whole picture of the child. Think of observation notes and records as snapshots in the classroom lives of children. Teachers want notes to show all the angles: front, side, back, and three-dimensional. Choosing one or several of the ways to record observations suggested here and using them regularly for all the children in the program ensures "full-color portraits."

In summary, the questions that teachers ask and answer while teaching include the following:

What does Jon know about the alphabet?

What can Helen do in math?

How does Marvin get along with other children?

How does Paul get along with teachers?

How does Brad get along with his parents?

How can I help Juanita learn to tie her shoes?

Does Carol understand how to sum two-digit problems?

Can Alan illustrate his understanding of the story?

Shall I put all the three-year-olds together for finger painting?

Should I put the story time before lunch?

What memories does the class have about our trip to the apple orchard?

My class seems to be humming along; shall I make any changes?

The answers to these questions come from observing the children. In fact, teachers make assessment decisions several times a day to inform their practice.

Insights from observation are the basic tools of assessment for early childhood education. Further testing of a formal nature may be necessary in some cases. Insights gained through observation will help decide when, whether, and how to use formal tests as part of the program. Observation records serve as a "check" on formal tests or as a valuable baseline for deciding whether to refer a child for formal study. Teachers gather important insights from observations to share with parents in conferences and in reports. With parents, teachers use observational insights to decide whether to refer an individual child for further assessment that may lead to the provision of special services for a particular child.

Summarized observational information on all the children in the program provides important evidence for administrators and other decision-makers. Such material can help in program evaluation that shapes and directs plans for the future. These summaries can serve as documentation of effective practice and prove the need for continued or enhanced funding of programs.

Because teachers want to make these decisions and reports effectively, they must develop assessment plans that are comprehensive, yet realistic. Not every procedure suggested in this chapter is necessary for every child. However, the plan for each child must represent techniques that will provide insights on all aspects of each child's development and learning in the program. To ensure that a plan is comprehensive, use many methods (multiple measures) to observe each child in multiple settings. This practice also enables the teacher to gather insights about how the group is behaving and learning. For each child, report on the basic areas of development: motor skills, language, intellect, social skills, and self-esteem. More detail will be required if there is a specific concern about David, Walter, Jose, Esther, or Chelsea.

Practicing Being a Better Observer

Observation is a skill sharpened with practice. Teachers have already had considerable practice in it. Teachers observe children in a variety of situations throughout the day. To practice observing more keenly, begin in a small way by watching the children's interaction—for instance, in the block corner—for 5 or 10 minutes a day or at the science learning center. Also, be aware of what

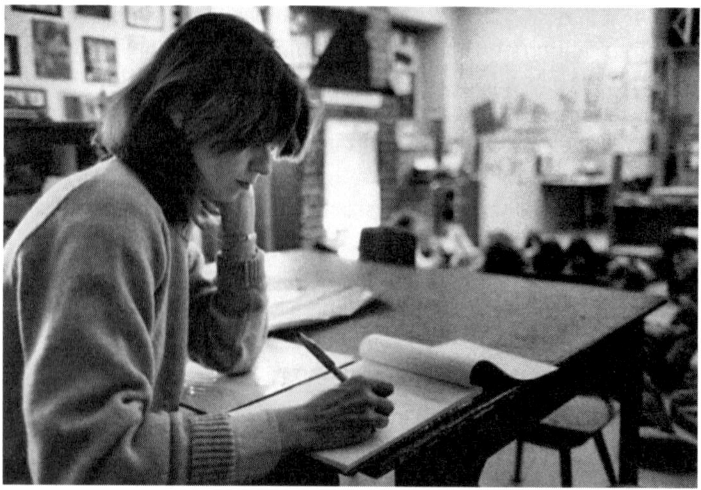

you bring to the situation—your culture with beliefs about child-rearing, appropriate ways to communicate, child independence, and so on; your personality, your temperament, interests, and feelings; and your professional experience (Jablon, Dombro, & Dichtelmiller, 2007).

Thus, as Ms. Wolf watches and records what she observes in good detail, she considers whether she is objective as she writes notes about Albert, Pablo, and Keisha, who are building in the block corner. She asks Ms. Brown—as a second teacher, a supervisor, or a teacher aide—to observe the scene with her and to listen to the report. Through the discussions, Ms. Wolf sees whether she observed similar behavior as the second adult and whether their conclusions match. This is a good check on the accuracy of the data. Almost certainly one of them will pick up a detail or two that the other missed.

To sharpen your observation skills, imagine that you are looking at a video recorded on your first birthday. At first, the camera shows the whole party scene: the balloons, grandparents laughing and watching, and the older children at play. Then it moves closer to capture you diving into the cake with two hands. With this favorite scene on DVD, you can review it and enjoy the experience all over again, seeing things that you may have forgotten—the color of the napkins and balloons, the exact expression of Aunt Mimi, and so on.

Think of yourself as that camera. First, note the complete "party" of your classroom. Then observe smaller groups of children involved in various activities. Then move in on the group in the doll corner, with close-ups of the individual children. At even closer range, you record one child's facial expression and wonder about the emotions reflected by it. At this natural level of observation, you are primarily noticing and describing. Your observations will be of great use when it comes to discussing a child with parents. However, your observations will be of use long before that. Observations will reinforce (or perhaps lead you to question) your general impression of the child—individual style, peer relationships, problem-solving skills, and so on. Observations will contribute to your appreciation of each child in your care as a unique individual, and to your empathy for each child—even for a misbehaving child. In addition, the observations will teach you much about your class as a group—material that can be applied to future planned activities. Your observations help you to read situations and children.

Planning for Observations

To plan for observations, first list your questions. Decide what insights you want to be able to write down about all the children in your program. Decide which children you may want to learn more about. Examine the performance standards or outcome statements required by your program, agency, or state. What outcome evidence will you need to support reports on specific children to document development and learning? Here you are defining what to observe and the focus of your observation. Is Jeanie really in constant motion? Can Elton work by himself on a writing project? Is Anita pinching other children? How long does Charles work in the block corner? Is Erica directing the play in the doll corner? How is Christopher doing as chair of the social studies project? Decide what you want to be able to tell parents at report time. Decide what information your principal or director will require about the children in your class. Determine which "lens" you will use for observation. Examples of observational focus include:

1. ***Learning climate*[1]*:*** The personal interactions—the ways in which the members of the classroom community interact. These include student-to-student interactions, teacher-student, and teacher-multiple-students exchanges (Berry & Mindes, 1993). You will assess whether the personal interactions are working for your class by observing with this focus. Are the children relating to each other with respect? Do you manage conflict so that children are empowered to settle matters between and among themselves effectively? Is everyone cooperating in group-based activities and projects? Is there a sense of caring in the classroom community?
2. ***Classroom management:*** Routines facilitate efficient accomplishment of everyday tasks and promote a sense of structure and predictability about the days and weeks of school. These include activities such as hanging up coats, distributing papers, lining up, and reporting attendance. With this focus, you observe whether your class has a relaxed, efficient flow. With a focus on rules and expectations, are the predictable consequences providing for the security of classroom citizens? Are the behavioral guidelines reflecting the values of the school community? Are there ways that you might involve students in the creation and modification of classroom rules that will ensure the practice of classroom democracy? (See Berry & Mindes, 1993.) Are the learning centers working well?
3. ***Lesson clarity, variety, task orientation, and engagement:*** With this focus, children are following directions, staying on task, and engaged in learning. You can document that you are offering varied activities and scaffolding learners for success. In addition, you can determine that the schedule is working for the whole and individuals. Do you have the right balance of large group, small group, and individual activities? Is the sequence of activity right?
4. ***Child or student achievement success:*** Focusing on child progress toward program outcomes will be an on-going focus of your observations. You will be documenting student achievement as well as identifying problems that may be occurring. From the documentation of problems, you will develop interventions to try, so that individual children and the group of children can be successful in their learning and developmental progress. Observational notes will help you think through solutions for modification of tasks and structure of learning for the group as well as individuals.
5. ***Evidence of higher-order thinking:*** As a check on child progress, you want to document evidence that the activities and engagement of class members show cognitive sophistication appropriate for the developmental stage. Do the activities require creativity and cognitive sophistication? Over the academic year, do children show deepening knowledge, skills, and dispositions? Is there evidence of appropriate logical reasoning and concept acquisition?

After you have the questions in mind, choose the ways to record that will give you the insights you want.

The outlines in Boxes 3.1, 3.2, and 3.3 highlight the kinds of questions you may want to keep in mind so that you can report completely on each child. You do not have to answer all questions for every child, but use the questions to help you pinpoint descriptions for each child.

---

[1]Lens are adapted from Borich, G. D. (2008), *Observation skills for effective teaching* (5th ed.), Upper Saddle River, NJ: Pearson/Merrill, pp. 16–17.

BOX 3.1

Suggested Observation Outline

General Overview

- Expressions: cheerful, bland, angry, and so on?
- General tempo: active, plodding, and so on?
- Alert, energetic, or listless and apathetic? Variable? If so, why?
- Dressed well or disheveled?
- Runny nose, eyes, and so on?
- Specific personal habits you notice (e.g., chewing hair, sucking thumb, and so on)?

Gross-Motor Skills

- Seems agile?
- Uses climbing apparatus well?
- Runs smoothly?
- Jumps on two feet?
- Hops on one foot?
- Gets up and down stairs?
- Throws and catches a ball?

Fine-Motor Skills

- Strings beads?
- Grasps a crayon, marker, or pencil well?
- Stacks a tower of blocks?
- Manipulates a puzzle?
- Chooses small manipulatives to work with (small blocks, and so on)?

Speech and Language

- Uses language to express needs?
- Speaks clearly or mumbles?
- Speaks both to children and adults?
- Understands what you say?
- Follows directions?
- Answers questions?
- Speaks only one language or parts of two languages in a bilingual home and/or school environment?

Cognitive Skills

- Can identify objects?
- Can identify objects in pictures or books?
- Can name some colors?
- Can count to 2? 10? 20? 100?
- Can learn new words quickly?
- Can recognize letters or numbers?
- Can solve problems: reflective, impulsive?

Relationship to Adults

- Discriminates between teachers and visitors?
- Calls teachers by their names or calls them "teacher"?
- When asked, knows teacher's name?

- Seems overdependent on adults?
- Appears defiant toward adults?
- Is cooperative, resistant, too compliant?

Relationship to Other Children

- Plays cooperatively?
- Shares materials?
- Becomes anxious when other children want to share?
- Teases or provokes other children?
- Hits or behaves in an aggressive manner?
- Is withdrawn or uninvolved?

Relationship to Self

- Appears self-confident?
- Appears to know who he/she is?
- Can tell own full name?
- Can tell about own likes and dislikes?
- Can tell about own family? house?
- Possesses self-help skills?

Free Play or Self-Selected Activities and Interests

- Finds occupations during free time or self-selected time?
- Plays with other children (solitary, parallel, cooperative, games with rules, rough and tumble)?
- Stays with activity or flits frequently?
- Uses materials appropriately, creatively?
- Requires an adult to initiate activity?

Group Activity

- Makes required oral or movement tasks?
- Sits with group during activities?
- Is attentive and cooperative?
- Needs the help of an adult to attend?

Transitions

- Moves easily from one activity to another?
- Requires frequent reminders from adults?
- Responds to prewarnings or announcements that a change of activity is coming?

Routines

- Follows schedule?
- Is self-reliant?
- Remembers structure?
- Challenges rules and expectations?

General Impressions

- General areas of strength?
- Any weakness?
- General areas of skill?
- Any particular impressions?

Modification of Baumann, McDonough, & Mindes, 1974.

BOX 3.2

Infant and Toddler Observation Categories

Object Manipulation

- Play with toys? Which toys? How?
- Uses specific features of the toy (pulls string, pushes buttons)? Which? Ignores other features (e.g., lifting lid)?
- Combines toys or real objects (spoons, cups) in pretend play? How?
- Imitates actions observed in the environment (pushes stroller with dolls)? How? What kind?
- Users any strategies to solve problems? How? Amount of persistence?

Derived from Higginbotham & Pretzello, n.d.

The categories of focus in Box 3.3 are broad and will require additional definition as you organize for a particular observational lens. That is, what is the question that you want to answer? Do you need to know whether your class can assume the responsibility of a longer-term cooperative assignment? What evidence will you need to establish this perception? Is Leonard ready to work independently on a week-long project? Is Cora ready to write a summary of her science experiment? Has she shown the ability to observe carefully? Does she have the handwriting and communication skills that are necessary? And so, you shape the observation and documentation process depending upon purpose.

In addition to developing your own observations systems as shown, you may wish to collaborate with colleagues to utilize a standardized instrument such as the Classroom Assessment Scoring System (CLASS) (Pianta, LaParo, & Hamre, 2008). CLASS is "a system for observing and assessing the quality of interactions between teachers and students in classrooms. (It) measures instructional and social interactions proven to contribute to students' academic achievements and social competencies" (http://classobservation.com, accessed June 17, 2009). The

BOX 3.3

Observation of Individuals in Primary Classroom

Shows evidence of:

- ability to classify concepts using graphic organizers, worksheets, and class discussion
- identifies similarities and differences in concepts, stories, experiments and other academic situation
- can summarize knowledge on a topic
- responds to reinforcement of effort by persisting in academic activities and projects
- can represent knowledge in words, pictures, charts and other written products
- uses cooperative group productively to accomplish assigned tasks
- engages in problem-solving for projects and activities
- shows ability to organize learning in words, pictures, charts
- demonstrates specific knowledge in subject areas as required by the curriculum outcome goals

Derived from the principles discussed in Marzano, R. J. and others (2005), *A handbook for classroom instruction that works*, Alexandria, VA: Association for Supervision and Curriculum Development.

system is also frequently used (and required) by program administrators as part of teacher and program evaluation. This standardized systems offers the following descriptive categories for observation and assessment:

1. Positive climate; relationships, positive affect, positive communication, respect
2. Negative climate: negative affect, punitive control, sarcasm/disrespect, severe negativity
3. Teacher sensitivity: awareness, responsiveness, addresses problems, student comfort
4. Regard for student perspective: flexibility and student focus
5. Behavior management: clear behavior expectations, proactive, redirection of misbehavior, student behavior
6. Productivity: maximizing learning time, routines, transitions, preparations
7. Instructional learning format: effective facilitation, variety of modalities and materials, student interest, clarity of leaning objectives
8. Concept development: analysis and reasoning, creating integration, connections to the real world
9. Quality of feedback; scaffolding, feedback loops, prompting thought processes, providing information, encouragement and affirmation
10. Language modeling: frequent conversation, open-ended questions, repetition and extension, self-and parallel talk, advanced language. (Pianta, La Paro, & Harme, 2008, p.16)

The observer records impressions on a seven-point Likert Scale with notes to support the ratings. "The CLASS is a multifaceted observation system that requires in-depth training for appropriate use" (http://www.brookespublishing.com/store/books/pianta-class/index.htm, accessed June 17, 2009). This instrument is a holistic observation approach that can be used by teachers to reflect upon practice, as well as by administrators to evaluate teacher effectiveness. Before embarking on this kind of multi-faceted and complex system or when you do not have access to such a system, you may wish to think about linking your own purposeful observations to various ways of recording and reflecting upon your experiences with children in your care.

Recording Observations

There are many ways to record observations, varying from brief notes to extensive running records. Some ways require lots of time, so teachers need to plan what the children will be doing while they are observing. For example, it is very hard to record detailed observations while you (as a teacher) are telling a story, leading a song, or taking children on a walk. The detailed observations are best conducted during free play or while primary children are engaged in project work. If there is extra help in the classroom, a teacher can sit and record details during large-group time. Also, teachers can train assistants and others to help in this kind of observation or invite a supervisor or colleague to help with the task.

Some observational records can be done more casually and even by reflection. In planning for observational assessments, you need to be sure that you include different kinds of observations for each child. The *first rule* of any assessment plan is to make multiple measures, so be sure to collect several samples of observations on all the children. Three of the most common methods for recording observations—anecdotal notes, running records, and logs or notebooks—are described in the next section.

These are naturalistic observations: "live" recordings that allow you opportunities to look at the same notes at different times and to gain new information or insights about what you saw each time. The following guide in Box 3.4 was created from ideas presented in various forms by early childhood professionals who have worked hard to make observation a skill that is available to our field. Included are ideas from Almy and Genishi (1979); Cohen, Stern, Balaban and Gropper (2008); Cook, Tessier, and Klein (2008); and Greenspan (2003).

anecdotal notes brief notes of significant events or critical incidents in a particular child's day.

ANECDOTAL NOTES **Anecdotal notes** are brief, accurate notes made of significant events or critical incidents in a particular child's day. For example, if a child who has never talked in

BOX 3.4

What Should I Do to Record Anecdotes and/or Running Record Observations?

1. Look at one child or situation. Be sure to observe all children at different times in the day over the course of the year. By the end of the year, you can probably answer questions about each child and how the child fits into the routine of your classroom. Questions that you may wish to answer to give a complete description of Gene, Lorraine, Bernadine, or Stephen include the following:

- **a.** description: physical appearance, expressions, agility, general tempo, moods, problem-solving style, and communication style
- **b.** attendance and arrival: start of the day, response to overtures from friends and teachers
- **c.** relationship to teachers and children
- **d.** relationship to materials
- **e.** relationship to routines
- **f.** approach to tasks

2. Write down exactly what a child is doing. You should be like a camera, recording what you can see. All the details should be recorded so you can remember later what happened and can interpret the behavior. For example, "Joshua played in the block corner for 20 minutes" is a sparse note. All that you can interpret from this note is that Joshua can concentrate. Details describing what he built, whether he constructed things by himself, and whether he was using a theme or merely stacking blocks and knocking them down gives you much more information to work with in figuring out later what Joshua's development is like.

3. Focus on one child at a time, recording peer interactions as they affect the focus on that child. It may be hard to write down the language of several children. They are all talking at once and may not be talking to each other. It is also easier to file materials about one child and to be sure that you have a range of material on one child if you focus on one child at a time. Occasionally, however, when two children interact, the observation can serve a dual purpose.

4. Be sure to record the observation in the same order that events occurred. For example, "Sara cried, threw a doll at Marcia, and grabbed her arm in pain." What really happened is that Marcia socked Sara, Sara grabbed her arm in pain, cried, and then threw a doll at Marcia. The interpretation of Sara's behavior will be different depending on the order in which the events are recorded.

5. If group dynamics are the focus of the observation, do not try to record every word said. Record key phrases and use arrows to show action between children. You probably will use this approach when you are trying to solve a classroom grouping problem or a social-behavior problem. That is, can Kevin and Arthur ever be placed in the same small group? How can I get Sylvia and Rose to broaden their jump rope group to include Suzanne?

6. Record in a style that is convenient for you. You may wish to develop your own abbreviations and symbols to help you in writing quickly. For example, T for teacher, first initials for children's names, and shorthand for objects (e.g. hse for house, blk for block, bk for book, and so on).

The purpose of the observation will shape the way you record. For example, if you wish to keep a record of all your 35 third-graders using art media, you will need to know which students you have observed. One way to remember is to write each child's name on a flag that you put around a pencil—one pencil for each child. Place all the pencils in a cup on your desk; have an empty cup beside the full one. As you record a note on each child, move the pencil to the empty cup. Watch your progress as one cup fills and the other empties (Greenberg, 1991, personal communication).

The major advice in keeping observational records is to make the system easy for you. Keep pens and pencils handy—in your pocket, around your neck, in magnetic boxes attached to furniture, and so on. Notebooks and papers of various kinds should be readily available. Some teachers like to use sticky notes on the spot and place them on paper for filing. Various-sized cards can be arranged and rearranged with notes for the summarization process.

Letter-size paper can be divided into sections for four to six children. After observations are entered, the paper can be cut into pieces for filing.

7. Collect regular information on a child; observe the child at different times in different settings. Avoid recording only negative incidents or only positive behaviors.

8. Be sure to schedule observations. Plan to observe only a few children each day. It is too hard to teach and record lots of observation notes each day. You want to participate in the play or discussion, so you have to think about what you are teaching, as well as the effect of the teaching on each child. Four children are a suggested number to observe in a whole day. Four observations on each child each month will give you 36 to 48 notes for the year. You then have many rich details

Dot	Harold
Ryan	Elsie
Jon	Gavriela

to share in reports to parents and information on which to base trend statements about each child in your program. For example: Veronica enjoys putting puzzles together. She has put puzzles together every day for the last six weeks. Donna organizes the play in the housekeeping corner. She decides whether the girls will be ballet dancers or whether they will be psychologists and then gives everybody a part to play. The girls cooperate with her.

Avoid recording running records on stressful days (e.g., parent night, first day after vacation, field trip days, and so on). Of course, if a critical incident occurs, by all means jot down the anecdote.

9. Another way to organize the scheduling aspect of observations is to pick a subject. Observe art one week, science the next, math the next, and so on. Collect information on Keisha, Andy, Arnold, Alex, and Otto for each subject.

10. Be discreet when observing. That is, record your notes so that the child's work or play is not disturbed. If children ask what you are doing, you can say that you are writing, because you like to write about children's play or work, and you are making notes to help you remember.

11. Be aware of your reactions as you are observing. What are you feeling about the action that is occurring? In a separate section of the notes, jot down these notions. Refer to them later as you try to understand what your opinion is about an individual child. For example, as I watched Luz-marie struggle to communicate with Tom, I felt pleased that she was making an effort to make her self understood. Or, as I watched Leo flit round and round the room, bumping into things, I felt exhausted and frustrated. These notes to yourself will help in the interpretation of the observations.

12. When you finish an observation session, jot down any question, ideas, and conclusions that pop into your mind about the observation. These notes will be useful for the summarization.

13. Maintain confidentiality of notes. Don't leave them out where the casual visitor can find them. Stress the need for confidentiality to all staff and volunteers who may be involved in recording observations.

class begins speaking, the teacher writes down what she said and under what circumstances she spoke.

- Valerie, age 3, arrives breathless, having run from the corner of the street. Valerie's mother trails a few steps behind, smiling broadly. Valerie jumps up and down in front of you, yelling "puppy, puppy." Her mom confirms that indeed the family now has a new puppy at home. Valerie's teacher, Ms. Sizemore, records this dated and timed note on the notebook in her pocket and makes a note to add books about puppies to the book corner. She does all of this while listening to Valerie, her mother, and the other children who are arriving. Alternately, Ms. Sizemore records the incident as soon as she can, keeping track of all the relevant details for Valerie's file.
- In another case, Ms. Weffer is working with Maureen, who often hits other children. One day Maureen and Peg are playing in the block corner. Maureen has used almost all of the blocks of

the foot-length size for her house. Peg has been asking her for some of them to complete her own house structure. She gives up on asking and begins to pull her foot back, as if to kick at Maureen's house. Maureen screams at Peg, "STOP, don't you dare knock my house down! I told you to get out of my way." Maureen starts to march toward Peg with her hand outstretched. Peg, anticipating the slap, retreats hastily away. Ms. Weffer moves quickly to the block corner before Maureen has a chance to swing. She commends Maureen for talking about the problem (though it was at scream pitch) and tries to help the girls figure out an agreeable way of sharing the blocks. Ms. Weffer records this anecdote as soon as possible for Maureen's record, so that she can begin to mark her progress toward verbal problem-solving strategies.

- For science time in first grade, the class divides into groups to make charts about caring for the classroom plants, fish, and gerbil. You notice that Rhoda is sitting silently in her group. Roger, a member of the group, asks Rhoda a direct question. She doesn't answer. Rose asks her a question and she answers. You make a note of this *anecdote*. You will want to follow up on whether Rhoda only responds to the girls in the room, had some special stress that day, whether she habitually daydreams, or whether the observation is a isolated experience not seen in other small- or large-group experiences.

The anecdotes serve as notes for further substantiation, documentation, and ways to explore behavior for patterns. (See Boxes 3.5 and 3.6 for sample blank forms to use in your program.) A more detailed form of this kind of observation is the running record.

BOX 3.5

Example of an Anecdotal Note Form

Anecdotal Note Form

Name of child observed: __________

Date: __________ Time Period: __________

Context (who is involved, where, what preceded the event)

____

____

What exactly is happening? Be sure to record in the order of the events. Write down exactly what is said. Use abbreviations to be sure to get the detail.

____

____

____

Questions that you have. Ideas to explore. Tentative conclusions—to be verified with other observations or sources.

____

____

____

____

Teacher's signature __________

*When observing interactions among children, list all children. Use arrows and other abbreviations to show interactions and conversation.

BOX 3.6

Example of an Anecdotal Note Observation Form

Anecdotal Note Observation Form

Name of child: __________

Time: __________ Date: __________

Objective for this observation:

____

____

List of others in the context (by initials to protect confidentiality; only for reference in determining any patterns of interaction, friendships): ______________________________

____

Context (when, where, etc.): ______________________________

____

____

Notes (What did you see? Record rich detail, but not conclusions):

____

____

____

____

____

____

____

Preliminary thoughts regarding observation (Do you have any conclusions, more questions?):

____

____

Teacher's signature: __________

RUNNING RECORDS **Running records** are narrative notes made of routine functioning of an individual child or a small group of children. For example, Ms. Ryan plans to observe Rachel for 10 minutes during the free-play period. She then writes down everything that Rachel does or says; she does not participate or interact with Rachel while writing. Ms. Ryan collects the record at different times throughout the year. Ms. Ryan saves each record for later analysis.

running records notes made of routing functioning of an individual child or a small group of children.

In another instance, a group of second graders is planning a way to use attribute blocks for a new game. As they establish rules, Mr. Sanchez observes and records the process in detail, using good descriptive words. When he analyzes this record, he makes decisions about child progress and grouping plans and gains information about what further details he should provide to the group about attribute blocks, game development, and so on. (See Box 3.7 for a template to use to create running records.)

This running record approach to note-taking is a widely used method for documenting reading progress (Clay, 2006). Ms. Anderson watches Bonnie read a passage, and uses a blank

BOX 3.7

Example of a Running Record Template

Running Record Template

Name: ___________ Date: ___________

Objective for this observation: ____

____

____

Context (who is involved, where, what preceded the event): ______________________________

____

Reflections/Questions	Notes

Continue on text sheet as needed.

Teacher signature at the bottom of last page. Initials and page numbers on all other.

BOX 3.8

Running Reading Record

Text	**Bonnie's Record**
Humpty Dumpty sat on the wall Humpty Dumpty had a great fall All the kings horses and all the kings men Couldn't put Humpty Dumpty together again ✓ Read correctly SC Self-corrected T Told a word TTA Try that again / Mispronounced ○ Asked for word	

paper and a code to note any problems that Bonnie has with the passage. Ms. Anderson will want to note substitutions, attempts, omissions, insertions, self-corrections, and repetitions; instances when she must tell Bonnie the word; times when she asks Bonnie to try again; and times when Bonnie asks for help (Gunning, 2008). Box 3.8 shows some of the symbols for this approach and Box 3.9 provides a blank template for your use. You can adapt one-to-one work with children on other subject areas in a similar manner.

BOX 3.9

Example of a Reading Running Record Form

Reading Running Record Form

Name: ___________
Date: ___________

Copy of text read attached or duplicated here.	**Child's Record**

✓	Read correctly
SC	Self-correct
T	Told a word
TTA	Try that again
/	Mispronounced
○	Asked for a word

Box 3.10 Running Record for Chato's Kitchen shows a teacher's observation and recording of Samantha's oral reading using the literacy running record technique.

Recording Narrative Notes. Before beginning to record an observation on a child or a situation, you should make a few notes that will help in remembering important issues and details. This includes a sketch or mention of the part of the room where the action takes place and

BOX 3.10

Reading *Chato's Kitchen*

By Gary Soto

Page of text	Printed text	Notes	
	Title page, glossary	*Look there's some Spanish here. K: Seems like it might be important to know that it is there.*	
1	Chato, a low-riding cat with six stripes, was slinking toward a sparrow when he heard the scrape of tiny feet coming from the yard next door. . . . His tail began to swing to the rhythm. He felt the twinge of mambo in his hips . . .		✓✓✓✓✓✓✓ ✓✓ ✓✓✓✓✓✓ ✓✓ scrap/scrape ✓✓✓✓✓✓ ✓✓✓ ✓✓✓✓✓✓✓ ✓✓✓✓ tw twinge/twinge ✓ ✓✓✓✓
2	. . . Through the narrow slats, his eyes grew big as he spied five mice the color of gray river rock.		✓✓✓✓ split/sc / sprd ✓✓
3		*She's like saying, "I'm talking on the phone."*	
4	Yes, it was a whole family of fat, juicy mice moving into the house next door. Chato ra-raked his tongue over his lips and mewoed a deep growling meow. The mice froze with the belongings on their backs. They began to shiver like leaves in the wind. Chato was the tallest cat they had ever seen! . . . "No, *de versa, hombres*. I'm ok" Chato reassured. But the yard was empty. Another meow rumbled in this stomach just barely suppressed.	*Is he thinking of eating them?*	ra-raked/raked ✓✓✓ ✓ R^3 ✓✓✓. ✓✓✓ tail, tail, tallest/tallest reserged/reassured
5	Chato thought for a moment as he stabbed his face into his furry shoulder and chewed the daylights.	*Look at that airplane, it's shiny.*	

a note about the context (i.e., who is playing, acting, where, and so on). Record the date, time, and any relevant preceding events. For example, if you are recording that Theda is crying, note what happened before—that Ronald hit her, she smashed her finger, or you saw nothing that tells you why she is crying. Box 3.11 illustrates a naturalistic observation.

Impressions From This Observation. Record your impressions from the observation. For example, Ronald seems to have had an "off day"; that is, he was quiet and subdued and tried to resist the offers of others to play. He is usually so peppy. (Is he feeling well? Did something

BOX 3.11

Sample Observation (in a Child-Care Center) of Two Boys at Play

This center is in a large house. It is a cozy, warm old house with many nooks and crannies for children to explore. During the free-play period, children can be inside or outside as their play takes them.

On this day, Ronald is inside in the living room of the house. This is the area where the housekeeping equipment is set up. Besides the standard equipment of wooden stove, refrigerator, and sink, there are large cardboard boxes set up in the area. The boxes are there to invite creative play. The boxes vary in size, but most will easily hold one or two children.

Ronald is a tall, slender, well-coordinated four-year-old. He is dressed in a T-shirt and comfortable cotton pants. Ronald is always clean and neat. He is regarded as a leader in this program. Most of the time, he leads children in a play activity of his choice. Today, he is playing alone in the housekeeping corner. His expression is bland today, although he is usually peppy and expressive. He appears to be a little bit tired, not his usual energetic self.

9:09 Ronald is sitting on the table pulling knobs off the stove. He is waving the knobs in the air, as if they were airplanes. He announces, "Take off, take off."

He pauses in his play to command Jon, who has strolled near Ronald at the stove, "You ain't playing here." He states this not in an angry way, but to clearly show that he wants to be alone and that he has the authority to direct the play of his peers.

Brad tries to join the play by handing Ronald a large cardboard box the size of an orange crate. Ronald tosses the box back to Brad.

Brad kicks the box around the housekeeping area. He really seems to want Ronald's attention. They usually play together. Ronald continues to ignore Brad and Jon. Jon wanders away.

Ronald continues his airplane play alone, with much buzzing sound.

He then declares, "Take off, man." He continues "flying" the stove knobs. He is becoming more excited and enthusiastic about the flying. His voice is louder, clearly imitating his notion of airplane sounds.

9:13 "BBBBBBBBBBBBBBB"

"uum oo oo"

"Buzz—"

"5 4 3 2 1 blast off." (Have the knobs become a rocket?)

Brad, who is sitting near Ronald in one of the boxes, turns to Ronald and entreats, "Pow, your turn to drive. Ronald, your turn to drive the car."

Brad, with resignation, says, "OK, I'll drive one more time."

Brad continues to badger Ronald, "Your turn to drive the car."

Pleadingly, Brad turns to Ronald, "Would you drive the car for me?"

Ronald finally climbs into the box with Brad. (Brad smiles broadly. He seems pleased to have finally recruited his friend Ronald into play.)

Ronald asks, "Where we going to—your house?" (He seems to be enjoying himself and seems good-naturedly going along with Brad in the shift to the car play.)

Brad exclaims, "Go real fast." They scoot around the floor in the box. Ronald hops out.

9:15 Ronald grabs some dishes from the stove.

Brad asks with puzzlement, "Ronald, what are you doing?"

Ronald responds matter-of-factly, "Putting gas in it."

Brad pronounces, "Just drive the car." Ronald hops back into the box.

Ronald sits in the box with Brad, but does not begin to drive. He turns his hands over and over (like wings).

Brad, frustrated, says, "Will you drive the car?" Ronald ignores Brad, and continues making wing-like movements.

Brad agrees reluctantly: "OK, I'll drive the car."

Ronald jumps out of the box.

(*continued*)

9:16 Ronald throws more dishes into the box.
He turns to Brad and announces, "OK, we'll throw these out as we go."
Brad says excitedly, "I got my foot on brake. We gotta get more food."
Ronald adds more dishes to the box.
Brad drops in a telephone.
Ronald throws in another phone.
Ronald shouts, "Get cover, get cover."
Both boys throw blankets in the box. (They seem to be getting a little silly. They are giggling and laughing. The play has shifted from driving a car to throwing things into the box.)
9:17 Ronald turns to Brad and shouts as he gives him toy fruit, "Here, Mr. Smith. Here Mr. Smith."
Brad rejoins, "My name is Cool Joe."
Ronald says commandingly to Kevin, "Don't play with us." (Kevin has come in and sat on the table.)
Brad falls on Kevin and laughs. Kevin joins the laughter. Brad and Kevin are rolling playfully on the floor.
9:20 Ronald threatens Kevin, "You better not laugh, kid."
Tony calls Kevin from across the room. He runs to join Tony.
Ronald and Brad settle back to the initial car game. They seem to have calmed down.
Together, they plan a trip in the car to Brad's house

happen at home?) Brad finally succeeded in dragging him into play. He seems to have a way of pulling Ronald out of his withdrawn mood. The other children really seem to depend on Ronald's leadership skills. Both boys could pull themselves together when the play was beginning to get out of hand. They are developing good self-control. Ronald's play shows a good imagination (use of dishes as gas); Brad is more concrete in his play (dishes as symbols of food).

The teacher, Ms. Perez, saves this running record for Ronald's file. Ms. Perez may also summarize her impressions of Brad and place them in his file. When doing this, Ms. Perez will want to protect Ronald's and Brad's privacy as she uses the files. She collects notes on each child in the program once or twice a month. At the end of the year, or when she wishes to report to parents, she reviews the notes to help clarify her thoughts about the developmental progress of each child in the program. Running record observation is the most time-consuming kind of observation. As you can see from the previous example, Ms. Perez's primary occupation during the 10 minutes is recording notes about Ronald and Brad. She sits close to the boys and watches and records their play. The rest of the group is playing in their respective areas of the classroom. Ms. Cobbler, the assistant teacher, is keeping an eye on the total group. This kind of observation may not always be possible in a program. The children in the class may need all the adults in the room to help them maintain smooth play. Sometimes, teachers may also need to collect observations while they are one of the participants in the action. Running records will not work then. Alternatives include making notes in logs or notebooks or on sticky notes or cards as soon as possible after the action, discretely during the action, or asking an assistant, volunteer, or child to help remember an incident. For example, you turn to the four-year-old at your elbow during story time and say, "Keisha, let's write down your comment. It added so much to our discussion." Then jot a note on the sticky note in your pocket. This serves to remind you of the high-level cognitive functioning of Keisha that you want to note with examples.

LOG OR NOTEBOOK Logs or notebooks are records accumulated throughout the year on each child. For example, Ms. Myers gets spiral notebooks for each child. She keeps the notebooks in a basket on the side of the room with a pen handy. Nearby, she hangs a calendar with the names of four children written on the days of the week when the program is running regularly. The calendar is her appointment schedule for recording observations for the children in the program. Therefore, she does not schedule observations on days when the class will be on a field trip, the day before or

Time	Week of February 15, 2011					
	Mon	Tues	Wed	Thurs	Fri	Notes
9:00–10:15	Indiv. Activities	→	→	→	→	Observe Anthony
10:15	Snack	→	→	→	→	
10:30	Story Time	→	→	→	→	Observe Lakesha
10:45–11:30	Outdoor Play	→	→	→	→	
11:30	Dismissal	Call Ms. Johnson	Bring Fish Food		Look for Pix for Train Theme	

FIGURE 3.1 Observation in the teacher's schedule.

after vacation, or at other high-stress times in the life of the program. Throughout the year, Ms. Myers collects observations on each child in the various areas of the room. The log is a developmental progress record. Ms. Myers records in her lesson plan book when she will collect these developmental progress records (Figure 3.1).

Some teachers like to make notes about each child on each day of the year. Teachers complete these daily logs at the end of each day, and then summarize at the end of each week. These are collected anecdotes like the previous examples. They are brief, filled with one's own notes and abbreviations, sketches, and so on. You write enough information so that you can remember the event, but the notes do not have to be so complete that their completion wears you out. These are impressions or memories of what children have been doing for the day rather than live observation notes. The impression or memory material can be useful, but "live" observations must be included as well. Keep in mind that impressions and memory material are interpreted or filtered, and conclusions drawn.

Written notes are not the only observational method for the busy teacher. The following sections describe some additional methods for recording information. These methods do not provide the rich insight data, but they do help teachers collect information. For example, Mr. Psujek, the third-grade teacher, plans a science project. He wants to be sure that everyone in the class uses the telescope at some point in the eight weeks. It is not necessary for him to record anecdotes or running records to assess the accomplishment of this goal—he can keep a checklist. As teachers, we do not always need to use the most complex method to assess children. We must match the knife to the purpose (e.g., a butter knife for bread, a steak knife for steak). For example, if you are interested in formative evaluation of your curriculum or of the day, you may wish to keep a class journal.

JOURNALS FOR THE CLASS **Class journals** are records that teachers make at the end of the day. In a few minutes at the end of the day, teachers jot notes of the events of the day with attention to salient details. These notes offer time for teachers to reflect on the curricular, instructional, and behavioral events that took place. The notes are subject to bias, as a few hours have passed, specific details are lost, and you solidify impressions before writing. For example, think about a traffic accident at an intersection. When it happens, you see which car turned left and hit the mailbox and newspaper stands and how the light pole went through the back of a second car. If you were there, in a few hours you may forget whether a taxi was involved, how far the

class journals diaries that teachers keep about a group's progress toward meeting educational goals.

BOX 3.12

End of the Day Formative Evaluation

As you think about the day, what worked well?

____

____

____

____

List three or four ideas or concerns that you will ponder:

____

____

____

____

What additional information do you need to solve any concerns or teaching issues?

____

____

____

____

mailbox leapt in the air, and whether the pavement was wet or dry. This is because you have other things on your mind. The formative evaluation form in Box 3.12 illustrates a series of focus questions for directing your class journal reflections. No matter which method you choose to use for observing and recording child behavior, you will need to make a plan to incorporate the time in your day.

checklists forms for recording the skills or attributes of the children in a class.

CHECKLISTS AS RECORDS **Checklists** are useful for recording the skills or attributes of the children in your class. Choose checklists that are commercially available, if these are compatible with your instructional goals. These are increasingly available as test companies try to capture the performance assessment market. Make checklists that match your teaching plans for the class. Make checklists to record progress that Zachary is making toward the goal you have set for him.

frequency records checklists for recording the presence or absence of, frequency of, or quality of selected behaviors.

Frequency records are teacher-developed or commercially designed checklists that teachers use to record the presence or absence of selected behaviors, how often a certain behavior occurs, or the quality of the behaviors. For example, you may want to know how often Mary Irene drinks milk at lunch. You make a list for this and check off the days Mary Irene drinks milk. Your colleague wants to know which students can add single-digit numbers. As she observes their play at the math center, she can check off which children can accomplish this task (Figure 3.2).

As teachers develop checklists, they must be aware that they are developing "assessment" instruments. Thus, the instruments must be derived from the philosophy and curriculum. The lists must describe skills (Figure 3.3) or target behaviors in a way that reflects the appropriate

		Yes	No
Adds single digits:	Ellen	X	
	Toni	X	
	George		X
	Albert	X	
	Bernard	X	

FIGURE 3.2 Addition skill checklist.

developmental sequence and subject matter progression. Otherwise, these seemingly benign lists become a biased instrument. Sources for the development of checklists include program goals, child development milestones, and district-wide scope and sequence charts.

Because we value the program goal of independence, we operationalize the goal for the age of the child we teach. For example, Ms. Potenza, a second-grade teacher, operationalizes the independence goal for her students as follows: Second graders arrive, hang up their coats, and choose an activity from their file of "things to do." Children may work together on their projects and share experiences. During this time, Ms. Potenza collects lunch money, conducts writing conferences, and provides individual guidance for those requesting assistance. At 9:45, the class meets to review the status of projects, to plan the day's agenda, and to listen to a story.

If Modesto, California, teachers want to assess the development of the children referred to their early intervention program, they check a child development milestone list to remind themselves of the typical sequence for the development of communication skills. They use the list as one indicator of progress, with interpretation dependent on the nature of each child's particular special need and with understanding of the issues involved in bilingual language development.

Math teachers at Middle Sized City have studied the National Council of Teachers of Mathematics (NCTM) Guidelines (2000) and invited experts to visit. They created a chart with skills identified for each age level, K–12. Ms. Park uses the kindergarten list to record which skills Kelly has developed. She finds that Kelly has mastered all of the skills. It is October. What next? Ms. Park can consult the first-grade scope and sequence material and state standards, and use the first-grade list to record Kelly's accomplishments.

Teacher's Name ______________________ Week of ______________

	Puts jacket in cubby					Washes hands before lunch				
Name	**M**	**T**	**W**	**T**	**F**	**M**	**T**	**W**	**T**	**F**
Shirley	X	X	X	X	X	X	X	X	X	X
Elly	X	absent	absent			X	absent	absent		
Laurita	X	X	X	X	X	X	X	X	X	X
Charles	X					X				

FIGURE 3.3 Self-help checklist for the Main Street School.

Activity checklists are lists of activities that teachers prepare to record which child engages in an activity during a given period. For example, you may wish to know who is using puzzles, clay, blocks, the easel, books, geoboards, and so on. List the activity across the top of the page. Then, down the side of the page, list the children in your class. You check or date when each child is doing one of the activities (Figure 3.4). Widerstrom (2005) includes checklists and matrices as part of the tools for developing a play-based curriculum. These prepared checklists may be useful as you learn to develop those keyed to your curriculum.

Name	Puzzles	Small Blocks	Books	Clay	Geoboards
Laurita	1/2	1/3			2/15
Regina			3/1	1/3	
Cheryl			3/2		
Mary			2/4		
Lisa			1/2		
Larissa					2/10
Nancy				3/15	
Jack	2/1				
Dennis		1/4	3/5		
Duncan		2/6			
Rosalind			3/6	3/7	
Sam	2/1				
Susan				2/10	

FIGURE 3.4 Activity checklist.

EVENT SAMPLING **Event sampling** is a record of skills or behaviors that you want the children in your class to know or to do in a specified amount of time. For example, you may want to know how often William asks to share a toy during the 40-minute play period; how often Lonnie is writing at the writing table during the 30-minute choice time; and how often Perry is at the computer center during the hour allowed for self-selected activities. Additional skills and attributes that can be observed and recorded in this way include:

- ***Social skills:*** cooperation, group cohesion, sense of fair play, competitiveness, and loyalty
- ***Affective expressions:*** joy, pleasure, satisfaction, self-confidence, shyness, and fear
- ***Cognitive attributes:*** decision-making, problem-solving, expressive language, and exploration
- ***Creativity:*** divergent response, fluency of ideas, spontaneity, flexibility, and originality
- ***Enhancement to self:*** sense of humor, leadership, and curiosity

event sampling record of skills or behaviors a teacher wants the children to know or to do.

Note that these skills and attributes are important life skills—ones not assessed with tests. Observation, therefore, is a critical method for assessing developmental progress. For example, Mr. Zuckerman, a second-grade teacher, values creativity and wants to assess whether children in his room are showing creative behavior (see Box 3.13).

TIME SAMPLING **Time sampling** is a way to check to see what is happening at a particular time with one or more children. For example, you may wish to know what is happening between

time sampling checklist for determining what is happening at a particular time with one or more children.

BOX 3.13

Cognitive Event Sample Record

Name	Divergent	Fluency	Spontaneity	Original
Arthur	3/5	3/6	3/8	3/12
Herb	3/5			
James	3/5	3/9		
Tom				
Betty				
Susan		3/6		
Dick			3/12	
Jane				3/12
Sally	3/7			
Frances		3/8		
Joey		3/8		
Marilyn			3/13	
Debbie				3/15
Billy				
Shawn	2/28			
Sharon				
Tony				
Melissa			3/25	
Deanne			3/24	

1:00 and 1:15 on Mondays. You collect this information by using a running record on Martin or by using a checklist to record the activities of several children. This technique may be helpful when you feel that the program is not working smoothly. There may be a lot of running about, bickering, or waiting in line. By sampling the period, you get an idea of who is where and begin to make some different plans. This technique also works to assess concentration and persistence for Mari. Ms. Carr is curious whether Mari can stick to one activity on the playground, so she makes the time sample chart shown in Box 3.14 to check whether Mari can concentrate in outdoor play.

rating scales methods of recording whether children possess certain skills or attributes and to what extent.

RATING SCALES **Rating scales** require teachers to judge child performance on some predetermined behavioral description. For example, "Hermes matches English color words to color swatches: never, some of the time, all of the time." Frequently, rating scales are part of a report card. As teachers, we are asked to decide whether an individual child possesses a particular skill or attribute and to what extent. For example, Clarence turns in homework on time (always, often, seldom, never); Arnetta writes clearly (excellent, satisfactory, needs improvement). Such procedures are subject to error and bias. For example, as teachers, you may hesitate to use the extreme positions of *never* and *always.* Unless, of course, Clarence, a third grader, needs to get a "wake-up call." Never turning in homework may be a serious problem. It may also mean that the homework is irrelevant, and Clarence knows it. These rating scales may lack a common definition in the minds of teachers. What does it mean that Gloria, a four-year-old, has emerging or accomplished conversation skills? What are the expectations in conversation for a four-year-old? Do all the teachers in the center have a shared definition? Do Gloria's parents know that "emerging" may be a problem at age 4? Is it a problem at age 4? Meeting with colleagues to establish common definitions for required skills and concepts in your program is one way to ensure common definitions and understanding for checklist categories. Another way to establish definitions for checklists is to utilize those available from publishers. Examples of these materials include the Child Observation Record (High Scope 2003), CC-PORT: The Creative Curriculum Progress and Outcome Reporting Tool (Teaching Strategies 2000–2009), Work Sampling System™ (2001). These assessment systems are discussed in the following chapters. Knowing how to establish definitions and keep records of observations assists you in selecting the published measures that match your program goals.

When developing or using rating scales, look for well-defined categories and those that are observable behaviors; for example, "recognizes five words (yes, maybe, not reading)," or "asks

BOX 3.14

Example of a Time Sample Record

Time Sample Record **Week of April 15**

Playground Activities for the Hummingbird School

Fifteen-minute record. Observer samples once each minute.
Observer watches one child at a time.

Child's Name	Big Wheel	Climber	Ball	Jump Rope	Not Playing
Judy	*x—15*				
Vincent	*xxxxx*		*x–10*		
John		*xxxxx*	*x–10*		
Mari	*xx*	*xx*	*xx*	*xx*	*x–6*

questions about the story (often, sometimes, never)." You can quickly observe each of the children in your class and "rate" each child's performance on these criteria. Keep in mind, then, that the more complicated the behavior is to rate, the greater the chance of error unless you and your colleagues have participated in extensive training to learn the definitions for the complicated behaviors to be rated.

USING PHOTOGRAPHS, VIDEOTAPES, AND AUDIOTAPES Photographs enhance observational notes. These are particularly useful in recording sculpture, block designs, and group dynamics. Videotape and audiotape are very helpful in recording storytelling and dramatic play. Use tapes sparingly, however, especially if you will transcribe the material to paper when the material is used for accountability. Transcription frequently takes two to three times as long as the original observation. For instance, a 10-minute observation may take 20 to 30 minutes to transcribe. As a permanent record of a child's work, tapes can be a rich source of information, because they show not only the words, but also the effect and group dynamics as well. The environment is as important as the players in video recordings. Revisiting videotapes and digital video may be an important adjunct to therapeutic interventions by therapists, diagnosticians, teachers, and parents when solving knotty problems (Guidry & van den Pol, 1996; Suarez & Daniels, 2009). As well, videotapes or other electronic recordings can be used to revisit an activity with children to review and reinforce learning or solve a class problem (Beaty, 2010).

Portfolios

Technically speaking, **portfolios** are one type of performance-based assessment, a strategy for deciding the competency of children in a particular area or areas. The portfolio is the place to keep all the information known about each child. Observational notes form the foundation of the portfolio. To enrich the observational record, add to the collection of each child's work. A collection of children's paintings, drawings, and stories shows what children know. Besides these artifacts, include lists of books read, transcripts of discussions with children about their work, and other products collected throughout the year to provide a good progress report. Save these materials in places such as individual file folders, portfolio envelopes, file boxes, scrapbooks, or other convenient containers. Collect the materials to answer questions about progress in developmental areas: social/emotional skills and attitudes, language/cognitive knowledge, and gross- and fine-motor coordination. Pictures and sketches of projects that you make aid in illustrating child progress. Be sure to include reflection as part of the process for selecting child work. Why is this work/artifact in the portfolio? What does it show about Monte's work? How would Monte improve or change the document if it were to be done again? These and other questions prompt children to consider learning as a process with stopping points—judgment spots along the way. Interviews of children about their interests, such as their favorite books, games, and activities, add details of each child's year in the program. Notes of parent conferences and questions add to a well-rounded picture of each child.

portfolios places, such as folders, boxes, or baskets, for keeping all the information known about the children in a class.

WHY USE PORTFOLIOS? The first and most important reason to use portfolios as part of an assessment plan is that these documents involve the teacher, parent, and child in the system. Some reasons to use portfolio assessment to support children as readers and writers are that the process itself:

- Increases language learning
- Emphasizes both content and performance, or holistic learning
- Links between learning across the curriculum
- Facilitates children's learning about audience awareness as they write
- Is individualized (Farr & Tone, 1998; Johnston, 2005)

DECIDING WHAT TO INCLUDE IN THE PORTFOLIO When first choosing what to include, you may collect a "laundry basket full of stuff." To be useful, however, the portfolio should contain selections carefully matched to answer the assessment question. You need to think about a number of things before filling a milk crate for each child, which is a common tendency for early portfolio builders. Will the portfolio represent a child's best work, selected drafts, a random sample of work, or only child-chosen or only teacher-chosen items? Will you develop several portfolios for each child, such as an ongoing portfolio and one for the end-of-the-year? The answers to these questions vary depending on whether the portfolio is:

- ***A working one***—to be used by you and the children during the course of a unit
- ***A formative one***—to show parents at the end of six weeks
- ***A summative one***—to pass to the kindergarten teacher

Some questions to guide you and your students in the selection of work include (Shanklin & Conrad, cited in Gullo, 2005):

- Will the work samples tell the consumer—child, parent, teacher—about the level of development or academic progress?
- Will the sample show what to modify in the curriculum or what to individualize?
- How do the selected products help the consumer—child, parent, teacher—understand the developmental or academic progress?

There are no right answers to these questions, only answers that match the purpose for collecting the information. (A sample portfolio template is shown in Appendix F.)

INVOLVING CHILDREN IN THE PORTFOLIO PROCESS As children grow older, they will want to be involved in the process of portfolio development; even preschoolers can begin judging their work (Shores & Grace, 2005; Fogarty, Burke & Belgrad, 2008). When you hold writing conferences with primary-aged children, you can ask them to select writing samples for their permanent record. Marcia can choose the math paper that shows that she has learned to add single digits. Eloise can select the painting that shows a complete story. At conference time with children, you can involve them in writing notes about their progress in social studies. Jacob may tell you that he is more comfortable in his assigned social studies project than he was at the beginning of the assignment. Then you translate the conversation into a note that says, "Jacob is feeling more comfortable in small-group assignments." Harvey may tell you that he enjoys reading "bigger" or "longer" books. A conference note is included that says, "Harvey is reading books of 15 pages now." By involving the children in the selection of work to be included in a portfolio and by showing them some notes that you make at individual conferences, you are showing how to conduct assessment. You collect samples of work that show skills, collecting multiple pieces of information, and demystify the assessment process for children. As well, you show them how to assess their own progress. Regularly examining the portfolio and setting new goals shows children that learning evolves. Children can be proud of their accomplishments and will help decide where they want to go next.

To help children select work products that document their learning, some questions include (Hebert, 2001):

- How has your writing changed since last year? Since January?
- What do you know about numbers that you didn't know in October?
- Let's compare a page in the book that you read in first grade with one that you are reading now.
- What is special or unique about your portfolio?
- What do you want to show your parents about your learning? How can you organize your portfolio to show this?

You are helping children understand assessment and evaluation at their developmental level by choosing questions that focus on the process appropriate to their age and stage of development.

This kind of review sets the stage for programs that want to move toward involving children in decision-making and responsibility for their own learning, including student-led conferences specifically in the primary years (Bailey & Guskey, 2001). Another approach to documenting child progress, called the **documentation panel**, has gained favor in preschools across the country. This is part of the philosophy and practice of education known as *Reggio Emilia* (Edwards, Gandini, & Foreman, 1998).

documentation panel is the part of the Reggio Emilia process that shows, publicly, the learning accomplishements of young children.

Documentation Panels

The application of the Reggio Emilia documentation panel (Helm, Beneke, & Steinheimer, 2007; Krechevsky et al., 2003; Lewin-Benham, 2008) to the classroom provides a focus for the accounts of individual child growth and for whole class summaries of knowledge, skills, and dispositions. This is a technique much like that used in program evaluation and is commonly called formative and summative evaluation. **Formative evaluation** is a review of the program or work as it is in process. "Major reviews of research on the effects of formative assessment indicate that it might be one of the more powerful weapons in a teacher's arsenal" (Marzano, 2007, p. 13). The research supports frequent formative assessment, as well. **Summative evaluation** is the decision, judgment, or opinion regarding the work at the end of a project or term. Thus, the visual display of work in progress serves to show all constituencies—children, teachers, parents, administrators, and community—what children know and are able to do. The panels include pictures, narratives, charts, and illustrations that show children's experience, memories, thoughts, and ideas. Assess these artifacts during the implementation of the curriculum—formative evaluation—and as a reflection later—summative evaluation. Whenever using observation and the related tools, you must remember that there are some limitations to the application of the method. As an early childhood teacher who practices an ethical approach to the collection and use of observational products, you will want to be aware of some of these limitations.

formative evaluation an approach to examining young children that holds that assessment is an ongoing process. It is similar to the scientific approach, in which a query is generated, validated or not, and then another query is formed.

summative evaluation reports the final results of a given assessment. For teachers, this often means the end-of-the-year summary of child progress.

VOICES FROM THE FIELD

Head Start Master Teacher with Comprehensive Plan for Assessment

Our centers begins the year with screening, using ESI-R Early Screening Inventory-R 2008 (http://test.pearsonassessments.com/esir.aspx) or the Ages and Stages Questionnaire AGQ-3 (http://www.agesandstages.com). My frustration with this requirement is that based on scores, we need to classify the children as OK, retest, or refer them for intervention. Many of our children come to school with no knowledge or limited knowledge of English. So, if I didn't have to refer them, in three or four months, they would be fine, since they would have learned English. It's hard to begin the year with parents saying that their child has special needs, based on this screening.

One hurdle that we face with parents when we refer children is the cultural interpretations that immigrant families apply. That is, in some cultures that we serve, having a child referred for special assistance is shameful and embarrassing. We work hard to help parents understand the U.S. school system and the benefits of referral for ongoing child progress.

Regularly, teachers record anecdotal notes with the program requirement that once a week they must observe one child for 15–20 minutes during free play—recording conversations and play activities. These observations go in each child's working portfolio. Throughout the year, we add work samples to this portfolio to share at parent conferences held in December and July. At the beginning of the academic year, we make home visits to meet parents and again at the end of the year to celebrate the child's accomplishments.

Finally, we are using the Reggio Emilia approach in our classrooms and integrating more and more of these practices. Examples of lessons that I have demonstrated for teachers include:

Art Studio

- *I brought small white canvases to class and asked the children to make self-portraits. During the process and afterwards, I talked with children about the choices they made in their portraits. Why did you choose this eye color? Hair color, style, etc.?*

Science Project

- *I brought clay for exploration and formation into shapes. During the project, I took four or five pictures of one child as he explored and added my notes on his responses to thinking that occurred as he explored.*

Limitations of the Observational Method

Appropriate use of observational methods depends on skillful, knowledgeable teachers. Teachers must know and understand child development milestones. They must be sensitive to cultural, individual, and situational variations for the attainment of these milestones. Teachers must know curriculum and instruction principles. That is, they must know how children learn and how subject matter is organized. Teachers must also avoid the following observer traps:

- Overinterpretation of behavior
  During an hour visit in a child-care home, Otto cried the entire time. He cried when the caregiver held him.
  Interpretation: Otto is ill.
  You do not have enough information to sustain this interpretation. If the observer considers other factors (too many children in this facility, five infants and one caregiver, length of time in the setting, and other unknown factors), Otto may be behaving appropriately for a stressful situation.

- Making inferences from global behavioral descriptions
  While the children were reviewing their Japanese words, Barbara was excited to answer the questions, but during free play when she was playing in the doll corner, she wanted to play alone.
  Interpretation: Barbara seems to be an outgoing person when it is necessary, but when she has more of a choice, she prefers to be by herself.
  Answering questions in large group is not necessarily "outgoing", nor is playing alone a reflection of isolation. There is no information about antecedent events. Did Barbara fight with friends? Do her classmates function cognitively at a different level? Is this behavior a regular occurrence?
- Observer's personal bias
  Maria, age 4, chatted with friends at the kitchen table in the house corner. Alicia suggested that the table become a diner. Maria, "No, I was here first and I want it to be my home."
  Interpretation: Maria sure is bossy. Alicia is much more cooperative.
  It sounds like this observer expects girls not to be assertive. The observer may not like Maria as much as Alicia and thus interprets Alicia more favorably.
- Wrong focus
  David, age 3, is playing with blocks. He is talking very softly to himself. Occasionally, he directs a remark to his companion, Ari, in the block area. He has built a large structure. Now he seems to be hiding the small cars and animals in the structure. Ari asks him what he is doing. David doesn't answer.
  Interpretation: David is an isolated child who is not social.
  Other possibilities: David is absorbed in the play. He is concentrating. He doesn't hear Ari. The observer misses the cognitive sophistication of what David is doing because he is not speaking.
- Inaccurate recordings
  George ran around the room, then dumped blocks on Sally and another girl who were playing at the small-group table. He then settled to work on a puzzle.
  Interpretation: George is hyperactive and aggressive.
  Other possibilities: George is playful. Sally and Keisha dumped his puzzle immediately before. The three engage in playful teasing and cooperative assistance in picking up puzzles. The three are working on learning to cooperate.
- Failure to record times of beginning and ending of behavior
- Failure to show the names of all the children involved in a segment of behavioral observation

- Preconceived notions
  Ms. Clark is sure that Danny is hyperactive. She wants his parents to take him to the pediatrician to get a pill to calm him down.
  Interpretation: Danny is a problem.
  Ms. Clark records notes on Danny when he is very active in the room. She does not record Danny at times when he is absorbed in an activity, even while he is moving. She neglects the language and cognitive aspects. She does not look at her schedule and routines.

Planning and Scheduling Observations

"(A)ssessment and curriculum are integrated, with teachers continually engaging in observational assessment for the purpose of improving teaching and learning" (Bredekamp & Copple, 1997, p. 21; Copple & Bredekamp, 2009). Your observations naturally include brief, casual observations of various children throughout the day. You adjust your teaching based on these casual observations. You record significant events as *anecdotal notes* on children. Periodically, you need more in-depth *running record* observations. Finally, you need a *systematic plan* for observing and recording the behavior of all children within your program.

Your assessment plan must include regularly scheduled running records so that you can plan appropriate learning activities based on the needs, strengths, and interests of the children in your program. Anecdotal notes document special events in the lives of individual children. Reflections of conversations and interactions with children allow you opportunities to think about individual strengths and interests of the children in your program. Checklists of developmental milestones help you see the progress of individual children and provide a group summary. Records of conferences with parents assist you in building a total picture of each child in the context of family.

In these ways, you are constantly gathering observational information to provide the best program possible for all of the children. This is a difficult and exhausting task, and it is not the only task that a teacher faces. You must also make, set up, and prepare materials; talk to children; help them settle into routines; and empathize with them. You must lead the group in song, story, and fun. You are a model of curiosity, good humor, and enthusiasm. You must set the tone for your assistant and parent volunteers, meet with parents, and handle crises as they emerge. Often, you are alone in the classroom, so you will need to develop a system that works for you. This may involve collaborating with a colleague during your respective planning times, if you need a second set of eyes in your room. It may mean that you plan for certain, more demanding note-taking to occur while children are engaged in projects. Note-taking should never preoccupy you so that chaos occurs in your class. Being alone in the room is not a reason to discard observation as an assessment method.

THE REAL WORLD OF EVERYDAY TEACHING Observation is the partner of instruction. You cannot teach well without observing. For example, as you set out finger paints every day for a week, you notice that Jimmy will not touch them. Popping a sticky note out of your pocket, you record an anecdote. Ms. Regan, a third-grade teacher, has index cards for each of the children in her class that are taped together in bunches and fastened to a clipboard (personal communication, 2005). She carries the board everywhere, making notes and jotting reminders of what to assess or

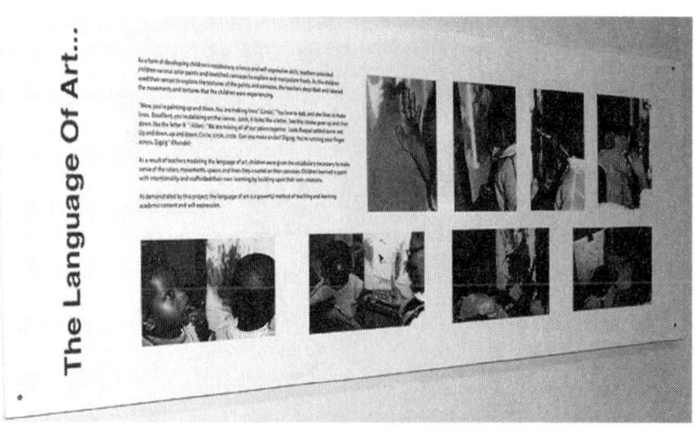

teach. At quarter's end, she has anecdotes and documentation for report cards and parent conferences. This is just one way to keep track of the data that you need to teach well. Additional ways to structure your classroom for observational success include leaving small notebooks and pens around the room so that you can record "in the moment" child behaviors and insights. Prepare a calendar for each child in a folder or on a ring-binder; record your assessment notes and summarize monthly. Dictate your notes in a pocket recording device. Use your Personal Digital Assistant (PDA) to record or save observations and watch for especially designed educational products to use with the PDA; at present, most software produced for PDA is for business applications (Meisels, Harrington, and others, 2001).

In another method, six weeks after the beginning of the year, you sit for one afternoon with your favorite checklist. For the next week, while the children are napping or participating in an informal group activity at lunch or recess, you reflect on each child and check the list accordingly. When you run into questions you cannot answer, you plan to find out whether a particular child "uses two or more sentences to tell me something" by engaging this child in conversation.

Using the schedule you have made for yourself, you systematically gather running records on everyone throughout the year. You file them away to use as you prepare reports and meet with parents. Obviously, when an emergency occurs and staff is short, the schedule is changed.

Foremost, you have a responsibility to plan systematic observation to answer the questions you have for each child in your program. Systematic observational plans are those that help you to be sure that you have answered all of the assessment questions about individuals and groups that must be answered so that all stakeholders know that learning is occurring, and if learning is not occurring, what some of the obstacles might be for individuals and the group. Thus, just as you plan what you teach—which activities, structure of the room, schedule for the day, and staff interactions with children in a developmentally appropriate way—you must plan how to collect observational information on each child regularly, covering all aspects of development and learning. You must write some information down. Your plan must reflect the philosophy and realities of your program. Practical suggestions for collecting the information have been included in this chapter. You must decide how many running records, anecdotes, logs, and checklists to collect on each child. You will need a balance of observations for each of the methods so that you will have the material you need to confer with parents and to write developmental reports.

SUMMARY

Keeping track of your observations on the children in your class makes it easier for you to teach them well. Recording observation notes and using checklists takes time in an already busy day, but it makes you a prepared teacher. Observations supplement standardized tests and provide the flesh for the description of complicated behaviors: language competence, social skills, and problem-solving approaches.

Observation is the tool you use to make teaching decisions, regardless of whether you write them down. Writing the notes, making the checks, or otherwise keeping track of your thoughts on the children in your class helps you be the best teacher for all the children in your care. In the end, you will be better organized. You will know which methods are working with which children. You will be able to answer questions about cognitive, social/emotional, motor, and language development, as well as academic progress, with precision and examples. You will feel more confident about your judgments and insights, because you have organized and planned for your assessments. You have made the link from the curriculum to assessment and completed the circle—teach, evaluate, reteach.

FIELD ACTIVITIES

1. With a partner, go to a grocery store, park, fast food restaurant, or mall where you can observe children. Each of you should watch the same action for 10 minutes at a time. Record the details. Discuss your results with your partner. What were the similarities and differences? Which presents the more accurate picture? See what you missed and try again.
2. At the local supermarket on the weekend, station yourself in the cereal aisle. Watch parent and child interactions. Record details. Develop a checklist based on your initial observations. Collect information on several children. What patterns did you observe?

3. Go to the park or other community location where you can find primary-aged children. Draw a sketch of the area. Develop a checklist of the areas: basketball, climber, swings, benches, and so on. Record the ages and sexes of children who participate in the diverse areas of the playground. Use this information to make after-school teaching plans based on your observations of the usage patterns and the goals for the after-school program.
4. In a classroom, record your observations of children at learning centers, during story time, or working on projects. Compare your observational notes to developmental guidelines and state learning standards. Use this information to determine what you know that will help you teach. Analyze what is missing from your notes so that you can plan the next observation.
5. Interview teachers in preschool and primary settings about how they use observation and records in planning for instruction. List each specific type and the purposes related to each type. Discuss ways the materials can be used to solve teaching problems, to talk with parents, and to refer young children for any special intervention that may be necessary.

IN-CLASS ACTIVITIES

1. Using an available DVD of children playing, watch 10 minutes of the children's interactions. Each participant should record a running record on one child or situation. Divide into pairs. Discuss the results of the observation. Examine the notes for objectivity and completeness of detail.
2. Using available state content guidelines for second grade, in groups of three, review the guidelines and develop a list of suggested artifacts to collect for the year. Describe how you will include children and parents in the collection and evaluation.

STUDY QUESTION

1. How can early childhood teachers recognize and utilize observation records most effectively? Why are observational records so highly regarded in early childhood settings?
2. How can early childhood teachers include observational records in class schedules? What are the assessment decisions that teachers frequently make through daily observations?
3. In which situations will anecdotal notes provide a comprehensive assessment? How will the teacher use anecdotal notes?
4. Why should running records always include analysis or reflections on the observation?
5. What types of information will be gathered through running records? How can this information be used in classrooms?
6. What are the components and types of checklists? Checklists are most effective for the early childhood teacher in gathering what type of information?
7. How are event and time sampling used differently in the classroom?
8. What factors will make rating scales most effective? How do rating scales differ from checklists? Frequency records? Running records?
9. What are the components of a portfolio? How can portfolios be incorporated into the curricula?

REFLECT AND RE-READ

- I know what the role of observation is in a well-crafted early childhood program.
- I can identify some ways to record and summarize information.
- I know how observation fits into the portfolio process or other record-keeping system.
- I know why observation alone is not enough for a fully developed assessment system.

CASE VIGNETTE

My interest in Carlota, a four-year-old enrolled in Head Start, came when I discovered that she is Argentine and speaks Spanish fluently. (I was reminded of my own childhood, growing up in an all-English-speaking child-care environment and speaking my home language the rest of the time.) In the beginning I was intrigued by her shy personality, and then I noticed she was having trouble communicating with classmates and teachers. She seems to understand what is going on but seems to lack vocabulary to express feelings or wants. In one such instance, I noticed her shaking her head "no" and repeatedly saying "no" to the teacher who was asking her to "go biz." At first glance, it appears that Carlota is refusing to cooperate with the teacher in going to the washroom. Another teacher interrupted to say that Carlota had already visited the bathroom. It was clear that Carlota understood the first teacher, but faced an obstacle when having to reply in English. What are the next steps in observation/assessment for Carlota? How will you gather evidence to plan/modify instruction? How will you sort out the behavioral, personal, and academic issues?

Source: From Y. Jacome, 2002, submitted in partial fulfillment of T&L 411, Assessment in Early Childhood Education: DePaul University. Used by permission.

TECHNOLOGY LINKS

http://www.aacap.org

American Academy of Child and Adolescent Psychiatry. Public information pamphlets related to mental health and links to a wide variety of additional websites.

http://www.aap.org

American Academy of Pediatrics. Position papers and publications affecting the lives of young children.

http://www.colorincolorado.org

Colorin Colorado has suggestions for assessing and teaching young children who are English Language Learners (ELL).

http://www.hhs.gov/children/index.shtml

U.S. Department of Health and Human Services. Public information for families.

http://www.kidsource.com

The KidSource™. This site covers a broad spectrum of issues related to assessment, observation, and teaching.

SUGGESTED READINGS

Beaty, J. J. (2010). *Observing development of the young child* (7th ed.). Upper Saddle River, NJ: Merrill/Prentice Hall.

Gronlund, G., & James, M. (2005). *Focused observations: How to observe children for assessment and curriculum planning.* St. Paul, MN: Red Leaf Press.

Owocki, G., & Goodman, Y. (2002). *Kidwatching: Documenting children's literacy development*. Portsmouth, NH: Heinemann.

Pellegrini, A. D. (2004). *Observing children in their natural worlds: A methodological primer* (2nd ed.). Mahwah, NJ: Lawrence Erlbaum Associates.

Scheinfeld, D. R., Haigh, K. M., & Scheinfeld. S. J. (2008). *We are all explorers: Learning and teaching with Reggio principles in urban settings.* New York: Teachers College Press.

Shea, M. (2000). *Taking running records: A teacher shares her experience on how to take running records and use what they tell you to assess and improve every child's reading.* New York: Scholastic.

Wood, C. (2007). *Yardsticks: Children in the classroom ages 4–14.* Turner Falls, MA: Northeast Foundation for Children, Inc. http://www.responsiveclassroom.org.

CHAPTER 4

Using Basic Concepts of Measurement

TERMS TO KNOW

- raw score
- mean
- range
- standard deviation
- normal curve
- standardized test
- norm-referenced test
- population
- normative sample
- norming
- norms
- criterion-referenced test
- derived score
- age-equivalent score
- grade-equivalent score
- interpolated score
- extrapolated score
- percentile ranks
- standard score
- scaled score
- deviation quotients
- normal-curve equivalents
- stanines
- reliability
- test-retest reliability
- interscorer reliability
- correlation coefficient
- standard error of measurement (SEM)
- validity
- face validity
- content validity
- criterion-related validity
- concurrent validity
- predictive validity
- construct validity
- convergent validity
- discriminate validity
- social validity
- absence of bias

In this chapter, all the basic concepts needed to use tests and other standardized measurement devices in a developmentally appropriate manner are fully described so that teachers and child-care workers can communicate confidently with parents, administrators, psychologists, and other professionals about all aspects of tests and other assessment tools and what they mean in the lives of young children. Most importantly, these are the concepts that you must understand to appropriately administer and interpret the standardized tests used increasingly in both the preschool and primary years. Throughout the chapter, practical examples are included to demystify the statistics of testing.

ASSESS AS YOU READ

- What do I already know about statistics in everyday life? How do these concepts translate to measurement?
- Why should assessment be a central focus of my instructional practice?
- How are tests developed?
- How can tests be an appropriate part of a multidimensional assessment plan? What are the limitations of these instruments?

NEW PARADIGMS IN ASSESSMENT

Assessment, particularly testing, continues to be a "hot topic" in education today. Some educators describe examples of holistic approaches as new paradigms. However, early childhood educators historically focused on assessment as inquiry (cf. Serafini, 2001; Delandshere, 2002). Yet, in the primary grades assessment as inquiry departs from assessment as measurement—comparison of children to standardized measures; assessment as procedure—using qualitative data gathering such as portfolio assessment to supplement standardized measures. Assessment as inquiry also has roots in the constructivist view of learning (cf. Goffin & Wilson, 2001), in which data on child behavior is gathered to obtain information to solve a learning or developmental issue. Constructivist view of learning is often called inquiry-based learning. This is the approach in which the teacher sets the learning stage for the learner to discover knowledge. More recently, the approach is described as "emergent" curriculum. Regardless of the measurement paradigm—holistic or based on test instruments—early childhood teachers must understand the statistics of testing. You must be able to know when the results are technically sound and programmatically useful. In addition, you must be able to explain standardized test results to parents and children. Thus, knowledge of the statistics of testing will help you know the strengths, limitations, and values of all approaches to measurement. Here the focus is on the statistics that apply to tests that are widely used with young children today. Dive into this chapter without fear; though you may think of statistics as math-based, hard, dreaded, or whatever, statistics are logical concepts that will give you a new language to embrace. You will be able to understand why certain instruments are good ones and why certain ones are not so good. Think of yourself as the knowledgeable investor who will be able to invest wisely in the high-stakes measurement of young children.

IMPORTANCE OF BASIC CONCEPTS OF MEASUREMENT FOR TEACHERS

Do not join the "(m)any teachers (who) see no need for training in testing and assessment because they believe these activities are supplemental or peripheral to the instructional process . . . (because) it is frequently the classroom teacher who must administer and then organize and interpret high-stakes and teacher-constructed test and assessment data, including performance and portfolio data, to curious and sometimes hostile parents and other concerned parties" (Kubiszyn & Borich, 2009, pp. 13–14). Fundamental to understanding tests is the understanding of measurement and all of its components. However, what exactly is *measurement?* According to Linn, Miller, and Gronlund (2009), it is "the assigning of numbers to the results of a test or other type of assessment according to a specific rule (e.g., in original counting correct answers or awarding points for particular aspects of an essay or writing sample)" (p. 26). In order for you, as a teacher, to understand how to evaluate tests, interpret test results adequately, and make appropriate use of other types of assessment (inventories, observation techniques, functional assessment, portfolio, authentic assessment, and so on), you should be familiar with some concepts and terms of measurement. Some of them will already be familiar to you from other contexts; others are more specific to tests. You will need to understand this vocabulary to be a good consumer of tests. By understanding tests and their properties, you will know when it is appropriate to use one and whether you have found a good one. As you read this chapter, keep in mind the five core concepts for understanding testing:

1. Tests facilitate understanding of students' behavior and learning.
2. Tests cover specified samples of behavior and knowledge.
3. Test validity is the premier important variable among test properties.
4. Test reliability is essential for appropriate use and understanding of tests.
5. Test bias is a factor that influences interpretation and use of tests. (Popham, 2000)

According to the National Association for the Education of Young Children, program stakeholders are responsible for assessment that "make(s) ethical, appropriate, valid, and reliable assessment a central part of all early childhood programs . . . making sound decisions about teaching and learning, identifying significant concerns that may require focused intervention for individual children, helping programs improve their educational and developmental interventions" (NAEYC, 2003; Copple & Bredekamp, 2009). Tests are only one part of a multiple-measures system. But, because they are widely used, teachers must understand the purpose, characteristics, interpretations, and appropriate application of the measures. To assist you in understanding the complexity of tests, you will need to be familiar and comfortable with the technical vocabulary explained in this chapter.

TERMINOLOGY

In the following pages, you will review the definitions of terms commonly used to describe the properties of tests. It is important to develop a working understanding of these terms so that you will know the strengths and limitations of the tests that you develop or use. Knowledge of assessment and appropriate uses of tests is part of an ethical commitment to young children and their families (NAEYC, 2005; DEC, 2000). The first term is one most familiar to you—how many right answers?

Raw Score

raw score the number of items that a child answered correctly on a test.

The first score you obtain on either a published test or a teacher-made test is the **raw score**, the number of items that the child answered correctly. Knowing each child's raw score is the first step in changing the child's score to a standardized score. However, raw scores provide little information about a child's performance in comparison with other children. These scores are not in a form that allows comparison between performances of children. Therefore, if Paul has a score of 10 and Nell has a score of 15, you do not know that Paul is less successful on the tested concept. So that you can make comparisons between Paul, Nell, and the other children in your class, the scores are standardized. This part of the standardization process is most important—turning scores into numbers for comparison. One of the first standardized scores that you need to tell you more about your class is the average score—the average number of right answers for most of the children in your room.

Mean

mean the arithmetic average of a group of scores.

Everyone is familiar with the word *average,* which is the **mean**, the arithmetic average of a group of scores. To calculate the mean age of one of your reading groups in which the children are 70, 72, 73, 76, 78, and 81 months old:

1. Add all the ages (450)
2. Divide by the number of children (6)

Thus, the mean of these numbers is 75.

$$70 + 72 + 73 + 76 + 78 + 81 = 450/6 = 75$$

Let's say that you want to check the understanding that your second graders have of subtraction facts. Over a number of days, you establish how many of the facts each child knows. You record their names and total facts known, as shown in Figure 4.1. You add their total scores (624) and divide by the number of children in your class (24). Now you know each child's score as well as the mean for the group (26). You can also see whether each child is above or below the mean. Besides knowing where most children are achieving, you will want to know whether the learners in your room are very far apart in their scores—how many scored very low and how many scored very high?

Child's name	# of facts	Child's name	# of facts
Alex	25	Lola	19
Ben	27	Maria	15
Christina	20	Martin	30
David	29	Norris	18
Dina	29	Paul	22
Ilana	31	Peter	12
Jerry	28	Ruth	28
Josiah	32	Sam	33
Juan	36	Sarah	11
Katie	30	Tara	17
Kim	40	Winston	29
Liz	23	Yolanda	40

FIGURE 4.1 The number of subtraction facts known by children in Miss Take's class.

Range

When you are dealing with the scores of your class, the next measure you want to determine is the variability of the scores, or how different they are from each other. The **range** is the "spread" of the scores or the difference between the top score and the bottom score. In the example where we calculated the mean chronological age of the reading group, the range is 11. This is the difference—or distribution of scores—between the lowest number (70) and the highest number (81) in the group (81 – 70 = 11). The range is not a very sensitive measure, because it is dependent on only two scores in the distribution, the highest and lowest. It merely tells you how far apart the achievements of your lowest- and highest-ability students were on a particular test. For more precision, you can statistically determine the variability of scores: Is a 29 different from a 42? Maybe; maybe not. The statistical determination tells the story for each test. So, to know whether 29 is different from 42, you must find out how far each score is from the mean by calculating the standard deviation.

range the spread of the scores or the difference between the top score and the bottom score on a test.

Standard Deviation

A very important measure that helps us quantify the "spread" of the distribution is the **standard deviation**. It measures the distance scores depart from the mean. If a distribution of scores is large enough, the scores will usually form a bell-shaped curve, known as a normal distribution (Figure 4.2).

standard deviation the distance scores depart from the mean.

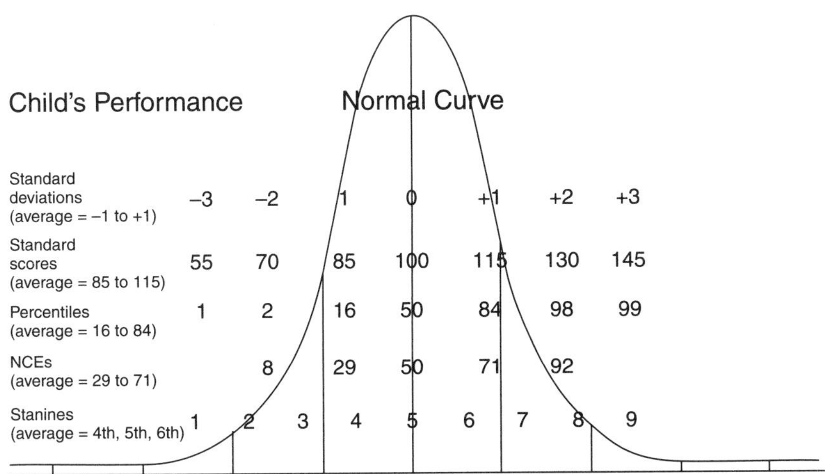

FIGURE 4.2 Different types of standard scores on the normal curve.

normal curve bell-shaped curve representing the usual distribution of human attributes.

This bell-shaped or **normal curve** represents the distribution of a large number of human attributes, including height, weight, and for our purposes, test scores. A normal distribution is hypothetically the way scores on a test would cluster if you gave the particular test to every single child of the same age or grade in the populations for whom the test was designed. The pattern shows that most children are about average, a few are slightly above or below average, and even fewer have extremely high or low scores. The mean score, by definition, is in the middle of this hypothetical normal distribution so that half of the scores will be higher than the mean and half will be lower. The standard deviation is a unit of measurement that represents the typical amount that a score can be expected to vary from the mean in a given set of data or on a particular test.

Looking at Figure 4.2, we can see that a large number of the scores fall near the mean or the "hump" part of the curve. Approximately 34 percent of the scores fall between the mean and one standard deviation above the mean; approximately 34 percent of the scores fall between the mean and one standard deviation below the mean. Thus, two-thirds of the scores (68 percent) fall between one standard deviation above the mean and one standard deviation below the mean. This means that two out of every three scores are within this range; this is certainly the "average" or, to use another term frequently applied in early childhood education, the "typical" range. Approximately 14 percent of the scores fall between one and two standard deviations above the mean and another 14 percent fall between one and two standard deviations below the mean. If we go from two standard deviations below the mean to two standard deviations above the mean, we have taken into account approximately 96 percent of all scores (14 + 34 + 34 + 14). That leaves only 2 percent at the low end and 2 percent at the high end of the distribution.

Later in this chapter, you will apply your understanding of these terms, and their importance will become even clearer. For the moment, keep in mind that the bell-shaped curve applies only to standardized instruments and is not a concept that you can apply directly to your classroom. Now that you have a basic overview of important statistical terms used in describing tests, let's turn to the description of how tests are created and standardized.

STANDARDIZATION AND NORMS

standardized test (norm-referenced test) test that interprets a child's performance in comparison to the performance of other children with similar characteristics.

Unlike teacher-made tests, most published tests are **standardized tests** or **norm-referenced tests**. Such measures have undergone a lengthy and often costly process in their development. Standardized tests are indispensable for clinical and psychoeducational assessment (Urbina, 2004), and increasingly these instruments play a more definitive role in most early childhood and primary-grade settings. Thus, early childhood educators should understand how such tests are developed and what the scores mean. When developers design tests appropriately and educators use them properly, standardized tests eliminate bias in the assessment of individual children as well as provide data to combine, allowing comparisons of groups to a standard (Hills, 1992; Linn, Miller, & Gronlund, 2009). Test publishers develop tests to reflect current learning theory, educational practices, and accountability demands. To develop the specific instrument or test, they conduct research on best practices and learning materials. This means that developers will consult national and state standards to identify the knowledge and skills required at different ages or grades. After the research is finished, then developers write test items, try them out, and send them to various experts for review. Finally, the developers begin the standardization process. This process necessitates choosing populations of children for piloting and on-going statistical analysis so that the test possesses technical soundness. Thus, all of these developmental efforts contribute to an instrument that works for the identified purpose, if you adhere to the following principles (Airasian, 2008; Goodwin & Goodwin, 1997):

- Match the test to the question you want to answer.
  If you are teaching children about the difference between fruits and vegetables, you want to ask children to identify, recognize, or name fruits and vegetables. The presentation of the standardized measure should correlate with the age of the child—writing for eight-year-olds,

identifying plastic objects for three-year-olds. The level of comprehension or skill development should match the curriculum. If it is the end of the first week or a pretest, the expectations are different than end-of-year or other summative points.

- Use standardized measures according to the designed purpose.
  Suppose you want to know whether your second graders are creative thinkers. Asking these kids to take a reading test will show you who knows reading skills and comprehension, but these tests will not give you information about creative thinking.
- Choose tests that are valid and reliable.
  If the math test you choose reports a reliability score of .40, it means that the test is inconsistent enough that you cannot trust the results. Although this may seem obvious, establishing reliability and validity statistics with young children is difficult, because young children grow and develop so quickly.
- You must follow the directions of standardized tests exactly.
  If the test directions say that you may repeat a dictated word only once, you can only repeat the word once. This is really hard for teachers who usually respond to children's questions, even the 25th time they are asked.
- Be sure you understand what the test reports and the statistics generated.
  If you do not know what a stanine is, you cannot explain it to a parent.
- Use multiple assessment methods to evaluate children and programs.
  If you check achievement of third graders with an achievement test and you still want to know about social/emotional adjustment, creativity, and problem-solving ability because these items are part of your third-grade curriculum, you will need to choose some performance measures to supplement your assessment program.

Following these principles when choosing standardized tests assures good practice. What, then, is a standardized test?

According to Popham, "a *standardized test* is a test either designed to yield norm-referenced or criterion referenced inferences, that is administered, scored, and interpreted in a standard, predetermined manner" (2008b, p. 282). A test provides a scale of measurement for consistent individual differences regarding some psychological concept and serves to line up people according to a concept. Think of tests as yardsticks, but remember that they are less efficient and reliable than yardsticks. A test yields one or more objectively obtained quantitative scores so that, as nearly as possible, each person is assessed in the same way to provide a fair and equitable comparison among test takers. Thus, a standardized (norm-referenced) test interprets a child's performance in comparison to the performance of other children with similar characteristics. The key to the use of these instruments is being sure that the child assessed is similar to those who comprised the samples when the instrument was developed. This factor is at the heart of the debate regarding the extent of the use of these materials with young children. Thus, how do these instruments come about; what is the process that produces standardized tests?

In designing a standardized test, test developers must first determine its rationale and purpose. Second, they must explain what the test will measure (there are many types of standardized tests, such as achievement tests, readiness tests, developmental screening tests, diagnostic tests, and intelligence tests), whom the test will be given to, and how the test results will be used. Test developers try to adhere to the standards jointly developed by the American Educational Research Association, the American Psychological Association, and the National Council on Measurement in Education (1999), which sets standards for test users as well as test developers. According to the National Association for the Education of Young Children (2003) "assessments (used in programs) are valid and reliable. (As well,) accepted professional standards of quality are the basis for selection, use, and interpretation of assessment instruments, including screening tools . . . and adhere to the measurement standards published by AERA in 1999." In following these professional and ethical principles, one of the first important considerations in choosing a test is determining whether the test developer included children similar to your class members, so you need to know about the norming sample.

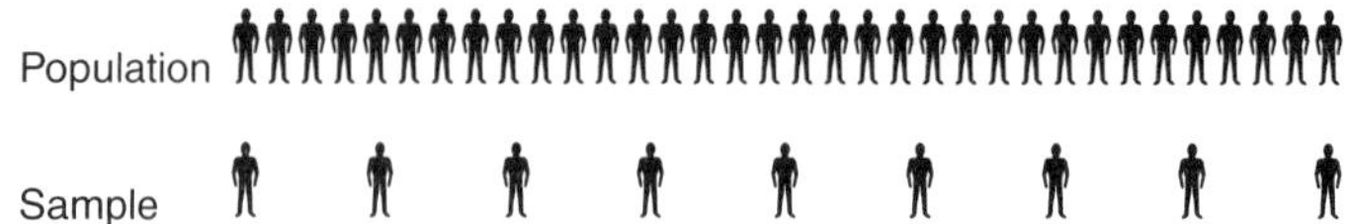

FIGURE 4.3 Relationship between a population and a sample.

population group of individuals on which a standardized test is normed.

normative sample subset of a population that is tested for a standardized test.

The **population**, or group of individuals, on whom the test is normed is of utmost importance. Even if it were possible, it is not necessary to test everyone in a particular population to make the norms applicable. The characteristics of a population can be accurately estimated from the characteristics of a subset of the population as long as the subset closely resembles the population in terms of specific characteristics. These characteristics must also be present in the subset in the same proportion that they are present in the population for this subset to be representative. Such a subset is the **normative sample**. Inferences based on what the developers learn from the sample (subset) can be extended to the population at large so that inferences can be made about the population (Salvia, Ysseldyke, & Bolt, 2010).

Figure 4.3 illustrates the relationship between a population and a sample. Frequently, test developers use U.S. Census figures for determining the percentages of children by age and ethnicity in planning a sample to generalize to a population.

Therefore, in a sample of 1,000 six-year-olds, in the development of the Shoe-Tying Test, the developer will want to be sure that there are appropriate numbers of African American, Asian, Caucasian, Latino, and Native American 6-year-olds so that when the test is published, the results can be a good predictor of where children in Mississippi, Boston, and Idaho will function in comparison to the national norm, which is representative of the population of six-year-olds across the country. Before publishing the Shoe-Tying Test, the developers will try it out on the 1,000 children and determine the scores for describing variations in performance for six-year-olds. This is the phase of development called norming.

norming the process of finding out what score most children of a given age will earn on a particular test.

Norming is the process of finding out what score most children of a given age will earn on a particular test. Take, for example, the Shoe-Tying Test, where the results might be as follows:

- Most four-year-olds cannot tie their own shoes.
- Some five-year-olds can tie their own shoes.
- Most six-year-olds can tie their own shoes.

By testing 1,000 children in a systematic and consistent way, the developers obtained these results. The 1,000 children were a representative sample of those who would likely take the test once it is developed. The norming process shows whether there is any regional, gender, racial, or other salient variables that might affect results. **Norms** are the scores obtained from testing the normative sample (Urbina, 2004). The adequacy of these norms (Salvia, Ysseldyke, & Bolt, 2010), is dependent on three factors: the representativeness of the norm sample, the number of children in the sample, and the relevance of the norms in terms of the test's purpose.

norms scores obtained from the testing of a normative sample for a standardized test.

When looking at the representativeness of the norm sample, it is common to look at the following factors: age, grade (for children in kindergarten or above), gender, geographic regions, socioeconomic status (a factor that shows a consistent relationship to how children perform on intellectual and academic tests), and racial or ethnic cultural differences. Recently, publishers are paying attention to English language learner population, as a growing number of young children come to school with English as a second language. The importance of this last factor cannot be overemphasized. "Assessment strategies that are not sensitive to cultural differences in learning style and rate and those that are not designed for children from linguistically diverse backgrounds cannot provide an accurate picture of children's strengths and needs" (Hills, 1992, p. 48; see also, Rhodes, Ochoa, & Ortiz, 2005; Grigorenko, 2009; Suzuki & Ponteroto, 2007). The Individuals with Disabilities Act (IDEA) of 2004 mandates nondiscriminatory assessment; this requires fair and objective testing practices for students from all cultural and linguistic backgrounds.

BOX 4.1

Kindergarten Sorting and Graphing Criterion Task

	Beginning	Established
Recognizes and names eight basic colors		
Recognizes and names six basic shapes		
Sorts manipulatives by color or shape		
Places shape or color symbol appropriately on a bar graph		
Indicates which column or bar has most		

The number of children in the normative sample is also important. One hundred subjects per age or grade is the minimum acceptable size.

You, as the test user, must be prepared to determine the relevance of the norms for the child or group of children you intend to test with the instrument. Generally speaking, for early childhood educators working with children in regular classrooms, preschools, or child-care settings, national norms would be the most appropriate. However, states and school districts are creating local norms, particularly for primary grades.

The date of the norms is also significant, because we live in a rapidly changing society. For a norm sample to be appropriate, it must also be current. Norms that are more than 15 years old are out of date (Salvia, Ysseldyke, & Bolt, 2010).

There is another category of standardized tests, **criterion-referenced tests**, which compare a child's performance to individual progress in learning a set of skills or behaviors arranged according to difficulty level. Such a test does not need to be normed. These are measures that contain a list of developmental or academic skills that a teacher must either observe or assess to see whether a child has obtained the concept, skill, disposition, or attitude. The results of the inventory are used to plan further instruction. For example, think about swimming and the lessons you had as a child. There were descriptors or criteria for tadpoles, beginner, and swimmer. You could measure your success against the criteria for each level. The principles for center and school criterion-referenced tests are the same. Examples of these tests include Brigance measures described in the Appendix C and on the Curriculum Associates website: http://www.curriculumassociates.com. Box 4.1 shows an example of a sequence for sorting and graphing in kindergarten.

criterion-referenced test a standardized test that compares a child's performance to his or her own progress in a certain skill or behavior.

Now that you have an understanding of the process of test development and some information about basic kinds of tests, what about the all-important test score? How are test scores developed and expressed? Which are good ones to use? How do the developers prevent or minimize test bias? These topics will be covered in the next section.

DIFFERENT TYPES OF TEST SCORES

It is relatively simple to determine whether a child has learned all the addition facts of single-digit numbers through direct assessment in the classroom, because there are a finite number of these facts. However, most information that we wish to assess is not finite, even for young children, so we ask a few questions and base our decisions on the assumption that what we learn from assessing a sample of behavior will give us an accurate picture of performance for the entire topic. As well, test developers strive to discriminate the performance of children with these instruments. Developers establish the ability to discriminate among learners performance by piloting instruments on large number of children. With a few items, the standardized test needs to demonstrate clear differences in performance across children. When you choose standardized tests (see Appendix C for guidelines to choosing tests) to use, you will want to be sure that the test matches your purpose for assessment and that a test is the most efficient and effective way to gather the information you need.

The most important reason for assessing a child's performance or behavior is to enable the teacher to develop appropriate lessons based on what the child can and cannot do. Because you need to know if the learning activity is suitable for a child of a particular age, test scores enable the teacher to determine the amount of difference that the child exhibits in a particular area from the expected level for his or her age or grade. In addition, you must understand how to use information provided in test manuals. Thus, before using a test with a child, you must be thoroughly familiar with the manual. You must know how to give the directions and how to score the measure.

Remember, the first score obtained from a test is the raw score, the number of items on either a published test or a teacher-made test that the child answered correctly. When you are using a standardized test, this score is compared with the performance of a group of children of known characteristics (age, gender, grade, and ethnicity) that are described in the test manual. These comparison scores are **derived scores** and you obtain them by using the raw scores along with tables in the manual. Many tests today also come with software packages that perform the calculations for deriving scores for you. However, when learning a new test, it is a good idea to practice with the hand calculations so you get the "feel" of how the items work. The three types of derived scores frequently used with young children are developmental scores (age-equivalent and grade-equivalent scores), percentiles, and standard scores. The first derived score, developmental scores, seems user-friendly but has the most limitations.

derived score score obtained by comparing the raw score with the performance of children of known characteristics on a standardized test.

Developmental Scores

Developmental scores—**age-equivalent scores** and **grade-equivalent scores**—have been widely used in the past and are reported in test manuals mainly because they enjoy a false reputation of being easily understood and useful scores (McLean, Wolery, & Bailey, 2004; Urbina, 2004). Currently, grade-level equivalents are used by school districts and states to determine whether children in third grade have made adequate yearly progress according to the requirements of the No Child Left Behind Act (NCLB) of 2001. These scores may or may not relate to the curriculum in particular school districts or child-care programs, although increasingly school districts modify the curriculum to align it with achievement measures used. As well,

age-equivalent score derived score giving a child's performance as that which is normal for a certain age.

grade-equivalent score derived score giving a child's performance as that which is normal for a certain grade.

grade-equivalent scores do not mean that a first grader who has a score of 3.9—third grade, ninth month—should be moved forthwith to third grade. The score only means that achievement is well above the average for first graders. An example of a developmental age-equivalent score is 3–2. This score means that the child's performance on the test is considered to be the same as an average child who is 3 years, 2 months old. This score would then be compared with the child's actual chronological age. An example of a developmental grade-equivalent score is 3.2 (the same numerals as the previous example but separated by a decimal point instead of an en-dash). This score means that the child's performance on the test is considered the same as an average child who is in the second month of the third grade. This score would then have to be compared with the child's actual grade placement. Developmental scores are obtained by computing the mean raw score made by children of a given age or grade. That point is recorded on a graph that has raw scores along one axis and age or grade levels on the other axis. Points are plotted for the scores obtained at different ages or grades and a line is drawn to connect these points so that one can easily determine what age or grade corresponds to each raw score. Figure 4.4 shows a graph for assigning raw scores to children in kindergarten, grade 1, and grade 2 on the fictitious Amerikan Reeding Test.

The graph in Figure 4.4 indicates that only children at the beginning of the school year, three months into the school year, and six months into the school year participated in the norming. The squares indicate the mean score of the children in the normative sample. This information is found in a table in the manual, so you would know, for instance, that the derived

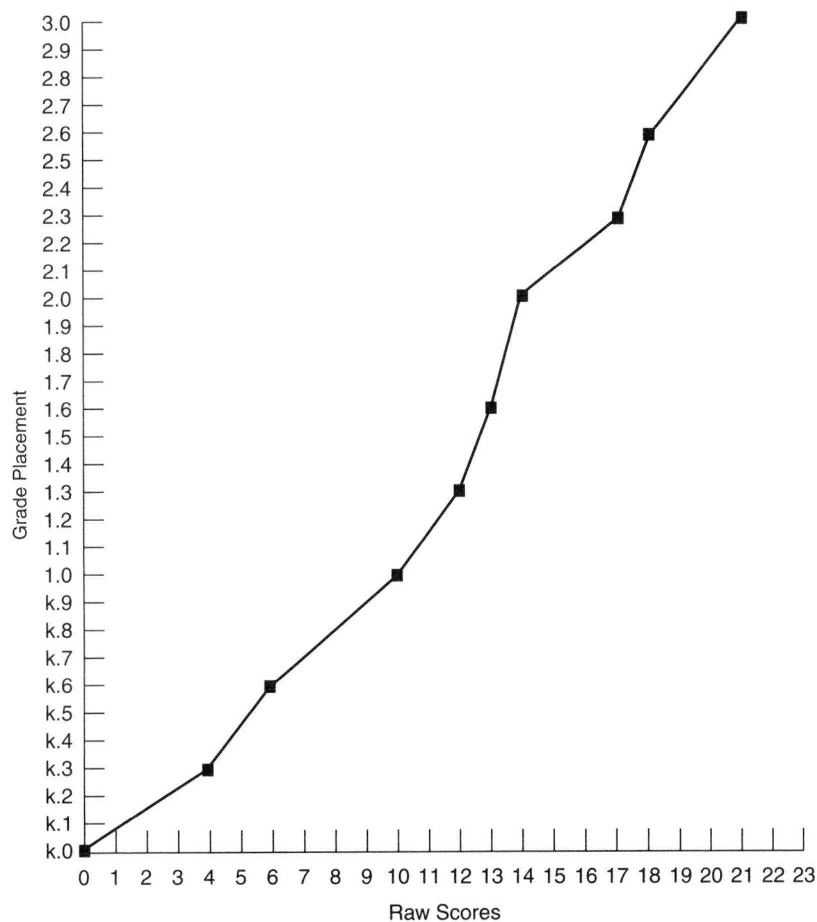

FIGURE 4.4 Raw scores earned by K–2 samples on the Amerikan Reeding Test.

grade-equivalent score for a raw score of 11 is 1.4. Such scores obviously are not based directly on evidence collected for children of a particular chronological age or grade but are estimated—interpolated or extrapolated. An example of an **interpolated score** would be if we tested a child whose derived score is between two points where data were actually collected, as in the previous example. The derived score in the manual is interpolated because no children at that grade placement (1.4) were actually tested to establish that score. An example of an **extrapolated score** would be if we used this test with a child whose raw score was beyond 21. We would have to extend the hypothetical line to determine the grade placement. Thus, we are estimating scores in both cases based on the hypothetical line of scores. These grade-equivalent scores seem to be useful, but do we really know what reading at 1.4 means for teaching on Tuesday?

interpolated score derived score estimated from norm scores because no one with that particular score was actually part of the normative sample.

extrapolated score derived score estimated from norm scores because the raw score is either less than or greater than anyone in the normative sample.

There are at least four other types of problems with using developmental scores (Salvia, Ysseldyke, & Bolt, 2010). For example, there is no such entity as an average 3–0 child (a child 3 years old) or an average 3.0 child (a child entering third grade), just as there is no such entity as an average family of 1.2 children. They are merely statistical abstractions and should be dealt with as such. In fact, both the International Reading Association (1980) and the Committee to Develop Standards for Educational and Psychological Testing (American Educational Research Association, American Psychological Association, & the National Council on Measurement in Education, 1999) recommend that developmental scores be abandoned. However, if you are going to deal with developmental scores, remember that age-equivalent results are written with hyphens (2–3, 4–11, 6–9, and so on) to represent the number of months in a year, whereas grade-equivalent results are written with decimal points (K.7, 2.3, 3.5, and so on) to represent months in a grade, which assumes that the school term is 10 months long. Thus, the developmental standard score may not be the one that will give you the best information. A more useful standard score is the percentile rank.

Percentile Ranks

percentile ranks derived scores indicating the percentage of individuals in the normative group whose test scores fall at or below a given raw score.

Percentile ranks are more useful as scores. They are derived scores that indicate the percentage of individuals in the normative group whose test scores fall at or below a given raw score. The percentile rank is not the same as percentages; it is not the percentage of correct answers. Rather, it is the percent of people who obtained the same number of correct answers. For example, if a child in your class receives a percentile rank of 84 on a particular test, it does not mean that she knew the answers to 84 percent of the problems on that test; it means that she scored as well as or better than 84 percent of the children in the sample for that test. Looking at Figure 4.2, you can see that the 84th percentile is at the top end of the average range.

Percentile ranks are not equal distances from each other. If we were to draw 100 vertical lines through the normal curve, with each line representing a percentile rank, the lines would be very close to each other near the center of the curve and get progressively farther apart from each other as they moved to either end. Thus, there is a big difference between being in the 98th percentile as opposed to the 99th percentile, yet there is a very small difference between the 50th percentile and the 51st percentile. In addition, because they do not represent equal differences, you cannot add, subtract, multiply, or divide them. To overcome the limitations of these derived scores, statisticians and test developers create scores to compare across the nation or other normed population. These scores are called *standard scores*.

standard score is created statistically. This process converts raw scores to numbers that can be used to compare child progress on a particular dimension.

Standard Scores

A **standard score** is the general name for any derived score that is transformed or changed in some way so that the mean and standard deviation have predetermined values. These are sometimes called **scaled scores**; they are used to derive other scores and for statistical analyses. Unlike percentiles, these derived scores are separated by equal distances on the normal curve. Although there are five commonly used standard score distributions—z-scores, T-scores, deviation IQs, normal-curve equivalents, and stanines—only the last three will be discussed, as these are the three most commonly needed by early childhood educators.

scaled score statistically determined scores that are used to derive total scores or that refer to results on subtests of an instrument.

A deviation IQ is a misnomer, because it is a derived score obtained from many different types of tests, not just an IQ or intelligence test. It has this name merely because it was first transformed for this type of test. More recently, this type of score is termed a *deviation quotient.* **Deviation quotients** are standard scores with a mean of 100 and a standard deviation of 15, usually. This type of score is widely used on *individually* administered tests of all types—intelligence, achievement, motor, language, and so on.

deviation quotients standard scores with a mean of 100 and a standard deviation of usually 15.

Normal-curve equivalents (NCEs) are standard scores generally found on *group* tests. Unlike percentiles, this scale divides the normal curve into 100 equal intervals with a mean equal to 50 and a standard deviation equal to 21.06. Figure 4.2 indicates that NCEs within the average zone range from 29 to 71.

normal-curve equivalents standard scores for group tests; scale has 100 equal parts, mean is usually 50, and standard deviation is usually 21.06.

Stanines are also standard scores that are less precise than the other two standard scores just described. The word "stanine" is a blend of *standard* and *nine*. Stanines divide the distribution into nine parts or bands. The middle stanine, the fifth, is .25 standard deviations above the mean and .25 standard deviations below the mean. The second, third, and fourth stanines are each .5 standard deviations in width below the mean, respectively, and the sixth, seventh, and eighth stanines are each .5 standard deviations in width above the mean, respectively. Finally, the first and ninth stanines are each 1.75 standard deviations or more below and above the mean, respectively. As a rule of thumb, the first, second, and third stanines represent below-average performance (23 percent); the fourth, fifth, and sixth stanines are average performance (54 percent); and the seventh, eighth, and ninth stanines represent above-average performance (23 percent). These percentages must be applied cautiously, because children with scores near the borders of stanines may be more alike than different. With a score of 29 and stanine 6, Sally may be very much like Suzy who has a score of 30 and is in stanine 7. Parents may understand stanines easier than any other type of standard score, if they have some knowledge of the broad concepts associated with this standard score. Thus, although it is not as precise as other standard scores, the usefulness of the stanine lies in the fact that it is a single-digit score and easily understood by parents. Stanines are also useful for comparing scores across subject areas. For example, suppose Alice has a stanine of 7 in math and a stanine of 3 in science. We know then that her achievement is better in math than in science. To investigate possible problems, we compare the test to the curriculum, if these are aligned, then we look to see whether there are other curricular or instructional issues that prevent Alice from mastering the science content, if these are aligned, then we look to see whether there are other curricular or instructional issues that prevent Alice from mastering the science content. Besides knowing about the scores, you will want to know whether the test works consistently. Does it work every time, giving similar scores for the same child? This, too, can be determined statistically.

stanines standard scores with nine unequal bands; bands four, five, and six represent average performance.

RELIABILITY

Reliability refers to consistency, dependability, or stability. A test needs to be reliable so that teachers and others can generalize from the current test results to other times and circumstances. If a test can generalize to different times, it has **test-retest reliability**. We can assume that we would get the same results tomorrow or next week. The typical length of time between the first test administration and the second is two weeks. If a test can generalize to other similar test items, it has *internal consistency, split-half* or *alternate form* reliability. We can assume that different test items would give us similar results. If a test can generalize to other testers who administer the test, it has interrater or **interscorer reliability**. We can assume that if other testers would administer the test, they would obtain the same results. Box 4.2 shows examples of test-retest reliability and interscorer reliability as you see them in the classroom.

reliability consistency, dependability, or stability of test results.

test-retest reliability ability to get the same results from a test taken twice within two weeks.

interscorer reliability ability of a test to produce the same results regardless of who administers it.

Test manuals report these different types of reliability as **correlation coefficients**, so you need to know what a correlation coefficient is. Without knowing how to compute it, it is still possible to understand it. A correlation is simply a measure of how things are related to one another; it is a measure of whether there is an association between two variables and if so, how much. The

correlation coefficient degree of relationship between two variables.

BOX 4.2

Reliability

Test-retest	When Charles takes the test today and in two weeks, he will have similar scores, assuming no instructional intervention.
Interscorer	Ms. Keno and Ms. Hausman give the Apple Test to Bonnie, and each gets similar scores.

degree of relationship between two variables is a correlation coefficient that can range from +1.00 to −1.00; no relationship at all is in the middle or .00. The number of the correlation coefficient tells us the strength of the relationship (the closer it is to one, the stronger it is) and the sign (+ or −) tells us the direction of the relationship. If the relationship is positive (+), as one variable goes up, so does the other. However, if the relationship is negative (−), as one variable goes up, the other goes down. An example of a positive relationship is the age of a child and his or her height. Generally speaking, as the child gets older, the child gets taller. An example of a negative relationship is the distance between the source of a sound and the ability to hear it. As the distance you are from a ringing phone increases, the ability to hear it decreases. An example of no correlation is the number of permanent teeth a child has and readiness to read, as reported by Gredler (1992). Most correlation coefficients reported in test manuals are positive.

When considering correlations, remember that correlations do not indicate causality. Just because two variables correlate, it does not mean that one has caused the other. For example, it is possible to correlate the sale of boxes of margarine with the purchase of motor scooters, but few of us would assume a relationship between the two variables. In an educational context, scores on intelligence tests and scores on achievement tests usually correlate. However, in this case, one cannot say that high intelligence scores cause high achievement scores or that high achievement scores cause high intelligence scores. Another variable may cause either or both of these results. As there are at least three possible interpretations, we should never draw causality conclusions from such data. Figure 4.5 shows correlations of subtests on the Ever-Read Test for Ms. Columbo's first grade. Besides knowing whether a test is reliable, based on the reporting of correlation coefficients, we will want to know what the error factor is.

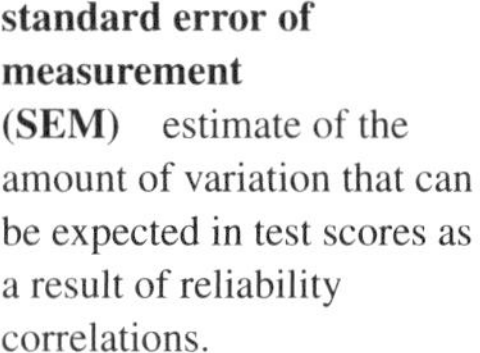

standard error of measurement (SEM) estimate of the amount of variation that can be expected in test scores as a result of reliability correlations.

The error factor statistic that tells about the score that may occur due to chance is the **standard error of measurement (SEM)**. Commonly, developers acknowledge that no test, no matter how well designed, is free from error. The reliability of a test depends on the size of the

Child	Subtest	Score	Correlation of subtest scores	Teaching implication
Ragnar	Phonemic Vocabulary	10 10	1.0	Balanced development; test is not challenging
Glenn	Phonemic Vocabulary	10 5	.5	Vocabulary development needed
John	Phonemic Vocabulary	7 10	.7	Work with rhyming and other phonemic awareness activities
Matt	Phonemic Vocabulary	0 10	0	Investigate auditory perceptional skills
Lisa	Phonemic Vocabulary	10 9	.9	Balanced development; needs attention in challenging
Erika	Phonemic Vocabulary	5 5	1.0	Balanced development; needs attention in both areas
Katie	Phonemic Vocabulary	3 6	.5	Needs skill development in both areas
Alissa	Phonemic Vocabulary	9 9	1.0	Balanced development; test is not challenging
What have you learned by reviewing the scores and correlations for the Ever-Read Test? Would you use it with your first-grade class? What additional information would you need to decide?				

FIGURE 4.5 Reading subtest report for the Ever-Read Test for Ms. Columbo's first-grade class.

SEM. The larger the SEM, the less reliable the test—this is true because the SEM is the estimate of the amount of variation that can be expected in test scores as a result of reliability correlations. Let's say a child in your class took an individual intelligence test that yielded a standard score of 88. The mean of this test is 100 and the standard deviation is 15. At first glance, this score suggests that the child is in the average range of 85 to 115, where 68 percent of the normative population would score. However, the SEM for this particular test is 10. That means the confidence band for this score is that two out of three times, this child's true score will be between 78 and 98 (88+ or −10); one out of three times, it will be above or below this band. If the SEM for this test was 3 instead of 10, you would have more confidence in the results, because then the confidence band would be 88 (+ or −3) and the true score would fall between 85 and 91 two out of three times. The smaller the SEM, the more reliable the test is because the scores fluctuate less. Thus, you can have more confidence in its stability. Figure 4.6 illustrates this example with the two confidence bands.

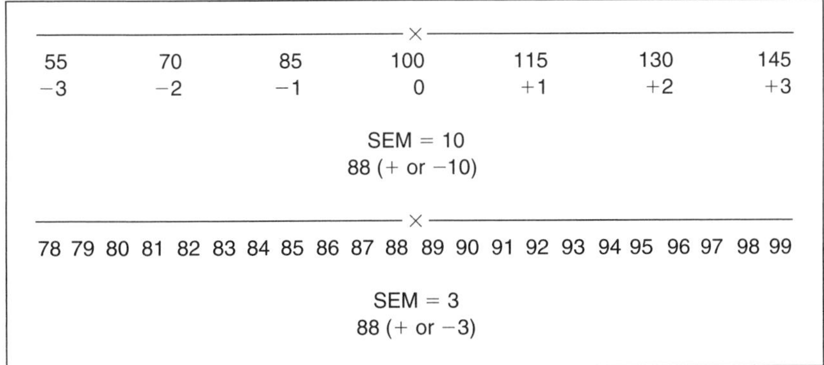

FIGURE 4.6 The influence of confidence bands (SEM) on the interpretation of a score.

The top line shows the derived standard score of 88 on the normal curve without considering any SEM. Above the second line, you can see the range where the child's true score would fall two out of three times if the SEM is 10. Below the second line, you can see the range where the child's true score would fall two out of three times if the SEM is 3. Besides the SEM, there are other factors that affect the reliability of tests—test length, time interval between testing, and size of the norming sample.

All of these variables affect reliability, and thus can inflate or deflate the reliability coefficients. The longer the test, meaning that it has more test items, the more reliable it will be. This is one of the main reasons that diagnostic tests are more reliable than screening tests. Screening tests, by their very definition and purpose, are shorter tests with fewer items. Another factor to check is whether the test has a sufficient number of items at each age or grade levels. Sometimes developers say that the test will work for children from birth to age 8, but when you look at the items for the 0–3 and the 5–8, you find that there are very few items. Thus, the test will be reliable only when used with the children aged 3–5, because at either end of the test, an individual child has fewer opportunities to demonstrate ability. In other words, the difficulty level at the beginning of the test is too steep, which affects its reliability. At the end of the test, the difficulty may be too easy, which affects its reliability. When standard scores increase or decrease as a function of a child's success or failure on a single test item, the test is less sensitive to small differences in the child's abilities. Thus, a test should have enough easy items to discriminate properly at the lower end of the range (and enough challenging items at the top of the range) to fully evaluate children in that range.

The shorter the time interval between two administrations of the same test, the higher the reliability coefficient. Thus, when looking at this statistic in a test manual, the amount of time between the two test administrations must be stated and taken into account.

The larger the norming sample, the more reliable the test will be, and this is a good reason for adhering to the minimum recommended size of the normative sample. Finally, the range of test scores obtained from the normative sample can also affect the test's reliability. The wider the spread, the more reliably the test can distinguish between them. In this way, you are sure that the test is reliable. You will also want to be sure that the test measures what it says it will measure, as discussed in the next section.

VALIDITY

validity the extent to which a test measures what it is supposed to measure.

Validity refers to the extent to which a test measures what it is supposed to measure. It tells how meaningful the test results really are. Developers do not measure the validity of a test per se; rather, they judge the test by its reliability and the adequacy of its norms. There are descriptions of a great many types of validity; however, validity "integrates various strands of evidence into a coherent account of the degree to which existing evidence and theory support the intended interpretation of scores for specific uses" (AERA, 1999). Developers try to determine whether they are measuring what they think they are measuring. Depending on a person's knowledge of research and reason for administering the test, an individual can consider various aspects of validity.

face validity whether a test looks as if it is testing what it is supposed to be testing.

Face validity is whether the test looks as if it is testing what it is supposed to be testing. This type of validity is very superficial, yet it is important to both the child taking the test and the person selecting the test. For example, if a mathematics test did not have addition, subtraction, multiplication, and division problems, it would not have face validity even if it were a very valid mathematics test based on other types of validity.

content validity extent of how well a test tests the subject matter it is supposed to test.

Content validity is established by evaluating three factors: how appropriate the items are, how complete the item samples are, and the way in which the items assess the content (Salvia, Ysseldyke, & Bolt, 2010). This type of validity is especially important for achievement and adaptive behavior tests. When utilizing this type of validity, the user must keep in mind the appropriate use of the test. For example, one would not use a mathematics test for determining reading ability. Nor would one use a T-ball test to measure soccer skills.

Criterion-related validity is the relationship between the scores on a test and another criterion measure. Of course, this criterion must itself be valid if it establishes the validity of a test. This type of validity is usually expressed as a correlation coefficient between the test and the criterion. The criterion does not have to be a test but often is. For example, on the Making Peanut Butter Cookies Test, you would need to find a recipe that serves as the criterion for effective peanut butter cookies, and then measure the effectiveness of the cookie product against the recipe. This kind of reliability is often used by developers seeking to show the relationship of the criterion-referenced test to state standards or typical developmental norms.

criterion-related validity relationship between the scores on a test and another criterion measure.

Concurrent validity is the relationship between a test and the criterion when the evidence is obtained at approximately the same time. During the development of the Kaufman Assessment Battery for Children (K–ABC; K–ABC II), children in the sample were administered the Wechsler Intelligence Scales for Children–Revised (WISC–R; WISC III), a well-established intelligence test for children. If the scores on the new test correlate highly with the scores on the well-established test, then the new test has concurrent validity. The concurrent validity of a screening test is usually judged by the amount of agreement the scores have when a sample of children are given an intelligence test.

concurrent validity relationship between a test and another criterion when both are obtained at about the same time.

Predictive validity refers to how accurately the child's current test score can be used to estimate performance on some variable or criterion in the future. For example, you administer a reading–readiness test to your kindergartners. The test should have established predictive validity when designed so that you know, by means of a correlation coefficient, the relationship of your children's scores to reading scores at the end of first grade or second grade on a specific reading achievement test (the criterion). Predictive validity strongly suggests that if a child currently has a score that indicates a developmental delay, the likelihood is that the child is at risk of future school failure.

predictive validity how accurately a test score can be used to estimate performance on some variable or criterion in the future.

Construct validity refers to the extent to which a test measures a theoretical characteristic or trait such as intelligence, creativity, scientific thinking, or reading comprehension. These traits are theoretical because they are not directly observable behaviors that can be seen or measured straightforwardly. As such, this may be the most difficult type of validity to establish. This kind of validity is established experimentally by test developers who use theories and learning standards to create test items. Through statistical analysis, they establish that the items relate to the theory. The analysis demonstrates convergent validity—meaning that the items relate to the construct. For example, suppose you are interested in a test of self-empowered learner, the items on this test might include the following:

construct validity the extent to which a test measures a theoretical characteristic or trait.

- Asks critical questions
- Justifies work product characteristics compared to standard
- Recognizes areas needed for improvement
- Sustains attention to independent tasks

So, to the extent that you agree with the test developers that these attributes relate to the theory of self-empowered learner and the statistics holdup, the measure has construct validity.

By examining the items for the developers examples of **convergent validity**, you can see whether the information from the instrument is of a quality to be helpful to plan an intervention (Bagnato, Neisworth, & Munson, 1997, p. 11). Shoe size, weight, and height do not provide much guidance for planning intervention. However, performance scores on language scales or

convergent validity is demonstrated when similar instruments measuring similar constructs yield comparable results.

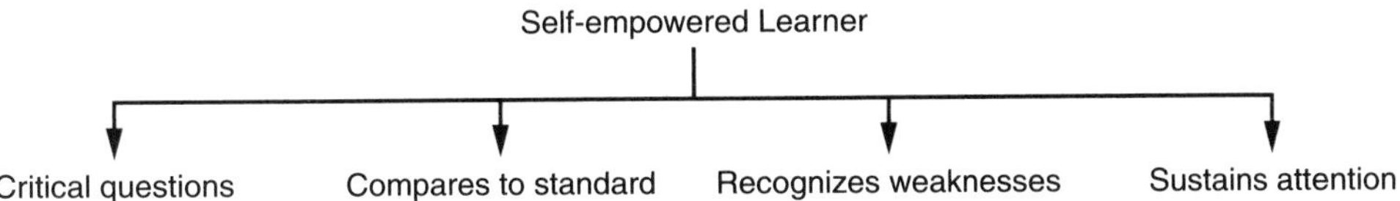

FIGURE 4.7 Characteristics of a Self-empowered Learner.

discriminate validity is demonstrated by showing that items that should be unrelated to a theory or construct are indeed unrelated to the construct.

motor development scales that can translate to the development of activities are useful to early interventionists. The companion of convergent validity is **discriminate validity**. In this case, the developers show that items that should not be related to the construct are indeed not associated. To go back to the construct of the self-empowered learner, for example, suppose the test has the following items:

- Requires constant assurance from the teacher
- Fails to start tasks promptly

To the extent that you believe that these items are not characteristics of the self-empowered learner and the developer statistically shows that these items are not associated with the construct, the test has discriminate validity.

social validity describes the usefulness of assessment information for the teacher in the educational setting.

Social validity represents the value and use of the information obtained from the instrument (McLean, Wolery, & Bailey, 2004). IQ scores and other developmental scores are often available, but these provide limited information for what to do in the classroom or in treatment interventions for children with disabilities. In addition, these tests have been widely misused in the past to stigmatize young children.

All of these different kinds of validity are useful constructs for understanding whether tests measure what they say they are measuring. Each kind of validity is more important depending on the purpose of the test and the planned administration. The chart in Box 4.3 gives practical examples of each of the defined validities.

Just as there are factors that affect reliability, there are factors that affect validity of the experience for a given individual. First, there are test-related factors such as anxiety, motivation, understanding of instructions, rapport between the examiner and the examinee, degree of bilingualism, unfamiliarity with the test material, and differences in other experiences from the

BOX 4.3

In the Real World Validity

Face	When Ms. Zelitzky examines the Apple Test, she determines that the items seem to represent the ones she includes in her curriculum.
Content	The Second-Grade Science Wizards Test seems to have the concepts that the State of Missouri requires for second graders.
Criterion	The New Test of Reading uses (similar items at similar levels as the well-established Amerikan Reeding Test).
Concurrent	The San Francisco Test of Reading compares favorably to the Early Reading Diagnostic Assessment®, Second Edition (ERDA® Second Edition).
Predictive	The History in America Test shows which third graders will be successful in the third-grade social studies curriculum.
Construct	The Whole-Child Screening Inventory for 3- to 5-Year-Olds contains items that represent the best practices articulated by professional associations such as the National Association for Education of Young Children and the National Center for Infants, Toddlers, and Families.
Convergent	The scores on the Infant Aptitude Test help Mr. Miller plan activities for Mr. and Mrs. Krasnow to try with their baby, Paul, who shows some delay in language development. Discriminate the scores on the Perkins Test of Algebra Knowledge Pre-K–2 does not contain counting activities. It does have items on pattern recognition and problems requiring mathematical relationships using symbols.
Social	The Wheat State Achievement Test provides information that will help third-grade teachers plan effective curriculum. Although the Test of Flower Knowledge gives interesting information, it is not useful in planning what to do on Thursday.

norm of the standardization group. Obviously, the test is not valid for children who are uncooperative, highly distractible, or who fail to understand the test instructions. Other moderator variables for test validity applied to the individual include interest, gender, and the social values of the child being examined (Urbina, 2004). Finally, the reliability of the test affects validity. A test cannot be valid unless it is reliable, so reliability is a necessary, but not the only, condition for validity.

A standardized test that covers a good sample of a subject, but not the subject or course as taught in a particular school, would have content validity, but not curricular validity. A test that reflects the knowledge and skills presented in a particular school's curriculum has curricular validity. In such a test, the items adequately sample the content of the curriculum that the students have been studying. In recent years, the consideration of the consequences of the use of standardized tests has suggested that the validity of the assessment relates to the way it is used (Linn, Miller, & Gronlund, 2009). In sum, validity is a unitary concept and the most important consideration when choosing a standardized test (AERA, 1999, p. 17). Curricular validity is more appropriately termed *alignment*. That is, the test aligns or matches the curriculum. Further, the use of the test should not exceed its developed purpose. In this regard, validity is a joint responsibility of the developer and the test user—choosing a test for its intended purpose (AERA, 1999). In the high-stakes, No Child Left Behind environment that you are entering as a teacher, the validity of tests relates to whether tests used are appropriate for the purposes originally intended.

You will also be concerned with whether the test can be said to have **absence of bias**, that is, whether the test is not offensive or unfair to certain children. Most test developers establish absence of bias by submitting the test to a review panel to see if the test, as a whole, will offend or unfairly penalize any group of children on the bias of personal characteristics, such as gender, ethnicity, religion, race, linguistic background or disability. Formally defined, bias "in tests and testing refers to construct-irrelevant score components that result in systematically lower or higher scores for identifiable groups of examinees. . . . Evidence (may be found) in content, comparisons of internal structure of the test responses for different groups, and in relationships of test scores to other measures" (AERA, 1999, pp. 76–77). Test developers report how they created the test to minimize bias in the technical manuals. The best way to prevent bias besides panel review is to administer the pilot instrument to large numbers of children from diverse backgrounds. Thus, as a consumer, you will want to review tests to be sure that a bias panel review occurred and/or that the norming sample is representative of the children in your program.

absence of bias assures that the test is not offensive or unfair to certain children

VOICES FROM THE FIELD

Beginning the Second Year in Third Grade

The hardest thing for me was the district required writing assessment. There was a district-required five-point rubric. It was easy to distinguish a 1 from a 5, but the distinction between a 2 and a 3 was more difficult for me, so I got other teachers to help me. For reading we used the textbook tests at week 2, 4, and at the end of the unit. The tests included new reading selections, multiple-choice tests, short and long essays. At each report card period, we were required to turn our gradebook in to the principal with the cards. Each week, we sent the week's packet of tests home with children. Parents signed to confirm that they reviewed the tests, and then we filed the packets. For the intensive reading program, as part of Response to Intervention (RTI) we dibbled (administered the DIBELS test, commonly referred to as "dibbling"; see https://dibels.uoregon.edu) every week; it was helpful to track child progress that way.

With all of this technical information in your mind and in the test manuals available, how do you decide which is the best test for your purpose? How will you know whether your program or school district chooses appropriate measures to answer questions about the children in your program? First, you will want to know where to get more information beyond the publishers' claims.

GUIDELINES FOR TEST EVALUATION

Thus, when you are expected to serve on committees for the purpose of selecting a standardized test, particularly a developmental screening test or a group achievement test, you will need to be knowledgeable about where to find reviews and what to look for in such reviews. Early childhood teachers should be able to evaluate standardized tests, both in terms of their technical adequacy (norms, reliability, and validity) and their appropriateness for a particular group of children. The principles followed in the evaluation of a test should always be in congruence with the NAEYC position on *Early Childhood Curriculum, Assessment, and Program Evaluation* (2003; Copple & Bredekamp, 2009), the NAEYC *Code of Ethical Conduct and Statement of Commitment* (2005), the DEC Recommended practices in early intervention (2000), and the Interdisciplinary Council on Developmental and Learning Disabilities (ICLD) *ICLD Clinical Practice Guidelines* (2000).

Evaluating tests is not a simple proposition. Even though there are standards developed by a joint committee of three prestigious and knowledgeable organizations—the American Educational Research Association, the American Psychological Association, and the National Council on Measurement in Education (1999)—not all standards will be uniformly applicable across the wide range of instruments and uses that currently exist. However, just as test developers have a responsibility to provide adequate information in the test manual, test users who need the scores for some decision-making purpose, such as teachers and administrators, have an ethical responsibility in selecting appropriate tests that meet the necessary standards for making decisions about children.

Using the previous standards as a guide and recommendations from other sources (cf. Salvia, Ysseldyke, & Bolt, 2010) for quantifying the standards, criteria for evaluating the technical adequacy of norms, reliability, and validity are shown in Boxes 4.4, 4.5, and 4.6.

Other criteria include an adequate description of test procedures in sufficient detail to enable test users to duplicate the administration and scoring procedures used during test standardization and a full description of tester qualifications. The skills specific to a particular test should be enumerated. Finally, evidence showing the appropriateness of the test for children of different racial, ethnic, or linguistic backgrounds who are likely to be tested must be stated. Due to the multicultural attributes of American schools, this is not easy. However, test developers must make every effort to avoid scores that vary as a function of race, ethnicity, gender, or language.

BOX 4.4

Technical Adequacy of Norms

1. Norms should be available in the manual or in an accompanying technical publication in the form of standard scores.
2. The test manual needs to define the standardization of the normative sample clearly so that the test user can determine the suitability for a particular population. Such defining characteristics should include five or more of the following variables: ages, grade levels, gender, geographic areas, race, socioeconomic status, ethnicity, parental education, or other relevant variables.
3. The norm-sampling method should be well defined. If the norm sample is based on convenience or readily available populations, it is not acceptable.
4. For each subgroup examined, an adequate sample size should be used, with 100 subjects per age or grade considered the lower limit. In addition, there should be 1,000 or more subjects in the total sample.
5. The test's norms should not be more than 15 years old.

BOX 4.5

Criteria for Evaluating the Realibility of a Standardized Test

1. The test manual should supply an estimate of test-retest reliability for relevant subgroups. A correlation coefficient of 60, 80, or 90 or better for group tests, screening tests, and diagnostic tests, respectively, is a current best practice criterion.
2. The test manual should report empirical evidence of internal consistency with a correlation coefficient of 90 or better.
3. Reliability coefficients as well as standard errors of measurement (SEMs) should be presented in a tabular format.
4. Reliability procedures and samples of at least 25 subjects should be described.
5. Quantitative methods used to study and control item difficulty and other systematic item analyses should be reported in the manual.
6. Measures of central tendency and variability (means and standard deviations for the total raw scores) should be reported for relevant subgroups during the norming procedures.
7. Empirical evidence interrater reliability at .85 or better should be reported in the manual.
8. The steepness of the test items should be controlled by having a minimum of three raw score items per standard deviation. The range of items for the youngest children should span two or more standard deviations below the mean score for each subtest and for the total score of the test.

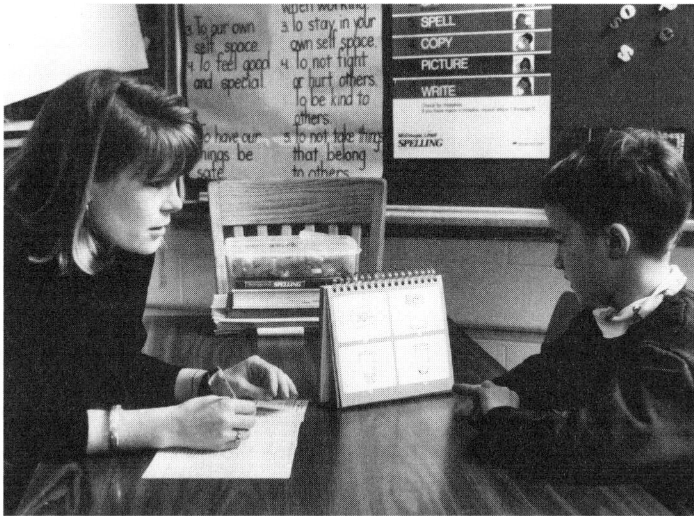

In addition to using these criteria, formal evaluations of tests, written by experts, are found in the *Mental Measurements Yearbooks*. The most recent yearbook (Geisinger, Spies, Carlson, and Plake, 2007) is available on CD-ROM and online. For many early childhood tests, the best sources of information are the journal articles that report the research associated with the development and use of the tests. See also the *ICLD Clinical Practices Guidelines* (2000) for the birth–3 population.

The importance of using only technically adequate tests cannot be overemphasized. In many places, tests control what we teach, what children learn, and what their future holds. These high-stakes tests have assumed almost biblical powers. They determine who will fail and who will be promoted; who will graduate and who will be prevented from graduating; who will attend summer school and who will be able to make choices for themselves. The outcomes influence which teachers will be rewarded or punished; which principals will be commended or punished;

BOX 4.6

Criteria for Evaluating the Validity of a Standardized Test

1. The test manual must define what the test measures and what the test should be used for.
2. Evidence of at least one type of validity should be provided for the major types of inferences for which the use of a test is recommended (i.e., content, criterion-related concurrent, or predictive construct).
3. For content validity, the manual should define the content area(s) and explain how the content and skills to be tested were selected. Tests that are based on content validity should update content on revised forms.
4. For both types of criterion-related validity, that is, concurrent and predictive: (a) the criteria should be clearly defined; (b) validity of the criteria should be reported; (c) samples should be completely described; (d) correlation coefficients with other tests should be reported; and (e) for predictive validity, a statement concerning the length of time for which predictions can be made should be included.
5. For construct validity, the manual should clearly define the ability or aptitude measured.
6. For tests for which there is a time limit, the manual should state how speed affects scores.

which families will be disappointed or be proud; which children will feel intact or feel deficient (Meisels, 2000, p. 16; Meisels, 2007).

Thus, if a standardized test is not technically adequate, it should not be used—no matter how well it meets the needs of your testing program from a nontechnical standpoint. You may think that using a poorly normed test is better than making a decision without any comparative data. On the contrary, if the measure cannot show validity for your purpose, you have no idea what is being assessed. The results will be meaningless. However, once you find a test that is deemed technically adequate, other considerations are appropriate before making a decision between one or more technically adequate standardized tests. Now is the time to consider administration and scoring characteristics such as time required to administer and score the test; age and/or grade range; ease of administration; the match between the content on the test and the content in your curriculum; examiner qualifications; and the appropriateness of the test format, how the items are presented and how the children are to respond, for your population.

According to the *Standards for Educational and Psychological Testing* (AERA, 1999), test users should select tests that meet the purpose for which they are to be used and that are appropriate for the intended test-taking populations. It is the responsibility of the test user to read the test manual, examine sample sets, become familiar with how and when the test was developed and tried out, read independent evaluations of a test, ascertain whether the test content and norm groups are appropriate, and select and use only those tests for which the skills needed to administer the test and interpret scores correctly are available.

Information on specific standardized screening and diagnostic tests used with young children is located in Appendix C.

SUMMARY

This chapter emphasizes the importance of basic concepts of measurement for the competency of the professional working with young children. In order to increase that competency, basic terms are defined and examples are provided. Then more involved terms such as *standardization, norms, validity,* and *reliability* are fully discussed. These terms are then applied to evaluating tests. Guidelines are listed so that teachers may determine the technical adequacy of the norms, reliability, and validity of any given standardized test.

FIELD ACTIVITIES

1. Turn to Appendix C, which describes specific tests, at the end of this text. Select two tests from any of the categories (e.g., screening, reading, giftedness). If possible, select two tests used in your school or community so that you can borrow the actual test and manual. Evaluate each test's technical adequacy following the guidelines in this chapter. Determine which of the two tests is more technically adequate. Check your decision with expert opinions from the most recent *Mental Measurements Yearbook* or journal articles in your college or university library.
2. Interview two experienced teachers working with young children of different ages who use tests for making decisions about children. Ask them which tests they use, which they like best, and why. Later, determine the technical adequacy of their choices.
3. Choose a test. Review it according to the principles suggested in this chapter and with the guidelines given in Appendix C. Explain the test to a colleague or teacher in one paragraph.

IN-CLASS ACTIVITIES

1. Pretend that you are teaching a group of children in which a small subgroup consists of children who speak Spanish both at home and with each other. Your administrator wants to use a standardized test with them that is not available in Spanish. Develop a list of arguments indicating that such a test would not be appropriate for these children and a list of possible solutions to resolve this problem.
2. Bring a test to class, and then in pairs, role-play the administration of the test to a child. After that, shift gears and role-play interpreting results to a child's family.

STUDY QUESTIONS

1. What does NAEYC hold as an early childhood teacher's responsibility in the assessment process?
2. How can teachers assist parents in understanding means, averages, and ranges for their child's test scores?
3. What information will a grade-equivalent score or age-equivalent score provide? How do they differ?
4. When will early childhood teachers need developmental scores?
5. How do percentile scores and standardized scores differ? Suppose that a child scores a standardized score of 50 (mean 100, standard deviation 10) and a percentile score of 60. What does this tell the teacher?
6. How do interpolated and extrapolated scores differ in classroom use?
7. Why is it important for teachers to examine correlation coefficients when reviewing assessment tools?
8. What factors will influence test reliability? What are the types of reliability in assessment? What types of reliability are teachers most concerned with?
9. How can teachers help parents understand and grasp the concept of stanine scores?
10. Why can't teachers conclude causality in the relationship between high intellect and high standardized achievement test scores?
11. Name the different types of validity. How is each type used in the early childhood classroom assessment program?
12. What factors will influence validity?
13. List the qualities that make a test technically efficient. What issues will need to be evaluated beyond technical efficiency?

REFLECT AND RE-READ

- I can define the important measurement terms and know what they mean in practice.
- I know how to explain the role of tests to parents and others, including strengths and limitations.
- I can outline a multidisciplinary approach to assessment that includes the appropriate use of tests for each of the following: infants, toddlers, preschoolers, and primary-age children.
- I am familiar with the ethical and social issues that apply to the development and use of tests with young children and their families.

CASE VIGNETTE

Makalo is a second grader in your class. He is 7.9 years old. It is November and the two of you have had many discussions about math; Makalo maintains that he doesn't like it! You administer the Key Math, Revised (Connolly, 1988) to see if Makalo has any particular strengths or weaknesses. The test has three subsets. Makalo's scores are as follows:

	Basic Concepts*	Operations†	Applications‡
Raw Score	23	19	30
Standard Score	101	102	107
Percentile Rank	53	55	68
Grade/Age Equivalent	7–11	7–8	8–3

*Numeration, rational numbers, geometry
†Addition, subtraction, multiplication, division, mental computation
‡Measurement, time and money, estimation, interpreting data, problem solving

As a mathematician skilled in interpreting statistics, what do you now know about Makalo? What else do you need to know to be able to understand these assessment results? What are the next steps in teaching Makalo?

Source: From N. Roberts, 2003, submitted in partial fulfillment of T&L 411, Assessment in Early Childhood Education: DePaul University. Used by permission.

TECHNOLOGY LINKS

http://www.unl.edu/buros

Buros Institute on Mental Measurements. This site is the on-line link to the series of *Mental Measurements Yearbooks*. It is the place to find reviews of published tests.

http://www.ctb.com

CTB/McGraw-Hill. A corporate site related to standardized tests. It contains a glossary and position papers as well as test descriptions.

http://www.ecehispanic.org

National Task Force on Early Childhood for Hispanics. A research and policy organization that distributes research reports and policy briefs.

http://www.ets.org

Educational Testing Service. In addition to test descriptions, this site has position papers and research related to tests and testing.

http://www.aera.net

American Educational Research Association. Policy linked to research and practice issues.

http://www.wida.us

World-Class Instructional Design and Assessment (WIDA) Consortium. "A consortium of states dedicated to the design and implementation of high standards and equitable educational opportunities for English language learners."

SUGGESTED READINGS

McLean, M., Wolery, M., & Bailey, D. B. (2004). *Assessing infants and preschoolers with special needs* (3rd ed.). Upper Saddle River, NJ: Merrill/Prentice Hall.

Popham, W. J. (2008). *Classroom assessment: What teachers need to know* (5th ed.). Boston: Allyn & Bacon.

Salend, S. J. (2009) *Classroom testing and assessment for all students beyond standardization.* Thousand Oaks, CA: Corwin.

Salvia, J., Ysseldyke, J. & Bolt, S. (2010). *Assessment* (11th ed.). Belmont CA: Wadsworth/Cengage.

CHAPTER 5

Testing: Choosing the Right Measure

TERMS TO KNOW

- tests
- norm-based instruments
- criterion-based instruments
- screening tests
- inventory
- curriculum-based measures
- diagnostic tests
- criterion-referenced measures
- performance assessment
- formative assessment
- mastery learning
- portfolio
- artifacts
- performance
- IEP goals
- IDEA
- technical issues
- rubric
- interrater reliability
- authentic assessment

CHAPTER OVERVIEW

This chapter begins with a discussion of the role that tests play in early childhood education. Appropriate uses of tests for accountability, screening, diagnosis, and Individualized Education Plans follow. Next, using performance-based measures to answer some important assessment questions is discussed, as well as technical issues regarding the use of performance measures. Coordination of testing programs with instructions and cautions concludes the chapter.

ASSESS AS YOU READ

- When is a good time to use a test?
- In addition to achievement tests, what are some other instruments for teacher use?
- What can I learn from the diagnostic process that will help me individualize instruction?
- Why bother with tests, now that we have performance-based assessment?
- How do I choose the right test for a child or a class? How do I know if the test is appropriate?
- What state and federal laws regarding assessment will affect my classroom practice?

TESTS IN THE ASSESSMENT SYSTEM

Tests serve an important function in early childhood programs when used for a specific, suitable purpose. Some reasons for testing include the following:

test instrument for measuring skills, knowledge, development, aptitudes, and so on.

- To give objectivity to our observations . . . instruments that record behavior from a neutral vantage point so we can apply . . . standards and values in evaluating it.

- To elicit behavior under relatively controlled conditions . . . (that is, the child is performing without help and without consulting the book) . . . by controlling some conditions, the teacher can eliminate the influence of many variables that may bias the outcome.
- To sample performances . . . (for efficiency we gather evidence of skill or knowledge possessed by setting it up).
- To obtain performances and measure gains relevant to goals or standards . . . (creating a situation for the learner to demonstrate mastery).
- To apprehend the unseen or unseeable . . . cannot fully see attitudes or values, developmental levels or social patterns . . . need instruments.
- To detect the characteristics and components of behavior . . . opportunity to isolate behavior, to explore the performances of which a (child) is capable.
- To predict future behavior . . . if we can detect characteristics . . . can predict related behavior.
- To make data continuously available for feedback and decision making . . . to facilitate (child) learning and growth. (Tuckman, 1988, pp. 3–5; see also Mertler, 2007)
- To describe commonalities among students for effective planning.
- To provide feedback to stakeholders, especially parents and children, about progress toward learning outcomes and developmental milestones (cf. Nitko & Brookhart, 2007).

Thus, tests serve teachers and decision-makers as an efficient and objective way to gain information about learner progress. The real issues in using tests for young children are purpose and use. That is, why is the test being given? What are the anticipated results? How will the results be used? Does the test have the technical qualities necessary to be useful and appropriate for the purpose? Most teachers use tests to help understand ways to teach children better and to substantiate learning and development. So, when you are choosing tests, examine them for their technical qualities, stated purpose, and alignment to your goals. In addition, be sure that they are appropriate for the children you serve. Finally, be prepared to follow the directions established in test manuals carefully. Given these prerequisites, when is it okay to use tests? What are some of the problems associated with testing young children? In the following sections, these issues will be addressed.

Responsible Use of Tests

Reeves (2004) suggests four straightforward questions that answer the needs of parents and policy-makers. Parents and policy-makers want to know:

1. How's my kid doing?
2. Are the schools (or early childhood programs) succeeding or failing?
3. What works best to help students learn?
4. Do test scores prove the effectiveness of educational programs?

Reeves then delineates the elements of an accountability system that will answer such questions: congruence with curriculum, respect for diversity, accuracy, specificity, feedback for continuous improvement, universality, and fairness. As you read more about assessment and the limitations of various strategies, these principles will come into play. You will need to think about the classroom level—can I answer all these questions? What data do I need to make an informed decision? When should I use a test to help me gather the information? What other information sources will I use to complete the picture about individual children or my program?

The term *standardized test* describes the fact that test administration, scoring of results, and interpretations follow specific standards and are referenced to a concept of *normal or*

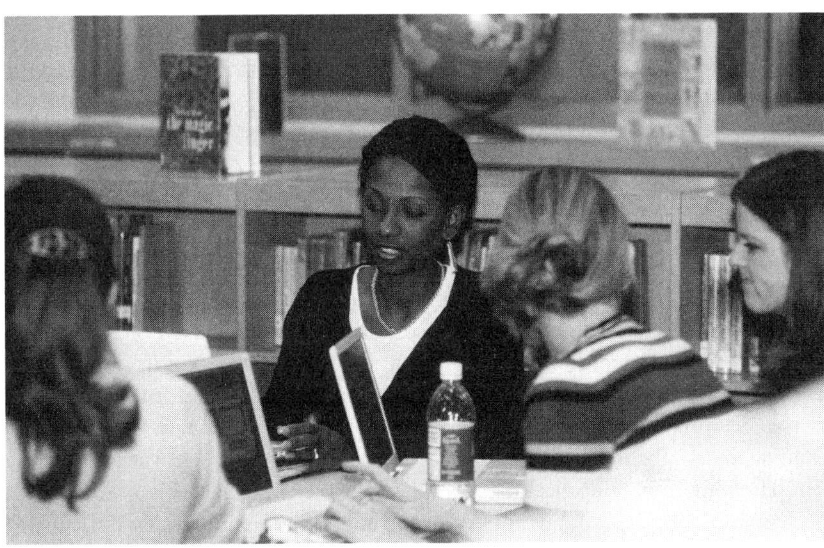

typical. Everybody who administers a particular test is supposed to do it the same way. Thus, the results for everyone assessed will be treated in the same way.

When using standardized tests, you must present the instructions in a specified way, according to the manual. You must record and score the child's responses to test items according to standards described in the test manual. The directions in the manual guide the method for interpreting the results. In the same way, you derive scores and statistics from the procedures outlined in the test manual. Good tests include cautions and limitations for using the particular instrument in the manual. Accordingly, before administering any standardized test, you must be thoroughly familiar with the procedures required for administration.

Errors in Testing That Influence Results

Inexperienced examiners often commit two types of *leniency* errors: (1) coaching—assisting the child beyond that permitted by the instructions; and (2) giving the child a break on the scoring when the child seems to know an answer but cannot provide a creditable response. If teachers take liberties with administration and scoring procedures, the testing situation is no longer standard for each child and results are no longer comparable across children. Leniency errors in assessments may result in the failure to refer children who are in need of special help. Young children thus lose an opportunity for enhanced development.

To be effective, fair, and efficient, teachers must devote time to learning the administration and scoring rules for specific instruments they choose. Directions in the manual tell teachers to read instructions, word for word, but there are various other aspects of test administration—arranging materials, doing demonstrations, applying scoring rules, and so on—that must become second nature to the examiner. You must practice doing the test before administering it to children so that you can administer it smoothly and correctly.

While following standardized testing procedures, the examiner—you—must also ensure that you elicit the child's optimal performance. Unless the examiner maintains the child's cooperation, a test will not yield a valid measure of performance. Goodenough notes that this will sometimes be the case "even under the best conditions and with the most skillful examiner" and proposes that "the safest procedure to follow is not to give any test at all, rather than to give a poor test" (1949; see also Mertler, 2007). Goodenough suggests also that the child return at a later occasion if the child doesn't cooperate. Of course, then, you document the "failed" experience as part of the assessment process.

Using Test Scores

Test scores act to supplement information known about children. Tests are not infallible. Scores require interpretation in the context of the child's life. This is why the requirements for standardized achievement testing should not be applied to individual children for high-stakes decisions—promotion, retention, enrollment eligibility—but rather such measures, if used, should be applied to curricular evaluation and program adjustment. In a recent position statement, *Empowering Schools and Improving Learning: A Joint Organizational Statement on the Federal Role in Public Schooling Vision of Public Education* distributed by Fair Test (2009) and signed by 84 national education, civil rights, religious, disability, parent, and civic organizations, the section on assessment states, "Assessments must be based on state standards and the local curriculum, assess higher order thinking and other 21st century skills, and provide multiple approaches for students to demonstrate their learning. The primary use of these assessments is to improve instruction and enable teachers to better address each student's strengths and needs . . . for all students, including English language learners and students with disabilities." Thus, there is widespread acceptance for the idea that tests used for accountability must be fair, appropriate, and developed for the context in which they will be used. In classroom situations, you will also need to conduct a contextual review of tests. The contextual review of test scores includes awareness of the individual child's personal, cultural, social, and emotional context, as well as the school context. Information gathered from a parent interview and teacher observation is the lodestone; test scores are the glittery specks. Unfortunately, teachers sometimes pay more attention to the glitter, particularly in these days of high-stakes testing decisions made in public education. A child is not a score on a test or a level of performance. A child is an individual: Lisa, Larissa, Peter, Jose, or Stephen, each with a particular family, a culture, and a personality, who uses diverse strategies to cope with the social-emotional and cognitive demands of the school setting.

VOICES FROM THE FIELD

Special Education Inclusion Teacher

I work with another "regular" teacher in a self-contained first grade. We're required to implement the district-developed assessments for reading and math. I modify these measures for the children who are identified as special education. At the district-required intervals, I take the district tests and make accommodations for the identified children. The accommodation I use most often is reading questions to children, so they can answer the questions orally—rather than being required to answer by filling in the blanks. I love the math assessments, because they can be done with manipulatives.

For 30 minutes at the beginning and end of the day, we divide children into groups according to DIBELS scores—I take the children with special needs and others who are functioning at the lower levels. DIBELS is really hard for most of the children with special needs; the timing doesn't leave enough cognitive processing time for them. During the beginning and end of the day Target Time, we work on skills. I love the Wilson Foundations® (http://www.wilsonlanguage.com) program for this—it's so hands-on and tactile. The children love getting out their drawers of tools and working on the white board. This year, the 30 minutes at the end of the day will be used for math intensive instruction. I plan to use these cool tools from http://www.thinkfun.com. I love the Thinkfun Block by Block.

Our science units are derived from the Smithsonian Institute's (http://www.smithsonianeducation.org) lesson plans for teachers. I like the lessons, but find the suggested test questions too hard, so I develop games for the children to play so that they can show understanding of the concepts.

For social studies, we use a district-developed guide. The units for first grade are school, family, and community. We incorporate history, civics, economics, and geography and use projects to assess learning progress for our students. I also use the techniques from http://www.loveandlogic.com. This system helps me empower children to be in control of their behavioral choices. The routine of the set statements for rules and conflict issues helps children learn to assess and think for themselves.

My co-teacher and I plan carefully to be sure that the Learning Centers in our room support the skills needs of our children. We use math in a Flash computer game. I am looking forward to using the newly installed white board.

EARLY CHILDHOOD TESTS AND THEIR USE

Early childhood tests vary in many ways. The most important issues are their *content relevance* and *practical utility* to early childhood teachers. Some tests are *comprehensive,* covering all the major developmental domains including gross-motor skills, fine-motor skills, language, and cognition. Others are limited to one or only a few domains, such as tests of language development or understanding of concepts. Some educational tests are curricular content measures used to assess the child's understanding. Educational tests are *norm-based* or *criterion-based.* **Norm-based instruments** (Box 5.1 describes one such instrument) compare children to others of similar age, grade level, or other important characteristics, whereas **criterion-based instruments** identify the list of skills or milestone markers that *all* children will presumably pass on their way to successful mastery of the developmental stage or academic subject. Such tests evaluate a child's performance on a specific standard. A teacher checks to see whether a child can count to five, hop on one foot, and so on. Some tests cover a broad age range; others target a specific age group,

norm-based instruments tests that compare children to others of similar age, grade level, or other important characteristics.

criterion-based instruments those based on a learning goal or standard. Finite steps in the learning of particular concepts are measured.

BOX 5.1

Norm-Based Test

The Iowa Test of Basic Skills (ITBS; Hoover et al., 2003) is an achievement test that compares children on a number of academic tasks. At the primary level, this test yields information about vocabulary, word analysis, reading, listening, language, math concepts, math problems, and math computation. At the upper levels of the primary battery, the test yields information about social studies, science, and using information. It takes about two hours over several days to administer the complete battery. Results can be used to plan the program and to monitor individual progress. Various standard scores are available. Electronic scoring and analyses are available from the publisher. The publisher outlines appropriate use of the primary level as follows:

> "to help determine the extent to which individual students have the background and skills needed to deal successfully with the academic aspects of an instructional program or a planned instructional sequence;
>
> to estimate the general developmental level of students so that materials and instructional procedures may be adapted to meet individual needs;
>
> to identify the areas of greatest and least development to use in planning individual instruction for early intervention;
>
> to establish a baseline of achievement information so that the monitoring of year-to-year developmental changes may begin;
>
> to provide information for making administrative programming decisions that will accommodate developmental differences;
>
> to identify areas of relative strength and weakness in the performances of groups (e.g., classes), which may have implications for curriculum change—either in content or emphasis—as well as for change in instructional procedures;
>
> to provide a basis for reports to parents that will enable home and school to work together in the students' best interests." (http://www.education.uiowa.edu/itp/itbs/itbs_about_5–8_prp.aspx)

such as infants or pre-kindergarten children. Tests vary greatly in length, as well as in the time and skill it takes to administer, score, and interpret them.

At issue is the use of these instruments for high-stakes decisions (Box 5.1) and other similar standardized achievement tests. As stated, the Iowa Test of Basic Skills (2009) are inappropriately used when they are used "(to) evaluate the effectiveness of an early childhood program, (because) the amount of emphasis given to academic objectives in an early childhood curriculum varies substantially among schools. All programs give attention to students' cognitive, physical, social, and emotional development, but the balance among the curriculum components in any given school ordinarily will depend on the nature of the students' background experiences, the philosophy of the teachers and administrators, and the demands of the community. Since achievement batteries can assess only a limited part of the total curriculum, test scores alone cannot describe the relative success or effectiveness of the entire program. Especially for programs that maintain a nonacademic or play-centered curriculum for the early years, scores on achievement tests provide only partial information about program effectiveness." So, even test publishers remind teachers and administrators to use tests wisely and appropriately.

Four Purposes of Tests

It is useful to think of tests as serving four purposes: (1) accountability reporting; (2) screening; (3) diagnosis; and (4) educational planning. State and federal legislation usually prescribe accountability-testing requirements. One such measure that requires links to curriculum, standards, and multiple measures is the No Child Left Behind Act of 2001 (P.L. 107–110). The passage of this legislation draws attention to the development of approaches to assessing young children for reading and mathematic achievement at third grade. Thus, early childhood teachers will need to be aware of state and local approaches toward assessment of this achievement and will need to be thoroughly familiar with the multiple ways for documenting academic progress prior to third grade. In addition, teachers must be vigilant at the local and state level to ensure that third-grade achievement measures do not become high-stakes assessment, relying on one measure for individual child enrollment or placement. Advocacy action on the part of early childhood educators is effective. One example is when the developmental screening tests initially were misused for the identification of children for special programs, a practice now prohibited in publicly funded programs.

Measures that are intentionally brief and provide a global index of developmental delay or normality are appropriate for developmental screening tests. These measures should be play-based when used for babies, toddlers, and preschoolers. At the primary level, these are the informal reading or mathematics assessments conducted by teachers. Diagnostic-level measures are more in-depth and time-consuming assessments that provide more specific information about an individual child's profile of abilities and disabilities, as well as contribute to developmental diagnosis and identification of educational disabilities. The most in-depth measures are those instruments intended to provide specific education-related information tied to curriculum goals and individual educational planning. Psychologists, special education teachers, speech therapists, and others who must identify children with disabilities most often use diagnostic instruments. However, there are diagnostic instruments that early childhood teachers may find useful in planning for instruction. As you choose appropriate diagnostic instruments to use with your students, you will want to remember the fundamental aspects of choosing the right tools.

The cornerstone of test standardization is validity. The question is, "How well does the test do the job it claims to do?" For a developmental screening test, "How accurate are screening test results when compared to the results of more in-depth developmental testing?" For diagnostic measures, "How well do they relate to results of other test measures, to evaluation based on professional observation, parental reports, and school performance? Have trustworthy studies been done to decide these relationships?" Most detailed curriculum-based measures lack research evidence of validity. The presumption is that they are valid because educational specialists design them in detail. This assumption could cause problems, particularly when you choose such instruments without consideration about whether they match the philosophy, curricular goals, and developmental levels of the children in your program.

Choosing Tests

To learn the relevance and utility of various measures for the children you work with, start by listing the characteristics of these children. Include age, sex, social/economic background, cultural and language backgrounds, and any other factors you consider relevant. Are these children assumed to be normal or are they "at risk" by virtue of environmental factors, developmental delay, or identified special disability? Next, why are you searching for a test? To help identify young children who may be in need of/entitled to early childhood special education services? To monitor the developmental progress of presumably normal children? To further assess children with identified developmental problems? Then ask, "Is this test designed to serve the purpose I need to accomplish?" At the most basic level, "Is the item content of this instrument addressing the developmental or academic issues that are appropriate for my program and the children who I serve? Are there sufficient numbers of items (e.g., questions, tasks) to adequately screen or assess these areas of development?" See the Test Evaluation Guidelines in Appendix D for a complete format to use in evaluating particular instruments. Box 5.2 illustrates teacher assessment decision-making in action.

BOX 5.2

Choosing Test for Purpose

Ms. Wynette needs to find out which of the 10 three-year-olds in her room know colors and numbers, geometric shapes, basic direction words—*over*, *under*, *above*, *below*. She can, of course, observe carefully, but she will need to make sure that she checks everyone. It may be easier to choose a criterion-based curriculum instrument to assess the knowledge of the three-year-olds because there are so many. It seems efficient to use a prepared instrument.

Mr. Nelson needs to know whether the third graders can multiply numbers from 1 to 10 in problems that are single-digit. He could, of course, administer a test that would answer this question and probably identify many other mathematical skills. It seems more efficient to use a worksheet or other classroom-based activity to assess the third graders.

Using Screening Tests

screening test test used to identify children who may be in need of special services, as a first step in identifying children in need of further diagnosis; focuses on the child's ability to acquire skills.

Screening tests are efficient for surveying large numbers of children. In a screening situation, you are trying to take a quick look at many children. You do not know these children or their parents very well (or at all). You choose a technically sound test designed for screening. Most of the children you see will pass through the screen to the other side.

The following two example scenarios highlight issues that often arise during a screening process. Specialists conduct these screenings in consultation with early childhood teachers.

ROUTINE VISION SCREENING You want to know how many children in your class need glasses. A nurse asks all the four-year-olds in your class to identify letters or bunny rabbits, according to the directions she gives. Steven fails the screening. Before you ask Mr. and Mrs. Green to run out to get glasses for Steven, you consider whether Steven seemed to follow directions given by the nurse. If he did not follow directions easily, you might suggest a rescreening in six weeks. If he followed directions and his parents are concerned about his vision, you could recommend that an optometrist or ophthalmologist see him for a diagnostic assessment.

ROUTINE SPEECH AND LANGUAGE SCREENING At first-grade level, a speech therapist comes to your class to screen children for articulation or other speech impairments. You schedule this evaluation to ensure that all children will have every available chance to continue early literacy development. You are concerned about Carter, who does not always speak clearly. Following the screening, you learn how to help Carter with articulation errors he makes. The speech therapist also decides, based on the results of the screening, to come to your room Thursday afternoons to interact with Gregory, Laura, and Stephan to help them with articulation. She will see them in her office on Tuesdays.

CHILD-FIND SCREENING You conduct educational screening the same way, using a technically sound instrument. You plan a day or more to screen three- and four-year-old children to find those children who may need a special service or to find out how the children in your community compare to the established standards. After screening 200 children, you find that 10 fall into the category of "risk" and 15 fall into the category of "watch." You let the parents of the 175 children who passed through the screen know that, currently, readiness for learning seems to be in place for their children.

For the 15 children in the "watch" category, you look at the results of screening to see whether there is one area of concern or low-performance areas across all the parts of the test, and compare the information that you have about each of the individual children and their families. You share the results of the screening with the parents personally and show that they can bring Robbin, Gloria, Constance, or Larry back for screening or seek diagnostic assistance if they are still worried about progress in a few months.

For the 10 children who fell into the "risk" category, you look at all available materials and discuss the next step with each child's parents. For instance, you might refer Mr. and Mrs. Whitewater to Easter Seals for a diagnostic assessment for Ashley, as you are worried about Ashley's gross- and fine-motor performance. You may suggest to Luzmarie's mother a bilingual preschool program, as you believe she may not understand all of the English directions. Mitchell Oxford appears to be quite isolated in a world of his own. You refer Ms. Oxford to a mental health or child guidance clinic. Erick was a terror in the screening situation; Mrs. Ross, his mother, seemed frustrated and embarrassed that she could not calm him down. You refer her to a special education diagnostic team or Response To Intervention (RTI) team (IDEA, 2006). These are teams of special educators and allied personnel who are charged with assisting teachers and administrators in providing suggestions for classroom teachers in providing differentiated teaching and learning opportunities to young children before an "official" diagnostic intervention is planned. The intent of the concept of Response to Intervention (RTI) is to support children in the typical classroom, providing "just in time" service for successful learning. If 100 of the 200 children

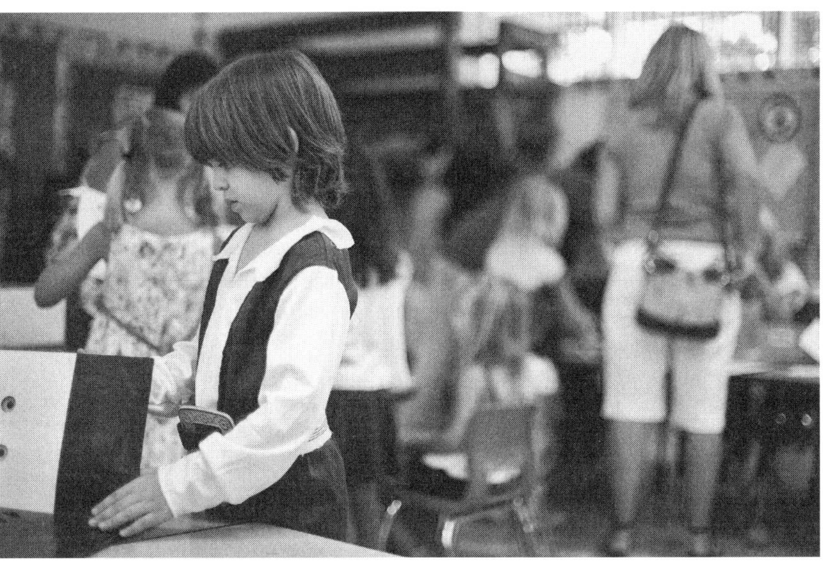

screened fail the test or otherwise show up as "at risk of academic failure," you *change the curriculum*. Although such an event is unlikely, the point is that screening instruments catch the few who need special assistance. If the screening net is catching many children, then plan educational interventions or programs according to the needs of the children. Tests used in this way inform teachers as they make teaching decisions about how to carry out the curriculum. Screening should occur responsibly at all age levels. In addition to developmental and preschool curriculum screening, there are opportunities for screening at the primary level. For example, the teachers may wish to know the achievement level of a given grade level in math or reading. These teachers would conduct an inventory.

READING COMPREHENSION INVENTORY Third graders in your school might complete a reading comprehension **inventory** conducted by the reading specialist or by the third-grade teachers. Those who score below the school cutoff points are involved in special reading tutorials planned to bridge the reading gap so that they will be successful in the independent work required in fourth grade. If only two or three in each class are eligible for this special assistance, the program is working well for most children. If half the class needs remediation, the teachers will change the curriculum by examining the results of the test; that is, they will look at the failure patterns and plan teaching strategies to help the children be successful. Besides using a locally development option, your school may choose an assessment system that links assessment to reading instructional level. One system is the Fountas and Pinnell Benchmark Assessment System (2008), which promises to enable instructors to:

inventory test to assess overall ability in a given area.

- Determine your students' independent and instructional reading levels
- Group students for reading instruction
- Select texts that will be productive for a student's instruction
- Assess the outcomes of teaching
- Assess a new student's reading level for independent reading and instruction
- Identify students who need intervention and extra help
- Document student progress across a school year and across grade levels
- Create class profiles
- Inform parent conferences

(http://www.fountasandpinnellbenchmarkassessment.com/aboutBenchmark.asp; accessed June 21, 2009)

These are screening situations in action. In these examples, tests are appropriate. The tests are gathering information quickly and in a standardized manner. The test score is only part of the data used to make a decision. Teachers must responsibly make decisions that affect the educational lives of children.

DIAGNOSTIC TESTING

Qualified professionals administer individualized intelligence tests, speech and language tests, and other specialized instruments based on a referral question from a parent, teacher, physician, or other person concerned with the developmental or learning progress of a particular child. **Diagnostic tests** provide an in-depth examination of a child's performance in cognition, language, hearing, and so on. The psychologist, psychiatrist, speech therapist, physical therapist, or neurologist tries to answer the questions that lead parents, teachers, and others to seek further information to optimize child growth.

diagnostic tests tests used to identify a child's specific areas of strength and weakness, determine the nature of the problems, and suggest the cause of the problems and possible remediation strategies.

Teacher's Responsibility on Multidisciplinary Team

The *teacher's responsibility* related to these tests is as a *multidisciplinary team participant*. Following the regular screening, a diagnostic evaluation, or watching the participation of children in their classes, teachers raise questions about those children who seem to be significantly different in their functioning than other children. When such an identification is made, teachers make a plan for further evaluation and appropriate experts conduct the diagnostic assessment. In this process, teachers report observations, impressions, and use academic checklists, and academic test scores as the occasion demands.

After consulting the family and reviewing the tests administered, the experts, the family, and you—the teacher—meet to make a plan to serve the child and family. The models of service delivery include (McWilliam, Wolery, & Odom, 2001; Raver, 2009) the specialist—speech therapist, occupational therapist, or other—who:

- Takes one child out of the room for 15 to 30 minutes or so
- Takes a small group of children out of the room for a short period
- Comes into the class and works with an identified child for a short period
- Teaches the whole class or a group of children
- Participates in class routines with the target child and others
- Consults only

To make these models successful in meeting the needs of young children, the team considers both classroom environment and specialized procedures as instructional intervention strategies (McWilliam et al., 2001; Widerstrom, 2005; McWilliam & Casey, 2008). When developing IFSPs and IEPs, be sure that the outcomes are broad, propose teaching skills in logical order and with appropriate intensity, be sure that instruction includes data collection (e.g. charts, graphs of progress), and consider involving peers in instructional intervention. Finally, think about important intervention strategies beyond the classroom that might include mental health professionals, medical personnel, and parents (Hooper & Umansky, 2009; McLean, Wolery, & Bailey, 2004; McWilliam, et al., 2001).

Teachers serve as informed observers prior to individualized diagnostic assessment. Afterward, teachers bear the responsibility for carrying out the specialists' individualized recommendations for service to the child and the family. Teachers can use diagnostic procedures as an outgrowth of the IFSP and IEP process or in preparation for it.

Diagnostic Curricular Measures

Teachers in early childhood use individualized diagnostic procedures to solve teaching problems. Such instruments are generally individualized **curriculum-based measures**. For example, if Sally seems to read with great difficulty, Mrs. George, the third-grade teacher, may use an

curriculum-based measures diagnostic tests for specific subjects.

individualized reading test to supplement her observations about the progress that Sally is making. She can then change her teaching approach. An example of a published curriculum-based measure for reading is the Diagnostic Assessments of Reading (DAR) (Roswell, Chall, Curtis, & Kerns, 2005). With this measure, you can determine whether individuals possess the following: print awareness, phonological awareness, letters and sounds, word recognition, word analysis, oral reading accuracy and fluency, silent reading comprehension, spelling, and word meaning (Roswell et al., 2005). On the other hand, if Ms. Maloy wonders whether 18-month-old Mateo is making appropriate social progress, she can refer to a list of social skills for the age range of birth to age 2 and see how his skills compare to the progression on this list. An instrument that Ms. Maloy might use for this purpose is the Infant-Toddler Child Observation Record (COR; High Scope, 2002). This standardized instrument will help Ms. Maloy in making comparisons about Mateo to benchmarks and will supplement and complement the observational data she collects.

Diagnostic tests help answer questions about children. Sometimes, they entitle children to services. For example, only children with the diagnosis of a particular condition, such as learning disabilities, are entitled to receive special assistance from the teacher of the children with learning disabilities. Although the teacher of the children with learning disabilities might consult with other teachers about issues relating to learning, only diagnosed children are entitled to be included in the regular caseload.

Individualized Educational Planning

Traditional academic achievement tests are the forerunners of curriculum-based assessment. Curriculum-based assessments arose from the recognition that diagnostic measures, such as intelligence tests, were too general and not closely related to children's development and learning or to their learning-related abilities and problems. What was needed, then, were clearly defined educational outcomes (goals and specific behavioral objectives) so that teachers could measure each child's progress toward those specific objectives to evaluate both children's progress and the program's effectiveness; in other words, individual learner outcomes and general program outcomes (Deno, 1985; see also Hosp, Hosp, & Howell, 2007). Box 5.3 shows a teacher's planning for individualized instruction. This is similar to the more formal IEP process.

Curriculum-Based Assessment

Over the years, Deno and his colleagues incorporated two key assessment features in curriculum-based assessment: (1) "measurement methods are standardized; that is, both the critical behaviors to be measured and the procedures for measuring those behaviors are prescribed" and (2) "the focus of the measurement is long term: the testing methods and content remain constant across relatively long time periods, such as one year" (Fuchs, 1993, p. 15). "Curriculum-based assessment

BOX 5.3

Sample Individualized Planning in Process

Background

Ms. Boneck describes Ralph, a four-year-old, as very active, friendly, and talkative. She finds that he is eager to please and receive affection. Ralph is a biracial (African American and Caucasian) child being raised by a single mother (age 26) and live-in boyfriend (age 37). Both are employed in sales. Ralph attends the child-care program from 8:00 to 6:30. Ralph and his family are eagerly awaiting a baby; he hopes for a sister. He has no contact with his biological father and regards his mother's boyfriend as his father. There are no particular medical or other problems for Ralph.

Test Administered

The Expressive Vocabulary Test (EVT-2) is an untimed individually administered screening tool used to quickly assess expressive vocabulary. Ralph performed at the 92nd percentile on this measure.

Intervention Recommended

Based on the results of this assessment, Ms. Boneck will plan enrichment literacy activities for Ralph. For example: Ralph will keep a new word log that he will share with classmates. Initially this may be completed by dictation.

(Dori Boneck, DePaul University alum, clinical activity in Autumn 2000 as part of TL 411 Assessment in Early Childhood.)

can be used to create functional goals . . . (and) provides (teachers) with baseline data to determine the progress a (child) is making and overall efficiency of program (Macy & Hoyt-Gonzales, 2007, pp. 43–44). Curriculum-based measurement breaks the demands of the curriculum into measurable pieces so that appropriate requirements for learners are developed. An example of a published version of such a measure is the *Brigance Comprehensive Inventory of Basic Skills–Revised* (see Appendix C for publication details), which can be used to assess basic reading, writing, listening, and mathematics skills. You can use the instrument to assess one skill or all. Electronic support for this instrument is available. This curriculum-based assessment instrument is a form of criterion-referenced assessment. Often the approach requires special recordkeeping, commonly enhanced by technology. New technology, especially the computer or personal digital assistant (PDA), permits the teacher to track the students' progress and allows the teacher to record detailed diagnostic data. This data can provide a wealth of information to help personalize and customize teaching and learning. These instruments are particularly useful in linking assessment to instruction.

When the curriculum-based instruments are organized by developmental domain—cognitive, social–emotional, gross- and fine-motor skills—the profile for particular children may assist in picking IFSP or IEP goals (Bricker, 1989; Macy & Hoyt-Gonzales, 2007). An example of such a system is *Assessment, Evaluation, and Programming System (AEPS®) for Infants and Children, Third Edition* (Bricker, 2009), which assesses six key developmental areas in young children: fine motor, gross motor, cognitive, adaptive, social–communication, and social. The system is available for ages birth to 6. Today many published curricular programs also include itemized checklists for use in assessing goal accomplishment. An example is *The Creative Curriculum® for Infants & Toddlers* (Dombro, Colker, & Dodge, 2006). This program guide is also available in Spanish. With the conscious link of tests to curricula and curricula to assessment, the teaching-learning-assessment process is in harmony and in action, just like the babies and young children you serve.

As used in special education, the curriculum-based approach handles those situations in the primary years where teachers have specific academic goals that can be specified clearly, analyzed in component parts, and assessed. Such measures are similar in philosophy to performance measures. That is, the goal is to find a "test" that is "the same" as the "task." This is so that you treat the learner fairly and so the teacher will have concrete information about how to teach on any given day. The crucial difference between curriculum-based assessment and performance-based assessment is the underlying theoretical approach of the methods. Curriculum-based measures depend philosophically on the view of behavioral science as applied in observable, measurable terms. Consider this: Ms. Mountain wants to know how Robert is progressing through the second-grade reading program. The second-grade program specifies many word attack and comprehension skills. Children work in workbooks and read with the teacher to develop these skills. Robert gets most of the pages wrong. Ms. Mountain chooses a curriculum-based reading test that evaluates the skills taught in the second grade. She gives the test to Robert, reviews the results, and revises her teaching strategies.

Thus, curriculum-based assessment can be of value to young children, and in particular to young children with special needs who require more specific individual educational planning. If such an approach could truly bridge early developmental milestones and educational benchmarks and provide for instruction helpfully informed by relevant assessment/progress information, young children could benefit greatly. The danger in this approach is that the child and the broad understanding of how children develop might get lost in all the specifics and particulars and that teachers could be overwhelmed in the process. A comprehensive developmental perspective is basic to planning and implementing sound assessment and intervention strategies. Without this general knowledge, the specifics of any assessment or intervention plan are meaningless.

Curriculum-based assessment traces a child's achievement along a continuum of objectives within a developmentally sequenced curriculum. In curriculum-based assessment, assessment and instruction link closely, both initially and over time, to find progress, or the lack of it, and to plan for appropriate educational help. The process is very useful as part of the assessment that seeks to entitle young children for special education, particularly when comparative data is available about the performance of peers in the context from which the child is referred. For example, if Mr. Spring refers Catherine, a second grader, because she lacks writing skills—cannot make a diagram, write a sentence, or outline a story—it is important to compare Catherine's skills to the other second graders in the school before deciding whether her performance is atypical. Mr. Spring could make this comparison by reviewing the aggregate scores for second graders at the McCoy School.

The foundation of curriculum-based assessment is a sequence of developmental objectives, sometimes called learner outcomes, that constitutes a program's curriculum. An objective may vary from landmark goals in a developmental domain (e.g., walks independently) to finely graded sequences of skills that lead to the achievement of the end goal. Such in-depth measures go beyond assessment for the diagnosis of some type of disability. They can pinpoint individual strengths and weaknesses and specific teaching objectives. Also, they provide for close monitoring of the child's progress and the program's effectiveness.

McTighe and Wiggins (2006) outline ways to incorporate curriculum-based assessment through a process called *backward design process.* The process includes three stages:

- Stage 1: Identify Desired Results
  - enduring understandings
  - essential questions
  - knowledge and skills
- Stage 2: Determine acceptable evidence
  - performance tasks
  - quizzes, tests, prompts
  - unprompted evidence
  - self-assessment
- Stage 3: Plan learning experiences and instruction
  - sequence of activities

Thinking through the elements in each stage ensures that assessment and instruction match. In this plan, curriculum-based assessment is formative, integral, and organized. Applied with care, backward design assures that learning goals, instructional activities, and assessment practices will be inclusive and substantive. This approach can also help you think through ways to differentiate instruction for young children with special needs (Tomlinson & McTighe, 2006).

In defining the curriculum, schools and programs identify certain skills to master. In determining whether mastery has occurred, you compare each child to the yardstick that your philosophy deems important as well as state other standards that you must meet. You set absolute standards that everyone must meet. Examples of these **criterion-referenced measures** in action include:

criterion-referenced measures tests that compare performance in certain skills to accepted levels.

- Kindergarten teachers specify self-help, beginning literacy, problem-solving skills, and social skills as the curriculum goals. They choose a published criterion-referenced instrument that provides a record-keeping system that matches these goals for quarterly recording of child progress.
- Third-grade teachers choose a reading skills inventory that matches their goals for literacy instruction. The inventory includes a list of word-attack skills, writing practice, and comprehension skills. They record child progress in six-week increments and teach accordingly.

These measures answer specific questions: Does Harold solve the problem 2 + 2 correctly? Does Bruce know which part of the book is the title page? Can Rita count to 10? An example of one widely used published instrument of this kind is the *Learning Accomplishment Profile–Third Edition* (Sanford & Zelman, 2004), which assesses across the domains of cognition, language, fine- and gross-motor skills, self-help skills, and personal-social skills. It assesses children functioning in the 36- to 72-month age range and is available in English and Spanish. Another example is the BRIGANCE® Inventory of Early Development–II (IED–II) (Brigance, 2004). This instrument includes curricular skills and developmental functions and is designed for children age birth to 7.

Sometimes school districts develop criterion-referenced procedures in district-wide curriculum committees. A committee establishes overall goals by reviewing the literature on the subject. Then, the committee identifies the component skills. This creates a criterion reference against which to compare each individual child's progress. It serves both as record-keeper and standards list. Increasingly, school districts are selecting or developing data management systems that coordinate with state goals and link to teacher lesson plans, often with the capacity to link to the preparation of parent reports. The systems are usually inclusive of assessment and record-keeping. One example of this kind of system is SuccessMaker®, which for "reading reinforces concepts and skills to address a variety of instructional needs within the five major components of reading for K–5 students. The mathematics course enables teachers to give one-to-one support to a wide spectrum of K–8 students who have difficulty with grade-level math concepts. Behind it all, the powerful Learning Management System provides on-demand reports for quickly assessing progress by classroom or student." (http://www.pearsonschool.com/sm21century; accessed June 21, 2009). Consequently, there are many ways that publishers assist teachers in electronic access to goals, objectives, state standards, and other outcome measures with links to planning and assessment tools. As you begin teaching, you will need to judge both the technical aspects of assessment system—particularly validity—and evaluate the necessary technical ease of use and hardware requirements to be sure that you are prepared to integrate the system and the technology effectively for the children you serve.

COORDINATION OF TESTING PROGRAMS

When using tests responsibly, make a plan. Choose tests to match the purpose and to match the population. Consider the tests from the point of view of usability for the faculty and staff. Such consideration includes factors such as special training required, possibility for breaking the procedure into several days, hand scoring, and so on. Make distinctions regarding screening, diagnosis, instructional, and accountability uses of measures chosen.

Factor teacher-observation and parent-interview sources into the plan. Include performance-based measures. Link to curriculum, institutional, local, and state mandates, as your program requires. The result of this coordination avoids both undertesting children—relying on one high-stakes measure for decision-making—and over-testing—so many assessments that teachers and children feel that they can't engage in the learning activities. Choose electronic assessment records with care so that they reflect the program's philosophy and instructional approach.

PERFORMANCE ASSESSMENT

A developmentally based view of the educational needs of young children does not lend itself to the formation of finite lists of skills for mechanistic assessment. You may ask: How will I know whether Pauline can read, compute, solve problems, and think creatively? How will I know whether Jeff can work cooperatively in a group? How will I know whether he can work independently? How will I involve Therese in the assessment of her own learning?

You can answer these questions based on observations of children in the classroom situation. In addition, you can plan special problems or situations that will tell you the answers to these and other important developmental questions. This approach to assessment is termed *authentic, direct, alternative,* or *performance* because the child's "test" closely resembles the classroom situation (cf. Eisner, 2002; Kohn, 2004; Bagnato, 2007; Popham, 2008b). **Performance assessment** seems to be the broadest and most descriptive term. Performance-based measures depend philosophically on the view of a constructionist approach to education. An example of a performance-based measure follows: Ms. Knapp wants to know whether Paul can complete a third-grade project on pioneers. The project in part requires that each child read various materials and write a report at the end of two months. Ms. Knapp pulls a book from the third-grade shelf, asks Paul to read a chapter and to then write a summary. She observes how he handles the process and revises her subsequent teaching plan accordingly.

performance assessment determining developmental progress of children through a variety of means, including observations and special problems or situations.

A key aspect of performance assessment is defining ahead of time what to assess. So Ms. Knapp will use definitions for successful comprehension of third-grade material as well as key components of summary writing in judging Paul's performance. The rubric for judging Paul's writing of a summary is shown in Box 5.4. Ms. Knapp is practicing formative assessment to adjust the intervention necessary for Paul.

BOX 5.4

Rubric for Writing a Summary

	Accomplished	Developing	Not Evident
Main Idea	Main idea is correctly and clearly identified	Most of the main idea is correctly and clearly identified	Details identified, but not main idea
Supporting Details	Two or more are stated in own words	Uses some of own words and some paraphrasing	Does not paraphrase and/or unnecessary details
Conclusion	Clear statement of conclusion	Somewhat clear statement of conclusion	No conclusion
Mechanics and Grammar	Few errors	Several errors	Readability is inhibited due to errors

Formative Assessment

(F)ormative assessment occurs when teachers feed information back to students in ways that enable the student to learn better, or when students can engage in a similar, self-reflective process. If the primary purpose of assessment is to support high-quality learning, then formative assessment ought to be understood as the most important assessment practice (Fair Test, 2007). Thus, **formative assessment** is described historically as the concept of providing feedback to students who are working toward **mastery learning**—the implementation of a curriculum that requires the specification of goals, developing formative assessments, organization of corrective activities, planning enrichment activities, and developing summative assessments (Guskey, 2001). Characteristics of good formative assessment are that the tasks should have (Guskey, 2001):

formative assessment an approach to examining young children that holds that assessment is an ongoing process. It is similar to the scientific approach, in which a query is generated, validated or not, and then another query is formed.

mastery learning the philosophy that promotes the idea that everyone should learn particular concepts or skills and that teachers are responsible for teaching toward this level of accomplishment for all children.

- Clear information, and if written, be legible for all students
- Precise directions in clear and simple language
- Minimal amount of class time—a snapshot, not a retouched photo
- Spiraling possibilities—referring to previous learning—linking to future learning
- Clear match with curricular outcomes

Therefore, formative assessment that utilizes curriculum-based, criterion-referenced methodology as well as other holistic approaches is congruent with the early childhood ideal of good practice that uses an inquiry approach to education. In this approach, assessment—not just tests, but a multiple-measures approach—is at the center of instruction, and you view the classroom as having these characteristics:

- A learning culture with instruction, learning, and assessment integrated to serve particular student needs.
- A place with dynamic, ongoing assessment, with assessment feeding back to the teaching–learning process regularly and routinely.
- A place to start teaching by assessing student's prior knowledge. For example, what does my class of four-year-olds know already about turtles and frogs? Do the third graders know what a "paragraph" is?
- A place that gives feedback on errors to scaffold the learning rather than paying attention to the mistakes for the virtue of identifying these alone. This includes ignoring minor

mistakes that do not interfere with the result, as well as giving hints to the learner so that learner avoids mistakes.

- A curriculum that uses explicit criteria for the evaluation of assignments. For example, "When you go to your seat, each of you must finish reading the story and prepare to discuss it with a partner. The partners will decide how to demonstrate their knowledge. Each demonstration must include the main idea and new vocabulary words."
- A place that involves students in self-assessment to help students assume responsibility for their own learning and demystify the assessment process.
- Utilization of self-evaluation and peer evaluation of teaching to help all keep the focus sharp and on target. (Shepard, 2000; see also Shepard, 2005)

In these ways, formative assessment is a process that makes learning goals explicit to children. "From the student's point of view, the ideal 'script' for formative assessment reads something like, 'Here is how close you are to the knowledge or skills you are trying to develop, and here's what you need to do next.' The feedback teachers give students is at the heart of that script. But feedback is only effective when it translates into a clear, positive message that students can hear" (Brookhart, 2007/2008). This process approach to assessment embodies the principles that ensure that "there is no final mark on the paper and no summative grade in the grade book. Rather, assessment serves as practice for students, just like a meaningful homework assignment does. This is formative assessment at its most valuable. Called assessment for learning, it supports learning in two ways: Teachers can adapt instruction on the basis of evidence, making changes and improvements that will yield immediate benefits to student learning. AND students can use evidence of their current progress to actively manage and adjust their own learning" (Chappuis & Chappuis, 2007/2008; see also Stiggins, Arter, Chappuis, & Chappuis, 2006).

Across the country, states and school districts are employing the holistic approach to assessment and reducing reliance on high-stakes measures. For example, Vermont uses portfolio assessment as well as multiple-choice measures for accountability measurement (Sacks, 1999; Vermont Department of Education, 2009). "Besides the New England Common Assessment Program (NECAP) mathematics, reading and writing assessments are administered in grades 3–8 and 11 each October and the NECAP science assessment in grades 4, 8 and 11. Schools also assess student performance in additional subject areas and at additional grade levels using portfolios (collections of student work), norm-referenced standardized tests, and locally developed assessments" (Vermont Department of Education, 2009). A suburban Chicago district reports the process of philosophical commitment to implementation of multiple measures (Schroeder & Pryor, 2001). The process was a multiyear project and required parent and school board education. Inspired by Rothstein's (2000) description of a composite index of school performance, the district changed focus. "Americans want students with proficiency in math and reading. But schools also should teach citizenship, social responsibility, cooperative problem solving, a work ethic and appreciation of the arts. And youth should leave school in good physical and emotional health, with habits and knowledge to sustain that health into adulthood" (Rothstein, 2009). "Work in the Process Portfolios is chosen by both teachers and students, as it demonstrates learning that they feel is significant. Video clips of students speaking Chinese, performing in plays, etc. demonstrate learning that cannot be captured on paper. PowerPoint is used to display these clips, with older grades creating their own presentations. Students learn how to manage their Electronic Portfolios in technology classes. Students write brief reflections (also called "work tags") for the pieces they choose. In May, each student makes his/her final selections for the Selected Works Portfolio and organizes it for Portfolio Day" (Cambridge Public Schools, 2008, http://www.cpsd.us/MLK/portfolio.cfm#top). With these examples of good practice in action, we can keep in mind the call to action by Popham, who says that "U.S. educators have been thrown into a score-boosting game they cannot win. More accurately, the score-boosting game cannot be won without doing educational damage to the children in our public schools. The negative consequences flowing from a national enshrinement of increased test scores are both widespread and serious" (2001, p. 12; see also Popham, 2008a). Though we must be accountable, we must have the courage to collect information systematically and with multiple data sources. Finally, any single measure—including criterion-referenced or performance-based task—can become high-stakes if status-changing educational decisions (e.g., retention in grade, eligibility for gifted program, enrollment in remedial program) are made on the basis of one single measure. The key to authentic assessment is regular, formative assessment with multiple measures leading to any summative decisions. Box 5.5 shows examples of performance-based measures.

Systematic Collection of Information

The teacher's responsibility as an educator, then, is not to just say no to testing and accountability requirements, but to develop measures that reflect and affirm an understanding of children and a philosophy of education. As a teacher, you do this through the systematic collection of information on each child in your care. You record using checklists and interviews: child interests, thinking, conversations, children at play, children following routines, and otherwise showing developmental progress. You keep anecdotal notes, logs, diaries, and samples of children's work.

BOX 5.5

Performance-Based Measures

1. To assess early literacy development, you might examine the way that children use written materials related to themes in the housekeeping corner. For example, you turn the housekeeping corner into a travel agency, bringing in travel posters, tickets, appointment books, and so on. You observe how much written material each child incorporates into dramatic play. This tells you the child's understanding of the functions and uses of written language. Another place to observe early literacy is at the writing table. By looking at the child's drawings and stories, you assess each child's familiarity with the features of written language (e.g., vocabulary, devices, rhythm, and intonation), spelling and decoding strategies and composing strategies. When you are reading stories to children one on one, you see which children have the concept of a story and individual progress toward sound/symbol relationship and so on (Teale, 1990, pp. 53–55). Additional elements of emergent literacy include awareness of sound patterns, individual sounds in words, specific features of letters, differences among letters, and ability to create narratives, as well as the concept of "book language" and book-related concepts such as title, front, back; developing concept of how "to read" and "to write" (cf. Otto, 2008).

2. To assess the mathematical understanding of young choung children, you might observe them during routines such as setting the table for snacks. When a child must be sure that there is a cookie for everyone, he is showing you whether he has developed the concept of one-to-one correspondence. You could also introduce group games involving logical–mathematical thinking. For example, young children love to play card games such as War (who has more cards), Go Fish, Old Maid, and so on. You could watch them at play to assess math concepts. In discussions of numbers, you have a chance to see which children have developed some ideas about numbers. Examples of these opportunities include judging how many marbles are in a jar, graphing which children prefer red jelly beans, and recording how many people are in each child's family (Kamii & Rosenblum, 1990, pp. 146–162; See also Kamii, 2000; Clements & Sarama, 2009).

3. Examples of science probleence problems for primary grades include activities called Whirlybird and Sugar Cube (Educational Testing Service, 1993; see also Harlan & Rivkin, 2008). In the Whirlybird activity, students watch an administrator's demonstration of centrifugal force and then respond to written questions about what occurred in the demonstration. Students need to make careful observations about what happens as the administrator puts the steel balls in different holes on the Whirlybird arms, and then infer the relationship between the position of the steel balls and the speed at which the arm rotates.

In the Sugar Cube experiment, students observe the effect of warm water on different states of sugar cubes, raw sugar, and fine granules.

Portfolios

You can combine these collected materials into comprehensive portfolios. A **portfolio** is a folder, box, basket, or other container that serves to collect work samples from children throughout the year. You collect a wide variety of materials, or **artifacts**—pieces of child's work—to document child progress. Portfolios are "the best vehicle to show us what a child learns and how schoolwork fits into that child's personal universe of knowledge" (Hebert, 2001, xiii). As well, there are commercially available electronic portfolios that you may wish to consider for compatibility with your curriculum. One example is the ClassLink Portfolio System™. "The ClassLink Portfolio System provides every student with an electronic collection of their achievements, assessment, and feedback. Teachers, administrators, and parents can review a student's portfolio and determine how to better support their learning. Tied to rubrics and standards, the portfolio identifies student skills, subject area proficiencies, and achievement of state and national standards" (http://www.classlink2000.com). In addition, some school districts and child-care programs develop electronic portfolios using the administrative data systems (or open-code source ware) already in place for monitoring attendance and other demographic information.

portfolios places, such as folders, boxes, or baskets, for keeping all the information known about the children in a class.

artifacts the materials that children produce to demonstrate knowledge, skills, or dispositions.

Thus, portfolios are systematic collections that document the **performance** of the children. Because young children think differently than adults, you must watch them to see how they solve problems and set up assessment situations for them to display such skills. Examples of ways to assess naturally and to pose problems for assessment purposes are discussed in the following section.

performance refers to actions on the part of learners that can be assessed through observation, review of child-produced documents or other learning products.

Link to Individualized Education Plan

In the past, much of the discussion at multidisciplinary staffings related to presenting symptoms, norm-based test results, and the development of **IEP goals**. Often, there was limited information about performance on standardized high-stakes achievement tests because school districts frequently excluded special education students from the district's testing program. Since the reauthorization of **IDEA** in 1997 (and continuing with the reauthorization of IDEA 2004), such exclusion is no longer possible; districts are required to include students with disabilities in high-stakes testing programs (No Child Left Behind, 2001). The issues related to this requirement are complex. How should children with disabilities be accommodated? What procedures and/or materials must be modified? Do we overprescribe accommodation? How are district-wide and statewide results influenced (Thurlow, 2001; Thurlow, Elliott, & Ysseldyke, 2003)? "Recognizing that many students with disabilities need accommodations in order to participate in high-stakes assessments, IDEA requires that students' individualized education programs (IEPs) delineate testing accommodations for state, district, and teacher-made tests. These testing accommodations help incorporate the principles of universal design for learning into the testing process, fostering the design and administration of testing materials that are accessible to students of a wide range of ability levels and unique strengths and challenges" (Salend, 2008; see also Kochhar-Bryant & Shaw, 2009 and Turnbull, Turnbull & Wehmeyer, 2010). This approach to accountability links testing, instruction, and the IEP process more directly to the curriculum and learning. That is, what are we going to do on Monday to help Bill in the classroom?

IEP goals the specified learning goals for children with disabilities. These are established by a multidisciplinary team that includes the child's parents.

IDEA federal law that governs the practices for delivery of educational services to all children with disabilities.

Technical Issues

Technical issues regarding performance assessment are emerging. Just because performance assessment seems user-friendly and connected to a holistic philosophy of curriculum and assessment, are the measures necessarily benign when used for accountability purposes? Probably not! The variables of task, learner, and context are each multidimensional. The consequences of errors in the interpretation of results are thus geometric rather than linear in proportion. For example, if four-year-old Matilde fails to give each child a napkin at snack time, does her teacher, Ms. Stone, assume because of this one observation that Matilde has not accomplished one-to-one correspondence? Most early childhood teachers would consider such an interpretation an overinterpretation and come up with several alternative reasons for the omission on Matilde's part. This

technical issues variables of task, learner, and context that can cause problems with performance assessment.

example is obvious and simple. In other instances, the accountability stakes are high and children may pass or fail based on the accumulation of evidence.

For example, when developing local standards or outcomes for children to meet, consider whether teachers share similar definitions for the items to be used:

- Do kindergarten teachers agree on the definition of "conversational skills" as expected?
- Do third-grade teachers know what "addition skills" are for the seven- and eight-year-olds in their charge?
- Are expected self-help skills for three-year-olds uniform across cultural/family groups?

The point is that these items require operational definitions. Teachers need to train on agreement for the definitions. To do less risks the repetition of the well-known abuses of standardized assessments in the performance arena. Consider the following analogy of two gardens. One garden has wildflowers with no path. There are also many weeds. The second garden shows paths along defined schemes with small stones to set off the flowers. There are no weeds. Which garden is beautiful? What definitions of *garden* and *beautiful* are used? Which garden should "flunk"?

Rubrics

rubrics Scoring criteria for performance tasks.

One way to address the issue of operational definition is to create scoring criteria to use with the performance tasks. These scoring criteria are **rubrics**. Teachers and others who develop performance tasks create standards and rules for judging the performance. In some cases, the criteria are points along a scale so that the criteria guide the teacher and the student in the teaching and learning process (Marzano, Pickering, & McTighe, 1993; Musial, Nieminen, Thomas, & Burke, 2009). The best rubrics give the steps in the assignment or task in explicit language for the learner, identify the process that the learner must use, and describe what the final product or performance will look like (Brookhart & Nitko, 2008). Thus, the rubric guides the learner in the acquisition of the skill, process, or knowledge required. Often, rubrics include gradations of quality—excellent, adequate, and below par—or gradations showing approximation toward mastery such as novice, intermediate, advanced, and superior (Arter & Chappuis, 2007).

Stiggins (2008, pp. 164–177) suggests the following steps for rubric development:

- Discover—that is, watch children at work on the learning task and identify distinctive characteristics of the work that meets the learning objective.
- Condense all of the ideas into key attributes of success.
- Define simple definitions for success and the continuum leading there.
- Apply the rubric several times so that you can be consistent when it counts.
- Refine the rubric as necessary.

In this way, Stiggins argues that you will create rubrics that specify important content with sharp clarity and that are fair as well as practical (2008). Groups of teachers best carry out rubric development for performance assessment because the work is time-consuming, important, and vital to linking assessment to curriculum and instruction.

Small school districts may decide to examine the way they teach and assess math in the primary grades. After reviewing curricula, consulting the learner outcomes for their state, and considering the National Council of Teachers of Mathematics standards, the teachers choose a sequence of instruction for K–3. They match activities to the goals. As the teachers work, they choose tasks that they believe are checkpoints along the continuum of problem-solving. These will be the performance tests. When they choose the performance tasks as tests, they must identify clear criteria for judging performance and progress toward the "ultimate" or top performance.

To ignore the rubric development or to adopt haphazardly a task outside the philosophy–curriculum–assessment system offers a serious opportunity for disaster. Vague, subjective, and unspecified criteria for evaluation result in unfair practices for children. Boxes 5.6 through 5.11 show sample rubrics. In addition to clear, defined, and operationalized criteria, other technical issues face teachers when using performance assessment.

BOX 5.6

Book Report Rubric for Second Grade

	Yes	No

• I read the whole book.
• The report tells:
  • Title of the book.
  • Author of the book.
• I wrote two or three paragraphs about the book.
• The paragraphs tell:
  • What the book is about.
  • Who the main characters are.
  • What I liked about the book.
• I checked the writing according to the class editing guidelines.		

BOX 5.7

Class Discussion Rubric for First Grade

	Very Well	Most of the Time	Need to Work on This
• I can sit and listen to my classmates. • I can wait for my turn when I am eager to add a comment. • I can say something related to the topic. • I can speak up loud enough to be heard by everyone. • I can appreciate the comments of my classmates even when I think that they are silly or not related to the topic.			

BOX 5.8

Science Drawing Rubric for Kindergarten

	Yes	No
• I drew the picture to represent the item viewed (e.g., leaf, rock, bug). • I used realistic colors for the drawing. • I labeled the drawing.		

BOX 5.9

Class Presentation Rubric for Third Grade

	Yes	No	Superb	OK	Needs Some Improvement . . .
• I made a graphic organizer to show the main points. • The organizer is neat. • Spelling is final-draft accurate. • There are details to support the main idea. • I made pictures to illustrate my topic. • The pictures are neat. • They are related to the topic. • I thought about questions that my classmates might ask. • I practiced my presentation. • I am ready for my classmates to judge my work.					

BOX 5.10

Oral Presentation Rubric

Name: ___________ Date: ___________

Attribute	Evident	Not Evident	Emerging
On topic			
Organized			
Creative			
Transitions			
Eye contact			
Loud enough			
Involved audience			
Visual aids			

Comments: ____

____

____

BOX 5.11

Group Skills

Name: ___________ Date: ___________

	Exemplary	Adequate	Needs Improvement
Uses quiet voice			
Takes turns			
Shares decision-making			
Respects others			
Contributes to conflict resolution			
Follows directions			

Listens	Often	Sometimes	Never
Helps others understand peer's ideas			
Asks questions to help group understand			
Shows interest in other ideas			

Additional important technical issues include reliability, consistency of the application of standards, and intrarater and interrater reliability. When using performance assessment for accountability purposes, it is critical to establish standards such as **interrater reliability**—statistically determined agreement of multiple raters observing the same task performance by a number of children. If the procedures are used simply to guide teaching, there is little question of validity. Questions of validity and reliability emerge when using the measures for high-stakes decisions. Such high-stakes decisions are those regarding promotion, placement in special programs, and identification as a special learner. This is due to the complexity of establishing reliability regarding these assessments.

interrater reliability ability of a test to produce the same results regardless of who administers it.

Currently, there is limited research on high-stakes performance measures that include questions of individual differences, task specificity, and the level of difficulty of the task (Elliott, 1993; Thurlow, Elliott, & Ysseldyke, 2003). Although these issues affect formally identified children with special needs, they are important considerations for all children. Whenever you make important decisions about children, you must be sure that every effort protects the rights, the best interests, and the integrity of the individual child. The tests must match the purpose of assessment, no matter what the form. A performance measure is not inherently better if the items are not congruent with the curriculum, if the child does not understand the directions, if the time limits are too rigid, or if bias exists in the material.

"When used for accountability purposes, the assessments must be conducted with many students, there must be consistency in the domains of knowledge being assessed, and the assessments must yield adequate samples of student performance within those domains. Costs and time associated with administration of the assessments to numerous students are also major considerations" (McLaughlin & Warren, 1994, p. 7). Performance assessment tasks must meet the same demands for efficiency, effectiveness, and fairness as other conventional testing approaches (cf. Popham, 2008).

Some practical guidelines for school districts using performance assessment include:

- Use the standards of NAEYC (National Association for the Education of Young Children) and applicable professional associations for defining expected performance at different age levels.

- Gather some definitions or descriptions of expected performance.
- Gather samples of children's work that illustrate varying quality.
- Discuss the work with colleagues.
- Write your own descriptions.
- Gather another set of student work samples.
- Discuss with colleagues and revise criteria for judging performance. (Herman, Aschbacher, & Winters, 1992; Arter & Chappuis, 2007)

Authentic assessment, when compared to conventional testing, makes far greater demands on both students and teachers. Some critics believe that it takes so much time that instruction is short-changed. However, this point of view misses the symbiotic relation between instruction and assessment. Within the best models of authentic assessment, teaching and evaluation become virtually indistinguishable: an assessment that teaches students how to monitor their work is a vital form of instruction (cf. Stiggins, 2008b).

authentic assessment determining developmental progress of children through a variety of means, including observations and special problems or situations.

The use of **authentic assessment** and a holistic approach to teaching and assessment considers the teaching–learning process as one that proceeds through the following steps:

- Learner outcomes—what do I want my students to know and be able to do?
- Outcome indicators—how will I know that the learner has achieved the outcome?
- Learning opportunities—what activities will support the learner and facilitate learning?
- Assessment tasks—what documentation of learning must I collect?
- Performance criteria and scoring rubrics—how will the learning be documented and evaluated? (Martin-Kniep, 1998, p. 27; see also Brookhart & Nitko, 2008)

These steps are consistent with the National Association for the Education of Young Children (NAEYC) and National Association of Early Childhood Specialists in State Departments of Education (NAECS/SDE) *Position Statement on Early Childhood Curriculum, Assessment, and Program Evaluation* (NAEYC & NAECS/SDE, 2003; see also Copple & Bredekamp, 2009). The profession and its stakeholders: make ethical, appropriate, valid, and reliable assessment . . . (a) central part (of programming), assess(ing) young children's strengths, progress, and needs; use assessment methods that are developmentally appropriate, culturally and linguistically responsive, tied to children's daily activities, supported by professional development, inclusive of families; connected to specific, beneficial purposes; (1) making sound decisions about teaching and learning, (2) identifying significant concerns that may require focused intervention for individual children, and (3) helping programs improve their educational and developmental interventions.

Accordingly, all assessment plans are treated systematically, seriously, and ethically, no matter how "teacher-friendly" the performance assessment measures, screening measures, or curriculum-based measures may look.

SUMMARY

Consider these final comments about testing in early childhood education. Ask yourself, "Why am I doing this?" Remind yourself of the uses and limitations of standardized tests and of their possible misuses and abuses. One common abuse is the misuse of a developmental screening test as a basis, by itself, for making placement decisions concerning educational programs. Remember that testing definitely does not equal assessment. Developmental assessment is a *process* for detecting the developmental progress of a child that may include testing. The child's parents know more about the child's development and functioning than any single test will ever reveal, and so do you as the child's teacher. Use the observations well in the service of both the child and the child's parents.

Tests are efficient and important tools used in the service of young children to provide educational opportunity (entitlement for service), instructional enrichment (diagnosis of special educational needs), and accountability (documentation of program outcome achievement). Misuse occurs when teachers and others pick the wrong tool or use one tool for everything. There is no one "food processor" that fits all of the required assessment tasks of the classroom.

FIELD ACTIVITIES

1. Visit a child-care center near you. Ask teachers at the center how they screen young children. Match their procedures to the practices described in this chapter. Are there any missing pieces?
2. Interview the special education coordinator in your area. Ask how the community uses tests.
3. Examine the contents of screening batteries. Try one or more of the measures on your classmates and on volunteer children. Discuss the problems you had in administering the measures and compare them with your classmates' experiences.
4. Interview a primary-grade teacher about achievement testing in your state or school district. Find out what is required at each grade level. Look at the instruments at the school or in the library.
5. Visit a school or center that uses a portfolio assessment system. Ask what material the teachers collect and how they use the portfolio, plus what role, if any, the child plays in the process. Discuss with classmates whether you found any potential technical problems in the system and whether the school makes high-stakes decisions using the portfolios.
6. Interview one or two parents of young children. What are their experiences with assessment? What do they know about the instruments and tasks used to evaluate their children? What is their understanding of the scores or reports?

IN-CLASS ACTIVITIES

1. With a partner, outline a complete yearly assessment plan for a preschool program. Then, plan an assessment program for second grade using copies of your state's standards for instructional outcomes.
2. Think about a child you know (or remember from childhood or field experiences). Describe this child to a partner. Identify any particular learning or developmental concerns. Plan a way to document this child's learning. For any questions that you cannot answer about the child's development, make a diagnostic testing agenda to carry forward.
3. Read *Testing Miss Malarkey* (Walker Books, 2003) by Judy Finchler (author) and Kevin O'Malley (illustrator). Discuss how you might use this children's book with children, parents, and other teachers.

STUDY QUESTIONS

1. What role do tests play in the assessment process?
2. How can teachers avoid stigmatizing children in the assessment process?
3. Why is it important for teachers to become skilled at the administration and scoring of each assessment tool they use?
4. How do norm-based instruments and criterion-based instruments compare? In which situations will the teacher use each?
5. What information do screening tests provide?
6. What role will the teacher play in the multidisciplinary conference?
7. Diagnostic tests answer questions about children. Why are these tests useful for specific stakeholders?

REFLECT AND RE-READ

- I know what tests can do to make planning for students more efficient.
- I know about the limitations and potential biases of performance-based assessment.
- I can plan some informal assessment strategies for use in my classroom.
- I know the key ingredients for developing rubrics.

CASE VIGNETTE

Sharlene is a bright, happy, enthusiastic four-year-old (3.11 actual age) who moved to Denver recently from Provence, France. She has a two-year-old sister, Shanae. Sharlene's parents are Mrs. Pierre, who describes herself as German American, and Mr. Pierre, who is French. The family speaks French at home; books and movies are available for both children in French and English. Sharlene attends an after-school French Academy. Until six months ago, if asked a question in English, Sharlene responded in French.

To determine Sharlene's English progress, her teacher, Ms. Shea, administered the Preschool Language Scale, 3rd edition (Zimmerman, Steiner, & Pond, 1992). The scores* for Sharlene follow.

	Raw Score	Standard Score	Percentile Rank	Age Equivalent
Auditory Comprehension	41	86	18	4.6
Expressive Language	44	98	45	5.6
Total Language Score	184	91	27	5.0

*Only the scores described in Chapter 4 are shown. The assessment instrument yields additional statistics.

What did Ms. Shea learn about Sharlene from this assessment conducted in English? What are the next steps for kindergarten instruction for Sharlene?

Source: From J. Shea, 2003, submitted in partial fulfillment of T&L 411, Assessment in Early Childhood Education: DePaul University. Used by permission.

TECHNOLOGY LINKS

http://www.ctb.com

CTB/McGraw-Hill. This corporate website publishes excerpts from achievement tests, a test glossary, and white papers on assessment issues.

http://www.rand.org

RAND® is a nonprofit institution that helps improve policy and decision-making through research and analysis.

http://www.riverpub.com

Riverside Publishing. The publisher of the Iowa Test of Basic Skills. The website includes information about testing and reports on testing.

http://www.pearsonschool.com

Pearson School. Assessment Information contains research reports and white papers on important assessment topics; publisher of many tests.

http://www.naeyc.org

National Association for the Education of Young Children. The website regularly presents position statements and links to policy related to the assessment of young children.

http://www.ncela.gwu.edu

National Clearinghouse for English Language Acquisition & Language Instruction Educational Programs. "Collects, coordinates and conveys a broad range of research and resources in support of an inclusive approach to high quality education for ELLs."

http://www.ed.gov

The Department of Education. Posts highlights of legislation so that you can read firsthand about assessment requirements.

http://www.rti4success.org

National Center on Response to Intervention. Clear description of the concept with resources for teachers and others.

http://www.altec.org

ALTEC. A center devoted to the integration of teaching and technology. One of its resources is an online rubric maker.

SUGGESTED READINGS

Gullo, D. F. (2005). *Understanding assessment and evaluation in early childhood education* (2nd ed.). New York: Teachers College Press.

Meisels, S. J. (2005). *Developmental screening in early childhood: A guide* (2nd ed.). Washington, DC: National Association for the Education of Young Children.

Salvia, J., Ysseldyke, J. E. & Bolt, S. (2010). *Assessment* (11th ed.). Boston: Houghton Mifflin.

Widerstrom, A. (2005). *Achieving learning goals through play: Teaching young children with special needs* (2nd ed.). Baltimore: Paul H. Brookes.

CHAPTER 6

Using Alternative Assessment Strategies

TERMS TO KNOW

- intrinsically motivating
- task analysis
- presentation mode
- response mode
- dynamic assessment
- mediated learning experience (MLE)
- ecological assessment
- functional assessment
- behavioral intervention plan
- strength-based assessment
- resiliency
- curriculum-based language assessment
- multiple intelligences
- Child Find
- inclusion
- response to intervention (RTI)
- peer-mediated intervention
- personal efficacy

CHAPTER OVERVIEW

This chapter surveys a variety of alternative assessment strategies employed by early childhood teachers. The use of each strategy is dependent on the particular skill or skills that you wish to assess, as well as a number of other variables such as the age of the child, the amount of time you can invest in the assessment, and the number of children assigned to your class who may have special needs. These are the strategies that form the basis of individualization of instruction, as well as forming the foundation for the classroom teacher's role in Response to Intervention (RTI).

ASSESS AS YOU READ

- What assessment methods can I use when I am worried about a child's social behavior?
- What can I do when a child is not responding to the usual methods of instruction?
- What can I learn from watching children play?
- What are some practical implications of multiple intelligences for the assessment system?
- What is my role in Response to Intervention? How will specialists help?

ROLE OF ALTERNATIVE ASSESSMENT STRATEGIES IN THE CLASSROOM

There are a number of reasons for considering the use of alternative assessment strategies. First, norm-referenced tests often have little direct overlap between skills and knowledge assessed and the curriculum in the typical classroom. Second, published norm-referenced tests measure relative standing—how a child compares to other children. This is different from measuring change—how a child develops over time. Teachers usually are more interested in the changes children demonstrate. Third, there is wide variability in how children perform on published norm-referenced tests, depending upon the specific test used. For example, if a child has a chronological age of 6–0 and labels letters correctly but reads no words, the child's standard score can vary from one test to another. As a result, there is a high likelihood that intervention teams and teachers will disregard the data collected from published norm-referenced tests in educational planning. Yet educational planning is the ultimate reason for conducting an assessment. Often, there are limited resources of time and specialized personnel in most schools and child-care centers. Therefore, classroom teachers must become adept at specialized techniques to facilitate learning in all children. Growing numbers of young children come to school with limited English proficiency. You must learn ways to assist them in learning English as well as the learning outcomes for your program. Finally, more children with disabilities are now included in the mainstream of early childhood classes. Each teacher must individualize instruction and behavioral management for these children with identified disabilities as well as other children who may require special diagnosis from time to time. Thus, early childhood teachers must have strategies for teaching a variety of particular children. Some of the special techniques that teachers must know about and be able to use include those discussed in the following pages. The first of these is at the heart of early childhood education—play and its interpretive properties.

PLAY-BASED ASSESSMENT

Most teachers believe that they can recognize play when they see it. However, play is easier to recognize than it is to define (cf. Fromberg, 2002; Fromberg & Bergen, 2006). Often theorists describe play as the natural learning medium of the child. From a competence perspective, play is defined as a complex process that involves social, cognitive, emotional, and physical elements and relates to an aspect of reality as not "serious" or "real." For the child, this characterization makes it possible to relate to things that might otherwise be confusing, frightening, mysterious, strange, risky, or forbidden and to develop appropriate competencies and defenses. The active solution of developmental conflicts through play thus enables the young child to demonstrate and feel competence (Mindes, 1982, p. 40). Through play, children develop many capabilities. Examples of child accomplishments include improvements in communication skills, physical agility, independence, social judgment, cooperation, impulse control, and so on. Play activities must be voluntary and **intrinsically motivating** to the child; otherwise, they are not play. By watching children at play, teachers can gain insight into the developmental competencies of infants, toddlers, and young children. Play is systematically related to areas of development and learning (Linder, 2008b; Widerstrom, 2005). Play influences language usage, cognitive understanding, social/emotional development, and physical and motor development. Because children's play is rooted in cultural understandings and beliefs, teachers must be sensitive and knowledgeable about the cultural meanings attached to toys, appropriate play activities, themes, and adult-child interactions during play when teaching and assessing young children so that bias does not enter the process (Gil & Drewes, 2005; Gosso, 2010).

intrinsically motivating causing a child to do something or continue doing something because of the nature of the thing or activity itself.

Intervention programs and child-care settings serving infants, toddlers, and preschoolers frequently describe programs as play-based. Thus, play is the curriculum in these child-constructed, teacher-enhanced adventures in learning. In such programs, children play and teachers facilitate learning by judging when to intervene. The teacher's role in play-based early childhood classrooms is complex. The teacher is a watcher, observer, and assessor, as well as a stage setter, stage manager, mediator, player, scribe, and planner (Jones & Reynolds, 1992; Johnson, Christie, & Wardle, 2005). The assessor role is the one that makes the approach work. It separates the benign, neglectful—"let the children play"—classrooms from the ones where children learn, grow, and develop. In the assessor role, the skillful early childhood teacher makes numerous decisions, such as when to change the props, when to add stimulation to the theme, when to mediate between and among children, when to "play with" the children, and when to call time

BOX 6.1

Play Skills in Active Classroom Life

Skills	Interactions	Potential Assessment Question
Social	Parents Siblings Classmates Isolate	Compatible, reciprocal relationship Cooperative, age-appropriate Leader, follower, collaborator, timid
Cognitive		Problem solver Persistent in the face of difficulties Engaged and focused Classifies and organizes Sequences
Creativity		Ideational fluency Music or artistic accomplishment
Language		Eye contact Use of gestures Vocabulary and grammar
Motor		Grasp of objects Crayon and market use Capacity to use scissors, hammer, stapler Climbing, running, jumping, hopping Balance Throwing and catching ball
Academic	Interested in	Writing and drawing, labeling Spelling, stories, and books Numbers One-to-one correspondence
	Aware of Curious about	Geometric figures and spatial concepts Natural world of plants and animals Approaches materials appropriately
Emotional		Self-regulated Appropriate affect for the situation Resilient Responsive Reflective

outs. Effective early childhood teachers are enacting this assessor role routinely and regularly. By watching the children play, you can learn about social skills, cognitive and language skills, motor skills, and beginning academic competence. Therefore, if you teach babies or two-, three-, and four-year-olds, you will need to know about play, its developmental sequence, and how to intervene to facilitate development. In Box 6.1, examine some of the developmental (cf. Fewell & Glick, 1998; Johnson, Christie & Wardle, 2005; Frost, Wortham & Reifel, 2008) and academic variables that you can document while children are playing.

Using play as an assessment tool is not a new concept, but what is new is that play scales are now refined enough that they have practical applications for young children (McLean, Worley, & Bailey, 2004; Gitlin-Weiner, Sandgrund, & Schaefer, 2000; Weber, Behl, & Summers, 1994). However, the best approach for regular early childhood educators would be informal assessment of play that is appropriate for the entire age range and utilizes ordinary but interesting and age-appropriate toys to assess general aspects of a child's development through direct observation.

BOX 6.2

Role-Playing Checklist

Role-Playing Checklist	Frequency		
Uses props in traditional ways (i.e., an apple is an apple; a car is a car; a block is a block)	Sometimes	Always	Never
Uses props in creative ways (i.e., a block is a hamburger; a scarf is a cape)	Sometimes	Always	Never
Pretend play follows script of story or family scene: Three Billy Goats Gruff, dinner at home	Sometimes	Always	Never
Pretend play shows creativity (e.g., Snow White goes to space)	Sometimes	Always	Never
Plays alone	Sometimes	Always	Never
Gives and takes in pretend roles with others	Sometimes	Always	Never
Uses gestures to communicate	Sometimes	Always	Never
Uses only a few words to move the play along	Sometimes	Always	Never
Uses four- to five-word sentences to communicate with appropriate vocabulary for the scene	Sometimes	Always	Never
Varies linguistic expression with the mood of the play	Sometimes	Always	Never

In addition, the detailed analysis of older children's conversations as they engage in collaborative make-believe can reveal information about interactive skills, social cognition in action, and the knowledge of practical language use that young children bring to their play (Garvey, 1993; Pellegrini, 2004; Van Hoorn, Nourot, Scales, & Alward, 2007).

One of the easiest ways for early childhood teachers to begin assessing play behavior is to use lists of critical skills and to match these to the curricular plan. Van Hoorn, Nourot, Scales, and Alward (2007) provide several examples of these matches: (a) Keep a play observation diary keyed to learning contexts and social contexts. That is, where is a particular child playing in the classroom? In each area where the child plays, is he alone, with one friend, or with several friends? Over time, examine the charts for patterns. (b) List block play stages (Chalufour & Worth, 2004; Hirsch, 1984; MacDonald, 2001) on a table with each child's name. Keep track of whether a particular stage is emerging or is at mastery level for each child in the program. (c) Chart role-play activities, including the use of props, make-believe, interaction, and verbal communication to keep track of child developmental progress through the stages of sociodramatic play. For toddlers, consider documenting explorations with clay showing their work as mathematicians and collaborators with others (Smith & Goldhaber, 2004). These charts (an example is given in Box 6.2) assist you in focusing observations, planning curriculum, and documenting child and program progress.

Based on a Vygotskian approach to the interpretation of play, Bodrova and Leong (1996; see also Van Hoorn et al., 2007) outline a way to gather observational information about spatial perceptions of young children using construction paper and blocks. The activity involves the development of classroom maps. Asking children to use the blocks to represent people and things in a specific environment offers rich possibilities for ongoing documentation of problem-solving strategies, perceptions of space, and perceptions of personal interactions. Repeat this activity throughout the year—say, in October, February, and June—forming a record of growth for each child. Mapping offers a window into each child's understanding of accuracy in spatial relationships, ability to use symbols to communicate to others, and understanding of the formal structure of maps and charts.

Similar approaches for charts are useful for individualizing instruction for infants and toddlers with special needs. Chart categories suggested include fine motor, gross motor, self-care, cognitive, social communication, and social (Bricker & Squires, 2009; Widerstrom, 2005). A numerical rating adds the potential to assess progress of individual children on very specific aspects of the target behavior. In this way, play-based assessment becomes an integral part of the planned learning activities. Planned activities meet individualized goals for particular children. Teachers employing this approach can document individual progress, select children appropriately for group intervention, and simplify record-keeping by using the chart as a combination curricular/assessment tool.

In addition to these curricular approaches, play scales are commercially available for infants, toddlers, and young children throughout the early childhood age span. Teachers can selectively match these to the population of children they serve and to their curriculum. The use of these instruments may assist in program planning and in the documentation of child progress. The key in picking these scales is "do they answer the questions you need to ask?" (See Box 6.3 for an example.)

BOX 6.3

Checklist for Play Assessment

1. Choose a relevant variable: a cognitive play stage, a social play stage, or an activity variable—block building, clay exploration, or drawing.
2. List the relevant stages at the top of the page.
3. Leave a space to document the evidence for your assessment of each child.

A sample template for a play assessment is provided next.

Cognitive Play Stages

1. ***Functional.*** Simple muscular activities and repetitive muscular movement with or without objects are used. The child repeats actions or initiates actions.
2. ***Constructive.*** The child learns use of play materials, manipulation of objects to construct something or create something (e.g., drawing a person, building a play-dough house, measuring with beakers).
3. ***Dramatic.*** The child takes a role; pretends to be someone else, initiating another person in actions and speech with the aid of real or imagined objects.
4. ***Games with rules.*** The child accepts prearranged rules and adjusts to them, controlling actions and reactions within given limits.

Social Play Stages

1. ***Solitary.*** The child plays alone with toys different from those used by other children; although the child may be within speaking distance, there is no attempt at verbal communication with the peer group. The child is center of his or her own activity.
2. ***Parallel.*** The child plays independently but among other children. The child plays with toys that are similar to those the other children are using. In short, the child plays beside rather than with other children.
3. ***Group.*** The child plays with other children. The children are borrowing, following each other with play things. All engage in similar if not identical activity. For *cooperative play*, the child plays in a group that is organized for making some material product, striving to attain some competitive goal, dramatizing situations of adult or group life, or playing formal games. There is a division of labor, a sense of belonging, and an organization in which the efforts of one child are supplemented by those of another.

(continued)

Not Play

1. ***Unoccupied.*** The child is not playing in the usual sense but watches activities of momentary interest, plays with his or her own body, gets on and off chairs, follows the teacher, or merely glances around the room.
2. ***Onlooker.*** The child watches the others play and may talk, ask questions, or offer suggestions to the children playing but does not enter into the activity.

Checklist for Play Assessment

Name: Peter Date: 2/22/11 Time: 11:00 to 11:20

	Solitary	Parallel	Group	Context or materials*
Functional				
Constructive				
Dramatic			With Mallory Quintin	Block corner to building airport with Starbucks, ticket counter, shoe shine stand, etc.
Games with rules				
Not play: onlooker or unoccupied				

Note date and duration of time.
*Note here relevant details to support creative or other significant observation.
Source: Adapted from G. Mindes, "Social and Cognitive Play of Young Handicapped Children in a Special Education Preschool Center," unpublished doctoral dissertation, Loyola University, 1979.

STRUCTURED QUESTIONS TO IDENTIFY STUDENT-LEARNING PROCESSES

Before turning to prepared instruments and scales to identify student-learning problems, you want to be sure that you are making the most of the instructional process by developing and using questions to "see" inside the child's learning strategies. For example, suppose you wonder why Lisa hates math and makes many mistakes. Over a week or so, you may wish to ask Lisa some questions while she is working on math problems. One area that you may wish to examine is problem comprehension. So, you may ask Lisa:

- What is the problem about? What can you tell me about it?
- How would you interpret that?
- Would you please explain that in your own words?
- What do you know about this part? Do you need to define or set limits for the problem?
- Is there something that you can eliminate or that is missing?
- What assumptions do you make? (Stenmark, 1991, p. 31)
- What do you think you should do first?
- Please tell me more about that.
- Show me how you got your answer.
- Tell me why you think that is the answer.
- Was there a rule you were following when you did that? Tell me which rule.
- Can you do that another way? What would that be?
- Draw a picture that shows that idea.
- What do you do when you run into a problem you can't solve?

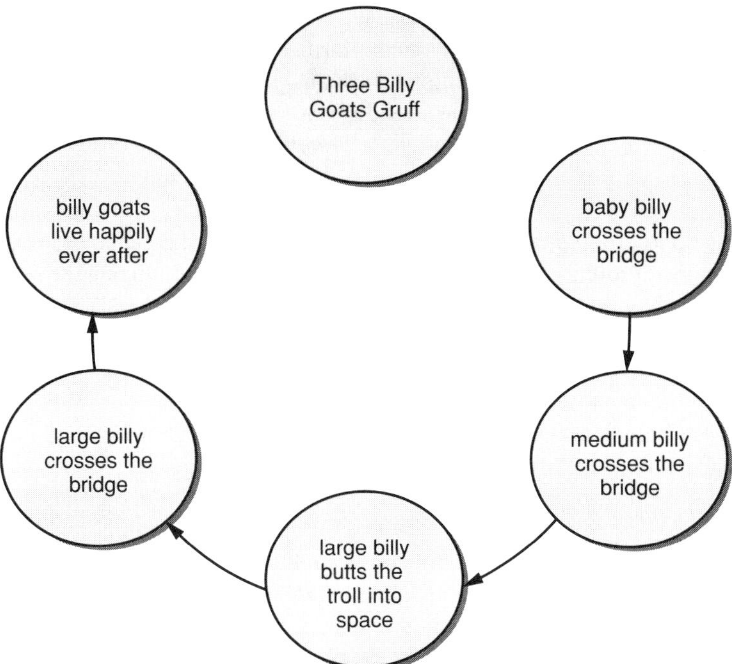

FIGURE 6.1 Sequence organizer.

- What do you do when you run into a word you don't know? (Kuhs, Johnson, Arguso, & Monrad, 2001, pp. 150–151)
- What evidence supports?
- What ideas or details can you add?
- In what other ways might you show/illustrate? (Fisher & Frey, 2007)

Other areas of potential learning difficulties that you may choose to explore in solving Lisa's problems with math include approaches and strategies, relationships, flexibility, communication, curiosity and hypotheses, self-assessment, equality and equity, solutions, examining results, and mathematical learning (National Council for Teachers of Mathematics, 2005; Stenmark, 1991). Questions related to each of these areas correspond to the National Council of Teachers of Mathematics (NCTM) Standards. You can use prepared questions from the NCTM's *Illuminations* lessons on the Web or develop your own for this curricular area or others to focus your attention and your students' attention on identifying learning strengths and problems. To assist in understanding whether young children have developed the concept of a story, you may wish to use a sequence organizer. In a conversation, you ask the child to tell you the story, filling in the blanks as you go. See Figure 6.1 for an illustration of this technique. You can also learn about children's problem-solving skills and strategies by observing them with the task.

TASK ANALYSIS

Task analysis is a process in which large goals are broken down into smaller objectives or parts and sequenced for instruction. Task analysis is the process of developing a training sequence by breaking down a task into small steps that a child can master more easily. Tasks, skills, assignments, or jobs in the classroom become manageable for particular children in ways that more generalized instruction may be missing their individual needs.

task analysis process in which large goals are broken down into smaller objectives or parts and sequenced for instruction.

Often, task analysis is informal. Jorge, a six-year-old who is having trouble buttoning his shirt, may be unsuccessful because (you notice informally) he usually wears T-shirts and sweatshirts. Thus, he lacks experience with buttons. Task analysis may be a more explicit and detailed process that you use with seven-year-old Brenda, who is showing limited writing fluency. The teaching question is *What can you do to facilitate Brenda's writing?* To answer this question, you list all of the steps in writing a story. For example, sitting in a quiet place with writing materials, paper, and some stimulus (picture, discussion, or thought-provoking questions); grasping pen or pencil; applying appropriate pressure to create legible marks on the paper and writing letters together to form words; grouping the words together in sentences; organizing the sentences to convey a story idea; and so on. After you list the component parts of the task, you watch Brenda at work. You see what parts of the task she can't do—maybe it's writing letters, maybe it's organizing her thoughts, or maybe it's leaving enough space between words to make it possible to figure out what she's trying to say. At any rate, once you have identified the problem, you can decide what to do to help Brenda in your class. You may also have enough information to refer Brenda for a more specialized assessment.

presentation mode way the task or learning situation is presented to a child as part of instruction.

response mode how a child responds to a direction or instruction.

One way of conducting a task analysis is to examine both the **presentation mode** and the **response mode** of any given task. You know that some children require you to tell directions; some to show directions; some to write directions; and some to tell, show, and write directions. Even if you habitually use multiple demonstration modes for tasks, skills, assignments, and jobs, you may find that a few children still do not understand what to do. In that case, through a task analysis of the presentation mode, you can decide why Joey is not singing at circle time. You may find that he requires more than multiple presentation modes (tell, show, or write). Maybe you have to repeat yourself several times or say it louder, more slowly, or using different words. You may find that Alexandra requires dual methods of presentation—for jumping rope, you must show her and tell her—but after several weeks of jumping rope with her, the skill becomes automatic. Alexandra can now show and tell Mimi how to be an Olympic jump-roper. Task analysis of the presentation mode focuses on why children are not doing what you require by looking at how you tell them to do it.

When you task analyze the response mode, you look at what you expect Jerome to do, say, write, or show to you. What you see may show that Jerome cannot tell you about the trip to the pumpkin farm but that he can show you what he enjoyed most, may be able to demonstrate how to pick pumpkins, or may be able to draw a picture about the trip. Agatha, by contrast, can't stop talking about the trip. When asked to draw a picture about the trip, she scowls and hastily scrawls a thin orange line around the edges of the paper, then scratches across a few lines to fill in the circle and dumps her work in her cubby. By knowing how Jerome and Agatha are comfortable in responding, letting you know that they have the skill, know the concept, and so on, you can set goals that will be appropriate for each of them. That is, you can let Jerome demonstrate what he knows by showing you, while working with him to describe verbally his experiences, knowledge, and attitudes. Thus, Jerome feels successful while moving forward in your program. Agatha can dictate a long tape to you to describe her experiences. You may sit beside her while she draws; she may need just the tiny bit of reassurance that her pumpkins can be interpretations of pumpkins rather than the true representation of the pumpkin of her mind's eye.

In addition to these informal uses, task analysis is a technique for determining the steps in accomplishing a goal on a child's IEP or IFSP. One way to use this approach is to use the process of forward chaining or backward chaining through a task. *Chaining* means identifying the first step in a process (or the last) and all subsequent steps that are each based on successful accomplishment of the one before. An example may be putting on a cardigan sweater, which requires a series of steps—taking out the sweater, identifying the front with the buttons or zipper, sticking one arm in one sleeve, then sticking the other arm in the other sleeve, and finally buttoning or zipping it closed. This task analysis method is useful in naturalistic early

childhood settings for both assessment and for planning subsequent instruction of complex self-help skills or other complicated concepts (Cook, Klein, Tessier, 2008; Noonan & McCormick, 2006). Chaining through a task means starting with an activity that a child has failed. Think about what happens before or what should happen afterward to determine where the failure occurs. Consider the following analogy: Mr. College Freshman is always getting overdraft notices from the bank. He must review the steps of checking account operation to ascertain the key to the task failure. Does he enter all the checks he writes in the ledger? Does he enter bank charges? Does he add and subtract regularly? Does he write numbers clearly? Does he follow the steps that the bank outlines for balancing? Once he has identified the break in the chain of steps to successful bank account management, he can make a plan to avoid overdrafts.

In early childhood settings, teachers focus task analysis on activities necessary for successful participation in the setting. For example, in many early childhood centers, children must brush their teeth after lunch. If Javier is not successful with this task, you can review the steps to success and figure out how to help him be a champion brusher. What you need to do is watch him closely, see which step or steps he cannot do, and then offer prompts or coaching until he can do the task by himself. See Box 6.4 as an example of this type of task analysis.

Four ways to develop the particular steps for a task analysis include watching a master, self-monitoring, brainstorming, and goal analysis (Cegelka & Berdine, 1995; see also Mercer & Mercer, 2005). Early childhood teachers can use each of these approaches to identify and record the incremental steps, as follows:

- Watching a master: To know how to help children walk the balance beam, watch someone who is doing this task well.
- Self-monitoring: To know how to help children make a papier-mâché turkey, review the steps that you follow in accomplishing the task.
- Brainstorming: To know how to help children plant a garden in a school plot, ask all the children to give you ideas.
- Goal analysis: To know how to help children develop conflict resolution strategies, review the observable and nonobservable aspects of this task and identify ways to see how it is accomplished.

All approaches to task analysis link assessment to instruction and involve the step-by-step breaking down of tasks into teachable increments.

BOX 6.4

Selected Steps for Teeth Brushing

1. Locate the toothbrush, toothpaste, and water source. These may be three steps, if necessary.
2. Apply the paste to the brush.
3. Brush the teeth in sequential order, front, sides, backs, and so on. These may be listed as more steps, if necessary.
4. Rinse the mouth.
5. Rinse the toothbrush.
6. Dry mouth and hands.
7. Return the materials to storage.

If a task analysis was successful with one child, it may well apply to another (McLean et al., 2004). Hence, teachers should compile a *task analysis bank.* Over time, teachers may find that their task analyses fall into certain patterns related to the children they typically teach or the particular curriculum they are using. When teachers are aware of these task-analysis patterns, it is easier to write new task analyses.

Not only do you need to analyze the task, but also you need to observe the child who is to learn the task in terms of what he or she can and cannot do. The number of steps in a task analysis depends upon the functioning level of the child as well as the nature of the task. There are a number of questions to answer about the child that enable the teacher to determine the functioning level (Lerner, Lowenthal, & Egan, 2002; see also McLoughlin & Lewis, 2008; Bayat, 2011). How does the child receive, store, and retrieve information? Which avenue of learning does the child seem to prefer: visual, auditory, or tactile? Does the child avoid certain pathways of learning? Does the child do better if more than one pathway is used simultaneously in the teaching process? Is intrusion necessary? How much assistance does the child require to master the step? Are scope and sequence lists available for academic subjects to use as hypothetical sequences for tasks? Answers to these questions will enable the teacher to blend the task analysis of the skill or behavior to be mastered to the current capabilities of the target child. In addition to task analysis, another teaching-related assessment activity that is gaining popularity in classroom use is dynamic assessment, discussed next.

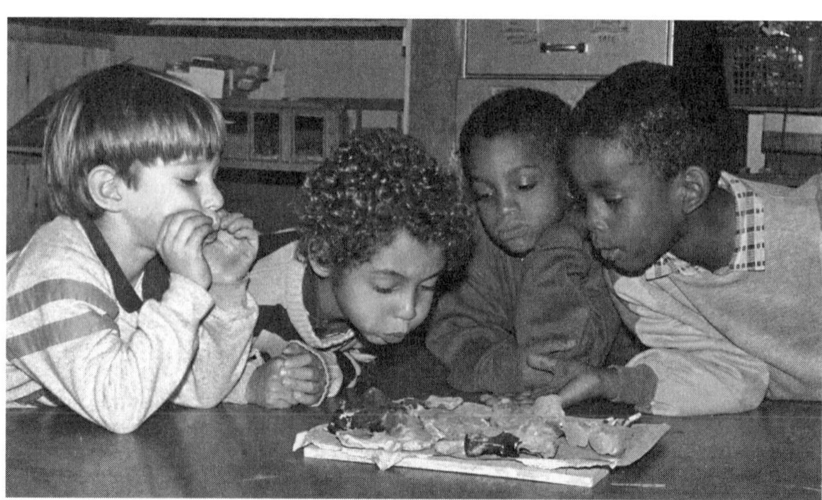

VOICES FROM THE FIELD

From the Private School Principal's Chair

Today's grads know a lot more about assessment than I did 20 years ago. They're not experts on the portfolio, but they have a handle on it. Besides, there's so much out there, not just tests; they seem to be trained in a variety of assessment methods.

Grading is a challenge for new teachers. How do you translate portfolio contents into grades? New teachers need help with this concept. It's easier with rubrics. We specify the number of work products so that grades will be based on a well-rounded judgment.

New teachers struggle with being objective, fair, and accurate. They should come to our school ready to collaborate with other teachers in the grade, so each class at a grade is using the same assessments.

I find new teachers to be biased against standardized tests and worried about the high-stakes consequences of testing. I don't think they are looking at the benefits of standardized tests.

DYNAMIC ASSESSMENT

Dynamic assessment is an approach that combines formal testing and teaching. Conduct a one-to-one interview with an individual child to learn more about that particular child as well as what the formal test may be missing. This method is particularly helpful for learners with diverse cultural backgrounds, because the formal test may contain biases or language and concepts that are unfamiliar (Sternberg & Grigorenko, 2002). The approach is being used as a theoretical framework for assessing and teaching children who are learning a second language (cf. Poehner, 2008). In this approach, the teacher uses available assessment information and tries to teach a specific skill. The available test data serve as the foundation of a task analysis for the skill or competency. The theoretical work of Vygotsky (1978, 1986) and Feuerstein (1979) are the underpinnings for this method. Quite often, speech and language therapists use dynamic assessment in their work with children who have communication disabilities (cf. Otto, 2010). In implementation of the technique, the therapist or teacher uses intuitive reasoning as well as conventional thinking in ferreting out why the young child is not successful with a particular skill or competency. The teacher observes as the teaching occurs and modifies the task in the process, so that the child can be successful.

dynamic assessment one-to-one interview approach between teacher and student using available assessment information for teaching a specific skill.

How does a teacher proceed with this technique? First, give or acquire test information about the skill or competency in question. Next, try to teach the child the missing pieces, according to the task analysis (or test data), observing and modifying during the teaching process. Finally, retest to document progress. This process of teaching is the mediated learning experience, (Haywood & Lidz, 2007). The **mediated learning experience (MLE)** involves the teacher's use of questions, suggestions, and cues to prompt the child to think more consciously about the task and to expand learner expertise.

mediated learning experience (MLE) teaching approach in which the teacher uses questions, suggestions, and cues to prompt the child to think more consciously about the task and to expand learner expertise.

For example, you may wish to encourage Morgan to elaborate her concept of stories. The available data shows that Morgan knows that stories have beginnings and endings. Your objective is for Morgan to know that stories have action that moves the story from the beginning to the end and that by changing these actions the story changes. At a quiet time, you sit with Morgan and read a short, unfamiliar story to her. Then, through a process of questions and answers, you help Morgan understand what you mean about action as part of the story concept. Later, you assess whether Morgan has maintained the skill or whether she needs reteaching.

This avenue of assessment is promising for teachers who wish to link instruction to learner outcomes for early childhood settings. The approach links test results to task analysis to teaching to individualization of instruction. It is an opportunity for making the learning process apparent to those children who may need special assistance in linking thinking to academic requirements, whether these requirements are preschool or primary. Sometimes, you need to consider not only the learner and the task, but also the environment. Then, you engage in a process called ecological assessment.

ECOLOGICAL ASSESSMENT

ecological assessment an approach that includes the classroom environment, personal interactions, and the learning tasks as variables in the collection of evidence for the measure of learning for individuals.

Ecological assessment is a tactic that utilizes focused observations of young children at home, in the center, in the community, or at school. As an assessment approach, variables such as culture and beliefs of the child and family; teaching style; time allocations for activities in the classroom; academic, behavioral, and social expectations; as well as class tone become important features to observe *in situ* (Brown-Chidsey, 2005; McLoughlin & Lewis, 2008). Such observation enables the teacher to assess what social/emotional variables influence successful completion of learning tasks in a particular situation. For example, sitting in a circle to listen to a story is a frequently planned early childhood activity. So, if Dana cannot listen quietly to stories, you observe what she does in the situation—interrupts to ask questions, pokes the children next to her, and shows great interest in the pictures for the story, often elbowing her way forward to look. After several days of observation at story time, you develop instructional supports that will help her sit quietly. Instructional strategies that support young children with special needs in the classroom include modeling, prompting, error correction, as well as repeated practice and incentive strategies. However, the critical variable for any instructional intervention is individualization for a particular child. For Dana, the solution might be a conversation before story time about the expectations for listening. For Ryan, the solution might be the opportunity to sit next to his best friend, Horace.

The roots of this assessment process come from Bronfenbrenner's (1979) view that various issues within and across the child's social contexts influence learning. The child-care setting and school are particularly important contexts that influence child learning and development. "Classrooms that benefit children and enhance academic performance share similar characteristics such as positive approaches to instructional planning, management, and delivery" (Sheridan & McCurdy, 2005). An additional critical aspect of this view of assessment that supports young children's development in context is that the observation is ongoing rather than a one-time event (cf. McLean et al., 2004). Thus, the method connects to curricular planning and intervention as individual children progress in a situation with appropriate developmental and instructional support. Pierangelo and Guiliani (2009, p. 39) offer questions to consider in the social context of school that may be particularly useful to teachers in the primary grades when children must move from class to class, or to preschool teachers concerned with supporting young children during "choice time" or free play:

- In which environments does the child show difficulty with the expectations?
- Are there instances where the child is successful?
- What are the behavioral and academic expectations in each situation?
- What are the differences between or among the situations?
- How can instructional planning support the child in the different situations?

Ecological assessment is dynamic, not static in nature. The focus is on the child, the situation, and the interaction between the context and the child. Thus, a number of variables are considered when reflecting on best approaches, including resources and materials, child behaviors, social relationships, and family/adult behaviors in relationship to the individual (cf. Howard, Williams, & Lepper, 2010; Hooper & Umansky, 2009). The process often assists in bridging home and center/school relations when observations of both situations are available. Thus, the ecological procedure creates an opportunity for home–school collaboration and definition of IFSP goals (cf. Cook et al., 2008). The approach, in sum, considers the whole child and the needs of the whole child—academic, social/emotional, and behavioral. There are situations that may require a focus on behavioral issues in particular. In these situations, you will want to be aware of ways to assess and facilitate social/emotional behavior so that young children with challenging behaviors can participate in the group life of the classroom setting. One specialized approach that serves this purpose is functional assessment.

FUNCTIONAL ASSESSMENT

Functional assessment is a focused observational method that links individual assessment to behavioral intervention for one student. The method is most appropriate to use when you are concerned about a young child with a serious problem that interferes with successful experiences in the regular classroom. "This model does not focus on typical sequential development but rather on age-appropriate expectations for functioning as independently as possible in specific environments. A functional model of assessment requires that both the individual's skill and the environment be evaluated. Because people function in several environments, each one must be evaluated" (Hoy & Gregg, 1994, p. 240; see also Chandler & Dahlquist, 2010).

functional assessment focused observational method that links individual assessment to curricular intervention for one student.

The method requires careful observation of small pieces of behavioral interludes. Divide the observation sequence into an ABC order—antecedent, behavior, and consequence. Thus, you observe the problem behavior (B) and then look more carefully to see what precipitates the event, the antecedent (A), and note the consequence (C). Before the careful observation, usually you have noticed either the problem behavior or the naturally occurring consequence. As a teacher, you seek to intervene or change the behavior by manipulating the antecedent or the consequence that in turn diminishes or extinguishes the targeted inappropriate behavior. The method comes from the behavioral analysis tradition of assessment and intervention (cf. Chandler & Dahlquist, 2010). Although historically the method was used in situations where children showed many problem behaviors that prohibited or limited their participation in mainstream or **inclusion** settings, the method has broader applicability. It is potentially quite useful as a tool to use in situations that require intervention, such as kicking, screaming, pinching, biting, cursing, or other behaviors that present group management and social acceptance concerns. The most important caveat for the method is to understand the meaning of the behavior for the child, that is, what need the child meets by employing the challenging behavior.

inclusion all children regardless of ability or possible risk or identified disability participate in typical classroom. Thus, they are included in childcare and education programs.

For example, suppose that when Martha, a three-year-old, approaches the children in your class, they run away from her. You do not understand why this is occurring. You are

concerned that it may be because Martha doesn't talk, because she walks with an uneven gait, or because she frequently arrives at school with her hair in a mess. Your tentative conclusion is that the children are fearful of Martha because they have limited experience with nonverbal children, that perhaps they are intolerant of her physical limitations, or that they are judging her on her messy appearance. You want to help the children in your class to be accepting of differences. You want to assure them that even though Martha doesn't talk, she is a worthy playmate. You plan a time to observe, so that you can learn what will help Martha approach children confidently and/or what will help the children in your group include Martha in their play.

You watch Martha. You see that she approaches Everett, gets very close to him, then puts her hand palm-down on his cheek and pats it. Everett looks at her warily, but continues to mold with play-dough while Martha leaves the area. Why, you ask yourself, did Everett look at Martha warily? Why do the children sometimes run and scream when Martha pats their cheeks? If you stop the assessment at this point, you may never know, or you may conclude that it is Martha's appearance or some other historical experience that the children have had with Martha that creates this reaction on the part of her classmates. In fact, you may talk to Everett and say, "Martha is your friend. She wants to use the play-dough. You, Everett, should invite her to join you." However, you continue your assessment before planning an intervention.

You continue to watch Martha. She approaches Kenneth, moving close with her open palm to his cheek. All of a sudden, instead of patting his cheek, Martha reaches with her nails and scratches a deep gouge in Kenneth's cheek. He screams in rage; Martha tries to pat his cheek; he runs away. You handle the crisis and later plan an intervention to stop the inappropriate social behavior of cheek scratching. An intervention strategy will not be easy to develop, because Martha sometimes pats and sometimes scratches. It is also difficult to develop an intervention that will be meaningful to Martha. Martha is "coping" (cf. Sandall & Schwartz, 2008); she is showing behavior to affect her environment. The fact that the teachers and peers do not perceive it as effective is not apparent to her. She is doing the best she can, even though it seems erratic to others. She is not learning from the typical techniques of modeling, rule reminding, and so on. You, her teacher, must intervene so that she no longer harms the children in her class and so that she may develop a more adaptive behavior style that will serve her in inclusive environments.

To use this approach, you must observe carefully to see what happens first—the *antecedent;* what she does next—the *behavior;* and then develop a suitable intervention—the *consequence*. In Martha's case, the *antecedent* is an open palm to the cheek of a classmate; the *behavior* is a pat or a scratch; and the *consequence* is currently that children stare warily, run away, or scream.

You wish to improve Martha's functioning in class, so you must develop an intervention to change the consequence and extinguish the patting and scratching behavior. You must stop Martha from touching children's cheeks. With your colleagues you plan an intervention strategy, keep records about how the strategy works, and continue through a process until you find a strategy that stops Martha from patting or scratching the cheeks of classmates. You may need to be by her side for several weeks to prevent this behavior. You may choose to reinforce Martha's keeping her hand at her side with a positive consequence. Or you may choose a negative reinforcer when she sticks her hand toward a child. You may also help the other children learn cues to steer Martha to a more appropriate path (e.g., "NO, Martha, you can't touch me. You can play here."). The key is that all the children use a consistent phrase.

McLean et al. (2004) discuss this assessment/intervention approach in the context of form and function. Form refers to the behaviors of children—self-injurious, aggression, tantrums, property destruction, social avoidance, and self-stimulatory behaviors—and function refers to the effects of those behaviors for the child—obtain desired outcome (teacher attention) or escape undesired outcomes (leaving favorite activity to transition to another one). This analytic approach to assessment and instruction is quite useful when teachers cannot always easily judge

what the behavior, or form, is trying to affect. That is, what is the young child trying to do? What does he want? For example, Kevin, an eight-year-old whose speech is difficult to understand, says in an agitated and excited fashion, "Mumble, mumble, mumble, mumble" (to your ears) at show and tell. You respond, "That's nice," because you are reluctant to embarrass him in front of the group. He then says, "NO, THEY STOLE!" You adjust your teaching strategy (in private) so that Kevin comes to show and tell with shorter sentences, pictures, or pantomime. As his speech becomes more articulate, you encourage him to use longer sentences.

Howard, a six-year-old, goes to the chalkboard at playtime. He picks up an eraser and runs the eraser up and down the chalk tray. He does this every day for the whole play period. What does this behavior mean to Howard? What can you do to change it so that he plays with other children, or so that he uses toys? It will not be easy to intervene. Howard doesn't talk and he screams if you try to take away the eraser. You must plan an intervention that will expand Howard's repertoire in small steps.

When using this assessment approach, you must consider both the child and the behavior, as well as the environment, schedule, routines, rules, personal interactions, and materials—the "baseline of the program" (Berry & Mindes, 1993). You examine the antecedents to see whether some aspect of the baseline of your program can change to support the behavior that you want to increase. For example, suppose your routine is that everyone must sit in a circle for large group time. Katie, a three-year-old in your class, does not want to sit in the circle. She resists when the teacher assistant tries to hold her. She gets up and runs away. She doesn't participate. What if you change the routine so that Katie can come to the circle when she wants to and when she is ready? If she does not come to circle, she must play quietly with her doll or play-dough or whatever. You have prevented a disruption to circle, and Katie can come to circle when she feels comfortable.

Or suppose Marc, a seven-year-old, cannot sit for a half-hour in the discussion period. You change the rule that desks must be clear for discussion. Marc pays attention to discussion while drawing pictures.

What you have to do in these situations is manipulate or change the baseline so that problem behaviors of children do not interfere with their social experiences (function) in the classroom. These changes are not always straightforward. Think about a dieter who knows that chocolate donuts should not be in the house (antecedent). The ingredients for brownies are in the cupboard. The dieter makes the brownies and eats them. The diet suffers! The dieter must develop other strategies for overcoming the weight gains by examining all of the variables that influence eating patterns, and choose behaviors and consequences accordingly. In the case of young children, the teacher or parent must choose the behavior to change so that the young child can function as well as possible in inclusive situations.

In summary, consider this assessment technique for situations where individual children show annoying behavior, yet conventional methods of observation and interventions have not been effective. It is important to remember that this assessment technique is for use with troublesome social behaviors that interfere with a young child's ability to cope or *function* in the classroom. To be effective, apply this technique to particular situations for individuals. It is a precision teaching tool to assess, intervene, and reassess. It is a tool to find the meaning for behaviors that initially are hard to figure out. By using this system of microscopic observation and personalized intervention, children can adapt more effectively to inclusive situations. The approach is often the first step in a **behavioral intervention plan** for a child who is or will be identified as one with special needs. To support the plan, you may implement a reward for accomplishing specific classroom goals. The first step in this approach is to choose a goal that can be quantified. For example, most teachers have a classroom rule related to respect for others. What does respect look like? How do you quantify it? In one example, consider this situation: Joan is always late to the circle time. She dawdles while putting away her toys or books. She stops to chat with her friend Harriette about what she watched on TV last night. She wanders around the circle trying to decide whether she will sit by Joyce or Arleen. She finally sits down. This episode is just one of her behaviors that disturb the class routine and flow. In a conference with Joan, you set the quantifiable goal that showing respect for others includes timely participation in circle. You set the goal for Joan being on time to circle; she will receive one point for each day she makes it to the circle on time. At the end of the week, she receives a reward, personalized to her interest. The reward might be a note home with praise for her behavior. It might be a sticker in a book. The reward should be small. In this approach, you can offer bonuses for several weeks running of on-time behavior. As this respect behavior becomes established, you can move to other disturbing points. In using this approach, you pick the most annoying behavior, quantifying it so that you can assess success. Sometimes, it may be useful to involve Joan's parents, as well so they can partner with you regarding dawdling at home (Mah, 2007). More serious situations and those in which all of your classroom interventions have failed may require the involvement of specialists. Mah (2007, p. 136) lists some behaviors that teachers notice and that will require interventions from specialists:

behavioral intervention plans plans made based on assessment of young children who present troubling behavior. Modifications to the regular program are made and monitored.

- Shows awkward body postures and movement when a physical disability is not involved
- Makes odd associations with words or thoughts
- Does not retain or learn concepts
- Shows irregular learning or developmental pattern beyond the typical

Each of these characteristics are described as "outside" the usual and customary behavior for a child of a particular age. Note that the characteristics are cast in the negative. Another approach to the ongoing assessment of children with special needs shifts the focus from deficit to strength. The approach is a core principle in the assessment of families and the strengths that they have that will support the development of a young learner with special needs. It is useful to think of the concept as applied to young children as the approach to assessment changes focus from a primary emphasis on "identification" and "treatment" toward a philosophy of inclusion—everyone welcome in typical early childhood programs—toward scaffolding for the success of all learners.

STRENGTH-BASED ASSESSMENT AND INTERVENTION

strength-based assessment requires the assessor to focus on a child's capacities to plan intervention.

resiliency capacity of children and families to overcome odds in spite of obstacles that developmental and environmental factors may place in the way of individuals.

In the past and in some cases today, teachers and others often focus on the troubling and dysfunctional deficits of children with disabilities. For example, IEP language, multidisciplinary staffings, and classroom modifications of lessons focus on Eric's inability to sit for long periods and his poor reading and writing skills. **Strength-based assessment** shifts the focus to the abilities, talents, and skills of the child with disabilities. This assessment/intervention focuses on developing **resiliency**—the capacity of children and families to overcome odds in spite of obstacles that developmental and environmental factors may place in the way of individuals—(cf. Stormont, 2007; Turnbull, Turnbull, & Wehmeyer, 2020; Heward, 2009). When you look at Eric again, you notice or assessment results document that he has a large oral vocabulary, draws imaginative pictures, and responds to teacher nonverbal cues. Which Eric do you want in your classroom? The core beliefs of this assessment method include:

- All children and families have strengths.
- Child and family motivation is higher when strengths are the focus.
- Failure of a child or family to demonstrate strength reveals absence of an opportunity for practice rather than a deficit.
- IEPs must be based on strengths. (Epstein, 1998, p. 25)

All of the special assessment methods discussed in this chapter lend themselves to application when you are trying to solve a classroom problem with a particular child. To solve the problem effectively, follow the principles and avoid common pitfalls (Kerr & Nelson, 2010):

- Pinpoint the behavior that is most important to monitor or that is the most disturbing to the class.
  - Is the behavior running around the room? Getting up to sharpen one's pencil without permission? Punching the kid next in the line?
- Don't collect answers to questions that don't apply to the problem.
  - If everyone is experiencing difficulty with sitting still for a half-hour, why single out this fact for the records that you are keeping on Vince?
- Count observable behavior; note the results of the behavior for more accurate information.
  - Count the minutes of in-seat behavior rather than the stars awarded for five-minute increments.
- Collect and organize data to use to affect the modification of a child's environment.
  - If the problem behavior is talking out, a chart summarizing this will be useful. Collecting information about roaming around the room and storing this data in a file won't help.

Peer-mediated intervention is a strategy that promotes child understanding of diversity and respect for peers. In this approach, children help each other with tasks and activities. Peer-mediated instruction (PMI) generally consists of four characteristics that create supportive and mutually beneficial relationships. These interventions:

peer-mediated intervention children are selected to model specific tasks for other children so that they may successfully learn how to do activities or routines in the classroom.

- Address a comprehensive set of target skills across classroom activities and routines
- Are intense, providing a sufficient number of learning opportunities
- Serve as a practical tool for teachers
- Increase a child's active involvement during daily activities.

In sum, the technique involves the modeling of tasks by the typical peer for the young child with special needs. To be effective, the tasks identified for intervention should include all of the expectations for a given age, the tasks must have multiple opportunities for performance, the tasks must be practical, and the task must actively involve the peers.

In addition to social/emotional issues and curricular adjustment issues, teachers are often concerned about the functional language of particular children. In these cases, the approach of curriculum-based language assessment may be quite useful.

CURRICULUM-BASED LANGUAGE ASSESSMENT

Curriculum-based language assessment is a special technique to use when you are not sure that a child has the linguistic capacity to understand the curriculum. With this assessment, you can plan to bridge the gap between the child's capacity and the demands of the curriculum. Suppose that Henrika, a five-year-old native Polish speaker, does not seem to follow directions well. Through a series of special steps, you can find out whether her problems are linguistic

curriculum-based language assessment a process for determining a child's functional language skills and vocabulary related to the subject matter being studied.

rather than behavioral. Aspects of linguistic functioning to investigate by observation and interview include (Losardo & Notari-Syverson, 2001; see also Baca & Cervantes, 2004; Klinger, Hoover & Baca, 2008):

- Does Henrika know how to match objects with words (blocks, crayons, chalk, pencils, and so on), identify objects by sound or touch, label and describe objects, and remember objects and information about them?
- Can Henrika use categorization skills to group objects, describe their characteristics, and see similarities and differences?
- Is she able to reorder information, such as what happened before and what may happen next?
- Can she draw conclusions based on inferences from previous learning and experiences? For example: What does it mean to be "afraid"?
- Are there differences that you see when Henrika is functioning in context—with objects and pictures? Or when she is asked to imagine or recall experiences with objects?

As you think about Henrika's difficulties and explore these and other questions, you will want to keep in mind the curriculum's specific vocabulary and experiences that she has had with English and school. Learn about her culture and the ways that language is typically used at home as well as "traditional" expectations for language in "school" settings. Keep in mind that cultures vary in the ways that communication is used orally and nonverbally. "Manners" and ways to address teachers, parents, and other children vary by culture. Rules for the ways that children communicate and interact with adults vary by culture. Conversational roles for children vary by culture (American Speech & Hearing Association, 2005). Compare what you discover to your own expectations and routines. Gather data on Henrika's performance in various academic situations—small group, large group, individual activities. While becoming aware of Henrika's language issues vis-à-vis curriculum, you may wish to be sure that your teaching approaches contain a wide variety of instructional strategies and ways to view learning. Ask yourself if words and sentences are the best way to tell whether Henrika can identify shapes and concepts in science. Could she select answers from an array of objects or pictures (Sadowski, 2004)?

In addition, be sure that your academic English instruction includes vocabulary and the argument structures required for justifying answers (Bielenberg & Fillmore, 2005; Haynes, 2007). See Box 6.5 for a starting point checklist for English language learners. This brief chart draws attention to the complexity of language learning by separating as much as possible the language processes of

BOX 6.5

Checklist for English Language Learners

For each of the language process areas, rank each child separately on the variables listed.

Name: ____________________ Date: ____________________

listening	speaking	writing	reading	**English**	emerging	functional	proficient
				Social vocabulary			
				Informational vocabulary			
				Academic vocabulary			
				Fluency			
				Grammar			

listening, speaking, writing, and reading. It offers three categories for rating performance in each of these areas. An important paradigm used by several states preparing for large-scale assessment is the one developed by the WIDA Consortium.

> *WIDA's English Language Proficiency Standards for English Language Learners in Kindergarten Through Grade 12: Frameworks for Large-Scale State and Classroom Assessment* is the first published product of an enhanced assessment system being developed and implemented by a consortium of states. Federal grant monies available under the No Child Left Behind Act of 2001 were awarded to Wisconsin (the lead state), Delaware, and Arkansas (WIDA), the original partners, in early 2003. Within the first half-year of the project, the District of Columbia, Maine, New Hampshire, Rhode Island, and Vermont joined the team, followed by Illinois in October 2003 (Illinois State Board of Education [ISBE], 2005).

The WIDA Consortium proposed five levels of language proficiency: entering, beginning, developing, expanding, and bridging (ISBE, 2005). Box 6.6 shows a checklist to consider when planning for the instruction and assessment of English language learners in your classroom. One useful approach for this focus is the applied aspects of multiple intelligences. This view of learning and teaching grows from the theories describing intelligence and the testing of intelligence.

MULTIPLE INTELLIGENCES

Gardner describes "human intellectual competence . . . (as) a set of skills of problem solving—enabling the individual *to resolve genuine problems or difficulties* that he or she encounters and, when appropriate, to create an effective product—and must also entail the potential for *finding or creating problems*—thereby laying the groundwork for the acquisition of new knowledge . . . (in a) cultural context" (2004, pp. 60–61). Gardner cautions that the intelligences he delineates do not "exist as physically verifiable entities but only as potentially useful scientific constructs" (2004, p. 70). The multiple intelligences perspective enhances teaching by

- Providing powerful points of entry to student learning—catching multiple ways to introduce and begin the study of a topic.
- Offering apt analogies derived from different dimensions and appealing to various intelligences.
- Providing multiple representations of the central or core ideas of the topic of study. (Gardner 1999, pp. 186–187)

BOX 6.6

English Language Learners (ELL) Checklist for a Welcoming Classroom

Our room:

1. Talks in normal tone of voice to our ELL classmates; we don't shout to make English harder to understand.
2. Invites our ELL classmates to share words of greetings or other phrases, if they wish to do so.
3. Pairs ELL classmates with helpers for some tasks; we each get to help, if we wish.
4. We ask our ELL friends if there is a special school name we should call them by.
5. We have books in all of the languages spoke by the children in our room.
6. We sometimes practice conversations about the weather and about our favorite books and TV programs so we all share our understanding and learn about appropriate social behavior and the social rules of a "polite" society.

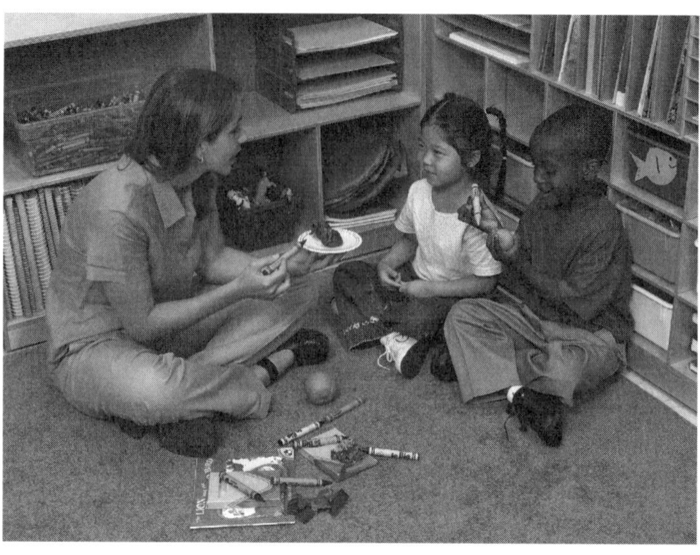

In practice, Gardner (1999; see also Gardner 2006; Gardner, 2009) suggests that teachers must provide various ways for students to become engaged in a topic, provide multiple opportunities for developing understanding, and permit diverse products and processes for assessment and documentation of work. This does not mean that you need to represent all the intelligences all the time, but that you provide diverse learning assignments and measures so that you tap the best in each child.

multiple intelligences theory that children have seven areas of intellectual competence that are relatively independent of each other.

Gardner has attempted to do just that by developing a comprehensive framework based on his theory of **multiple intelligences** (MI). He posits that the areas of intellectual competence (intelligences) are relatively independent of each other. The intelligences are linguistic intelligence, musical intelligence, logical–mathematical intelligence, spatial intelligence, bodily kinesthetic intelligence, and personal intelligences (Gardner, 2006). It is possible to provide classroom learning centers for each of the different abilities (language center, math and science center, music center, movement center, art center, working together center, personal work center) that would help children learn subject matter content while utilizing their own relative strengths. However, you should not assume that the centers are promoting learning in a direct way; the intellectual process is much more complicated.

An example of a research and practice project based on MI theory is Project Zero, implemented at a center where Howard Gardner serves as one of the principal researchers. "Project Zero's mission is to understand and enhance learning, thinking, and creativity in the arts, as well as humanistic and scientific disciplines, at the individual and institutional levels." The center's principal researchers are involved in a variety of projects. Two projects of interest for early childhood educators involve the "creative learning" project that seeks to promote creative thinking in classrooms and the "making learning visible" project that links the practices of Reggio Emilia to MI theory and practice (Project Zero, 2009). These projects promote holistic views of children and an integrated assessment/teaching approach. For the purposes of thinking about assessment issues in the classroom, MI theory offers support for the notion of the complexity of learning/thinking. MI theory does not provide support for assessment of particular intelligences—only the notion that problem-solving in all its permutations is complicated. In addition to assessing children for instruction, teachers are responsible for referring those who may be at risk or those who may have disabilities. MI theory and the specialized techniques discussed in this chapter help you understand that young children possess unique characteristics, abilities, and strengths and that you need a variety of techniques to be able to assess, evaluate, or see in young children so that you will be able to teach each of the individuals in your class. As a teacher, your responsibility for individualizing education is codified in the IDEA 2004 with the 2006 regulations calling for an approach know as Response to Intervention (RTI) (IDEA, 2006) and theoretically supported by the principles contained in *Developmentally Appropriate Practice in Early Childhood Programs* (Copple & Bredekamp, 2009). The next section explores RTI as well as the prerequisite curricular approach to support inclusion of young children with disabilities.

RESPONSE TO INTERVENTION (RTI)

response to intervention (RTI) a problem-solving approach to classroom practice that begins with screening of all children and continues with a three-tier intervention protocol to individualize instruction for all children.

"**Response to Intervention (RTI)** integrates assessment and intervention within a multilevel prevention system to maximize student achievement and to reduce behavior problems. With RTI, schools (and child care centers) identify students at risk for poor learning outcomes, monitor student progress, provide evidence-based interventions, and adjust the intensity and nature of those interventions depending on a student's responsiveness, and identify students with learning disabilities" (National Center on Response to Intervention, http://www.rti4success.org; accessed June 25, 2009). The process is required by IDEA regulations (IDEA, 2006) and is designed to identify children with learning disabilities for specialized services. Before children are classified as children with learning disabilities, the school district or child care program must go through a series of interventions to modify the learning situation so that an individual young child can be successful in a typical early childhood program. You begin the RTI process with high-quality instruction and universal screening of all the children in your classroom. In this way, you are aware of the standards and outcomes required by your program and armed with knowledge of where you class members stand in regard to meeting goals. As a teacher, your role is to provide struggling learners with modified approaches and structures toward the accomplishment of these goals, keeping track of progress on individual children, and documenting alternatives tried. As you need more help, a team of specialists assist with interventions at increasing levels of intensity to accelerate their rate of learning. The interventions are called tiers of support. The process begins with a referral by a teacher to the school's RTI support team, when you are concerned about a particular child. A key characteristic of the RTI process is collaborative planning with parent/family involvement in supporting the learner. The team then decides what kind of intervention might be helpful. With slight modifications to tasks or class structure, the intervention is described as Tier 1 support. At the Tier 2 level, more extensive modifications are made to an individual child's learning experience and environment, including the involvement of specialists such as speech and language therapists, occupational therapists or others on the special education staff. Tier 3 support is more specialized. In Figure 6.2, see an illustration of the hierarchical

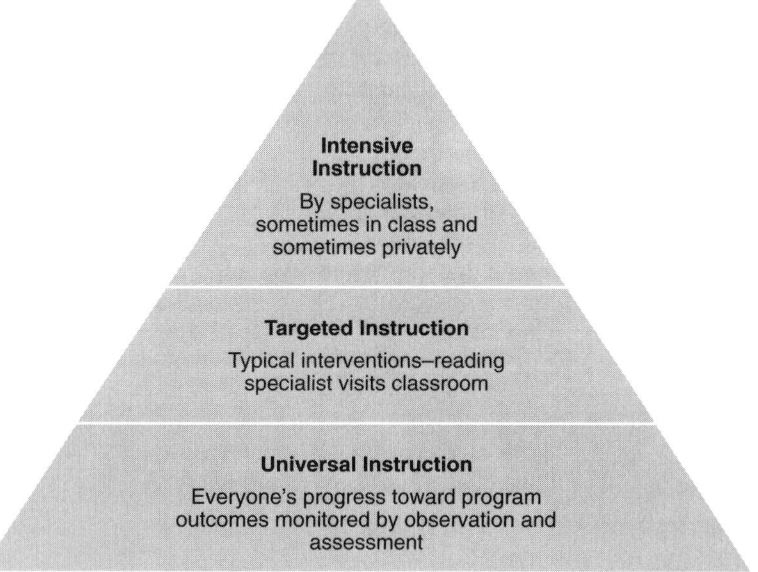
Intensive Instruction
By specialists, sometimes in class and sometimes privately
Targeted Instruction
Typical interventions–reading specialist visits classroom
Universal Instruction
Everyone's progress toward program outcomes monitored by observation and assessment

FIGURE 6.2 Response to Intervention (RTI).

relationships of the tiers of service for individual children. Note that at the top of the pyramid, the most intensive intervention occurs.

In each tier of intervention, plans are made for data gathering, data interpretation, and revision of the teaching/learning environment. So RTI is a data-based process approach to intervention with the emphasis on scaffolding young children for success. Interventions are intensive and targeted. The techniques used by teachers and specialists are many of the same special techniques described in this chapter. The techniques support early childhood inclusion, which "embodies the values, policies, and practices that support the right of every infant and young child and his or her family, regardless of ability, to participate in a broad range of activities and contexts as full members of families, communities, and society. The desired results of inclusive experiences for children with and without disabilities and their families include a sense of belonging and membership, positive social relationships and friendships, and development and learning to reach their full potential. The defining features of inclusion that can be used to identify high-quality early childhood programs and services are access, participation, and supports" (Copple & Bredekamp, 2009). As a successful teacher who uses RTI, you will need to be a skilled observer as well as an organized data-gatherer—all of the best practices of early childhood education delineated in *Developmentally Appropriate Practice* (NAEYC, 2009). One key component of RTI is prevention; that is, if universal screening and skillful teaching identify potential problems for young children early, then specialized assistance or intervention can provide scaffolding for individuals to stay within the typical classroom and learn. To be sure that your classroom is ready for inclusion and the process of RTI, you need to set the stage for learning.

Setting the Stage for Success—Attending to the Classroom Climate

Successful classrooms provide security for young children. You provide this security by attending to the baseline: the room arrangement, the schedule, the routines, the rules and expectations, the personal interactions, (Berry & Mindes, 1993). Embedded in this structure is the bones of the classroom, which promote child understanding of the way the environment and expectations will be predictable and enduring. Ritchhart and Perkins describe the classroom culture that supports learning as one where there are:

1. Routines and structures for learning
2. Set language and conversational patterns
3. Implicit and explicit expectations
4. Appropriate time allocation for engagement
5. Modeling by teachers and others
6. Supportive physical environment
7. Relationships and patterns of interaction
8. Creation of learning opportunities (2008, p. 58)

With this foundation, teachers make thinking visible to children. Some strategies include techniques called:

- "Headlines"—what is the summary headline for our discussion about grandparents in our lives?
- "Connect-extend-challenge"—how does the information today connect to what you already know? What new ideas make you think in new directions? What are you still wondering about or still puzzling over? (2008, p. 59; see also Project Zero's Visible Thinking Website (http://www.pz.harvard.edu/vt)).

Other ways to support making learning visible is the use of charts and/or graphic organizers. Box 6.7 shows some popular forms to consider for various uses in your class.

The well-organized classroom also includes learning centers for students to practice skills, learn from each other, and document their learning progress. A planning scheme as shown in Box 6.8 helps you think about how to set up centers for learner success.

BOX 6.7

Graphic Organizers

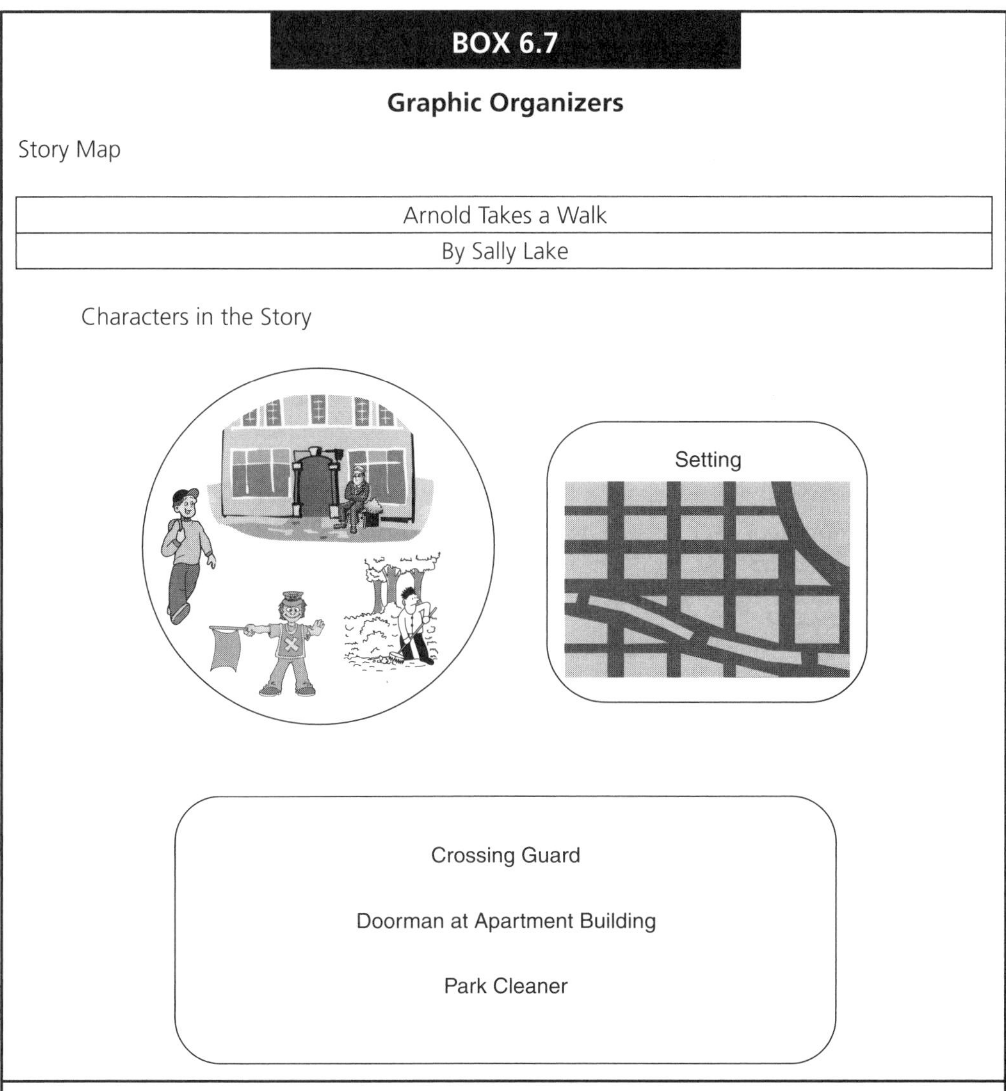

What we Know about homes	What we Want to know	What we Learned
People live in homes	How do people build homes?	
Homes give shelter	How do people repair homes?	
Some homes are made of bricks	Are homes in MT like homes in FL?	
Some homes are made of wood	Why do some people not have homes?	
Some homes are made of concrete		

(continued)

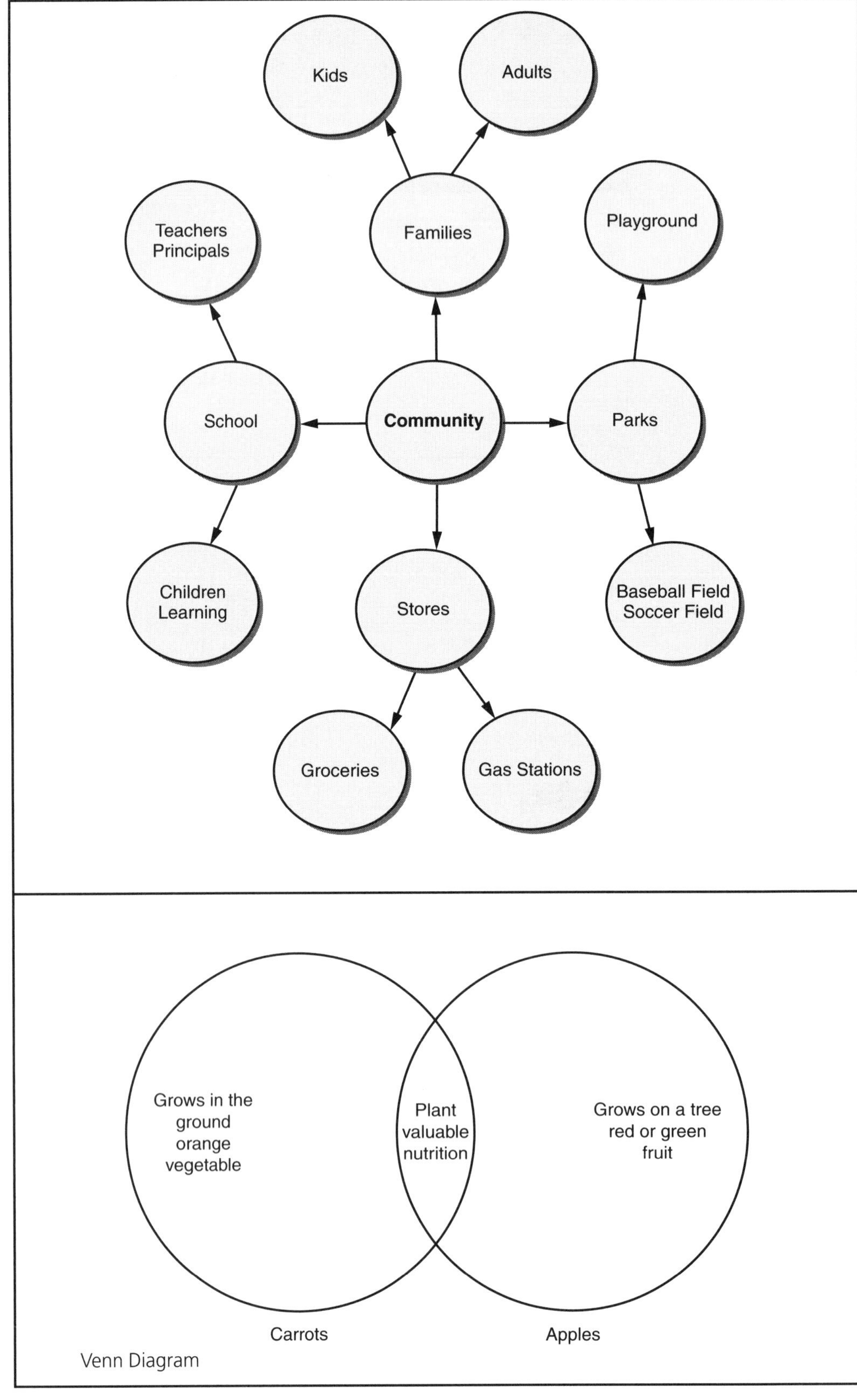

Venn Diagram

BOX 6.8

Planning Scheme for Learning Centers

Center	Independent or Interactive	Location and Seating	Materials	Stationary or Portable
Read relate and respond	Independent	Table near the class library	Books Worksheets Markers/pencils	Stationery
Problem-solve	Independent	Box	Attribute blocks Recording sheet	Portable

Adapted from Southall, M. (2007) *differentiated literacy centers.* New York: Scholastic, p. 46.

Grouping for instruction is another important element of a successful inclusive classroom. Important points to keep in mind:

- Avoid "static" groups—always the same learners in one group.
- Base groups on assessment results—who needs to practice identifying shapes?
- Make groups that support independent learning as well as teacher-directed activity.
- Think about grouping by pairs.
- Organize the movement and expectations for "group" behavior.

An illustration of a teacher's record-keeping system for writing is shown in Box 6.9.

BOX 6.9

Small-Group Observation Form for Tracking Writing Progress

Names	Notes about the craft of writing	Notes about the conventions of writing	What's next?	How to implement?
Dolores	Writes what she knows	Uses mostly uppercase letters	Using lowercase letters	Provide opportunities in learning center to manipulate magnetic letters
Al	Re-reads and makes corrections	Listens to sounds and applies to writing	Provide more challenging stories to read and respond to	Conference to discuss reading interests
Irene	Includes small specific details about the story	Labels independently	Work on summary	Mini-lesson on summary with others: Baila, Rae, and Gail

Adapted from Horn, M. & Giacobbe, E. (2007) *Talking, drawing, writing: Lessons for our youngest writers.* Portland, ME: Stenhouse.

One of the difficult times in this predictable structure for some children is the transition from one activity to the next. In planning for transitions that will support your group's adherence to the routines, you may ask yourself whether any transition can be eliminated. This question follows your examination of what is happening during transition and whether children have something to do while waiting for the next activity. With your group, you teach acceptable transition behavior. For example, when moving to large group activity in a preschool, suggest that children move in a certain way—as if they were moving through peanut butter, wiggling though Jello, marching in a band, bird flying to a nest, in a car driving down the road (Hemmeter, Ostrosky, Artman, & Kinder, 2008, p. 21). This gives the group a focus and a way to concentrate on moving from centers to large group. Some children will not be able to do this easily. For these children, you make an individual plan. Perhaps it involves a "pre-signal" for Peter that you model, cue, or provide pictorial support for. Essentially you are teaching Peter how to clean up and leave activities. This approach includes focusing on a targeted transition, examining why the behavior occurs, developing ways to prevent the problem, responding to the problem, with the result that Peter adds a skill to his repertoire of "successful" learner (Hemmeter et al., p. 24).

Teacher language is another important way that you can support learners effectively. In the words you use with children, you affect the child's sense of identity. Suppose that Jeff is excited about the goat cheese he tasted for the first time. He starts to tell you about it, but he begins to stammer; you say, "Slow down, I can't understand you when you're in such a rush." What's the probability that Jeff will want to share excitement with you again? You have effectively "shut him down." Why not instead, listen, then respond with, "Wow, what an exciting new taste; I loved hearing about it." In another example, you promote writing skills for third grader Paula by saying, "Your words show me exactly what the old house looks like, you used such wonderful description." Paula takes away the impression that her writing is valued. Denton (2008) outlines five principles for using positive language with children:

1. Be direct, say what you mean and use a kind, straightforward tone, so children learn to trust you. "It's time to listen now."
2. Convey faith in students' abilities and intentions. "Show me how you will follow the rules in the hall."
3. Focus on actions, not abstractions. Rather than reminding children to show respect during discussions, focus on the observable, required behavior. "When someone is speaking, we are listening."
4. Keep it brief. "What should we do when we get to Morning Ex (assembly)?"
5. Know when to be silent. That is, wait for children to respond to questions. (pp. 28–31; see also Denton, 2007).

inclusive classroom affirms and welcomes children from diverse backgrounds and abilities

Each of these strategies focus on a positive, welcoming classroom community that is required to truly have an **inclusive classroom**. "In truly inclusive classrooms, teachers acknowledge the myriad ways in which (children) differ from one another (class, gender, ethnicity, family background, sexual orientation, language, abilities, size, religion, and so on) value this diversity and design and implement productive, sensitive responses (Sapon-Shevin, 2008, p. 49). To see whether your classroom meets a positive, inclusive environment, review whether you are:

1. Building community throughout the year
2. Teaching positive social skills
3. Explaining and illustrating the concept of "community"
4. Adopting a policy of confronting negative comments and behavior
5. Using materials and bulletin boards, songs, and activities that highlight the value of inclusion of everyone
6. Sharing your childhood experiences with diversity so that children can learn appropriate language to use when discussing differences
7. Seizing teachable moments to discuss words or behaviors that may "hurt" children's feelings and show respect for values of different cultural practices

8. Providing opportunities to work together with everyone and to appreciate the assistance of others
9. Creating an atmosphere where everyone is valued
10. "Keep(ing) in mind that (children) will remember only some of what you taught them but everything about how they felt in your classroom" (adapted from Sapon-Shevin, 2008, p. 51).

The inclusive classroom climate relies also on a sense of **personal efficacy**—"deep-seated belief in our own capabilities" (Sagor, 2008, p. 28). We communicate to children that they can be successful learners by permitting them to talk about what they are learning, by permitting them to describe and document their learning, and by allowing them to present their accomplishment in portfolios with reflections and at parent conferences.

personal efficacy also called self-efficacy, this concept refers to a child's sense that as a person or learner, the child can be successful.

PREREFERRAL SCREENING

This referral process is **Child Find** (IDEA U.S. Department of Education, 2004). Child Find is the process of identifying young children who may be at risk for disability, previously unknown to the parents or to the school. As you carry forward your responsibility in this endeavor, you want to keep careful records of your concerns about the problems or limited progress of the few children in your room who may need the skilled diagnosis of a psychologist or other member of the multidisciplinary team member that serves your school or program. As part of this record-keeping procedure, you may find that a checklist of student classroom behaviors will be an efficient way to check your judgment of need for intervention (Busse, 2005; Schmid, 1999; see also Pianta, LaParo, & Hamre, 2008, discussed in Chapter 5). For example, your impression is that Josefina has difficulty with the social routines of first grade. As a result, you might list the behaviors that you expect on a checklist, then observe Josefina for a week or so and complete your checklist on her comparison to school standards. Ms. Firestorm developed the list shown in Box 6.10 Kindergarten Classroom Behavior Checklist for her class.

Child Find federal requirement for teachers (and others working with young children) to identify young children with disabilities so they may receive appropriate services and interventions to ameliorate such disabilities.

When you are watching a young child whose first language is not English, you will want to be extra careful as you try to decide whether Sofia is presenting a behavior problem or whether she is still in the midst of learning English while maintaining her first language. So you will need to look at all areas of development, find a speaker of her language to assess Sofia's abilities in her first language, as well as note her capabilities in English-based tasks. If Sofia is beginning to learn English, she may show behaviors that you think are problems—nonverbal, difficulty in following directions, difficulty in expressing ideas and feelings, and difficulty in responding to questions consistently. Thus, what looks like a problem may merely be a child who needs time to learn English (Santos & Ostrosky, 2005; Garcia, 2005).

Again, you have applied functional assessment or other individualized assessment appropriate for the problem evidenced in the classroom, as part of the referral process of young children who may be eligible for services to ameliorate their cognitive, emotional, or behavioral disorders. The

BOX 6.10

Kindergarten Classroom Behavior Checklist

Kindergarten Classroom Behavior	1 (not at all) to 5 (most of the time)				
Raises hand for class discussion	1	2	3	4	5
Stays in line in the hall	1	2	3	4	5
Works on seat assignments with minimal assistance	1	2	3	4	5
Sits in the circle story time and so on	1	2	3	4	5

identification of these young children is complex due to issues of definitions of the disorders, issues related to cultural norms, effects of poverty on learning opportunity, and problems related to the role of norm-based assessment in identifying children who experience these disorders (cf. Howard et al., 2010; Raver, 2009). As the lines of regular and special education continue to blur and teachers assume increased responsibility for supporting young children while individualizing behavioral expectations for success in the regular classroom, functional assessment continues to be a useful tool.

SUMMARY

This chapter describes the most common alternative assessment strategies in use today. Their use depends on a number of variables, such as the age of the child, the amount of time the teacher can invest in the assessment, and the particular skill or skills you wish to assess. These measures are often play-based methods for babies, toddlers, and preschoolers. This chapter's discussion incorporated the description of seven alternative assessment strategies: play-based assessment, task analysis, dynamic assessment, functional assessment, ecological assessment, curriculum-based language assessment, and multiple intelligences as a framework for understanding the complexity of human intelligence. The chapter concludes with a discussion of inclusion, response to intervention, and setting up the assessment/teaching connection for the success of all young children.

FIELD ACTIVITIES

1. With a partner, go to a local park or playground. Between the two of you, see if you can find examples of solitary play, parallel play, group play, cooperative play, functional play, constructive play, sociodramatic play, games with rules, unoccupied behavior, and onlooker behavior. Use the checklist in Box 6.2 to record your observations or take anecdotal notes. Discuss your findings with each other to see if you can reach total agreement.
2. In a child-care center, watch a child who is off-target for the social group expectations. Try out the steps of functional analysis.
3. Visit a class with children who are English language learners. Watch one child in an academic activity. Try to identify the vocabulary that may be academic and possibly unfamiliar to the child.
4. Sit with a child who has difficulty with completing a worksheet, while teaching the child, and identify through reflection afterward some difficulties that might have contributed to the child's failure with this sheet. Discuss these with colleagues.
5. Go to a school or child care center. Ask the teacher how they are implementing RTI. Come back to class and compare notes with your colleagues.

IN-CLASS ACTIVITIES

1. Select a long-term objective that you think would be worthwhile to teach to a young child. Identify the steps involved in learning the objective.
2. With a partner, pick a task that is unfamiliar to you—peeling a pineapple, putting on eye makeup, washing a car—and analyze the number of steps in the task.
3. Watch a video clip of preschool children playing. Using the definitions of play, watch the tape again. With a partner, select a child to watch and make notes about regarding the play categories. After the viewing, review your assessment with your partner. Resolve areas of disagreement and share your findings with the class.

STUDY QUESTIONS

1. What are some critical skills that a teacher may incorporate into a curriculum plan? List strategies that the teacher may implement to assess progress.
2. How will a child's play activity provide extensive information about his personal developmental level?
3. Why is it important for teachers to include alternative assessment strategies into planning for the children?
4. What are the components of a task analysis? What skills can an early childhood teacher assess with a task analysis?
5. Create a task analysis by developing a long-term goal for a preschooler. For instance, the parents and teachers would like to see a child's play include increased appropriate exploration at the art center with manipulatives such as paintbrushes and crayons. Break this goal into steps for task analysis.

6. Consider situations throughout a school day where a teacher may use mediated learned experience and functional analysis.
7. Correlate the assessment/intervention approach to form/function.
8. What are the components of functional assessment? How will the teacher use this information over time?
9. What does multiple intelligence theory contribute to your understanding of the complexity of assessment tasks?
10. What are the critical elements of Response to Intervention? Why is this process an important concept for teaching and learning in early childhood?

REFLECT AND RE-READ

- I know how to structure observational questions to help solve a social or behavioral problem.
- I am familiar with the general principles of play-based assessment and its usefulness to the teacher.
- I have some strategies for solving tough teaching problems.
- I can apply multiple intelligence theory to activities for my students.
- I know how what my role in RTI should be as a classroom teacher.

CASE VIGNETTE

Ms. Archibald, mother of Adriana, came to school one day to say that Adrianna, a three-year-old, wished to go on a diet. Ms. Archibald was worried because Adrianna was refusing breakfast, eating only a bite or two at dinner, and refusing her favorite after-preschool snack of frozen yogurt—she even looked in a mirror and declared herself fat. This behavior occurred for about a week. Adrianna and her five-year-old sister, Marla, are bright, energetic, active children with no previous social/emotional, cognitive, or school adjustment issues. There are no particular family stresses. Ms. Archibald wants to know what actions or behaviors the preschool teachers are seeing that relate to Adrianna and food. What do you do at school to discover why Adrianna is refusing to eat and is thinking that she is fat? How might you use play-based assessment?

TECHNOLOGY LINKS

http://www.cec.sped.org/AM/Template.cfm?Section=Home

Council for Exceptional Children. This is the ERIC Clearinghouse for information about children with disabilities. Descriptions of publications that facilitate teaching are included.

http://www.ldonline.org

LD OnLine. A site with information for teachers, parents, and other professionals.

http://pzweb.harvard.edu

Project Zero at Harvard University. The site is a source of research and information about applied multiple intelligences applications.

http://www.responsiveclassroom.org

The Northeast Foundation for Children, Inc. Provides ideas and publications directed toward safe, challenging, and joyful classrooms for elementary-aged children.

http://www.crtiec.org

Center for Response to Intervention in Early Childhood (CRTIEC). The mission of this center is to provide resources and conduct and disseminate research.

SUGGESTED READINGS

Diller, D. (2007) *Making the most of small groups: Differentiation for all.* Portland, ME: Stenhouse.

Frost, J., Wortham, S., & Reifel, S. (2008). *Play and child development* (3rd ed.). Upper Saddle River, NJ: Merrill/Prentice Hall.

Gould, P. & Sullivan, J. (2005). *The inclusive early childhood classroom: Easy ways to adapt learning centers for all children.* Upper Saddle River, NJ: Merrill/Prentice Hall.

National Center for Learning Disabilities. (2009). *Roadmap to PreK RTI* (available at http://www.rtinetwork.org/images/stories/learn/roadmaptoprekrti.pdf).

Schiller, P. & Willis, C. (2008). *Inclusive literacy lessons.* Beltsville, MD: Gryphon House.

Sprenger, M. (2005). *How to teach so students remember.* Alexandria VA: Association for Supervision and Curriculum Development.

CHAPTER 7

Record Keeping, Reporting, and Collaborating with Families and Others

TERMS TO KNOW

- confidentiality
- student-led conferences
- grades
- report card
- standards-based
- screening results
- RTI conference
- initial referral conference
- Individualized Education Plan (IEP) conferences
- multidisciplinary staffing
- stakeholders
- accountability

CHAPTER OVERVIEW

This chapter discusses the record-keeping, collaborating, and reporting issues for the teacher role in relation to all stakeholders in the assessment system for young children. Highlighted is the importance and role of routine parent–teacher conferences as part of a comprehensive assessment system. The chapter begins with issues and suggestions surrounding recording, storing, and maintaining child files. The topics of parent permission and parent participation in the assessment process are included, as are examples and issues related to report cards and portfolio assessment reporting procedures. Special procedures for partnerships with parents as clients are a special feature. Suggestions for involving children as partners in the assessment and reporting process are included. The chapter describes the teacher's role and responsibility in Response to Intervention (RTI) and multidisciplinary staffing. Finally, there is a section on issues and suggested report procedures regarding the other stakeholders in the assessment system—administrators, boards, legislators, and the public.

ASSESS AS YOU READ

RTI conference the conference with one or more specialists to discuss Tier 1 (modified tasks in the typical classroom), Tier 2 (specialized intervention), Tier 3 (intensive intervention).

- What kinds of reports are useful for reporting to parents?
- What is the role of report cards?
- Where do children and parents fit in the portfolio process? Is there a difference when portfolios are electronic?
- How should I prepare for **RTI conference** or multidisciplinary staffing?
- What do principals and other stakeholders want to know?

RECORD KEEPING AND REPORTING IN THE ASSESSMENT SYSTEM

Collaboration and communication between families and teachers begins at enrollment. If parents view the entrance of their child to the care and education system positively, then subsequent contacts at conference and report card times will start favorably. Families will enter the conference with the expectation of respect, cooperation, and mutual discussion about the best interests of their child. Engagement of families in the process improves student achievement as well, according to a review of 50 studies on parent, family, and community connections (Mapp & Henderson, 2005). The National Association for Elementary School Principals (2006, p. 24) affirms this research with the expectations that effective principals for young children and their families adopt the following principles:

- Acknowledge and support families as children's first and most influential teachers.
- Provide early education experiences that are informed by young children's cultural and community experiences.
- Act as a bridge between schools and community-based supports for young children and their families.
- Build coalitions with community organizations to strengthen learning for children from birth to the start of fourth grade.

This "best practice" statement gives teachers and families support for placing families at the center for decision making about their young children. Thus, as teachers, you need to establish the first conferences and reports—whether in child-care or school settings—as the best experiences for all stakeholders. The conversations should be reciprocal with families. This includes "(maintenance of) frequent, positive, two-way communication (planned conferences and messages sent home are important, as is day-to-day communication" (Copple & Bredekamp, 2009, p. 45) Active listening is the key to building a reciprocal relationship with families. Techniques for active listening are illustrated in Box 7.1.

Thus, through your verbal and nonverbal support, you make it possible for families to feel that the conversation is real and personal. Additional active listening ideas include reflection—your point about Eugenia being excited about counting; I can see that in the math center where she loves to count the blocks (cf. Grant & Ray, 2010).

Conference and report card periods are the summative opportunities for parent–teacher communication. It is a time when all parties in the assessment system—parents, child, teacher, and other professionals—share information from their diverse perspectives. It is a time to reflect on the past and to prepare appropriate intervention, teaching, and learning goals for the future.

BOX 7.1

Illustrations of Active Listening

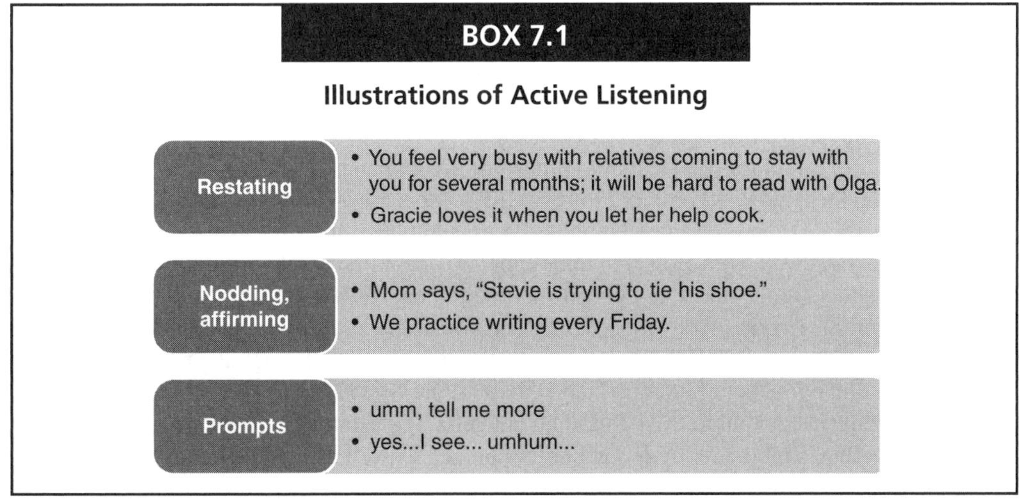

Restating
• You feel very busy with relatives coming to stay with you for several months; it will be hard to read with Olga.
• Gracie loves it when you let her help cook.
Nodding, affirming
• Mom says, "Stevie is trying to tie his shoe."
• We practice writing every Friday.
Prompts
• umm, tell me more
• yes...I see... umhum...

In preparation for these times, teachers must formally reflect about each child in the program, collect records, and prepare for the conference or translate the material to a child-study or report-card format. These efforts must match the philosophy, curriculum, and parent program.

MAINTAINING CONFIDENTIALITY OF ASSESSMENT INFORMATION

confidentiality allowing a child's assessment and other records to be available only to school personnel, agency officials, and parents.

As teachers prepare written records for these conference intervals, careful attention is required for the ethical and legal responsibilities for confidential child progress records. Teachers maintain **confidentiality** by treating assessment and other child records as private documents. Only authorized school or agency officials and the child's parents know the contents of these materials. Official school or agency records should be stored in only one place (P.L. 93-380, the Family Educational and Privacy Rights Act [FERPA], 20 U.S.C. § 1232g; 34 CFR Part 99). This includes demographic information, family and social history, academic history, attendance records, medical data, test scores, anecdotal notes, and report cards (narrative or checklist). Schools and centers house these records in a locked file. Authorized school personnel (principal, teacher, specialists) may view the records; these personnel maintain the records. Parents may see the records by appointment within 45 days of the parent-initiated request.

In the classroom, before records become *official,* teachers must safeguard notes, scores, and drafts of reports. Teachers must also choose with care the words that they use in recording notes and progress. Describe behavior of note or concern, specifically. Label judgments, opinions, and hypotheses clearly as such. Avoid broad, sweeping generalizations and value judgments. Teachers and other professionals may only write about observations and experiences that they have the credentials to assess; for example, teachers are not qualified to judge mental health and intelligence. However, teachers may appropriately discuss observable concerns and problems in performance. Box 7.2 shows illustrations of appropriate and inappropriate practices.

Teachers prepared the notes shown in Box 7.2 prior to parent conference time. The notes represent the reflections of the teachers. Parents can be similarly involved by asking them to bring notes or observations of their children doing particular activities at home.

INVOLVING PARENTS IN ASSESSMENT

Before parents come to school to hear the report at the conference, teachers can suggest real assessment partnerships for parents:

1. Ask parents for their goals for their children. This will provide an opportunity for you to talk with parents about the curriculum and their child.

   Ms. Berkeley, the parent of a kindergartner, believes that her son, Seth, is gifted. She bases her assessment on Seth's early talking. Ms. Berkeley wants Seth to read at the end of the first quarter of kindergarten. Ms. Myers, the kindergarten teacher, explains the developmental stages of literacy to Ms. Berkeley. She shows Ms. Berkeley evidence of Seth's progress and invites Ms. Berkeley to keep a log of stories and other literacy activities that occur at home over the first quarter of the year.
2. Ask parents for their opinion about homework assignments.

   Ms. Donohue asks children in her third-grade class to interview a senior citizen, relative, or friend. Children must be prepared to summarize their interviews in a paragraph. The Robins moved from Houston; they know no one in the neighborhood. Their daughter, Sylvia, is distraught that she will fail the assignment. Sylvia attended a developmentally inappropriate second grade with stress placed on completion of assignments according to exacting directions. Ms. Donohue learns of Sylvia's distress through the return of the parent questionnaire about homework and can reassure Sylvia before the problem casts itself into a concrete mountain. Ms. Donohue suggests, for example, that Sylvia can interview Ms. Donohue's mother, who is a school volunteer, as well as the chief engineer, the security guard, or other friendly adults around the school.

BOX 7.2

Teacher Comments on Report Cards

Inappropriate Practice

- Garfield has caused me a lot of concern.
- *Very hyperactive and immature.* He needs a medical exam and perhaps something to calm him down!

Appropriate Practice

- Ms. Taylor collects notes and checklists that she developed for use with the kindergarten. At report time, Ms. Taylor notices as she reviews her notes that Garfield spends an average of five minutes on drawing, painting, and puzzle activities. He spends an average of about 10 minutes in the block corner. At the circle times, Garfield wiggles, but listens attentively to the stories. In writing, Ms. Taylor can report the facts of her observations and notes. She may then interpret the facts with a sentence or two. Garfield prefers block play. This activity seems to hold his interest more than other available areas in our room. He seems to enjoy story time. He follows the story line well. Whether Ms. Taylor initiates a discussion about unusual activity level will depend on additional information available (e.g., family has new baby, Garfield responds to structure and limits offered). Garfield is probably functioning within typical limits for four-and-a-half-year-olds.

Inappropriate Practice

- Patty is lazy and shirks responsibility for getting work done. She must be prodded to do neater work.

Appropriate Practice

- Patty is a third grader in Mr. Merrill's class. Mr. Merrill assigns work at the beginning of the week. Each third grader is responsible for personal time management. Assignments include small group project work, individual worksheets for math, and reading books by interest and level. Science, art, music, drama, and physical education are separate subjects taught by subject area specialists. Students who do not finish assignments at school must take them home. Mr. Merrill notices near the end for the quarter that Patty has many worksheets that are incomplete. He notices that the ones that require writing are written in a haphazard fashion. Stories prepared by Patty are short, one or two sentences. Mr. Merrill reflects that this behavior is new for Patty. In second grade, she completed assignments and seemed enthusiastic about school. Mr. Merrill plans an open-ended parent conference, rather than a narrative report summarizing his findings. He plans to ask Patty's mother, Ms. Jones, questions about school from Patty's perspective and from Ms. Jones's perspective. Then he will ask Ms. Jones if there are unusual stresses at home. Following this discussion, Mr. Merrill will make a teaching plan to assist Patty.

  If required to write a narrative report for the quarter, Mr. Merrill can state the following: Patty has not finished assigned work at school. She has written very short essays. This approach to school work is very different than her approach in second grade. Ms. Jones, let's meet to discuss how we can assist Patty in becoming a successful third-grade learner.

Inappropriate Practice

- Alan doesn't copy from other children anymore, but he lacks original ideas. Goes home for lunch and forgets to come back from the playground.

Appropriate Practice

- Alan, a first grader, seems to like to work with friends. He thrives on their simulation. He likes active play. Lunchtime is his favorite time of the day. He needs some assistance in remembering to return to the room after lunch. We are developing a plan with Alan.

3. Provide checklists or open-ended question sheets for parents to record their own experiences with their children's progress in a subject area.

   Mr. Lester, the science teacher, suggests several take-home science experiments for young children attending Bowman Early Childhood Center, which serves children birth to age 8. Parents and children are encouraged to try the experiments at home. Parents, with their child's help, record the experiment results. They are encouraged to keep a notebook of experiments, results, any problems, and a record of concepts. At conference time, parents share with teachers the observations and solicit suggestions for associated readings. Teachers can comment on the observations from school. Thus, the partnership becomes solid.
4. Use the written parent comments at conference time: My child . . .
   a. understands more of what he/she reads.
   b. enjoys being read to by family members.
   c. finds quiet time at home to read.
   d. sometimes guesses at words but they usually make sense.
   e. can provide summaries of stories read.
   f. has a good attitude about reading.
   g. enjoys reading to family members.
   h. would like to get more books from the library.
   i. chooses to write about stories read.
   j. is able to complete homework assignments. (Fredericks & Rasinski, 1990)

You can develop similar questionnaires for any subject or developmental area. These items serve as suggested activities for parents and involve parents in the assessment process. Ms. Jewel can develop a list of questions for parents of the three-year-olds in her program about favorite play activities. For example, my child . . .

- enjoys pretend play with dolls and small figures, cars, spaceships.
- enjoys water play at bath time or in kitchen sink with parent or responsible older sibling.
- likes to go to the park to run and chase friends.
- loves to act out favorite stories.
- sings songs from school.

All of these procedures provide meaningful, personalized opportunities to involve parents in the regular child-care and educational lives of their children.

Sometimes, the results of these regular contacts, or initial contacts, will require specialized assessment to develop appropriate planning for children with special needs. In those cases, parent involvement is not only recommended but also required.

Parent permission is required for any specialized assessment of children. This includes any measure beyond the usual and customary actions of teachers and caregivers—for example, a speech therapist screening Lori for a lisp, an in-depth assessment by a school psychologist on Bartholomew, or a physical-therapist review of Daniel. Obtain permission as an outgrowth of a routine or special conference with parents. This is part of the Response to Intervention (RTI) process, as well as sometimes an outgrowth of routine screening at the time of enrollment or during the program year.

CONFERENCING WITH PARENTS

Preparing Parents for the Experience

Preparing parents for conferences is an important teacher role. Use many approaches to communication of expectations due to the diverse needs of parents. Parents themselves may have ideas about good preparation strategies. The parent community may be especially helpful in those situations where cultural and linguistic differences between teachers and parents affect basic communication. Of particular importance in early childhood programs is familiarity with child-rearing practices and how these will affect the reciprocal family/center or school partnership. Points to know about your community of families include the following:

- "Ways children demonstrate respect/disrespect for adults, including whether children are expected to make eye contact as a sign of respect; whether children are expected to ask adults questions, engage in dialog, or make jokes with adults; and the names adults are called by children. . . .
- Relative value placed on play and academics, including whether play is viewed as an important task . . . or distraction and whether academics are viewed as the most significant type of learning." (Feeney, Moravcik, Nolte, & Christensen, 2010, p. 421)

Eggers-Pierola suggests bringing pairs of parents to class to observe the activities (2005, p. 43). As the parents watch the activities and observe the environment, they will focus on any number of program variables that you identify. Then, you can discuss with individuals or in small groups such issues as:

- What behaviors, activities, or practices do you encourage at home that you see (or don't see) here?
- What did you notice about the personal interactions here—among children, between teacher and child? Were they respectful?
- Did you notice something new about your child?
- What is missing from our program that might assist your child?

This pre-observational procedure serves to identify potential value conflicts that influence parent perceptions of child progress and program effectiveness, and is one of many techniques to consider for diverse settings. Therefore, in preparation for conferences, teachers continue their parent communication through various formats, including casual conversations, telephone calls, and e-mail contacts (Box 7.3 shows some guidelines for communicating by e-mail).

BOX 7.3

Communicating by E-mail

When using e-mail with parents, think about the following:

- Remember that email is very *public* and can be deceptively friendly.
- Be concise and to the point when you send notes. Use correct spelling, grammar, and punctuation so that you appear professional.
- Write personally to parents, using the "Dear all" only if the message applies to everyone (e.g., write only to the parents who did not send in a permission form rather than to everyone). Blanket messages such as "for those of you who haven't," etc., lead parents not to read any messages—blanket or individually specific.
- If parents write to you, decide whether e-mail is the best way to discuss the question or comment. Do not, for example, e-mail test results or concerns about child behavior and learning. Invite the parent to schedule a phone or in-person appointment about serious issues. You might ask yourself: Is this a message I would like to receive by e-mail (or voicemail)?
- Develop templates for regular items.
- Let parents know when you will respond—perhaps once per day and not all day because you are teaching their children.
- Avoid using "high-priority" indicators and never write in all capitals.
- Use carbon copies sparingly.
- Be sure to include a relevant message heading so that you don't wind up in the spam drawer.
- Be sure to proofread before sending.

Teachers create a welcoming environment by being available to parents before and after school. During these informal chats, a comfort level is established. Teachers can also set times to be available by phone. They communicate with parents by notes and in newsletters, dialog journals, or websites; increasingly, school districts have customized websites for parent–teacher and teacher–student communication. At conference time, teachers may make suggestions in the newsletter or on the class website concerning effective conference participation. Dietel (2001) offers specific suggestions from the parent perspective:

- Know what is expected in the school or center for the age of your child.
- Know how well your child is reading or what interest your child has in books and stories.
- Understand test scores (see Teachers and Families First for a Primer for Parents at http://www.teachersandfamilies.com/open/parent/scores1.cfm) or be prepared to ask.
- Ask the teacher for information and opinions on your child's progress.
- Know about your child's homework and work products sent home.
- Be aware of your child's social skills in other group situations.
- Ask your child about school perceptions and listen to responses.

When meeting parents from cultures different from your own, prepare ahead to be sure that you know about the cultural concepts of family and family roles, expectations for behavior and academic performance, and important customs and traditions (Jordan, Reyes-Blanes, Peel, Peel, & Lane, 1998; Feeney, Moracvik, Nolte, & Christensen, 2010).

Regular—weekly or monthly—newsletters (cf. Berger, 2008) to parents often contain information about class activities, wishes for volunteers, and recyclable material, as well as parent-education pieces such as those shown in Box 7.4.

Preconference Survey to Parents

Child-care programs and public schools may wish to develop a survey to send to parents. This may be particularly useful when parents are entering a program. A survey gives parents time to clarify their goals for their children and an opportunity to solidify their knowledge. It may serve to prepare them for the world of child care or school. This also may help a teacher guide the discussion. Parents feel empowered because they have had an opportunity to prepare for their first encounter with the school.

BOX 7.4

Newsletter Suggestions to Parents

- Think about your child before meeting with the teacher. What do you know about the school schedule, routine, and curriculum? What do you want to know more about? Jot down a couple of notes. Identify any particular developmental issues that you think the teacher may have suggestions for.
- Think about what your child tells you about school. If your child is old enough, ask what the child expects to happen at the conference. Ask if there are any problems with the curriculum or peers.
- Come prepared to learn about ways to help your child at home. Besides supervising any homework, find out what you can do to further the school objectives. Listen to suggestions about ways to volunteer at the school. If you are not free during school hours, find out what you might do in the evening or on weekends. Remember that parents who participate in schools show their children that school is important. The children respond by achieving.

BOX 7.5

Preconference Survey

Child's name: ______________________ Date: __________

Family member responding: __________

	Most of the Time	Sometimes	Rarely
My child loves to come to school			
He/she feels that the activities support his/her learning			
He/she understands "school"			
Homework is easy for him/her			

Other things to think about before our conference:

____

____

____

____

____

____

See you on October 15 at 4:30 as planned.

Primary teachers may survey parents about experiences with school, using open-ended questions such as the following:

- When you think about it, what excited Willard most about second grade? Were there assignments or activities that he seemed excited to do and couldn't wait to go to school for that day?
- Which projects seemed most difficult for Willard?
- Did Willard enjoy cooperative assignments with classmates?
- Are there some children that Willard has difficulty working with?
- How do you describe Willard as a learner? Worker?
- What are the most important learning goals for third graders from your perspective?

Teachers will want to develop the questions so that they focus and relate to their school goals. Writing style and language should be suited to the school community. (See Box 7.5 for a suggested form to use as a preconference survey.)

When developing guidelines for parents, you will want to pay attention to the developmental issues that may concern the parents in your community. Useful materials include suggestions for health and nutrition, television management, story reading, and sleep routines. You may want to illustrate academic skills used at home, such as locating information, organizing information, recalling information, adjusting reading rate, formalizing study methods, using graphic aids, and following directions. It is useful to include age-appropriate expectations with illustrations for preschool and primary ages. Skills included in checklists, posters, or newsletters serve to help parents invest in a partnership with the school. Progress on home activities shared with teachers assists teachers in responsive programming for individual children and families. Such materials also serve to empower parents as experts in the lives of their children. This may be particularly important in situations where parents are uncertain or insecure about their own levels of educational attainment (Maxwell & Clifford, 2004; Ohio Department of Education, 1990a, 1990b; see also Scholastic for Parents, http://www2.scholastic.com/browse/parentsHome.jsp, and Head Start, http://eclkc.ohs.acf.hhs.gov/hslc/For%20Parents/).

BOX 7.6

Pre-planning Conference Form

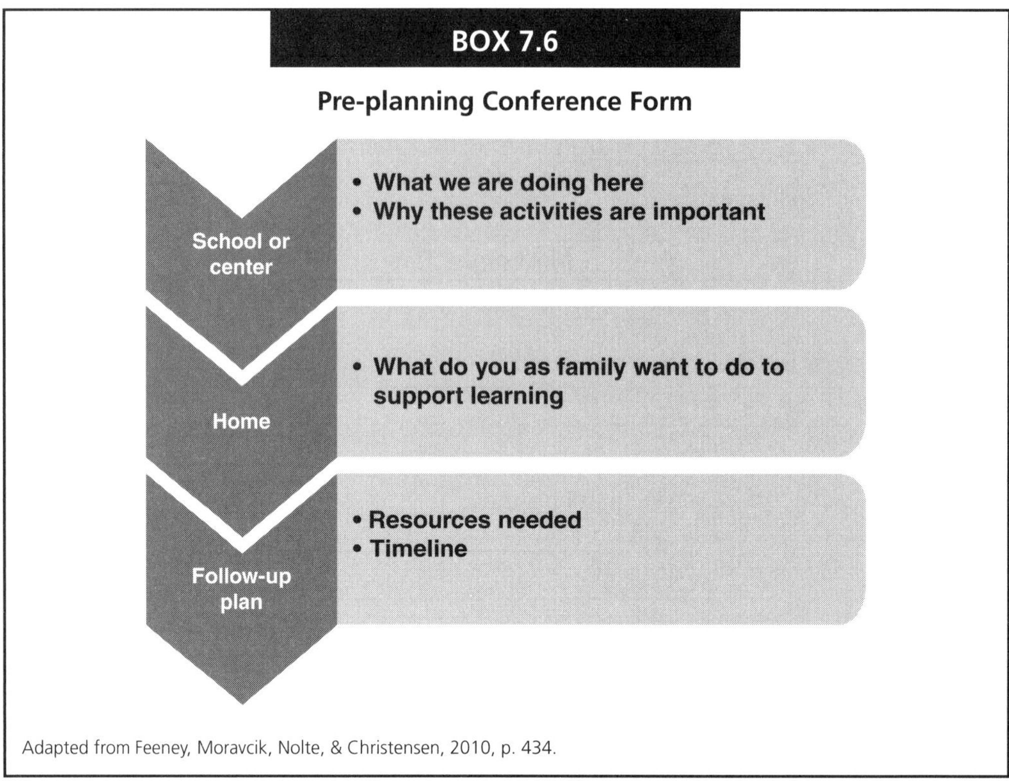

Adapted from Feeney, Moravcik, Nolte, & Christensen, 2010, p. 434.

In addition, to gathering ideas from parents, you will want to prepare for the experience yourself. Box 7.6 illustrates a Pre-planning Conference Form that can be prepared for each child before you meet the families.

Also, be sure that your program or school has not created barriers for parent participation. Perceptions that the parents or families often have are that the school is not welcoming, that the school treats families like clients rather than as partners, that the school will not help them help their children, that teachers use jargon and other intimidating tactics, and that the school will not alert them promptly when there are problems (Wherry, 2009). An example of parent disappointment follows:

> Mrs. Singer, parent of second-grader Burt, goes to the conference after the first quarter to discover that Burt will be failed in handwriting. Mrs. Guilford, Burt's teacher, shows Mrs. Singer several very messy papers and says, "These are unacceptable in second grade." Mrs. Singer is astonished on two counts—one, that this is the first time she heard about the problem, and two, because Burt has an IEP requiring assignment modification for fine-motor activities. The problem is solved through consultation with the occupational therapist and special writing paper. Burt feels happier about school and Mrs. Guilford has learned two valuable lessons—to pay attention to IEP requirements and what they mean, and to alert parents early when concerned about child progress.

To avoid such disasters and the creation of a less than positive parent conference, plan ahead from the beginning of the school year, utilizing best practice guidelines, and then set up the conference for success.

Staging Effective Conferences

The seating and room arrangement will influence the success of a conference. For the first conference of an academic year, it is helpful to hold the conference in the classroom so that you can show the living walls of your room. Be sure that your classroom has enough adult-sized chairs so that parents and teachers sit equally. Late in the year or for problem situations, if possible, choose a small conference room for the conversation so that quiet may be preserved. Be sure that everyone can see each other at the conference and that there is appropriate space. Too much open space may be intimidating. Constant brushing against participants may also be disconcerting. At the end of the conference held elsewhere, be sure to invite parents to visit the room to see displayed work, bulletin boards, and other important environmental supports to instruction.

Greet parents at the door and introduce yourself by first and last name or by following the conventions of the community for formality. It is inappropriate to call parents by their first names and to call yourself Ms. Teacher. Some parents prefer the formality of the address of Mr. and Mrs. Parent and are comfortable if you introduce yourself as Ms. Teacher. Others will prefer first names on all sides—parents and teacher. In addition to following conventions regarding addressing parents, you will want to respect parent norms regarding time and formality of dress.

Observe appropriate time-keeping customs for the community in scheduling and holding conferences. Hold conferences when parents can come to school conveniently. Provide child care, if necessary. If parents view the starting time as a target time to arrive at the meeting, then allow appropriate latitude in keeping with the cultural community perspective.

Provide opportunities for parents to participate in decision-making about their child's educational plan. Some parents will come with questions and suggestions. Others will have limited information about school. Some will remember with horror their own negative experiences. The structure of the meeting may intimidate some; that is, the number of professionals may threaten parents who are insecure with their own development or educational attainment.

Suggestions for effective parent–teacher conferences are as follows:

- Notify (or invite) parents about the purpose, place, date, and length of time.
- Offer a flexible conferencing schedule.
- Allow enough time and be sure to schedule at least 10 minutes between appointments.
- Provide a welcoming atmosphere.
- Identify any parent concerns.
- Start with descriptions of the child's strengths, interests, or abilities, and be personal.
- Concentrate on priorities.
- Be honest in your descriptions of learning and behavioral progress.
- Show that you care.
- Use parent-friendly language (i.e., "Michael shows strong ability to put objects together by group" rather than "Michael has great classification skills").
- Help children understand that conferences are routine.
- Collect relevant materials.
- Use examples of children's work to support your points.
- Listen carefully and be tactful in presenting information that parents may regard as threatening or may respond to with distress. For example, Mrs. Lawyer may not be delighted to hear that her daughter has failed the second-grade math test.
- Be aware of the time, so that you have time for everyone; schedule an extra conference if necessary.
- Don't respond to seemingly hostile or threatening comments.
- Make notes of relevant information after the conference is over or secure parent permission to make notes.
- With the parents' assistance, summarize the conference. If the conference plans a discussion of written reports, test scores, and grades, share a copy of these materials.
- Seek parent input for any next steps.
- Plan follow-up activities, interventions, and conferences with parents.

- Suggest simple activities for at-home educational enrichment (e.g., arranging socks in pairs and counting them by twos).
- Make notes for yourself as well as send a short summary of key points to families. (Bell, 1989; Million, 2005; Potter & Bulach, 2001; Seplocha, 2004; Grant & Ray, 2010)

These suggestions apply to preparation for conferences with all parents.

In addition, teachers must be sensitive to the individual needs of parents. For example, a sit-down conference may be difficult for a young mother who has a new baby and a preschooler in your program. She may prefer to visit by phone. She may likewise invite you to her home. Teachers, however, must be sensitive to parent preference about the location of the conference. Some parents may prefer not to have the privacy of their home invaded by the school. Others may feel that it is their responsibility as a parent to go to the school. It is a demonstration of their perception of the *good* parent. For example, Mrs. Cobb, a mother of 10 children who did not have a car, categorically refused to have her youngest child's teacher come to the home, in spite of the one-hour bus trip necessary for Mrs. Cobb to arrive at the school. She cared for her children, and going to school was a demonstration of care.

There may also be times when you need to schedule special conferences to resolve issues about learning or behavioral issues. In these cases, Grant and Ray offer the following guidelines: show parents that you are distinguishing the "problem" behavior from the child—you appreciate Mabel; keep in mind her strengths—besides being very active in the classroom, she is cheerful and friendly; outline a plan for supporting Mabel and listen to suggestions from Mabel's family; see what you can work on together and keep in touch (2010, p. 260). If you and Mabel's family share different cultural values and these may be clashing, be sure that your conversation is a dialog and not an argument. Gonzalez-Mena contrasts the differences as follows:

- In a dialog the purpose is to gather information; in an argument there is a winner.
- Dialogers ask; arguers tell
- Arguers try to persuade; dialoguers seek to understand
- Arguers cast the discussion into win/loss; dialogers entertain multiple views (2009, p. 142)

Survey parents to obtain suggested procedures for further individualization of conferences to determine their preferred level of participation:

- How much time do you spend at night discussing your child's day at school? (de Bettencourt, 1987, p. 26)
- How many hours a day do you work? (de Bettencourt, 1987, p. 26)
- Do you find it stressful to help your child at home with school-assigned tasks?
- What do you do with your child that is fun?
- Which other family members are available to help your child with school-related activities?

Seligman (2000) suggests that teachers work at establishing rapport with parents, or be aware of why the rapport is difficult; for example, if you are preoccupied with your own personal crisis, very fatigued, or if there is a reason that you may not respect a parent who may have a history with drug addiction, child abuse, or whatever. If there are cultural differences between you and the family, Seligman (2000) suggests that you inform yourself of special terminology of other languages and speak in straightforward English, avoiding the use of slang and jargon. In addition, be aware of the role that nonverbal behavior plays cross-culturally so that you are not inadvertently offensive to families. Finally, know when to be supportive—for example, with the young mother who is exhausted with the care of three children and a new baby—and when to be firm—for example, telling a parent that he or she must be sure that George comes to school on time with his homework completed. At the end of a conference held about an achievement issue or a behavioral problem, consider creating a summary form. (Box 7.7 shows an example.) In addition to the parents, another key stakeholder

BOX 7.7

Example of a Parent Conference Summary Form

Parent Conference Summary Form

Date of conference:

Name of child:

Family members responsible:

Purpose of conference (e.g., regular, special problem, parent request):

Documents related to the conference (portfolio, work samples, screening results, checklists, parent questionnaire, etc.):

Significant input from family members:

Summary of the conference:

Plans, next steps:

Parent signature: ______________________ Teacher signature: ______________________

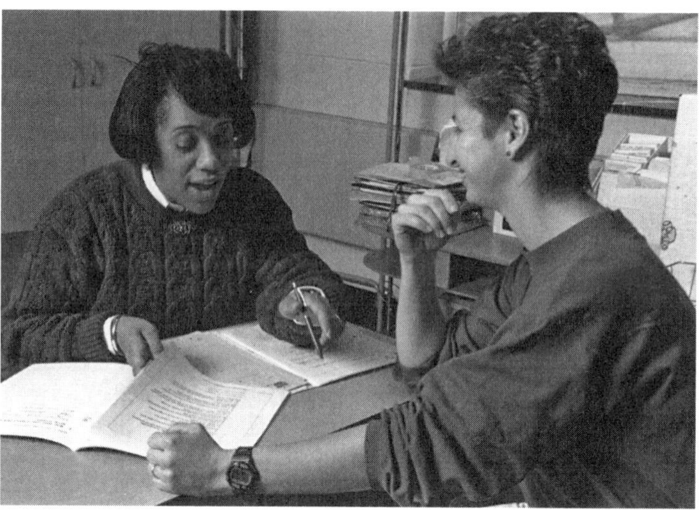

in the reporting process is the child. More and more, as an outgrowth of authentic assessment in the classroom, children can be involved in the parent–teacher conference process.

Involving Young Children in Student-Led Conferences

student-led conferences are those meetings between teacher and child where the learner holds the responsibility for reviewing and judging self-progress in relationship to class standards and teacher judgment. May include parents.

As part of a schoolwide emphasis on student responsibility for authentic learning and assessment, you may wish to explore the development of **student-led conferences** (cf. Bailey & Guskey, 2001; Shores & Grace, 2005). This approach leads to the possibility of following the 3 Rs of assessment—relevance, responsibility, and reliability—for you are helping children see the link from learning to evaluation to communication to others, and therefore, you are removing some of the mystery of the accountability process. In addition, students learn at an early age to assume responsibility for their own progress and the display of it. The benefits include helping children to:

- Assume responsibility for documenting their own learning
- Practice organization skills
- Become empowered assessors of their own learning
- Practice communication skills
- Involve their families in their learning
- Demonstrate goal setting and accomplishment
- Demonstrate progress toward program outcomes and state goals (Bensen & Barnett, 2005, p. 16)

Of course, you must help children organize their work for presentation. It is easy to accomplish in programs where you are using portfolios (cf. Benson & Barnett, 2005) and holistic approaches to instruction; for example, if children are accustomed to preparing for class presentations including evaluation: "This story about my camping trip works well, but it might have more details to support the moves from the campsite to the water hole and back. I know this because my classmates asked so many questions—showing that I was not clear." Then, they can begin to learn to organize a presentation for families reporting their personal learning progress:

- "I want my parents to know these things about my progress in ___________. They need to know that I can now work in a group cooperatively. I can document this by including evidence of ___________."

A good place to begin thinking about student-led conferences is in the portfolio display process. Even if the child's responsibility for the conference is minimal, the portfolios allow a beginning step toward this authentic assessment approach. Besides academic performance, you will want to help children report on social/emotional behavior. To help children report on social/emotional, character, or other student traits in this process, Austin (1994; see also Kostelnik, Soderman, & Whiren, 2007) suggests the use of concept maps.

- Pick a value, such as cooperation, then ask children to give examples of how they fulfill this goal; or
- Ask each child to rate personal performance in "collaboration" and illustrate the rating.

This focus builds on reflective learning for all aspects of being a student and gives voice to student accomplishment. The portfolio can be a useful adjunct to this process.

Using Portfolios Effectively at Conferences

Prior to the first set of parent conferences, think about the way you use portfolios in your program. Define for yourself or in consultation with others the purpose of portfolio assessment. Is this the only information collected? What other sources of information are available? How are students and parents involved in deciding what stays in the portfolio?

One possibility for younger children is to share portfolios with parents biweekly (Hill, Kamber, & Norwick, 1994). Children look through the collection of their own work. Then they dictate or write a letter to their parents about what they have studied. As well, children might choose samples of work to go home. In Hill's suggested format, parents review the work over the weekend. Then, they send comments to their child and teacher about their impressions. Donovan (1995) developed a two-way form for the Chicago Public Schools Project of Erikson Institute, as shown in Figure 7.1.

Gronlund and Engel (2001, p. 194; see also Fogarty, Burke & Belgrad, 2008) describe a systematic reflection for teachers using portfolios with parent conferences that suggest a number of questions for consideration:

- What do I know about the interests, accomplishments, progress, and challenges for each of the children in my care?
- How can I encourage family members to share important information about their child's development with me?
- How will the conversation affect my planning and teaching strategy choices after our conference?

Using these questions as a focus assures that you approach conferences and reporting as formative steps in the assessment process. The reflection also offers you the opportunity to think about children holistically and your program organically. You can engage in this thinking even if you are required to give grades to young children in the primary years.

Parent Response Form		Teacher Reply Needed?
Date Initials	Comments from Teacher	Yes No
	Comments from Parent	

FIGURE 7.1 Parent response form. *Source:* Donovan, M. (1995). *Parent response form for the Chicago Public Schools Project.* Chicago: Erikson Institute on Early Education. Used by permission.

Shores and Grace (2005, pp. 129–130; see also Kingore, 2008) suggest that a conference with portfolios takes at least 30 minutes per family. In addition to sharing school or center information from both the child and teacher's perspective, you may invite parents to contribute written home information. Writing prompts for families include "tell me about your child's favorite game"; "tell about times when your child enjoys talking with one or more family members"; "tell about chores your child does"; and "tell me about a favorite book that you read or a favorite TV program that you watch together." To promote additional demonstration of organizational competencies as well as to demonstrate the capacity to use software effectively, some teachers suggest that young children prepare electronic representations of their work using Microsoft PowerPoint™ or Kid Pix Deluxe version 4.2. Such electronic presentation may be reassuring and affirming for the "nervous" kid. Though sharing portfolios supports a holistic approach to care and education, some systems are requiring grades or summary evaluation as part of the drive toward accountability, with the idea that grades are somehow more objective and concrete.

GRADING IN THE EARLY YEARS

grades letters or numbers ascribed to child-performance, based on a summative judgment by the teacher regarding child accomplishment of a task, a course, or a marking period—quarter, semester, year.

Progressively more school districts require letter **grades** for the K–3 years. If this is happening in your area, you will want to advocate for change. Young children do not understand marks for academic accomplishments and grades act to summarize work that is complex and evolving. Nevertheless, if you are required to use them, try to help parents and children see that the scales report to other stakeholders and that these simplify very complex accomplishments for a point in time. This kind of reporting is clearly out of alignment with a holistic approach to instruction and highlights the need for a report card that matches the program philosophy. In addition, schools use grades for a variety of purposes that create a validity problem. Various purposes include ranking of children, reporting academic progress, and motivating children to try harder (Brookhart, 2008). None of these purposes are particularly useful in developmentally appropriate practice. However, in many primary school settings, you will be required to grade young children and to prepare report cards. The form of the report card grades many vary from letter grades to pass/fail to a checklist of objectives. If you are preparing letter grades, keep in mind the points outlined in Box 7.8.

PREPARING REPORT CARDS

The form of a report card must match the philosophy and educational approach of the school or program. That is, in developmentally appropriate preschool and primary settings, parent conferences, narrative reports, portfolios, and checklists are appropriate. Letter grades and arbitrary rankings are not appropriate for young children, but they are often used in elementary schools. If school districts move toward the philosophy of holistic instruction and performance assessment, new report processes must be developed. **Report cards** are formal, written documents that form a legal academic history for each child in your program. In modern public schools, report cards are often **standards-based**. Standards-based reporting involves using local, state, or national standards as outcome statements. The standards may be content standards that describe the knowledge and skills expectations for a given grade, or performance standards that identify a level of proficiency that a student must obtain. Many school districts, parents, and teachers find that these systems are often much too detailed (Popham, 2008, p. 347). In standards-based grading, teachers compare performance of children to both the content and performance standards, noting accomplishments or absence of progress toward meeting the standard. In preparing report cards as part of a reporting system addressing standards, Carr and Harris (2001, p. 106) suggest that report cards answer the following questions for parents:

report card formal, written documents that form a legal academic history for a child.

standards-based teaching an approach to teaching that requires teachers to coordinate instruction to specified standards or goals.

- What is my child doing at school—activities, units?
- What standards—knowledge and skills—is my child learning?
- What evidence—products or performance—is available to show my child's learning?

BOX 7.8

Preparing Grades for Report Cards

Develop a gradebook.

- Clearly delineate scores that will be used for the report card
- Think about these as end product or summative assessment
- Separate these from process and progress items that you communicate in notes and conferences

Develop a plan for collecting information to be used for grades.

- Refer to outcome assessments required
- Assign points to each assessment element
- Communicate the plan to children and parents

Base grade assignments on:

- Using the same assessment for all children
- Separating dispositions and academics for grading
- Comparing child performance to a standard or criterion
- Practicing objectivity, using rubrics for the assignments

Grades are a permanent record.

Adapted from McAffee & Leong, 2007, pp. 205–206.

- How is my child's behavior in class?
- Is my child making progress or is assistance needed?
- What can the family do to support my child's progress?

Regularly, parents pick up report cards, receive a mailed copy, or perhaps view them on the web. One system is MarkBook® 2009 (http://www.asyluminc.com); the system automatically calculates summaries for attendance and grades, if necessary. The system includes options to enter comments on student progress. Other companies with similar products include Thinkwave (http://www.thinkwave.com), Filemaker (http://www.filemaker.com), and Rediker's Administrator's Plus (http://www.rediker.com). As well, many school districts use total data management systems that are integrated to prepare school attendance reports, analyze and prepare special achievement testing reports, coordinate lesson plans, and report cards. One such system is PowerSchool 6 (http://www.pearsonschoolsystems.com/products/powerschool/). Many large school systems custom build such data management systems. Chicago Public Schools describe the goals for this system as follows:

> Goals:
> We strive to provide Chicago Public Schools with the very best information and analysis that not only is accurate and timely, but also is useful and actionable. We support our district's goal that every child in every school is on track at every stage in his or her CPS career to graduate prepared for success in post-secondary education and employment. We:
>
> > Develop accountability and performance measures to meet district, state and federal goals and requirements
> >
> > Establish and manage high-quality student assessment systems

Conduct research and evaluations that can guide the decision-making of program and district leadership

Produce reporting on student and school outcomes to keep internal and external stakeholders informed of CPS' performance

Ensure compliance with local Board of Education policy and state statutory requirements (http://research.cps.k12.il.us/cps/accountweb/; accessed January 07, 2010)

Often, the electronic report card is part of a larger administrative management information system adopted by child-care centers or school districts. Renzulli (2005) describes the accomplishments of a Philadelphia program in providing administrators and teachers with one-stop access to student demographic and assessment data linked to the district's core standards-based curriculum. Parent and child access to the Web-based system began in Autumn 2005. It is now embedded in a special link for families, and described as follows:

> Welcome to the School District of Philadelphia's FamilyNet allowing families to access their child's progress data, report card grades, attendance, test scores and instructional resources. (http://phila.schoolnet.com/outreach/philadelphia/parents/)

If your center or school does not have a system-wide electronic report card and you want to use one, there are some packages available or you can create useful forms using Adobe Acrobat®. To see examples of these documents, visit *http://www.adobe.com/education/instruction/acrobat/pdfs/reportcards_ss.pdf* (accessed June 28, 2009). Whether you use paper forms or electronic ones, teachers and schools must be clear about the criteria and choose criteria according to the evidence available for report cards. Kovas (1993; see also Stiggins, 2008a) describes the following three categories:

1. Product criteria: What can the child produce at a particular point in time? Does the product match expected developmental or academic progress?
2. Process criteria: How does the child function as a learner? Is his or her progress appropriate for age, stage, or grade?
3. Progress criteria: What gain has the child made in relation to his or her previous performance at a point in time? Individual evaluation is key. Comparison to the group is not a part of this approach.
4. Standards-based: How do the child's knowledge and skills compare to the expected outcomes of local, state, or national standards? (cf. Carr & Harris, 2001; see also Brookhart & Nitko, 2008)

Many districts use a combined method. The combination yields a fuller picture and provides opportunities for a description of special needs and social context in relation to the criteria. A combined method follows the principles of multiple data collection to give a more accurate portrait of child progress. A complete system might include the following: report cards, notes attached to report cards, assessment reports, phone calls to parents, regular progress reports, open house, newsletters, personal letters to parents, comments written to students/parents about projects completed, portfolios exhibited, homework assignments and hotlines, school web pages, and conferences (Guskey & Bailey, 2001). If notes are attached, you must keep in mind that these will be part of the child's permanent record. Notes on report cards must be—formal, professional, and based on data. Box 7.9 shows some ideas to consider.

In school districts that use electronic systems, often the comment portion of the report card comes from a district-approved list that you must use. There are also many comment lists found on teacher lesson plan websites. If you choose to these, keep in mind that the goal of the comment section is to elaborate on the grade—to present amplification for understanding. Finally, comments should of course be cautiously and judiciously worded. Good rules of thumb are to ask: "Is this the best way to present this information? Would a two-way dialog be better? Am I following school district policy regarding these comments?"

BOX 7.9

Writing Comments on Report Cards

Positive view

- Is thorough
- Shows commitment
- Improving
- Best work this quarter
- This quarter_____challenged himself by
- Attentive in large group

Needs help

- Finds difficulty with
- Has trouble at times with
- Could profit by
- Seems to need ample supervision when...

Use these words not at all or with caution

- Can't
- Always
- Struggling with
- Uncooperative

Adapted from Spinelli, *Tips for Teachers*, 2006, p.113.

It is possible to key modern report cards to standards with performance-based descriptors that include both achievement descriptors and behavioral descriptors. Some categories used in Kentucky include *distinguished, proficient, apprentice,* and *novice*. Nebraska uses *advanced, proficient, progressing,* and *beginning* (Guskey & Bailey, 2001; 2009). When choosing the descriptors, it is important to choose words that the parent population understands and that are clear to the teachers who must interpret the distinctions to parents. An example of such a procedure is one in which teachers use academic state standards to report performance in learning. For each grade, there is a checklist in Microsoft Excel™ format for teachers to download. In a Microsoft Word™ document, there are phrases that teachers can use to report on learner qualities such as *demonstrates perseverance, shows initiative, communicates effectively, takes responsibility, contributes to group effort, uses conflict-resolution techniques,* and so on. When grading children with these descriptors, it is important that you do not allow non-achievement factors such as effort, participation, cooperation, and the number of assignments completed, etc., to be included as part of the academic grade. Dispositions should be reported separately.

Some school districts use the following reporting categories for social behavior, writing, and reading: Secure (S), Progress (P), and Needs Improvement (I) for social behavior. In grades K–2, teachers report progress on a continuum of skills for the year. Teachers mark the quarter (fall, winter, spring) that students meet the standard. Teachers identify reading progress as "on target," "below target," or "above target." Box 7.10 shows examples of outcomes and report card entries.

Whichever report card you use as part of a reporting system, each requires a four-step process to preparation. Gather the evidence needed to support that the child is accomplishing the

BOX 7.10

Kindergarten Outcome: Counts to 20

- Not yet
  - counts 1 to 5
  - counts to 10, but skips one or more numbers
  - may be able to count along with someone else
- Developing
  - counts from 1 to 10 but cannot court from 11 to 19 without errors
  - counts to 20 but skips one or more numbers
  - when asked for the next number; may need to start counting from 1
- Achieving
  - counts orally from 1 to 20 without any errors
  - automatically knows the next number
- Extending
  - counts beyond 20
  - counts by 2s, 5s, and/or 10s
  - counts backward

outcomes you are reporting. Store the information in a grade book, folder, secure computer disk, or other suitable locked storage. Summarize the information that you have. Then report the information clearly and fairly (Stiggins, 2008). Report cards are powerful communicators with parents. They are familiar; most parents received them when they were students. In the primary years, they are ever more complex as school districts strive to create standards-based reporting systems. As new systems fall into place, teachers do not want to repeat the errors of the past that sometimes served to stifle self-esteem and promote child/parent/teacher conflict due to the ambiguity or inappropriate yardstick measure applied.

- Suzy was an A student in all subjects—reading, science, math, and social studies—when she was eight years old. Nevertheless, no matter how hard she tried, she could not produce uniformly round, slanted, and looped handwriting as required by the teacher. The teacher gave her an F in handwriting. Thirty years later, as her child enters third grade, she shudders about this nightmare.
- Leroy remembers whippings for low marks in "effort." At age 7, he could read and compute well. However, he did not choose to do all the worksheets required by the teacher. The worksheets seemed boring to him.
- Mrs. Stewart comes to school at the end of the year for a final conference. She wonders why her son, Everett, received a D in math. The teacher, Mrs. Packard, had sent home papers with shiny faces and stars all year. At the midyear conference, Mrs. Packard assured Mrs. Stewart that Everett performed in math in accordance with expectations. The fact that Mrs. Packard thought Everett was "a bit slow" never entered the conversation.

Communicating Fairly

As report cards and reporting systems evolve, educators must communicate in fair ways with parents. Report cards should clearly indicate:

- How a child's performance compares to local and national norms
- Child progress toward learner outcomes
- Child progress compared to previous achievement level
- Progression of learner goals from grades K–3 so parents have a perspective of the big picture

- Enough subdivisions of learner outcomes so that parents can clearly see the scoring or evaluation criteria
- Descriptions of learner development that include quality of work and comparisons to expectations for long-term goals. (Wiggins, 1994; see also Brookhart, 2008)

Whenever teachers report to parents in conferences, in report cards, or casually at the drop-off/pick-up time, goals for the report should be clear. Keep the frame of reference in mind. Families want to know the following:

- What is my child's present achievement level?
- Is my child functioning at average, above-average, or below-average level for his or her developmental age or grade level?
- How do my child's work samples compare to his or her previous work and to those of other children?
- What can I do as a parent to help my child be a better student?
- Are you, as a teacher, doing everything you can to assist, challenge, and encourage my child?
- Does my child get along with friends and peers in the setting?
- Is my child making progress (i.e., does my child have weaknesses? What strengths does my child have)?

In addition, at report time invite parents to analyze their own efforts and to seek suggestions for ways that they can meaningfully provide help to their child. As teachers prepare for reports to parents, reflective questions include:

> Are you confident about the reliability of the data that you plan to report to the parent?
>
> Did you use an appropriate method to gather the data?
>
> Is the material stated in objective or appropriately qualified terms?
>
> Is the information appropriate for the problem?
>
> Is there evidence to support the interpretation of the data?
>
> Do the data provide new information?
>
> Do the data fairly represent the child as a learner or as an achiever in a content area?
>
> Are there any circumstances that would cast doubt on the accuracy of the information? (Guerin and Maier, 1983, p. 139)

In addition, Brookhart (2008, pp. 123–124) suggests that you examine the format of the report card. Are the instructional targets traditional subjects: reading, math, and so on, or lists of performance criteria, such as "can complete one-to-one correspondence tasks"? The form of the report card influences the value and kind of information that the school district or agency wishes to communicate. If locked into a system that communicates letter grades, you may wish to supplement the communication with a parent letter.

Common Errors

Teachers should also check that their reports do not make the common types of errors—computation or recording errors—and do not overlook important developmental information and situational factors (Guerin & Maier, 1983, p. 142). For example, Victor, a two-year-old, has difficulty holding a crayon. He was a premature baby who is small, but is making good progress in language and other cognitive and social/emotional areas. Allow developmental latitude for Victor in acquiring fine-motor skills. Also, Aretha, a five-year-old, is the only survivor of a house fire. She doesn't talk to the teacher and begins to suck her thumb. It is not an appropriate time to interpret this behavior as socially immature.

Writing Notes on Report Cards

Lee and McDougal (2000) suggest general rules of thumb to be sure that the written communication you send to parents preserves the partnership that you seek to foster. These principles include:

- Be personal. "Dear Parent" implies that you don't have a relationship with a child's family.
- Be sure to use the actual names of the parents or foster parents or appropriate family members. For a widow, getting a letter addressed to Mr. and Mrs. Calvin is not only rude, but also painful.
- Personalize the report so that you are talking about Katie, not the generic "your child."
- Sign the note or letter with your first and last name, not "Mrs. Wishe."
- Be sure to type or write neatly, proofread, and re-read, particularly before hitting the send button on e-mail. Review to see if you have been tactful.
- Think about whether writing is the best way to deliver the message, particularly when the parent may perceive the information as threatening. That is, if you see a serious problem, and did not discuss it with the parents, a conference is probably a better venue.

These rules of thumb remind you of the weight of your words. Of course, you have to follow ethical principles as well as program and school district policies when writing notes. For example, if there is a possibility that a second grader will be retained and you've tried unsuccessfully to reach his or her parents, a tactful note may not only be necessary, but required.

WHEN FAMILIES ARE CLIENTS

Sometimes, parents seek early intervention or education experiences that involve the whole family. These situations include the times when there is an at-risk birth of an infant, when parents are concerned about the development of their child, and when others recommend to parents that an educational experience may assist the family. When the family is the client, the family must be involved in assessing priorities and planning interventions (cf. Turnbull, Turnbull, Erwin, & Soodak, 2006). As part of the process for working with families in these situations, it is again helpful to focus on the strength-based assessment of the family unit. Some characteristics of strong families include the following:

- One or more caring adults in child's life
- Family encourages trust, independence, and initiative
- Family is warm and has high expectations for the child
- Harmony is present between family and school/center and other caregivers involved
- Family possesses positive energy
- Family is stable over time
- Relatives and neighbors support the family
- Family values are shared among the members
- Sense of family oneness
- Sibling relationships are strong and positive (Stoneman, Rugg, & Gregg, 2009, pp. 468–469)

In working with families who are clients, the following principles are regarded as best practices:

- Families and professionals share responsibilities and work collaboratively.
- Practices (interventions, supports, resources) strengthen family functioning.
- Practices are individualized and flexible.
- Practices are strengths-based. (DEC, 2007)

A tool that may be useful to families in identifying and documenting their strengths is the "Take a Look at Me!" strengths-based portfolio (*http://strengthsbased.com*, accessed June 27, 2009).

Sometimes, it may be useful to involve the family in record-keeping. Family record-keeping involvement offers the potential to educate parents as well as involve and inform them about progress in the program. One particular technique that serves as communication device as well as record is the dialog journal. You as teacher send a note in a notebook home every day with Samantha about the progress that she made on listening at circle time (or other mutually established goal); the family responds with a note the next day about Samantha's progress at the dinner table. In this way, you are communicating and dialoging. With some families, it may be possible to convert the paper journal to email. Remember it is informal and for special situations where families are collaborating on target goals. Other specific ways to involve families in assessing their children include research in Early Head Start programs and in Family Literacy programs.

Early Head Start, a program to serve infants and toddlers, generated increased research related to working with the hard-to-reach family. When mothers have their own histories of abuse, trauma, loss, and current family violence, they are at-risk as first-time mothers. That is, they need special help with mothering and child care. Home visiting is a promising method of support for these families (Spieker, Solchany, McKenna, DeKlyen, & Barnard, 2000; see also Shonkoff & Meisels, 2000; Cook, Klein, Tessier, 2008). As teachers, focus on helping families play with their children in a way that will facilitate development and that will be comfortable for the parents. These plans grow from a collaborative partnership and can include such programs as toy lending, book sharing, or other clearly academically focused ventures.

Family literacy projects are one such venture. For example, collect portfolio material reflecting parent and child growth. Examples of the portfolio contents include a page of the storybook that the parent and child are writing; a photo of holiday activities, such as stuffing a turkey, and a written paragraph about it; drawings illustrating a parent reading a story; songs written by parents and the child; photos of activities that the parent and child enjoy; and videos and audiotapes of activities. Parents and the teacher can review these items to develop plans for future program participation (Popp, 1992; see also http://www.famlit.org, the website of the National Center for Family Literacy, for other ideas for your community).

To the extent possible, in situations where the teacher is part of a team working with a multiproblem family, the parent should be part of the assessment process. Sometimes, parents may be involved with a social worker or psychologist to assist with parenting or personal issues. Part of that process will include parent self-assessment. Teachers will be responsible for communicating and eliciting appropriate cooperation in the assessment of children involved at the level of readiness that the parents possess.

In the Women's Treatment Center in Chicago, a state preschool program involves parent participation in the classroom. Women in the program are concentrating on rehabilitation of their lives, previously dominated by substance abuse. Some of the women have a history of child abuse and neglect. Teachers work carefully with the therapeutic staff to pick a good time for moms to participate in the classroom. The assessment aspect involves teachers pointing out to the mother the appropriate play of the young child. As time goes by, the mom can recognize appropriate limits and play activities. She can then be involved more concretely in the assessment of her child.

In this scenario, parents are involved in assessment of themselves as well as their children. This can demystify the assessment process for them and provide positive empowering opportunities that can counter any previous negative experiences that they may have had.

VOICES FROM THE FIELD

Building-Level Literacy Coach—A Reading First School

We use DIBELS in September, January, and May for all children. For those children showing difficulties, we ask teachers to assess them twice a week. In the classroom, for instructional purposes, children are assessed with DIBELS once per month. Until last year, we didn't do the monthly assessment on Benchmark children; now we DIBEL everyone, every month. DIBELS guides instruction—we use results to form small groups and target instruction. We reform groups three times per year based on DIBELS. Otherwise, a child here or there might be moved, based on teacher recommendation.

Each teacher has a DIBELS notebook with graphs for each student. As they monitor progress, they graph so they can visualize the progress or lack of it. Parents get DIBELS reports four times per year.

In the past, we also administered the Gates-MacGinitie (http://www.riverpub.com/products/gmrt/index.html) twice a year, but that was too much testing, so we now use it in Spring only. For kindergarten, we use the pre-reading test; level 1 was too hard for kindergarteners.

If children fall below the aim level on DIBELS three times, I test them on the Diagnostic Assessment of Reading (DAR; http://www.riverpub.com/products/dar/index.html). This helps us zero in on what each child needs so that we can plan accordingly. I write notes and suggestions for teachers and parents. Parents get a letter from me with my phone number, so that if they have questions or want suggestions, I can help.

Teachers also use the unit tests supplied by the reading series publisher, Scott Foresman. We used to use Reading Counts twice a year (http://teacher.scholastic.com/products/readingcounts/management.htm), but the children didn't perform well on this—they didn't take it seriously, so we stopped giving this.

We use DIBELS and DAR results at Response to Intervention (RTI) meetings.

Advice to new teachers:

- *DIBEL the children yourself—don't rely on the paraprofessional to do it. While you're interacting—testing—you learn about the child in ways that don't show in scores. Make notes; use the information to improve your teaching.*
- *Use the literacy coach's notes from DAR or another diagnostic measure.*
- *Be open to take suggestions—you didn't learn it all in teacher ed!*
- *Think about giving an inventory of likes and desires; I did this as a teacher, and I learned so much about my first graders. "If you could go anywhere in the world . . .": one child said, "I'd go to Kmart in Boston"—which is about a 15-minute drive from our school. I really had to stop and think about this child's experiences with travel.*
- *Teaching doesn't end at 3:00 . . . there will be homework.*
- *Ask to visit other classes at your grade level; learn from colleagues.*

MULTIDISCIPLINARY STAFFING

Staffing conferences are potentially stressful times for parents. The conference thrusts parents into the school or agency turf and frequently outnumbers them with an array of experts who have evaluated their child and who have begun to make preliminary plans for services for the child. The most stressful times are those when the parents have just completed an initial evaluation. Each of the professionals who participate in this meeting must prepare to report assessment results in a way that will honestly describe the scores and impressions, but each must sensitively recognize the parents' perspective. This requires judgment of the social, educational, emotional, and economic context of the family. It requires empathy. Often, teachers are the people that parents are most comfortable talking with about the results of assessments. Therefore, you need to become familiar with the ways that you may be involved.

Teacher Role

screening results documentation of broad-based, quick overview of child's developmental or educational progress on a set of objectives/milestones.

As a teacher, you report **screening results** because these instruments assess developmental and educational territory that you know. When you discuss screening results, think about the following points:

- Remind families that screenings tests are *not* a diagnostic instrument; screening results give you a roadmap to explore.

- Be sure to communicate strengths, as well as issues that may concern you, based on the screening results.
- Describe how you will monitor and provide support to facilitate child growth and learning.
- Listen to the family and make plans to work together.
- Communicate how you will be available for follow-up conversations—in person, by email, or by phone.
- Be available to answer questions about any planned referrals and explain who on your team will coordinate or facilitate the referrals, including resources for diagnostic assessment.
- Empathize with family concern and conclude with invitation to family for regular conversation. (Adapted from Meisels and Atkins-Burnett, 2005, p. 48.)

In addition, if you notice an issue or problem and need to work with the parents to solve it, you will need to schedule an **initial referral conference.** In talking with parents about screening results or a perceived problem, you need to be sensitive and respectful as well as involving the families in reciprocal conversation prior to referral; it is, after all, possible that you and the family may solve the problem. RTI is in the end a collaborative process involving family, child, and teacher. Some guidelines for the RTI conference:

initial referral conference the meeting where teachers and parents meet to share concerns about a child's progress in the learning situation.

1. Be sure that families know the purpose of the conference, e.g., "I'm worried about Michael's progress in math."
2. Observe the courtesies expected by families, e.g., "Hello, it's great to see you again," and so on.
3. Use open-ended questions, e.g., "Would you share the routine for getting Michael ready for school?"
4. Reflect sensitivity when you sense family is worried, e.g., "I see you are worried about the interview with the speech therapist."
5. Talk to siblings and other significant family members when it will help you understand Michael better or when the family asks you to do so.
6. Start with general discussions of behavior and funnel to gather and discuss more details. (Banks, Santos, & Roof, 2009, p. 16)

To prepare effectively, your child study should have the following components: Identification and description of concept development, relation of concepts to theories and expected program outcomes, and support of your data with observations and work samples (Ahola & Kovacik, 2007). Included in your supporting documentation will be anecdotal notes, checklists, and other observational documents, as well as child work products with your interpretation of approximation toward the program outcomes. Depending on the nature of the referral planned, you may call upon the principal, a social worker, or other professional to assist you with this conference. Finally, you have a responsibility for preparing written and oral reports for annual **Individualized Educational Plan (IEP) conferences** that summarize the classroom interventions and outcomes accomplished in your work with individual children with disabilities. These roles are described in the following sections.

Individualized Educational Plan (IEP) conference the multidisciplinary meeting where parents and those involved in intervention with a young child with disabilities meet to assess progress or review initial assessment results, and plan educational interventions to support the child's learning.

REPORTING SCREENING RESULTS Teachers are responsible for knowing the technical characteristics of the measures that they are administering. They must then explain the process and the results of the assessment to parents. Teachers must understand the process of typical child development and variations due to social, cultural, and economic conditions.

For example: Mrs. Jenkins is a member of the Child Find team in Local School District, New York. Local uses the DIAL3 to screen children in the spring and in the fall. Mrs. Bond brought Carrie to the spring screening. Carrie is 3. She is the third child in the Bond family; her siblings are 10 and 6. Mrs. Bond is concerned that Carrie doesn't talk very much at home.

Mrs. Jenkins reviews the procedures and limitations of the DIAL3. Mrs. Bond was an observer and participant in the process, so this review is a refresher. Then, Mrs. Jenkins interprets the results of the screening.

Carrie's performance is within developmental limits. Mrs. Jenkins and Mrs. Bond examine opportunities for Carrie to talk. Maybe older siblings are talking for her. Mrs. Jenkins tells Mrs. Bond about a weekend program for parents and tots. They agree to meet in three months or sooner if Mrs. Bond is still worried.

INITIAL CONFERENCE OR REFERRAL CONFERENCE At an initial or referral conference, early childhood teachers appropriately listen to evaluation results presented by professionals who have assessed the child. Teachers also listen to parent perceptions and concerns. You should also recognize parent/family rights beyond the legal ones for notice, due process, and confidentiality. It is a family's right to worry and be concerned about their child and what the future may bring as Dee, their child, negotiates the educational system. Consider the following to be the family rights:

- Right to feel angry that their child may face lifelong challenges.
- Right to seek another opinion from someone outside the "school" or "center" so that they can feel more in control or that they have exhausted all options for assisting their child's development.
- Right to stop trying home intervention due to the overall stress of the parent/child relationship, i.e., making the child perform a detested 10-minute routine may really take 20 minutes and 2 aspirins for the family member.
- Right to be annoyed at their child without feeling guilty—the child is a kid first.
- Right to be a parent—not the "teacher". (Raver, 2009, pp. 40–41)

Consider also the needs of families for support in meeting Maslow's (1943) hierarchy of basic human needs—beginning with basic needs for shelter, food, and other physiological needs. In addition, as a teacher, you need to recognize the family members' capacity to be effective in parenting and their need for current information about best practices. When you don't recognize these basic needs of families and appreciate family strengths, the reciprocal relationship is off to a bad start. Families may treat you with disdain or disrespect. (Cook, Klein, & Tessier, 2008, pp. 38–39).

It is particularly important to develop reciprocal communication and responsiveness to family cultures, values, and languages that are different than yours. Ways to show responsiveness include:

> **1.** Respect for the values and practices of all (family) members;
> **2.** Encouragement of multiple viewpoints to enrich the (center or school);
> **3.** Seeking ways to extend competence (of teachers) . . . with regard to differences in family cultures, values, and languages; . . .
> **4.** Encouragement and support of the development and dissemination of products that address family cultures, values, and languages;
> **5.** Meetings and conferences . . . that incorporate the impact of family cultures, values, and languages in all early childhood activities and services (DEC, 2002; see also NAEYC, 2009).

In addition, teachers must be prepared to describe their program. Each must identify modifications to incorporate easily for an optimum inclusion experience. Teachers are responsible for identifying necessary support services for the program.

For example: Ms. Seefeldt has 25 kindergartners in a developmentally appropriate play-based kindergarten class in Baltimore. She needs to be able to describe her program. What are the routines and schedule? How does she plan? What modifications does she make for the three children with special needs in her room now? For example, Betty has a diagnosis of spina bifida with some cognitive delays. What assistance will Ms. Seefeldt need to provide so that Betty receives a developmentally appropriate program, yet Ms. Seefeldt is allowed to continue her fine work with the 24 other kindergartners? Ms. Seefeldt may appropriately request a teacher assistant to care for Betty's medical needs. She will be able to describe the justification for this request.

Ms. Seefeldt will listen to the psychologist's suggestions about appropriate cognitive intervention. The speech therapist will schedule regular visits to the classroom. Ms. Seefeldt will implement suggestions for follow-through into her regular curriculum.

Ms. Seefeldt will express a welcoming attitude toward Betty's parents. She will assure Mr. and Mrs. Columbus that kindergartners will treat Betty fairly and kindly. She will invite them to visit the room before enrollment and during the first weeks of school.

ANNUAL INDIVIDUAL EDUCATION PLAN CONFERENCE At annual IEP conferences, teachers are responsible for reporting progress on the annual goals derived for every child with special needs. As in the RTI and initial referral conferences, you are expected to bring data about child progress and to speak knowledgeably about how you are scaffolding for success. This conference is a **multidisciplinary staffing** that includes all of the professionals involved and the parents of children with special needs. They must state and justify deviations from the plans that have occurred through the year at the classroom level. Teachers must report progress in all the ways that they have gathered the information. Progress data may include observations, checklists, screening results, achievement scores, curriculum progress, and diagnostic assessment test scores. Teachers must listen to the concerns and issues raised by parents and other professionals at this conference. In addition, they must have thought through the next steps for the children in their care. What are appropriate educational goals? Where do these goals fit in the normalized environment and routine? Does an effective program plan require additional assessment information?

multidisciplinary staffing group of professionals involved in the assessment of children with special needs, the teaching of these children, and the evaluation of their progress.

For example: Baby Stacie, the firstborn daughter of Mr. and Mrs. Hewlett, is 18 months old. She and Mrs. Hewlett have regularly attended the infant-stimulation program for children with cognitive delays and Down syndrome. The facilitator–teacher of the program is Mrs. Meadows. The program meets weekly for one hour. During the program, Mrs. Meadows plans gross-motor activities, songs, and exploration of infant toys. Parents assist their own children throughout the morning. Mrs. Meadows, her assistant, the physical therapist, the occupational therapist, and the speech therapist join in the play as individual demand dictates.

At the multidisciplinary conference, Mrs. Meadows reports that Mrs. Hewlett and Stacie have attended regularly. Mrs. Hewlett has learned the songs. Stacie smiles and laughs when she sings the familiar songs. Stacie is following along with the circle activities, happily ensconced in Mrs. Meadows' lap. Preferred toys for Stacie are foam blocks and water toys.

Mrs. Meadows suggests that Stacie seems to be making fine-motor progress—her grasp is improving. She is prepared to state that Stacie should participate in the program for another year. She will listen to suggestions from the physical therapist, occupational therapist, and language therapist. Otherwise, she has no strong recommendations for a program change.

Another example is as follows: Kevin, a three-year-old in the Mother Goose Child-Care Center, has finished his first year of inclusion placement. Mrs. Gardner, the head teacher for the three- and four-year-olds, presents his progress. Kevin's mother, Ms. Wood, who is 18 and enrolled in a work-study program, the district mainstream coordinator, and the child-care center director attend the multidisciplinary staffing.

Goals for Kevin for the year include:

1. Following the center's routines with support.
2. Beginning to use words to express needs.
3. With support, using words to solve disputes.

Mrs. Gardner reports with the assistance of checklists and anecdotal notes that Kevin does not follow the center's routines. He wanders from the group at circle time and from the playground. Kevin does not speak in intelligible language to the staff. Kevin continues to take toys away from peers and hits children when they will not give them up.

Mrs. Gardner reports that Ms. Wood has regularly volunteered with the program. She has taken a leadership role in identifying speakers and parent needs.

Mrs. Gardner likes Kevin. He is warm and affectionate in her one-on-one contacts with him. She wants to keep him at Mother Goose, but she is worried that other children and parents are beginning to complain about his combative behavior. Mrs. Gardner asks whether the mainstream coordinator can give additional specific suggestions for modifying the structure for Kevin. She asks whether there are ways that Ms. Wood and she can work together to maintain Kevin's enrollment in the Mother Goose Child-Care Center.

Also consider this final example: Jose, a second grader with a learning disability, lives in a school district that plans to move from self-contained special education to inclusion. Mr. Decker is Jose's second-grade teacher. The resource teacher for children with learning disabilities, the inclusion administrator, the school psychologist, the speech therapist, and Mr. and Mrs. Castillo (Jose's parents) attend a multidisciplinary staffing conference.

Mr. Decker reports that Jose is cooperative and well liked by his peers. He seems to pay attention in small-group activities. When working with a partner, Jose completes written assignments quite well. In large-group discussions, Jose frequently stares out the window, fidgets, looks into his desk, and sometimes rolls his pencil on the desk. Mr. Decker and the children have learned to ignore this distracting behavior. Mr. Decker prepares written notes for Jose when necessary. Jose pays close attention when he knows something about the subject at hand.

Mr. Decker and the team make plans for third grade. They identify goals for developing and enhancing note taking and other supports for large-group discussions. Mr. Decker knows that Jose will be fine in Ms. Heather's third grade. He will talk with her about the cuing and mediation strategies that he has developed with Jose.

Mr. and Mrs. Castillo will help Jose with organizational skills in the summer, including color-coding notebooks, folders, and a planning calendar for third grade. They will send him to an art program for part of the summer. Part of the program will help Jose enhance fine-motor skills and develop his interest and skill in art.

The preceding examples show the teacher's role in the assessment system with children and parents. Another important role for teachers is reporting to additional stakeholders in the educational lives of children and families. These include administrators, boards, school councils, legislators, and the public at large. (See Box 7.11 for an example of an IEP conference summary form.)

REPORTING TO OTHER STAKEHOLDERS

stakeholders people important in the lives of children, especially regarding the assessment of children.

The importance of reporting to other **stakeholders** has acquired new urgency as teachers seek to preserve the child's best interests in the face of greater demands for high-stakes performance results—No Child Left Behind and Head Start Outcomes Report, for example. Teachers must assume responsibility for reflecting, recording, and reporting group assessment results according to their holistic philosophical beliefs regarding developmentally appropriate practice. Otherwise, measuring the progress of young children may continue according to test scores and test reports alone.

One method for reporting results to these other stakeholders is to use illustrations of the progress of individual children to validate the method of teaching that you are using. For example, if your goal for first grade is to show that the children in your program can write a simple story, review individual child reports and tally how many children can write a story. Then, use samples from the reports on individual children to illustrate the different levels of sophistication of stories written by the children in your program. Thus, you have shown that children are reading and writing and that they have achieved these skills without the use of workbooks.

Another method for teachers to use to demonstrate child accomplishment is to use displays of work samples. Work samples are the products of daily classroom activities. Thus, you collect the products to show the work: the graphs that children are making; the write-ups of scientific experiments conducted by children; and the solutions generated for performance-based tasks in social studies, such as interview transcripts, family trees, and cause-effect drawings.

BOX 7.11

IEP Team Meeting

Date____________

Child's name____________

Family members participating

Team members present

Purpose of the meeting (initial placement, ongoing planning, transitional to different program)

Meeting notes

Next steps

Lesson adaptations required

Expected learner outcomes

Products or processes that show competence

Modifications
Presentation of tasks
Time for completion
Support strategies

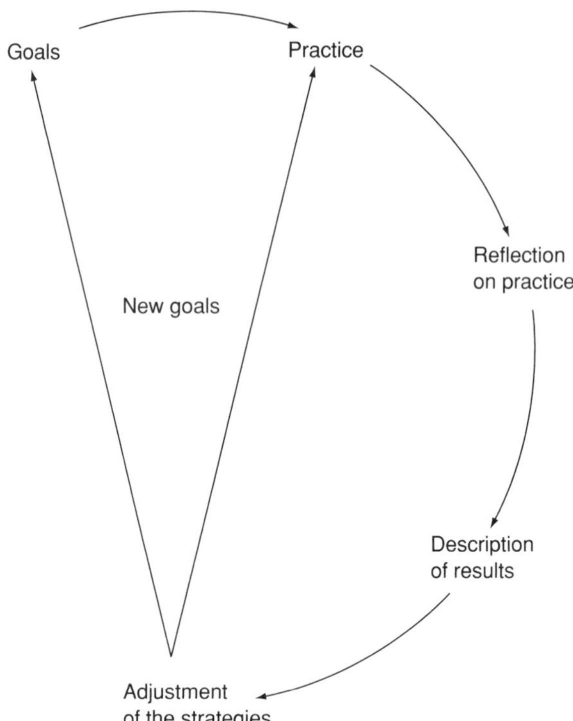

FIGURE 7.2 Accountability through reflection on goals and practices resulting in changes.

The most comprehensive way to demonstrate child and class accomplishment to other stakeholders is through work sample assessment information. You should be able to address thoughtfully the following issues in nontechnical language:

- philosophy of the program
- program goals
- teaching methods
- ways that child progress is monitored
- how adjustments are made to accomplish child goals
- ways to see the precursors of reading, writing, math, and other learnings

These are, after all, the questions that you answer in collaboration with parents. The difference in the two reports—parents/others—is the emphasis shift from an individual and particular child to a group of children. The process for preparation of an **accountability** report is the same as that illustrated in Figure 7.2. Recording and reporting assessment results to parents and others is one of the integral roles of the teacher.

accountability being responsible for the proper education of all children.

SUMMARY

Reporting assessment and progress to parents and other stakeholders is a key part of the educational process. The technique for reporting must match the purpose. Each teacher must have a repertoire of methods. At the beginning of programs, teachers describe the philosophy and curriculum to parents. Teachers report casually to parents in daily chats, telephone visits, or e-mail conversations. Teachers report at regularly scheduled times through conferences and report cards. Teachers report when problems arise. On each of these occasions, the teacher must be sensitive to the emotional and social context of the child and his or her family. Teachers must respect parents' individuality. Teachers must be prepared to articulate clearly and concisely orally, in writing, and on websites. Finally, teachers must understand the role and limitations of the diverse assessment methods that are included in their program. Assessment procedures and reporting must match the philosophy and the curriculum. This includes the use of any software or Web-based programs.

FIELD ACTIVITIES

1. For a grade level of your choice, develop a performance task to address one of the required reporting areas. If possible, try the task on a child. Report and discuss your results with colleagues.
2. With permission, interview parents about their experiences in receiving information from child-care centers and schools. Discuss your experiences with colleagues. Are there any improvements that you might suggest?
3. With permission, sit in on a parent conference. After the conference discuss your observations with the teacher who conducted it. Ask any questions that may have concerned you about the proceedings.
4. With a classmate, visit a school board or local school council meeting. Observe the proceedings. Pay particular attention to issues of accountability that arise in the meeting. With a classmate, plan how you might address the requests for information that might arise if you were teaching in the school.
5. Review a website for a school data management system that includes links to reporting to parents. Identify ways the system might be helpful to you and to parents.

IN-CLASS ACTIVITIES

1. Using collected sample report cards from the communities in your area, or from the Web, examine the criteria that teachers must address. Develop an assessment plan to help you answer the questions.
2. Develop a timeline for holistic reporting system for preschool and for primary grades. Include the relevant standards addressed. Identify what information to collect as well as when to collect. Identify summary points and procedures. Specify regular conference times for all stakeholders.
3. Design a developmentally appropriate report card for an age level of your choice.
4. Brainstorm comments that teachers or parents might make in conferences. Design a way to counter or respond to these comments in a conference (e.g., "I don't know if I should tell you this, but my wife is a meth addict." "What's the best way to get my kid to eat broccoli?" "Do you think Spruce will ever learn to add numbers? I know I hate math.").

STUDY QUESTIONS

1. What are the steps that teachers must take to ensure confidentiality in the classroom?
2. How can teachers and school professionals ensure parent involvement in assessment and diagnosis? How can teachers ensure that parents will feel comfortable and confident in advocating in the interests of their children?
3. What strategies will help teachers prepare for conferences with parents? How do you integrate portfolios into the parent–teacher conferences?
4. How can teachers lessen the ambiguity of report cards? How do report cards stifle the self-esteem of children? How can teachers circumvent this potential downfall?
5. What are some situation factors not reflected on report cards? How can teachers include these in the child's assessment?
6. How can you link curriculum, assessment, and reporting through the use of standards?
7. Why is it useful for teachers to consider families as "clients"?
8. How can teachers prepare for a multidisciplinary conference? What role does the teacher play in the Individualized Education Plan?
9. What are the methods teachers utilize to report results to stakeholders? How can these be included in accountability reports?

REFLECT AND RE-READ

- I know several ways to report to parents and how to involve them in the process.
- I can prepare my students for the reporting process.
- I know how to be a responsible team participant in the multidisciplinary staffing.
- I can design a report card to match my teaching philosophy.

CASE VIGNETTE

The following is an excerpt from the June report card for Mina, a first grader:

Work Habits	First Marking	Second Marking	Third Marking
Follows directions	N	N	S
Works in a group	N	N	N
Works independently	U	N	S
Listens attentively	U	U	N
Organizes time, area, and materials	U	U	N
Works to ability	U	N	N
Demonstrates effort	N	N	N
Completes class work	U	N	S
Completes homework	U	U	N

Mina continues to be unfocused and careless in her schoolwork and when it comes to homework, forget it. She needs to improve her behavior.

Code: Unsatisfactory; Needs Improvement; Satisfactory; Excellent

What do you know about Mina's experience in first grade based on this report card excerpt? What do you imagine her achievement is like? As you prepare to welcome Mina to your second-grade class, what will you do? What assessment plan will you make?

TECHNOLOGY LINKS

http://www.aasa.org

American Association of School Administrators. Short articles that examine current trends from the administrative perspective with links to relevant websites.

http://www.ascd.org

Association for Supervision and Curriculum Development. Searchable database on topics such as report cards and other instructional issues.

http://dadsdivorce.com

Dad's Divorce. Resources for dads who are divorced, including a chat opportunity.

http://kidsturn.org

Kid's Turn. A not-for-profit organization with links for children, parents, and "others."

http://www.marchofdimes.com

March of Dimes. Public interest information on babies and children with disabilities.

http://www.naesp.org

National Association for Elementary School Principals. Reproducible bulletins on current topics to share with parents. Some are translated into Spanish.

http://www.psparents.net

Public School Parents Network. Resources for issues that affect parents in public schools.

http://singlemothers.org

National Organization of Single Mothers. Discusses all of the issues facing the single mother; includes a chat room.

http://www.beachcenter.org

The Beach Center on Disability. A resource for families and professionals dedicated to the promotion of research and practice on high quality of life for families of children with disabilities.

SUGGESTED READINGS

Davis, C. & Yang, A. (2005). *Parents & teachers working together.* Turners Falls, MA: Northeast Foundation for Children, Inc.

Edwards, C. A. (2009). *Tapping the potential of parents: A strategic guide to boosting student achievement through family involvement.* New York: Scholastic.

Keyser, J. (2006). *From parents to partners: Building a family-centered early childhood program.* St. Paul, MN: Red Leaf Press.

CHAPTER 8

Building a Child Study

TERMS TO KNOW

- Apgar score
- child study
- primary responsibility
- Child Find team
- diagnostic evaluation
- referral questions
- typical development
- atypical development

CHAPTER OVERVIEW

This chapter shows how a child study serves as a summary point in a comprehensive assessment system. The first part of the chapter identifies the purposes of child studies. Then, the discussion delineates the elements of child studies and gives suggestions for writing child studies. Finally, there are examples of child studies with analyses and issues to ponder.

ASSESS AS YOU READ

- What can I use, in addition to tests, to create a child study?
- When will I need to conduct a child study?
- What are some important elements of a child study?
- When I write my report, what are some limitations that I must keep in mind?

CHILD STUDIES IN THE ASSESSMENT SYSTEM

child study in-depth look at a particular child at a specific point in time.

A **child study** is an in-depth look at a particular child at a specific point in time. A study summarizes the information available from all sources: child, family, teacher, and specialist. In addition, the study raises and answers questions through the process of gathering the material for the report of the child study. Some studies are brief and geared to one developmental or teaching issue. Other studies are complex and include formal assessment.

primary responsibility the person expected to perform a certain task.

Apgar Score screening test given to newborn infants 1 minute and 5 minutes after birth.

diagnostic tests tests that delve deeply into achievement in one domain or subject. Often these are administered individually.

PURPOSES OF CHILD STUDIES

Child studies serve diverse purposes. A study summarizes available knowledge about a child at a moment in time. In early childhood, different professionals may assume **primary responsibility** for the preparation of this summary report, depending on the age of the child and any questions about learning, behavior, or development.

- *At birth*, Sheila—who received a low **Apgar score**—will have a case study summarizing available medical and social history information. Plans derived from the known information delineate the proposed medical intervention. The physicians plan **diagnostic tests**. If necessary, social workers gather further family history and plan social service intervention.

- *At preschool*, the **Child Find team** summarizes screening results on Oswald. Oswald shows no difficulties. Thus, the child study ends.
- Ricardo displays speech and language problems. After screening results and Response to Intervention (RTI)–specified classroom modifications substantiate the teacher's perception, the Child Find team refers Ricardo and his family to a speech therapist for **diagnostic evaluation**—an in-depth, specialist-conducted assessment related to the developmental or learning aspect in question. The child study then evolves. First, the Child Find team assumes **primary responsibility** for summarizing Ricardo's available history and screening results. Then, the speech therapist adds diagnostic assessment results and addresses any questions that may occur during the assessment process. If the speech therapist questions Ricardo's intellectual capacity, then a referral to a psychologist occurs. The evolution of the study continues. At any point in the process, the Child Find team members discuss a summary of the available information and results with Ricardo's parents so that permission for diagnostic assessment can be obtained and so that plans for Ricardo can be made.

Child Find team group of professionals whose responsibility it is to determine children with special needs.

diagnostic evaluation *see* diagnostic tests.

The following are examples of the different situations in which a **child study** might evolve:

- Ms. Hayes, who teaches at Merry Mack Preschool, meets twice a year with parents. She collects observational material and samples of each child's work and writes a narrative report to share with parents. There is a child study of progress at Merry Mack for each child in the program.
- Mr. Anastasiow worries about Albert, a second grader. Albert seems sad. He has no friends at school. He watches everything and seems to know answers when called upon, but does not complete any projects or write in his journal. Mr. Anastasiow gathers any available achievement test scores and his own observations and contacts Albert's family to share his concerns. He summarizes the material. A child study evolves.
- Ms. Zecker visits a first-grade class to observe the dual-language learners. She spots Sarah, whose first language is English. In conversation with Sarah, conducted in Spanish, Ms. Zecker concludes that Sarah will require tutoring in Spanish vocabulary related to school topics. She wonders if this vocabulary limitation relates to other learning problems and suggests that the school conduct a bilingual learning disabilities assessment. A diagnostic child study evolves.

In each of these examples, the reasons for developing the child study are different. The procedures are the same: summarizing and organizing information for effective screening, assessment, and intervention planning for children.

ELEMENTS OF A CHILD STUDY

Items to consider in answering questions about a child's development include those listed in the following section. Whichever professional is initiating the study or whoever is the case manager should comment on known information in these areas. When information is unknown or when there are different perceptions about available facts, summaries serve to identify questions for further investigation. What are the **referral questions**—the questions from various stakeholders about problems or learning and developmental progress? A child study is a dynamic process. The process begins with basic demographic information that is pertinent to the questions at the time. As available and for serving the child and family, items to consider include the following:

referral questions questions posed in a child study to aid in the determination of the specific problems and needs of a child and the assessing of the developmental progress of the child.

- Identifying information: name, age, sex, birth date
- Description of the child: appearance, general physical characteristics, personality, position in the family

- Questions, concerns, problems
- Family background: siblings, family's social/economic status, known family problems, concerns, family crises or tragedies, parental attitudes, separation issues, home, neighborhood
- Medical history: circumstances of child's birth
- Early developmental milestones
- Current functioning: self-help and daily living skills; handling of body functions; body movement and use of body (motility, energy); facial expressions; speech and language; emotional reactions (expression and control of emotions and feelings, imagination and fantasy, self-concept, self-management skills); reaction to other children; reaction to adults; play or school activities; thinking and reasoning; problem-solving skills; health; developmental progress for social, emotional, cognitive, and physical skills; communication skills; school adjustment (attendance and arrival, reaction to routines, following directions, taking turns, response to support and individualization)

When a child study or summary is prepared because there is an educational or group care issue or concern, the child study may include items and descriptions related to a child's adjustment to this group setting. In addition, an observer may record, suggest, or include any ideas about any changes that may assist teachers in preparing a more suitable environment.

CONDUCTING A CHILD STUDY TO DETERMINE TEACHING OR INTERVENTION STRATEGIES

When a child study is prepared because there is a question about learning or socializing in a child-care or educational setting, consider the following factors:

- Physical environment of the group setting
- Snack, lunch, naps, toileting, routines
- Scheduling and planning
- Individualization
- Curricular expectations
- Activities
- Record-keeping
- Teacher style and interactions
- Family communication and activities

Once all the material for a child study is gathered, the teacher or other professional writes a summary report. The first step before writing the report is becoming familiar with the information available. Next, organize it to address the purpose of the study—report, referral, or summarization of a year. A checklist for preparing the report is given in Box 8.1

BOX 8.1

Writing the Report

1. Start the report with a statement of why it is being written.
   For example, Chris, a four-year-old in my class, seems to have difficulty with the algebraic concepts, so I administered the TEMA 3. The report that follows describes the testing experience as well as the classroom observation and child-work analysis that led to the testing.
2. Include all relevant demographic information.
3. Summarize the classroom observation and child–work product analysis.
4. Describe the testing experience. Include descriptions of Chris's behaviors during testing. Did any behavior change during the administration? Did particular items or types of activities appear to influence the behavior? Why? How did Chris handle frustration?
5. Report the scores. Interpret the meaning of the scores.
6. Make recommendations for interventions that you will try.

Writing Style and Mechanics

- Did you include specific and descriptive information?
- Are your interpretations of behavior free from bias—based on repeated observations on separate occasions?
- Have you differentiated fact from impression?
- Is the report clear?
- Review the flow of the report. Does it move from question to conclusions logically and fairly?
- Are the conclusions reasonable, based on the test you used and the classroom observation as well as child-work that you have available? Did you go beyond the data?
- Did you make thoughtful, reasonable recommendations?
- Review test scoring for accuracy.
- Prepare neatly and proofread.

EXAMPLES OF CHILD STUDIES

In the following pages, a variety of child studies are shown. Each shows a picture of a baby, toddler, preschooler, or primary-age child at a moment in time. Some of the studies have rich amounts of background; others show only an assessment situation with limited background material. Some of the studies use and report diagnostic testing results with examples of reports completed for various stakeholders. Some of the studies employ informal and authentic assessment with interpretation by the teacher candidate completing the studies. As you read the studies, put yourself in the teacher's seat. What have you learned about each of these young children and their families? What more do you need to know? Are there alternative interpretations to the data or opinions? What will you do if you meet the young children in a teaching situation? What plans for intervention and teaching will you make? Besides the families, are there others to involve in implementing optimum learning opportunities for these young children?

CHILD STUDY 1

Bradley Howshaw, 4 years 11 months, Home-Schooled

Background Information

Bradley is a four-year-old Caucasian child of average height and weight. He is fair in complexion with blond hair. There is no history of medical problems, and from observation, it seems that he is at expected levels for physical and cognitive development. The observer finds that he has an outgoing and pleasant personality. Bradley is the oldest of three children, with two sisters, ages 3 and 12 months. Bradley lives in an apartment in a middle-class Chicago neighborhood with his father and mother. Mr. Howshaw works full-time while Mrs. Howshaw is a homemaker. Bradley is home-schooled, but will be attending kindergarten next year. Mrs. Howshaw works with Bradley daily and says she reads frequently to him, and has done so since birth. Mr. Howshaw plays with him after work. Mrs. Howshaw tells the observer that she is looking forward to her son starting school because she feels that he is bored at home. She feels that being in a classroom will keep him more structured and appropriately motivated. Bradley's parents expect him to go to college; thus, the family engages in many mentally and physically stimulating activities together. They visit the zoo and museums, and go to plays and parks often. The family's apartment is also well suited for his appropriate development. Bradley has a large collection of books, many developmentally appropriate toys such as blocks, Lincoln logs, Legos, an easel and paint, and play-dough. From all appearances, Bradley seems to have a happy home life. Mrs. Howshaw says Bradley has friends in the neighborhood who will be attending his school, so she imagines that separation anxiety upon entering kindergarten will not be an issue with Bradley.

Question for This Study

The central question is whether Bradley is developmentally equipped to succeed in a kindergarten program. Because Bradley is home-schooled, the assessor was interested in determining whether he would be ready and well-enough equipped to achieve success.

Formal Assessment

The assessor administered the Woodcock-McGrew-Werder Mini Battery of Achievement (MBA) to Bradley one afternoon before his dinner. Bradley was excited to take the test because his mother told him he would be looking at pictures and numbers. The MBA is a brief, wide-range test of basic skills—reading, writing and mathematics—and knowledge designed for use with children and adults ages 4 through 90+. Factual knowledge is also tested. On the basic skills portion of the test Bradley scored within the high average range of scores obtained by others at his age level. His writing and mathematics scores were within the very superior range of others at his age level. His reading scores were within the high average range. The factual knowledge portion of the test is a measure of science, social studies, and the humanities (art, music, and literature). Bradley's performance on this section of the test placed him in the high average range compared to others his age who took the test. Bradley was very strong in the factual knowledge portion of the test. He named the pictures and symbols before the assessor could finish reading the question.

Bradley performed well in the identification section of the reading test, identifying correctly all letters, both upper- and lowercase. During the dictation portion of the writing section, Bradley was able to print all upper- and lowercase letters asked of him. In the comprehension section of the reading test, Bradley did not answer any questions correctly because he cannot read; Mrs. Howshaw told the assessor this prior to the administration of the test. Bradley does possess some decoding skills, as demonstrated by his determined efforts to sound out all the words he saw. He struggled to identify the letters *b* and the cursive *u* in the identification section. It is developmentally appropriate for him to be struggling in these areas.

In the mathematics section, reasoning and concepts, Bradley really surprised the observer with his ability to tell time by looking at a clock. Mrs. Howshaw claims he can't really tell time but is able to recognize the hour hand on the appropriate number. He failed to read the correct time on a digital clock. Bradley failed to name the days of the week, although he was able to recite correctly up to Thursday. Bradley is able to identify and print all numbers up to 10 and do basic single-digit addition. He doesn't know how to subtract. Bradley showed no problems discriminating between largest/smallest, last/middle, and most/least.

Bradley separated easily from his mother for this assessment, not bothering to notice his mother watching from across the hall. He enjoyed the test, and told the assessor that some of the questions were way too easy for him. At one point when he was puzzled, he tried to stump the observer by asking a random riddle. Bradley was extremely determined and performed with complete attention with only minimal squirming during the approximately 35 minutes of assessment.

Informal Assessment

The informal assessment of Bradley is based on an interview conducted with him on a previous visit a week prior to the formal assessment. During the conversation, Bradley said he liked being read to and is learning how to play the guitar with his uncle. He stated that he is looking forward to starting school so he can learn how to read to himself and his two sisters. He also said he wants to join the school band and play guitar. When asked what he likes to do, he said watching television, playing outside, and going on walks to the park. His favorite color is blue and his current favorite book is *Squarehead.* He stated that he knows how to write his name and all the letters in the alphabet. He was very talkative during the interview, easily volunteering information and skills he has learned and things he has heard, such as songs and jokes.

Summary of the Child Study

Bradley is on-level developmentally across every area based on formal and informal observational assessments. Mrs. Howshaw's only concerns are that recently he has become very disruptive around the house. She hopes this is because he is bored from not being challenged enough socially and somewhat academically. Mrs. Howshaw says she runs a very structured and routine-based schedule with their daily instruction. She feels this will help him adapt to the regular routine of a classroom next year. Bradley performed in the high average range on the Woodcock-McGrew-Werder battery and has demonstrated normal social skills in all meetings. Based on these assessment measures, Bradley will succeed wonderfully in kindergarten.

Comments on the Child Study

This study of a typical four-year-old boy shows that he is academically and developmentally on-target for kindergarten in the autumn. What suggestions would you make for Mr. and Mrs. Howshaw to begin the partnership with his kindergarten teacher? If they plan to home-school the sisters until kindergarten age, what, if any, suggestions would you make for modification in Mrs. Howshaw's approach?

CHILD STUDY 2

Beatrice Jewel, an Adopted Toddler

Beatrice is a 5.2-year-old African American child who was adopted at 18 months by Mr. and Mrs. Jewel (also African American). She currently attends kindergarten at the neighborhood public school. Prior to entering kindergarten this fall, she was in a preschool program at a for-profit commercial child-care center. She was the youngest child in the family until the birth of her little brother in 2002. She has an older brother who is nine years old. She lives with her mother, father, and brothers in an affluent suburban community. Not much is known about Beatrice's biological parents or health and family history, but Beatrice's adopted parents are both college-educated, having attained master's degrees in their fields of study. English is the only language spoken at home. Mrs. Jewel is a stay-at-home mom, having elected to do so after the birth of her son in 2002. She values the importance of schooling, and thus is very involved in her children's education and facilitates literacy activities in the home at every opportunity. She loved to read as a child and into adulthood, and subsequently obtained a B.A. and M.A. in English. Prior to electing to stay at home, she was employed as a technical writer.

Beatrice is very sociable, talkative, inquisitive, and accommodating, as noted in various interactions with her. She is confident and secure in her role and position in the family. Her hygiene is well maintained, and she is always dressed cleanly in conservative clothing. She possesses typically described normal self-help and daily living skills. Her emotional status appears to be intact and normal (appropriate affect, happy, playful, etc.). Her overall health and development appears to be normal as observed via sentence structure and language skills, conversational skills, listening skills, and math one-to-one correspondence skills. Mr. and Mrs. Jewel believe that Beatrice is developing normally and have even been told that Beatrice is above average for her age, as documented on numerous teacher assessments from the preschool. Mr. and Mrs. Jewel are

somewhat curious about this, and thus supported the idea of doing an assessment, specifically in reading skills or reading ability.

The Test of Early Reading Ability—Third Edition (TERA-3) was chosen for three reasons: one, appropriateness for the type of assessment to be done; two, ease of administration; and three, quickness of administration—Beatrice is 5.2 years old and generally cannot sit still for long periods of time. Form B of the TERA-3 was administered to Beatrice at her home, 20 minutes after arriving from school at 3:40 P.M. She had been told by her mother two days before that I would be coming over to administer the test. Beatrice was excited and eager to take the test. The test was conducted in the well-lit kitchenette area at the family dining table. The testing area was free from distractions because her older brother and mother were in another part of the house working quietly, her younger brother was at child care, and her father was at work. In addition, the ringers on the phones were turned off. The total test time was 30 minutes. Beatrice began to drift toward the end of testing, specifically toward the end of the third subtest, which assessed meaning. Beatrice was praised and encouraged throughout the testing period per the guidelines set forth in the TERA-3 Examiner's Manual.

Beatrice scored equally well in Conventions and Meaning, receiving a standard score of 10 in each section. This translates to average for both subtests. Thus 50 percent of the standardization sample scored the same or below Beatrice in each of these two sections. Alphabet was Beatrice's strength, as evident from a standard score of 15, which was superior. Thus, 95 percent of the standardization sample scored the same or below Beatrice in this section. Her Composite Quotient was above average at 111.

Based on Beatrice's test results and the interpretation guidelines of the TERA-3, she appears to be good at phonics and decoding words in print. She generally understands how to hold a book and where to start reading. She exhibits some difficulty in knowing when to turn a page at times, and appears to not have a clear understanding of different parts of a book or different functions of punctuation marks. She exhibits difficulty in recognizing signs and knowing their meaning, but appears to grasp logos and their meanings.

It seems that Beatrice has benefited from an aggressive in-home literacy program along with her natural abilities. A continuation of emphasis on literacy will continuously propel Beatrice forward and enhance learning potential and skills in all developmental domains (language arts, math, science, art, music, physical/motor, social/emotional). Suggested activities might include reading stories aloud and having her summarize them; choosing books that have numbers corresponding to pictures, books with science themes, and books with heart themes; visiting the American Heart Association's website; and singing nursery rhyme songs.

Case Comments on the Child Study

Beatrice seems to be a typical first grader in terms of overall development and progress in reading. It is November; what should her first-grade teacher do to support Beatrice's growth? What recommendations do you have for Mr. and Mrs. Jewel?

CHILD STUDY 3

Angela Flores, a Second Grader

Angela, seven years old, has been observed three times and interviewed once by an outside consultant to her second-grade classroom. Ms. Kim describes Angela as a friendly with peers, sensitive, and shy with adults. Angela attends an urban public school in a predominantly Puerto Rican neighborhood. The school divides students into classrooms based on English-language strength in four levels and by parent request. Angela's home language is Spanish; she is in the English-only second grade by parent request. Angela, her mother, her older eight-year-old brother, and her mother's boyfriend, Jose, live in the home. Jose works as a janitor and her mother stays home with the children. Angela has no contact with her biological father. Angela's mother uses an authoritarian discipline style with her children. Angela has no history of medical problems and seems to be at expected developmental levels for physical and cognitive development. She seems shy in large-group classroom situations, but is comfortable in small-group activities. Her mother comes to school daily to drop off and pick up her children and asks about Angela's progress; communication with the second-grade teacher is limited by her mother's English fluency issues and the second-grade teacher's limited Spanish vocabulary.

Ms. Kim wanted to see what progress Angela was making in language arts. She describes the classroom as a literacy-rich one where there are many opportunities for all language arts, with many books available and accessible to students.

In the first observation, Ms. Kim spent the morning observing Angela using the four language processes: reading, writing, listening, and speaking. She showed no difficulty with reading, speaking, and listening. The writing assignment required children to write three things that go together; the class was studying comma usage. Angela had difficulty with this assignment. Ms. Kim asked her the following questions: What are three things that you like to eat? What are your favorite zoo animals? What are your favorite things to do at school or home? Angela wrote: I live at home with my mother, Jose, and my brother.

For observation two, Ms. Kim observed Angela in a class discussion activity. The teacher would read a page on animal tracks, and all of the other children tried to guess the animal. Angela tried to hide behind other students to avoid answering the questions raised by the teacher about a story on animal tracks.

During the last observation, Ms. Kim led a small group of children in a guided reading activity that included Angela. First, the children took a picture walk through the story. Angela was able to describe pictures in detail. Page reading by each child in the group followed. Then shared reading occurred. Angela performed successfully in both situations, reading with enthusiasm and confidence.

Ms. Kim administered the Developmental Reading Assessment (DRA) (1994), using the story *The Wagon*. Angela's running record shows 98.5 percent accuracy. She was able to determine story meaning from the context. She used sight word recognition strategies. She replaced sight words with other high-frequency words when she made errors. She tried to use pictures for clues in these situations and used pictures as a problem-solving strategy. In the retelling analysis, Angela was able to tell the story in her own words, including characters, important details, special phrases from the story, the setting, and the major events in the correct sequence. Angela enjoys reading before she goes to sleep, and when she has difficulty sleeping she reads to her stuffed animals. Her favorite books are the Arthur series by Marc Brown.

Ms. Kim recommends that Angela continue to read. She further suggests that the third-grade teacher promote and encourage Angela to speak Spanish with her peers who also speak her first language.

Reflections

Ms. Kim finds this performance assessment effective and efficient. It is not an in-depth measure, and Ms. Kim thinks another measure that focuses on language development would be a wise next step.

Comments on the Child Study

Ms. Kim is very concerned about the language development of young children. She wants to be assured that a child's culture and language is respected. As well, she wants to be sure that an English-only situation supports Angela's learning. Do you think she is justified in her perception that Angela is well served in this program? Why do you think Ms. Kim and Angela's mother have different opinions about English-only education?

CHILD STUDY 4

Matilde Sanchez

Ms. Wolf conducted an evaluation of Matilde, a six-year-old, in her home setting. She administered the Stanford Early School Achievement Test (SESAT) (1989).

Background Information

Matilde attended half-day preschool programs from the time she was 3. She began all-day kindergarten in a suburban private school, where she continues in first grade. Matilde has one older brother in fourth grade and a younger brother in kindergarten. She is fluent in Spanish and English, although she reads and writes in English only.

The SESAT was administered after dinner at the kitchen table in Matilde's home, while her mother and brothers were occupied in another room. The test took some time to administer and toward the end, Matilde tired. She also did not like doing the silent reading portion.

Matilde's performance is summarized as follows:

- She did well on the sounds of letters portion, matching correctly the sounds of letters to pictures and words. She used picture clues to help.
- She did have some difficulty in putting letters together to form words, after sounding them out.
- She seems to have a short attention span related to reading.
- She did not remember the minor details from stories, although she could tell me the main ideas.
- In math, Matilde understands one-to-one correspondence, number sense, shapes, and patterns. She enjoyed the nonroutine math problems.
- She has good initial understanding of time and currency.

Reflections by Ms. Wolf

"I felt comfortable with the test and chose it because the norms are based on a diverse population. The directions were clear and precise; I felt prepared after running through it three or four times, before administering the test."

Comments on the Child Study

This report contains no standard scores, so we must rely on Ms. Wolf's interpretation of the strength of Matilde's performance. What would the next assessment step be for this first grader who, according to Ms. Wolf, is on-target? Does she have the requisite skills for the first-grade curriculum in your district/state?

CHILD STUDY 5

Baby Ralph Brown

Ralph is a 12-month-old who receives monthly early intervention sessions to monitor his development in all areas. He lives with his mother, father, and seven-year-old sister, Tracey. Services were initiated following the death of his three-year-old brother, Michael, in a home accident. Michael was involved in a preschool special education program before his death. Tracey had been scheduled to be screened by the school district to determine if she had special education needs before Michael's death and her own injuries in the home accident.

Ralph's mother, Connie, is 21 years old. She received special education services for the mildly mentally retarded from elementary school through the beginning of high school. She quit high school in her first year due to an unplanned pregnancy. Connie is quiet, often looks depressed, and holds her head down when spoken to. She makes little eye contact. She says that Ralph is smarter than Michael was and she is not sure why Ralph needs this program, yet she comes each month and calls if she has to miss. She loves her children. She does make eye contact with them and provides them with food and clothing. She does not talk to them very much.

Ralph's father, Arthur, age 29, has a high school diploma and works seasonal jobs. Ralph's parents do not view him as having any special needs. Child assessment revealed that Ralph is approximately six months delayed in personal, social, and communication development. Qualitative concerns exist with fine- and gross-motor development.

Ralph receives health care through the County Hospital Medicaid Program. Extended family members assist with financial needs. Tracey receives treatments for her burns in a large Los Angeles hospital 35 miles from home. Prior to Michael's death, Connie received birth control services and counseling from a California Public Health Program, but services were discontinued due to funding cuts. Connie pursued her GED but discontinued the program due to learning difficulties. Homemaker services were also being investigated but were discontinued at the parent's request. Connie has expressed an interest in obtaining a job.

Parent Requests

A job for mother; a second-grade program for Tracey.

Providers' Assessment of Need

Parenting skills; parent-child interactions; homemaker skills; financial planning assistance; special education screening for Tracey; tutoring for GED courses, vocational assessment, assistance in placement; and health care management.

Comments on the Child Study

The writer is an early intervention specialist who has summarized notes of an initial conference with Connie, Ralph's mother. She has identified the problems that the family presents, both from the record and from the interview. She has made notes of what the family wants in further early

intervention service. In addition, she has prepared her own list of suggested services. At a multidisciplinary staffing, she will choose which of the suggestions to share immediately and relate those to parent goals. The effectiveness of future collaboration will depend on the sensitivity of the specialist in weaving the different agendas—parent and early intervention—together.

CHILD STUDY 6

Ted Miller

A physician who, along with Mr. and Mrs. Miller, was concerned about a possible language delay and the quality of Ted's walking had referred Ted, a 21-month-old and his mother, Mrs. Miller, for assessment. The doctor's report stated that Ted had been suffering from upper respiratory problems and ear infections since one month of age. Ted's mother filled out a family form that stated that the oldest sibling, now 10 years old, was an apnea baby. The five-year-old sibling has no hearing in one ear, and the three-year-old sibling is in an early intervention program due to a developmental speech delay. Mrs. Miller drives the three-year-old to therapy appointments three times per week.

Developmental History

The Shaker Heights Child Find program was responsible for screening Ted a day after his first birthday. At that time, the Denver Developmental Screening Test results indicated a slight language delay. All other areas were scored within normal limits. However, during this time frame Ted had eye surgery due to one eye turning inward. He is to wear prescription lenses with bifocals. Mrs. Miller reported that she has been busy with her other children and cannot buy the glasses until next month.

The Battelle Development Inventory was used to determine if Ted was eligible for services six months ago when he was 15 months old. At that time, Ted performed well in the cognitive domain and passed in the area of gross-motor skills. He passed, even though he could walk only 2 feet before falling down, as reported by the nurse. The occupational therapist explained that the quality of the walking is not a consideration with this test. Ted scored at 11 months in expressive communication and at 9 months in receptive communication. Once again a discrepancy seemed to exist, as Ted used no speech imitations, no word sounds, and could not follow any directions. However, at the same time, Mrs. Miller reported that Ted said a few words. The developmental specialist who did the testing was confused by the results and recommended an arena assessment, so that other specialists might contribute insights.

Mrs. Miller scheduled an appointment within a month but did not keep the appointment. Mrs. Miller reported that her mother was ill and that she had assumed care of her. This care included having her mother move to the family home. For the next five months, all attempts to reach her were unsuccessful. Finally, Mrs. Miller initiated contact with the center and reported that in the interim her husband had walked out on her, the four children, and her mother. At this point, she had contacted a lawyer to file for maintenance support.

Arena Assessment

Ted, on the day of the arena assessment, was wearing his shoes on the wrong feet to correct a "toeing in" problem. Mrs. Miller also had not bought the corrective shoes that were prescribed months ago.

Ted held up well throughout the one-hour session. The occupational therapist used a fine-motor adaptive checklist that combined items from the Bayley Scales of Infant Development, the Revised Gesell Developmental Schedules, and the Denver Developmental Screening

Tests—Revised. At 21 months, Ted vocalizes but does not talk. He does a lot of "mouthing" of objects. He enjoys putting objects into a container and taking them at. He turned his head to sounds made behind and to each side of him but he did not seem to comprehend the words. Sometimes he responded to gestures or demonstration. He did not respond to a loud, firm "no" from the therapist who tried to get him to stop an activity. There was no eye contact made and Ted appeared to have difficulty focusing on objects.

The physical therapist concluded that Ted is unstable when walking, has difficulty getting into and out of a chair, trips himself when attempting to run, cannot step on an object on the floor, cannot shift the weight of his feet, and cannot climb stairs. According to the physical therapist, Ted's problem seems to be solely in his feet: "His hips are in place and structurally he looks good."

The speech therapist seemed to feel that the inside of Ted's mouth looked intact, but she could not continue her assessment because Ted was ready for a nap and began to cry.

Discussion

The members of the team met for an hour after the assessment session. They completed a checklist and summarized as follows: Ted was content throughout the session. Although unaware of the situation, he was friendly, cooperative, and moderately active. He adapted to the tasks required. He was tolerant of handling. Socially, Ted showed poor responses to interaction and initiated no interaction. He was not distracted by visual or auditory stimuli. Even though he did not understand the tasks presented, he was not easily frustrated. The reliability of the test results were judged to be "average."

Comments on the Child Study

This team is just beginning to work with the family. They have identified a number of problems through observation during the arena assessment. In addition to the developmental problem, they have a record of the family emotional problems, based on the interview with Mrs. Miller. They have a history of the Millers' previous involvement with the agency. The next step will be the development of a plan that addresses the mother's emotional needs as well as Ted's early intervention needs. They have the basis of referral for social services and interagency collaboration.

CHILD STUDY 7

Jorge Sanchez, a Kindergartner

Background Information

Jorge is a five-year-old child enrolled in a full-day kindergarten class at an urban public school. Jorge is of average height and weight for his age. His has a medium-to-dark complexion and dark hair. Jorge's parents were born and raised in Mexico. Mr. & Mrs. Sanchez moved to the United States three years before Jorge was born. Jorge is an only child. Jorge's parents mainly speak English at home but do speak Spanish with other family members occasionally. Jorge learned both languages simultaneously as he grew up. He speaks English slightly better than Spanish due to the fact that he uses English more often. Each summer the family returns to Mexico for a few weeks, during which Jorge speaks only Spanish.

Jorge has been enrolled at the school since he was in the state pre-kindergarten program at age 4. I have numerous opportunities to meet with and observe Jorge, because his mother is my classroom assistant. Jorge helps his mother every morning and afternoon with cleaning and preparing my classroom. He often talks to me about his school day or what books he read. Jorge willingly helps his mom with any task but especially loves putting the books away. Jorge and I talk often about books and his schoolwork. Every day at 2:30 he comes down to my classroom to meet his mom and announces that he received a 100 percent on his test or homework. He also pulls all his papers out and displays them to his mom and me. Jorge obviously takes great pride in his work. Jorge recently received an award for reading the most Accelerated Reader books in the kindergarten!

Jorge's mother is very involved in her son's education. She speaks with his teachers every day and often requests extra work for him at home. Jorge's parents have limited formal education—the equivalent of a high school diploma. However, they would like to see Jorge go to college. Jorge and his parents engage in many stimulating activities together as a family. They often go to the zoo, museums, and parks. Jorge replays these events for me each morning while preparing the classroom. Jorge's home environment is also very suitable for his development. He has a large library of books, numerous appropriate and open-ended toys such as blocks and Legos®, and a wide array of art supplies and play-dough. Jorge is very well spoken for his age. I observed his vocabulary to be well above that of most of his peers. I have often observed Jorge to initiate conversations with adults in topics ranging from his school day to his most recent outing to the zoo. His extended family includes numerous cousins his age whom he frequently spends time with. There are also a few families with children his age living on his block. This allows Jorge frequent opportunities to socialize outside of school with children close to his age.

Developmental History

Jorge's mother reports **typical development** throughout infancy and toddlerhood. He was walking by 12 months and talking in sentences by age 2. Characteristic of boys, his toilet training began at age 2 but he was not fully trained until he was 30 months old. She reports that he has always been especially interested in animals and clearly spoke words such as *cow* and *dog* by age 1!

typical development the usual or expected developmental pattern of children.

Jorge's mother is concerned because his teacher, Ms. Swenson, is reporting that Jorge is talking too often and at inappropriate times during class. Mrs. Sanchez is concerned that Jorge needs some extra attention or maybe more playtimes with children his own age at home. Ms. Swenson has observed that Jorge disrupts students working around him to talk to or laugh with. Mrs. Sanchez also thinks that maybe Jorge is too bored in school and possibly needs to be in the next grade or needs more advanced work.

Mr. Sanchez expressed the opinion that Jorge is functioning at a higher cognitive level than the rest of the children in the kindergarten. Both parents reported that he is reading books at home with very little adult assistance. He also adds money and counts change for his piggy bank at home. If Ms. Swenson continues to have difficulty with Jorge, they do not want to transfer him to the half-day kindergarten because they have very limited resources for child care for him. Mr. and Mrs. Sanchez feel that Jorge is more advanced than the rest of the children in the class and this is causing his disruptive behavior. They feel that putting him in a first-grade classroom will keep him more focused and attentive to his more-challenging work.

When questioned about his behavior, Jorge stated he spoke to the other children because he was finished with his work. His parents have also talked to him about this and expressed to him that this may be the cause. Jorge responded that he normally talked to two specific friends about schoolwork or other people in the room. He also said he thought the work was really easy.

Question for This Study

Based on Mr. and Mrs. Sanchez's concern, the basis of this clinical study is to determine the readiness of Jorge for first grade at this November date. The results of the study are intended to assure the parents that Jorge is in the most appropriate class. The study will include interviews with teachers, interviews with the parents, interviews with Jorge, informal assessments, and the results of the Metropolitan Performance Assessment.

School History and Academic Progress

Jorge attended the pre-kindergarten class at our school last year in the mornings. Ms. Cooper, his previous teacher, reported that Jorge's play and social behaviors were all appropriate for his age. She noted his exceptional language and cognitive development. Jorge loved reading about animals he had seen at the zoo, such as lions and flamingos. His knowledge about specific zoo animals was more extensive than she had ever seen from a child at his age. He appropriately labeled all animals in her books. He had also learned to spell certain animal names, such as bear, lion, flamingo, turtle, snake, and so on. Ms. Cooper informed me that Jorge often played with other children in associative or cooperative play without teacher direction. He had two specific male friends and they would play together most days. Their favorite activity was building a tent in the block area. They told the teacher they were sleeping in the tent in their backyards! Jorge often led these boys around the class and chose what activities to engage in during center time. Jorge spent most of center time playing with other children. He rarely painted or went to the art table independently. The teacher often prompted him to make pictures or go to the art table, because he would not choose them otherwise. He did enjoy painting and coloring but usually would complete one picture then go to the blocks or truck area. Occasionally Jorge would sit in the book area and ask the teacher to read books with him. Jorge was "reading" his favorite books through memorization. He used no decoding skills. Ms. Cooper reported that he was able to dictate the sounds of specific letters, displaying emerging phonetic awareness. He was still at the pre-reading level. He was writing all uppercase letters and random lowercase letters.

At kindergarten, Ms. Swenson asserts that Jorge is on-level developmentally across every area based on informal observational assessments. Ms. Swenson's only concerns are Jorge's frequent disruptive talking behaviors during class. She expects most children to need time to adjust to a full-day kindergarten. Ms. Swenson's class follows a clear visual schedule that is reviewed each day. The school day is structured based on specific routines. The children have certain specific times when they are allowed to talk to the people at their tables. During other times the children are required to sit quietly and listen to the teacher. However, Jorge seems to be having more trouble adjusting than the rest of the students. Ms. Swenson notes that he is often the first to finish his work. He will talk to other children or get up from his seat and walk around the room without permission. Typically Jorge will finish his seatwork, stand up from the table, and walk around the room to the other areas even when instructed to sit in his seat. Ms. Swenson believes that Jorge's phonemic awareness skills are developing on-level according to the kindergarten guidelines for classroom work. Jorge often requests reading books and asks to go to the listening center to listen to books on tape during free time.

I observed Ms. Swenson's interactions with the children at different points throughout the day. She spoke with them during center times. She listened to their stories and concerns attentively. Most interactions involved Ms. Swenson "talking at" the students. Ms. Swenson's style of teaching is very structured and teacher-directed. The children are expected to sit quietly and follow her commands frequently throughout the day.

Interview of Jorge

Jorge said he liked to read and he wanted to be in the first grade so he could read better. I asked him what he liked about school and he responded that he liked playing with his friends, reading books, and the listening center. His current favorite book is Dr. Seuss's *ABC* and his favorite animals are baby lions. One day Jorge plans to be a veterinarian or work at a zoo.

Formal Assessment

The formal assessment used in this child study was the Metropolitan Readiness Test MRT (1995). I administered the Performance Assessment for Level 2. The test assesses objectives taught at the end of kindergarten or early in first grade. The test gives a holistic score for the child along with scores in the areas of Language/Literacy and Quantitative/Mathematics. This is a performance-based assessment that will give a measure of Jorge's readiness for first grade. The tasks are integrated within a specific theme. I decided to use both the "Pizza Party" and "Birthday Surprise" for greater reliability in results. I also wanted to have numerous documents to show his parents the results of the examination. The validity of the test is reported to be high across all measures. The author of the scoring booklet also notes that the Metropolitan Readiness Test (MRT) is an authentic measurement. The test measures the ability of the child to independently perform tasks introduced in the classroom. The behaviors necessary for the completion of each task are seen in the regular classroom. Predictive validity is not relevant in the MRT, because it measures the developing concepts and strategies used by the children. The test can be administered to a group. The teacher and children are expected to interact throughout the test with the teacher observing the children to see what they are answering and how they answer. The MRT is designed to help the teacher understand what strategies and concepts the child has mastered thus far.

I completed the examination over four sessions. Jorge was very compliant and eager to finish the work with me. He insisted on taking the work home with him, so we made a copy of it together. Jorge takes great pride in his work. The most interesting aspect of the interview was watching the strategies he employed to solve the problems. Because this is a performance-based assessment, I was able to observe how he processed the problem more than I was able to do with other assessments in the past. Jorge is very strong in the areas of computation. He solved the fractions problems without waiting for me to finish the explanation in the manual. He easily worked through the patterns and addition problems. The first page shows he is not wasteful with the pizza! He obviously did not fully understand the concept of splitting the pizza into four separate slices.

Jorge completed the addition problems quickly and easily. The subtraction problem took more time but he finished successfully. He finished the pattern problems with no trouble. The only area of concern was the story writing. Jorge was hesitant to even begin writing the story. He stated, "I do not know how to write." I urged him to do his best and he sounded out "pepperoni" and copied "pizza party" from the book cover. He shows phonemic awareness of a kindergarten level with only the beginning and ending syllables represented in the invented spelling of pepperoni. Overall this assessment clearly places Jorge at the kindergarten level for reading and writing but at the beginning first-grade level for math.

I also administered the "Birthday Surprise" edition of the Metropolitan Performance Test. He did very well with the patterns but had some problems with the story writing, as in the "Pizza Party" test. This shows the reliability of the test. Jorge again proved very efficient in math. His reading and writing skills place him on-level for his age. He clearly falls above average in math for a kindergartner. His reading and writing skills are average. I have a feeling Jorge has more math experience throughout his day than writing. He seemed very unsure of his abilities in reading and writing. He hesitated and wanted assistance with each reading and writing problem. His reading comprehension was shown to be higher than writing, delineating the fact that Jorge needs more writing opportunities.

Jorge has very clear strengths and weaknesses as previously discussed. Through the observations and testing procedures I have determined Jorge to be a very gregarious, communicative five-year-old. He enjoys school and especially enjoys math. It is not atypical for a child to perform better on math than reading. Frequently, this may be the sign of a learning disability in children. Jorge, however, performs average for his age in writing and slightly higher in reading comprehension. Thus, Jorge does not need further testing. He will succeed fabulously in kindergarten proceeding with the curriculum in place. Ms. Swenson may consider providing more writing opportunities and integrating reading with math. Jorge will benefit from more proactive writing. This will give him more confidence to attempt this skill.

Jorge displays greater strength in math than reading. He has practiced at home using a number line for addition and used a number line during this test. He has not had any experience with money and values in school, but uses money at home. His reading skills are at level for a kindergartner. He had some problems with sequencing and story comprehension. He is not yet able to write word sentences, although he had no problem writing the math sentences! He was not yet able to sequence the "Birthday Surprise" story with pictures after listening to part of it. This is a first-grade skill. Additionally, he had difficulty answering the questions with pictures on the third page of "Birthday Surprise." Overall, he had more difficulty with the "Birthday Surprise" than the "Pizza Party." Both are Level 2 assessments, meaning they are meant for the end of kindergarten or the beginning of first grade. Interestingly, he had no problems with the phonemic awareness skill of matching initial sounds on the first page. I am certain he performs numerous tasks similar to this each day in school, thus explaining his ease with this task. He demonstrates definite skills in identifying the initial sounds of words as evidenced through his invented spelling of *pepperoni*: "Pronee." Overall, Jorge exhibits clear cognitive strengths. He is an exceptional student; however, Jorge would not benefit from skipping kindergarten for first grade. Kindergarten will provide him with the social and language-enriched base to help him move successfully through school. Jorge's parents are aware of a gifted program at a school in the district. They would like him to remain at his current school due to proximity and the fact that his mother works there. They do not want to pursue this school at this time.

Recommendations for Mr. and Mrs. Sanchez

Jorge's parents can encourage Jorge to write stories about their trips through pictures or words. Jorge should keep a journal of his trips with his family and even present them to the class. This would provide a great learning experience for Jorge and his peers. Ms. Swenson might also include journaling in the daily routines. Jorge is progressing well in his current placement and should do the same next year. Mr. and Mrs. Sanchez should be encouraged to allow Jorge to use invented spelling and pictures through his journals. They may even begin their own, as a model for Jorge.

Recommendations for Ms. Swenson

Jorge will need ample opportunities to write and share his writings. He excels at math and may be useful as a peer tutor for children struggling through math. Jorge enjoys helping others and often finishes his work quickly. This may provide time for Jorge to help around the classroom in such tasks as cleaning the fish bowl, organizing the library, or providing journaling time. Ms. Swenson can work with the fact that Jorge loves helping adults and peers. He takes every job his mother or I give to him with great seriousness and diligence. I am confident this will transfer into the classroom. At this point, I do not feel that Jorge is academically ready for first grade, especially having missed the first quarter. I feel both Jorge and Ms. Swenson will benefit from thinking creatively and working together to help Jorge continue developing into a productive, successful student. Mr. and Mrs. Sanchez should be part of the process and remain the teacher's best resource for working with Jorge's strengths.

Jorge's parents agree that journaling is a fabulous idea for him. They would like to work with Ms. Swenson to see if he can work on a journal after finishing his class work. Jorge agrees that he can do this. Jorge feels he will not talk as much if he has more to do!

Comments on the Child Study

This study shows the interaction of formal knowledge with informal assessment. It also raises some issues regarding peer-teacher review. How can teachers work together in Jorge's interest? What additional curricular or instructional suggestions might you have for Ms. Swenson? Are there cues that you might suggest for Jorge, so he can perform well in a teacher-directed classroom? Do you have any other ideas about how Mr. and Mrs. Sanchez might support their son in school?

CHILD STUDY 8

Mary Ellen Luby

Background Information

Mary Ellen Luby is aged 6 years 2 months and of average size for a six-year-old; she has red hair, fair skin, blue eyes, and freckles. Mary Ellen's older sister, Bernadette, is in third grade. Mary Ellen comes from an upper-class family whose parents are highly involved in her academic career. Mrs. Luby is a room parent and always picks Mary Ellen up and drops her off at school. There are no known family problems, concerns, or family tragedies. When Mary Ellen entered kindergarten, she was adamant about starting school and had no separation issues. After seeing Bernadette go off to school, Mary Ellen was excited to begin her journey in elementary school. Mary Ellen was born on time and was delivered naturally. She has never been hospitalized and is an overall healthy child. There do not seem to be any developmental delays.

Throughout the eight months I have known Mary Ellen, I have found her to be social and always in a good mood. She follows directions in class and listens to her teacher, does her work with the utmost care, and is respectful of her peers. Mary Ellen has beautiful printing and is currently teaching herself how to write her name in cursive. She has a few friends but hangs out with one girl more than the others. She does not often cry when hurt or when she is upset.

Child Study Question

Although Mary Ellen works well with her classmates and works hard in school, she has some difficulties with word and number reversals and seems to have a difficult time learning to read. How can I help Mary Ellen learn to read fluently and become more social with other children in the room? How can I help Mary Ellen become autonomous?

Description of Classroom Setting and Test Administration

The *Brigance® Inventory of Early Development* was administered at Mary Ellen's school in Brooklyn during nap time/rest time for a total of five days for 30-minute increments. We went to a private table in the back of the room, while the other students were working independently and lying on mats. There are fifteen other classmates: seven girls and eight boys, consisting of two Indian children, one African American, one Pakistani child with polio, and the rest Caucasian. Peers seem to get along well with Mary Ellen and listen attentively when she displays her show and share objects. Through the day, the students move from their tables to the carpet several times. The teacher explains the lessons on the carpet and has the students complete their work at tables. Once Mary Ellen moves to first grade, she will be placed in a single-sex classroom through eighth grade. She sits with one other girl and two boys at a round table. She has her own supply bin with crayons, scissors, pencils, and markers with her name on them. She brings her folder to class every day with notes from her parents or notes from her teacher, Mrs. Jones.

The classroom has four tables, a sink, one back table for students to work at, a computer center, science center, reading center, and art center. Mary Ellen shares a cubby with another girl, where she puts her lunch, winter clothes, and backpack. Mary Ellen is dressed in uniform like the other children, but always wears some kind of brightly colored bow in her hair that makes her stand out. Mary Ellen is nearing the end of kindergarten year, where they are currently studying a unit on money and participating in writing workshop. Mrs. Jones is kind and strict. She expects children to be on task, yet always gives them plenty of free choice time and has fun with them in transitions and during activities. Mrs. Jones is always goofing around with her students and reading funny books to them. The class seems to adore her and really enjoys being in her company. Mary Ellen has a great bond with Mrs. Jones. Mrs. Jones calls on her quite often in class and always comments on her beautiful printing in front of the class.

When I asked Mary Ellen if I could interview her for a class of mine, she was very excited and delighted to help me. She sat in her seat and answered every question with thought and effort. There were times when other students would come over to our table and ask what we were working on, but Mary Ellen gave me her full attention and was never distracted by her peers. Her best friend walked over and asked if she could be interviewed next and Mary Ellen looked at me and said, "Can Rita have a turn? I don't want her to be left out!" I thought it showed Mary Ellen's kindness and sincerity for her friends.

Self-Help and Daily Living Skills

Mary Ellen holds her utensils with care and ease. She uses a knife to spread peanut butter on sandwiches but likes it better when her mom cooks for her. She serves herself at the table and knows how to prepare dry cereal. She set the table once with the help of her mother and is learning how to set the table on her own now. She proudly told me that she can dress herself and picks out her own clothing. She puts on shoes successfully, yet has a bit of trouble tying her shoelaces. Occasionally I need to assist Mary Ellen in zipping up her jacket or her friend may do it for her. When Mary Ellen and I talked she told me that her mother brushes her hair and does her hair in the morning, but she assured me that with assistance she can brush her own teeth. Mary Ellen does not shine her own shoes or clean her nails on her dominant hand (right). I did notice, however, that when Mary Ellen coughed she did not cover her mouth. Currently Mary Ellen is practicing to snap her fingers like some of the classmates.

Body Movement and Use of Body

Mary Ellen has excellent gross-motor skills. When I asked her to play a game with me, Simon Says, she perfected each task that I asked. She stood up straight, stood still for 20 seconds and jumped and hopped on each foot. Mary Ellen's locomotor skills consist of walking and running, running up stairs, kicking, catching, and sitting with enough balance and support to free her hands for an activity, and can sit erectly for five minutes. Mary Ellen carefully walks up and down stairs while holding her backpack every day and always holds on to the railing. Her gym teacher, Mr. Polaris told me that she can throw a tennis ball a distance of 15 feet and can toss a beanbag, but cannot seem to get the beanbag into the wastebasket yet. She was successful in the gymnastics unit on the balance beam and had to stop and think before she walked backwards on the beam. But she performed well walking forwards. She loves to jump rope outside at recess and is still working on her mastery of jumping more than two times without fail.

Mary Ellen is right-handed and demonstrated how to fold a paper diagonally for me. She divided the sections and creased the paper in the form of a triangle. She can print her first and last name and uses an eraser when she sees an error in her work. When I spoke with her art teacher, Ms. Custer, she explained to me that Mary Ellen loves art and is very sensitive in her class. She discussed with me that when she critiques Mary Ellen's work or asks her to add color, she gets upset and offended. She has trouble with negative feedback yet does beautifully with positive feedback, as most children would. Mary Ellen makes definable shapes and animals when using a paintbrush. She selects her colors with care and shares her opinion about pictures and other artistic items with her art teacher. Mary Ellen also likes to complete puzzles when asked, but prefers to draw during her free time in class. When putting a puzzle together, Mary Ellen will use a lot of trial and error yet remains patient throughout the process. When I asked Mary Ellen to draw a picture of a person with lots of detail and all the body parts, she included all except for the nose and ears.

Speech and Language

Mary Ellen on occasion, has talked like a baby with her girl friends. Her speech skills are satisfactory and she participates in conversations without monopolizing them. She does not answer the phone in her house and always uses words related to sequence. She does not use tomorrow and yesterday in her vocabulary, nor does she answer "when" questions. The length of sentences Mary Ellen uses is appropriate for her age group. When I asked her to tell me about her personal data, she knew her birthday, parent's names, and telephone number. She could not seem to remember her address, an intersection near her home, or the name of her doctor. She can describe differences in objects and can define simple words, like bike, school, or map. I gave Mary Ellen a picture vocabulary assessment where she had to point and name the items in the book. She completed this assessment with flying colors. Mary Ellen's verbal directions were spectacular when I asked her to show me under, over, next to, around the, besides the, etc. When I asked Mary Ellen to describe to me receptive body parts she was able to list them up to the point when we hit the word "waist."

Emotional Reactions (Expression and Control of Emotion and Feelings, Imagination and Fantasy, Self-Concept, Self-Management Skills)

Mary Ellen described to me her imaginary friend when she was four years old. She can read stories aloud with assistance and can read many sight words. She has trouble distinguishing between fantasy and reality. Mary Ellen appears to be extremely sensitive when it comes to her artwork or handwriting. She takes her work seriously and criticism is hard for her. Mary Ellen manages to keep on task with her work and is in complete control of her behavior skills.

Reactions to Other Children

Mary Ellen plays well with other children. She seems to pick other playmates that are quiet and calm. She keeps to herself and it appears that she is happy that way. Until a few weeks ago, Mary Ellen hung out alone or would transfer from group to group. Her classmate Rita was always playing one-on-one with other girls until she began hanging out with Mary Ellen. Now they are inseparable and finish each other's sentences. Mary Ellen seems to get along better with girls than boys. The boys in her class are outgoing and social, but she seems to prefer not to interact with them. Mary Ellen takes pleasure in doing favors for others. She takes pride in her accomplishments and companionship with her friends. Mary Ellen tends to fabricate and exaggerate stories with her classmates. I have discussed the importance of sharing with Mary Ellen on many occasions. She has trouble sharing markers, glue, or paper. Mary Ellen does play games by the rules and cooperatively plays with one or two children for extended periods of time.

Reactions with Adults

Mary Ellen has a great relationship with her sister and her mother. Every time her mom comes to pick her up from school or helps out in the classroom she shyly walks over and gives her a hug. Mary Ellen seems to love her teachers and the adults in the classroom. She knows all of the room parents well and appears to enjoy her special classes: gym, art, music, library, French, movement, and religion. Each of those teachers explained to me that they highly enjoy Mary Ellen's company as well as her charisma that she brings to the class. When I spoke with her French teacher, he explained to me that her attention was out of focus and she would talk a lot during his lessons. He seemed to think that she was not interested in his class and felt that he could not keep her interested. He also explained to me that Mary Ellen never memorized her vocabulary words and would not participate in class.

Play or School Activities

When I observed Mary Ellen at lunch and recess she was always eager to sit with me or ask me questions. She loved to tell me stories and would always keep the teachers around her laughing. She would play nicely with others, yet she kept close to her friend Rita the majority of the time. They would ask to go to the bathroom together, go to the nurse together, read the same free choice books, and even get a drink of water together.

Thinking and Reasoning

Mary Ellen and I discussed what we do in different situations. She explained to me that when she is sleepy she reads a book and that when she is cold she hugs her body tightly. When I asked her "what do you do?" when she breaks something that belongs to someone else she said, "I will give it to a teacher." When asked what she does when strangers offer her candy, she replied with, "I would never say yes!" Mary Ellen and I also spoke about the use of objects. She knew that clocks were used to tell time and that airplanes are used for travel. When we spoke about the community, she knew immediately that nurses were meant to help the sick and that firefighters were there to "help from fires." We went into some more expressive questions about the community and her eyes widened when asking these questions. She knows that "farmers have food and animals, teachers teach us, painters paint pictures, and grocery stores help us live." She looked at me blankly when asked about carpenters and mechanics. Mary Ellen also described to me that when she gets her haircut she goes to the "hair place" and that she goes to the bookstore when she wants to read a new book with her mom. Mary Ellen also knew that in order to buy stamps she had to purchase them at "the store."

Developmental Progress for Social, Emotional, Cognitive, Physical Skills

Mary Ellen knew each color of the rainbow as well as pink, gray, and white when colors were shown in front of her. She was able to name each shape that was placed in front of her: circle, square, rectangle, diamond, and heart. She classified animals, furniture, musical instruments, and tools beautifully as well. Her directional/positional concepts were perfect, bottom/top, over/under, center/corner; however, she had trouble distinguishing between her right and left.

Mary Ellen can neatly cut construction paper, cloth, and angles; however, when I asked her to cut an enclosed area from a picture by punching a hole in the paper and cutting out the enclosed area she could not complete it. Mary Ellen holds her pencil beautifully. She likes to draw hearts on everything and takes her time when printing her name and her schoolwork.

When I asked Mary Ellen about some quantitative concepts she was able to explain to me the meaning of long/short, large/small, and all/none. She could not describe to me the meaning of deep/shallow, thick/thin, wide/narrow, and many/few. After watching many observations of Mary Ellen, it seems that she is comfortable with herself and offers apologies for unintentional mistakes. Mary Ellen likes to pretend that she is a housewife, actress and singer with her friends.

Communication Skills

Mary Ellen always accepts help from adults when she is hurt or upset. She performs simple errands for her teachers and enjoys being called on in class. Mary Ellen seems exceptionally dependable.

School Adjustment (Attendance, Arrival, Reaction to Routines, Following Directions, Taking Turns, Response to Support and Individualization)

Mary Ellen appears to be a follower in her classroom of students. She tends to go with the flow and adapt to whatever games are being played or to whatever her friends want to play. She takes turns and follows directions to a T. However, she seems to be more of a loner type of child.

Summary for Stakeholders

For Teacher

Mary Ellen is a mature and hard-working student. She enjoys listening to stories, participates in classroom activities and is the first person to raise her hand to volunteer. Mary Ellen listens to directions and seeks approval from her teachers. She takes criticism seriously and tries to improve her skills every day. Mary Ellen seems to know what to work on and how she can accomplish her goals. Her parents are extremely involved in her education and are adamant about helping Mary Ellen's education. Mary Ellen is currently struggling to read short books, yet she seems to have phonemic awareness skills and is consistently working on them. Mary Ellen is an athletic child who enjoys art, music, gym, and religion. She has developed close relationships with all of her teachers and values their opinions. Mary Ellen is a strong-willed student and a great asset to any classroom. Mary Ellen's biggest weakness is her reading skills. Mary Ellen scored a 99 in her raw score of her assessment. This score suggests that Mary Ellen is an average to above-average student and is on the correct path in academics.

For Parent

I am pleased to tell you that Mary Ellen has been an extreme delight in class. She follows directions, is respectful of her peers and puts forth effort and energy in the classroom. Mary Ellen loves to write in her journal and is currently working on strengthening her reading skills. She is always eager to learn in class and asks questions. She is very persistent and always tries her best in each subject. Mary Ellen is kind to her classmates, yet seems to stick to one child more than others. She seems to be quiet but has opened up towards the end of the year. Mary Ellen is an excellent listener and communicator. Over the summer, I recommend that Mary Ellen write in a journal about her summer activities or family members and read some first- and second-grade leveled readings. This will give her excellent practice to develop as a young reader and writer.

Questions to Think About

1. Do you think that Mary Ellen has reading delay? Why or Why not?
2. What would you do to enhance Mary Ellen's learning to read?

Do you see any other issues that might concern you, if Mary Ellen were to be in your first grade class? If so, how will you assess and track progress for these issues?

CHILD STUDY 9

Edgar Abercrombie, a seven-year-old who loves the outdoors

Background Information

Edgar Abercrombie is currently seven years old; Edgar lives in Shawnee Mission, where he's lived since he was born. Edgar's family includes mom, dad, four sisters—Quinn, Kelly, Christine, and Megan, as well as one brother, Pat. The age range of the siblings is from 19 years old down to Edgar, who is the youngest. The upper-middle-class family is very close and connected. Edgar seems to be a very happy, well-adjusted second grader. Edgar's siblings are all protective of Edgar and clearly look out for and care for him—especially his older brother Pat, who is 17 years old. Mrs. Abercrombie said Edgar is in great health and is very physically active. Edgar tends to play outside with many neighborhood children whenever he gets the chance. He loves sports and so far has been involved in soccer and baseball for organized sports. Mrs. Abercrombie said Edgar is already quite independent and can take a shower, get dressed, fix his own breakfast, and so on without any assistance at all. He is very confident in his abilities as far as life skills and academics are concerned. Edgar has no problem communicating with adults, although he's just a little shy, at first; he's not shy at all with his peers. My overall impression of Edgar is very positive; he seems to being progressing developmentally and academically as appropriate for his age. Edgar appears to be an extremely likable boy, who seems happy and self-assured.

Academic History and Functioning

It was not surprising at all to me to find out Edgar is a very bright student who does well academically. Edgar attends a private K–8 elementary school in Shawnee Mission. He loves school and takes it very seriously. In first grade, he received straight A's the entire year and for the first quarter of this year, he received all A's except for one B in penmanship. Mrs. Abercrombie said he was upset about getting a B and is now working hard to improve his penmanship. Edgar even checks his grade online each week to see if his grade went up! I couldn't believe how much he cared about grades at this young age! I asked Mrs. Abercrombie how the other siblings were doing in school and she said they all have A to high B averages. No wonder Edgar is following in their footsteps. I felt like sending my own kids over to their house! I asked Edgar's mother about his study habits and she said Edgar does his homework (if he has any) right when he gets home from school each day without being asked. He likes to get it out of the way so he can play before dinner. I asked Edgar if he usually finishes his work in class before the class period ends and he said yes. He said that he gets a reading or math packet to work on when he finishes his daily work. Edgar's mom said his favorite subject is reading and he is a good reader. He is now reading chapter books and reads pretty quickly. I asked Edgar if he liked his current teacher and he said yes. He feels comfortable asking his teacher questions now, but at the beginning of the year he was a little hesitant asking questions or talking to her.

Questions/Concerns

Although Mr. & Mrs. Abercrombie are very happy with Edgar's progress in school, they do have a couple of concerns. The first one is regarding Edgar at school. They are a little worried that Edgar is not being challenged enough, as he gets packets to work on only once he's finished with his regular work in the classroom. Mrs. Abercrombie said she would hate to see him get bored with school, since up to this point he loves it and is motivated to do well. The second concern is his penmanship and sloppy work. Edgar tends to race through his homework after school so he can play with his friends. His work at school is also in need of improvement as far as neatness goes.

Central Question

Is the school Edgar attends providing enough challenging and interesting work for Edgar? My next step was to make sure, through assessment, that Edgar was performing at advanced levels and then I could make my recommendations to his parents, his teacher and to Edgar.

Assessing Edgar

The first test I administered to Edgar was a math test called the TEMA-3: Test of Early Mathematics Ability—Third Edition. It is a good test for screening or to see what level a child is at in terms of mathematics. It is also useful in helping guide instruction or showing whether the individual needs more support. The test was easy to give and I found it very clear with the directions. I gave Edgar the test at his home when his mom was there, though she was not in the same room. We sat at the dining room table and I was seated across from Edgar. He seemed pretty relaxed but was taking the test seriously. I started the test with problem #A32, since Edgar was 7 years, 7 months, and 7 days old on the day of the test. The testing went well and Edgar answered almost all of the answers correctly. He missed one occasionally but overall, he did a great job. When I got to problem #A64, he started to get a little tired and he missed a few questions. On problem A66, he looked bored and asked if he could stop now. I said yes and told him he did a great job on the test. The raw score on the test was a 63 that had a grade equivalent of 8-9. Edgar tested in the 91st percentile and his math score ability was 120 out of a range of 117–123. The SEM was 3 and the confidence interval was 68%. The basal was from problems A59–A63. The ceiling was right after that since Edgar wanted to stop testing. I feel Edgar could have probably scored more correctly on the test if we had continued. He is excelling in math and the TEMA-3 test confirmed this. I have confidence in the TEMA-3 test, especially after comparing it with the DIBELS test that I also researched. The TEMA-3 test was not difficult to administer or score at all. It was not confusing like the DIBELS was for me. I also have confidence in the test because research shows the test has internal consistency reliabilities all above .92 and the alternative form reliabilities are in the .80s and .90s (ProEd Inc.com, 2008). The internal consistency reliability was important, since I was giving Edgar the test only one time. I believe I will use this assessment test when I am a teacher because of its ease and reliability.

The second test I administered to Edgar on a different day was a performance test. I was trying to see whether Edgar had good comprehension skills, since his mom told me he was a good reader. Edgar was currently reading the chapter book called *Mr. Popper's Penguins* by Richard and Florence Atwater. The book has 139 pages and is written for children ages 9–12. Edgar had read up to chapter 7 already. I asked him to read chapter 8 to me, which he did. The chapter was six and a half pages long and Edgar read it in 7 minutes 22 seconds, which I thought was pretty fast for his age. He read very well and had trouble with only a few big words, but was good at sounding them out. I asked him several questions relating to the chapter like, "Was Captain Cook (the penguin) happy to be on a leash?" and "What was Mrs. Callahan's response when she saw the penguin and why?" Edgar was able to answer all of my questions correctly. I was pleased to find that not only was Edgar reading above his grade level but that he was also comprehending what he read.

Recommendations

Through observation, standardized testing, and performance testing, I have found that Edgar is performing above grade level in both reading and mathematics. Edgar was given the TEMA-3 and scored in the 91st percentile and almost reached the nine-year-old level of ability. Thus, he seems capable of performing well above grade level. In reading, Edgar was given a performance test to evaluate comprehension. Edgar did very well on the assessment and is reading above grade level. He did a fine job comprehending a book that typically 9–12 year olds read. Although Edgar is very happy with school and his progress so far, there is a little concern that he may need more challenging work. Because Edgar finishes class work quickly, he then works on math or reading packets. These are good supplements, but I would recommend that Edgar be given a few more options of activities/work. Edgar has expressed that he likes the computer and would be interested in computer activities. There are many fun, worthwhile activities online that enhance learning. Some popular sites are http://www.brainpop.com, http:/kids.nationalgeographic.com, and http://www.coolmath.com. In addition to computer activities, Edgar could read books in class that he has chosen and then write a book report or do some writing activity that would measure comprehension and improve writing skills. Edgar could also work on his penmanship at this time, since that is one area of weakness for him. I think giving some choices to Edgar for "extra" work could greatly add to his love of school and learning.

Summary/Recommendations to Edgar's Parents

After observation and testing, I have found that Edgar is performing above grade level in both reading and mathematics. He is just under a nine-year-old level of ability for math and his reading ability is also above grade level. He is doing well comprehending books that typical nine- to twelve-year-olds would read. Although Edgar is enjoying school and happy at this point, I would recommend that Edgar have additional choices at school when he finishes his class work. Computer time would be a good option, since Edgar has said he likes the computer. There are many wonderful sites that Edgar could access that will enhance learning, such as http://www.brainpop.com, http:/kids.nationalgeographic.com, and http://www.coolmath.com. In addition, I recommend that Edgar bring books from home to read in class. He could then do some written activities that could show comprehension while also improving his penmanship skills. At home, I would offer Edgar these same choices of activities and whatever else you would feel could enhance Edgar's learning. I would also watch Edgar when he does homework and make sure that he is not speeding through it too fast so that his writing suffers. The goal should be for Edgar to continue progressing in school while giving him choices of activities he would enjoy that he can work on after he is finished with his regular work. This will foster Edgar's love for school and also enhance his learning at the same time. You might also encourage investigation of non-fiction topics at the library—e.g., "Would you like to learn more about 'real' penguins?" and so on.

CHILD STUDY 10

David McMillan, 4 years old

Background Information

David McMillan is a four-year-old male who is in good physical condition. He is tall and big for his age; bright and inquisitive. He is knowledgeable about neighborhood locations such as the library, parks, and the children's museum. David also loves to read books, play outside, and go to Little Gym. His favorite season is fall because he loves the color orange.

David and his family live in an upper-middle-class suburb outside of Denver. David's parents own and run two small businesses in their neighborhood. David's father works full-time and travels for business at least once a month. David's mother works part-time and has a nanny who comes in two or three days a week. David is the youngest of three boys. Chad is 10 years old and is in the fourth grade, and Bruce is 8 years old and is in the second grade. Bruce has an IEP for a behavioral issue. Bruce has a hard time dealing with his emotions. Often Bruce is set off by little interactions with other people. He gets overwhelmed easily and usually needs time alone before he can calm down and talk about what upset him. Chad has no developmental or behavioral issues. David exhibits some separation anxiety, especially when his routine or schedule has been interrupted. For example, when David's father leaves for business trips, David latches on to his father and won't let him go. He also cries, screams, and sometimes hyperventilates. David is not receptive to others helping him while his father is still in the house. Once his father leaves, David returns to his normal state in a matter of minutes. Another instance of David's anxiety occurs in the beginning of this past school year: David would not let his mom leave after dropping him off at preschool. Mrs. McMillan stated that he often cries when there is a break in his routine.

To the best of my knowledge, David has no medical circumstances during birth or hospitalizations and injuries. David seems delayed in hand and finger skills. He is unable to draw circles or squares. He also has difficulty holding a pencil correctly. For example, he will hold his pencil while making a fist. He also has a difficult time communicating with other children. He goes to Gym for Fun once a week, and his class is very small. One of his friends also attends the same class and often times David will not immediately talk to his friend or want to leave me, the teacher assistant at the preschool, to go play with his friend before class starts. However, once the class begins, he will play with his friend. David is on track in other developmental milestones such as cognitive skills, movement, language, social, and emotion.

David is preparing to go to preschool five days a week next year; he goes three days this year. He is on track in several of the developmental milestones. David is able to tell stories, he is able to count to 10, and he engages in fantasy play. David also understands the concept of time; however, he still does not understand the order of days. In language, David is able to form sentences and questions using five to six words, using articulate speech. Emotionally David views himself as a whole person. When he plays by himself he usually creates different voices for his imaginary characters. Some concerns observed in David's behaviors are ignoring other children, clingy behavior around parents, cannot draw circles or squares, and cannot grasp pencils/crayons between thumb and fingers.

Test Administration and Learner's Behavior

The Bracken Basic Concept Scale-Expressive (BBCS-E) is a test that evaluates children's basic concept development. The test has 10 subtests/categories that are assessed. These include Colors, Letters/Sounds, Numbers/Counting, Sizes/Comparisons, Shapes, Direction/Position, Self-/Social Awareness, Texture/Material, Quantity, and Time/Sequence. The first five subtests assess a School Readiness Composite (SRC), and educational concepts children need to know in order to be ready for an early formal education. The test was created to assess children ages 3–6 years old. The results of the assessment can used by early education teachers, speech pathologists, and psychologists to determine and assist in identifying language impairments, curriculum interventions, identifying concepts the child has not obtained, and determining whether the child has acquired the basics concepts for school readiness. The purpose for this assessment is to determine David's school readiness and to find areas for improvement.

The BBCS-E was administered at the library in two 15-minute sessions. David and I sat on the same side of the desk looking directly at the BBCS-E flip book. The first session administered the first five subtests to determine the SRC score. The second session administered the last five subtests. I initially intended to test David in one 30-minute session, but I observed his behavior throughout the test and decided to have another session at a later time. I work with David and am familiar with his abilities. There was one point in the assessment where he needed to count and tell me the number. I know he can count to at least 10, but I could tell he was getting tired and carelessly counted the items. Also, I could tell that David was losing patience as the test items got more difficult. The second session was also conducted at the library. I noticed the same behaviors as the first session, where David would lose interest in more difficult items and tired easily with answering questions. However, we were able to complete all of the subtests.

Recommendations and Summarization for Stakeholders

Teacher

For the SRC (subtests 1–5), David scored a raw score of 50. The SRC consists of colors, letters/sounds, numbers/counting, sizes/comparisons, and shapes. The descriptive classification of this score places David at a very advanced level. For this section, he is at a concept age level of 5 years and 6 months. David is knowledgeable in these categories. I would recommend working on sizes/comparisons, and three dimensional shapes such as cubes, pyramids, etc. On subtests 6–8, David's scores reflected a descriptive classification as average. The concept age level ranged from 3 years and 3 months to 4 years and 1 month. David needs improvement in textures/materials, and social awareness. David did very well in the category of direction/position. I would recommend extending his knowledge with more difficult directions and positions such as rising/falling, around/through, and alone/together. I would also work with David on distinguishing between emotions such as smiling/frowning/laughing. In subtests 9–10, David scored a descriptive classification as delayed. His concept age for this section reflected a score of 3 years and 0 months. David did not understand quantity and time/sequence concepts easily. He was not able to set a basal starting point for both of these two subtests. I would recommend working on these two categories to improve his knowledge in these two concept areas. Overall, David is on track in most of the subtests. I would start next year working on extending on knowledge in subtests 6–8, and developing concepts in quantity, and time/sequences. I would create learning centers where David and other children can explore different textures, as well as quantities and time/sequences.

Parent

Mr. and Mrs. McMillan, David completed the Bracken Basic Concept Scale assessment. He did very well in the following categories: colors, numbers/counting, letters/sounds, sizes/comparisons, and shapes. He demonstrated that he is knowledgeable and comfortable with these concepts. Some areas for improvement include distinguishing between different textures, quantities, and time/sequence. My recommendations for next year's teacher included extending on the knowledge he is comfortable with. I also recommended that next year's teacher create some new learning centers to help him in these areas. For example, he is very good with two-dimensional shapes; the next step would be to work on three-dimensional shapes. When David is not in school, I would recommend taking him to the library to get picture books on three-dimensional shapes. Or, if you are able to get three-dimensional block shape toys and label them, it would help David understand the differences between a triangle and a pyramid. You can also play games with him at home to help him understand sequences.

For example, you can line up some of his toys and create labels that state: first, middle/in-between, and last. Next, show him the sequence of where those labels should be placed, then have him try it. I know that David is capable of learning these concepts; he will just need exposure and encouragement to develop these skills.

I found the results to be accurate. I have worked with David for the past year and knew some of his strengths and weaknesses, but the assessment clarified and pinpointed areas where he is lacking. If I were his teacher, this assessment would be beneficial in planning instruction and tracking achievement.

Bracken, B. (2006). *Bracken Basic Concept Scale-Expressive: Examiner's Manual.* PyschCorp: San Antonio, Texas.

Questions to Consider

1. Are you worried about David's social/emotional progress? If so, how might you support development?
2. What might you do to facilitate fine-motor skills?

CHILD STUDY 11

Joy Cross, a First Grader

The child being studied is Joy Cross. She is seven years old and was born in Charleston, South Carolina. Joy is the older of two girls in her family. She is of average height and weight with straight sandy blonde hair and tanned skin. Joy is sometimes shy, but upon getting to know her, she is quite vibrant and bubbly. Joy likes humor and uses her sharp wit as a way of joking with peers and family. After observation of Joy with her family, it is clear that she learned her sharp wit from her parents, as they use it frequently with each other and their children. This humor seems to translate well into her friendships in class. Joy is considered one of the girls everyone wants as a friend, and she has had no problems with other students in school. Joy attends gymnastics and swim classes on a weekly basis. Her grandparents are a big part of her life and she sees them at least twice a week. Joy is interested in popular culture and her parents limit the amount of television she watches each day. She is allowed to watch only children's shows on public television.

Questions, Concerns, Problems

Academically, I believe Joy to be exactly where she is supposed to be, if not slightly above average for her age and grade level. However, her parents have shown concern for Joy's recalcitrant behavior when it comes to homework. Mrs. Cross says she must bribe Joy to do her homework and has to battle with her on a nightly basis. Currently this behavior is being seen only at home and not in school. My suggestion is that Mr. and Mrs. Cross work together with Joy and her teacher to resolve the homework issue before Joy begins the second grade, as homework will be more challenging then. The good news is that Joy can do the work. Her grades in class show that she is quite capable.

Family Background

Joy comes from a middle-class family; Mr. Cross works full-time and Mrs. Cross stays at home full-time. Joy's younger sister, Ellen, is four years old. Joy has never been hospitalized, nor has she sustained any significant injuries. Mrs. Cross said that Joy passed all the normal developmental milestones at the appropriate times. There are no known family problems or concerns.

The only unusual aspect of Joy's family life is the fact that the whole family sleeps "family-style" in one bed. This is a practice some parents follow to strengthen the family bond. Joy has never spent a night away from her family. Joy's family is also vegetarian. Her parents make it a point to buy and eat locally grown organic foods and use locally made organic products. Mrs. Cross insists on knowing what type of cleaning materials and pesticides are used at the school and on the school grounds outside.

Current Functioning

Joy functions very well as a seven-year-old girl preparing to enter the second grade. She uses facial expressions a great deal to convey emotion. Joy tends to let her emotions take over when she fails to get her way and this is something her parents say they are working to resolve. Joy has temper tantrums at home, but not at school. Mr. and Mrs. Cross are evaluating their home rules and will be addressing the issue of control over emotions and feelings along with appropriate reactions to situations in which Joy does not get her way.

Joy is good at problem-solving, but seeks approval of her actions from adults before she can put her ideas into action. Joy does not seem self-confident at home or at school. According to Mr. and Mrs. Cross, she acts immature at home and she does not use words to communicate feelings. Mrs. Cross says she is bossy toward her family and is often disrespectful. Joy's teacher does not notice any signs of disrespect in the classroom or among Joy and her peers. Taking turns, following routines and obeying directions are all strong areas for Joy in school. However, at home Joy is said to be quite different. Mrs. Cross says she becomes extremely argumentative and challenges authority at every turn. Because this is not happening at school, I wonder if parenting issues can explain in large part why it is happening at home and not in school.

Because of the attitude Joy is said to display at home I suggest that Joy's future teachers have a strong hold on the rules and classroom environment. Joy, as most students, seems to do well when rules and expectations are clearly laid out from the start, as they were in her current first grade classroom.

The Test

Joy Cross was given the TEMA-3 (Test of Early Mathematics Ability—Third Edition). She appeared to have no test anxiety or apprehension and took the test with ease, eagerly awaiting the end when she could go out and play! Joy scored well on the TEMA-3, with a raw score of 63, an age equivalent of 8-9, a grade equivalent of 3.7, and a math ability score of 121. Joy scored in the 92nd percentile.

The reason Joy was picked for this math assessment was because her parents were concerned about the math instruction at her school. Joy goes to a Spanish magnet school, in which half of the day is taught in Spanish. Math instruction in Joy's school is done only in Spanish. Mr. and Mrs. Cross expressed concern that she would not be able to apply math skills in English, but the results of the TEMA-3 demonstrate that she is doing well. The TEMA-3 was conducted in English, not Spanish, and Joy had no problem with the wording of the test, even though it was not in the same language used for her math instruction. Joy was strong in most of the areas in which a first grader should be strong and answered the majority of the items correctly. Joy did not know multiplication and was not as strong in mental number line of three- and four-digit numbers. Also, I noticed the items that involved money took Joy longer to compute in her head.

Once we moved to the mental subtraction, Joy mentally checked out of the test. She stated that she wanted to pass and grew quite antsy. Joy's younger sister was outside and the neighborhood children had all gathered in the back yard. We stopped the test at item 64. I believe that Joy could have gone further, but it was apparent that her attention was being drawn outside on a beautiful day.

Summary for Joy's Teacher

(A) ***What areas of learning strength did you discover? What are the child's relative weaknesses?*** Joy seems to be strong in math abilities. Mental math in the single and double digits is extremely quick. Joy did not have to think for long to do any of the addition facts up to 9 or the counting by 2s and 10s. Joy had to put more thought into answering the questions about the three- and four-digit mental number line and missed a few. I noticed Joy's hesitation when I asked her item B57, which was adding multiples of 10, but in terms of money. Joy did fine on adding multiples of 10 previously, but when I added the words "dollar bill" to the mix, it took her longer to compute. The same observation was made during item B64 when she had to subtract multiples of $10 bills. Having worked with Joy previously with money, I know that she is neither interested in nor comfortable using it and is not as strong with money sense as she is with other areas of math.

(B) ***What instructional implications can be drawn from these testing data? Where should the teacher "begin," in your estimation?*** After going over the results of this assessment, I believe that Joy is ready for the second grade and has mastered the majority of first-grade math skills. I would make sure to give Joy extra instruction with money and with three- and four-digit number sense. I also would ask her parents to work closely with her on money and set up a steady stream of communication about her progress over the summer and during the school year. Because Joy enjoys doing so many things well, looking for the little details of her weaknesses and setting a goal to work on them in school and at home will ensure her further success in math. Joy loves to go to the mall and shop. I believe planning lessons with "shopping" in them will motivate Joy to practice using money and making change.

(C) ***Tests scores and the interpretation of these scores.*** Joy had a raw score of 63 on the TEMA-3 form B. Her age equivalent was 8-9 and her grade equivalent was 3.7. Her math ability score was 121 and she scored in the 92nd percentile. Joy is performing above the average level of mathematical ability for children her age. Joy did well on the TEMA-3 and has mastered her first-grade math skills.

Questions to Consider

1. What recommendations do you have for the second-grade teacher regarding homework plans for Joy? What factors might be contributing to Joy's current difficulties with homework?
2. Do you have other suggestions for fostering knowledge and skill with money?

CHILD STUDY 12

Timothy Callaghan, Assessing Motor Skills of a Four-Year-Old

Background

Timothy was chosen to participate in the Inventory of Early Development II to determine whether his motor skills are being appropriately supported by his school and at home. Timothy's parents, Anita and Louis, were concerned that tasks presented to him were below his zone of proximal development and that he was not being challenged to improve motor skills. Based on observations, Timothy's parents believed that his motor skills were more advanced than those of peers.

At a private school in Atlanta, Timothy is one of the oldest students in his class. Teachers emphasize motor skills most relevant for children ages 3-0 to 3-11. Timothy has adjusted well to the school environment. He has a twin brother, Trevor, who goes to school with him, and they spend most of their time together. Timothy's social skills with other students are also very good. Timothy willingly and eagerly participates in class learning and play activities and displays excellent communication and thinking/reasoning skills. For example, after a story, Timothy is able to answer "why" questions posed by the teacher.

Timothy has control of many daily living skills, such as dressing himself, using the restroom, and feeding himself. His current functioning shows no sign for concern, and there is no evidence of developmental delay in his medical history. Timothy's body movements are fluid and purposeful.

Timothy and Trevor have one older brother, Brendan (6 years old), and one younger sister, Amyra (2 years old). The family lives in an upper-middle-class neighborhood. Timothy does have some separation issues from his family and sometimes brings a pacifier to class to calm himself.

Referral Query

Do the motor tasks presented to Timothy—at school and at home—fall within his zone of proximal development, and do they challenge him to improve?

Tests Administered

BRIGANCE® Inventory of Early Development-II (IED-II); Motor Domain

Environmental conditions were taken into consideration before performing the assessment. The IED-II was administered early in the day so that Timothy would be refreshed (Standardization and Validation Manual, pp. 18–19). Sub-domains of the IED-II were presented to Timothy as "games" rather than tests. The assessment was administered in a quiet hallway outside of Timothy's classroom. For familiarity, we used a desk from the classroom during the assessment. During administration of the Fine Motor domain of the IED-II, we used paper from his classroom, with which he was familiar to ensure more accurate results. As recommended by the Standardization and Validation Manual (pp. 18–19), rapport was created to remove anxiety. Stickers were also utilized as rewards and wiggle breaks were given to bring back focus.

According to IED-II test administration guidelines, examiners are not expected or encouraged to assess all areas of the IED-II comprehensively in a single session. Rather, professional judgment should be used to select the most relevant skill area(s) for assessment and to consider the appropriate length for each child's assessment. In light of this, the Motor developmental domain was administered to Timothy during his testing session, which lasted approximately 45 minutes. The Motor domain includes the sub-domains of Fine Motor and Gross Motor skills. The standardized version of the IED-II was administered to determine how Timothy's motor skills scored relative to his peers.

Test Results

Subtest/Domain	Quotient		Percentile	Age-Equivalent Range (in months)
Total Fine Motor	119–122		90–33%	58–60
Nonlocomotor		83–102	13–55%	41–43
Locomotor		89–103	23–58%	38–44
Total Gross Motor	92–100		29–50%	43–46
TOTAL MOTOR DOMAIN	114–122		82–93%	58–59

All scores are provided with a 90% confidence rating.

Behavioral Observations

Timothy was eager to participate in the assessment process. He entered the assessment with his typical outgoing, mischievous, and active personality. He was willing to take risks and needed little encouragement to take on difficult tasks or guess when the answer was unknown. During testing, he was eager to participate in the gross motor tasks and enjoyed that he was able to get up and move. Despite showing some anxiety, he even tried to walk heel-to-toe without encouragement. Timothy also was eager to write his name. However, when it came to writing letters or numbers that he did not know, he needed some encouragement to try.

Result Interpretation for Teacher and Parent

Fine motor skills are strong for Timothy within the Motor skills domain. He was able to stack nine one-inch cubes, copy basic and more advanced shapes such as a circle and a square, and he was also able to hold a pencil correctly and consistently with his right hand. He was proud of drawing a person with a head (including ears, eyes, a nose, and a mouth), legs, arms, and hands. He was able to write his name unquestionably, and the sequence of letters was correct. Timothy was able to write the numbers one through six, but many of these numbers—2, 3, 4, 5, and 6—were reversed and/or sideways. He was also able to write the first three letters of the alphabet *A*, *B*, and *C*—the *C* reversed.

Timothy's results indicate that he performs the above-mentioned fine-motor tasks better than 90%–93% of his peers in the standardized sample. His quotient scores range from 119–122, demonstrating that his fine-motor skills are above average to superior. These scores are reported with a 90% confidence rating. For fine-motor skills, Timothy's instructional range or zone of proximal development includes tasks for children ages 4-10 to 5-0. Fine motor tasks at the 4-10 age equivalence should be easily accomplished; skills at the 5-10 level would be at Timothy's frustration level.

Gross-motor tasks were a relative weakness for Timothy within the Motor skills domain. Timothy was able to stand on one foot for five seconds, and he was able to stand on one foot with his eyes closed for a few seconds. However, he was unable to do either task with his other foot. He hopped on one foot for more than two hops and was able to do the same for the other foot. He was able to jump backward on both feet for two consecutive jumps but was unable to jump backward for five consecutive jumps. Timothy ran fluidly with symmetrical motions and was able to start and stop on command. He walked backward four steps and was able to walk on his tiptoes for four steps. He is not yet able to walk heel-and-toe. Timothy was able to walk up and down stairs with alternating feet while holding the rail.

Timothy performed the gross motor tasks mentioned above better than 29%–50% of his age group in the standardized sample. His quotient score range 92–100 indicates that his gross-motor skills are average. These scores are reported with a 90% confidence rating. Currently, Timothy's zone of proximal development for gross motor tasks is age 3-7 to 3-10.

Overall, Timothy's results for the Motor domain—combining Fine Motor results with Gross Motor results—show that he performed better than 82%–93% of his peers in the standardized sample. The Motor domain quotient ranging from 114–122 shows that his combined motor skills are above-average to superior. These results are reported with 90% confidence. Timothy's zone of proximal development for motor skills is 4-10 to 4-11.

Instructional Implications

To continue to advance Timothy's current above average to superior performance on motor skills, it is important to remain focused on fostering both his fine-motor skills and gross-motor skills at and slightly above his current level of achievement. By using his zone of proximal development in both sub-domains—as reported in the IED-II score sheet, Timothy is able to stay in his current classroom and his teacher can continue to develop his motor skills in a more efficient and focused manner.

The following recommendations were drawn from the criterion-referenced portion of the IED-II. Skills sequences were selected at and slightly above Timothy's current level of achievement (IED-II Standardization and Validation Manual, p. 51).

Fine-Motor Skill Recommendations

- Allow ready access and free time to work with inset puzzles of 13 to 16 pieces and then 17 to 20 pieces (Evaluation Binder, p. 68).
- Allow ready access and free time to work with puzzles (not inset) with 9 to 12 pieces and then 13 to 25 pieces (Evaluation Binder, p. 68).
- When painting, encourage Timothy to focus on the process rather than just the end product (Evaluation Binder, p. 68).

- When painting, encourage Timothy to evaluate and criticize his own painting (Evaluation Binder, p. 68).
- Provide access to clay and encourage Timothy to make refined objects that are recognizable by others (Evaluation Binder, p. 68).

Gross-Motor Skill Recommendations

- Provide opportunities to play with a ball. Encourage Timothy to bounce the ball once and catch it with both hands (Evaluation Binder, p. 44).
- Provide opportunities to play with a ball. Encourage Timothy to bounce the ball two or more times with both hands (Evaluation Binder, p. 44).
- Allow Timothy to practice swinging at a stationary ball. Ask him to stand to the side of the ball and swing in a horizontal plane (Evaluation Binder, p. 44).
- Allow Timothy to practice swinging at a stationary ball. Have him practice swinging by rotating his trunk and hips and shifting body weight forward (Evaluation Binder, p. 44).
- Play music for Timothy and ask him to move separate body parts to the music (Evaluation Binder, p. 44).
- Play music for Timothy and ask him to walk in rhythm to the music (Evaluation Binder, p. 44).
- Provide access to a tricycle. Encourage Timothy to pedal the tricycle around a corner or obstacles (Evaluation Binder, p. 44).
- Provide access to a wagon. Encourage Timothy to ride and steer the wagon with one foot (Evaluation Binder, p. 44).
- Have Timothy practice performing a basic forward roll (Evaluation Binder, p. 44).
- Ask Timothy to practice spinning in a circle on one foot (Evaluation Binder, p. 44).

Interpretation of Results for Timothy's Parent(s)

The IED-II assessed Timothy's fine-motor and gross-motor skills. Fine-motor skills are skills that "require the use of hands and fingers in grasping and manipulating" such as stacking blocks or writing (Evaluation Binder, p. 45). Gross-motor skills are skills "required to move the body effectively and efficiently within the environment (Evaluation Binder, p. 17). Gross-motor skills include capabilities such as coordination, speed, agility, power or strength, and balance and are used in tasks such as running, hopping on one foot, and climbing stairs (Evaluation Binder, p. 17).

IED-II Developmental Profile

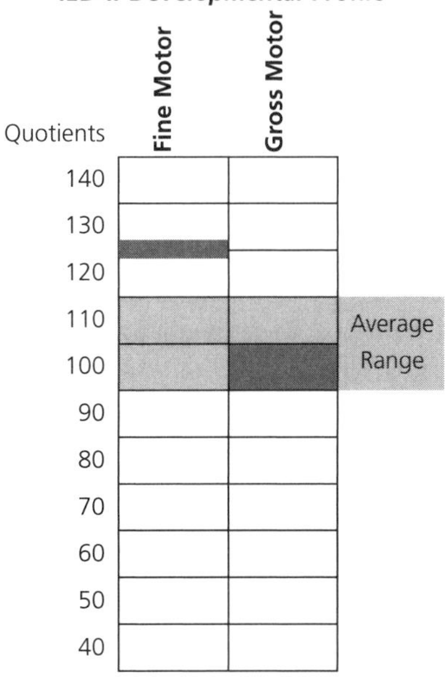

Fine-motor tasks are strong for Timothy. The results indicate that he performed better than 90%–93% of children his age on tasks such as writing and drawing. Timothy's quotient results are considered above-average to superior for his age (refer to chart). Timothy performed better than 29%–50% of his age group on gross-motor tasks such as hopping on one foot and walking heel-to-toe. His quotient results are considered average for his age (refer to chart).

Overall, Timothy's combined results (in the Fine Motor and Gross Motor sub-domains) show that he performed better than 82%–93% of his peers. These results are considered average to superior.

At home, you can encourage Timothy's fine- and gross-motor skills growth by providing opportunities for him to play with puzzles, write, and draw. To work on his gross-motor skills, Timothy can play sports, dance, or do an obstacle course.

References

Brigance, A., & Glascoe, F. (1978, 1978–2004). BRIGANCE® Diagnostic Inventory of Early Development-II Evaluation Binder. North Billerica, MA: Curriculum Associates, Inc.

Brigance, A., & Glascoe, F. (1978, 1978–2004). BRIGANCE® Diagnostic Inventory of Early Development-II. Retrieved March 2, 2009, from Mental Measurements Yearbook database.

Brigance, A., & Glascoe, F. (n.d.). BRIGANCE® Diagnostic Inventory of Early Development-II. Retrieved March 2, 2009, from Tests in Print database.

Brigance, A., & Glascoe, F. (1978, 1978–2004). BRIGANCE® Diagnostic Inventory of Early Development-II Standardization and Validation Manual. North Billerica, MA: Curriculum Associates, Inc.

Questions to Consider

1. Are you concerned about Timothy's social/emotional adjustment? How might you assess?
2. What plans would you make to facilitate handwriting skills for Timothy?
3. Why do you think Timothy's family is concerned about motor development? What questions might you ask to elucidate and understand their concern?

CHILD STUDY 13

Marilyn Jones, at Kindergarten Screening

Marilyn is a five-year-old African American kindergarten student who is currently enrolled at a small, private Catholic elementary school in Chicago. She was exactly 5 years and 2 months at the time of the test administration. Marilyn comes from a middle-class family that lives in the southern city limits of Chicago. Mr. & Mrs. Jones have been divorced for approximately three years and Marilyn is the younger of two children, with an older sister, Eloise, who is currently in the fourth grade. Marilyn spends the majority of her time living with her mother and sees her father every other weekend. Marilyn's schooling prior to kindergarten was at a child-care center. Marilyn appears to be within average height and weight for her age group. She has an enthusiastic personality and loves to smile. She is also descriptive in her oral language expressions and emotions. Marilyn is affectionate with teachers and other adults and is extremely sensitive. Marilyn does not socialize with peers as often as other children and tends to choose independent activities that she can perform alone. Marilyn interacts with her peers when other children approach her; she rarely seeks out others. In times that she does interact with her peers, she is empathetic to them. Marilyn also tends to be introverted and shy in uncertain situations.

Test

For this child study, I chose to administer the Early Screening Inventory-Revised (ESI-R) test. The ESI-R is a developmental screening instrument that is individually administered to children between three and six years of age. Marilyn was given the kindergarten version of the test for students between four-and-a-half and six years old. This test is designed to identify children who may need further evaluation to determine if they require special education services. This test is only used to identify the *possibility* of a learning condition that would affect the child's overall potential success in school. The test includes three sections: visual motor and adaptive, language and cognition, and a gross motor evaluation. There is also a supplement parent questionnaire, but I was unable to receive that information from Marilyn's parents.

Why Marilyn?

Marilyn was chosen for this evaluation because of her consistent tendency to perform all activities slowly. In observation, from eating her lunch to putting a box of toys away, Marilyn is often distracted, sometimes is unaware of what is going on around her, and is always one of the last children to finish. She is constantly being reminded to keep moving. She is also slow with hand writing, and other classroom projects.

Marilyn's extreme sensitivity to when things don't go perfectly for her is concerning. Marilyn works very hard on her work, but if it is not exactly how she wants it, she tends to emotionally fall apart. The shy traits, lack of seeking out peers to play with, and tendency to not want to participate in certain social activities was another observable behavior that made me curious in determining how her development was progressing.

The final reason why Marilyn was selected for this evaluation was due to her ability to already read almost fluently. She can phonetically spell out words, and when she writes upper- and lower-case letters, she is correct most of the time. Ironically, though the letters are usually correct, numbers are often transposed and written incorrectly. This made me wonder if there were a delay in number understanding.

Test Conditions

The ESI-R test was conducted in Marilyn's regular classroom after school. The room was quiet with no other children around, which I expected to have no distractions, but Marilyn had trouble focusing at first because she wanted to show me a painting she had done that day, her weekly classroom job, and the Flat Stanley map her class was creating. The test was administered at a round table where I sat next to Marilyn and had her perform the various tasks. Marilyn was given a snack prior to the taking the test. The test began at 2:30 and ended around 3:00.

Learner's Behavior During Testing

It took Marilyn a few moments to focus her attention on me, sitting in her chair without squirming, and listening to my directions. Once the building blocks activity began, Marilyn suddenly became engaged, because she thought the test was a fun game. Overall, Marilyn was cooperative and seemed to enjoy participating in the screening. She was talkative during the test and said things like, "Is this a special project just for me?" and often commented with, "This is fun!" She also said, "Oh that's so easy," when she knew how do the activities I asked her to perform. I was concerned Marilyn would be tired after a long day of school, but she did not seem affected by that at all.

Results

(A) ***Visual Motor/Adaptive Skills*** Marilyn was able to build with the blocks easily and almost constructed the gate building perfectly and constructed it perfectly after she copied it from the model. Drawings were accurate, except when she had to draw a cross. Short-term memory in the visual section with the picture cards was easy for Marilyn.

(B) ***Language and Cognition*** In the verbal expression activity, Marilyn easily discerned the pattern of naming the objects, giving the colors and shapes. She was incredibly expressive and had a lot to say about each one. Marilyn could not count to 10, but was able to count five blocks. She also accurately answered three out of the four verbal reasoning sentences. Marilyn showed that she has no problem with her auditory sequential memory, as she easily relayed three-digit number series back to me.

(C) ***Gross Motor*** The gross-motor tests gave Marilyn no trouble at all. She was able to skip in a consistent pattern, hop on each foot, and keep her balance on each foot for 10 seconds.

Overall, Marilyn scored a 23 on the ESI-R test for kindergarten-age students. In the ESI-R kindergarten test, there are three subgroups for ages 4.6–4.11, 5.0–5.5, 5.6–5.11. The score range for Marilyn's age required her to score 18 or higher to be considered OK, which she easily achieved. If Marilyn had scored between 14 and 17, she would have been in the referral category that requires readministration in two weeks of the same ESI-R test. If she scored 13 or less, then she would have been referred for more testing to see whether she would require special education assistance.

Teacher

According to the test results, Marilyn is at a level that is developmentally appropriate for her age. There is no need for further testing for Marilyn. She has proven that she is not at risk for special education modifications, based on this screening inventory at this point in time. Her fine- and gross-motor skills are at age expectation. Marilyn's visual motor and adaptive skills are incredibly strong, verbal language is expressive, and vocabulary is well advanced for her age. Marilyn can already read and is beyond age peers in word recognition. She should be faced with reading challenges to increase fluency and begin strengthening her comprehension.

From observation, Marilyn could use additional opportunities to expand cognitive skills in number concept and counting abilities. She had trouble counting 10 blocks, but could easily count five for me. Based on observation, even though there was not a portion of the test that evaluated her handwriting, I would also practice correct transformation of numbers when Marilyn writes, since she has a tendency to confuse her numbers and write them backward. Marilyn makes minor articulation errors, which should be monitored throughout the school year to make sure that her phonological development continues. I expect her speech pattern to adjust as she develops throughout kindergarten.

Due to observed behavior, Marilyn should also be given more opportunities to socialize with her peers and be exposed to language modeling to help with articulation errors. Even though Marilyn is expressive, she communicates with adults more easily than children. Becauseacceptable range for her age group in this ESI-R test, her performance is without concern and I expect her to continue in her academic development and performance with further exposure to kindergarten.

Meisels, S., Marsden, D., Wiske, M., & Henderson, L. (2003). *Early Screening Inventory-Revised.* New York: Pearson.

Questions to Consider

1. What specific ideas can you suggest for Marilyn's teacher to scaffold speedier work completion?
2. Are you worried about the way numbers are formed? If so, what might you do to help Marilyn?
3. How can you help Marilyn make friends in class?

CHILD STUDY 14

Charles Taylor, a Five-Year-Old

Background

Mary Taylor was 20, unwed, and a college student when Charles was born. Mary and Charles live with Mary's parents in a suburban home. Charles's father is completely out of the picture. Mary has held several minimum wage jobs and now works as a teller at a bank. Charles is her only child.

Based on observations, Mary seems disengaged with her son and appears to see him as more of a responsibility and burden than as an intelligent child. Most of her discussions with him are commands or reprimands, such as "Pick up your toys" or "Go play in another room." I saw little interaction between the two in terms of conversation or game-playing, although on one occasion Charles repeatedly asked for his mom to play T-ball with him. Instead, she directed him to a set of his building blocks in another room while she continued written work of her own.

Mary's parents, Scott and Laura, appear to have taken on more of a nurturing, parental role. Through their influence, Charles has had a traditional childhood; their photo album is full of photos of Charles dressed in Halloween costumes, watching fish at the aquarium, dressed for soccer practice, sitting at a Lakers game, or receiving his first bike. They frequently babysit for Mary, take Charles to child care, make his dinners, and fulfill other daily necessities. Charles is particularly enamored with his grandfather, who he calls "Papa." Scott was the one who took Charles out to play T-ball and reminded him to use good manners. Scott expressed a feeling of being caught in the middle; he knows he isn't Charles's father and doesn't want to impinge on his daughter's parental duties, but on the other hand, he knows that Mary isn't giving Charles what he needs.

Charles will be entering kindergarten in August. Mary applied for Charles to be in a bilingual program where he learns Spanish and English. She explained that Charles's father is Mexican, and she wants to expose Charles to that part of his heritage. She also believes knowing Spanish will make Charles more employable, eventually.

Charles currently attends a full-day child-care program every day. Mary says it is less structured than a typical preschool, but that students are exposed to the alphabet and identifying letters on a daily basis, although she admitted, "I'm not sure all they do."

According to Mary, Charles is extremely social and has many friends in his class. She said she took him to a birthday party last week and all the other moms said how their children talk about Charles frequently and "love him." On one occasion, I observed Charles playing with a female family friend, who was a year younger than him, at his house. Although Charles had never met her before, he immediately began talking to her, showing her his toys, and chasing her around the house. The two connived a way to sneak candy purposefully hidden. The little girl complained at several points that Charles was being "too bossy" and would not let her be the seeker in hide and seek. Mary affirmed that Charles has a hard time sharing and hates to lose a game (and will dramatically pout when that occurs).

Charles shows little shyness around strangers. He is an extremely energetic, gregarious child. Each time, from the moment I walked in the door Charles was trying to pull me outside to play or telling me stories. He has a hard time sitting still and has to be frequently reminded not to run or talk so loudly in the house. Charles is easily excited and shows energy and vitality in his facial expressions; he also motions and uses his hands while talking. Charles can carry conversations with adults, and likes to be included on what's going on, showing a natural curiosity. He understands jokes and demonstrates a good sense of humor. Overall, he seems to be a happy, upbeat, energetic, and humorous child.

Charles does not have a notable medical history (no hospitalizations or significant injuries). Mary was unable to note any early developmental milestones, reinforcing the idea that she is detached from her role as a parent. "I think he was walking early, but I'm not sure what it should have been," she said. Mary says that Charles has an "attention problem. He can't focus." She was worried Charles would be distracted and unable to complete the assessment.

Test Conditions/Learner's Behavior

I administered the test in Charles's home. We sat at the kitchen table and turned the radio off, so it was quiet. I told Charles he was helping me practice to become a teacher and that now was the time to show me how smart he was. I promised him it wouldn't take long and he could play afterward.

Charles was selected for the child study because his family and mine are acquaintances. I selected the Peabody Picture Vocabulary Test Fourth Edition (PPVT4) for Charles, as I was particularly interested in testing one aspect of Charles's readiness for kindergarten.

During the training exercise of the PPVT, Charles intentionally missed the first question. Before I could respond, Charles threw his head back to laugh and said, "I was just kidding!" After explaining why it was important for him to tell me the right answers, he did not try joking again.

As we progressed to the first set of vocabulary words, Charles tried to stop in between each word to tell a story or ask a question. Comments ranged from stories ("It was my birthday last week. See my birthday sign? I had a Superman cake.") to questions ("Are you married?", "Want to move in with us?") to reflections on the vocabulary word ("Tearing. He is tearing the paper."). I frequently had to redirect Charles to the task at hand. I also found that Charles needed frequent affirmation. As per the test instructions, I was not allowed to tell Charles whether he had gotten the question right, which was extremely difficult. Instead, I had to give general affirming statements.

Midway through the test, the novelty of it had worn off and Charles was bored. He slumped in his chair, tried to walk outside, and had to be coaxed to finish. Charles began "pointing" to answers with his nose, wiggling his head around until his nose was above the answer. Mary was sitting in the kitchen also and firmly asked Charles to pay attention.

The test was only supposed to take 10 minutes, but because Charles was so advanced and kept getting answers correct, the test was much longer, around 20–25 minutes. With the PPVT, learners continue to answer sets of questions until they get eight or more errors in a set. If I had been his classroom teacher and aware of his advanced vocabulary, I would have chosen a higher set to begin with. As completed, Charles's basal set was set 4, for children aged 5. But the manual allows test administrators to start testing with a higher set than a child's age if the child is advanced, so test fatigue does not occur. Charles didn't make his first error until set 8.

As I realized how long the test was taking after the first two sets, I tried to move through it more quickly by eliminating some of the chit-chat in between questions. But as it was, near the end of the test Charles was antsy.

After the test was complete, Mary said she was worried that Charles had just randomly given answers toward the end because he wanted it to be over. I had another take. I did notice that in the last set Charles was randomly giving answers, but I felt it was because he did not know the answers, so was just guessing. "What's that?" he asked after nearly every vocabulary word in the last set, before putting his finger on an answer.

Test Results

Charles's raw score was a 125. This was calculated by taking the ceiling item number (the number of the last question in the set where Charles made eight or more mistakes) and subtracting the number of errors total he made on test.

This raw score translated into a standard score of 130, which was determined by following a chart in the back of the test manual. A standard score shows how the learner's score differs from the average. On this test, a standard score of 100 is average. Because Charles received a standard score of 130, that means he is above average.

The standard score can be used to determine a percentile. Charles's percentile score was 98, meaning that he performed as well or better than 98 percent of the children the same age as him.

Charles's normal curve equivalent, or NCE, was a 92. The test manual describes a NCE as a way to "communicate the distance between the examinee's raw score and the average raw score in the normative reference group." NCE are used primarily for government reports, the manual notes.

Charles's stanine was a 9, the highest possible. Stanines, which range from 1 to 9, are a way to group ranges of percentile scores, and can be used as a general descriptor of performance when precision is not needed.

The growth scale value was a 156. This number can be used in the future if Charles is given the same test again to measure change over time.

Using Charles's raw score, an age equivalent and grade equivalent can be calculated. Charles's age equivalent was a 7.6, meaning that he scored the same as the average seven-and-a-half-year old. His grade equivalent was 1.9, meaning that he scored the same as the average first-grader midway through the year.

Stakeholder Summary

Teacher

Charles demonstrates advanced vocabulary knowledge. His standard score of 130 on the Peabody Picture Vocabulary Test places him in the 98 percentile, meaning that he scored as well or better than 98 percent of children his age taking the test. He is in stanine 9, the highest grouping of percentiles. His testing age equivalent (7.6 years) and grade equivalent (1.9) make him about two years advanced compared to his actual age and grade.

The PPVT measures receptive vocabulary. Based on Charles's scores, he will most likely be the most advanced student in the class when it comes to vocabulary. There is a strong relationship between advanced verbal development and reading comprehension, so another one of Charles's strengths most likely will be reading.

Vocabulary acquisition is an important indicator of a child's cognitive development and readiness for formal schooling. In this case, Charles appears primed for kindergarten.

Although the test did not require it, Charles was extremely expressive during the test, often stopping after each word to use it in a sentence or share a story involving the word. This could possibly demonstrate advanced linguistic and expressive ability, although that would have to be formally tested.

Despite his high score on the PPVT, administration of the test indicated some weaknesses. Charles was easily distracted and had difficulty focusing. If Charles is not personally engaged, he quickly loses interest. Also, if he is not challenged he becomes bored. It will be essential for a teacher to keep Charles challenged and engaged, or he has the potential to cause serious behavior problems in the class.

In the classroom, the teacher should read advanced books to Charles, so that he's exposed to new vocabulary and continues to grow his vocabulary knowledge. Vocabulary should be explicitly taught, with Charles's growth measured. The PPVT offers a scoring mechanism for measuring growth. He should be exposed to synonyms, antonyms, and analogies as a way to challenge his vocabulary skills.

The teacher should have extension activities for Charles if he finishes his work early. Charles will distract other students, be out of his seat, and cause disruptions if not properly directed. Hands-on, engaging lessons will keep Charles interested, and he should be provided plenty of mental breaks. He needs encourage and firm reminders to stay focused, and should be rewarded for saying on task.

Parent

At home, you can challenge Charles by reading advanced books to him, stopping frequently to ask him questions about the characters, plot, and new vocabulary. You can also play the synonym game, where you say a word and ask Charles to come up with another word that has the same meaning. Encourage Charles to focus while completing homework and praise him when he is focused.

Questions to Consider

1. What community resources might assist Mary, as a mother?
2. How will you involve Charles's grandparents in school activities?
3. What are the extension activities that you might plan for Charles after he finishes his work?

CHILD STUDY 15

Gerald Sutton, a Kindergartener, Assessed Informally

I assessed Gerald, a five-year-old kindergartener attending private church school in Austin, Texas. Gerald's family lives in the city and appears to come from a middle-class background. Gerald and his mother constitute the family. Gerald's father died of cancer a few years ago. Mrs. Sutton is a Sergeant in the Salvation Army, which means that approximately every four years, she moves to a different location within the county. This is their second year in Austin. Gerald is in a class of approximately 16 students: nine are girls and the rest boys. Gerald's teacher suggested I assess him in language arts/phonemic awareness abilities, as he is still having some difficulties in this area and she thought it would be a good exercise and practice for both of us. Mrs. Apple, the teacher, wanted me to use the materials they used to assess all of their students and provided me with them. I was allowed to change some of the words that were given during the assessment to vary what he has been given before. The assessment isn't solely a published version, but rather a mix of assessment tools used widely across the country. I observed Gerald two separate times, for approximately 30 minutes each time, right after school in the library. I then subsequently observed him one more time to ensure my accuracy. Each of the times I met with Gerald, he appeared to be extremely friendly and very articulate, especially for someone his age. I learned that he loves to be read to, especially books that are of interest to him. Besides books, he enjoyed playing on the computer and phonics videos instead of actually reading himself. When I first began assessing him, he seemed to be a little nervous, stating he wasn't good at taking tests. I assured him that I wasn't testing him but instead was going to ask him a group of questions he is already used to seeing and that there was no right or wrong answer he would be penalized for. This seemed to ease him up a bit and he was ready to get going. By the third visit, he was extremely comfortable and more confident.

To begin my assessment, I started with understanding of phonemic awareness—a series of rhyming patterns. After modeling several examples, I asked Gerald to say either "yes" or "no" if he thought the two words I was saying to him rhymed or not. When I assessed him the first time, I gave him six different word pairs. Overall, I found this to be a bit difficult for him. He was able to recognize the rhyming patterns in words such as cat/hat, pig/wig but struggled with words such as hike/bike and box/fox. On my subsequent visit, I asked him an additional 10 word pairs (listed below). He did significantly better this time versus the previous assessment. I have marked "yes" or "no" next to each pair of words representing whether he correctly answered or not.

Thick	Brick	(Yes)
Pencil	Stencil	(Yes)
Ball	Bat	(Yes)
Ding	Swing	(Yes)
Fox	Box	(Yes, this was one he previously got incorrect)
Lock	Key	(Yes)
Boy	Toy	(Yes)
Pig	Farm	(Yes)
Free	Tree	(Yes)
Hike	Bike	(Yes, this was one he previously got incorrect)

To continue the original assessment, I presented Gerald with a rhyming activity. I started the activity by telling him that I was going to say a word and after I say that word he should say a word to me that rhymes with the word I stated. After modeling a few examples, he was successful at giving me three- and four-letter words that rhymed with the words I was stating. When I said the word cake, he said rake. I said hat. (He said bat.) Man. (He said pan.) Dig. (He said pig.) For wide, (he said dide). Even though dide isn't necessarily a word, he was able to produce for me a word that rhymed with the word said to him.

I then moved on to another rhyming exercise. This time I told him that I was going to say a pair of words that rhymed and his job was to come up with another word that rhymed with the pair of words I stated. His answers are represented below in bold.

1. rack, sack, **dack**
2. pop, hop, **lop**
3. wing, king, **fling**
4. goat, coat, **cat**
5. wide, hide, **dide**
6. bake, lake, **snake**

I gave another rhyming assessment then to see if he would recognize rhyming words if I presented them in a different manner. I told him that I was going to give him a series of four words (listed below), and he should tell me the word that sounded different from the others. He was able to detect the correct answer each time.

mat	hat	**march**	cat
ball	fall	mall	**man**
box	ox	fox	**swim**
man	**fish**	fan	pan
swing	ding	**dog**	thing

I went on to perform an oddity task with Gerald, to see if he was able to detect the beginning and ending sounds of words. I started off by displaying in sets of three picture cards for the word sets (all listed below) on the table and asked him to find the two pictures whose names begin with the same sound. I provided him with some examples to get him started. The picture cards he chose within each set are bolded below:

1. **sun** **sock** fish
2. **mop** sun **man**
3. pig **leaf** **log**
4. **pig** **pan** dog

Next, I assessed phonemic segmentation. I started by saying single words as a whole such as: cat, hat, mat, dog, log, did, and mom. I asked him to first repeat the word as a whole. He did very well on this. After he said the word, I asked him to break it into syllables. I did this by asking him to clap the number of syllables he heard in each word. When doing this, he had a difficult time recognizing syllables. I then told him to break the word into sounds starting with eliminating the first sound he heard. He did an excellent job at this as well. I then explained the difference between the sounds he hears and the syllables and gave him another chance at the words I first presented and he did much better the second time around.

I presented Gerald with a series of picture cards given to me by the teacher. I displayed the picture card set and asked him to find the two pictures whose names began with the same sound.

Some of the sets were: sun/sock/fish, mop/sun/man, pig/leaf/log and pig/pan/dog. He did a very good job recognizing the same initial sounds. After that, I asked him a series of words again and told him to tell me which one out of the bunch did not begin with the same initial consonant sound as the others and he did extremely well and was able to tell me all the word that did not belong.

I then presented him with the same exercise, except the words all ended the same sound; except for one, he again did very well. Some of the pairs I offered to him were: bat/rock/nut, sock/cup/rake, bus/glass/bat, and ten/fan/cup. It took him several times of sounding out each word to hear the ending sound to eventually come up with the correct answer. Even though he was able to detect the correct answer, I found that listening for the ending sound was more challenging for him than listening for the initial sound.

I moved on to assess his phonemic blending awareness. This time I again said six different words but separated the phonemes and asked him to tell me the word I stated. He was able to detect all six words I presented him with. I then gave him same words and asked him to segment the words like I did. He had a more difficult time with this than when I said them but he was able to distinguish once he felt comfortable doing it and saying words in this manner.

Next I gave stated separate words/sounds and asked him to put them together for me. cow/boy, moon/light, blue/berry, etc. He was able to do this very easily and tell me tell me that cow/boy equaled cowboy and moon/light equaled moonlight.

To assess his phonics skills, I laid cards on the table that each had a letter of the alphabet on them. I first went through all the upper- and lower-case letters to see how well he knew how to detect them and he did extremely well being able to recognize them all. Then, I told him that I was going to say a word and I wanted him to grab the card that represented the beginning sound he heard. For instance, when I said cat, he picked up the card displaying the letter "c". For bat, he picked "b". For hike, he picked "h". He did really well with detecting the sound to the appropriate card. I then did the opposite. I pointed to a card and had him tell me a word that began with the sound I pointed to. He was able to come up with correctly sounding words for each card.

Once I completed the previous exercise. I picked up the cards and put them in random order and asked him to name the sounds associated with the card I am presenting. Overall, he did really well with this exercise. However, he got confused with "C" and originally said /S/. With "G" said /J/. With "M" said /W/.

The final assessment I did with Gerald was reviewing concepts about print. I started this assessment using a list of guideline given by the teacher. I asked him to grab a book he felt comfortable reading to me. He chose one of his readers, *The Nap* by Helen Foster (Pearson Publication, 2004). When he brought the book over to me, he knew how to hold the book correctly and knew the front from the back. When I told him to begin reading it to me, he positioned it correctly and immediately stated the title. He then turned to the first page and began reading from left to right. He knew every word in the book and turned the pages at the appropriate times. However, when he pointed along to the words he was reading, he knew where the spaces between the words were, but I noticed he wasn't necessarily pointing to the correct words/sounds at the right times. It then became apparent that he was not truly "reading" the words in the book; instead he had memorized the sounds and patterns of the story. I realized that he chose what textbooks would call a "predictable book." This was a book he read and reread several times and now knows what comes next in the story. He used the storybook's illustrations, wording, and expression to sound like he was indeed reading the story. He used his knowledge of the specific events of the story to help him recall, which appeared to be memorizing to me to help him recall the specific words in the story.

I then decided to choose a book for him, one that he was not familiar with. I chose *Oh Cats* by Nola Buck (Pearson Publishing, 2004). When I told him that I was going to choose the book, he automatically got nervous and doubted his abilities to read it to me. Consistent with the first book, he knew how to handle and navigate through the book. Except this time instead of guiding fluently through the pages he pointed to each word and attempted to sound each word out, since he hadn't mastered the pattern of the book yet. This book gave me a better indication of whether he knew which words were what and where the spaces between words were as well as the punctuation. From what I observed, he did know where the words, spaces, and punctuation were and knew when to move on to the next page. Unlike the other book, he didn't know all of the words but demonstrated he knew the basic concepts of print.

After the reading practice, I gave him a set of flash cards given to me by the teacher, containing some of the common high-frequency words presented in kindergarten. He was able to recognize many of them, like colors, a, am, I, and, the, it, in the, you, and me. I also showed him some cut-outs of cereal boxes and canned goods that would be familiar to him like Cheerios, Frosted Flakes, peanut butter, and so on, and he was able to identify these words.

To end the assessment, I asked him to write anything he would like for me to know about his experience in kindergarten, and he did a very good job. He was able to distinguish between words and spaces and punctuation, even though the spelling wasn't correct. He was able to collect his thoughts and write them down in a manner that was understandable.

Summary

Overall, I felt Gerald did a great job in responding to my questions and evaluations and provided me with a better understanding of how to assess literacy in the early grade levels. He was very able and eager to tackle all of the assessments and challenges I provided him and helped me gain further understanding. I learned from this assessment that Gerald was strong in identifying and recognizing letters, basic words, and sounds; however, he struggled putting all of these concepts together to read. I feel many of his weaknesses were based on a lack of confidence on his part, as it was easier for him to detect when they were standalone questions vs. being asked to read (on-level) print materials. The teacher scored the assessment as number of right answers.

I thought this assessment was in line with others I found when I began to research the one I gave to Gerald. The informal assessment uses a mix of phonics, phonemic awareness, segmentation, and concepts about print to determine a full spectrum of a child's reading skills and level versus using just one of these.

Questions to Consider

1. What family context variables might account for Gerald's hesitant approach to academics?
2. How do you evaluate this informal reading assessment? What might you add? Would you change any of the measures?

CHILD STUDY 16

Bonnie Jackson, in Second Grade with DIBELS

Background Information

Bonnie Jackson is a seven-year-old second grader at a public school in Milwaukee. She is one of the younger children in her class. Bonnie is petite with long blond hair, two new front teeth, and blue eyes. Friendly, sensitive, social, and confident describe her personality. She has no siblings.

Bonnie's parents, Barney and Harriette, are well educated and active in their community. Barney works long hours as an information technology executive. Some of his week is spent working from his home office; otherwise he commutes to an office in the suburbs. Harriette volunteers at Bonnie's school and plans to re-enter the workforce sometime in the next few years. Their large and nicely appointed condo is in an urban neighborhood that is considered to be middle to upper-middle-class.

Bonnie was born in the southern United States, where the family stayed until she was three before relocating to Milwaukee. Bonnie's birth was a normal vaginal delivery with no trauma. When she was eight months old, Bonnie bit her tongue, severing an artery. She was hospitalized for three days. Her tongue was cauterized, which her parents believed for a while may have affected her speech. Last year, Bonnie's first-grade teacher recommended a speech evaluation; however, the result of the evaluation was that Bonnie did not require speech therapy. Harriette has noticed an improvement in speech in the last year. Throughout her young life, Bonnie has appropriately reached emotional, cognitive, physical, social, and developmental milestones.

Described by Harriette as "always having her head in a book," Bonnie is an avid reader at home. She currently is fascinated by the Nancy Drew mystery series, and just finished the first two books in the Harry Potter series. Bonnie enjoys independent play, doing arts and crafts, playing with her dollhouse, or pretend play as an animal or fairy, although she does not enjoy playing "dress-up." Mr. and Mrs. Jackson believe she thrives at independent play because she is an only child. Many of Bonnie's closest playmates in her grade also do not have siblings. She has play dates with these friends several times each month, including sleepovers on occasion. Bonnie uses language well to express her feelings with friends and adults. The Jacksons cancelled their subscription to cable television a few years ago. Bonnie watches very little television on the Internet and plays about 30 minutes of computer games each day. She enjoys watching a movie or two on the weekends.

Earlier in this report it was mentioned that Bonnie is petite. This has caused some frustration for her in social situations. For example, at a winter festival she recently attended with friends, her height was below that required to partake on certain carnival rides. Also, although she is coordinated, many of her friends are faster at running and other sports. Harriette speculates that Bonnie may have hypoglycemia, because she becomes irritable and lethargic when she is hungry and returns to regular, predictable behavior after eating a snack. This is chronic and the Jacksons plan to talk about it with their pediatrician.

The Jacksons take Bonnie to museums at least two times each month. She is enrolled in Girl Scouts and tae kwon do. Last year she was in gymnastics and various art classes, which she also enjoyed. A favorite family activity involves all three of them reading their own books together in the master bedroom's bed, which usually occurs a few times each week.

Bonnie's second-grade teacher, Ms. Delaware is a nationally board-certified teacher with over 25 years of experience. Homework is generally not too great of a challenge for Bonnie; she can usually perform language arts assignments independently and often needs assistance with math assignments. She performs at or above grade level in all subjects.

Observing her recently, I noticed that it took Bonnie some time to transition into the school day. The children entered the classroom, unpacked items, and were prompted to write in their journals. After the Pledge of Allegiance and announcements, Bonnie fiddled with a hair ribbon she found in her desk and looked around for about 10 minutes before opening her journal to write.

The classroom could be described as active and moderately noisy at this time of day. Barney and Harriette have expressed concern over loose classroom management applied by the teacher. For example, there is a lot of activity going on in the room throughout the day, not just in the first hour of the day when I was observing. There is also a student who is loud and often disruptive; he is assigned to a full-time aide.

Bonnie's teacher describes her as a good reader who could do better at spelling if she applied more effort; she considers her to be a B-speller. I read Bonnie's journal with her. It was full of detailed stories of past birthday parties, her cats, a trip to the pizza store, and some math stories. I noticed some misspelled words on every page, although I am not certain this is unusual. Bonnie was eager to have me look through her journal with her. She is generally quiet and cooperative in class, according to my observation and feedback from the teacher. Harriette shared that once or twice each month Bonnie handles frustration at school by crying.

I also observed Bonnie in a tae kwon do class. Here, Bonnie followed all instructions. She looked tired, which is understandable as the class is right after a full school day. Finally, I met with Harriette to learn more about Bonnie's childhood, habits, and routines.

I chose to work with Bonnie because she is a predictable child whom I know well. I chose to administer the DIBELS test because I want to know more about it, having heard a lot about DIBELS from this class and knowing this test is administered to my son. I chose to supplement the evaluation of Bonnie's reading with an Informal Reading Inventory to bring depth to my understanding and analysis of Bonnie as a reader.

The DIBELS Oral Reading Fluency (ORF) and Retell Fluency (RTF) Assessments

On Thursday, February 19, I administered the DIBELS Oral Reading Fluency test to Bonnie. We worked in the school library after school, with permission from the librarian. Harriette said Bonnie was so excited to be chosen to help me become a teacher that she insisted on bringing along a special dress and changing from her school uniform before the test. After changing, she ate a snack of red grapes, goldfish crackers, and a juice box that I brought along, and we spent 10 minutes talking. She shared information about her day and I asked her some questions about her favorite things like animals, her friends, and her cats.

Bonnie was eager to get started with the testing. I performed all tests according to the directions. I prepared for the test by reading the directions at home several times and once minutes prior to meeting with Bonnie. The first reading was titled "Mom's New Job." Bonnie read 140 words with 8 errors for a total score of 132 in the time allowed. For the second reading, titled "My Handprints," Bonnie read 116 words with 5 errors for a score of 111, and for the third reading, "Meals on Wheels," she read 99 words with 9 errors for a score of 90. Bonnie's mean score for the 3 readings is 118 words read in one minute, with 7 errors, for a mean oral reading fluency score of 111 words read in one minute.

Many of the words Bonnie read incorrectly or omitted were "my," "the," and "to." She seemed to get ahead of herself, then get confused and would try to re-read. In the first reading, she missed the word "cereal" the first time but read it correctly later in the passage.

After reading each passage, I quickly recorded the score and performed the Retell fluency test. Bonnie scored 51 on the first test, or 39% of the oral reading score. On the second passage, 39 or 35% of the oral reading score and on the third passage, the retell total was 40 words for 44% of the oral reading score. Her average on the retell fluency is 39%. The directions on the test indicate that most children score around 50% and it is unusual for children who read 40 words in a minute to score under 25% on the Retell Fluency portion of the test. Further, if the Retell Fluency score is under 25%, then the oral reading fluency score alone may not be providing a good indication of the child's overall reading proficiency. There is nothing in the directions to indicate how to interpret a student's status if the score is between 26% and 50%, where Bonnie scored.

Reflections on Administering the DIBELS Assessments

The library was unexpectedly not an appropriate place to administer Bonnie's assessment. We were granted permission to work there; however, the librarian was loud in her discipline to children working on some after-school projects on the computers. I found the atmosphere to be distracting. Bonnie was cooperative, able to stay on task, and cheerful during our entire time working together. She seemed to get tired by the time we read the third passage. I recognize that working together at the end of the school day may have affected her performance. Our total time working together on this day was 45 minutes.

The Oral Retell Fluency assessment was problematic for me. I felt like I was trying to do too many things at once: count the number of words she was saying while discerning if her retell corresponded with the passage. I was also concerned about the stopwatch. It seemed like the experience went by quickly and could be open to mistakes in keeping track of and my interpretation of the score.

Bonnie reads well. As stated earlier, she enjoys reading and chooses to spend much of her free time with books. Based on her mean score of 111, her oral fluency exceeds the benchmark goal set forth for second graders in the spring, which is a score of 90. Her reading comprehension scores are lower than what is listed as typically average; however, they are not in a range low enough to trigger a comprehension concern.

Informal Reading Inventory (IRI)

On March 5, I met Bonnie after school to administer an Informal Reading Inventory (IRI). The IRI was a Level 2 (second-grade) narrative passage assessment protocol. Again, she changed in to a skirt for the test; she wanted to wear something special. Before commencing the test, I gave Bonnie a snack and we spoke for 10 minutes. We chose a quiet place to work; an area with a work table near the third-grade classrooms in the school, away from after-school program traffic. This assessment took less than 15 minutes and involved Bonnie reading a passage silently followed by retelling important details from the story. I prompted her as instructed on areas she did not discuss during the retelling. She correctly answered seven of the eight silent reading comprehension questions, which indicates per the directions that this passage was easy for her.

During the Oral Reading Accuracy section, Bonnie missed four words scoring in the "adequate" range per the directions. She omitted two words "the" and "her" and mispronounced the words "swept" and "carport."

Reflections on Administering the Informal Reading Inventory (IRI)

The IRI assessment went very well. I felt more comfortable administering the test, because the directions were detailed and I did not feel like I was multitasking. Bonnie's reading comprehension score was very high and her oral reading accuracy score was adequate; these are slight contradictions from our DIBELS experience.

Conclusion

My assessment is that Bonnie is reading at the high end for a second grader or at the low third-grade level.

It was a worthwhile experience to administer the DIBELS test. There was a lot of attention given this test last year at my sons' school. Last month I spoke with two teachers whom I respect and admire. Both have to use DIBELS in their reading assessment three times each year and they use the STEP assessment for reading comprehension two times each year. One teacher said that DIBELS does not assess comprehension properly and the other referred me to the book *The Truth about DIBELS*. Although I did not have time to read the entire book, which is a collection of articles that critique DIBELS, I read the introduction and one article by Sandra Wilde.

Wilde's article, "Is DIBELS Scientifically Based?", examines the findings of two studies linked to DIBELS. She concludes that DIBELS does not serve as a strong indicator of whether a child will fail to learn to read. She does claim that it would be reasonable to use DIBELS as a screening tool by which to identify students that need further assessment.

Meanwhile, the DIBELS website has over one dozen articles in the technical section in support of their assessment tool. The two articles critiqued in the Wilde article are posted as resources.

My experience is limited; however, I believe from my time with Bonnie that DIBELS or the IRI can serve their purpose as reading measurements if they are supplemented with other means of assessment. For example, the Diagnostic Assessment of Reading (DAR) that I analyzed is a very detailed standardized test that can pinpoint issues in reading. Perhaps there is no single assessment tool that can help us fully understand the true status of a student. However, taking the time to utilize multiple tools and perspectives can surely give depth and knowledge to an educator so they may meet the various needs of the learner.

References

https://dibels.uoregon.edu

Flynt, E., Cooter, R. (2007). *Flynt-Cooter reading inventory for the classroom.* Upper Saddle River, NJ: Pearson/Merrill Prentice Hall.

Gunning, T. (2008). *Creating literacy for all students*. Boston: Allyn & Bacon.

Wilde, S. (2006). "But isn't DIBELS scientifically based?" In *The truth about DIBELS: What it is—What it does,* ed. Kenneth Goodman. Portsmouth NH: Heinemann.

Questions to Consider

1. Where will you start third-grade reading for Bonnie?
2. Do you think there are additional interventions that might be important for Bonnie's social adjustment?

CHILD STUDY 17

Clarence Cooper, an Eager Kindergarten Reader

Clarence is kindergarten student, age 5 years, 10 months. He is an only child and currently lives at home with his mother and grandmother. Clarence was born following a full-term and straightforward birth and met developmental milestones appropriately. Clarence attended preschool prior to kindergarten and was identified as performing above average on a kindergarten screening test. Clarence was assigned to a regular kindergarten classroom. Clarence is neat and presentable in his school uniform, which consists of navy-blue pants and a light-blue button-down shirt. He is of average height and weight compared to the other kids in his class. He is very friendly, outgoing, and is eager to help classmates and talk with adults.

Questions/Concerns/Problems

Clarence functions academically at a higher level than his classmates. His teacher and his mother would like to know how advanced his reading and writing skills are. In order to answer this in part, I will administer a Comprehensive Test for Phonological Processing (CTOPP), which is suitable for testing ages 5–24.11 years.

Academic History

Clarence attends a neighborhood school in Cleveland. Clarence is in kindergarten and, therefore, does not have an extensive academic history; however, he was successful in preschool and continues to be a stand-out student in kindergarten. The exact classification of Clarence's family's socioeconomic status is not known; however, a majority of the students in this school appear to be living at a lower-middle-class status, at best. According to his teacher, Clarence's mother has high expectations for him and is very involved and supportive of her son's education. She attends conferences regularly and keeps in contact with the teacher and the school. Clarence comes to school appropriately dressed and cared for. However, his mother is described as being "young" and I am not sure of her exact age. The teacher believes Clarence has a good home life. It is the neighborhood that is a concern for her. The school and many of the students' homes are in a very poor, run-down, crime-infested area of town.

Early Developmental Milestones

Clarence has always been a bright and inquisitive child, according to his preschool and kindergarten teachers. He was identified immediately as a leader. According to his mother, Clarence has always learned quickly. Both his mother and his grandmother work hard to foster his learning at home and encourage him.

Current Functioning

Clarence functions as well as can be expected for a five-year-old child. His energy levels and movements appear to be appropriate. He does not need help with daily activities and living skills. He uses accurate facial expressions, speech, and language. He seemed slightly nervous to meet with an unfamiliar adult, but he was friendly and engaged. He has a positive self-concept and is aware of his advanced reading and writing skills and likes to use them and show them to others. He is very helpful to classmates and offers guidance or suggestions to help them find correct answers. He is respectful of adults. He is friendly and likes to talk about his favorite things such as books, games, toys, etc. He is a healthy child and enjoys playing with other children. He is thoughtful and communicates often and clearly with others. He is a critical thinker and uses problem-solving skills to sound out and predict words he does not know while reading. He responds well to routine. He arrives to school on time and dressed appropriately. The school has specific rules about the dress code, bathroom breaks, hallway behavior, and lunch times. Clarence is respectful of these rules and even helps other kids remember them if they seem to have forgotten.

The Test

The Comprehensive Test of Phonological Processing was administered over a two-day period. It consists of eight short assessment sections: Elision, Rapid Color Naming, Blending Words, Sound Matching, Rapid Object Naming, Memory for Digits, Non-word Repetition, and Blending Non-words. The test was administered in a room that was separate from the regular classroom. This was in an attempt to avoid distractions from classmates or others passing in the hallway. The test can be used to test persons ranging in age from 5 to 24.11 years. The curriculum emphasis is Language Arts, specifically phonological processing. Clarence was chosen for this study because he is one of the few students in his class who can afford to spend time away from the regular instruction of the class and both his mother and his teacher would appreciate additional assessment of his fundamental reading abilities.

Behaviors

Clarence was friendly and eager to participate in the assessment. I asked him to bring a favorite book to our session. He brought a book titled, "I Love Trucks!" (Sturges & Halpern, 1998). Discussion of the book helped us break the ice and helped me learn more about his interests and abilities. We had a long discussion about trucks and cars, specifically police cars. Clarence concentrated very well during the testing. He did seek approval from me, which I was not allowed to give during the test. At the end, I explained that he did a great job! He was pleased when asked to name the colors and items. He found this to be very easy and felt as though he must be doing very well on this test. When we were done after day two, he was disappointed that it was over. He was enjoying the process.

The Stakeholders

Teacher

(A) ***Strengths and Weaknesses*** Clarence scored very well on the CTOPP assessment. His age and grade equivalent scores are high; however, these are not recommended scores to share with parents because they do not signify that Clarence should be in a higher grade or is as smart as an older child, and they are an estimation, not real test-score data, and should be "taken with a grain of salt (Popham, 2008, p. 290). Clarence's highest standard score was 14 on the Elision section. His weakest score was an 11 on the supplementary subtest—Blending Non-words. All other subtests had the same score of 12.

(B) ***Instructional Implications*** According to these scores, Clarence is performing above average in phonological processing. He has mastered the fundamental skills for his age and grade level. And there is no doubt that he will continue to succeed academically. Instruction may not change significantly in terms of Clarence's long-term academic goals; however, this assessment can be compared to future progress monitoring assessments to decipher whether Clarence is maintaining the level of learning that is currently taking place. Proficiency in phonological assessment can indicate that he will or has learned to read easily. Instruction should be focused on enhancing his reading skills and opportunities. It will also be important to encourage reading regularly and help Clarence continue to enjoy it so he will not lose ground and will continue to develop his phonologic and reading skills at this high level.

(C) ***Test Scores and Interpretation*** Raw, age equivalency, grade equivalency, and standard and composite scores are given for this assessment. Clarence consistently scored well above his actual age and grade. Therefore, his *phonological age* far exceeds his actual age, but is still considered only slightly above average. Please refer to Appendix A to see a copy of the scoring booklet.

Clarence's standard and composite test score are listed below. The tables in Appendix B show the makeup of the categories.

Subtest	Clarence's Score	Range
Elision	14	(above average 13–14)
Rapid Color Naming	12	(average 8–12)
Blending Word	12	(average 8–12)
Sound Matching	12	(average 8–12)
Rapid Object Naming	12	(average 8–12)
Memory for Digits	12	(average 8–12)
Non-Word Repetition	12	(average 8–12)
Blending Non-Word	11	(average 8–12)

Clarence scored highest standard score of 14, above average, on the Elision subtest, which indicates this as a relative strength. For the remaining sections, he was at the very top half of the average range. For example, the average range is 8–12 and Clarence scored 12 consistently. Clarence did not show signs of weakness and his standard scores are not deficient in any subtest category.

The Phonological Awareness Composite Scores (PACS) compile the subtest scores in three areas: Elision, Blending Words, and Sound Matching for five- to six-year-olds. "Children with well-developed phonological awareness learn to read more easily than do children with poorly developed phonological awareness" (Wagner 1998, 46). Clarence scored 117 which is in the above average range for PACS.

The Phonological Memory Composite Score (PMCS) includes the standard scores of the Memory for Digits and the Non-ward Repetition subtests. Clarence also scored in the above-average range here with a composite of 112.

Finally, the Rapid Naming Composite Score (RNCS) includes the Rapid Color Naming subtest and the Rapid Object Naming subtest. Clarence scored 112, above average for RNCS.

Parents

(A) ***Strengths and Weaknesses*** Clarence is a very friendly, courteous student. He enjoys helping classmates that are struggling with concepts. He scored well on this test and ended within the above-average ranges consistently. He was particularly strong on the Elision test. This test measures the ability to remove segments from spoken words to form other words (Wagner, 49). Clarence will undoubtedly be an excellent reader and writer if we continue to encourage his love of books and his reading talents.

(B) ***Summary of Recommendations to Teacher*** I have recommended that the teacher focus on Clarence's enthusiasm. He has exhibited signs of great potential as a successful student in the future, if he is given materials that maintain his interests. He is proud of what he learns so we will all continue to guide him in the right direction.

(C) ***How Can Parent Help at Home?*** We want you, Clarence's mother, to continue to be a part of his "teaching team" (Berger 2007, 211). Because Clarence enjoys reading as much as he does, and has mastered the basic skills to move forward as a successful reader/student,

I encourage regular reading times at home. He should be consistently exposed to books that are above his reading level and give him challenges to consider and work through. Perhaps we can develop and maintain a reading log between home and school to verify that adequate time is being spent fostering his talents.

References

Berger, Eugenia Hepworth. (2007). Chapter 7, in *Parents as Partners in Education: Families and Schools Working Together,* 7th Edition. Upper Saddle River, NJ: Prentice Hall.

Lennon, J. E., Slesinski, C. (2002). *Comprehensive test of phonological processing (CTOPP): Cognitive-linguistic assessment of sever reading problems*. Retrieved from the Fairleigh Dickinson University website on March 5, 2009, http://alpha.fdu.edu/psychology/comprehensive_test_of_phonologi.htm.

O'Connor, Ken. 2002. "Communicating with students about grades." In *How to grade for learning: Linking grades to standards,* 2nd ed., pp. 176–184. Arlington Heights, IL: Skylight Professional Development.

Popham, J. W. (2008). *Classroom assessment: What teachers need to know*. Boston: Pearson Education, Inc.

Questions to Consider

1. What specific interventions at school will move Clarence forward in reading?
2. What community resources might be available for Clarence and his family to advance academic goals?
3. Are there technological resources that Clarence might find exciting to use in school or at the library?

CHILD STUDY 18

Brenda Ryan, Third-Grade Math

Brenda, a third grader who is age 8 years, 9 months, lives in an upper-middle-class neighborhood in the suburbs of Phoenix. She has one sibling, a twin sister, Belinda. Brenda's mother describes her pregnancy as difficult, since she was put on bed-rest for a while, and the twins were born five weeks early. However, Brenda and Belinda are developmentally average today. Mrs. Ryan, the twins' mother, told me that even though Brenda and Belinda are the same age, Brenda has definitely taken upon the oldest sibling role in the household. Mrs. Ryan describes Brenda as very outgoing, helpful to everyone, and states that she has no difficulties with current self-help skills. After speaking with Mrs. Ryan about Brenda's academic abilities, she told me that Brenda is doing well in school. She told me that Brenda seems to enjoy doing math.

Record of Scores on *TEMA-3: Test of Early Mathematics Ability*

- Raw Score: 68
- Age Equivalent: >8-9
- Grade Equivalent: >3.7
- Percentile: 84%
- Math Ability Score: 115
- SEM: 3
- Confidence Interval: 68%
- Math Ability Score Range: 112–118

Testing Conditions

I tested Brenda on a Saturday afternoon in a quiet environment. First, I engaged her in brief conversation and she told me that she loves math and is happy to be working on math with me. She seemed to have a positive attitude about math and participating in this assessment tool with me. We worked in her kitchen, while the rest of her family was in another room, so the testing conditions were quiet and comfortable for her to work. She was very eager to work with me, which was excellent. When she knew an answer, she replied to me in a confident tone of voice. Even for questions that she told me that she was unsure as to how to do the problem (e.g., multiplication, in which she said that she has not learned yet), she still guessed on each problem.

The reason that I chose this assessment tool was because I am very interested in working with the primary grades and I thought that this would be a great assessment tool to learn about and use with a child. I was hoping to learn how to figure out exactly how to use this tool and I found that it was very simple to learn, since everything that was supposed to be said by the examiner was written in red. Also, the examiner's manual was very easy to use, especially for finding how to score the child; the book explained the steps in simple terms and easy-to-follow language. I was also interested in working with this particular child in a math assessment tool, because I know that she loves math and I was eager to see what level that her math skills were at, and it was interesting to see the results.

Interpreting this Data

According to the Examiner's Manual, Brenda is performing above the average level of mathematical ability for children her age. She can do addition and subtraction facts with ease, yet does not have the concept of multiplication. Therefore, as far as follow up instruction, I recommend continuing to practice her basic addition and subtraction facts and beginning to start practicing multiplication facts. Since she seems to have core understanding of addition, I feel confident that her multiplication facts will come easily to her. Also, throughout the testing, it seemed to me that Brenda was demonstrating strengths throughout the entire assessment. She was attempting every problem and guessed when she did not know the answer. As far as activities that you can do at home with Brenda, you can ask her mental math problems (addition and subtraction) often. Also, make math fun at home. Play games such as a dice game with two dice and take turns adding the dice together. Keep score to see who reaches 50 first. Also, since she will be introduced to multiplication soon, practice with flashcards.

Questions to Consider

1. How might you assess Brenda's problem-solving skills?
2. Do you agree that multiplication instruction should be postponed? Why or why not?
3. What other assessment measures will help you understand Brenda as a learner?

CHILD STUDY 19

Sharon White, a First Grader

Background Information

For the last several weeks, I have been observing Sharon (age 6), her classmates, and her teacher, Ms. Brown. Sharon, is a delightful and bright child who loves to learn, produces excellent work, and gets along well with her classmates. She has long brown hair, brown eyes, fair skin, pink cheeks, and freckles. Sharon is thin and stands at the average height of a first grade student. She has one younger sibling—a two-year-old brother, Harold. Sharon is extremely well-behaved, a good listener, and a hard-working student who listens to and respects her teacher and stays focused when she does her school work. She is very organized and detail-oriented, and she has a great memory. A few weeks ago, I was conferring with her about reading workshop documentation about a one-room schoolhouse book. We were comparing old-fashioned schools to those of today, and Sharon remembered that a week earlier, I had told her about some interesting characteristics of a one-room schoolhouse that I had visited as a child. I did not even remember telling her that! Sharon is a creative artist and writer. A few weeks ago, during a writing workshop, she produced an "All About" book on riding a bicycle using only one hand. She included a cover with an illustration, a table of contents, a "how to" page with instructions and illustrations for riding a bicycle using only one hand, a safety tips page, and more. Sharon is very talkative and enjoys sharing her work, ideas, and real-life stories with others. She is enthusiastic and full of energy. Sharon's eyes light up when she speaks, and she always has a smile on her face.

I chose the *Peabody Picture Vocabulary Test*, Fourth Edition, for my assessment tool. According to the *Peabody Picture Vocabulary Test, Fourth Edition Manual*, the test "measures the receptive (hearing) vocabulary of children and adults" (p. 1). The test is available in two forms: Form A and Form B (p. 1). Each form contains "training items followed by 228 test items, each consisting of four full-color pictures arranged on a page. The examinee selects the picture that best illustrates the meaning of a stimulus word spoken by the examiner" (p. 1). The items are grouped into 19 sets of 12, and "the sets are arranged in order of increasing difficulty so that the examiner can easily administer only the sets appropriate for the examinee's vocabulary level (the *critical range*)" (p. 1).

When I selected the test, I knew I would be assessing one of Ms. Brown's students, but I was not sure which one. Because Ms. Brown teaches emerging readers, she focuses many of her lessons and student assignments on reading comprehension and finding meaning in reading. According to the *Peabody Picture Vocabulary Test, Fourth Edition Manual*, "vocabulary is strongly related to reading comprehension ability, as a person must know the meaning of the words he or she is reading in order to understand the text, and the remediation of vocabulary deficits can be a useful part of a reading improvement program. Finally, for individuals whose primary language is English, vocabulary correlates highly with general verbal ability" (p. 1). I took this into consideration when selecting the test. I also considered that all the students in Ms. Brown's class have recently been given other assessments, including DIBELS, and I did not want to cause any more test anxiety than the students may have already been experiencing. I was hoping that this test, because it uses pictures, would not be a source of anxiety for Sharon. Another factor I considered when selecting a test was the time. According to the test manual, it takes 10–15 minutes to administer the test (p. 1). I wanted to use a fairly quick test so that I would not disrupt the student's school day and learning.

Administration of the PPVT

I administered the test at Sharon's school, Harriet Tubman Elementary School, a San Diego Public School. Ms. Brown suggested that I assess Sharon, because she is a "typical first-grade student." Ms. Brown said that Sharon's reading abilities are average. I conducted the assessment in the hallway outside Sharon's classroom. This environment was fine at first, because there is not much traffic in this particular hallway of the school. However, the test went much longer than I expected, and it was toward the end of the school day, so a few students walked through, which was somewhat disrupting. Nevertheless, Sharon did very well on the test.

To introduce the test, I began with two training items, and Sharon got both right without any help, so I began testing at Set 5, the start for age 6. Hours after I had administered the test, I realized that I administered the wrong training items. Before I administered the test, I had read about the training items for ages 4 through adult, and how if the examinee responds correctly to two items, the examiner can move to the appropriate age set. But I administered two training items for ages 2:6 through 3:11 and then moved to the age set. Thus, I followed the correct directions for

Sharon's age but used the training items for younger children. If I were to give this test again, I would put a sticky note on the correct page of training items, ahead of time, so I would not make the same mistake twice.

We began with item 49, the first item in Set 5, as the *Peabody Picture Vocabulary Test, Fourth Edition Manual*, states that "the recommended Start Item is the first item in the item set recommended for the examinee's age" (p. 10). Sharon made no errors in this set. Because this was the first set I administered, and because Sharon made one or zero errors, the Basal Set was established—Set 5. I moved on to the next set—Set 6, the start for age 7. Here, she made only one error. I continued with Set 7, the start for age 8, in which Sharon made no errors. She made no errors again in sets 8 and 9, the starts for ages 9 and 10, respectively. At this point, I was very impressed. We had already been through five sets, and we were going to continue. According to the *Peabody Picture Vocabulary Test, Fourth Edition Manual*, "on average, examinees take approximately 5 sets of 12 items each, or 60 items out of 228 (26% of the test)" (p. 10). In Set 10, the start for ages 11–12, Sharon made one error, and she made one error in Set 11, the start for age 13. We moved on to Set 12, the start for ages 14–16. Here, she made three errors. In Set 13, the start for ages 17–18, she made six errors. Finally, in Set 14, the start for ages 19–adult, Sharon made nine errors. At the end of this set, we stopped, as the test manual states that "the *Ceiling Set* for an examinee is the *highest* set of items administered containing eight or more errors" (p. 11).

Sharon was very patient during the testing. Toward the beginning, she was smiling, laughing at some of the pictures on the test, and making comments about some of the pictures and words that I presented her. She also seemed confident in her abilities and very relaxed. I mentioned earlier that the test went much longer than I expected. I began the test at Set 5 and ended at Set 14. So, Sharon had to sit through 10 sets of 12 words. Over time and with the traffic in the hallway, Sharon began to lose interest, and as the words increasingly became more challenging, she seemed a little discouraged.

Scoring and Interpretation

To begin scoring Sharon's performance on the test, I counted the total number of errors from all the administered sets—the Basal Set, the Ceiling Set, and all the sets in between. The total was 21 errors. Next, I subtracted the total number of errors from the Ceiling Item, which was item 168. In doing this, I calculated the raw score, which was 147.

The next step in the scoring process was to determine Sharon's standard scores, percentiles, stanines, and normal curve equivalents (NCEs). According to the *Peabody Picture Vocabulary Test, Fourth Edition Manual*, these "compare an examinee's vocabulary knowledge with that of a reference group representing all individuals of the same age or grade" (p. 21).

The standard score "indicates the distance of the examinee's raw score from the average for people of the same age or grade, taking into account the range of scores among examinees in that reference group. On the PPVT-4 scale, a standard score of 100 is the average score for the person's age or grade" (p. 17). The standard deviation is 15 (p. 17). To determine Sharon's standard score, I used tables in the appendix of the manual. These tables provide the conversion of the raw score to the standard score, depending on the student's age or grade level. For Sharon's age of 6 years and 9 months, her raw score of 147 converted to a standard score of 129. For Sharon's grade—Spring, Grade 1—her raw score of 147 converted to a standard score of 123. Therefore, the PPVT-4 scale indicates that Sharon's receptive vocabulary is above average for both her age and grade. It makes sense that her age-based standard score is slightly higher than her grade-based standard score. Being 6 years and 9 months old, Sharon is an "older" six-year-old, and because her birthday is in August, she is a "younger" first-grade student. Because percentiles, NCEs, and stanines are directly related to the standard scores, these reinforce that Sharon's receptive vocabulary is above average for both her age and grade.

According to the *Peabody Picture Vocabulary Test, Fourth Edition Manual*, "A percentile indicates the percentage of individuals in the reference group who performed at or below the examinee's raw score. Thus, a percentile of 50 signifies that the examinee's raw score is average for examinees of that age or grade" (p. 17). To obtain Sharon's percentiles, I used tables in the appendix of the manual to convert the standard score. Sharon's age-based standard score of 129 converts to a percentile of 97, and her grade-based standard score of 123 converts to a percentile of 94.

As for Sharon's NCEs, these, "like standard scores, communicate the distance between the examinee's raw score and the average raw score in the normative reference group" (p. 17). To obtain Sharon's NCEs, I used tables in the appendix of the manual to convert the standard score. Sharon's age-based standard score of 129 converts to an NCE of 91, and her grade-based standard score of 123 converts to an NCE of 82.

The Peabody Picture Vocabulary Test, Fourth Edition Manual states that "stanines are whole-number scores that range from 1 through 9, with a mean of 5 and an SD of 2" (p. 18). Each represents a range of percentiles (p. 18). To obtain Sharon's stanines, I used tables in the appendix of the manual to convert the standard score. Sharon's age-based stanine is 9, and her grade-based stanine is 8.

The standard scores, percentiles, NCEs, and stanines are graphed on the Graphical Profile of the score sheet. In the score summary and graph, I used age-based scores. The completed graph indicates that Sharon scored moderately high and has the potential to score extremely high.

Next, I determined Sharon's age and grade equivalent scores. "An age equivalent represents the age (in years and months) at which an examinee's raw score is the average score. Likewise, the grade equivalent signifies the grade (in tenths of a grade) at which a given raw score is the average score" (p. 18). These scores are based on average raw scores at different ages and grades, and they do not account for score variability (p. 18). Again, I used appendix tables, but this time, I used Sharon's raw score of 147 and converted that to her age equivalent of 9.6 (9 years, 6 months) and her grade equivalent of 3.9 (toward the end of third grade).

Using the same tables, I determined Sharon's growth scale value (GSV), which "is useful for measuring change in PPVT-4 performance over time" (p. 18). When I converted Sharon's raw score to both her age and grade equivalent scores, I continued reading the tables to find that her GSV is 174. According to the test manual, this score indicates absolute level of performance, rather than representing how an individual scores compared to other examinees (p. 205). An examinee's GSV will increase as his/her vocabulary expands (p. 21). Because this is the only time I administered this test to Sharon, I do not presently know what her GSV would indicate, in terms of her progress over time, but if she were to be tested again, a difference of 8 GSV points would indicate a significant change (p. 205).

I determined the confidence intervals for Sharon's standard scores, "to take measurement error into account when interpreting" her performance on the test (p. 20). "The confidence interval is a range of scores that has a specified probability of including the examinee's true score" (p. 20). To calculate Sharon's confidence interval, I had the option of selecting the 90 percent confidence interval or the 95 percent interval. The test manual states that the 90 percent interval "is often found to be useful for reporting purposes," so that is what I used (p. 21). I used another appendix table and found that the confidence interval for Sharon's age-based standard score of 129 is 122–134, and the confidence interval for her grade-based standard score of 123 is 117–128. I graphed the age-based confidence interval on the Graphical Profile of the score sheet. The test manual states that because the standard score, percentile, NCE, and stanine have a fixed relationship to one another, "by drawing two vertical lines. . . all three sets of confidence intervals are plotted" (p. 21). The PPVT-4 manual also states that the reliability of the test's scale is high, and "the chances are great that an individual's obtained score and true score are very similar" (p. 21). In addition, "because errors of measurement have a normal distribution, a person's true score is more likely to be near the middle of a confidence interval than at either end. Therefore, the obtained score is the best single estimate of the person's true score" (p. 21).

Finally, I performed a qualitative analysis of Sharon's PPVT-4 performance by utilizing a worksheet that can be used to classify incorrect responses by part of speech. "Each PPVT-4 stimulus word is classified as a noun, verb, or *attribute* (adjective or adverb) (p. 21). Sharon incorrectly responded to 14 nouns, out of 81; 5 verbs, out of 23; and 2 attributes, out of 16. According to the test manual, "a comparison of error types by part of speech could indicate where vocabulary instruction should initially be focused for the greatest benefit" (p. 22). I am not really concerned with Sharon's incorrect responses, as the majority of the errors were made in the last two sets, which are the starting sets for ages 17–18 and for ages 19–adult. Additionally, in comparing Sharon's answers, in terms of parts of speech, there did not seem to be a major problem in any one area. She answered incorrectly for about 17.3 percent of the nouns, about 21.7 percent of the verbs, and 12.5 percent of the attributes. The PPVT-4 indicates that Sharon already has the receptive English language skills of a 9-year-old and a third grader, and I think that in short time, as she ages, she will master the words for which she responded incorrectly.

Summary for Future Teacher

Adapted from "Report to Parents" (Peabody Picture Vocabulary Test, Fourth Edition Manual, p. 198).

The following table outlines Sharon O'Hara's scores on the Peabody Picture Vocabulary Test, Fourth Edition (PPVT-4), administered May 29, 2009. This test measured Sharon's level of oral vocabulary knowledge by evaluating how well she understands Standard English words spoken aloud.

Raw Score = 147 **Age Equivalent = 9.6** **Grade Equivalent = 3.9**	**Age-Based**	**Grade-Based**
Standard Score	129	123
Percentile	97	94
Normal Curve Equivalent	91	82
Stanine	9	8

The PPVT-4 provides a variety of scores that indicate Sharon's receptive vocabulary knowledge compared with the skills of children who are the same age or in the same grade.

The standard scores show how Sharon's raw score differs from the average. Sharon's raw score was converted to her standard scores, which are on a different scale than the raw score. A standard score of 100 is average; higher than 100 is above average; and lower than 100 is below average. Both Sharon's age-based and grade-based scores indicate that Sharon's receptive vocabulary is above average for both her age and grade.

The percentiles indicate the percentages of students who performed at or below Sharon's score. Sharon's age-based percentile of 97 means that she performed as well or better than 97% of children the same age. Her grade-based percentile of 94 means that she performed as well or better than 94% of children in the same grade.

The normal curve equivalent is a scoring method that is frequently used in government reports. These scores range from 1 through 99, and scores of 1, 50, and 99 correspond to percentiles of 1, 50, and 99. However, other values do not directly relate to percentiles.

The stanine scores are single-digit scale scores with bands ranging from l (lowest) through 9 (highest). Each stanine contains a range of percentiles. Sharon's age-based stanine of 9 indicates that she scored extremely high, and her grade-based stanine of 8 indicates that she scored moderately high.

Sharon's age equivalent of 9.6 represents the age (9 years and 6 months) at which her raw score is the average score. Her grade equivalent of 3.9 signifies the grade (in tenths of a grade) at which her raw score is the average score. Therefore, her grade equivalent is toward the end of third grade.

Sharon is an all-around good and well-behaved student who produces excellent work and easily understands new concepts. Sharon learns very well when she can produce something, such as a poster or book, to document her thinking and learning. She also learns well when there are opportunities for movement in the classroom and when repetitive activities, such as the PPTV-4, are kept to a maximum of 20 minutes. Sharon has an extensive receptive vocabulary that compares to that of a 9-year-old and a third-grader. She is also very skilled at making inferences and predictions while reading, as well as comprehending what she reads. I recommend that future teachers continue to challenge Sharon by introducing vocabulary that is advanced for her actual grade level, encouraging her to read more difficult books, and prompting her to think even more deeply about what she reads. I also recommend that future teachers place Sharon in cooperative learning groups and guided reading groups with students who are both more and less advanced in their vocabulary development. This may help Sharon expand her vocabulary even further, and it may help other students learn from her and expand their vocabularies, as well.

References

Dunn, L. M., & Dunn, D. M. (1959, 1959–2007). Peabody Picture Vocabulary Test, Fourth Edition. Retrieved June 2, 2009, from Mental Measurements Yearbook database.

Questions to Consider

1. What effect did starting with the wrong training item have on the results of this assessment, if any?
2. How did the assessor's experience with Sharon help her place the test results in context?
3. Do you agree that Sharon is a typical first grader? What variables shape your opinion?

CHILD STUDY 20

Lillian Bolden, 4 Years Old

Lillian is a 4.3-year-old, African American, and the only child of married parents. Mr. and Mrs. Bolden both graduated from college and work full-time. Lillian's mom, Mrs. Bolden, is the head of nursing at a local hospital, and Lillian's dad, Mr. Bolden, works at a school for troubled youth. Lillian's family lives in a house that they own in a south suburb of Chicago with a diverse demographic. Lillian's grandmother (father's mother) lived with her family until this past summer when she suddenly passed away. Lillian is in child care five days a week for nearly 10 hours a day, due to her parents' work schedules. She also is in ballet class one night a week. I have been Lillian's teacher at the child-care center since she was age 2-2.

Education Information

Lillian has been in full-day private child care since she was two years old. Since age 3, she has been attending the preschool program at her child care center. She was identified as "at-risk for school failure" by the screening process used for the preschool program. When screened as a 3-0 year old by the DIAL-3 tool, Lillian was deemed "at-risk" by the school's requirements for their preschool program.

Test Administered

The test used in this study was the TEMA-3 (Test of Early Mathematics Ability), Form A. The TEMA-3 was designed as an instrument to provide useful information about the mathematical strengths and weaknesses (in both formal and informal knowledge) of young children. The

TEMA-3 is described as a reliable, valid, norm-referenced test of early mathematical ability, focusing on children from ages 3-0 to 8-11. The TEMA-3 test has four chief purposes: (1) identify children significantly above of behind their peers in the area of mathematical development; (2) identify specific strengths and weaknesses in mathematical thinking; (3) suggest appropriate individualized instructional practices for children; (4) serve as a measure in research projects.

The TEMA-3 shows "that mathematical skills develop from a foundation of informal mathematical thinking that emerges before the child begins formal schooling" (Crehan, 2004).

Choosing This Test

I have been Lillian's teacher for the past two years. Working with her every day, I have a good sense of her developmental strengths and weaknesses, based on my observations of her performance in class activities and documented by the work products that she produces. Lillian has strong language skills, so I knew it would not be beneficial to further test that area. Lillian is a very verbally expressive child. She demonstrates the ability to converse with classmates and teachers. She is curious about many things and often asks me questions about my clothes, shoes, hair, personal life, and more. Lillian can answer questions from others in detailed multiple sentences of many words (over ten). She actively participates in Circle Time and often shares personal experiences with the group. She also shows many emerging literacy skills such as print concepts and letter recognition. From my other assessments of Lillian in the classroom, I thought that her mathematical skills were also on track for her age. She can count verbally past 10, she has one-to-one correspondence in counting (she volunteers to count the children present at school, patting them on the head with each number she counts), and she uses her fingers to correctly display numbers. Since I had never administered this type of comprehensive mathematical test to her before, I thought it would it would be beneficial to all stakeholders to learn more about her mathematical abilities. The TEMA-3 seemed like the right choice for this situation, because it is easy to learn to administer, mostly appropriate for Lillian's age, and it is easy to interpret the results.

Testing Conditions

I administered the TEMA-3 to Lillian at her child-care center on a day when preschool was not in session (since there are fewer children there those days). We sat together at one of the tables in the classroom, across the room from where the majority of the other children were playing. Two young girls were coloring at a table next to ours, and I asked them if they would please not interrupt us during the test. The classroom was remarkably quiet and peaceful that morning, so it seemed like a good and non-threatening testing environment. Since I do a lot of one-on-one games and activities regularly with the children, Lillian thought this was no different than any other day at school.

Lillian's behavior during the test was typical of her everyday behavior. She was not extremely fidgety or antsy. She sat patiently and listened attentively to the instructions. She did not ask any questions regarding the test. Lillian did not become obviously distracted by the other children.

Test Results

Lillian's age at the time of testing was 4-3. Lillian scored a grade equivalent of preschool with the percentile ranking of 37. Lillian's math ability score was 95. With an SEM of 4, that puts her math ability score range 91–99. Her math ability score translates as "average" performance for her age, according to the TEMA-3 Manual.

Lillian showed strengths in the mathematical areas of: perception of small numbers, producing finger displays to five, verbal counting to five perception of more (up to 10 items), enumeration of up to five items, cardinality, number constancy, producing sets of up to five items, and verbal counting to 10.

Lillian showed mathematical weakness in the areas of: nonverbal addition and subtraction, naming the number after (1–9), and reading numerals, all of which are skills for a four-year-old, according to the TEMA-3. In following the test regulations of testing her until she made five incorrect answers in a row, she also showed weakness in the five-year-old-level skills of: writing single-digit numbers, concretely modeling addition word problems, and part–whole concepts. Suggestions for developmentally appropriate follow-up instruction activities are listed in the parent and teacher reports.

Parent Report

Based on the results of the TEMA-3 test, Lillian showed mathematical abilities pretty typical for her age. Lillian showed strengths in many mathematical areas that are taught in her preschool class and are based on the Illinois Early Learning Standards (http://illinoisearlylearning.org/standards/index.htm). Specifically, Lillian has skills in counting (to 10) and producing finger displays of numbers up to 5. Lillian displays good one-to-one correspondence; that is, she can count the correct number of items in front of her. Lillian displays strength in "number constancy," which means that when shown three items in a line, for example, Lillian will still know that there are three items if you switch their positions or move them out of the line. She knows that the number of items did not change, only the positioning. Lillian can also produce the correct number of sets of items. For instance, when asked to hand me three tokens, she correctly placed three tokens in my hand. Lillian tends to use her fingers when counting, and sometimes she holds up a finger display of a number without verbally telling you the number. When asked, however, Lillian does tell you the correct number she is holding up. Lillian can also correctly identify more or less when shown two groups of the same item.

Lillian could not correctly complete the "nonverbal production" item on the test. For this item, I demonstrated the skill by placing a number tokens on a piece of paper, covering up that paper, then asking her to "make yours just like mine," as instructed by the test. Lillian completed this task two out of the three times (with three different numbers), but did not receive credit for successful completion. Although this specific skill is not related to our preschool curriculum, it would be a useful skill for Lillian to master before kindergarten. To promote growth in this skill at home, I recommend playing math games that involve this type of "hiding" the number, such as Concentration. In playing Concentration, the child has to determine the number of items shown on a card *and* where the card is located.

Lillian also showed weakness in a similar hiding game of "make yours just like mine" with the tokens. The format here was the same as the previously mentioned task, except that now another step was included—the adding or taking away of a number of tokens from the group. Lillian did not successfully complete any of these items. This kind of game can be practiced with any small items Lillian can manipulate (pennies, Cheerios, etc.). Simply practicing the simple addition to and subtraction from the group, without including the "hiding" aspect, should promote positive development in this area. Again, this skill is not directly related to preschool curriculum, but it is a useful math skill to have for the future.

Lillian can count to 10 out loud, an important skill she has success with, but when asked questions like, "What number comes next—4, and then comes ___ ?", she is unable to fill in the blank. The authors of the TEMA-3 guide recommend the following activity to enhance development in this area: "One (idea) is the 'Number-After Race,' in which the child rolls a die to determine how many spaces he or she can move a car on a racetrack. The child is allowed to move one more space than the number indicated. Thus, if the child rolls a 5, he or she must determine the number 'just after 5' and is allowed to move 6 spaces."

Lillian could not successfully read single-digit numbers. The best way to promote development in this mathematical area is to read children's books about counting. Any well-illustrated counting book is a way of exposing Lillian to these written numbers. We have many books of this nature in the classroom that I can read with Lillian, and there are also several appropriate books in the Family Library that Lillian can check out and read at home.

Overall, Lillian shows typical mathematical knowledge and skill for preschool. The games and activities suggested above should help her master the mathematical skills needed for success in kindergarten and beyond.

Reference

Crehan, K. (2003). "Review of Test of Early Mathematics Ability, Third Edition." 16th *Mental Measurements Yearbook*. Lincoln, NE: Buros Institute of Mental Measurements.

Questions to Consider

1. Where will you start with Lillian in math activities? What kinds of materials and activities might you include in a Math Center?
2. How will you incorporate Lillian's interest in ballet in plans for her?

CHILD STUDY 21

Martin Knox, in Pre-Kindergarten

Description

Martin and his family live in Shaker Heights, Ohio. The family is upper-middle-class (dad is an attorney; mom stays at home, but used to be an attorney as well). Both parents are very involved with their children and invested in their education. The children attend the public schools in, which generally have high scores on state tests. The neighborhood is very family-oriented and tight-knit, and the community is a safe, friendly one in which to raise children. Martin is six years old and attends full day pre-kindergarten. He is the middle child of three boys; his older brother, Seth, is in second grade, and his younger brother, Arnold, is two years old. Martin is very lively, talkative, and happy, and enjoys playing games and sports. Overall, he is an active young boy who has fun playing with his brothers.

Current Functioning and History

There are no concerns with Martin's childhood, upbringing, medical history, or development. He seems right on track and is just beginning to read in his pre-K class. I have known Martin since he was a baby and have never observed anything out of the ordinary. He has control over his body functions and movement, is emotionally stable, reacts well to both children and adults (enjoys talking and playing with everyone), has a good attitude towards learning and school, is physically active, communicates very clearly and well with adults and other children, and followed all of my directions perfectly during the assessment. Martin and Seth are both extremely well mannered and thoughtful young boys. This is Martin's first year in pre-K, so I do not have any report cards or teacher reports on his previous academic performance, but Mrs. Knox told me he really likes going to school and is doing well.

Environment

I conducted the test in Martin's living room; Mrs. Knox and Seth were in the room (Seth wanted to watch). We sat across from each other on a couch; it was a casual environment.

Time

We did the test at 1:30 P.M. on a Sunday, after lunch and during Arnold's nap time; the boys were playing on their Leap Frogs when I arrived. I chose Martin because I wanted to assess his print and phonological awareness. He is not yet in kindergarten, and while this portion was labeled as kindergarten level, he is in pre-K classes and I wanted to see where he stood in terms of reading skills. I am very fascinated with the process of learning to read and was curious to assess his current level.

Test Information

I gave Martin the kindergarten portion of the Diagnostic Assessment of Reading (DAR). He completed five mini tests as part of the larger assessment. I stopped administering the test when I noticed he did not understand the instructions (auditory blending). He started to get restless at this point and said he did not know what to do. I did not want to push him or make him feel like he was doing badly, so I stopped here. The booklet said to stop when the student misses two words, but since he did not want to try, I ended the assessment.

According to the Riverside Publishing website, the company that publishes the test, the DAR "provides an assessment of individual student achievement in print awareness, phonological awareness, letters and sounds, word recognition, word analysis, oral reading accuracy and fluency, silent reading comprehension, spelling, and word meaning" (http://www.riverpub.com/products/dar/index.html, accessed November 19, 2008). It is appropriate for use with ages 5 to adult and claims to be able to "identify areas of difficulty for struggling readers in 40 minutes or less."

Test Administration

Martin appeared a little nervous at first, but I assured him this was more of a test for me and he was just helping me on a school project. He relaxed and liked the idea of helping me. Seth wanted to watch so as to not feel left out, which I do not think was a distraction at all. Martin jumped right into the first test with no hesitation. During the word segmenting test, he thought the word "porcupine" was really funny and he and Seth laughed when he said it. It definitely seemed like he did not mind partaking in this assessment and was maybe even having a little fun. Based on the results, I think Martin is right on track, even though he did not attain "mastery" on the first subtest. I found the print awareness test to be somewhat confusing, and although his answers were not correct according to the response packet, they were understandable errors. I believe the layout of the print awareness test was very confusing and that the content was rather arbitrary—there was a sentence, then the name of the author, and then two words, which had nothing to do with the rest of the page, listed next to each other on the bottom. When I asked to point to a word Martin pointed to "sun," which is a correct answer. The next question asked him to point to where I would begin reading, and again he pointed to "sun." Then I said, "I am going to read a sentence that is on this page. Point to the last word in the sentence when I'm done reading." After this instruction Martin pointed to the end of the word "dandelion," which was written next to sun, on the bottom of the page. While this was incorrect according to the response packet, he did point to the last word on the page, making his mistake very understandable. Again, I think the overall layout of this page (which was a stark white page with purple writing) was perplexing. Taking the other tests he completed into account, I would say Martin is performing at, or even above, his age level based on the results of the five tests he completed.

He started to move around and get fidgety during the fifth test, but I continued onto auditory blending, the sixth test. We stopped here because he said he did not understand the examples and I could sense he was no longer in "test mode."

Teacher

Martin reached "mastery" on four of the five tests he took. I think Martin is right on track with phonological awareness but could perhaps use some work in print awareness. However, if he was given an actual book and not a piece of paper with arbitrary words on it, the results may have been different. I think more work with letter sounds, especially at the end of words, would be beneficial in addition to more handling of real books. Mrs. Knox said they just began reading in pre-K and I think that with more exposure to reading, Martin will improve in these areas. After some work with blending, I would re-administer that portion and see if he can move onto the subtests in letters and sounds.

References

Riverside Publishing website, http://www.riverpub.com/products/dar/index.html. (Accessed November 19, 2008.)

Roswell, F. G., Chall, J. S., Curtis, M. E., & Kearns, G. (2006). *Diagnostic Assessment of Reading,* Second Edition, Form B. Itasca, IL: Riverside Publishing.

Questions to Consider

1. What plans will you make for Martin to support facility with print awareness? What will be in your Literacy Center to support his development?
2. What specific activities on blending might be included in your plans for Martin?

CHILD STUDY 22

Minerva Reynolds, 8 Years Old

The child I chose to study for this project is named Minerva, and she is eight years old. Minerva is about 4½ feet tall, and has brown hair and hazel eyes. She lives in suburban Detroit and attends a Catholic grade school close to her house. Minerva has a very outgoing personality. She has many friends, and enjoys being the center of attention. She enjoys several extracurricular activities outside of school. These include such things as basketball, soccer, ceramics, and especially dance.

Minerva comes from a very affluent family. They live in a new house built three years ago. Mr. Reynolds is the president of a family business and Mrs. Reynolds is a home-maker. Both parents are college graduates, and education is very important to them. Someone is always around to help Minerva with her homework or encourage her to start studying for her spelling test. Minerva is the second of four children. She has an older sister, Isabella, who is 10, a younger brother, Arthur, who is 6, and a younger sister Lisa, who just turned 4. Minerva and her siblings have the usual rivalry and fights that any other family would have. Overall, they all play together well and get along.

Minerva has been on track developmentally. She is very independent in self-help and daily living skills. She is vocal and has no trouble getting her point across when speaking. She is mostly composed, but does sometimes have outbursts, as would any other eight-year-old child. She gets along well with children her age, as well as adults. Minerva's thinking and reasoning skills are where they should be for her age. She likes to have a schedule and be on time for things. For example, she does not like to be tardy for school. This can often cause a problem in the morning, because her sister or brother may not be ready on time.

Minerva's academic history is stellar. On first- and second-grade report cards, she was graded satisfactory or excellent for all her subjects. She just received her first third-grade report card, and though it measured some different things than the others, she still had an outstanding report. Minerva's report card did not contain letter grades; rather, it had a plus for excellent, a check mark for satisfactory progress, a minus for limited progress, and a T for taught not graded. One particular heading which caught my eye on the report card was that of "Personal and Social Growth." This measured such things as respects authority, respects peers, works well in group, completes work on time, works independently, and helps to create a pleasant environment. Minerva received all pluses and all checkmarks, which I think helps define her as a growing student. She also received pluses in Religion, Spelling, and Handwriting. She received checks in Reading, English, Math, and Social Studies. In Spanish, PE, Music, Computer, and Art, she received a "T".

Minerva obviously does well in school, but this did not really give me an idea about her feelings on assessment. I decided to ask Minerva a few questions about assessment:

ASSESSOR: What kinds of tests have you taken this year?

MINERVA: I have taken all kinds of tests—spelling, math, science, social studies—I feel like it is so many.

ASSESSOR: What do you think about before the test?

MINERVA: I think about the questions that may be on the test. I also think about the study guide and stuff I should know.

OBSERVER: How do you feel when you take the test?

MINERVA: I feel nervous because I want to do good.

ASSESSOR: Which tests do you find the most difficult?

MINERVA: I think science is hard. There are always questions on that test that were not on the study guide. Sometimes, I don't know the answers to those.

ASSESSOR: How do you feel if you don't know the answer to questions?

MINERVA: I feel sad. I feel like I am going to get a bad grade.

ASSESSOR: Which test do you think is the easiest? Why?

MINERVA: Spelling is easy. I just always know spelling.

Clinical Activity

I decided to give Minerva the Peabody Picture Vocabulary Test (PPVT). The PPVT is a test that measures receptive vocabulary achievement and verbal ability. Since vocabulary can be a strong predictor of school success, I thought this would be an excellent measure of her scholastic aptitude. The test was administered on October 30, at Minerva's home and took about 18 minutes. There were not any distractions during the test and the room was quiet and well lit. During testing, Minerva seemed very much at ease. She actually enjoyed taking the test for the first half, but as the questions became a bit harder to interpret, she started to get a little frustrated. At this time, it seemed as though she was not trying as much as she was towards the beginning of the test.

Minerva ended up scoring above average on the test. Her raw score was 144 and her standard score was 107. She was in the sixtieth percentile and her Normal Curve Equivalent (NCE) was 60. Her stanine was 6 and her Growth Scale Value (GSV) was 170. Her age equivalent was 8:10 and her grade equivalent was 3.4.

References

Dunn, L., & Dunn, D. (n.d.). *Peabody Picture Vocabulary Test, Fourth Edition*. Retrieved November 21, 2008, from Tests in Print database.

Dunn, D. (2008) *The PPVT(tm)–4 Test Delivers Contemporary Features for Even Better Assessment*. Retrieved November 21, 2008, from http://www.speechandlanguage.com/article/sept2006.asp.

Questions to Consider

1. As you review Minerva's behavior during the test, what are your predictions about how she might handle frustration when trying to learn new material? How can you support her development as a self-empowered learner?
2. What do the results of this assessment on receptive vocabulary tell you about Minerva? How will this shape your thinking about literacy activities for Minerva? What specific interventions will you plan?

CHILD STUDY 23

Juliana Jenkins, 4 Years Old

Child Background

Juliana Jenkins is a girl aged 4 years, 10 months, mousy brown hair and a fair complexion. She is of average weight, and slightly taller than her peers. Juliana lives in a three-bedroom single-family home with her mother, father, and twin sister, Melissa. Mrs. Jenkins has bachelor's and master's degrees in Elementary Education; she taught kindergarten for 10 years before resigning while pregnant with her twin girls. Mr. Jenkins has bachelor's and master's degrees in Business Administration and is a marketing executive at a large advertising firm in New York. Juliana's family would likely be described as upper-middle-class.

Juliana was diagnosed with Sensory Integration Disorder at around 18 months of age. According to Mrs. Jenkins' explanation (and from my own observations as her nanny the past two years), it affects her processing of sensory experiences, such as distain for loud noises, getting wet, or labels on clothing touching her skin. There are also times when she seeks out sensory experiences, such as moving around in her seat, chewing on different items (i.e., her blanket), or hugging people tightly. Juliana receives occupational therapy twice a month.

Juliana has attended educational and enrichment programs (focus on areas such as motor skills and social development) since about six months of age through the park district, as well as privately owned centers such as Gym for Tots and Dance n Play. At age 2½; she began attending a publicly funded preschool program (an hour-and-a-half program) two days a week. At age 3, she began attending preschool (a half-day program) at a neighborhood private school. She continued attending the public preschool simultaneously. By age 3½ she was attending the private school three days a week and the public program two days a week. This was in combination with various sports programs being offered by the park district, such as floor hockey and gymnastics. Mrs. Jenkins told me she believes it is best to keep her daughters engaged in many activities. Mrs. Jenkins takes Juliana and Melissa to various museums and community programs, usually on a weekly basis.

Juliana currently attends a half-day Junior Kindergarten program at the same private school she began attending at age 3. Mrs. Jenkins states that Juliana does well in preschool academically; however, teachers report that she needs to build self-confidence, as she is often hesitant to answer questions or raise her hand in school. Melissa often "overshines" Juliana by answering questions for her or instructing Juliana on what she should and should not do. To help avoid this problem, Mr. and Mrs. Jenkins have asked that the girls be placed in separate kindergarten classrooms.

Testing Conditions

I tested Juliana in her home at around 9:30 A.M. I sat on the floor and Juliana kneeled at a child-sized table in the office area of their open-floor-plan first floor, as this is where she requested to be tested. About 20 feet away, another graduate student was testing Melissa with the Peabody Picture Vocabulary test at their dining-room table. Testing began well and Juliana was very attentive and engaged. After a few questions she stated that she wished she had a chair, so I got a stepstool for her to sit on and she was satisfied with that. About five questions after that, however, I noticed that she began watching her sister and Harry, the other graduate student. I asked her if she would rather go somewhere else in the house so that she would be less distracted, but she did not wish to do this. I would gently remind her to pay attention when her eyes started to drift. A few questions later, Juliana requested that we move downstairs to the basement. She explained to me that she kept looking and listening to Harry and Melissa and so was having a hard time paying attention. We then moved the table downstairs to the basement. Once we were in the basement, she was moving around much more than she had been upstairs, even lying on the ground at one point, and began asking when the "test" was going to be over (I found it interesting that she referred to it as a test as I had only called it a "game"). I considered stopping testing at this point, but it was only a question or two later when it was time to stop testing due to test rules anyway. Total testing time was about 40 minutes. Upon completion, Juliana's mother asked me how it went. I explained that she was getting restless near the end of the testing. She said to me that that was likely due to her Sensory Integration Disorder and that testing is difficult for her.

Statement of Decision-Making

I used the TEMA-3 (Test of Early Mathematics Ability), to assess Juliana's mathematics abilities. It is designed for use on children age 4 years 0 months through 8 years 11 months. It is composed of 72 questions, and is individually administered with testing beginning at the age-appropriate question. Testing is discontinued when the child answers five consecutive questions incorrectly. An examiner's manual, picture book, manipulatives, and a worksheet for the child to place written responses are used to administer the test. Answers are recorded in a recording booklet. For some questions, the child can get one or two of several trials wrong, and still get the answer correct; other questions require all trials to be correct. Scoring is simple: correct responses receive one point and incorrect responses receive zero points. The basal is formed when the child answers five items in a row correctly, and the ceiling is reached when the child items five consecutive items incorrectly. Two forms of the test come in the test kit, so it is well suited as a pre-test and post-test. Another aspect of the TEMA-3 that I felt helped expand its usefulness is also described in its review from the *Mental Measurements Yearbook*. Crehan (2003) explains, "The TEMA-3 materials provide more than a test of mathematics. The accompanying Assessment Probes and Instructional Activities presents an item-by-item set of useful guides to the understanding of each task and the child's responses. The author describes the task, comprehension of the task, underlying thought processes, probes to stimulate response, and suggested instructional activities."

I decided on this test based on my prior observations of Juliana and her family. Juliana's home is full of children's literature. From the time they were newborns, they have been read to daily. When I began working with them—when they had just turned three years old—I would always read them five books before naptime (their mother explained that this is what they were accustomed to) and another five books before bedtime. So, although I have seen Juliana interact with literature on many occasions (noticing her ability to comprehend stories, hearing her expansive vocabulary and witnessing her beginning stages of writing), I realized I have rarely seen her doing math. Therefore, I wanted to assess her in this area. Also, math is one of my personal weak areas and I felt administering a math assessment would be good practice for my future teaching and testing.

Child: Juliana Jenkins **Test:** TEMA-3, *Test of Early Mathematics Ability*

Results Table

Correct Answers	Incorrect Answers
A1. Perception of small numbers	A9. Number Constancy
A2. Produce finger displays: 1, 2, many	A13. Number After: 1 to 9
A3. Verbal counting by Ones: 1 to 5	A15. Writing Numerals: Single-Digit Numbers
A4. Perception of *More*: Up to 10 items	A16. Concretely Modeling + Word Problems: Sums up to 9.
A5. Nonverbal Production: 1 to 4 items	A17. Part-Whole Concept
A6. Enumeration: 1 to 5 items	A18. Written Representation of Sets up to 5
A7. Cardinality Rule	A20. Choosing the Larger Number: Number Comparisons 5 to 10.
A8. Nonverbal (Concrete) + & –	A21. Verbal Counting by Ones: To 21
A10. Produce Sets: Up to 5 items	A22. Number After: 2-Digit Numbers to 40
A11. Produce Finger Displays to 5	A23. Enumeration: 6 to 10 items
A12. Verbal Counting by Ones: 1 to 10	A24. Verbally Count Back from 10
A14. Reading Numerals: Single-Digit Numbers	
A19. Choosing the Largest Number: Number Comparisons 1 to 5	

Questions were divided by age on the score sheet. They were divided as follows:

A1.–A6.: Age 3. Juliana answered all of these items correctly.
A7.–A14.: Age 4. Juliana answered 6 of 8 items correctly.
A15.–A21.: Age 5. Juliana answered 1 of 7 items correctly.
A22.–A31.: Age 6. Juliana did not answer any of the 3 items that she was tested on correctly. The TEMA-3 guidelines state testing should be ended when the child answers five items in a row incorrectly. As Juliana was incorrect in the last two Age 5 questions, I stopped testing after the third age 6 question.
Total Raw Score: 13
Age Equivalent: 4 years 3 months
Grade Equivalent: Preschool
Percentile: 32
Math Ability Score: 93
Standard Error of Measurement: 4
Math Ability Score Range: 89–97

Juliana's math ability score of 93 is considered average (the average range is 90–100 points). Her results place her in the 32nd percentile. Her age equivalency (or "mathematics age") was that of a child age 4 years and 3 months. Her grade equivalency is preschool. Details of items answered correctly and incorrectly are listed in the previous table. NOTE: The examiner's manual emphasizes that age and grade equivalency should be interpreted with caution. Test creators state that examiners should avoid using them whenever possible and that standard scores and percentile ranks is a far better procedure.

The items Juliana answered correctly measured the following mathematics abilities: perception of small numbers, producing finger displays to 5, verbal counting by ones: 1 to 10, perception of *more*—up to 10 items, nonverbal production of 1 to 4 items (i.e., counting out tokens), enumeration of 1 to 5 items, nonverbal addition and subtraction (using tokens), producing sets—up to 5 items, reading single-digit numbers, and choosing the larger number—number comparisons 1 to 5 (this last item was a five-year-old item). For the items that Juliana answered incorrectly, the test authors suggest activities parents and teachers can do with Juliana to help encourage her development in these areas. They are as follows:

- "Number constancy" is remembering that a group of items remains the same after changing their grouping (i.e., putting tokens in the shape of a circle) and not having to recount the items. One of the only ways to teach this skill is to simply remind them that when you move items around, the number does not change and continue to do practice trials.
- "Number after" refers to memorizing which numbers "come after" a given number. In order to perform this skill, they must memorize the order of numbers 1 through 10. Practice asking "what number comes just after . . ." can help with this skill.

All other items answered incorrectly were in the five- and six-year-old areas of the test and do not align with the Early Learning Standards, but rather with the Early Elementary Standards and therefore should not be a concern until kindergarten. Those areas were: writing single-digit numbers, concretely modeling addition word problems (sums up to 9), part–whole concept, written representations of sets up to 5, choosing the larger number—number comparisons 5 to 10, and verbal counting by ones—to 21.

Questions to Consider

1. Where will you begin math instruction with Juliana? What role will the diagnosis of sensory integration disorder play in shaping your plans?
2. How might you assist parents in supporting Juliana and Melissa in their separate growth and development trajectories?

CHILD STUDY 24

Howard Bullett, a First-Grader

Background Information

Over the last three months, I have observed a first-grade student named Howard. Howard attends Garfield Elementary School. He is one of seven boys in a class of 17. Howard did not go to kindergarten or preschool at Garfield Elementary School; he went to a Montessori school. Howard's parents, Mr. and Mrs. Bullett chose the Montessori kindergarten because it provided whole-day programming. Howard is a seven-year-old of average height and weight. From observing Howard, it seems that he is at the expected levels for physical and cognitive development. Howard's personality seems very shy or cautious. He does not talk unless you ask him questions. It takes some time to get to know Howard. It has been three months since Howard started school and he now is starting to make friends with his classmates and to open up with them.

Howard is the youngest of three brothers. The oldest brother, Steve, is 14 and the middle boy, Leroy, is 10. Howard says that he gets along with both his brothers and they are nice to him. He went on to tell me that some of his friends on their street do not get along with their brothers and he is glad that he does.

Every Friday, Howard goes to after-school gym at Garfield Elementary School. He occasionally has play dates with his friends. He has not had a play date with any of the peers in his class. Howard mostly plays with friends in the neighborhood.

Howard lives with both his mother and father in an upper-middle-class home in a northern suburb. Both parents went to college and have careers. Mrs. Bullett is an executive for a software company and Mr. Bullett is an executive for a sales company. Both of Howard's parents expect him to do very well in school and end up getting a good job just like they have. Therefore, they encourage Howard to do his homework on time and to get extra help on reading assignments.

Howard is involved in the reading recovery program at Garfield Elementary School. The reading recovery program works with Howard 30 minutes a day for 20 weeks on intense reading skills with a learning disabilities teacher.

Questions for This Study

The central question is what Howard's strengths and weaknesses are and why he scored so low on the initial tests in the beginning of the year. I was interested in knowing whether he made any improvements, or if he is still at the same level.

Conditions of the Test Administration

The first time I tested Howard, it was in the morning, at 8:45, when school starts. Howard was alert and ready to take the test. The test was administered in a room that was quiet and not distracting. There were no environmental factors that would have any influence on this test.

Behaviors During the Test

The first time I administered the test, Howard was energetic and ready to take the test. As Howard was reading, he would start to become frustrated and get distracted. At one point during the test, he was playing with his pencil instead of reading the test. I held the pencil for Howard to eliminate any further distractions. The second time he took the test I held the pencil until Howard had to use it. During both sessions Howard would become frustrated about the test questions and words that he did not know.

Although his breathing became louder and exasperated, he did complete the test. The second time I met with him, Howard's attitude had changed and he seemed like he wanted to try the test again. Howard's behavior changed when he was asked questions about the book he had just read. He was frustrated while reading the book, because he was having difficulty reading the words, but his attitude changed when I asked him comprehension questions about what he had just read. This was also the case for the second and much more difficult book. He became frustrated that he did not know how to read most words on the page, but he began to fully engage when I asked him question about what he had just read.

Furthermore, Howard's behavior changed when he was tested on Cloze questions. Howard could not read each sentence, but once I read each sentence to him, he was able to fill in the missing word. Howard's attitude changed once he was able to understand each word to fill into the sentence. Howard was frustrated in some areas and was fully engaged and ready to move onto the next question in other area.

Chosen Tests

I chose to do these three tests because I wanted to learn more about Howard's strengths and weaknesses. These where the appropriate tests in finding this information.

Teacher/Caregiver Report:

Total Words: 72	Total Micues: 4	Miscue Rate: 1:5	Total Self-Corrections: 2	Self-Correction Rate: 1:3	Accuracy Percentile: 71%
95–100% accuracy = Independent	90–94% accuracy = Instructional	Below 90% accuracy = Frustration	Total Words divided by Total Miscues = Miscue Rate	Miscues + Self-Corrections divided by Self-Corrections = Self-Correction Rate	Total Words + Miscues divided by Total Words = Accuracy Percentage

The results as shown in the table demonstrate how Howard did on the oral reading record from the Rigby Literacy Test. This test begins with reading level 5 for a first grader; I started Howard on level 5 of the test. Howard was to read the story *The Dentist* from the Rigby Series (Rigby Pearson Australia) and answer some questions after. It is evident that Howard has a miscue rate of 1:5. With this ratio, it makes it difficult for Howard to read fluently. Howard needs to work on his sight words in order to improve his fluency of reading.

Howard's accuracy is at 71% and he is well below 90% accuracy. Howard falls well below frustration level. He did become frustrated during the test, but he wanted to continue. This level needs to improve during the course of the year. This is well below average for this time during the year. This was at the first level of the test. This may be an indication as why Howard is in the reading recovery program.

The next test I gave Howard was the Fry Sight Words test. This test is composed of 300 sight words. There are 10 columns consisting of 10 words each in each grade level. The student must be able to read at least 7 out of the 10 words correctly. If the first grader knows 100 words by the end of first grade, then he or she is at the first-grade level. If the first grader knows 200 words, then he or she is in the second-grade level; and if the first grader knows 300 words, he or she is at the third-grade level. This time in the year, the average first grader should be at the third or fourth column of words. Mid-year, they should be in columns five and six, and by the end of the year, they should know all 10 columns. In the beginning of the year, Howard was given the Fry Sight Word test and only knew 2 out of 10 words in column 1.

In column 1, Howard read all the words correctly. In column 2, he could not read the words "on" and "of." In column 3, he missed the word "good." In column 4, he missed the words "about," "her," and "do." Because Howard missed three words, I stopped testing. Howard fell in the correct column for where he is in the year.

The third type of test I did with Howard was the Cloze test. This type is a type of test that deletes words from a passage according to a word-count or sight-word formula. The student is to then fill in the missing blank with the sight words that are listed.

The first test was a worksheet with all of Howard's sight words on it. I asked Howard to read all of the sight words. Then Howard was to read the first sentence and fill in the blank with the correct word. This was a very difficult task for Howard, because he could not read the words in the sentence. I read the sentence and asked Howard for the word that went in the blank. Howard could not answer this question. I continued by saying each sight word with the rest of the sentence until Howard picked the correct word. This continued though all of the questions.

Howard's strengths are that he knows how to use the pictures as clues to help him understand and comprehend what he is reading. He could tell me what the story was about, just by looking at the pictures. Howard is also good at individual sight words, as indicated in the Fry Sight Word test.

Howard's weaknesses are that he does not sound out the words correctly. Howard lacks the knowledge of certain letter sounds such as the long and short vowels and the blends th, ch, and oo.

Howard also does not understand how to read site words when they are in a sentence. He can read these sight words independently but when they are in a sentence, he is unable to read and pronounce them correctly. This was demonstrated in the Cloze test when Howard could not put the sight words into the blanks of the sentence. I needed to read each sentence and ask Howard each individual word to see which one was correct. Howard's peers are able to do this type of test.

I suggested that the teacher begin working on sight words, letter sounds, reading strategies, and comprehension skills. Howard needs to work on understanding and using sight words within a story. I suggest that the teacher work on the activities similar to the Cloze test to get Howard to use his sight words within a sentence.

More emphasis needs to be on letter sounds for Howard. He does not understand some of the letter sounds, as well as the long and short vowel sounds. The teacher needs to work with Howard to improve his letter-sound skills. Using books that have rhyming and the same letter sounds will help Howard improve his sounds. In addition, going over the alphabet sounds each day would be useful.

Howard also needs to work on reading strategies and clues that help him sound out words he does not know in the story. He does not have any of these strategies now except for using the pictures as clues to understand the story. Howard only used self-correction twice within the story, which makes his self-correction rate 1:3.

Conclusion

Throughout this study, I have learned many things about Howard. Howard still struggles in the areas of letter sounds and vowels, sight words within a sentence or story, and reading strategies and clues to help him read more fluently. Howard's strengths are that he knows how to use the pictures in the story to help him comprehend the story that he is reading. He also understands sight words when they are isolated. Howard should continue working in the reading recovery program and if these skills do not change, he should be considered for additional diagnostic assessment.

Questions to Consider

1. How will you work with the reading recovery teacher to assist Howard with letter sounds, sight words, and other reading strategies?
2. What software or computer-assisted programs might be valuable for Howard to use at school and at home or in the neighborhood library?

CHILD STUDY 25

Patrick Bennett, a First Grader

Background Information

For this child study, I worked with a young boy who lives in my neighborhood. Patrick is six years old and is in first grade at a local Catholic school. He will turn seven years old in January. Patrick's parents are married and the family is upper-middle-class. Mr. Bennett works downtown in marketing and Mrs. Bennett stays at home. Both parents read to Patrick, socialize with him, and provide opportunities for socialization with peers through organized sports and play dates. Patrick's sister, Melvina is four years old and has Down syndrome. Both Melvina and Patrick know how to use sign language and do so on occasion.

It is clear from my conversations with both Patrick and Mrs. Bennett, that Patrick truly enjoys school. Mrs. Bennett says that he doing very well in math and absolutely loves reading. Recently, she noticed that he is becoming increasingly expressive when reading aloud. Mr. and Mrs. Bennett attempt to make time to read together every night. Currently, they are reading the first book in the Harry Potter series. Mrs. Bennett said they started reading the book to him, but now Patrick reads to them and that he really gets into character while reading. Overall, I find Patrick to be very bright, outgoing, inquisitive, and very articulate.

Assessment Chosen

I have known Patrick and his family for a year and spent a great deal of time with him last winter for an "Emergent Literacy Observation" project, which evaluated phonological and phonemic awareness, phonics, concepts about print and reading, and writing. I feel that this project gave me great insight into his literacy skills, which is why I chose Dynamic Indicators of Basic Early Literacy Skills (DIBELS) as my assessment tool. DIBELS measures were designed to assess three of the five ideas of early literacy: phonological awareness, alphabetic principle, and fluency with connected text. These measures have been found to be predictive of later reading proficiency. I conducted the Benchmark 1 for the beginning of first grade, which should be conducted in fall. This includes Letter Naming Fluency (LNF), Phoneme Segmentation Fluency (PSF), Nonsense Word Fluency (NWF), and Word Use Fluency (WUF), which is optional.

For LNF, students are presented with a page of upper- and lowercase letters arranged in a random order and are asked to name as many letters as they can, and the score is the number of letters named correctly in one minute. The PSF is intended to assess a student's ability to segment three- and four-phoneme words into their individual phonemes fluently. The examiner orally presents words of three to four phonemes and the student is to verbally produce the individual phonemes for each word. The number of correct phonemes produced in one minute determines the final score. In the NWF measure, the student is presented an 8.5" × 11" sheet of paper with randomly ordered VC (vowel, consonant) and CVC (consonant, vowel, consonant) nonsense words and asked to verbally produce the individual letter sound of each letter or verbally produce, or read, the whole nonsense word. The final score is the number of letter sounds produced correctly in one minute. For WUF, the student is orally presented with a word and is asked to use that word in a sentence. The examiner records the number of words used in the sentence and the final score is the total number of words correctly used.

Because I am familiar with Patrick's oral reading ability from last winter's project, I chose to administer one test from Benchmark 2, which should be administered in the winter. I chose Oral Reading Fluency (ORF), in which students are presented with a passage appropriate for their grade level and asked to read the passage aloud. Student performance is measured by having students read a passage aloud for one minute. Words omitted, substituted, and hesitations of more than three seconds are scored as errors. Words self-corrected within three seconds are scored as accurate. The number of correct words per minute from the passage is the oral reading fluency rate. To accompany the ORF, there is an optional measure called the Retell Fluency. This measure is designed to assess the comprehension of the passage read in the ORF by asking students to tell the examiner everything they can about the passage they just read. The score is the number of words the child produces in his or her retell.

Predictions

Last year, I noticed that Patrick seemed to have a mastery of both rhyme and blending, and that segmenting or pulling apart words provided more of a challenge. Though separating words into syllables came easy to him, isolating the beginning and ending sounds was by far the most difficult task I presented to him. Patrick prides himself on his ability to spell correctly. I believe that he envisions or recites the spelling of words when thinking about sound. I think it is this analysis that prevented him from identifying sounds rather than the letter names. Patrick had a strong mastery of phonics last year. He was able to correctly identify consonants and vowels, both upper- and lowercase. He recognized many high-frequency words and was excited by the reading process.

Because I was concerned with Patrick's ability to isolate sounds and segment words, I wondered how he would perform for the PSF measure. If his PSF score indicated a low skill level, would the development of his reading comprehension suffer? When used as recommended, DIBELS results can be used to evaluate individual student development as well as provide grade-level feedback toward validated instructional objectives. I was curious to see how Patrick's results would compare to his current success in school and his current reading ability. Would he need additional help in segmenting phonemes in order to be a proficient reader?

Administering the Test

While Mrs. Bennett did laundry and Melvina napped, Patrick and I sat at his dining room to work without the distraction of television or computer. This is how we spent both visits. During our first visit, we just played and colored and talked about school. He is a child who clearly likes school and spoke about math class as his favorite subject. During our second visit, I administered the DIBELS Benchmark 1 for first grade. I am aware that Patrick is quite the perfectionist. Because of this knowledge, I told him that I was practicing how to give tests, so that the pressure would be alleviated. I did ask him about tests at school and they didn't seem to be the source of any stress for him.

Patrick enjoyed the DIBELS exercises and was confident and articulate in his answers. He performed very well on the LNF. The PSF measure was a bit more challenging for him. The last word we reached in that test was "fish." He correctly produced the first two phonemes, then produced the s sound before self-correcting (which earned him full credit). He then said, "Fish. That's a hard one because sh is a digraph." For the NSF, he could choose to provide either the sounds of the letter or the whole word. For each of the 15 words, he produced the sounds of the letter. I think this was an easier task than the PSF because he was able to see the letters, rather than just listening to my prompts. This seems to indicate that he is a visual learner. I was impressed with his word choice and sentence construction during the WUF. He chose words like "poisonous" and said each sentence with great emotion, as if he was reading a story or imitating someone. I was truly impressed with his fluency during the ORF. He seems to have grown in his reading skills since we last met. He only had one error ("through" instead of "though") and added one word ("very"). His comprehension was also impressive, as he was able to remember many of the details of the story during the optional Retell Fluency.

Scoring

LNF

A benchmark goal is not provided for LNF, because according to the DIBELS creators, letter naming is not a crucial concept of early literacy skills. However, a score below 25 is described as

At Risk, a score between 25 and 37 is described as Some Risk, and a score above 37 is described as Low Risk. Patrick scored 63.

PSF

The benchmark goal is 35 to 45 correct phonemes per minute in the spring of kindergarten and fall of first grade. Intensive instructional support is suggested for those students who score below 10 in the spring of kindergarten and fall of first grade. Patrick scored 23.

NSF

The benchmark goal for Nonsense Word Fluency is 50 correct letter sounds per minute by mid first grade. Intensive instructional support is suggested for those students who score below 30 in the middle of first grade. Patrick scored 43.

WUF

A benchmark goal is not provided for WUF, because additional research is needed to establish its linkage to other big ideas of early literacy. It is an optional test. Patrick scored 45.

ORF

The benchmark goals are 40 in spring of first grade, 90 in spring of second grade, and 110 in the spring of third grade. Intensive instructional support is suggested if students score below 10 in spring of first grade, below 50 in spring of second grade, and below 70 in spring of third grade. Patrick scored 107.

RF

It appears children's retell scores may be typically about 50% of their oral reading fluency score, and that it is unusual for children reading more than 40 words per minute to have a retell score 25% or less than their oral reading fluency score. Patrick scored a 44, which is 41% of his oral reading fluency score.

Stakeholder Summaries

Summary for Teacher (Who Does Not Know Patrick)

Patrick is a very bright child who seems to learn visually. His scores do not indicate any major areas of concern. He scored a 63 on the LNF. Since a performance above 37 is described as Low Risk, I would say that there is no problem. His performance on the PSF earned him a score of 23, which is described as Emerging. I am not concerned about this score, because his performance on the NWF clearly indicates his ability to provide letter sounds. He scored a 43 on the NWF; a score above 24 is considered Low Risk. On the ORF, he earned a score of 107, which is clearly above average. The expectation is for a score of 40 at the end of first grade and a score of 110 at the end of third grade. Based upon his performance, I would say that he is at a third-grade reading level. His retell fluency demonstrates that he is comprehending material, and though he is not at 50% of his ORF score, he is close at 41%.

I think selecting challenging text for Patrick is the key to his development as a proficient reader. I also think asking him to make predictions before reading and providing him with questions after reading passages will help develop his reading comprehension. I believe Patrick will be an excellent model for reading fluency and will benefit from reading to others out loud.

Though Patrick seems to learn better when he can read or see the text, I don't think any accommodations should be made at this stage. I would monitor this throughout the school year to see whether any instructional support is needed. If so, you could teach him to translate what he hears into images, and record those images using webbing, mind-mapping techniques, or pictorial notes. Again, I don't consider this a weakness, but something to monitor.

References

Riedel, B. (2007, October). The relation between DIBELS, reading comprehension, and vocabulary in urban first-grade students. *Reading Research Quarterly, 42*(4), pp. 546–562. Retrieved November 9, 2008, from Education Research Complete database.

Riedel, B. (2007, October). A response to Samuels. *Reading Research Quarterly, 42*(4), p. 567. Retrieved November 9, 2008, from Education Research Complete database.

Rouse, H., & Fantuzzo, J. (2006, September). Validity of the dynamic indicators for basic early literacy skills as an indicator of early literacy for urban kindergarten children. *School Psychology Review, 35*(3), 341–355. Retrieved November 9, 2008, from Education Research Complete database.

Samuels, S. (2007, October). The DIBELS tests: Is speed of barking at print what we mean by reading fluency? *Reading Research Quarterly, 42*(4), pp. 563, 566. Retrieved November 9, 2008, from Education Research Complete database.

Questions to Consider

1. If you are not familiar with DIBELS, how do you understand the results of this assessment? Do you have the information about Patrick to begin teaching? If not, what will you do?
2. Do you agree with the way the parent report is presented? How might you shape it? What additional suggestions will you make to Mr. and Mrs. Bennett?

CHILD STUDY 26

Lucille O'Malley, a Kindergartener

Description

Lucille is a very cute, very precocious five-year-old. She is the oldest child of my aunt, Jo, and her partner, Glenda. She was the only child until the birth of her twin brothers, Lester and Murray, 1.5 months ago. Lucille is very talkative and inquisitive. Because she was an only child for so long, she spent a lot of time around adults. The parents' progressive parenting style has Lucille acting much older than a typical five-year-old.

Questions, Concerns, Problems

With the birth of her twin baby brothers, the focus has shifted from just Lucille to all three. I think the new additions have produced some changes in Lucille's behavior as she struggles to gain the attention she once had. One thing that helps with the transition is that Lucille is currently enrolled in kindergarten. This "big girl" world helps give Lucille an outlet to what is going on at home.

Family Background

Lucille comes from an upper-class family. Her family is different from the typical family in that her parents are a lesbian couple. They recently added twin boys to the family. Although her parents are very hands-on and involved in the children's upbringing, Lucille had a full-time nanny before she entered kindergarten. Lucille is very close to her extended family and grandparents.

Current Functioning

Lucille is a very smart, high-functioning five-year-old. She says a lot of things that are wise beyond her years. Her jokes are very funny and I believe this is because she is such a smart five-year-old. She is very independent and has been raised with a lot of discipline. She can hold her own with adults, which she often does.

Lucille's parents are very involved with teaching her cognitive and communication skills at home and she has been read to every day since she was born. Lucille is involved in many different extracurricular activities including dance, cheerleading, and soccer. Lucille has a very good imagination and has a fun time playing "make believe." She recently started running make-believe stores, movie theaters, and zoos out of her basement, creating signs and inviting customers. I think this level of play shows her advanced intellectual ability and the evidence of how much her parents have worked with her.

Lucille spent two years at a private preschool where she began going every other day, but finished going five days a week. She is currently in an all-day kindergarten at a private school in the city. Teachers report that they always love her because she is very smart and well-behaved, but also because of how funny she is. She gets along well with others in her class but occasionally can have a tantrum or a meltdown. She is used to getting her way at home and I feel that sometimes she finds it hard to share or compromise with other children.

Clinical Activity K and 1 Brigance Screen II

I met with Lucille at her home. We met in her bedroom, where we sat on the floor to make her more comfortable. She was very interested in what we were doing and I told her I was "giving her a test made for kindergartners." I stressed that she was helping me with a project for my class and she was very excited to help.

I started by asking Lucille her personal information—name, age, address, birthday, and telephone number. She knew all of these. Sometimes when she answered, she kind of gave me a cute attitude, like "Why wouldn't I know my own name?" Her mom, however, was surprised that she knew her phone number.

We continued to the second section, where Lucille was to identify body parts. She got all of them correctly, except for waist. When I pointed to the waist, she simply said, "Stomach."

When we measured her gross-motor skills, the Brigance test said I was allowed to actively participate. It had her stand on one foot for 10 seconds, so we did that together. She liked getting up and didn't seem to act like she felt this was a "test." She successfully exhibited all of her gross-motor skills.

The next section measured her color recognition, which she did correctly. She answered all of the questions very quickly, with no hesitation. The next section measured her visual motor skills. She did a good job copying the shapes, although her triangle was a little iffy. It was hard to score this one, because it didn't look like the shapes the test classified as wrong, but it didn't look like the correct shapes either. I gave it to her because she knew what she was doing.

The next section of the test was the one where Lucille faltered the most. This section had the child draw a person. Lucille left out a couple of body parts of the person, including ears, neck, and hands. She was then asked to print her full name. She did a great job with this. Brigance says that if the child does this with ease, have them print other information. I had her print the names of her baby brothers, which she did correctly.

After this, I asked Lucille to "count as high as she could." She looked at me with the biggest eyes and said, "This could take forever!" I had her start counting and I stopped her right after she got to 100. I really think it could have lasted forever!

She excelled on the remainder of the test, which included numeral comprehension, number readiness, and reading uppercase and lowercase letters. I had her speak about herself at the end to measure her syntax and fluency, which is very good. She is quite talkative and demonstrates the ability to hold a conversation.

Lucille seemed very at ease during the testing. She was a little hesitant when we first sat down with the task at hand, but I believe that is probably because she is used to playtime when I come over. As she progressed with the test, she was serious and exhibited a studious side.

For the Teacher

Lucille was very proficient during the Brigance test, and excelled at most levels. I think her strong suit is definitely language arts and communication skills. She obviously excels at writing and speaking. Though Lucille was sufficient at every assessment, I could see her gross-motor skills being more of a weakness as she continues with her education.

I think to help Lucille in the classroom, one could strengthen her already strong point of reading and writing. Challenge her with more difficult books and have her show you what she has learned by administering performance-based activities. I think her gross-motor skills will improve with age and with participation in group sports.

References

Brigance, A. (2005). *K & 1 Brigance Screen II.* North Billerica, MA: Curriculum Associates.

Costenbader, V., Rohrer, A., Difonzo, N. (2000). Kindergarten screening: A survey of current practice. *Psychology in the Schools,* 37, 323–332.

Popham, J. (2008). *Classroom assessment: What teachers need to know.* Boston, MA: Pearson Education, Inc.

Questions to Consider

1. As Lucille's teacher, what will you do to support her acceptance of baby brothers? What books might you add to the library?
2. What will you do to help Lucille's gross-motor development?

CHILD STUDY 27

Frank Montgomery, a Third Grader

Frank is an eight-year-old healthy boy who loves sports and has a knack for making people smile. He is above-average in height with a thin build and chestnut-brown hair and piercing blue eyes. Adjectives such as kind-hearted, sensitive, empathetic, high-energy, and happy can be used to describe Frank's personality.

Family Background

Frank is the youngest of three boys. He has two older brothers, George (age 11) and Alvin (age 15). Frank and his two brothers are members of an intact nuclear family that is supportive and provides a nurturing home environment within the family residence. Frank's parents, Mr. and Mrs. Montgomery, follow a credo that they will help their children in any means possible as long it as it is ethical and conveys sound judgment. The high socioeconomic status of Frank's parents has allowed this second grader to have access to many support services and resources and other tangible goods such as books and toys. In terms of familial problems, I am not aware of any except the imminent death of his grandmother, although it appears Frank does not understand the magnitude of this evident, due to his young age.

Early Developmental Milestones

In regards to Frank's early developmental milestones and medical history, it is evident that Frank has not had the same development as the majority of his same-age peers. First and foremost, Frank did not start speaking until the age of 4. This is obviously a very late start for the use of oral language. Frank's parents choose not to label Frank with any syndrome or disability, but rather choose to talk about his behaviors merely for the sake of brainstorming the best educational practices for him. Nonetheless, Frank's late arrival at the oral language milestone coupled with Frank's present difficulties with communicating and understanding social conventions has led my fellow educators and me to believe that Frank may be suffering from Asperger syndrome or other communication disability. This is not a definite prognosis by any means, but merely a possible reason for Michael's behavior.

Self-Help and Daily Living Skills

In terms of his self-help and daily living skills, Frank is very reliant upon others for making his day run smoothly. Between his mother, babysitter, and academic staff, Frank is given constant assistance throughout the day and thus is not very independent. This is obviously not very uncommon for a second-grade student, but Frank does exhibit a bit more dependency on adults than many of his same-age peers. For instance, Frank does not lead his own morning routine or after-school homework routine. He is in need of many explicit directions in order for him to complete many of the functions that are necessary for living.

Social Skills and Reactions to Others

Despite early language difficulties, Frank enjoys social interactions and has a number of friends. Many of these friends are his classmates who, like Frank, have attended a private school since kindergarten. This school prides itself on fostering an environment of inclusion and also on small student to teacher ratios (under 20:1); therefore, Frank and his schoolmates have created very close bonds throughout their early school years. His empathetic reactions to other students are exemplary. A hug or a "are you okay?" are commonplace offerings made by Frank. Adults are also subject to this tenderness.

Emotional Reactions and Communication Skills

This sensitivity and emotionality are not always manifested in a positive manner. For instance, when faced with academic or athletic challenges, Frank's emotional reactions are amplified and can result in tears, yelling, drastic body movements, and/or excitability displayed through rapid motion of his hands. This happens particularly during team sports when Frank's team is not winning. Frank, although a determined and dedicated athlete, does not exhibit a lot of control over his body, and therefore can sometimes be described as awkward when partaking in physical activities. Also, Frank, although possessing an ability to sense and respond to others' emotions, is not able to understand perspectives, likes, dislikes, or opinions that are different from his own. Furthermore, Frank is not able to understand idioms or figurative language, although he is able to joke and laugh when humor is used. Frank, Frank's family, and an occupational therapist and speech therapist are all working to help him with communication, understanding others' perspectives, competitiveness, and life skills, and so far they have made great strides!

School Adjustment

Overall, Frank enjoys attending school, has a desire to please his teacher, likes to be successful, and dislikes challenging material. In terms of his learning environment, Frank thrives in routines and structured environments, gets very upset when routines are broken, and has issues following directions when given more than one directive at a time. Luckily for Frank, his second-grade teacher has created a very structured learning environment with a respectively structured schedule that includes times for mental breaks including snack time, lunch, recess, and P.E. This schedule has proved to be very beneficial for Frank, because it means that he follows a fairly rigid routine and grants him time to reorganize himself. In addition to a structured school day, Frank benefits from reminders, repetition of directions, priming, and encouraging words. As mentioned previously, Frank's school practices inclusion; therefore, there is no pull-out or resource room available for Frank. Most of Frank's in-school support or individualized instruction comes from me, his personal shadow. I do not follow any formal IEP, but I am present to help keep Frank organized, on-task, and emotionally stable. Furthermore, I give Frank one-on-one instruction during guided reading time in order to improve his reading comprehension. Individual attention is also provided during math and writing, but only upon Frank's request or when Frank is seen having difficulty with the material. The ultimate goal for Frank, as created by his parents and teacher, is for him to be able to complete his academic work independently.

Academic Functioning

As mentioned earlier, Frank attends a small private school. It is in this school environment that I have had the opportunity to work with him in the second-grade classroom since the beginning of this school year. Frank's biggest academic hurdle is his inability to focus for long lengths of time. He has a very difficult time staying focused and making transitions between subjects and tasks. This inattentiveness does not manifest itself via hyperactivity, but rather Frank appears to merely "zone out," for lack of a better term. Despite his attention issues, Frank is able to perform well on the second-grade curriculum in an inclusive environment. His strongest subject is math. Frank is fluent with computational exercises and mathematical procedures, but faces more difficulty with mathematical word problems. I attribute this difficulty less to Frank's mathematical capabilities and more to his reading capabilities. From spending extensive time observing and instructing Frank's reading, I can conclude that his fluency and phonics skills are extremely strong, but his comprehension skills are weak. Frank's strong phonics and phonemic awareness bring him much success in spelling, but not in the realm of writing. During writing exercises, Frank has trouble coming up with novel ideas, writing in length, and being detailed. His sentence composition and grammar are excellent, though.

Central Question

Due to my close relationship to Frank and the fact that his reading comprehension deficiencies are strongly affecting his performance in all subjects, Frank was a great choice for my child study. The purpose of studying him is to gain valuable information in order to help me answer the central question: Why is Frank not achieving the ultimate goal of reading comprehension? I intend to use the test results to inform my educational decisions related to Frank. More specifically, I intended to tailor his reading instruction to meet his needs as determined by a standardized reading assessment.

Assessment Method

In choosing the best assessment instrument for these intentions, I selected a standardized test that measures many skills related to successful reading including decoding, vocabulary, comprehension, and word recognition. This battery of norm-referenced reading and related tests is entitled the Gray Diagnostic Reading Test-2 or the GDRT-2. According to the Examiner's Manual, the GDRT-2 "was built to provide users with a comprehensive measure of reading skills." More specifically, the test is designed "determine strengths and weaknesses, document progress in reading programs, help diagnose specific reading problems, and serve as a research tool for use in the continuing examination of reading" (Bryant, Wiederholt, & Bryant, 2004, p. 4). The test is "appropriate for individuals ages 6 years, 0 months through 13 years, 11months" (p. 2). Due to the description of the test and its uses, the GDRT-2 appeared to be an excellent choice for answering my question concerning Frank's reading abilities. Mrs. Montgomery agreed that this test would be an outstanding way for us to diagnose and report on Frank's reading abilities.

Conditions of the Test Administration

The test was administered after school at approximately 3:30 in the dining room of Frank's home. During the one 90-minute testing session, the room was quiet, dimly lit, and the dining-room table provided ample workspace for Frank and me to take the test. Before administering the actual test, I primed Frank by telling him that I wanted to learn about how he reads so I could help him best during the school day. Frank gave me no complaints or hesitation. He approached the test with no apparent anxiety or fear, although hid did voice on a few occasions that the test material was getting challenging. I administered all seven subtests of the GDRT-2. The seven subtests are as follows, with the last three being considered supplemental subtests because "their content represents only a correlative relationship to reading" (Bryant, Wiederholt, & Bryant, 2004, p. 4):

1. Word Recognition
2. Phonetic Analysis
3. Reading Vocabulary
4. Meaningful Reading
5. Listening Vocabulary
6. Rapid Naming
7. Phonological Awareness

Summary of Subtest Scores

Upon discovering the correct scoring procedures for each subtest, it was clear that the scores provided by the GDRT-2 were aligned with my observations of Frank's reading capabilities. In the table, Frank's scores are presented by subtest.

	Percentile Rank	Age Equivalent	Grade Equivalent	Scaled Score	Descriptive Rating
Word Recognition	**84%**	**11.0**	**6.0**	**13**	**above average**
Phonetic Analysis	**98%**	**13.9**	**8.7**	**16**	**superior**
Reading Vocabulary	**91%**	**11.0**	**6.0**	**14**	**above average**
Meaningful Reading	**N/A**	**N/A**	**N/A**	**N/A**	**N/A**
Listening Vocabulary	**75%**	**9.9**	**4.7**	**12**	**average**
Rapid Naming	**37%**	**7.9**	**2.7**	**9**	**average**
Phonological Awareness	**84%**	**11.0**	**6.0**	**13**	**above average**

Superior Rating

Frank received one "superior" descriptive rating on a core subtest. This remarkably high score was on the Phonetic Analysis subtest. According to this subtest, Frank's ability to correctly pronounce printed pseudowords is above that of an average eighth-grader in the seventh month of the school year and that 98% of the standardized sample scored at or below Frank on this particular subtest. This is quite impressive, but not a surprise. Frank has wowed me many times at his ability to decode long, phonetically complicated words and his corresponding skill at spelling these words.

Above Average Rating

On three of the GDRT-2 subtests, Frank received "above average" descriptive ratings. The three tests are Word Recognition, Reading Vocabulary, and Phonological Awareness. Word Recognition is nothing more than what its title suggests. Frank was asked to read aloud a series of printed words in this particular subtest. His performance on the Word Recognition subtest was similar to an 11-year-old or a sixth-grader at the beginning of the school year. These two normative measures indicate that Frank's word recognition skills are over two years above Frank's chronological age and 3.5 years above his grade placement. On a more interpretive, holistic level, these scores imply that Frank's sight word bank is large and that his reading comprehension issues are not due to his inability to recognize common words.

The Reading Vocabulary subtest asks children to use word recognition skills as well as their knowledge of word meanings. More specifically, Frank was asked to "select two words from the five that are meaningful opposites" (Bryant, Wiederholt, & Bryant, 2004, p. 3). On this subtest, Frank scored at or above 91% of the standardized sample, and again his equivalent scores were the same as an 11-year-old or a sixth-grader at the beginning of the school year. Frank's "above average" rating on this test indicates that he understands the meaning of many nouns and adjectives and also has a strong grasp on oppositional relationship between the same nouns and adjectives. Therefore, if using this test to determine Frank's strengths and weaknesses, his performance on this test suggests that his reading vocabulary can be placed in the "strengths" category.

The Phonological Awareness supplemental subtest has no printed component and is administered orally. In the GDRT-2 Examiner's Manual, the tests format is described as follows with two accompanying examples: "The student hears a spoken word, repeats it, and says the word again, deleting a designated phoneme sound or group of phonemes (e.g., store without the /t/ is sore; basketball with /ball/ is basket)" (Bryant, Wiederholt, & Bryant, 2004, p. 8). Although he initially was a bit confused about how I was asking him to manipulate spoken words, Frank soon caught on and exhibited a strong phonological awareness. His scores place him above 84% of other students his age that took the same test. As with the two previously discussed "above average" subtests, Frank scored as well as an 11-year-old or a sixth-grade student at the beginning of the academic year. These scores convey that Frank is able to delete phonemes from words with success, and more generally speaking, Frank understands that words are composed of individual sounds and that these sounds can be manipulated to create new word, or, more generally, Frank has a strong phonemic awareness.

Average

On two of the supplemental subtests, Frank received a descriptive rating of "average." These tests are Listening Vocabulary and Rapid Naming. Listening Vocabulary differs from Reading Vocabulary in that there are no printed words. Rather, the subtest uses pictures to measure an individual's receptive vocabulary. Frank nearly missed the "above average" mark on this test with normative scores such as a 75th percentile rank; an age equivalent of a 9 years, 9 months; and a grade equivalent of 4.7. Therefore, one can conclude that Frank's receptive vocabulary, like his reading vocabulary, is strong and is likely not the underlying cause of his reading comprehension issues that have been affecting him at school.

Rapid Naming is the sole subtest with a time component. In this supplemental subtest, students "view rows of known letters and words and says aloud as many of them as they can as fast as they can" (Bryant, Wiederholt, & Bryant, 2004, p. 4). Due to Frank's age, he was only shown words during his testing session. It was clear that the stopwatch instilled a bit of anxiety in Frank. The 89 seconds he required to read all the provided two- and three-letter words granted Frank a score above 37% of his same-age peers as well as an age equivalent of 7 years, 9 months, and a grade equivalent of second grade, seventh month. These scores are not worthy of excitement, considering that Frank's chronological age is older than the age equivalent yielded by the subtest. It is difficult to determine whether Frank's scores were muddled by his nervousness over the daunting stopwatch. If not, then this subtest would suggest that Frank would benefit from some fluency practice via timed readings.

Below Average/Inconclusive

The Meaningful Reading subtest provided no scores for Frank, because upon taking the Level B test, intended to assess "students' understanding of passages," Frank did not achieve a basal set. Following the test procedures, I then administered the Level A Meaningful Reading test, intended to measure "basic reading skills" (Bryant, Wiederholt, & Bryant, 2004, p. 3). Because this test tests only conventions of print, it does not yield a basal or ceiling set for any test subject. Thus, Frank achieved no score for the Meaningful Reading portion of the GDRT-2. The lack of score, however, did not prevent me from gaining valuable information from this subtest. Frank's inability to attain a basal set on the Level B indicated that these test items were too difficult for him and the Level A test , for children in grades K–1, would be a better indicator of his literacy. Frank did not miss one item on the Level A test, which asked him handle a book and questioned him on his knowledge of where to stop and start reading. Therefore, Frank has mastered concepts of print. In conclusion, Frank's performance on the Meaningful Reading subtest indicates that Frank's reading comprehension, as related to the Cloze procedure on short passages presented in the Level B test, is very low. As a second grader, Frank is expected to read longer expository and nonfiction texts; thus, if the Meaningful Reading subtest is a true indicator of his reading comprehension skills, it is evident that Frank is in need of a reading intervention focused on comprehension!

Summary of Composite Ability Scores for Core Subtests

	Ability Score	Percentile Rank	Descriptive Rating
Decoding	127	97	superior
Comprehension	82	12	below average
General Reading	105	63	average

In addition to providing five normative number-based scores for each subtest, the GDRT-2 also provides three composite ability scores for each subtest. By adding the scaled scores of particular subtests and translating those new scale scores into ability scores and percentile ranks, one is able to attain a descriptive rating for particular reading skills. The chart demonstrates clearly that Frank's performance on the subtests indicate that his Decoding is "superior." The GDRT-2 Examiner's Manual states that readers "with high DEC scores have excellent word identification skills, either by possessing an extensive sight vocabulary or by being able to recognize phonetic patterns in words and use that skill to identify words" (Bryant, Wiederholt, & Bryant, 2004, p. 25). Frank's Comprehension is "below average." This low composite score is due primarily to the "zero" he scored on the Meaningful Reading subtest. Referencing the Examiner's Manual again, "low COM scores mean that the student has difficulty with word meanings and/or with using content to identify missing words in continuous text" (Bryant, Wiederholt, & Bryant, 2004, p. 26). Because comprehension, not decoding, is the ultimate end goal of reading, it is evident that Frank needs individualized instruction in comprehension in order for him to be a reader who not only gains meaning from text, but also gains pleasure from it. Lastly, Frank's General Reading was calculated at "average," due to the balancing between his decoding prowess and comprehension difficulties.

Recommendations for Teacher

First and foremost, Frank is a kind, respectful, and dedicated student. His desire to succeed and his motivation to learn are quite impressive. After spending thorough time instructing, observing, and assessing Frank, it is evident he is a student who will benefit from individualized instruction in reading comprehension.

Since the beginning of this academic year, I have spent every day with Frank in his second-grade school environment as his shadow. From my academic interactions with Frank, it became apparent quickly that he experiences much difficulty with reading comprehension. I have seen him on several occasions read a text fluently and with expression, but with little to no understanding of the meaning of the text. Therefore, I thought it appropriate to administer a standardized assessment to Frank in order to better decipher if any particular reading skills, such as decoding or vocabulary, were the source of Frank's comprehension issues. I selected the Gray Diagnostic Reading Test-2, a norm-referenced assessment that was built to "provide users with a comprehensive measure of reading skill." The test is composed of seven subtests:

1. Word Recognition
2. Phonetic Analysis
3. Reading Vocabulary
4. Meaningful Reading
5. Listening Vocabulary
6. Rapid Naming
7. Phonological Awareness

According to the seven subtests, Frank's strengths, as related to reading, are phonics, phonological awareness, word recognition, and reading vocabulary. These strengths are conveyed by "superior" or "above average" descriptive ratings as well as age and grade equivalents that are well beyond Frank's chronological age and grade placement.

This standardized assessment also revealed that Frank is "average" in terms of his listening vocabulary and his ability to rapidly read common English words, entitled the Rapid Naming subtest. Thus, Frank's reading skills in relation to his receptive vocabulary and fluency could be sharpened via timed readings and the use of high-frequency vocabulary words when conversing with or giving instructions to Frank.

My observations in Frank's classroom environment and his inability to reach a basal set on the reading passages of the GDRT-2's Meaningful Reading subtest both indicate that Frank's apparent reading difficulties are caused by his weak comprehension skills. As you know, comprehension is a necessary tool for learning in second-grade and in later grades, and therefore, it is necessary for Frank to receive intense comprehension instruction so that he can be successful in all subjects.

The instructional implications for that can be drawn from Frank's performance of the seven subtests of the GDRT-2 are clear. Frank is in need of comprehension instruction. This instruction can be a part of guided reading time in which Frank reads short passages in the presence of a teacher and then completes activities that allow him to practice his literal comprehension skills. These activities can include short answers response questions, sequencing of events, story elements, and reader response. Furthermore, Frank would also benefit from priming before reading an unfamiliar text. Priming should include reviewing new or complicated vocabulary, scanning the text with regards to length and pictures, and pre-reading the material. This would help Frank become familiar with the reading selection and therefore better able to comprehend the story when read as a class or individually. Last, when reading with Frank, encourage him to make connections to the text. These can be connections to him, another book, or the world. The point is to make the text relevant to his life so that his interest is piqued and he has an attachment to the text, and thus his comprehension is likely to be greater.

Once Frank has shown improvement in his ability to comprehend text on a literal level, the next step would be to approach text on an inferential level. However, I will inform you that he has a difficult time understanding idioms and figurative language. These types of speech would be a great thing to practice in the future. I feel that by improving Frank's reading comprehension, his performance in other subjects with accordingly improve, because reading is an integral component to nearly every subject. I also suggest that after long-term instruction has occurred, the second form of the test, Form B, should be administered in order to gauge progress. I am confident that with precise, consistent, and engaging comprehension instruction, Frank will be a more confident reader and will find more success in second grade and beyond! Please contact me with any questions, comments, or concerns.

References

Bryant, B. R., Wiederholt, J. L., & Bryant, D. P. (2004). *Gray Diagnostic Reading Tests-Second Edition Examiner's Manual*. Austin: Pro-Ed.

Margolis, H. & D'Onofrio, A. (2004). *Review of the Gray Diagnostic Reading Test-Second Edition (GDRT-2), Seventeenth Mental Measurements Yearbook*, 866–872. Retrieved November 21, 2008, from EBSCOHost Mental Measurements Yearbook database.

Popham, W. James. (2008) *Classroom assessment: What teachers need to know* (5th ed.). Boston: Allyn & Bacon.

Questions to Consider

1. The teacher candidate, Frank's shadow at school, suggests that he may have an identifiable special education condition. How would the school verify this possibility? What collaboration from family would be required?
2. What strategies will you utilize to develop Frank's reading comprehension? What materials and software might you include in this work?
3. How is the relationship of the "shadow" with Frank a strength for him? What characteristics and strategies must you emulate as Frank's teacher?

CHILD STUDY 28

Rupert Armstrong, Three Years Old

I chose Rupert for this child study because he is a challenge in the classroom. Rupert has an extremely interesting home life and background, which some would say explains his behavior; however, my gut is telling me that there is an underlying problem with him. Rupert's speech is developmentally behind than most of the children, he attacks for no reason and has no understanding of why most the time, and moments after he pounces on a child he will be happy and cheerful on to his next activity. Rupert does not understand that the other children fear him; he calls them him friends. His smile is contagious, even though you want to be angry with him. He was, in my mind, the only real option for my child study, not only for this class, but because I want to be able to help him, his family, and teachers. "Nothing you do for children is ever wasted. They seem not to notice us, hovering, averting our eyes, and they seldom offer thanks, but what we do for them is never wasted" (Keillor, 2006).

Rupert is a usually happy boy, age 3 years, 3 months, who attends a private child-care center. Rupert is an only child, adopted at birth from Russia. His parents are an older couple in their early fifties. Both parents, Mr. and Mrs. Armstrong work full-time, leaving Rupert enrolled in the program's full-day preschool. Recently, the parents let go of Rupert's nanny and are currently going through a divorce. Despite the divorce, Rupert's parents are currently in the process of adopting a baby girl.

In class, Rupert is outwardly a happy child. He smiles, laughs, acknowledges, and hugs staff members that walk by. What is concerning are his violent tendencies towards other children: pushing and hitting other children without understanding the consequence. He will often give blank stares after hurting other children. Rupert becomes easily distracted while playing or performing simple tasks. Teachers describe him as often being in his own world. Rupert seems to understand some of what happens in class, but not all the time. Since there is a concern for developmental delay, the Brigance Preschool Screen II was chosen in hopes to initially find out whether Rupert showed signs of possible developmental delays or other underlying problems in order to resolve or seek further assistance. Mr. and Mrs. Armstrong, though not opposed to screening, do not understand the need for it. I explained to them that skills in this screen are at a level of review that most children develop or master by three years, zero months. Rupert is three years, three months. If he tested at a base score, then he would show no signs for developmental delays, and we would have to discuss options then.

I administered the test right after lunch, when I knew Rupert had a lot of energy. I invited him to play a new game with me in an empty classroom that he and I often played in. We sat at an empty table in an area free of toys and distractions. To keep his attention throughout the test, we took short breaks for him to ride a tricycle in the room or play "head, shoulders, knees, and toes." Throughout the test, Rupert wanted to talk and play, but with the incentive of the short breaks in between my "games," I kept him interested for short periods of time. The findings of the test were that Rupert scored high in the following areas: Personal Data Response, Color Recognition, Picture Vocabulary, Use of Objects, Understanding of Body Parts, and Prepositions and Irregular Plural Nouns. The areas he scored low in were Visual Motor Skills, Gross Motor Skills, Number Concepts, Building Tower with Blocks, and Repeating Sentences. Rupert's overall score was 66. The cutoff score for detecting developmental delays is 55. Rupert falls within the normal range according to the findings of this assessment.

What we were able to find were areas that Rupert can work on at home and in the classroom, like working on fine- and gross-motor skills and number concepts. His teachers can encourage him to play in the block area or at the sand or motor-sensory table. If an aide becomes available, it would be the best solution for Rupert to have a one-on-one at this point for the structure and safety of the class. The teacher should continue to work closely with the school's Family Services coordinator and continue to work toward finding possible alternatives and options for the classroom. In addition, I recommend maintaining close contact with Rupert's parents about what happens in the classroom. In reporting to Rupert's parents, I was able to tell them that he does fall in the normal range for children his age. He has a strong picture vocabulary and a very good self-awareness and body identification. Rupert was able to identify prepositions and plural nouns and ability to repeat four-syllable sentences; however, six- and eight-syllable sentences were more difficult. He has a weakness in number concepts, counting, and block building. One thing they can work on at home is building towers with blocks and counting how many blocks are in the towers, as well as reading books with repetition and multisyllabic sentences. Mr. and Mrs. Armstrong should also continue to work closely with the teachers on his progress and behavior issues.

Since the test, changes have been made to actual layout of the classroom, making it harder for Rupert to bounce from center to center, and although he has the same amount of energy, the amount of violence in the classroom has lessened. In addition to the physical change, throughout the day, small groups are taken out for short periods at a time for play. It was decided that the large size of the class, 16 to 19 (majority male) depending on the day, is too stimulating for Rupert. By removing a group of six or seven of the larger group, it makes for a calmer, less stimulating environment. Although Rupert still tends to need a constant eye, the classroom is running much better, for all children. It has been discussed that Rupert should be in a smaller program, though I do not think that will be the final answer for Rupert's problems. In my opinion, I think he will need much more testing down the road, but he might be too young to fully be diagnosed now. The classroom changes seem to support Rupert now. Mr. and Mrs. Armstrong will need to stay on top of his situation and I hope that the new baby will not get in the way of that. Ideally, he should be fully evaluated by an early interventionist. Though some would say Rupert is just a misbehaving kid, I cannot believe that. He has an underlying issue that needs to be addressed. The Brigance Preschool Screen II was able to tell me that he is developmentally where he should be for his age; however, his behavior tells a completely different story. He has had many stable forces broken in his life in the past year, which can attribute to some of the behavioral problems, but because of the severity I cannot believe that they are the whole reason. My hope is they do not move him to another school for fear of what this next change will do. The recent changes in his classroom have proven to be a good change and he has teachers that are fighting for him. Rupert is that kid that you never really want in your class, because he is going to be a challenge, but once he gets there, and every morning when he comes up and gives you that great big hug and shines his pearly whites, you couldn't imagine your classroom without him.

Resources

Brigance Preschool Screen II. (2005). N. Billerica, MA: Curriculum Associates, Inc.
Keiller, Garrison. (2006). Children Quotes. http://www.wisdomquotes.com/cat_children.html.

Questions to Consider

1. Do you agree that an early intervention assessment should be postponed? Why or why not?
2. What interventions do you recommend to help Rupert make friends? How might you structure peer-mediated help for Rupert?

CHILD STUDY 29

Ellen Kozinsky, a Second Grader

Description of the Child

Ellen is a young Caucasian American of Polish descent. A healthy, robust seven-year-old child with a slender frame and long curly brunette hair, she wears homemade pastel pink or purple dresses with flowers and butterflies, pink socks, shinny leather shoes, matching ribbons in her hair, and costume jewelry on her fingers and wrists.

The center of attention upon entering the room, she appears acutely aware of herself as she smiles, giggles, tilts her head, and shyly tucks her chin. Ellen is a bundle of restrained energy ready to rupture. Given any attention, a question or a game to play, she bursts forth unrestrained, talking, balancing on tiptoes, and taking command with requests to "Let me try, let's go here, let's play it this way." Fun-loving, curious, and creative, she will build a city from jelly and cream containers, sugar packets, and salt and pepper shakers gathered from the restaurant table. Clever and astute, she quickly learns and applies rule changes in a game of "I Spy" or "Parcheesi." Generally a happy, contented child, she can become sullen and pout when she does not get her way. Nonetheless, she is disciplined and cooperative. She soon regains her cheerful disposition in spite of having been scolded and not getting what she wanted.

Family Background

Ellen is an only child to a couple living in Michigan. In Michigan, she is surrounded by her extended family, including both sets of grandparents, aunts, and uncles. Mr. Kozinsky is a Mason and very involved with the local lodge, regularly attending meetings and the Friday night fish fry, where they see family and friends. Mr. and Mrs. Kozinsky are also very involved with their church, contributing time to the many charity activities.

Mr. and Mrs. Kozinsky are well educated, conservative, and hard-working. They are struggling with the present economy, like most Americans. Fortunately, their present job positions are stable. Mr. Kozinsky is a computer consultant for a subsidiary of an international company with its main office in Michigan. Mrs. Kozinsky does the accounting for her brother in his business and is a librarian at the local library.

Mr. Kozinsky has spent the past two years working in Cleveland during the week and spends only weekends, vacations, and holidays at home. Even at home, Mr. Kozinsky may continue to troubleshoot computer problems that arise, as he is available to co-workers by phone and online.

In spite of the absence of Mr. Kozinsky and Mrs. Kozinsky's busy schedule, there is every indication that Ellen's needs are the center of their daily concerns and she is not suffering any emotional stress as a result.

Ellen has many afterschool activities like piano lessons and Girl Scouts. She has ballet in the winter and softball in the summer and Sunday school on the weekends. She has many friends at school and from the neighborhood.

Medical History

Ellen does not have any unusual medial concerns. She has no allergies or asthma. She has had no more than minor or common childhood illnesses.

Early Developmental Milestones

By the age of 3, Ellen attended a mother–child preschool. Morning sessions with teacher-directed activities and learning centers for the children were attended with their mothers. By the age of 4, Ellen was attending preschool without her mother. At age 5, Ellen was in the kindergarten class at her present school.

Ellen has a large collection of books and has always enjoyed it when adults read to her. During a visit last year, she was observed sounding out words at every opportunity, on the sides of buses and billboards.

Current Functioning

At age 7, Ellen is very self-sufficient, dressing herself from a selection that she and her mother made. Ellen will tend to her bath and brushing her teeth with minimal supervision. Ellen will pack her backpack, which she will have her mother check. Her mother takes her to school and picks her up.

Ellen's motor skills are developing. While playing with a magnetic toy that requires a top to spin up and down a U-shaped piece of metal, she struggled to get her arm, wrist, and hand to mimic the movement necessary to keep the top spinning. Determined, she practiced throughout the day when she could. She could keep the top moving for almost a minute by the time she had to go to bed. Dancing together, Ellen imitated my movements step by step and followed the sequence as we continually added new steps.

Ellen has a large vocabulary and expresses her thoughts in conversational sentences. When she has trouble telling the complex story, she asks her mother to tell the story. Mrs. B. has always been very articulate with Ellen and does not limit her vocabulary. Mrs. B. will answer any question and is very precise in her instruction. Mrs. B. will define the moon as a satellite or the bird on the porch as a sparrow.

Ellen has good self-control; although her legs might swing, or shoulders and arms twitch, she is able to sit for long periods of time. Eventually, after 20 minutes of inactivity, she will begin to amuse herself but she is still within her seated area.

Ellen has had a stuffed monkey, Mooch, since she was a baby. Mooch has traveled with her everywhere. Occasionally Mooch has had a companion. Currently Mooch has a friend, Dewey, another stuffed monkey orphaned at the library. Mooch's friends have come and gone, but Mooch, worn out and sewed up, has remained her constant companion. The time has come when Mooch does not go to school regularly and Ellen is adjusting well to the separation.

Ellen is confident among adults. Putting in her request for attention, she wants to be a part of the conversation, she wants to hold the pet birds, and she wants to play a game. Although unable to witness Ellen with other children, she discussed her many friends at school.

Present Concerns

Ellen is in a private church school with seemingly limited faculty. This year Ellen is officially in the second grade. Unofficially, there are other arrangements. Ellen is one of eight second-grade students in a classroom with the seven first-grade students. The classroom has one teacher in the morning and another teacher in the afternoon. The afternoon teacher also attends to the four kindergarten students.

Last year, Ellen—as an official first grader—was in the joint first/second-grade class and accelerated in math and reading, as she was often grouped with and taught with the second-grade students. So far, there have been no accommodations for her advanced skills this year. There are no subjects where she joins the third-grade class. In fact, the students are often asked to assist with the kindergarten students on procedural matters such as where to hang up coats and putting away supplies.

Mr. and Mrs. Kozinsky are concerned for her academic progress. Even Ellen has expressed frustration with the arrangement. She complains that she is tired of hearing her afternoon teacher tell students to "get out the wiggles."

TEMA-3 Test

Ellen was selected for this case study because of the present concerns. Ellen has always excelled academically. It is a good time to determine her present abilities to see whether the present classroom situation will affect her progress.

Ellen and her family had come in to Chicago for a few days to visit the museums. They were staying at my house. On Sunday morning, we went out to breakfast and then returned to the house. The test was administered at the dining room table, which had been cleared of all books, papers, and computers. Only the test booklet, the manipulatives, and the score sheet were on the table. Her parents sat reading in adjoining living room.

Ellen volunteered to assist me by taking the test and did not appear to be uneasy until she sat down. Then she became inquisitive and a bit nervous about the test. I explained that I was learning to be a teacher. I explained that the test was not to see whether she knew math but whether I could give a test. This explanation seemed to put her at ease and any anxiety on her face left when she smiled.

The TEMA-3 test is simple but very precise regarding test instructions. I had read them several times and was determined to follow the instructions. However, the "no counting" and "less than 3 seconds" instructions I felt I may have slipped on occasionally.

I wanted to give her credit for using fingers or blocks on her own initiative in order to resolve the problem, but I knew that was not a part of the test. If she got the answer within five or six seconds, I wanted to give her the benefit of the doubt, but I tried not to sway from the instructions.

Ellen took the test very seriously. She was focused and concentrated on getting the answers correct. Only once did she make a remark to her parents when she noticed that some of the questions on the TEMA-3 worksheet included double-digit equations. I assured her that we probably would not get that far and she should not be concerned. She regained her focus.

I had never given her any indication from beginning to end when she had gotten a question right or wrong and praised her efforts on each question. However, at the point where she consistently got problems wrong, she began to get flustered. After she had gotten five questions incorrect, I went on for two more questions and stopped.

She is good with numbers and number sequences and counting by 10s. She can count into the three-digit numbers but must concentrate over 150. She is good with addition and subtraction of small numbers. She feels more confident using her fingers or manipulatives; however, when asked if she count on her fingers in her head, she could answer the questions almost as quickly. She remembers and uses number tricks.

She has not added and subtracted in the double digits. She has a little difficulty translating word problems into the numeric language when the problem was subtraction. She had difficulty with base 10, putting 10s into 100.

TEMA-3 Results

The Entry Point for Ellen was question 32, according to her age. Her basal was questions 38–42. Her ceiling was questions 47–51. According to the directions for scoring the test, all items below the basal level are scored correct and all items above the ceiling are scored incorrect. Therefore, her raw score was 42. Using Appendix C to convert her raw score to age and grade equivalent, she is age range 6-9 and grade range 1.7. Using Appendix A to convert raw score to math ability scores, she has a math ability score of 92. Using Appendix B to determine percentile, she is at 30%. Appendix D is the standard of error of measurement, which represents a 68% confidence interval. Using Appendix D, the math ability score is altered to plus or minus 3, which makes her math ability score 89–95. The TEMA-3 manual admits that the raw score has limited value. The math ability score indicates Ellen's overall ability. Percentile ranks represent a value on a scale of 100 that indicates the percentage of the distribution that is equal to or below that value. Therefore, a rating of 30 indicates that 30% of the standardization sample at her age scored at or below her raw score.

TEMA-3 Meaning for Teacher

To test only one child, the best use of this test is to determine what knowledge the student is missing and use the Assessment Probes and Instructional Activities to structure the curriculum to fill in those gaps.

Ellen did well in number sequence, counting by 10s, simple addition and subtraction. The questions where Ellen had difficulty were "symbolic additive commutativity" and base 10. The teacher should concentrate on reviewing with Ellen her thought process while doing math. The teacher should work with her on other methods of thinking about and working with numbers.

Academic History and Necessary Accommodations

Ellen is confident about her academic abilities that are within her range of ability. She will hesitate and smile nervously and ask for assistance when she feels she has gone beyond her ability.

The reports from school have been positive. She does well in spelling high-frequency words, vocabulary, reading, and math. Aside from the present classroom situation, Ellen has not had complaints about the class or the teachers. Most likely, her classmates are children that she has known for years through church activities.

The school needs to rearrange the classes to accommodate the kindergarten children in the afternoon. In addition, the first/second-grade teacher should work with the third-grade teacher to have the advanced student to join the class for certain subjects.

Summary and Recommendations for Next Teacher

Ellen is a model student, self-disciplined, enthusiastic, and academically motivated. She comes from a healthy home environment with supportive parents. She did well on the TEMA-3 test; she is at her age level. She should feel a bit more confident about her single-digit addition and subtraction; start with a review of these items and move on to double-digit addition and subtraction. Using the math in projects will keep math engaging.

Ellen will need to be continually challenged in the second and third grades to maintain her level of academic skill. With a few modifications to her present situation, she should maintain her progress. The third-grade teacher can try to assist the present teacher with these modifications.

A student like Ellen could be invited to join in some of the third-grade classes, especially at the end of the year, to challenge her and maintain her enthusiasm. In the third grade, continue a challenging academic curriculum. However, look for the signs that she is reaching her limits. She will hesitate and ask for more assistance. She will be honest if asked whether the work is too hard. Level off the work until she feels more confident.

Questions to Consider

1. Do you agree with the assessor's suggestion that Ellen should be included in third-grade activities? What else might teachers do to keep Ellen appropriately engaged?

2. What problem-solving activities might the teacher include at a learning center for math and science? How can these activities provide multiple entry points?
3. What might teachers in this school do to organize learning themes that are accessible from diverse skill points?

CHILD STUDY 30

Baby Charlene Spenser

Background Information

Charlene is a baby of average height and weight. She is eleven months and one day old. Charlene is the youngest child with an older brother, Gabe (age 3), and an older sister, Melinda (age 4). Melinda attends preschool five afternoons a week and Gabe is at home all day. Charlene's parents, Mr. and Mrs. Spenser are both very well educated, having post-graduate degrees. Mrs. Spenser is a professor at a university and Mr. Spenser is a lawyer. Charlene lives with her family in a home located in an upper-middle-class suburb of San Francisco. Charlene is at home throughout the week, either being watched by a nanny or Mrs. Spenser. The family engages in many developmentally stimulating activities throughout the week. These include trips to the children's museum, library, zoo, parks, music class, and outdoor play.

Charlene is read to quite often during the day. There are quite many books in each room for the children as well as adult books for the adults. Art supplies, toys, swings, and slides are available to the children throughout the day. Television is not encouraged and really only watched at night by Charlene, Gabe, and Melinda.

From observations, Charlene reached all of the physical and cognitive milestones. Charlene has just begun to walk and one can see in her face and demeanor that she is very proud of herself for doing so. She is also encouraged to explore and discover her environment in the home as well as in the neighborhood. Charlene gets put in the stroller for walks at least once a day and really enjoys getting into the pots and pans cabinet in the kitchen and making noise with them. Charlene seems very comfortable in her home and with her family. Charlene's needs are being met, and she is developing at her age level.

Question for This Study

I mainly just wanted to test to see if her development was on track and whether she met the developmental milestones. Charlene was born breech through a Caesarian section that was scheduled a couple of weeks before her mother's due date. Charlene reached all developmental milestones and is eager to move on to the next ones.

Formal Assessment

I administered Stanley Greenspan's Social-Emotional Growth Chart to Charlene after several daily observations of her behavior. The observations usually occurred between 11 A.M. and 2 P.M., in between her naps. The growth chart is a screening questionnaire for infants and young children. The test included a caregiver report that measured the baby's behavior frequency. Sensory processing and total growth were both given scores. Charlene fell into the full mastery stage. The full mastery stage means the baby has demonstrated proficiency or mastery of needed skills. All of the boxes were checked in the "all of the time" box except for a couple. Taking a calm and enjoyable interest in most sights, including colorful or bright things was checked "most of the time." So was the question, "Does your child reach for or point at things, or make distinct sounds to show you what he or she wants?" At the time I did the screening, Charlene was checked in "some of the time" for understanding my actions by returning the gestures, and using many consecutive actions in a back-and-forth way to show you what she wants or to have fun. However, in the past couple of days she has been playing games with me, including peek-a-boo, which she initiates. She also will take a hat or a pair of glasses and hand them to me. After I put them on I will take them off and put them on her. She then takes off the hat or glasses and gives them back to me. This game can go on for a solid 10 minutes.

The other questions focused on areas of social development. Charlene was checked in the "all of the time" boxes for these. Charlene calmly enjoys touching or being touched by different things. Swinging, dancing, or quickly lifting Charlene up is very enjoyable for her. She looks at interesting sights, such as a person's face or a toy. She responds well to people talking or playing with her by making sounds or faces. Charlene is also enjoys smiling and will exchange smiles with others. She has mastered all of the needed skills for her development. I would consider Charlene very social. She can get very upset when she is not around people, especially her family.

Informal Assessment

The informal assessment is based on observations of Charlene since her birth. I have watched her grow and develop since she was brought home from the hospital. It has been not only very interesting to observe Charlene reach developmental milestones, but I am also amazed at how much children learn and grow during their first year of life. Currently, Charlene is walking on her own, eating solid foods, and beginning to say words. She enjoys exploring everything from cabinets and drawers to toys and books.

Charlene also enjoys the company of her siblings. She is very interested in what they are playing with at the moment and communicates with them as well with smiles or screams.

Summary of the Child Study

Charlene has reached the full mastery stage of needed skills for her age. Her assessment was based on in-home observations over the course of a couple of days. I would recommend to Charlene's parents The Circle of Communication Game and The Copycat Game. These games are to prompt and develop communication in the baby. Charlene's communication is there; she may enjoy these games, which will enhance the development of communication. Charlene is full of energy, curiosity, inquisitiveness, and wonderment. She is developing socially and emotionally on track and would be ready for a infant child care setting if needed.

Questions to Consider

1. Why do you think the assessor recommends communication games? Do you share the perception for this need? Why or why not?
2. If Charlene enters your center, what plans will you make for her and family? What additional assessment will you plan?

CHILD STUDY 31

Melvin Lewis, a Second Grader

Description of Child

Melvin, 7 years old, is the middle child of three boys in his family. Older brother Arthur is 14 years old and his baby brother Frank is 16 months old. Melvin is an outgoing and athletic child who participates in organized competition of soccer, basketball, and baseball. Melvin also explains that he enjoys swimming in the backyard pool during the summer, but at times likes to play video games with older brother and friends. "I have an XBox and PlayStation 3!" Melvin has a very energetic personality and appears to be extremely talkative, as he demonstrated no reservations in answering any my questions. Melvin's overall appearance is a well-groomed child who wears well-kept clothes and Nike gym shoes.

Questions, Concerns, Problems

During a brief discussion with Melvin's father and stepmother, Mr. and Mrs. Lewis, they explained that he had a difficult first-grade school year (last year), behaviorally. According to his parents, he attended a public elementary school and continuously got into trouble. They expressed, "We were constantly getting phone calls from Melvin's teacher that he was always goofing around, talking too much, misbehaving, and not doing his work." Melvin's father went on to explain that over the summer before starting second grade, they made the decision to switch him to a more disciplined private, parochial school, which three of his cousins also attended. Melvin's stepmother, Michelle, then went on to suggest that the change for Melvin was excellent and that he has had a much better second-grade school year. Both parents were in agreement. "We are very happy that he made the switch." "He also seems to have done much better academically this year."

Family Background

Mr. Lewis and Melvin's biological mother initially raised him jointly but they got a divorce when Melvin was in kindergarten. Then, shortly after that, Mr. Lewis remarried while Melvin was in first grade. This was around the time when Melvin developed behavioral issues in school, explained his father. "He had a little adjusting to do with our divorce." Mrs. Lewis contributed that Melvin initially had a hard time with her existence as a family member. Today, Melvin lives primarily with his father and stepmother, but visits and lives with his biological mother, who also just recently remarried, every other weekend. Despite all of the divorce and remarriages, Melvin appears to be well taken care of and loved by all involved in his upbringing. He is also fortunate in that both sets of parents have lucrative jobs and have homes in affluent suburban neighborhoods.

According to his parents, Melvin has no significant medical history or birth complications to note. Per Melvin's father, there were no delays and Melvin met all developmental milestones. He commented that Melvin walked and talked at the appropriate months with no difficulties.

Current Functioning

The following information in regards to Melvin's current functioning was gathered during a conversation with his father and stepmother.

Skills	According to Melvin's Parents. . .
Self-Help and Daily Living Skills	Melvin is independent with the activities of daily living. He is able to make himself a snack after school and occasionally helps out in the kitchen to make other meals. Melvin is able to use the bathroom by himself but needs occasional reminders about taking a shower or brushing his teeth.
Gross-Motor Skills	Melvin is able to keep up with his peers. Per his father, most of his friends struggle to keep up with him. He is able to run, jump, climb, swim, kick a ball, catch a ball, etc. "My son is very athletic." "He plays soccer, basketball, and baseball."
Fine-Motor Skills	Melvin has just mediocre handwriting. His parents commented that he could probably use a little help in this area. But he has no trouble with scissors, buttons, zippers, opening containers, etc.
Coordination and Body Awareness	Melvin is occasionally a clumsy and rowdy seven-year-old boy, but overall he's pretty coordinated. He's extremely coordinated when it comes to sports.

(continued)

Speech and Language	His parents could not recall when Melvin said his first words and do not remember having any concerns when he was younger. They also commented that he has done fine in school and that his teachers have never had any concerns with his speech and language development.
Self-Concept	Overall, Melvin's self-concept in regards to school is that he is good at both reading and math. In regards to sports, he believes he is the best on the court or the field.
Self-Management Skills	Melvin does occasionally need reminders to do his homework, because he gets so busy playing outside, and going to sports practices. When asked about video games, his parents said that Melvin does enjoy playing them, but he would rather be outside.
Reaction to Other Children	Melvin is a very social kid and gets along with everyone at school.
Reaction with Adults	Melvin is a talker and has no problem with entertaining adults. But he would rather be with his friends or playing with his brothers.
Play or School Activities	Melvin enjoys being outside all the time and always wants to have friends over to play in the yard. He participates in organized sports including soccer, basketball, and baseball.
Thinking and Reasoning	When Melvin was in the first grade his teacher called us at least once a week to tell us that he was misbehaving in class. This was shortly after his parent's divorce and when he gained a new stepmother. Fortunately, the misbehaving resolved after switching him to a private, parochial school with his cousins. He loves his new school, has accepted the divorce, as well as the remarriage. Melvin does at times need adult guidance with some reasoning and higher-level thinking but overall he is able to choose the right thing to do in most situations. He occasionally gets in to trouble at home, but not too much anymore at school. He's really quite a good kid.
Problem-Solving Skills	Just like the comments above with "thinking and reasoning," Melvin is able to solve simple problems but needs some adult guidance with complex problems.
Overall Health	Melvin has not had any medical complications and is generally healthy.
Development of Social Skills	Melvin has never had difficulty in social situations. He is very outgoing and talkative and loves to be with people. He was able to make new friends at his new school right away.
Development of Emotional Skills	At times, Melvin can be like a typical seven-year-old boy who gets upset when he wants something and can't have it. Parents report that he sometimes shows his frustration with us by locking himself in his room for some time or trying to ignore us.
Development of Cognitive Skills	Melvin has done very well in school this year (second grade). He is one of the highest-level readers in his class and does well in math too. Both parents enjoy reading, and therefore, put a heavy emphasis on having their children read, too. During first grade when he was exhibiting some behavioral problems at school, the parents were afraid that his academics were going to suffer, but fortunately he made academic progress.
Development of Physical Skills	Melvin's parents expressed that they feel he has always been somewhat advanced in the development of his physical skills. He was able to walk, run, jump, climb, and so on well before his older brother ever did.
Development of Communication Skills	Melvin also did not show too many concerns when it came to his communication skills. He is able to hold a conversation with an adult and has pretty intellectual insights. "You would be surprised at some of the adult like expressions that come out of his mouth."
School Adjustment	Overall, Melvin had no issues with the adjustment of going to school. He looked up to his older brother and wanted to do everything that Arthur did, so he didn't mind starting school. He wanted to be like his big brother.

Academic Influences

Emotional Issue

After having a discussion with Melvin's father and stepmother, one can note from the documentation several outside factors that may have affected academics. First, Melvin was presented with the divorce of his parents, which is quite an adjustment for many children. He then had to deal with his father getting remarried in addition to gaining a stepmother. Both are very difficult situations and circumstances for a child to have to experience. I agree with his parents that Melvin's reaction to all of this started to present at his old school when he was in the first grade, in the form of misbehavior. Fortunately, he is a bright student and these behaviors did not take a toll on his academics. I was not sure how I felt about his parents switching him to a new school, because this too can be difficult on a child. But because Melvin is a social, energetic, and outgoing child, it was obviously okay, because he quickly made friends and had his cousins at the new school to also help him adjust. The new school offered the opportunity to have a "fresh start" where he was not known as "behavior problem."

Parental Influence

The second condition that I believe may have influence on Melvin's academics is the fact that his parents have set the example of being a reader at home. When children are able to see adults reading on a regular basis, especially their parents, they are more likely to want to develop reading skills. I also want to note that both sets of parents are successful professionals with high academic achievement. Parents who engage in conversations about academics help their child succeed in school. It was apparent that Melvin's parents put an emphasis on his academics when they suggested that they are always questioning him about what he has for homework, and whether it is done.

Friends and Popularity

A third influence is the fact that Melvin is a social, talkative, and outgoing child who does not have difficulty with making friends. Because he knows that the other children in his class like him, he does not have this as stress that could potentially affect his schoolwork.

Purpose of the Study

Melvin is nearing the end of second grade, so this particular study using the Fountas and Pinnell Benchmark Assessment was conducted as a summarization of the current reading level. This is a more beneficial study when it is administered with a student over the course of a school year. When given at the beginning, middle, and end of the year, one is able to observe the progress that a child makes in his reading with regards to reading processing, fluency, and comprehension.

Because there are no previous scores for this particular assessment with Melvin, the results will yield his optimal level for independent reading and instructional reading for this one point in time. These results can serve as a guide or starting point for the third-grade reading teacher as he begins school again in the fall. Additionally, the third-grade teacher could also administer the test again at the beginning of the year to see if any progress was made over the summer. The results can serve as a guide for parents so they are informed on what sort of help Melvin may need over the course of the summer in regards to his reading.

The Assessment

- ***Location, environment influences:*** The Fountas and Pinnell Benchmark Assessment System 1 was administered to Melvin in his home. More specifically, I administered the test to him after he had come home from school and had a little time to play in addition to eating a snack before participating in the test. We sat together at the kitchen table with no distractions from the rest of the family.
- ***General reading curriculum and emphasis of the Melvin's second-grade teacher:*** When asked about the emphasis that the second-grade teacher puts on reading, Melvin responded with, "My teacher, Mrs. Paul, makes us read every night! We have to

take a book home from the class library every day. But you don't have to read all the books by yourself. I can have my brother or my dad read it to me too."

- ***Describe the learner's behaviors during the assessment:*** Melvin was extremely well behaved and very cooperative for the administration of this test. He became a little fidgety toward the end of the assessment, mostly because he was ready to go back outside and play in the backyard. Melvin was attentive and cooperative and listened to all of the directions. He appeared very proud of his reading capabilities. He made several comments about the test being easy.

Starting Point

Where to begin? Because I was unable to speak with Melvin's teacher, I had to determine what level book to use to start the test. Fountas and Pinnell provide several great tips on how to choose where to start the test, with several charts that correspond with their books A–N and to the grades K–2 (Fountas & Pinnell Assessment Guide, 2008, pp. 18–19). According to the charts provided, a good starting level for Melvin is most likely book "K." This is true because Melvin is at the end of second grade and according to his parents' report, Melvin has been on track or on level in reading.

Fountas and Pinnell also provide a quick "Where-to-Start Word Test" to help identify a starting point with the child. I first administered the Level 1 word list, which is where one should start with a student in second grade. Melvin scored correct on all 20 of the Level 1 word list items, so I proceeded to administer the Level 2 word list; he answered 16 correctly. According to Fountas and Pinnell, if the child reads 10–20 words on a list correctly, then stop and begin the text reading at the appropriate level on their "Where-to-Start Chart" (Fountas & Pinnell Assessment Forms, 2008, p. 214). According to the authors' chart, Melvin should begin the test with book level "K."

The First Book

Edwin's Haircut by Susan McCloskey

- Level: K
- System: 1
- Word Count: 480
- Genre: Fiction

Melvin appeared to do well with this first book. He read with 98% accuracy, which correlates with four errors made over the entire reading of this text. Melvin's self-correction ratio can be expressed as 1:2, which indicates that he made one self-correction for every two errors made. When considering Melvin's fluency for reading this text, I felt that he read smoothly, with appropriate pausing and appropriate stress, and at a reasonable rate with very little slowdown. Overall, his comprehension of *Edwin's Haircut* was "excellent," as he had no difficulties with discussing the meaning of the story and answering all of the comprehension prompts correctly. He scored an extra point in this section, because he went above and beyond with his interpretation and explanation of the text.

The Second Book

Giants of the Sea by M. C. Hall

- Level: L
- System: 1
- Word Count: 436
- Genre: Non-Fiction

Melvin struggled slightly with this book in comparison to the Level K book. Overall, he stumbled on a few more words and needed to re-read parts of the text as he went along. His fluency and comprehension were also slightly lower than the previous reading. Melvin's results reveal that he scored with 96% accuracy, which correlates with 10 errors and his 3 self-corrections. His self-correction ratio to errors was 1:4 with this text, *Giants of the Sea*. In regard to his fluency, he read primarily in three- to four-word groups with occasional slowdowns. He demonstrated some difficulty with stress placement and pausing as he read. Finally, his reading comprehension was 8/10 possible points, which is considered "satisfactory" for this text. Melvin struggled with two of the prompts but was able to gain an extra point for an additional connection on understanding. The text prompted Melvin to be curious about what the second largest animal in the world is.

The Third Book

The Thing About Nathan by Sharon Fear

- Level: M
- System: 1
- Word Count: 624
- Genre: Fiction

If you examine the results of the previous book that Melvin read for this assessment, you will be able to gather that he experienced much more difficulty in the reading of this text. Melvin became frustrated and seemed to tire during the reading of *The Thing About Nathan*. His accuracy rate for this text fell to below 95%, according to the chart that Fountas and Pinnell provide. Melvin had a total of 18 errors and 3 self-corrections for this reading. His self-correction ratio was 1:7 for this particular time of reading this text. It was apparent during this portion of the assessment that his fluency fell as well as his comprehension. I scored Melvin a 1 for fluency because he was no longer reading smoothly but was very choppy with pauses and stresses at inappropriate times. His reading rate also appeared much slower, even though I did not time him. Finally, his overall comprehension of the text was characterized as "limited" according to Fountas and Pinnell. Melvin was able to mention a few facts and ideas but he did not express the important information.

- ***Scoring the Assessment:*** Overall, based on the Fountas & Pinnell Benchmark Assessment, Melvin's results correlate at Level K for his "independent reading level," and Level L for his "instructional reading level."

Recommendations and Summarization of the Assessment

Teacher

According to Fountas and Pinnell, students at the instruction Level L are characterized by being able to process easy chapter books, including some series books with more sophisticated plots and fewer illustrations (Fountas & Pinnell Guide, 2007, p. 148). Students at this level are also able to understand that chapters have multiple episodes related to a single plot. These readers are beginning to recognize themes across text and understand some abstract ideas. Because Melvin scored at Level L for his instructional level, this is where some of the goals should be related to his reading.

Parents

First, I would tell Melvin's parents that he is on level for his age and grade level in reading, specifically looking at accuracy, fluency, and comprehension. According to Fountas and Pinnell, Melvin is "on level," because at the end of his second-grade year, he is independent with a Level K book. The authors also indicate that at the beginning of the third grade, for a student to be "on level," he or she should be reading or receiving instruction at Level L.

It is also important to educate Melvin's parents on what it means for a child to be Level K for their independent reading level and Level L for their instructional level. In order to truly get the parents to understand these two levels, I would probably give them a copy of the descriptions of each of the levels. Detailed descriptions for each of the levels are provided by Fountas and Pinnell in their *The Continuum of Literacy Learning; Grades K–2, A Guide to Teaching.*

Additionally, it's important to educate the parents by telling them that this is just one moment in time. On this particular day, Melvin scored at these levels and he could change or progress beyond these levels very quickly or slowly. But these results give a good idea of what level he is reading at right now, which can help guide both his teacher and themselves on how best to help Melvin with his reading skills.

Finally, I would also refer to the descriptions of Level K and Level L, rather than just saying, "Melvin is a Level K or Level L." When discussing the results, I feel it's important not to assign a level to a child. Instead, you should truly get to know a child's strengths and weaknesses, therefore, guiding instruction. Basically, I feel that it's of greater value to discuss the descriptions of the levels so that all parties involved with Melvin's learning understand his strengths and weaknesses.

In conclusion, when ending a discussion about assessment results with a parent, I feel it is necessary to end on a positive note; therefore, reiterating his strengths and accomplishments at this point would be beneficial.

References

Fear, S. (2008). *The Thing About Nathan.* Portsmouth, NH: Heinemann.

Field Study of Reliability and Validity of the Fountas and Pinnell Benchmark Assessment Systems 1 and 2. Retrieved June 9, 2008, from http://www.fountasandpinnellbenchmarkassessment.com/fieldstudy.asp

Fountas, I. S., & Pinnell, G. S. (2008). *Fountas & Pinnell Benchmark Assessment System 1; Assessment Guide.* Portsmouth, NH: Heinemann.

Fountas, I. S., & Pinnell, G. S. (2007). *The Continuum of Literacy Learning; Grades K–2: A Guide to Teaching.* Portsmouth, NH: Heinemann.

Fountas & Pinnell. (2008). *Fountas & Pinnell Benchmark Assessment System 1; Assessment Forms.* Portsmouth, NH: Heinemann.

Hall, M. C. (2008). *Giants of the Sea.* Portsmouth, NH: Heinemann.

McCloskey, S. (2008). *Edwin's Haircut.* Portsmouth, NH: Heinemann.

Questions to Consider

1. If you were Melvin's first-grade teacher, what might you have done to support him while he was absorbing the family divorce and remarriage?
2. How might you use Melvin's interest in support to support reading?

CHILD STUDY 32

Erik Diaz, a First Grader

Erik is of average height and weight for his age group. He has dark skin, hair, and eyes. Erik is social with his friends and clearly looks up to the leaders of our classroom. It is apparent that he often feels competitive with his peers and often compares himself to others. Erik often appears anxious and nervous.

Concerns/Problems

Erik's self-esteem is a main concern, as he consistently compares himself to his classmates and often worries about what others around him are doing. Erik often fails to follow directions in the classroom. He lacks focus during whole group instruction. Additionally, Erik's reading is of concern. He is reading below grade level and continues to struggle with applying decoding skills. He is hard on himself during reading groups and becomes frustrated when he finds a particular book or passage difficult.

Family Background

Erik's father is Argentine and his mother is American. Erik was born in Argentina and associates very much with this culture. He enjoys reading books about Argentina and often refers to his time there. Erik's family is relatively affluent. The family lives in the city of Miami. Erik has one younger brother who is in his first year of preschool. His brother also struggles in the academic setting and is currently being screened for behavior and learning disorders.

Erik's home setting appears to be rather disorderly. His parents are continuously late to meetings. The parents are frequently late in getting the boys to school as well as picking them up. The parents are difficult to get ahold of and struggle to return permission slips, homework sheets, and notes in a timely manner.

It is clear that Erik's mother is worried about his problems academically. She understands that he is performing below his grade level and that he is very anxious at school.

Erik regularly suffers from headaches. When he has headaches, he often wants to lie down in the nurse's office.

Current Functioning

Overall, Erik is currently functioning fairly sufficiently. He is able to complete all, or most, daily living skills as independently as expected for his age. One concern is Erik's extreme change in voice inflection, particularly when reading. His voice will go from very loud to very soft and the tone will change rapidly and dramatically while reading and sometimes speaking. He often stands when reading at his desk, pushing his hands down hard on the table. When reading on the floor, he will often squirm a lot and hover over his book.

Erik rarely has conflict in the classroom and demonstrates problem-solving skills when necessary. He clearly looks up to strong leaders among his peers. He likes to play soccer at recess and runs and plays with the other children. He is very competitive, not only on the playground, but also in the classroom setting. He is frequently distracted by what his neighbor is doing and becomes very concerned if he feels he is being asked to do something different or modified.

Erik's lack of self-confidence is an additional concern. He is particularly aware of how difficult or easy different tasks are for himself and his peers. He becomes very down on himself if assignments take him longer than his classmates. It is clear that he wants very badly to do well in school and works very hard to keep up with his classmates.

Erik is very respectful and sincere when speaking to adults. He is friendly when he comes into the classroom each morning and looks you in the eye when speaking. Unfortunately, Erik often arrives to school late and struggles to follow directions. Instructions often have to be restated explicitly.

Although Erik's academic level is slightly below his peers, this would not be of great concern if it weren't for his additional issues of self-worth. He performed relatively average in both kindergarten and first grade. It appears that he is falling slightly behind in second grade.

Results of the Assessment

Name: Dynamic Indicators of Basic Early Literacy Skills, Sixth Ed. Grade 2

Authors: Roland H. Good III & Ruth A. Kaminski

Copyright: 2003

DIBELS is a standardized test intended to assess oral reading fluency as well as comprehension. The test is intended to monitor and screen students and provide information necessary for early intervention. It is used to identify at-risk students and provide information on which to base early intervention. The assessment allows the teacher to take a quick snapshot of how the child is performing and making progress towards grade level benchmarks.

Outcome

Because DIBELS is a very quick assessment, it took only one day to administer the assessment. I did, however, spend a few days taking notes on Erik's classroom behavior prior to administering the test. I used three different portions of DIBELS to test the following: nonsense word fluency, oral reading fluency, and retell fluency.

Nonsense Fluency

Although nonsense fluency is not typically tested in the middle of second grade, because I was particularly interested in Erik's ability to apply decoding skills, I was interested to see how he would perform reading nonsense words. In one minute, Erik was able to read 65 words, which is the level at which he is supposed to be. I allowed him to read the entire page beyond the one minute to see if any miscue pattern would surface. Erik made very few mistakes and read the whole page rather quickly.

Oral Reading Fluency

Because Erik is in the middle of second grade, I used benchmark 2.2 for the test. In the allotted one minute, Erik read 62 words with two errors, giving him an oral reading fluency score of 60. This would place Erik in the top 38% toward achieving second-grade goals and place him at "some risk." Based on the DIBELS performance descriptor, the instructional recommendation for Erik would be "strategic-additional intervention."

Retell Fluency

Erik's retell fluency score, meaning the number of words he used to explain what he had read, was 21. According to the DIBLES scoring guide, a retell score close to 50% of the ORF score is typical, and a retell of less than 25% of the ORF score may indicate cause for concern. Erik's score of 21 is roughly 35% of his ORF score. Although this score is not ideal, according to DIBELS it is not a score of particular concern.

Testing Conditions

The DIBELS assessment was administered to Erik at school, during his regular reading time. The assessment took place in a reading room, typically used for small reading groups. The only two people in the room were Erik and I. At the time of the assessment, Erik was 7 years and 11 months of age. Because one of our major concerns about Erik is his apparent stress brought on by reading, I chose to administer DIBELS in order to assess his oral reading fluency.

Per usual, Erik appeared very anxious when asked to read. He hovered over the paper with his palms pushing down hard into the desk. He gasped while reading and was clearly aware that he was being timed. When he was finished with the reading, he exclaimed, "That was easy."

Teacher

The result of the DIBELS assessment shows that Erik's ORF puts him at some risk and that he is in need of additional intervention. As far as causes or direct solutions, this is not information that DIBELS provides. It is up to the teacher to determine what is best for Erik, now that she has the information that he is performing slightly below his peers, or below where he should be performing. Erik's strength—the ability to decode nonsense words—was revealed in this testing. He did very well as far as words (or letters) read and also made very few mistakes. Additionally, Erik made few mistakes while reading the oral reading fluency passage. Although he read fewer words then desired, he was very accurate. Finally, Erik's retell fluency score was possibly a little lower then what would be desired. Similar to his ORF, he was very accurate in his retell; he just failed to go into great detail.

As stated, no real instructional implications can be drawn from this testing. No specific solutions are given or outlined. This information simply tells us that Erik's ORF is slightly below where he should be performing.

Parent(s)

The learning strengths stated above could all be shared with the parent. Erik's reading level is around the 35th percentile compared to his peers; therefore, he is in need of some additional instruction and practice in order to bring him to where he needs to be. This information is a great way to show parents where their son is performing in comparison to where he should be. Additionally, this is a great way to be able to track progress and growth over time. As a teacher, assuring parents that you will use this assessment again at the end of the year to compare growth is a very good way to use benchmarks with parents.

University of Oregon Center on Teaching and Learning. (2007). DIBELS. Accessed on March 3, 2009, from http://dibels.uoregon.edu.

Questions to Consider

1. If Erik is speaking both English and Spanish, do you interpret the results of this test differently?
2. What are relevant cultural factors to consider?

VOICES FROM THE FIELD

Getting Ready for the First Big Monday in First Grade

I had the advantage of being a Professional Development School PDS intern in two different grades in this early childhood center. I expect to use the required tests in the math text and the reading text. In addition, the first-grade teachers in my building developed common assessments for our grade. This will be a big help for me as a new teacher. I want to use portfolios for writing and reading—not sure how, yet, but I'll get help from other teachers. One thing that I learned as an intern that opened my eyes was using art activities to assess young children; I'll do that. I'm ready for differentiating instruction—I'll use centers and small groups and hope to work with other teachers to share students for targeted teaching as part of the Response to Intervention program in my school. As an intern, I got to observe parent conferences, so I'm ready to go. It was helpful to see how veteran teachers presented information professionally.

atypical development unusual developmental pattern of children.

SUMMARY

Each of these examples of a child study shows a summary point in the assessment process. Teachers and others conduct child studies so that all the information on a particular child is gathered in one place. Usually this summarization occurs when there are developmental or educational questions to be answered. Then, a team of parents, teachers, and other professionals will review the available material and plan the next steps in the process.

In each of these vignettes, the reader is allowed to see the dynamic process of child-study development. The observers report progress from their vantage points. Available history and school progress are included.

A diverse group of studies is presented—children in various settings, of various ages, ranging from typical to **atypical development**, in the sophistication of the reports—to help guide you in preparing your own reports and in reading those of others.

The notes following the child studies raise questions for further consideration and elaboration of the issues and concerns. The teaching-assessment-reteaching process continues.

FIELD ACTIVITIES

1. Observe a child in school or child care. Summarize your information in a child study in as much detail as available. Outline your next teaching, intervention, or assessment steps.
2. With permission, review a child study for a child in a center or school. Outline the next steps in teaching, intervention, or assessment.
3. Plan a parent interview for a child you are studying. What additional information will assist in the teaching, intervention, or assessment of the child? Compare your notes with colleagues.

IN-CLASS ACTIVITIES

1. Pick one of the child studies presented in this chapter for further consideration. Plan the next steps in assessment, intervention, or teaching. Compare your notes with a colleague.
2. Examine one of the child studies presented in this chapter with a classmate. If the child was in your class, what would you do differently at the outset? Compare your thoughts with those of your classmate.

STUDY QUESTIONS

1. What are the purposes of a child study for early childhood teachers? Who are the key people involved in executing and evaluating the child study? What elements of a child study are most important for teachers?
2. What role does the early childhood teacher play in the Child Find team?
3. What role do child studies play in the assessment process? How does the Child Find team use child studies?
4. Why must early childhood teachers have a clear understanding of child development before completing a child study?
5. Review the examples of child studies presented in this chapter. What are the strengths and weaknesses of each? Do they include all of the components necessary for child studies? Identify the extent to which each focuses on typical and atypical child development theory.

REFLECT AND RE-READ

- I can describe the important elements of a child study.
- I know how to use a child study to answer a behavioral or academic question.
- I know how the child study might help with RTI.
- After reading the sample case studies, I can think of ways to teach the involved children.
- I can identify more questions to ask about the children described and have some strategies for gathering more information.

TECHNOLOGY LINKS

http://www.zerotothree.org

Zero to Three. This site is concerned with assessment and intervention for infants and toddlers.

http://www.naeyc.org

National Association for Education of Young Children. This site covers topics related to the education and assessment of young children.

CONTRIBUTORS TO THE CHILD STUDIES[1]

Armour, S.
Barton, E.
Bavolek, L.
Boneck, D.
Brandt, C.
Bresse-Rodenkirk, J.
Cochran, K.
Daley, L.
Dass, M.
DeCoucey, A.
Fagel, L.
Fantroy, L.
Finlay, J.
Fishman, A.
Foxgrover, G.
Grasso, M.
Jarol, A.
Jump, K.
Lee, L.
Le Quesne, L.
Machemer, E.
McMaster, M.
Monticello, L.
Moore, L.
Nelson, C.
Noonan, S.
Reynolds, L.
Sachs, L.
Schroeder, A.
Schrodt, S.
Ull, J.
Varner, K.
Winkofsky, H.
Zeller, H.

SUGGESTED READINGS

Borich, G. D. (2008). *Observation skills for effective teaching* (5th ed.). Upper Saddle River, NJ: Merrill/Prentice Hall.

Daniels, D. H., Beaumont, L. J. (2008). *Understanding children: An interview and observation guide for educators* (2nd ed.). New York: McGraw-Hill.

Deater-Deckard, K. (2004). *Parenting stress.* New Haven, CT: Yale.

Gandara, P. & Conteras, F. (2009). *The Latino education crisis.* Cambridge, MA: Harvard.

Gronlund, G. & James, M. (2005). *Focused observations: How to observe children for assessment and curriculum planning.* St Paul, MN: Red Leaf Press.

Pellegrini, A. D. (2004). *Observing children in their natural worlds: A methodological primer* (2nd ed.). Mahwah, NJ: Lawrence Erlbaum.

[1]These case studies were submitted by students at DePaul University as a requirement for the coursework. The selected child studies have been edited and identities have been changed. Recognition is given here to those whose work was selected.

CHAPTER 9

Special Issues in Infant and Toddler Assessment

TERMS TO KNOW

- functional assessment
- prenatal testing
- amniocentesis
- ultrasound
- chorionic villus biopsy (CVS)
- precutaneous umbilical blood sampling (PUBS or cordocentesis)
- gestational age
- developmental delay
- established risk
- biological risk
- environmental risk
- Individualized Family Service Plan (IFSP)
- family collaboration
- fetal alcohol syndrome (FAS)
- outcomes

CHAPTER OVERVIEW

This chapter covers special issues in infant and toddler assessment, those aspects of assessment that are unique to the population of birth to age 3 (or even prior to birth). Some of the assessment methods used for preschool- and primary-age children also apply to this discussion. In order to identify problems in the development of infants and toddlers, it is especially important to understand the meaning of development, recognize developmental milestones, and grasp the factors that affect developmental change in the first three years of life. Included in the discussion is routine documentation of progress when infants and toddlers are in group care situations. An especially critical component of infant/toddler assessment is reciprocal family collaboration.

ASSESS AS YOU READ

- How do you assess babies? Why is this assessment important?
- How are parents and others involved in the assessment of babies and toddlers?
- How does assessment lead to intervention?
- What should I know about infant/toddler assessment if I am working in a child-care setting that serves typical children?

THE TOTAL ASSESSMENT PROCESS OF INFANTS AND TODDLERS

More and more infants are in child-care situations, because many women with young children are now working. In addition, with the requirement for services to infants, toddlers, and pregnant women through Early Head Start beginning in 1995, the issues related to curriculum and assessment gain increased importance. Early Head Start requires screening of infants and toddlers within 45 days of program enrollment (Head Start, 2002). The principles of appropriate practice

are the same—whole child, constructivist approach, safety, cultural sensitivity, and individualization (Copple & Bredekamp, 2009; Interdisciplinary Council on Developmental and Learning Disorders [ICDL], 2000; Sandall, McLean, & Smith, 2000; Zero to Three, 2005). Specifically, screening should follow the best practices, as follows:

1. Screening is part of intervention service, not just a means of identification and measurement.
2. Use processes, procedures, and instruments only for the specified purpose of each.
3. Incorporate multiple sources of information as part of the process.
4. Periodic screening is important because babies change developmental status rapidly.
5. Screening is only one approach to on-going evaluation.
6. Use reliable and valid procedures when choosing approaches.
7. Conduct screening in natural, nonthreatening environments.

And, of course family partnership is the cornerstone (Head Start, 2002; Ensher, Clark, & Songer, 2009). Families have the responsibility for child rearing and socialization of the baby and toddler into their own culture as well as the larger society. Families and caregivers share the responsibility for communication and participation with each other around the needs of the baby. Finally, families contribute to the development of literacy and linguistic acquisition initially and in partnership with caregivers. This practice leads to the development of social competence, academic and social skills, literacy development, and positive engagement with peers, as well as adults, and with learning (Weis, Caspe, & Lopez, 2008). Although the screening results do not provide direct links to curriculum, the observation of infants and toddlers during the process reveals trends in behavior that may allow you to choose among goals for emphasis during the coming weeks. Basic goals for teachers working in the mainstream with infants/toddlers include helping infants/toddlers to learn about:

- Themselves
- Feelings
- Others
- Communicating
- Moving and doing
- Thinking skills

An example of such goals in a curriculum, planning, and assessment system for caregivers created by Dombro, Colker, and Dodge is the *Creative Curriculum for Infants and Toddlers®* (2006), available in English and Spanish. The program integrates assessment and teaching/learning activities and provides opportunities to plan optimum learning opportunities for babies and toddlers. "High quality early learning experiences during the infant and toddler years are associated with early competence in language and cognitive development, cooperation with adults, and the ability to initiate and sustain positive exchanges with peers" (Zero to Three, 2005). But before infants and toddlers are enrolled in programs, they are often assessed by other professionals.

Assessment at birth and shortly thereafter is best described as a "snapshot" that will be revised following the rapid early growth of infants (Smith, Pretzel, & Landry, 2001; see also Ensher et al., 2009). Depending on the medical condition and the nature of family support needed, the assessment will focus more or less on the baby and more or less on the family. This is true particularly in the cases of HIV/AIDS or cranio-facial anomalies and other complex medical issues. That is, medical intervention occurs according to medical need, whereas assessment issues relate more to what support the family needs at birth and the first months following, rather than exclusive concentration on the baby.

The principles behind **functional assessment**, which include the requirements that the assessment be "contextually relevant, functionally appropriate, relationship-enhancing, (and) observationally based" (Meisels, 2001; see also NASP, 2009; Bagnato, 2007), describe the ways in which assessment, intervention, program, and intervention activities are linked to serve infants and toddlers, their families, and their caregivers. Thus, practitioners situate assessment in the developmental tasks, processes, and content of appropriate educational activities. With this approach to assessment, there is minimal need for parents, caregivers, and early interventionists to extrapolate from isolated tests to learn about infant/toddler developmental progress. Following these principles, Meisels, Marsden, Dombro, Weston, and Jewkes prepared the Ounce Scale™ (2003) with the "purpose to assist families and service providers in observing, collecting, and evaluating functional information about infants' and young children's development and provide a framework that helps parents and service providers use this information to plan curriculum and engage in relationship-enhancing activities and experiences. The Ounce Scale™ provides an interactive system of documentation, monitoring, and evaluation for Early Head Start and other early care programs for infants, toddlers, and pre-schoolers" (Meisels, 2001, p. 7). The Ounce Scale Kit includes an Observational Record, a Family Album, and a Developmental Profile. The Ounce Scale answers developmental questions about personal connections, feelings about self, relationships with other children, understanding and communication, exploration and problem-solving, and movement and coordination.

functional assessment focused observational method that links individual assessment to curricular intervention for one student.

> The Ounce Scale is organized around six major areas of development and six principal questions:
>
> Personal Connections: How does the child show that she trusts you?
>
> Feelings About Self: How does the child express who he is?
>
> Relationships with Other Children: What does the child do around other children?
>
> Understanding and Communication: How does the child understand and use gestures, vocalizations, and words to communicate?
>
> Exploration and Problem Solving: How does the child explore and figure things out?
>
> Movement and Coordination: How does the child move his body and use his fingers, hands, and eyes to do things?
>
> The Ounce Scale is distinguished by:
>
> - Multiple approaches to collecting information
> - Structured methods of keeping track of infants' and toddlers' accomplishments
> - Inclusion of family members in the assessment process. (http://www.pearsonassessments.com, 2009)

An example of the domains, areas of development, and aspects of development is shown in Figure 9.1.

Figure 9.2 shows the Ounce Family Album, which includes families in the assessment of their baby.

A sample Developmental Profile and a corresponding page from the Standards for the Developmental Profiles are shown below.

Toddlers I Developmental Profile

Age level
Toddlers I: 24 months
Standard domain title
Social and Emotional Development
Area of Development
I. Personal Connections: It's About Trust
Indicator comparable to observation question in the Observation Record and matched to indicators on the Developmental Profile
1. Seeks the support of familiar adults to try things
Rationale describes age-level expectations for this indicator
Toddlers depend on having the adults who are important to them in view while they are playing, exploring, and trying new activities. Although their increased mobility allows them to explore more actively and do more things independently, they need to be close to the adults who are important to them so that they can feel secure about moving away. For example, they might:
Developing as Expected:
• start moving toward the room where the toys are kept but come back to a familiar adult several times before finally entering the room
• explore the water table while their mother is sitting nearby, but stop playing, protest loudly, and follow her when she moves toward the door to leave
• pull the face of a caregiver toward them when he or she begins to talk to someone else
• want to eat the food from their caregiver's plate
• bring toys to a familiar person and pile them on his or her lap
• cry when they cannot have their caregiver all to themselves
• hand a piece of their cookie to a familiar person sitting nearby
• try the slide at the park after sitting beside their caregiver for a while watching the other children shriek with joy as they slide down
Examples of behavior for the rating "Developing as Expected"; rating to be matched to child's recorded behaviors in the Observation Record
Needs Development:
• refuse to try any of the swings or the slide even though they had been begging to go to the park earlier
• refuse to leave the side of their caregiver or parent, even to play with toys that
Examples of behaviors for the rating "Needs Development"

Page 42, Standards for the Developmental Profiles

FIGURE 9.1 Ounce Developmental Standards Profile.

I. It's About Trust

How Your Baby Shows Trust

What does your baby do when she sees you?

When you feed, change, bathe, cuddle, and talk to your baby, she gets to know you. She starts to feel comfortable with you and the other adults who regularly take care of her. When you are with your baby, she might:

- look into your eyes when you hold and feed her
- coo and smile when you talk gently to her
- fuss or cry to get your attention, then calm down when she gets it

What does your baby do when she sees you?

____

____

____

____

____

____

When your baby looks into your eyes and responds to your words and actions, she shows you how very important you are to her.

FIGURE 9.2 Ounce Family Album.

Other instruments that take this approach include the DIR®/Floortime™ (Developmental, Individual-Difference, Relationship-Based) instrument, designed for use by therapists and skilled clinicians (Wieder & Greenspan, 2001; see also Greenspan & Wieder, 2006a). The instrument assists in understanding both current functioning and how the baby functions. "DIR®/Floortime™ is a framework that helps clinicians, parents and educators conduct a comprehensive assessment and develop an intervention program tailored to the unique challenges and strengths of children with Autism Spectrum Disorders (ASD) and other developmental challenges. The objectives of the DIR®/Floortime™ Model are to build healthy foundations for social, emotional, and intellectual capacities rather than focusing on skills and isolated behaviors." The Ounce Scale and the DIR/Floortime are examples of assessment systems that set the stage for planning programs and services for infants/toddlers and their families, which are more commonplace in our world. In addition, "Parents' Observations of Infants and Toddlers– POINT– is a new rating scale for children 2 through 36 months of age. Using the observations of a child's parents and caregivers, POINT is designed to screen and identify infants and toddlers who have potential developmental problems and who may need further diagnostic assessments. Early identification of such children can lead to early intervention and the provision of effective services to those who are identified as at risk" (Mardell & Goldenberg, 2006; http://www.firstpointkids.com). All of these instruments share the goal of providing information for families and caregivers that will assist early intervention in potential child behavior that may inhibit or proscribe development without early attention.

Contemporary research identifies the importance of timing, individualization, cultural relevance, and sustained and intense intervention for best outcomes (cf. Mowder, Rubinson, & Yasik, 2009; Maldonado-Duran, 2002). Interest in the prompt and accurate identification of infants and toddlers with developmental disabilities, Autism Spectrum Disorders (ASD), or potential learning problems has increased significantly over the years (cf. Howard, Lepper, Williams, 2010). In addition to the influence of Early Head Start, other federal policies governing the changing nature of infant/toddler assessment are the evolving policies related to young children with disabilities.

The Individuals with Disabilities Act (IDEA, 2004) governs assessment and intervention practices for infants, toddlers, and children of all ages. Part C is the portion of this legislation that refers to early intervention; states govern the definition for eligibility for service, so you should check your state department of education to see your state's plan. Each state must at a minimum include the following provisions to satisfy the assessment dimensions of this public law:

- "A rigorous definition of the term "developmental delay"
- Timely and comprehensive multidisciplinary evaluation of needs of children and family-directed identification of the needs of each family
- Individualized Family Service Plan and service coordination
- Comprehensive child find and referral system
- Policies and procedures to ensure that to the maximum extent appropriate, early intervention services are provided in natural environments except when early intervention cannot be achieved satisfactorily in a natural environment (NECTAC, 2009)

IDEA is constantly evolving, so be sure to check with the latest federal and state government requirements and provisions (see the U.S. Department of Education website at http://www.ed.gov or the Division of Early Childhood website at http://www.dec-sped.org/ for the most current rules and regulations governing practice). Advocates for early intervention strive to ensure that the IDEA includes a system that will guarantee assessment so that all infants and toddlers and their families receive appropriate intervention services. Such practice involves "anticipating, identifying, and responding to child and family concerns in order to minimize their potential adverse effects and maximize the healthy development of babies and toddlers. . . . Services include evaluations of a child's strengths and needs; individualized educational experiences; special therapies such as physical, occupational, and/or speech and language therapy; family supports such as home visits; service coordination; and transition to supports to facilitate a smooth change from early intervention to preschool programs" (Zero to Three, 2005).

The values of best practice as outlined by McLean, Wolery, and Bailey (2004; see also Zero to Three, 2005) and shared by professionals, families, and legislation continue for infants and toddlers:

1. Quality of infant/toddler physical and social environment significantly influences behavior and long-term development.
2. Early intervention reduces the impact of disability conditions.
3. Family partnerships are essential.
4. Interdisciplinary teams are most effective.
5. Focus on infant/toddler strengths rather than deficits.
6. Developmental and individualized goals are the means to effective intervention.
7. Effective intervention requires individualized assessment.
8. Planning is integral for generalized effects of intervention program goals.

In addition, such values are congruent with IDEA 2004 (P.L. 108–446, the Individuals with Disabilities Education Improvement Act of 2004).

This legislation continues the following priorities of previous versions of the law:

- Statewide services for all infants/toddlers with disabilities and their families are encouraged.
- Coordinated services across public and private sources, including insurance, are encouraged.
- Enhance states' intervention services capacity.
- Special efforts to serve the underserved are necessary.

Infants and toddlers must receive service or intervention if they are:

- Experiencing developmental delays in
  - Cognitive development
  - Physical development
  - Communication development
  - Adaptive development
- Have a diagnosed physical or mental condition that has a high probability of resulting in developmental delay

States may also elect to serve babies and toddlers who are at risk of substantial developmental delays, although IDEA 2004 proposes stricter regulations regarding the definition of developmental delay. Thus, everyone involved in the lives of families—medical, educational, and child-care providers—must assume responsibility for assessing infants and toddlers who may be at risk of disabilities. The Division for Early Childhood of the Council for Exceptional Children (1998) endorsed a natural environments policy for the delivery of assessment and intervention (Sandall et al., 2000). What this means is that separation of babies and toddlers for special intervention from families and peers is inappropriate practice. Family involvement best practice follows these needs:

- To have multiple options for family participation
- To consider family involvement as a continuum, beginning with the family's first formal encounter with the early intervention or child care setting
- For smooth articulated transitions among and between services offered to families, infants, and toddlers
- To have culturally responsive practice at the forefront of all professionals' mindsets
- To partner across and between community agencies in the interests of families (Weiss, Caspe, & Lopez, 2008, pp. 13–15)

In establishing partnerships with families, consider the following imperatives:

- Listen first
- Reflect and acknowledge the emotional messages
- Reflect and acknowledge family expertise
- Use effective questions to elicit honest and problem-solving dialog (Winton, Brotherson, & Summers, 2008, p. 27)

One way to make the planning visually concrete for families is through the use of a technique described as *eco-mapping*. In this approach, all the potential players in a family's life sphere are identified and graphically organized according to contribution or role to the family's strengths (McCormick, Stricklin, Nowak, & Rous, 2008). The graphic organizer shows relationships between and among the players, identifying the functions and roles that all play. It documents the resources, nature of interactions, and potential conflicts among and between members. The map becomes the summary of reciprocal discussions of professionals and family and offers another "picture" of family strengths.

Another imperative that serves families and young children is IDEA 2004 special emphasis on the underserved (U.S. Department of Education, 1991). The 1991 reauthorization of IDEA required states and school districts to recruit underserved families from minority, low-income, inner-city, and rural areas for early intervention services that will promote learning and development. This emphasis continues with the 2004 reauthorization of IDEA. In reaching this population, intervention teams must be particularly aware of cultural and linguistic issues. Steps to developing a culturally sensitive Child Find program include:

- Promoting public awareness of early intervention services in the native language of all populations served
- Involving community members in planning early intervention services and referring families to services
- Involving the whole team—medical, child care, school—in services
- Developing conveniently located and culturally appropriate screening centers
- Recruiting and preparing professionals from the targeted population
- Developing a tracking system to monitor the progress of at-risk and identified children (Pavri, 2001, p. 5; see also Baca & Cervantes, 2004; NECTAC, 2009)

How do all these imperatives and best practices influence the teacher working with babies and toddlers in child-care or educational settings? First, you must be aware of the nature and types of disabilities in the birth-to-3 age range. As you may know, the first disabilities identified are usually medical or physical.

Following the identification of medical and physical disabilities that may be present at birth or shortly after, the most frequent symptom that parents and caregivers identify is difficulty with communication—talking. Communication is a complicated area to assess. It includes assessment of gestures, responsiveness, comprehension of language, and vocalization. This process view of communication assessment requires ongoing evaluation, multiple sources, sharing observations, and making interpretations to generate new hypotheses with the selective use of standardized instruments (Otto, 2010; Owens, 2010; Reed, 2005). Though communication may be the initial focus of assessment, the symptom may be indicative of another problem. Greenspan and Wieder (1997, p. 5; see also Greenspan, 2006) identify four truths that apply to assessment and intervention with young children:

1. Every child has a profile of development and requires an individualized approach.
2. Child symptoms and problem behaviors often stem from underlying problems in sensory modulation and processing, motor planning, and affective integration.
3. All areas of development are interrelated.
4. Child interactions in relationships and family patterns are the primary vehicle for mobilizing development and growth.

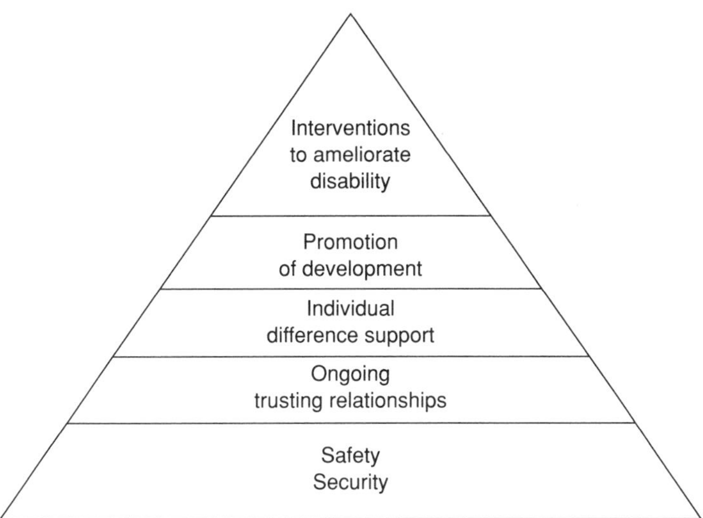

FIGURE 9.3 Integrated developmental services build on foundation needs.

These truths support the need for an integrated developmental approach in support of families. Greenspan and Wieder (1997, p. 7; see also Greenspan 2006) use a pyramid to illustrate basic services (see Figure 9.3). Safety, protection, and security form the foundation of the pyramid, next is the formation of ongoing trusting relationships, then the implementation of relationships geared to individual differences, then techniques to promote development, and at the top, specific interventions.

The rapid growth and early nonverbal nature of infants and toddlers complicates their assessment. In addition, our dependence on talking as a measure of understanding developmental progress, the inadequacy and/or inaccuracy of many standard measures, and the inextricably linked family and cultural factors that influence development also complicate the process. To determine infant and toddler competencies fairly and for best services to infants and toddlers in their diverse learning environments, base the assessment process on an integrated developmental model and involve multiple sources of information and multiple components. An assessment should proceed in the following sequence:

1. Establish an alliance of trust with parents. Listen to their views of the baby's strengths and challenges.
2. Realize that parents may not share all of the baby's developmental history at once. They will share more as they trust.
3. Initial observation should occur in a familiar or naturalistic setting with parents or caregivers present.
4. Later observations and assessments by clinicians should offer parental opportunity for participation.
5. Utilize standard measures and tests sparingly to answer specific questions that cannot be answered in another way.
6. Interpret all of the gathered material from observations, interviews, and formal assessments in a developmental framework that incorporates knowledge of child development in a social/cultural context. (Zero to Three, 2005)

These ideas are embedded in the Diagnostic Classification: 0–3R (Zero to Three, 2005), as well as the *Clinical Practice Guidelines: Redefining the Standards of Care for Infants, Children, and Families with Special Needs* (ICDL, 2000) and *DEC Recommended Practices in Early Intervention* (Sandall et al., 2000). These manuals should serve as a reference for all who serve the birth-to-3 populations so that the assessment of infants and toddlers can be systematic, comprehensive, and inclusive of diverse settings with various caregivers. The measure of humans begins at birth or before and continues lifelong. How, then, is assessment focused in infancy? The sections that follow elaborate.

The foundation of assessment in the early years is observation by the first caregivers—parents and others in contact with infants. To help parents think of important components of development, Greenspan and Wieder (1998, pp. 3–4; see also Greenspan & Wieder, 2006) identify six fundamental developmental milestones that lay the foundation for future learning and development. These include the abilities to:

1. Take an interest in the sights, sounds, and sensations of the world and to calm oneself down—take in and respond
2. Engage in relationships with other people
3. Engage in two-way communication
4. Create complex gestures, to string together a series of actions into an elaborate and deliberate problem-solving sequence
5. Create ideas
6. Build bridges between ideas to make them reality-based and logical

Biological challenges—sensory, processing, creating, and sequencing planning responses—affect these functional and emotional skills. In addition, interaction patterns with others, as well as family and social patterns, influence development (Greenspan & Wieder, 2006).

THE IMPORTANCE OF ASSESSMENT IN THE FIRST THREE YEARS

Not too long ago, when a baby was born, the primary questions asked, after determining the sex of the baby, were "How much does the baby weigh?" and "How long is the baby?" Nowadays, it is far more common to ask, "What is the baby's Apgar score?" Most hospitals across the United States use the Apgar Rating Scale (Apgar, 1953) to screen newborn infants. One minute after delivery the evaluation occurs, and then it is repeated 5 minutes (and sometimes 10 minutes) after delivery. Five easily observed signs—heart rate, respiratory effort, muscle tone, reflex response, and color—are scored on a scale from 0 (poor) to 10 (good). Total scores in the 0 to 3 range suggest extremely poor physical condition, are very serious, and indicate an emergency concerning the infant's survival. A score of 4 to 6 indicates fair condition, and a score of 7 to 10 implies a good condition. Color is the least dependable of the signs, as pink and blue tones do not apply to all babies. For all babies, physicians can see a darkening glow as oxygen flows through the baby (Berk, 2008). The purpose of this screening is to determine the developmental status of the baby at birth and to identify, as early as possible, infants who may be at risk for serious developmental problems. Most babies (97 percent) are born without major birth defects (American College of Obstetricians and Gynecologists [ACOG], 2007). Nonetheless, for the other 3 percent, early identification, screening, and assessment are integral parts of early intervention services. Recently, many newborn screening tests are included in routine deliveries. These tests consist of screenings for metabolic disorders, endocrine disease, cystic fibrosis, and other specific gene defect screenings, as well as hearing screening. If screening reveals particular risk issues, then families must decide upon an intervention strategy so that a healthier baby may result (Clark, 2009). Several tests before birth provide information to parents about the health and well-being of their expected baby.

Prenatal Testing

Prenatal diagnostic tests that identify a serious medical problem include maternal serum screening, real-time ultrasound, magnetic resonance imaging, fetal echocardiography, amniocentesis, chorionic villus sampling (CVS), diagnostic testing of fetal cells, and percutaneous umbilical blood sampling (Schonberg & Tifft, 2007, pp. 30–35; see also Berk, 2008).

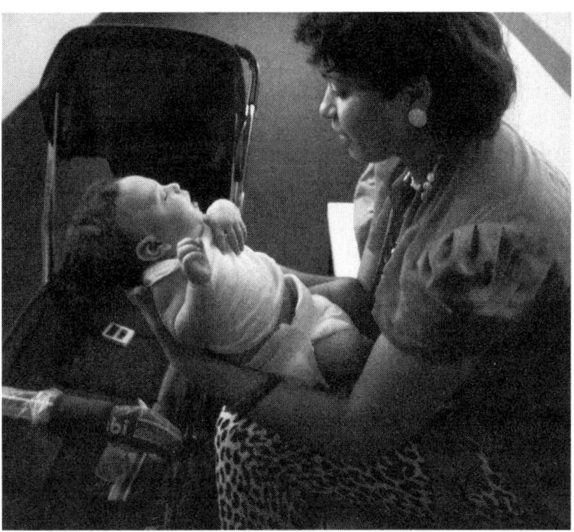

Many parents opt for **prenatal testing** such as **amniocentesis**, in which a slender needle inserted through the mother's abdomen into the embryonic sac surrounding the fetus in the womb draws a small amount of amniotic fluid for biochemical analysis (ACOG, 2007). The fluid contains fetal cells that when analyzed determine fetal maturity and chromosomal and metabolic abnormalities such as phenylketonuria (PKU) and congenital hypothyroidism, or 250 other genetic abnormalities such as Down syndrome, Tay-Sachs disease, and spina bifida. Usually physicians perform this procedure during the 15th to 18th week of pregnancy for women in the at-risk category—maternal age of 35 or greater, previous baby with chromosomal abnormality, positive carrier of known genetic defect, prediction from the maternal serum screening test, or abnormality identified by ultrasound (Schonberg & Tifft, 2007, p. 33).

prenatal testing testing done prior to the birth of a baby.

amniocentesis a prenatal test in which amniotic fluid is withdrawn from the embryonic sac of a fetus.

Ultrasound (sonography) is another less-intrusive screening method in which sound waves enable the technician to determine the fetus's development. In the first trimester, ultrasound can show the number of fetuses, the viability of one or more fetuses, and the placement of the placenta. During the second trimester, ultrasound images may show subtle findings associated with genetic disorders, as well as neural tube defects, facial clefts, renal anomalies, skeletal anomalies, hydrocephalus, and certain brain malformations (Schonberg & Tifft, 2007, p. 30).

ultrasound a prenatal test in which sound waves are used to determine a fetus's development.

Another method of prenatal testing that may eventually replace amniocentesis is **chorionic villus biopsy**, or CVS (Schonberg & Tifft, 2007, p. 33). This procedure is performed earlier than amniocentesis or ultrasound, usually in the first trimester (9th to 12th week of pregnancy), before the mother feels any movement of the fetus. The main advantage of this earlier screening is that a decision to terminate a pregnancy is usually emotionally easier and medically safer at this earlier stage. Guided by ultrasound, some chorionic tissue, which is the fetal component of the developing placenta, removed by suction is examined under a microscope. Because fetal cells exist in relatively large numbers in the chorion, they are analyzed directly, unlike the process in amniocentesis that requires two to three weeks for the fetal cells to grow in a culture medium. CVS has been used successfully to detect certain chromosomal abnormalities, measure the activity of specific enzymes, and determine the sex of the fetus.

chorionic villus biopsy a prenatal test in which chorionic tissue is removed from the developing placenta.

Precutaneous umbilical blood sampling (also called **PUBS** or cordocentesis) detects intrauterine infections, evaluates fetal anemia, and checks blood type in rhesus (RH) pregnancies (Schonberg & Tifft, 2007). At the 18th week, the test is performed under ultrasound guidance.

precutaneous umbilical blood sampling a specialized prenatal test performed during pregnancy. The test predicts the potential for biological disability.

The maternal serum screening happens at the 16th week (ACOG, 2007; Schonberg & Tifft, 2007). In this screening, blood is analyzed for alpha-fetoprotein (AFP) levels, estriol, human chrorionic gonadotropin, and inhibin A. A small amount of blood is drawn from a vein in the woman's arm during the first 15 to 18 weeks of pregnancy. The test results show whether there is an increased risk for neural tube defects, Down syndrome, trisomy 18, or abdominal wall defects (ACOG, 2007). These are multiple-marker screening tests, and the physician usually will perform three or four.

Prospective parents use these tests in consultation with physicians not only to satisfy their curiosity, but also to relieve their concern and anxiety over possible difficulties and to identify any deviations prior to birth that might cause the parents to elect aborting a fetus with serious, maybe even fatal, defects. Such procedures carry with them many ethical issues that must be resolved by the individuals directly involved.

Assessment at Birth

gestational age how long a baby had been developing in the uterus before birth.

A common measure that describes the infant's status at birth is the determination of **gestational age**, and a baby born before the 37th week is considered premature. From the 23rd week, babies are viable—capable of survival outside the uterus. Premature babies are born with underdeveloped organs. Depending on the gestational age, body systems affected are respiratory, cardiovascular, neurological, renal and gastrointestinal, muscular, skeletal, skin—in short, all of them. Babies of low birth weight and very low birth weight also are at risk for health problems and often cognitive or other disabilities (Howard, Williams, & Lepper, 2010). Thus, major prenatal hospital centers that serve high-risk infants often use infant development scales to plan intervention and family support.

One of these instruments is the Brazelton Neonatal Assessment Scale (BNAS; Brazelton & Nugent, 1995). This is a detailed examination designed to identify abnormalities in the central nervous system and sensory abilities, but it goes beyond a focus on neurological reflexes. It can describe the quality and level of the infant's behavior, detect changes in the infant's behavior, assess the impact of treatment interventions, and predict future development and function.

A screening mandated in most states before the infant leaves the hospital is a blood sample taken with a heel stick. Analysis of the blood seeks indications of metabolic diseases that may result in retarded growth and development. Among these diseases are phenylketonuria (PKU) and congenital hypothyroidism. Screening for the prediction of optimum development is not easy, for there are many developmental and social factors that contribute to a baby's welfare.

Principles of Child Development

No two babies, not even identical twins, are exactly alike. Each will develop somewhat differently based on genetic and environmental factors. Furthermore, there is no single theory of child development that all experts accept (cf. Feldman, 2010) However, there are a few general observations about very young children that are commonly accepted:

- Multiple factors determine development.
- Environmental influences support, facilitate, or impede developmental change.
- Parental figures mediate societal and cultural influences on the child.
- The family plays a unique role in and makes vital contributions to the child's development.
- Parenthood is a developmental and adaptive process. (Meisels & Provence, 1989)

When working with infants and toddlers, it is important to recognize the early childhood milestones. Teachers can find examples of milestones in the NAEYC Position Statement on Developmentally Appropriate Practice in Early Childhood Programs (Copple & Bredekamp, 2009) and in Appendix B of this book. (See Box 9.1 for an example of a checklist to use when modifying care in infant/toddler programs.)

Early Head Start publishes and distributes many materials for use in programs serving infants and toddlers (http://www.ehsnrc.org, website of the Early Head Start National Resource

BOX 9.1

Checklist of Developmental Considerations for Babies and Toddlers in Group Care

Modifications Needed	Developmental Aspect
Describe briefly what modifications are needed for group care situation.	
	Eating
	Sleeping
	Dressing
	Communicating
	Playing
	Muscle tone
	Locomotion
	Fine motor

Center) that will be useful for developing curricula and assessment programs for infants and toddlers. As well, *The Creative Curriculum® for Infants & Toddlers*:

> is a comprehensive and easy-to-use framework for planning and implementing a quality program, one where building relationships with children is central.
>
> The Curriculum outlines:
>
> - what children learn during the first three years
> - the experiences they need to achieve learning goals
> - what staff and parents do to help children reach these goals (Dombro et al., 2006)

Developmental principles are embedded in this program. Also, caregivers should consult milestone lists found in theoretical discussions of issues such as attachment, perception, emotions, language, and so on (cf. Eyer & Gonzalez-Mena, 2009). By being aware of these milestones, an early childhood educator can often allay unwarranted concerns of parents.

Answers to the following questions may help determine whether to refer a child for diagnostic assessment in the first year:

- Are the child's skills consistently delayed in a *number* of areas such as motor, language, and self-help?
- Has the one-year-old child started to *understand* some words?
- Are there any doubts about the child's hearing?
- Is the child's motor development significantly delayed in a *variety* of tasks, such as sitting, crawling, standing, and walking?

Risk Factors

Most infants and toddlers develop without developmental problems; however, several different factors put infants at risk. These factors, divided into four categories, are not mutually exclusive; thus, an infant may be at risk due to one or more of the following:

developmental delay term used by states to entitle infants, toddlers, and young children to intervention services.

1. ***Developmental delay:*** Each state defines this category differently, but it includes significant delays in the usual developmental milestones or unusual patterns in development.

established risk risk to infants because of gene abnormality, malformation or structural problems, or *in utero* drug exposure.

biological risk risk to infant because of prenatal, preinatal, or neonatal difficulty.

environmental risk risk to infants because of family or social stress.

2. ***Established risk:*** Infants in this category possess a gene abnormality, a malformation or structural problem with the brain or central nervous system, or received alcohol or illegal drugs in utero. These factors contribute to challenges in development.
3. ***Biological risk:*** Infants in this category have a prenatal, perinatal, or neonatal difficulty, including low birth weight, respiratory distress at birth, central nervous system infection, or difficult birth process. These difficulties are associated with challenges to development.
4. ***Environmental risk:*** Infants in this category may be affected by family or social stress. Factors that contribute to challenges in development include malnutrition during pregnancy or in the period immediately following birth. Additional difficulties include patterns of care by the primary caregiver that may be inadequate. Overall, family poverty contributes risk to this category.

These categories of risk create eligibility for service for babies, toddlers, and young children (under IDEA), although the services vary by state (McLean, Worley, & Bailey, 2004). Interactions across risk factors occur. In brief, poverty heightens the likelihood of established risk. Child abuse, malnutrition, and accidents also heighten the development of special needs identified before school entrance. Disability can range from visual and hearing impairment to complex mental and physical handicaps. Although risk conditions may create the possibility that infants, toddlers, and young children may need special intervention to foster growth and development, these factors cannot determine eligibility for early intervention services. Informed clinical opinion is the measure required for entitlement to early intervention. This clinical judgment must support the presence of a medical disability, other known disability, or a developmental delay. Definitions, by state, include percentage of chronological age demonstrated by performance, number of months of delay, score of one standard deviation below the mean on a norm-based instrument, and observed atypical behaviors. Some states have developed matrixes and charts to aid agencies, clinics, and programs in determining eligibility for early intervention (Shackelford, 2009). The thrust of best practice in all of these definitions is looking at the individual baby, toddler, or three-year-old in the context of family and community and judging whether the individual needs early intervention. In the next section, some of the factors that affect the assessment of infants and toddlers are highlighted.

UNIQUE ASPECTS OF INFANTS AND TODDLERS

What makes assessment of infants and toddlers different from assessment of preschool and primary-age children? Some of the distinctive characteristics of infants and toddlers that affect assessment are the following:

Babies and toddlers may

- Lack expressive skills
- Struggle with separation issues
- Demonstrate a limited attention span
- Be uninfluenced by extrinsic motivation
- Adapt slowly to new surroundings
- Fatigue easily and need naps
- Refuse to cooperate
- Exhibit a wide range of normal behaviors
- Demonstrate highly variable hour-to-hour behavior, although behavior and personality are globally stable over years
- Tend to put the testing materials in their mouths
- Show the effect of developmental overlay; that is, each area is influencing the total, so it's difficult to isolate particular problems
- Change rapidly
- Show cultural variations in behavior and consequent development
- Often demonstrate subtle developmental problems and require professional interruption (Head Start, 2002; Raver, 2009)

Another important difference is that although the term *development* implies a high degree of continuity and stability in behavioral change across time, in general the first few years are characterized by a lack of permanence in development and lack of smoothness in behavioral change (cf. Berk, 2008). This means that the infant or toddler may demonstrate a developmental milestone one day and never perform it again for days, weeks, or months. Or, the baby may progress on a regular basis and then reach a plateau and stay at that point of development for a long time.

VOICES FROM THE FIELD

Professional Development Planner on Infant/Toddler Assessment

As I visit home-care sites, I see little use of assessment instruments unless the homes are connected to special programs. Those connected to Early Head Start tend to use the Ounce (http://pearsonassess.com/HAIWEB/Cultures/en-us/Productdetail.htm?Pid=PAaOunce&Mode=summary).

The birth–3 programs in public schools use Creative Curriculum® for Infants, Toddlers & Twos *for instruction and are beginning to use* The Creative Curriculum® for Infants, Toddlers & Twos Developmental Continuum Assessment Toolkit *(http://www.teachingstrategies.com/page/IT2_Overview.cfm). For screening, these programs use Ages and Stages (http://www.agesandstages.com). Before using this complete curriculum and assessment systematic approach, programs used informal observation, various checklists, and developmental milestone comparisons. Now with the use of Creative Curriculum and Assessment, assessment will be connected to teaching and program goals. Creative Curriculum and its online resources are invaluable to programs (http://www.creativecurriculum.net). However, there are many teachers who are not yet comfortable with using the curriculum and assessment system. Often, this is because center directors do not provide opportunities for teachers to attend the regularly offered training. The centers located in not-for-profit community sites tend to send teachers for training. Many of the for-profit centers do not see training as a priority. There needs to be legislation or funding strings to require these centers to send their teachers to training. Even with training, many teachers are struggling with the assessment demands. Follow-up support (and initial) is offered to teachers—it's going to get better.*

One change that I've seen in programs is that past practice relied on activities to anchor the curriculum. In high-quality programs, the curricular shift is toward relationship building with infants and toddlers, using the assessment to plan appropriate activities for the babies and toddlers. Most teachers are quite able to identify infants and toddlers who have special needs; the more subtle issues in development often are harder for teachers who are not using, or just learning to implement systematic approaches to assessment.

In birth–3 programs, many teachers do not have teacher certification and few have special courses geared toward infants and toddlers. Colleges and universities should step up their offerings for infant/toddler teacher preparation.

Advice to New Teachers

- *Ground yourself thoroughly in child development so you will recognize behaviors that are typical of the age range rather than "misbehavior."*
- *Understanding of child development helps teachers maintain "cool."*
- *Connect with veteran teachers to get support and mentoring.*
- *Go to workshops to continue your lifelong learning.*
- *Observe individual children in your program so you learn about them and can build relationships as well as appropriate play-based activities for each of the children in your program.*
- *The most important piece: Teachings is a cycle—observe, assess, plan, implement the plan, observe . . . it never stops!*

Thus, an early childhood educator must consider a number of issues and trends to see the overall picture of infant and toddler assessment and the requirements and principles of IDEA Part C (2004). The outcome orientation of the law states that early intervention services should:

1. Enhance a child's development, minimize the potential for developmental delay, and recognize the significant brain development that occurs during a child's first three years of life . . .;
2. Reduce educational costs by minimizing the need for special education and related services after infants and toddlers with disabilities reach school age;
3. Maximize the potential for individuals with disabilities to live independently in society;
4. Enhance families' capacity to meet the special needs of their infants and toddlers with disabilities; and
5. Enhance the capacity of state and local agencies and service providers to identify, evaluate, and meet the needs of all children, particularly minority, low-income, inner-city, and rural children, and infants and toddlers and in foster care. (Turnbull, Huerta, & Stowe, 2006, pp. 38–39)

Individualized Family Service Plan (IFSP) specific plan for the assessing of needs and for the services needed for a child with a developmental problem.

Fortunately, the mandate also has procedural safeguards that include frequent parent and professional review of **Individualized Family Service Plans (IFSPs)**, as well as the right to appeal, the right to confidentiality of information, the right to prior notice to parents in their native language, the assignment of surrogate parents, and the establishment of procedures to ensure that services are provided while complaints are being resolved. The 2004 IDEA "proclaims the nation's goals are to preserve and strengthen the families of children with disabilities and the children themselves, while, at the same time, developing state and local capacities to serve them" (Turnbull et al., 2006, p. 39).

IFSPs must be written and must contain the following:

1. Statement of child's present levels of physical development, cognitive development, communication development, social or emotional development, and adaptive development, based on objective criteria.
2. Statement of the family's resources, priorities, and concerns relating to enhancing the child's development.
3. Statement of the measurable results or outcomes expected to be achieved for the child and family, including pre-literacy and language skills as developmentally appropriate for the child; the criteria, procedures, and timelines used to determine the degree to which progress toward achieving the results or outcomes is being made; and whether modifications or revisions of the results or outcomes or services are necessary.
4. Statement of specific early intervention services based on peer-reviewed research, to the extent practicable, necessary to meet the child's and family's unique needs, including the frequency, intensity, and method of delivering services.
5. Statement of the natural environments in which early intervention services shall appropriately be provided, including a justification of the extent, if any, to which the services will not be provided in a natural environment.
6. The projected dates for initiating the services and the anticipated length, duration, and frequency of the services.
7. Identification of the service coordinator from the profession most immediately relevant to the child's or family's needs who will be responsible for implementing the plan and coordinating with other agencies and persons, including transition services.
8. The steps to be taken to support the child's transition to preschool or other appropriate services (Turnbull et al., 2006, pp. 39–41)

Multidisciplinary teams write these IFSPs in collaboration with families. Services provided include family training and counseling, special instruction, speech and language therapy, occupational or physical therapy, psychological assessment, medical services for diagnostics and evaluation, social work services, assistive technology, transportation and related costs, and service coordination. In making the plans, teams follow the best practice principles for assessment and intervention described in the following section. One way to assure that the IFSP makes sense to families and interventions is described as "ROUTINE, which stands for Routines based, Outcomes-related, Understandable, Transdisciplinary, Implemented by family and caregivers, Nonjudgmental, and Evidence-based" (Jung, 2007, p. 3). This approach forces the team to think about how interventions will be implemented into the baby's daily activities, assures measurable outcomes, and organizes a task chart that is readily understood by all involved. When planning the IFSP in the context of a family's daily living, some questions that may yield a better picture of available strengths take into consideration the whole family rather than the toddler's identified problem. For example, shape your questions for family:

- "What is your typical day" rather than "how do you help your toddler with_____?"
- "How do you spend your holidays" rather than "do you take vacations?"
- "How do you work out your schedule" rather than "is it difficult for you to deal with ____'s problem?" (Xu, 2008, p. 15)

Telling families that they do not have to answer questions that they prefer not to address assures them that you will respect them and their judgment about appropriate information to share with outsiders—the child care center, school, or other intervention agency. To begin the conference and to create a sense of the family in cultural and social terms, consider questions like the following:

- Can you share your family background by telling me where you are from, originally?
- Where did you go to school? What is the last level that you completed?
- When you were a child, did you know any children with disabilities?
- Before now, have you heard of Kent's disability?
- Have you told other family members, neighbors, trusted friends about Kent's problems? (Seligman & Darling, 2007, p. 365)

These questions, asked at the beginning of a planning process, help you understand the sociocultural context of the family. You may wish to conclude this initial conversation with "Is there anything that I didn't ask that you'd like to share?"

PRINCIPLES THAT GUIDE INFANT AND TODDLER ASSESSMENT

Once it is determined that an infant or toddler should be referred, there are a number of principles that guide the assessment approaches with very young children. First, assessment is a continuing, evolving process rather than a discrete activity initiated and completed at a single point in time. Thus, assessment must be blended with intervention (Sandall et al., 2000; Bagnato, 2007).

Because infants display complex patterns of interaction with the world from birth, there has been a continuing movement to document their behaviors and reactions in some formal way. The most striking aspect of the evolution of infant assessment has been the logical shift from measuring what we think of as intelligence to assessment of a number of interrelated systems in very young children combined with a move toward interdisciplinary assessment (ICDL, 2000; Zero to Three, 2005).

As it is not possible to divide the infant's skills and activities along such lines as motor, social, and cognitive domains in the early weeks of life—and even during the first three years such a division remains somewhat artificial—it is necessary to assess the infant's behavior and capacity by considering the underlying internal organization that has been suggested by current developmental theory. Professionals should accomplish this with training in many diverse fields of study. Play-based assessment is most often used. Teachers and other observers compare baby and toddler play to typical developmental play aspects, through baby and family play interactions, and through peer play of toddlers. Often the observation of play includes comparison to a scale or checklist (Gitlin-Weiner, Sandgrund, & Schaefer, 2000). One well-known and commonly used checklist is the *Transdisciplinary Play-Based Assessment*, 2nd ed. (TPBA2, 2008). The system provides observational criteria for four developmental domains—sensori-motor, emotional/social, communication, and cognition. The observation is conducted while the baby or toddler plays with family, peers, and professionals. The easy-to-use observation guide has questions that focus observation, strengths to look for, examples of behaviors that may be of concern, ideas for next steps, and a space for notes (Linder, 2008). In a companion volume, Linder (2008) provides intervention guidelines, based on the initial assessment and through ongoing relationships with families. The volume includes worksheets and a record-keeping system for use in early intervention programs.

Another system that coordinates child-find or early identification of babies and toddlers with intervention guidelines is the *Assessment, Evaluation, and Programming System for Infants and Children (AEPS®)* (Bricker, 2002). The system includes software to provide coordination of assessment, intervention, and progress monitoring.

Thus, assessment of very young children involves the sampling of behavior. A specific task is presented and then analyzed to determine the baby's underlying competencies and ways of organizing the world. For example, if we roll an attractively decorated ball to a baby sitting on the floor and request that the baby roll it back, we learn about the baby's interest in the object and ability to roll it back as well as how the baby relates to requests. If we see whether the toddler can lick food from around his or her mouth, we are really observing sensory awareness, voluntary control of oral structures, and body awareness. If we engage the baby in playing peek-a-boo, we can observe social awareness, turn taking, role perspective, imitation, body awareness, cooperation, and anticipation or prediction. Identifying the critical functions underlying each task enables the assessment team to use the information for program planning purposes.

To get the most reliable results, assessment should take place in multiple settings—home, child care, or school—and on multiple occasions when the baby is awake and alert and when the parents are not anxious or under stress. This reduces the pressure to finish the assessment on a particular day and reduces the parents' feeling that the child failed any particular task (McLean et al., 2004). Above all, support the family priorities when planning any potential intervention.

Family Collaboration

family collaboration involving the family reciprocally in all phases of the assessment of a child with a developmental problem.

Therefore, family priorities and information needs shape the assessment process, as well as child characteristics and diagnostic concerns (ICDL, 2000). This necessitates **family collaboration**—the identification of the family's strengths and priorities, and the family's determination of which aspects of their family life are relevant to their child's development. The assessment process reflects family values and family styles of decision-making. It is particularly important that teams consider the traditional cultural values and traditions of the families that they serve. These factors include whom the families would traditionally respect for advice and help. Particularly important is the role of elders and spirituality in the traditional culture. A plan that does not consider these issues for the family is doomed to failure if it is in conflict with the belief system. Families have diverse opinions about disability and intervention that are based on cultural, religious, and social class experiences and beliefs. To work effectively with families from diverse cultures, it is a good idea not to come to the communication table with pre-conceived notions of family strength based on your perceptions or misperceptions of social and cultural status. Learn the family's language or involve professionals on your team with that skill. Depend on community experts as much as possible so that the cultural and social values are respected and you have a leg up on family trust. Provide information for families in a form and manner that they can access—in person, on the phone, or by email, for example. Secure the family's definition of the issues and their perception of the presence of problems or not. Recognize that the families' need for meeting basic human needs—food, water, shelter—may come before education in their priorities. Be flexible in your communication with families—including extend family members, avoiding direct questions, adjusting your posture and voice, and other subtleties of culture (Seligman & Darling, 2007).

Additional factors of importance to cross-cultural understanding include styles of interaction and communication, as well as the concept of cultural identity—there are many variables here regarding the perceived identity of the particular family (Hanson, 2004).

All aspects of infant evaluation should reflect interactions between the child, the family, the professional, and the setting (cf. Hooper & Umansky, 2009). Infant evaluation variables are infant endurance and states of alertness, responsiveness to new tasks and unfamiliar situations, spontaneous activity, unstructured discovery, levels of frustration and irritability, and interaction with varied objects and toys, in addition to the infant's interaction with caregivers.

When assessing preschool and primary-aged children, parents may sit and observe or may not even be present. However, parents are an integral part in the assessment of infants and toddlers. Why should we involve parents in the assessment? First, it acknowledges that parents know their baby best and are their baby's most important teacher. It implies that parents are most likely to get a typical response from the baby. Family involvement provides a more complete understanding of the child—how the child fits into the family. The collaborative assessment and interview process provides opportunity for the parental perspective. Family involvement provides a basis for planning intervention that fits within everyday routines and coordinates what occurs in the group setting with what occurs at home. Parents identify goal priorities from their perspective as well as in conjunction with the developmental status of the child. In this way, parents' anxiety is reduced and parents learn how professionals plan learning experiences and activities for their baby. Now parents are part of a problem-solving team in which intervention solutions evolve through the collaborative assessment–intervention process. This increases the parents' involvement and likelihood that they will believe the results and work with the team for the benefit of the child.

Special At-Risk Populations

Babies exposed prenatally to alcohol, drugs, cigarettes, and marijuana suffer physical or neurological harm (cf. Ensher, Clark & Songer, 2009; Howard et al., 2010). One of the most common risks is **fetal alcohol syndrome** (FAS). In this case, infants exposed to excessive amounts of alcohol during pregnancy develop the key features of growth retardation, characteristic facial features, and abnormalities of the central nervous system (Abel, 1998; Davidson & Myers, 2007). Medical personnel make the diagnosis with a checklist of relevant characteristics to entitle babies and their families to intervention and possible prevention of future cases, as the syndrome implies a familial issue (Morse & Weiner, 2005). Current research suggests that the incidence is .33–.40 cases per 1,000. Blood alcohol level determines heavy drinking; however, a rule of thumb is five or more drinks per day, although even weekly binges may affect fetus development. The greatest effect to skeletal structure occurs in the first trimester, with effects on the central nervous system highest in third trimester (Morse & Weiner, 2005).

fetal alcohol syndrome physical and mental abnormalities associated with infants born to mothers who consumed excessive amounts of alcohol during pregnancy.

Babies exposed prenatally to drugs, such as cocaine, are at risk for environmental and biological reasons. However, recent research shows that the long-term effect of cocaine exposure is not as once imagined (Howard et al., 2010). Newborns exposed to cocaine show symptoms of irritability, restlessness, lethargy, poor feeding, abnormal sleep patterns, tremors, increased muscle tone, vomiting, and a high-pitched cry; the symptoms last for up to 48–72 hours after birth (Winsch, Conlon, & Scheidt, 2002; see also, Ensher, Clark, & Songer, 2009). Long-term effects are most likely due to use of multiple drugs and environmental conditions that contribute to sustained parental drug use rather than cocaine per se (Howard et al., 2010).

"More than 10% of pregnant women smoke throughout their pregnancies . . . (leading) to an increased risk of preterm delivery, and infant death. Research also suggests that infants of mothers who smoke during and after pregnancy are 2–3 times more likely to die from SIDS than babies born to nonsmoking mothers. The risk is somewhat less for infants whose mothers stop smoking during pregnancy and resume smoking after delivery" (American Cancer Society, 2005; 2009). In addition, smoking during pregnancy contributes to the incidence of low-birth-weight babies. Smoking slows fetal growth (American Cancer Society, 2009).

There is little information about the effects of maternal marijuana use on babies prenatally. However, although there are no differences in miscarriage rate, Apgar scores, or fetal malformations in infants whose mothers smoked marijuana regularly during pregnancy and those who did not, there is an association with prematurity and decreased birth weight (Winsch et al., 2002).

The best intervention in these emotional/social issues of pregnant women is substance abuse treatment during and after pregnancy. If mothers do not receive assistance during pregnancy, the problems increase with subsequent pregnancies (Winsch et al., 2002). As well, early childhood intervention programs often support infants/toddlers and their families who are wrestling with these complex social/ environmental issues. "Effective interventions, however, increasingly require striking a fine balance among the characteristics of the participants, the characteristics of the services, and service use (especially participants' active involvement). Policy-makers, moreover, cannot expect early interventions to inoculate vulnerable infants to future difficulties. Rather, as a nation we must support multifaceted early intervention programs and evaluations that will, in turn, continue to shed light on enhancing development throughout the life span" (Berlin, Brooks-Gunn, McCarton, & McCormick, 2004, p. 147; see also Ensher, Clark, & Songer, 2009).

ECOLOGICALLY AND DEVELOPMENTALLY RELEVANT ASSESSMENT STRATEGIES

Assessment of infants and toddlers is a blend of testing, informal observation, and parental interviews over an extended period. Traditional instruments—norm-referenced and criterion-referenced measures—often have the goal of quantifying a child's abilities, which means attaching a number or score to the responses. However, they often fail to address the qualitative aspects of a child's abilities, such as appropriateness of movement patterns, social competence, and attention abilities (Barnett, Macmann, & Carey, 1992; Hauser-Cram & Shonkoff, 1988; see also Salvia, Ysseldyke, & Bolt, 2010). As a result, there is a definite trend in infant and toddler assessment away from traditional instruments toward more ecologically and developmentally relevant assessment strategies that lead directly to program planning (ICDL, 2000; Zero to Three, 2005).

The Team Approach

The fields of child development, early intervention, and mental health have a rich history of interdisciplinary work that has evolved in the last 40 years or so as the importance of early attention to developmental disabilities gained increased recognition. When assessing infants and toddlers, a set of interdisciplinary assessment principles includes the following:

- Validate scores from standardized instruments against the material gathered from naturalistic settings.
- Reevaluations should be routine, considered in context, and note that uncertainty may be an ongoing feature of the results.
- Testing should be coordinated and case histories collected to avoid redundant use of particular instruments or procedures.
- The assessment process itself is dynamic and may yield new information.
- Different disciplines bring various communication styles, protocols, and philosophies; thus, the team must operate from a perspective of respect for the diverse traditions in support of the particular infant.
- View each child in a cultural context that considers the definition of competence from the uniqueness of that culture.
- The family perspective is the central guiding force in assessing and planning for infants and toddlers.
- Include community providers in the assessment process when recommending special services and an IFSP.

- As part of assessment, inclusion and support of the family and infant are key. (Guralnick, 2000; Guralnick & Conlon, 2007)

IDEA (2004) also mandates that professionals from several disciplines need to work cooperatively to provide services to infants and toddlers with disabilities and their families. The purpose of the team is to determine eligibility and develop the IFSP. A number of disciplines mentioned in the law are involved in the assessment and program development of an infant or toddler. These include a special educator, nurse, speech and language pathologist, audiologist, occupational therapist, physical therapist, psychologist, social worker, and nutritionist. Of course, it is unlikely that all of these disciplines would be involved in any given assessment. The background and issues surrounding the particular child would determine the exact composition of the team. Besides the parent, others who might be directly involved are the early childhood educator, the building or program administrator, the counselor, and the adapted physical education specialist. These individuals make up the early intervention team.

What may best distinguish early intervention teams from one another is neither their composition, since they are all composed of some combination of the disciplines just mentioned plus the family, nor the tasks that include assessment and intervention, but rather the structure of interaction among team members. Family members participate as full members of the team in determining assessment results and in developing the program plan. The case manager, one member of the team, writes reports separately for the team and family (Hooper & Umansky, 2004).

THE INTEGRATION OF ASSESSMENT INFORMATION INTO PROGRAMMING

Infant assessment is in actuality infant intervention (cf. Bricker, 2002; Linder, 2008; Ensher, 2009). The continuous observation of the infant and toddler, along with talking with the parents, provides the opportunity to note the child's responses and blend the assessment into the intervention plan. As much as possible, the assessment process simultaneously serves as a guide to individual programming, program planning, and evaluation. Ensher concludes that "all aspects of evaluation in the early years must reflect interactions of child, family, professional and setting . . . (assessment) methodology (must be guided) by an understanding of immediate problems and dynamics . . . strategies need to embrace the goal of achieving a more natural, integrated, and flexible approach to evaluation (and intervention)" (2009, p. 105).

The assessment team needs to answer a number of questions in order to plan the most appropriate program for the child and the family (cf. McLean et al., 2004). Not only do teachers and other team members need to know *what* the baby/toddler can do, but also *how* the task is performed. In addition to examining the critical functions mentioned earlier in this chapter, team members need to examine the quality of the performance. Then team members need to determine what the infant or toddler needs to learn next, what the baby is unable to do and why, and, finally, how this particular baby learns best. The answers to all of these questions will enable the assessment team and family to develop the most appropriate program for the infant or toddler, including the daily planning that integrates the goals and objectives of the IFSP into the routines of the early childhood setting. Assessment measures "should include . . . (ways for determining) child endurance, temperament, various dimensions of play, attention-gaining and self-calming abilities, responsiveness to new tasks and unfamiliar situations, unstructured discovery and spontaneous activity, levels of frustration and primary modes of communication" (Ensher, 2009, p. 103). If all of these factors are considered at the outset, then comprehensive intervention plans can be made. Then, a structure is set in place for intervention and on-going assessment geared toward best baby and toddler outcomes, as outlined in the IFSP. Without a doubt, the most important purpose of assessment is program planning and monitoring of individual and group progress.

outcomes the specifications used by school districts, states, and professional associations to describe measurable educational goals.

Some important considerations for ensuring that the assessment information translates to **outcomes** that make a difference in the lives of infants, toddlers, and their families are as follows:

- Do we know why we're writing this?
- Does this outcome mesh with activities that the family chooses to do?
- Have we explored informal, natural, and community-based supports (i.e., those that are least restrictive)?
- Who will pay for or provide services?
- Can the family understand the language of the outcome?
- Does this outcome really matter to the family and the infant/toddler/young child who will be evaluated against it? (Rosenkoetter & Squires, 2000, pp. 4–5; see also Bagnato, 2007).

The answers to these questions are critical, for the most important outcome for early intervention is school success.

The characteristics that enable children to learn in school are now: curiosity, confidence, the capacity to set a goal and work towards its accomplishment, the ability to communicate with others, and to get along with them. Children who don't have these characteristics do not perform well in school. School readiness—or unreadiness—begins in the first years of life (Zero to Three, 2004; Copple & Bredekamp, 2009).

DOCUMENTING INFANT/TODDLER PROGRESS IN TYPICAL CARE SITUATIONS

As more families choose group care situations for their babies and toddlers, increased attention must be given to the curriculum for babies, which includes the on-going assessment of each individual enrolled in group care. Fundamentally, the curriculum is play-based, facilitated by caregivers who support and nurture babies and toddlers as if they were primary in the babies/toddlers lives. The group care environment to support this approach must be carefully constructed to permit baby and toddler exploration (West ED, 2009). The environment sets the stage for teachers to provide a culturally sensitive approach, which pays attention to the ways that families socialize their young children and supports this approach, recognizing the family's expertise. The caregiver's first responsibility is meeting basic care needs "in a relatively spontaneous and intuitive manner, without focus on planned learning experiences" (Bergen, Reid, & Torelli, 2009, p. 2). The curriculum becomes "a dynamic, interactive experience that builds on respect for and responsiveness to young children's interests, curiosity, and motives, and to their families' goals and concerns" (Bergen et al., p. 3). The infant/toddler curriculum is one that is individualized, emergent, and in tune with the baby/toddler's particular curiosities, learning style, and temperament. Good care is routine-based, so that the baby can learn to predict behavioral consequences. For example, "swaddling in a blanket, rocking, and a quiet sleeping song can be signals for a baby to relax into sleep" (Petersen & Wittmer, 2008, p. 42). Lally describes this approach to teaching with the idea of the teacher as researcher. The teacher is one who "observes and listens to children's ideas and actions, (then) reflects on what you see and names the children's interests, (next) creating learning encounters that will build on the children's interests and your observations" and implement, observe, and revise (2008). In this way, you "catch the infants in the act of fiddling around with things, experimenting, and constructing knowledge"; you are engaged in dynamic, inquiry-based curriculum for infants and toddlers.

Assessment follows this inquiry-based approach with techniques focusing on observation, functional, and dynamic assessment. Simple documentation of feeding, response to food, sleeping, and toileting are essential elements to record and to share with families (Petersen & Wittmer, 2008). The methods discussed earlier in the chapter are used with typically developing young children, but the intensity of the use of specialists and intervention planning are less formal and more routine as in the preschool and primary care and education setting. This does not mean that

BOX 9.2

For Communicating with Parents at Infant/Toddler Center

Notes from home...
When did Josephina last eat?
How much did she sleep last night?
- Any diapering issues to know about?
- Any other things we should know?

Notes from Cradle 'n Care Center
- Josephina ate at the following times:
- Sleeping
- Diapering/toileting
- We played...

you should approach assessment casually; documentation of progress toward program outcomes is important, as is the identification of potential learning or developmental issues. Besides parents, skillful teachers of young children serve as important "finders" of potential issues that can be addressed to improve child toddler outcomes for later school success. Because babies cannot "tell" what has happened at home or center, an important way to communicate as well as document daily feeding, sleeping, and activities from family to center reciprocally is through a paper or email note. See Box 9.2 for an example of this type of note.

The most appropriate assessment methods in typical care situations will include anecdotal notes, running records, developmental checklists, time and event sampling. By employing these techniques, as well as the "learning" or developmental logs exchanged daily with families, you will develop a portfolio of materials to share at regular intervals with families. Toddlers will, of course, have paintings and projects to share, as well. These child products can be collected in a portfolio.

SUMMARY

This chapter describes the role that assessment plays in the lives of all infants, often even before they are born. After describing the total assessment process used with infants and toddlers and the importance of assessment in the first three years, current assessment issues and trends, such as principles that guide infant and toddler assessment and the significance of family collaboration, are discussed. A short discussion on the integration of assessment information into programming is highlighted, as the most important purpose of assessment is program planning for individual infants and toddlers. Finally, an approach to documentation of infant/toddler progress in typical group care situations extends and ends the chapter.

FIELD ACTIVITIES

1. Visit the newborn nursery in your community. Observe the infants through the window. Note the difference in size, coloring, movement, and so on. Ask the hospital administrator or head nurse if you could observe any screening (e.g., Apgar, Brazelton).
2. Visit an early intervention program in your community. Observe the children to see if you can ascertain the reason they are in the program. Observe the speech therapist and the physical therapist as well as the early interventionist. Inquire if any of the children also spend time in another child-care program in the community.
3. Visit a neonatal intensive care unit (NICU). This facility will probably be further from home than the other two programs. Ascertain if you may observe any infant. Depending on the facility's policies and the amount of time you have to spend on this activity, there may be other roles for you to play in the NICU.

4. Identify the number and types of programs serving infants and toddlers in your community. Compare your findings to numbers of programs 10 years ago by consulting library copies of community resources for the previous decade.
5. Visit a toddler class; observe the way the toddlers are playing. Make notes and develop a potential record-keeping system for the development of friendships in toddlers.

IN-CLASS ACTIVITIES

1. With a partner, identify play activities for infants/toddlers at various developmental stages: 6 months, 1 year, 18 months, 2 years, and 2½ years. Describe how you might use these activities in a learning assessment.
2. In small groups, develop questions that you might use with families seeking to enroll infants and toddlers in your center. What questions would be included that might give you information about the baby's developmental state? How would you ask these questions with sensitivity?

STUDY QUESTIONS

1. Define *prenatal assessments* and list examples.
2. When and how is the Apgar Rating Scale used? What information does it provide?
3. What are five principles of child development? Why is knowledge of these necessary when thinking about infant/toddler assessment?
4. How do the three risk factors relate? Why do early childhood teachers need this information?
5. What characteristics of infants and toddlers make it imperative that specifically designed assessments be used before age 3? What principles guide these assessments?
6. How can family involvement reduce parent anxiety?
7. Why is it important to identify at-risk infants and toddlers?
8. What does IDEA state regarding early interventions and their purpose?
9. What role does intervention play in infant/toddler assessment?

REFLECT AND RE-READ

- I can list common prenatal assessment procedures.
- I know how infant/toddler assessment is unique.
- I understand the link from assessment to intervention.
- I can use developmental principles to identify at-risk babies.
- I know what is unique about the parent role in infant/toddler assessment.

CASE VIGNETTE

Setting up to assess a 28-month-old toddler, the assessor notes the following description of Deiondre and her family situation: On a bright day in November, Deiondre is wearing blue jeans with embroidered flowers, a pink long-sleeved shirt, and pink socks. Deiondre is a tall, thin, caramel-colored toddler with dark, curly hair braided in five French braids in back. Deiondre is the only child of Della Masters and Ronald Lark. When the observer arrived, Deiondre seemed to be a very active and energetic toddler. Ms. Masters and Mr. Lark report that they have a hard time keeping her out of things; she loves to rub on lotions and body oils. Last year she swallowed a Tylenol and her parents rushed her to the hospital for treatment.

Deiondre seems to speak very well for a toddler; she can hold a short conversation with an unfamiliar adult, using clearly understood words correctly. Occasionally, she uses swear words, a habit she picked up from family members who have since stopped swearing in front of her. Deiondre loves to mimic the activities of adults such as writing, dancing, typing on the computer, and washing the dishes. While in the kitchen with her family, Deiondre scoots a stool to the kitchen counter and stands on it to "wash the dishes." When someone takes away the stool, she simply pushes the kitchen chair to the sink and tries once again to "wash the dishes." Finally, after a lot of crying and pleading, and the help of Gerber fruit snacks, Ms. Masters gets her to stop.

If Deiondre enrolled in your infant/toddler program, what additional assessment information would you plan? What instructional plan would you make? How will you collaborate with Ms. Masters and Mr. Lark?

Source: From J. Darko, 2004, submitted in partial fulfillment of ECE 375, Early Childhood Assessment: DePaul University. Used by permission.

TECHNOLOGY LINKS

http://www.apha.org

American Public Health Association. Publishes material on mental health and health issues related to children.

http://www.aap.org

American Academy of Pediatrics. Position papers and publications affecting the lives of young children.

http://www.acog.com

American College of Obstetricians and Gynecologists. Information pamphlets on women's health and prenatal care and development.

http://www.brightfutures.org

Bright Futures at Georgetown University. Promotes health and mental health; site includes checklists and information about health assessment.

http://www.nectac.org

National Early Childhood Technical Assistance System. A clearinghouse for information on the education of young children, with technical papers and practical suggestions for programming and assessment.

http://www.pitc.org

Program for Infant/Toddler Caregivers. Resources to support a relationship curriculum for infants and toddlers.

http://babylab.uchicago.edu/welcome.html

Center for Research at the University of Chicago. Information on baby/toddler language development.

SUGGESTED READINGS

Bergen, D., Reid, R. & Torelli, L. (2009). *Educating and caring for very young children: The infant/toddler curriculum* (2nd ed.). New York: Teachers College.

Gonzalez-Mena, J., & Eyer, D. W. (2009). *Infants, toddlers, and caregivers: A curriculum of respectful, responsive care and education* (7th ed.). New York: McGraw-Hill.

Kessen, W. (2006). *Infant care.* New Haven: Yale University Press.

Sandall, S., McLean, M. E., & Smith, B. J. (2000). *DEC recommended practices in early intervention/early childhood special education.* Longmont, CO: Sopris West.

Wittmer, D. S. (2008). *Focusing on peers: The importance of relationships in the early years.* Washington, DC: Zero to Three.

Wittmer, D., & Petersen, S. (2010). *Infant/toddler development and responsive program planning: A relationship-based approach* (2nd ed.). Upper Saddle River, NJ: Merrill/Prentice Hall.

CHAPTER 10

Issues in Preschool Assessment

TERMS TO KNOW

- multiple intelligences
- project-based learning
- webbing
- Reggio Emilia approach
- documentation
- portfolios
- developmentally appropriate practice
- play-based assessment

CHAPTER OVERVIEW

This chapter traces the use of assessment systems in preschool settings. One use of such systems is selection of children for participation in limited enrollment situations. Using screening instruments for enrollment decisions and the important limitations of such an approach is a featured debate. Next is a focus on the issues surrounding the connection from assessment to curriculum, instruction, and the return. A segment is included regarding referral to special services. Included in the discussion are links to appropriate teacher roles in the process and play-based assessment. Finally, there is a spotlight on the issues of first-grade transition.

ASSESS AS YOU READ

- When and how do you assess preschoolers?
- What is the role of screening in the early childhood program? What are the limitations?
- What are the Head Start Performance Standards? Why is Head Start requiring educational outcomes assessment?
- Where does Response to Intervention (RTI) fit into preschool?
- How do I plan for outcomes assessment?
- How can I articulate with kindergarten-primary teachers?

PRESCHOOL ASSESSMENT SYSTEM ISSUES

At the preschool level, young children may attend a child-care center, family child care, a half-day nursery school, a part-time playgroup, all-day care, Head Start, or a regular or special education program. Teachers in each of these settings have similar demands for assessment measures. They plan instruction and keep track of child progress. Sometimes teachers participate in decisions that require consultation and professional assistance. The most common preschool assessment decisions include selection for the preschool program, planning for instruction, referral for special services, and transition to kindergarten/first grade. In each of these situations, preschool teachers are problem solvers who use assessment to teach.

SELECTION FOR THE PRESCHOOL PROGRAM

Family Convenience

Families often choose a program close to their home and enroll their children there. These programs usually accept children on a first-come, first-served basis. These community-based programs generally select children because of age, religious affiliation, ability to pay, or other demographic characteristics. A child's ability is not usually the basis for selection decisions.

Limited Enrollment Decisions

Choosing children deemed "academically at risk" currently proceeds in a manner dictated by the restricted public funds available for screening. However, across the nation, there is a move to increase public funding to provide universal preschool. "Universal access to publicly funded high-quality preschool education . . . policymakers and the public focus on the potential benefits from a universal preschool programs . . . potential benefits include lower intangible losses from crime and child abuse and neglect, averted, reduced reliance on public welfare programs, improved labor market outcomes for parents of preschoolers, improved health and well-being of preschool participants, and the intergenerational transmission of favorable benefits . . . and the distribution of economic and social well-being" (Karly & Bigelow, 2005). In states and communities where universal preschool is reality, there is no need to use screening instrument to select for the "most needy" of those who may be deemed "academically at risk." HR 555, the Universal Pre-Kindergarten Act, was introduced by Rep. Dennis J. Kucinich of Ohio with the following purpose:

- To assist States in establishing a universal prekindergarten program to ensure that all children 3, 4, and 5 years old have access to a high-quality full-day, full-calendar-year prekindergarten education.

The act is currently under consideration by the House Committee on Education and Labor.

In the meantime, selection criteria may apply to family and child characteristics. Family demographics included are poverty, limited English fluency, or teen mothers. After agencies and school districts collect a pool of demographically eligible children, they employ an efficient

method to choose those most in need of the special program. School districts frequently choose screening instruments for this purpose. These measures give a general overview of a child's ability and achievement in self-help skills, cognition, language, fine- and gross-motor skills, and social/emotional development. The opportunity for participation in screening should be open to all children to secure this developmental review.

Screening programs survey many children in a short period. Thus, most children pass through the screen and go to a regular program; they are not eligible for an at-risk program. The screening procedure acts as a selection device. Because screening procedures typically survey developmental milestones, the results have a short time of usability. The younger the child, the more limited the time frame. This is due to the rapid nature of developmental change in young children. When there is a long time delay between screening and program delivery, rescreening is necessary. The critical time delay varies with the age of the child, but a good rule of thumb is a delay of three to six months.

CHOOSING A SCREENING INSTRUMENT

When choosing a screening instrument or procedure, consider many factors. First, a developmental screening review should be comprehensive, reviewing all aspects of development: cognitive, physical, and social/emotional. Conduct activities with the children that they see as play; concrete materials ought to form the basis of the activity. The procedure must reflect the cultural diversity of a particular community. When screening young children at enrollment time, it is helpful to have speakers of the languages of the community available to make families and children feel welcome as well as to conduct any necessary translation. Familes should be involved in providing primary information about a child's history and perceptions of current functioning. Families can also give information that will help you know which languages young children use and under what circumstances. For example, it is not unusual that young learners will know some words in English and other words in the home language.

Questions that you might ask the child's family:

- When your child wants a cookie, how does he or she ask for it? Home language? English?
- When relatives visit, does your child follow the conversation in your home language? Fully, somewhat? Not all?
- Does your child speak your language with few errors? With some errors, like most children? Only has a few words?
- Can your child ask for help in English? Example: for tying shoe? Buttoning coat? Only some things? Not at all?
- Does your child use English to talk about TV? Toys?
- Does your family speak any English at home?
- Does your family watch your home language on TV?
- Do you watch any children's TV programs in English?

By asking these questions at the point of enrollment, you can plan the kinds of support that you will need for individual children. Perhaps you will need picture signs to demonstrate class areas, rules, and the schedule. In addition, you will want to stock up on picture books and picture dictionaries that have clear, unambiguous pictures so that young children can associate a name easily with a picture. Good sources for these are National Geographic http://kids.nationalgeographic.com and Heinemann/Raintree Classroom http://www.heinemannclassroom.com. You are looking for clear pictures with limited background so that you can see the apple, pear, orange, and not the tree, the supermarket or the grove. Besides talking with families and furnishing your classroom with good pictures and picture books to facilitate language learning, you will need to pay attention to the technical qualities of reliability, validity, and overreferral/underreferral when choosing a screening system and whether it is suitable for speakers of languages other than English. The procedure or plan must be quick to administer to individual children. Young children can give limited attention to formal screening tasks. Quickly administered measures function efficiently for the screening agency.

Head Start placed increased emphasis on screening with the passage of legislation requiring attention to performance outcomes. Screening of young children is required within 45 days of enrollment in the program. The screening focuses on the whole child—health and developmental assessment. The screening process identifies child strengths and any areas of concern to follow throughout the child's enrollment in Head Start. "Through this process, (teachers and parents) come to know each child's strengths, interests, needs, and learning styles in order to individualize the curriculum, to build on each child's prior knowledge and experiences, and to provide meaningful curriculum experiences that support learning and development. In these ways, staff, parents, and programs support each child in making progress toward stated goals. (This Head Start policy supports a national concern) . . . with the whole child, (including) social competence as part of school readiness" (Head Start, 2003, p. 15; see also current regulations in §1308.6 Assessment of Children). Of particular interest is the need to screen for behavioral problems, as these problems interfere with later school adjustment and achievement. Preliminary studies (Kaiser, Cai, Hancock, & Foster, 2002; Kaiser, Hancock, Cai, Foster, & Hester, 2000; Serna, Nielsen, Mattern, & Forness, 2003) show an overlap of language problems with parent-reported behavioral problems and classroom-observed behavioral difficulties, and difficulties with social skills. Thus, screening in Head Start must find those at risk for these difficulties while remaining fully aware of the potential stigmatizing effects of early identification and labeling and the contextual differences in behavioral expectations.

Limitations of Screening Instruments

Screening procedures and instruments have limitations. These tools cannot diagnose children. They can appropriately select children who may be at risk of academic failure. However, they cannot definitively decide individual developmental profiles. Further assessment is necessary to decide eligibility for special education placement or to plan for educational intervention. This is in keeping with best practice as defined by the American Educational Research Association, the American Psychological Association, and the National Council on Measurement in Education. Their joint Standard 13.7 states: "In educational settings, a decision or characterization that will have major impact on a student should not be made on the basis of a single test score. Other relevant information should be taken into account if it will enhance the overall validity of the decision" (AERA, APA, & NCME, 1999, p. 146).

Thus, "screening programs identify those children who may need special kinds of help to function well in school. They should not exclude them from a program for which they are legally eligible. Sound, ethical practice is to accept children in all their variety, identify any special needs they have, and offer them the best possible opportunity to grow and learn" (Hills, 1987, p. 2). "When a screening tool or other assessment identifies concerns, appropriate follow-up, referral, or other intervention is used. Diagnosis or labeling is never the result of a brief screening or one-time assessment" (National Association for the Education of Young Children and National Association of Early Childhood Specialists in State Departments of Education, 2003a; see also NAEYC, 2009). Finally, children who are chosen for special enrichment programs should not be labeled "at risk" or by any other label that may result in lifelong stigmatization. Program plans should include documentation of learning progress as well as rescreening when appropriate.

Using Screening Instruments Appropriately

At the beginning of the enrollment period or shortly after children are admitted to your program, you will make plans for teaching children based on the results of the screening conducted. So, as you look at the results and interpret the scores, ask the following for each child:

- Barely miss cutoff by a few points?
- Lose points in one domain or area?

BOX 10.1

Using the Screening Information for Orville, a Three-Year-Old.

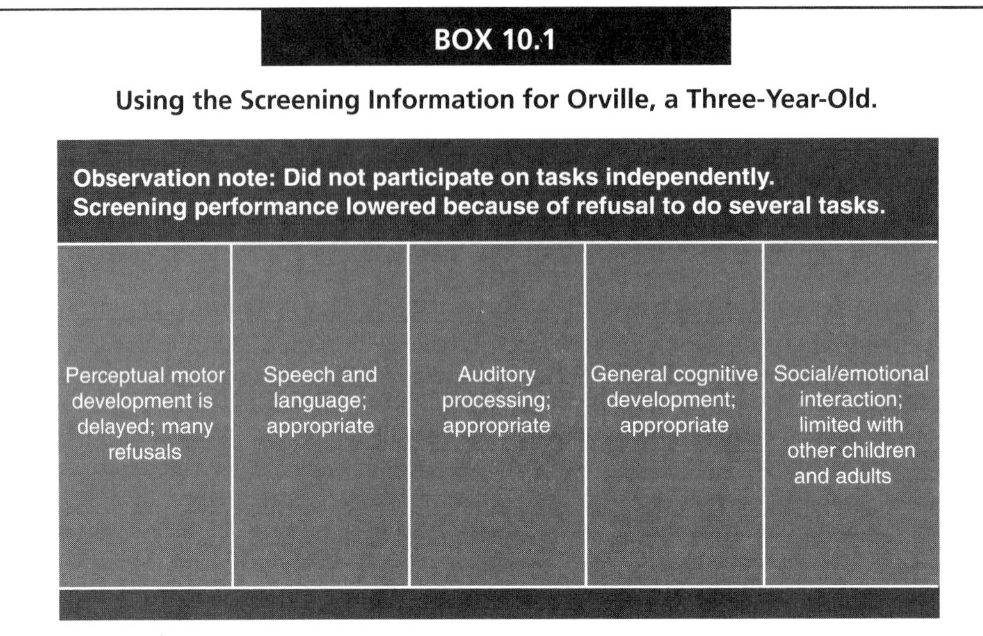

Observation note: Did not participate on tasks independently.
Screening performance lowered because of refusal to do several tasks.
Perceptual motor development is delayed; many refusals
Speech and language; appropriate
Auditory processing; appropriate
General cognitive development; appropriate
Social/emotional interaction; limited with other children and adults

- Points lost when directions were verbal?
- Points lost when sequencing visual or auditory memory required?
- Didn't seem to understand instruction?
- Just move to the next level for passing, then see what would happen if the test was a few days earlier (Meisels & Atkins-Burnett, 2005, p. 36).

When you have the answers to each of these questions about each of the children in your program, you can decide what to do next to teach each one. You can group children for instruction in small groups and/or plan interventions on the basis of areas that show relative weaknesses. If you have made charts for the skills covered or used the record sheets or software from the screening, you can document learning and rescreen as indicated. See Box 10.1.

Although this report does not give scores, you have information about Orville. You know that he seems shy both with children and adults. You know that he will need to be encouraged to try knew things, particularly activities that ask him to use crayons, blocks, puzzles, and paints. You do not know why he refused to use such materials at the screening. Is this the first time that he has seen the materials? So, you have a start for planning to meet Orville's needs. You might model using crayons—sitting beside him and drawing, talking about your picture. You might encourage Orville to join Tom in the block corner and so on. All the while you are trying these interventions, you are keeping track of your experiences with Orville to document his progress. The way in which you document Orville's progress and the way in which you teach will be guided by your program's philosophy.

PLANNING FOR INSTRUCTION

Once children enter a program, the program philosophy guides the curriculum and instruction. Assessment links the instructional strategies to individual children. *Observation* of children forms the backbone of the preschool assessment program. This assessment method is an integral part of the play-based curriculum found in preschool settings. Play-based curricula incorporate concrete experiential activities. In this approach, you plan projects grounded on the interests and needs of

BOX 10.2

Happy Valley Kindergarten Baseline Individual Profile of Progress (For Teacher Use Only) August–September

Student: ______________________ **Teacher:** ______________________

NY	B	D	S	Concepts/Skills	Criteria and Notes
				1. Name eight basic colors (red, green, brown, orange, blue, black, yellow, purple)	Show marker/crayon and ask, "What color is this?" NY = 0; B = 1–5; D = 6–7, S = 8
				2. Rote count to __________	Ask, "Can you count for me? Please start." NY = 0; B = 1–9; D = 10–19; S = 20+
				3. Count backwards 10 to 0	Ask, "Can you count backwards for me? Please start." NY = Cannot; S = Can
				4. Identify numbers 0 to 20	Use sheet to record which numerals are identified. NY = 0 numbers identified; B = 1–9; D = 10–19; S = 20–21
				5. Rational counting to __________	Spread out 10–20. Unifix cubes on the table and ask, "Can you count these for me? Please start." If the child wants to continue, spread out another set of 10.
				6. Write first name	Use boxed signature paper for four administrations during year. NY = Cannot; S = Can

Key NY = Not Yet; B = Beginning; D = Developing; S = Secure

Letter Identification*	Notes
Uppercase __________	
Lowercase __________	

Source: Developed by Marie Ann Donovan, DePaul University. Used with permission.
*Use master sheet to record which particular letter was identified.

the children. Commonly, the divisions for curricula are knowledge, skills, and attitudes. Knowledge is the content or subject matter for the program. Typically, curricular themes for preschool include those rooted in the immediate social world of the children—my family, my community, my friends, our garbage, and so on. The skills of the instructional process include problem solving; communicating in words, pictures, and writing; cooperating with friends; following schedules and routines; and so on. Attitudes include curiosity, risk taking, self-confidence, respect for others, and so on. Learning of knowledge, skills, and attitudes occurs in activities that tap the intellectual, creative, social/emotional, and physical domains (see Box 10.2).

Many programs use prepared curricular guides that include checklists to document child progress toward outcomes. An example is "*The Creative Curriculum® for Preschool*, (which) forms the basis of (a) fully integrated program for three- to five-year-old children. Nationally known for its forward-thinking, comprehensive, and rigorously researched model, (the) unique approach helps you successfully plan and implement a content-rich, developmentally appropriate program that supports active learning and promotes children's progress in all developmental areas" (http://www.teachingstrategies.com/page/CCPS_Overview.cfm; accessed June 29, 2009). The assessment instrument that accompanies this curriculum compares child outcomes to a developmental continuum. Each outcome is well illustrated. Then in Chapter 4 of the *Creative Curriculum for Preschool®*, the authors describe the integration of observation, guiding children, and assessing learning as part of the teacher's role. Illustrations are given for questions to use when talking with children about their work so that you can document their thinking and ability to think aloud, to observe, to make predictions, to discuss similarities and differences, to problem-solve, to consider consequences, and to evaluate (Dodge, Colker, & Heroman, 2002, pp. 165–209). When using developmentally based curriculum guides with associated assessment materials, you can have confidence that you are approaching teaching and learning holistically. However, if you are not using a prepared curriculum, you use theme the themes and projects organized around a topic provide children opportunities to develop in holistic fashion in each of the domains. Typical themes include families, school, community, farm, toys,and many others that appeal to children's interests as well as provide material for problem-solving and investigation by young children. Opportunities for children to experience the topics occur in small groups, at interest centers, individually, and with the whole class. The teacher provides the environment and activities for children to explore in their relationships with children, materials, and the teacher.

Thus, teachers plan activities around themes that offer multiple outcomes, so that they serve a wide range of child abilities and interests. These complicated activities accommodate the typical range of development found in any classroom. In addition, such activities work well with mixed-age groups and with children who have special needs. You will facilitate child-learning by choosing activities that accommodate the diverse social experiences of children permits the enrichment of their basic understanding of their broadening social world.

By starting with their interests, knowledge, and skills, teachers create an excitement for learning. This approach is often called inquiry-based or emergent curriculum. In such an approach, children learn by experimenting with materials, observing their environment, conversing with others, and sharing their insights. The teacher sets the stage for the integration of learning by starting with complex topics that lead in many directions. Questions that teachers ask to assess curricular effectiveness include whether they encourage children to:

1. Think divergently?
2. Seek alternate solutions for problems?
3. Be independent?
4. Develop foundational skills in literacy, numeracy?
5. See logically integrated curricular topics?
6. Participate in a balance of teacher-initiated and child-initiated activities? (Cromwell, 2000, p. 160; see also Wortham, 2010)

The child-initiated theme approach to curriculum is an example of a complex topic developed with multilevel experiences to meet the needs of the diverse group of four-year-olds in Ms. Berg's class, as discussed in Box 10.3. Draw parents into the process as the experience evolves. The theme offers opportunities to develop knowledge, skills, and attitudes in the intellectual, social/emotional, physical, and creative domains. Experiences in this theme are concrete and active (cf. Berry & Mindes, 1993; Wortham, 2010; Stacey, 2009).

An explicit outline and explanation of this approach is available in *Developmentally Appropriate Practice in Early Childhood Programs Serving Children from Birth through Age 8* (Bredekamp & Copple, 1997; see also DAP, 2009). One important principle of this approach is that process and presentation—the *how* of instruction—is as important as the specific content. Complex activities that have multiple outcomes form the content. The presentation of the activity and the teacher's interaction helps and stimulates the acquisition of content and/or skills. In this curricular approach, the teacher plays a critical role as "decision-maker," motivator, model, innovator, environmental planner, and evaluator (Berry & Mindes, 1993). The teacher shifts roles based on observation of the children in action.

BOX 10.3

Garbage in Our World

Ms. Berg's four-year-olds attend a school that recycles papers, magazines, glass, and cans. The children see recycling efforts made by the whole school in the cafeteria that uses donated silverware and dishes to avoid paper plates. The dishes don't match. One day at lunch, Kimberly asks Ms. Berg why the dishes don't match. From this discussion, the children decide that they want to explore other ways to help the school and their families conserve and recycle. Ms. Berg prepares a number of interest centers for the children that will elaborate the theme. The children develop a compost heap, interview their families about garbage awareness and recycling habits, read books about ecology, draw pictures representing a world full of garbage, and so on. The children begin a schoolwide drive to collect cloth napkins as a further recycling effort.

Teacher Instructional Role

As they observe, teachers change their roles in instruction from observer to validator, participant/converser, extender, problem initiator, model, instructor, and manager/organizer/provider (Lee-Katz, Ellis, & Jewett, 1993; see also Feeney, Moravcik, Nolte, & Christensen, 2010). Teachers use role-shifting based on inference through observation; teachers also ask children to describe and interpret their work. In this way, the teacher can explicitly understand a child's thinking and goals. Teachers design games, interviews, contracts for specific work, and directed assignments to gain a better understanding of children's development and to plan instruction (Hills, 1992; Yelland, 2000; see also Kostelnik, Soderman, & Whiren, 2007; Brown, 2008). Epstein (2008) gives practical steps for you to think about assessing and documenting child thinking through the following steps:

- Ask individual children—for example, Ruthie—what they will do during a self-selected activity time block, if they are showing some struggle with moving into materials. Use the words: What is your plan for writing a story about your new kitten? What is the kitten's name? Who will the story be about?
- Be sure that Ruthie can see all of the materials that might be useful for story development.
- Ask a few open-ended questions about the kitten's activities, using open-ended ones like, "How will you show that Buttercup is shy?"
- Accept Ruthie's answer and try to extend it; Buttercup hides under the sofa. When does she do this? Does she hear loud noises? Does Buttercup hide when big shoes get near?
- At the end of the self-selection time, invite children to reflect upon what they did. So, you might ask Ruthie: How did you tell Buttercup's story? Do you think there is more to tell?
- Comment on the plan and the actual activity.

With this emphasis on planning and reflection, you assist each child in getting the concept of thinking about their own work—making thinking explicit. As an assessor, you learn what each is thinking and gain anecdotes for documentation of learning progress.

Teachers establish the baseline for the program: routines, room arrangement, rules and expectations, schedule, and interpersonal relationships (Berry & Mindes, 1993). Once the stage is set and the theme chosen, teachers assess the curriculum effectiveness for individual children and for the group by watching the children. Teachers then adjust the baseline to meet the needs of children. For example, if an objective of the program is to increase knowledge of the functional uses of print, then how does a teacher know whether Maria understands? In a dramatic play setting, she observes Maria grabbing a message pad and scribbling as she listens to the phone call. Maria shows that writing is a substitute for oral messages (Tompkins, 2010). Teachers instruct and assess simultaneously. Focus questions for this kind of integrated teaching embrace the following developmental issues:

- Are children showing progress in relationships?
- Are they expressing joy, anger, jealousy, or fear in ways that facilitate coping?

- Do they run, skip, climb, and move with greater ability?
- Can they handle scissors, pencils, and tools more efficiently?
- Do they show increased knowledge about their world?
- Are they using language effectively?
- How do they solve problems?
- What new concepts do they seem to be exhibiting? (Seefeldt & Barbour 1998, p. 328; see also Krogh & Morehouse, 2008)

Teachers should adjust their interactions with children, create an environment that promotes self-discipline, and assist children in mediating their own interactions. Sensitive responses and adjustments to observed problems help children grow and succeed. Teachers can decide what to teach by watching the children. Who is interested in leaves? What do the children know about squirrels? Can they identify red, blue, or green? Checklists and discussions of materials, room arrangement, and activities are available in the child guidance and curriculum literature (cf. Beaty, 2010; Dodge & Colker, 2002; Hohmann & Weikart, 2008; Kostelnick, Stein, Whiren, Soderman, & Gregory, 2009). An example of how you can keep track of learning outcomes while teaching is shown in Box 10.4. On a particular day, use the form to record your assessment about one or more children, thus documenting progress toward outcomes.

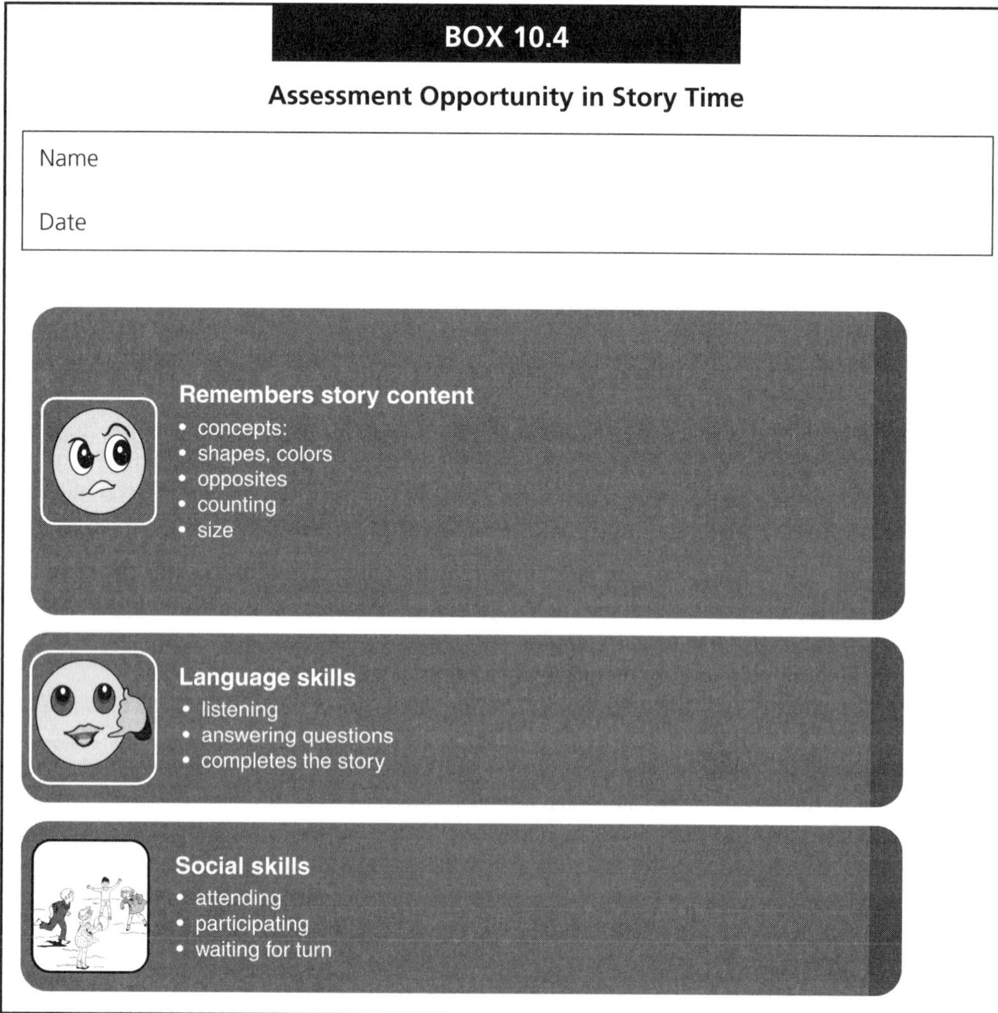

BOX 10.4

Assessment Opportunity in Story Time

Name

Date

Remembers story content
- concepts:
- shapes, colors
- opposites
- counting
- size

Language skills
- listening
- answering questions
- completes the story

Social skills
- attending
- participating
- waiting for turn

BOX 10.5

Story Cards to Support Story Concept

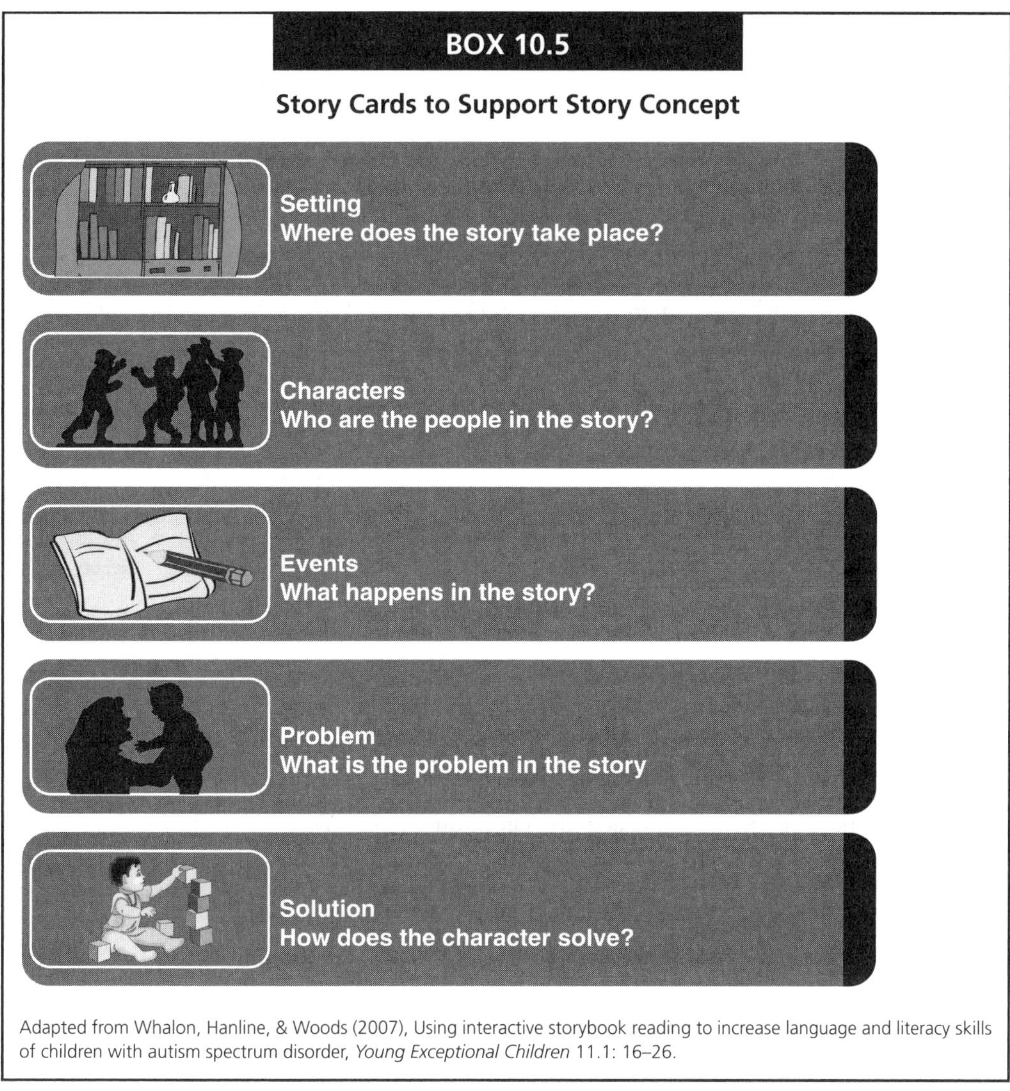

Setting
Where does the story take place?
Characters
Who are the people in the story?
Events
What happens in the story?
Problem
What is the problem in the story
Solution
How does the character solve?

Adapted from Whalon, Hanline, & Woods (2007), Using interactive storybook reading to increase language and literacy skills of children with autism spectrum disorder, *Young Exceptional Children* 11.1: 16–26.

When working with individual children on reading, you can use picture cards to cue them to successful conceptual development. See the example in Box 10.5.

In this situation, you are reading a story about a child going to school. To help Mildred understand the elements of stories, you provide the picture clues so that she can form the concepts. These documentations are used as part of a holistic approach to curriculum, based on the notion that young children learn through their experiences with materials and people in the classroom. As you choose record-keeping systems and ways to record observations, you will be considering the program's philosophy.

Link to Philosophy

Teachers should carefully select recording methods and the particular goal for observation based on the philosophy and goals of instruction for the program. You can find examples of different assessment traditions by reading ecological studies of teaching. Teachers talk about how they have incorporated assessment in the teaching-learning process. Teachers discuss how philosophy, planning, and assessment go together. Assessment is not an extra; it's part of what a teacher does (Dyson & Genishi, 2005; Paley, 2004; Stacey, 2009).

Assessment is developmentally appropriate to the extent that the processes are

- Continuous
- Directed to all developmental areas
- Sensitive to individual and cultural diversity
- Completely integrated with curriculum and instruction
- Based on a defensible theory of child development and learning
- Collaborative between teachers and parents
- Helpful to teachers in their planning to meet the needs of children and the goals of the program
- Unequivocally in the best interests of the children (Hills, 1992, p. 61; see also Gullo, 2005; NAEYC, 2009)

Thus, the preschool way of teaching is active, and involves problem-solving and decision-making. Teachers show children how to learn by observing, questioning, and developing interesting projects for them. Teachers establish what children can do through their interactions with them. Using their knowledge, teachers individualize instruction. This is possible in the optimum preschool setting because the activities and procedures are broad. Multiple outcomes and levels of success are possible. For example, a teacher plans a theme on *Where Do We Live? Houses and Shelter*. "This theme allows children the opportunity to develop knowledge of the physical properties of their immediate family and the home environment. In addition, the theme fosters scientific inquiry about building materials" (Berry & Mindes, 1993, p. 87). One of the activities for the theme is "4.3.6: Make House Structures—Use paste, liquid cornstarch, sticks, and so on to make buildings with paper and wallpaper samples. Glue on vinyl tiles for roofs. Discuss what makes these structures work or fall apart" (Berry & Mindes, 1993, p. 94; see also Kostelnick et al., 2007).

Every child who attempts this activity can be successful. There is no right answer to the "house" or the "apartment." Not all children are required to make a shelter. Some may choose to read about houses, some may choose to draw, or some may choose to build houses with blocks. Because you do not require that all children engage in the same activity, they can choose an activity rather than fit into a "one-size-fits-all" activity; all can be successful. Children build confidence in themselves as learners and dare to try new things. Teachers inventory knowledge, skills, and attitudes of children in the intellectual, social/emotional, and physical domains. They search for ways to stretch and encourage children as learners and achievers. Successful preschool teachers braid assessment and teaching into a smooth coil.

The Head Start Child Outcomes are a nationwide example of this approach. "Released in 2000, the Head Start Child Outcomes Framework guides Head Start programs in their curriculum planning and ongoing assessment of the progress and accomplishments of children" (Head Start, 2003). The Head Start Child Outcomes framework models a coordinated philosophy, holistic curriculum, and assessment framework. The framework contains 8 general domains, 27 domain elements, and 100 indicators of specific elements of child development and learning. The learning domains are language development, literacy, mathematics, science, creative arts, social and emotional development, approaches to learning, and physical health and development. By promoting growth in these areas, regularly measuring progress, and individualizing instruction, teachers can be sure that the young children in their care are ready for elementary school. Although this holistic framework addresses important learning outcomes for young children, it does not specify a particular model for delivering curriculum. Many models offer a holistic approach to curriculum including High Scope, Creative Curriculum™, Montessori, and so on. Examples of curricular approaches that promote a holistic view of the integration of assessment and instruction include those based on the theory of multiple intelligences (Gardner, 2006), the project approach (Katz & Chard, 2000; Helm & Beneke, 2003), and the Reggio Emilia (Edwards, Gandini, & Forman, 1998; Scheinfeld, Haigh & Scheinfeld, 2008; Lewin-Benham, 2008) approach.

Multiple Intelligences Curriculum

There are many interpretations of the **multiple intelligences** curriculum. Gardner (2006) identified at least eight forms of intelligence—linguistic, logical/mathematical, spatial, musical, bodily/kinesthetic, interpersonal, intrapersonal, and naturalist. Some curricular manuals seek to match "an intelligence" to "an approach" to instruction. More appropriately interpreted, Gardner's (2006) theory leads teacher to develop various tactics for instruction. Thus, instruction supports learners thinking from diverse perspectives.

multiple intelligences theory that children have eight areas of intellectual competence that are relatively independent of each other.

One of the best places to learn about such an approach is through the selection of readings from the Project Zero website. As an outgrowth of research in schools and elsewhere, Project Zero is the center at Harvard Graduate School of Education that seeks "to understand and enhance learning, thinking, and creativity in the arts, as well as humanistic and scientific disciplines, at the individual and institutional levels" (Project Zero, 2009). One product of this work is a handbook for teachers that identifies:

> five "pathways" or approaches . . . exploration, bridging, understanding, authentic problems, and talent development—represent(ing) the ways in which the multiple intelligence (techniques) can be implemented and nurtured across the elementary grades. The Pathways Model promotes and supports the development of a well-grounded understanding of multiple intelligences theory to inform goal-setting and planning for using multiple intelligences theory in the classroom. Each pathway addresses a different set of goals and provides appropriate guidelines and examples. (Baum, Viens, & Slatin, 2005; see http://www.pz.harvard.edu for additional or current information about Project Zero)

Starting with the theory that intelligence is not "a thing" but is composed of many specific "ways of knowing," a multiple intelligence curriculum intentionally links all aspects of intelligence—movement, language, mathematics, science, social, visual arts, music—and adds working styles to systematically stimulate growth and development geared to each of the ways of knowing. The resulting holistic approach to instruction links naturally to portfolios for documentation of child progress (discussed later in the chapter). Another holistic approach to curriculum and assessment is the project approach.

The Project Approach

Drawing from child curiosities and implementing with strategies that foster inquiry-based and **project-based learning**, or investigation of topic from multiple perspectives (cf. Katz & Chard, 2000; Jacobs & Crowley, 2006), teachers construct activities with children that enhance development of self-understanding, foster investigatory skills, and promote cooperative learning and enhanced appreciation of cultural diversity in the community of the classroom. One of the benefits of the approach is the promotion of communication skills as part of the small-group work that is a hallmark of the approach (Katz & Chard, 2000). The approach uses **webbing**—a graphic organizer that starts with a circle delineating a topic—say, cactus—in which lines leading from the cactus identify what children know about cacti—plant, requires little water, grows mostly in deserts, and so on. Then, children decide what else they would like to learn about cacti—can they survive in rainy places? How big do they grow? Are they all green? Do they have flowers? Next, children investigate using resources that teachers and parents provide. Finally, children document their learning with posters, stories, constructions, and so on. Box 10.6 illustrates a possible cactus web. The web and the processes and products generated during the projects serve to document learning (cf. Helm & Beneke, 2003; Curtis & Carter, 2008).

project-based learning curricula organized on the basis of child-generated curiosities.

webbing an outlining technique that shows graphically or visually the relationships among ideas.

Because projects frequently involve children working in small groups to investigate questions of interest, peer collaboration is a vital part of the method. "(T)he content of the social action rules will not be the same from classroom to classroom, but the need for a social participation structure to be co-constructed, explicit, and working well before productive projects can be

BOX 10.6

Cactus Webbing Example

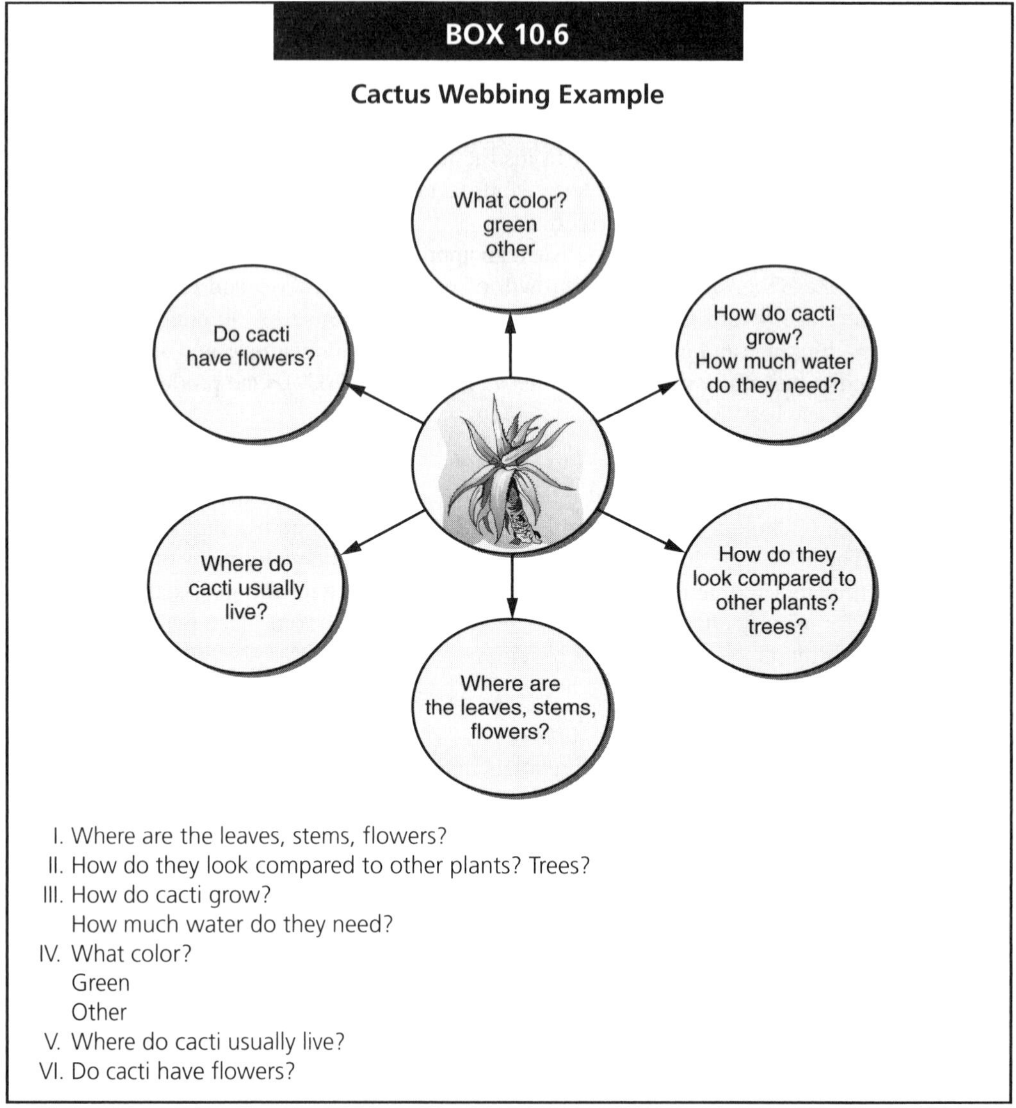

I. Where are the leaves, stems, flowers?
II. How do they look compared to other plants? Trees?
III. How do cacti grow?
How much water do they need?
IV. What color?
Green
Other
V. Where do cacti usually live?
VI. Do cacti have flowers?

accomplished is essential" (Williams, 2003). Therefore, when planning a project-based approach to instruction, you will need to assess your students' developmental and functioning social skills. Then work out meaningful ways for young children to work together—maybe it is only sitting beside each other and looking at a book, or maybe it is cooperating to build a model cactus. In these situations, teachers and children need to assess whether the group works well. A simple checklist serves as a rubric to document the way that four-year-olds work together to solve a problem. For example, the checklist might include: listens to everyone's ideas; uses respectful words; accepts group decision without complaint; does what needs to be done (Diffily & Sassman, 2002; see also Curtis & Carter, 2008). Another approach to project-based learning is Reggio Emilia.

Reggio Emilia approach holistic community way to develop early childhood programs that includes all stakeholders—child, parents, teachers, school leaders, and the community at large.

Reggio Emilia

The **Reggio Emilia approach**:

> fosters children's intellectual development through a systematic focus on symbolic representation. Young children . . . explore their environment and express themselves through "expressive, communicative, and cognitive language," whether they be

> words, movement, drawing, painting, building, sculpture, shadow play, collage, dramatic play, or music. . . . From the beginning, . . . explicit recognition of the . . . partnership among parents, educators, and children (is made). Classrooms . . . support a highly collaborative problem-solving approach to learning . . . use small groups in project learning, . . . sharing of culture through joint exploration among children and adults. (Edwards et al., 1998, p. 7)

Child, teacher, and family interest drive the curriculum through long-term projects that promote engagement in learning and child development. School schedules are flexible so that time matches activity rather than the reverse. The approach requires "constant reflection, collaboration, and questioning" (Wurm, 2005, p. 5) by teachers who plan and implement learning with/for young children. The assessment portion of the practice is **documentation**—the "process of gathering evidence and artifacts of what happens in the classroom . . . not only the process of gathering . . . but also a physical collection . . . the reflection on and analysis of the collection . . . in a way that makes children's learning visible" (Rinaldi, 1994, cited in Wurm, 2005, p. 98; see also Seitz, 2008; Wilford, 2009) to all stakeholders. Documentation begins with everyday observation of child learning. It includes child products that have grown from their investigations. All the tools for recording observations—including anecdotal notes, photos, and child work samples—are available for the documentation process. In the Reggio Emilia approach, a documentation panel shows the work formatively and in summation; the panel functions to display learning and offer opportunities for reflection about its meaning. (See Box 10.7 for an example of a documentation panel.) Thus, from an early age children engage in critical analysis of their work, enhancing their understandings and development. An additional way to collect child documents and to document learning is through the portfolio.

documentation collection of artifacts to support record-keeping of child progress in learning.

Collecting Assessment Information in Portfolios

Portfolios serve as documentation for assessment information. For portfolios, you collect, review, and share teacher observations, informal assessments, and student work products with parents and students. The portfolios are a more dynamic record of child practice than records of formal screening tests and other measures. To be effective, portfolios must contain representative work samples, reflect clear rubrics or outcomes, and be relevant for the learning documented (Borich & Tombari, 2004; Popham, 2008; Stiggins, 2008b). An accompanying reflection details why a particular product is part of the portfolio. Comments that teachers use to inspire reflection consist of the following examples:

portfolios places, such as folders, boxes, or baskets, for keeping all the information known about the children in a class.

- The process I went through to create this piece
- Who or what influenced me to create the piece
- New insights I gained about myself
- I have discovered that I am good at (Costa & Kallick, 2004, pp. 65–66; see also Burke, 2009)

Even young children can begin to be reflective learners (Smith, 2000) if they are given time to practice reflection. They can teach each other through sharing reflections. To become reflective learners, they need to be involved in decision-making. The reflective portfolio provides a common ground for children, teachers, and parents to think about learning holistically. "I have a picture to show you. You're a good drawer. The sun looks really good with the rays coming out" (Smith, 2000, p. 208). Some questions to promote thinking or reflecting include:

- Describe the process you used to complete this work? Did the process work? Were there problems? What would you change next time?
- Did you get any ideas from others that helped you revise your work?
- How can you see the differences between your best work and your not-so-good work? What does this tell you about how you have improved?
- What do you still need help with? What kind of help do you need? (Stiggins, 2008, p. 324)
- How is this project a celebration of learning progress?

BOX 10.7

Apple Picking Trip

We saw apples grow on trees. We picked the apples from the ground and baskets.

We drank apple juice. We ate doughnuts.

Apples

We cut the apple open. The apple has small black seeds. We planted the seeds in a flower pot. We will watch the pot.

We made special apples

Ms. Eldorado brought apples to school. We used a recipe to make special apples.

Recipe

30 apples
30 sticks
Caramel sauce
Waxed paper for the drying apples

Wash the apples. Dry the apples. With teacher's help, stick the stick in the center of the apple. Pour the caramel sauce in a bowl. Dip the apples in the caramel sauce. Swirl the apples carefully in the sauce. Move the apple to the wax paper next to the bowl. Let dry.

Collecting work over time helps you document progress. Examples of documents to collect include: art projects—drawings, collages, paintings; writing; story dictations, books made; graphs or drawings from science and math projects (Dodge, Colker, Heroman, 2002, p. 201). Besides collecting papers for portfolios, you can document work with photos; some activities to record at intervals include block structures, sculptures, and murals, as well as photos showing child progress with self-help skills and group participation (Dodge, Colker, Heroman, 2002, p. 202).

One promising use of portfolios is as a parent-education piece. That is, you review the portfolio with parents. In addition to seeing child progress, parents learn about **developmentally appropriate practice**—instruction that is child-centered and holistic—in a practical, specific way. You show them examples of the way that Deidre shows that she knows story concept. Horatio is ready to go to kindergarten, because—among other things—he can write his first and last name and can organize materials in space in three dimensions through construction (e.g., using Legos™), as well as solve science problems. All of this learning shows up in the portfolio work products, for example, in photos with dictated child reflection about the works. Examples of organizational categories for portfolios include products from a theme on personal growth, favorite stories, special science projects, or other materials chosen by the child and teacher to show the parent (Gelfer & Perkins, 1992; see also Shores & Grace, 2005; Nilsen, 2007). Portfolios are the paper or electronic storage frameworks for collected information. Regardless of the assessment measures required by the stakeholders, portfolios are appropriate even in such instances as the Head Start Outcomes requirement, where specific goals must be measured. Children produce the outcomes, but the measures and interventions show achievement in a variety of ways. Figure 10.1 gives you an idea of the kinds of documents that you might place in a portfolio to document progress toward outcomes. (An example portfolio template is given in Appendix F.)

developmentally appropriate practice planning instruction for preschool children around topics rooted in the children's social world.

Outcomes Teaching and Performance Standards

Released in 2000, the Head Start Child Outcomes Framework is intended to guide Head Start programs in their curriculum planning and ongoing assessment of the progress and accomplishments of children. The framework also is helpful to programs in their efforts to analyze and use data on child outcomes in program self-assessment and continuous improvement. The framework is composed of 8 general domains, 27 domain elements, and numerous examples of specific indicators of children's skills, abilities, knowledge, and behaviors (Head Start, 2003).

The domains are:

- Language
- Literacy
- Mathematics
- Science
- Creative arts
- Social and emotional development
- Approaches to learning
- Physical health and development

"The framework (is a foundation) of building blocks that are important for school success. The framework is not an exhaustive list of everything a child should know or be able to do by the end of Head Start or entry into kindergarten. (It is) intended to guide assessment of 3- to 5-year-old children" (Head Start, 2003). Head Start programs, then, must seek assessment materials that match the curriculum and the national framework. Common instruments used to support these efforts include the Work Sampling System™—including software options and Child Observation Record (COR)—with software support, and the Creative Curriculum® Progress and Outcomes Reporting Tool (CC-PORTTM)—a software product designed for use with the Creative Curriculum® Developmental Continuum Assessment Toolkit for Ages 3–5. In addition to routine assessment to improve the child outcomes and the program itself, sometimes you must assess and report your findings related to children who may need special services so that you can optimize an individual child's progress.

REFERRAL FOR SPECIAL SERVICES

Thus, after adjusting the baseline and the activities, teachers will find some children who need special services. The method used for referral today is Response to Intervention (RTI), which is

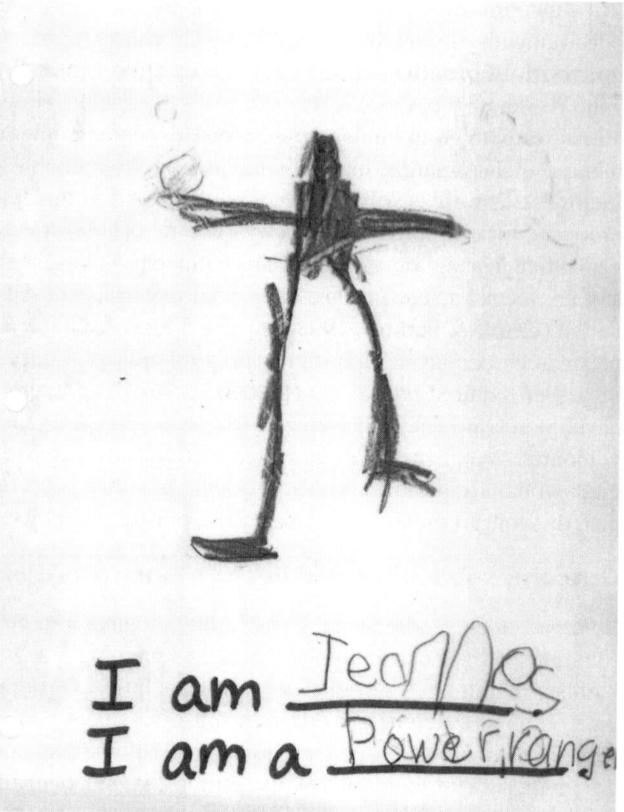

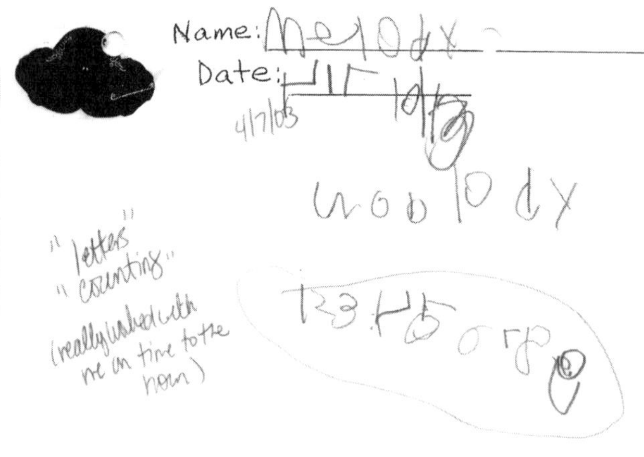

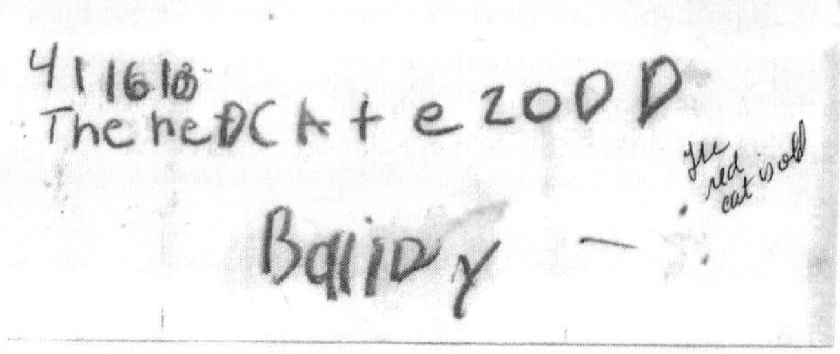

FIGURE 10.1 Examples of Portfolio Documents.

a tiered approach to delivery special educational intervention in the typical classroom; in special interventions adjacent to the classroom experience; and in the intensive provision of special services (IDEA, 2006 Regulations; National Center for Learning Disabilities, 2009). Beyond the Tier 1 intervention implemented by the classroom teacher in the typical classroom, the Tier Two services often include speech and language therapy, occupational therapy, physical therapy, play therapy, and other special services to the family. In such situations, teachers need to document their observations in a child study, as well as have evidence about child performance related to outcomes. The child study serves as a basis for communicating with parents and other professionals. Increasingly, children who need special services receive them in the regular preschool setting. Consequently, the preschool teacher is an integral member of the team serving the child and the family. Therefore, teacher observations serve as a source of information for choosing appropriate referral starting points and for ongoing assessment of the effectiveness of the interventions planned and carried out.

Standard ingredients in a child study and questions to ask include birth history, motor development, language history, family composition and history, interpersonal relationships, and medical history. Obtain this information by interviewing the parent. A social worker, psychologist, or counselor may conduct more in-depth interviews as the diagnostic process proceeds.

Teacher Contribution to the Process

The teacher offers observations, strategies used to modify the curriculum, and modifications to the instructional process, as well as work products. Strategies employed may address variations in classroom organization and instructional techniques. Instructional activity individualization considers the child's particular social responsiveness, cognitive style, interactive competencies, and developmental progress (Raab, Whaley, & Cisar, 1993; see also Wood, 2009). A qualified professional should then evaluate the child depending on the complaint presented or set of symptoms of concern. Qualified professionals include speech and language clinicians, occupational therapists, physical therapists, psychologists, and social workers. Sometimes only one specialist will be necessary. For example, if a teacher observes difficulty with the form of language that a three-year-old uses, an on-site evaluation by a speech and language therapist may be necessary. The teacher's role in this situation is to help the therapist pick a good time to visit the class to assess the target child's use of language in the play setting and to help the therapist in establishing rapport for an interview. Sometimes, the teacher may interview the child to obtain information for the therapist.

However, a social worker, psychologist, child psychiatrist, or counselor usually interviews a child with behavioral problems. The nature of the problem and the kind of services most conveniently available to the community and family will influence the choice of the mental health professional. For a child presenting severe symptoms such as hitting, kicking, screaming, or biting, a comprehensive evaluation by a team of professionals may be required.

Of course, for any evaluation, parents must give written permission. This is in keeping with good practice and federal law (e.g., IDEA 2004). Appropriate and best practice in preschool settings involves teachers in creating a regular dialog with parents about child progress and adjustment. Thus, parents and teachers form an ongoing partnership in the best interests of the child. To begin this partnership in a play-based program, one assessment method that is used is play-based assessment (Linder, 2008).

Play-Based Assessment

Play-based assessment utilizes an observation protocol with categories that include cognitive development, social/emotional development, communication and language development, and sensorimotor development. The team of professionals, including the preschool teacher, observes and records information according to a protocol. Parents are an integral part of the

play-based assessment relies on the teacher's knowledge of child's play to judge the social/emotional, language, cognitive, and physical development of a young child. This can be conducted in a natural situation or by interview.

BOX 10.8

Keeping Track of Head Start Outcomes for Social Emotional Development

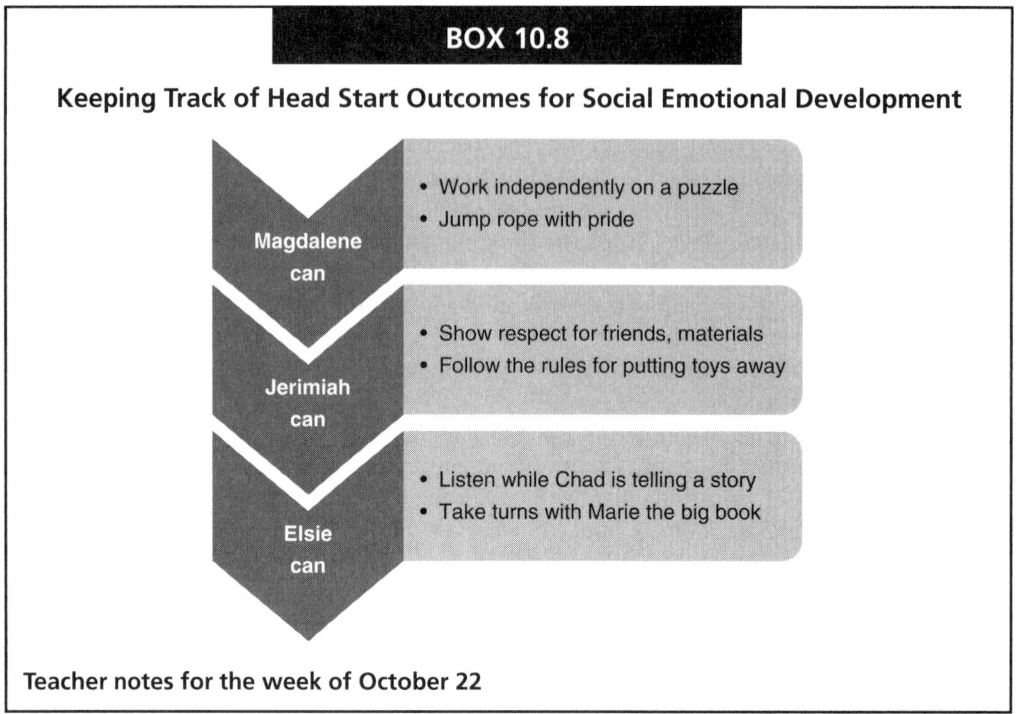

Magdalene can
• Work independently on a puzzle
• Jump rope with pride
Jerimiah can
• Show respect for friends, materials
• Follow the rules for putting toys away
Elsie can
• Listen while Chad is telling a story
• Take turns with Marie the big book

Teacher notes for the week of October 22

process (McGonigel, Woodruff, & Roszmann-Millican, 1994; Linder, 2008). Preschool teachers must be familiar with this approach to assessment as a possibility for their programs, as well as part of their responsibility for articulation with infant/toddler programs. It is an example of holistic assessment and it embodies the principle of multiple assessments to identify young children with disabilities. In addition, assessment of an individual child's play helps teachers plan activities for children who do not at present play well, either by themselves or with others. You can observe many important characteristics that will help with program planning by watching children at play. An example of a teacher's record keeping system for observational notes is shown in Box 10.8. For example, child contact with toys, toy preferences, play level (i.e., the cognitive and social sophistication that is present or not), typical ways of communicating with peers and adults, favorite activities over time, ability to sustain and engage in sociodramatic play activities, and so on (Garfinkle, 2004). As well, it offers opportunities for child-care settings to see concretely the continuum of development of young children and their special needs.

The Continuum of Referral

Referral of young children for special services operates on a continuum. At the beginning, teachers observe and interact with the children, adjusting various aspects of the program—routines, relationships, room arrangement, and activities. In these situations, the teacher seeks to individualize the preschool setting so the child can be successful.

Next in the continuum, teachers may contact parents to obtain suggestions and insights for helping a child participate successfully. Sometimes teachers will discover a family event or crisis that requires special support for the child and the family. Stressors for children include a new baby, the loss of a pet, a move, a change of child-care arrangements, an illness, a death, or a divorce. Whatever the situation, teachers and parents need to work together to support the child in adjusting. (See the National Association for Education of Young Children's website at http://www.naeyc.org for many articles on dealing with particular stressors that may affect the whole class, such as violence, turbulent times, and war.)

At the next step of the continuum, teachers and parents exhaust their ideas and resources for solutions to the child's symptoms. This is the beginning of the RTI process. After various classroom modifications are tried and progress evaluated, intensive intervention may occur. This part of the process frequently involves individualized assessment conducted with parent permission by a specialist. Then a specialist evaluates and makes suggestions for modification to the preschool program or special services. Speech therapy is a commonly required special service. It is critical that teachers and parents prepare young children for the experience of a formal assessment (diagnostic testing). Children will have many questions, such as "What will the examiner do?" "Can Mom or my teacher stay with me?" "Do I have to?" "Why me?"

Agencies and schools need to be sure that whoever conducts the examination is an experienced therapist with young children. To assist the examiner, teachers and schools must:

- Give a clear and specific referral question
- Supply information and materials that will help the examiner understand the history of the problem
- Identify all the relevant people to be included in the assessment
- Assist in identifying all areas that need to be emphasized
- Assist the examiner in developing an overall testing strategy (Romero, 1999, pp. 57–58; see also Lewis & Doorlag, 2006; Halverson & Neary, 2009)

On rare occasions, teachers, parents, and specialists will decide to remove a child from the typical preschool program. In these situations, a specialized setting may be necessary to help a child. Children with profound hearing loss, for example, may profit from a class with sign language as the instructional focus. At each point of the continuum, assessment results will suggest intervention modifications. Intervention modifications succeed or other strategies are tried. The process of intervention modification continues until something works.

Mrs. Martin cannot say, for example: "I tried seating Jerard next to me at large-group time and it doesn't work. He continues to get up and leave the group." You must try another modification. Maybe offering Jerard the opportunity to listen to the large group from the block corner, house corner, water table, or other favorite area would be more effective.

At the same time, communicate to the rest of the children that modifications made for Jerard as an individual in the group are just like modifications made for them as individuals. Mary Lou doesn't drink milk because she is allergic to milk. Muhammad doesn't eat pork because it is against his religion. Alice doesn't eat birthday cake because it is against her religion. Arnold doesn't run because he is recovering from heart surgery. Marta stays away from chalk because she is allergic to chalk dust. James doesn't have to count to 20 because he is still learning to talk.

A structured approach to curricular modification for children with special needs is an activity-based approach (Pretti-Frontczak & Bricker, 2004). In this approach, a specific analysis of child functioning matches to specific behavioral expectations for successful accomplishment of class activities. The structured activities grow from child interests and from needed skills. For example, for four-year-old Ethyl who does not use words to communicate, the intervention team will identify word approximations for her to use in expressing her needs to the teacher, then the children. Or, Iyor may need step-by-step help for successful puzzle completion. First, make the pieces right-side-up, then place the pieces, one at a time, into each space to see which fits, then try another, and so on.

The team of parent, teacher, and specialists strives to strengthen child successes in the preschool setting so that the child becomes a confident learner.

Formal Identification for Special Education

For any child identified and classified as a child with a disability, the provisions of IDEA (U.S. Department of Education, 2004) apply.

Assessment must:

- Be selected and administered so as not to be discriminatory on a racial or cultural basis.
- Be provided and administered in the language and form most likely to yield accurate information on what the child knows and can co academically, developmentally, and functionally, unless it is not feasible to so provide or administer.
- Be used for purposes for which the assessments or measures are valid and reliable.
- Be administered by trained and knowledgeable personnel.
- Be administered in accordance with any instructions provided by the producer of such assessments.

The evaluation process must:

- Include a variety of assessment tools and strategies to gather relevant functional, developmental, and academic information, including information provided by the parent, that may assist the team in making the two critical determinations: Does the child have a disability? Which disability?
- Not rely on any single measure or assessment as the sole criterion for determining whether the child is a child with a disability or determining an appropriate educational program for the child.
- Use technically sound instruments to assess the child across four domains: cognitive, behavioral, physical, and developmental.

In conducting initial and subsequent reevaluations, the team must:

- Review existing evaluation data on the child, including evaluations and information provided by the parents of the child, current classroom-based local or state assessments and classroom-based observations, and observations by teachers and related service providers.
- On the basis of that review, and input from the child's parents, identify what additional data, if any, are needed to reach the required conclusions about disability and special education needs. (Turnbull, Huerta, & Stowe, 2006, pp. 20–21)

Formal Planning and Documentation

Federal law requires an Individualized Family Service Plan (IFSP) for infants and toddlers (0–3) or an Individualized Education Plan (IEP) for older children. This document serves as a record of goals, interventions, and results. The child manager or teacher convenes regular meetings with the family to review and change this planning document. All records of assessment and intervention are confidential. The Family Educational Rights and Privacy Act (FERPA) of 1974 governs access and confidentiality specifications.

The planning may include modifications to the curriculum in a typical setting. Methods for individualizing and delivering curriculum in the mainstream program include (Lieber, Schwartz, Sandall, Horn, & Wolery, 1999; see also Gould & Sullivan, 2005; Cook, Klein, & Tessier, 2008):

- Environmental support
  This includes modifying the classroom baseline (Berry & Mindes, 1993)—room arrangement, personal interactions, transitions, and so on—to support a child with special needs.
- Adaptation of materials
  This includes clarifying boundaries with tape or lines, or consulting with occupational therapists to modify cutting, pasting, and other fine-motor projects, to support a particular child.
- Simplification of activities
  This includes looking at activities to remove extraneous steps, such as eliminating walking across the room to get supplies by delivering the supplies to a child who has difficulty with movement or who is easily distracted.

- Use of child preferences
  This includes knowing what will capture a child's curiosity or motive to learn and not expecting everyone to produce or be interested in the same activity.
- Adult support
  This includes modeling, giving extra cues, scaffolding the task, and stepping to ensure child success.
- Peer support
  This includes the practices of working with a collaborator and involving the classroom community in supporting each other differentially.
- Special equipment
  This includes the use of communication devices, specially modified puzzles, or other items to promote successful social and communicative integration.
- Embedded learning opportunities
  This is a more intrusive support that involves directed teaching of an individual within the mainstream, often at a time when this individual cannot participate effectively in the whole-class activity.
- Specialized instruction
  This may include Braille instruction or other support that is beyond the preschool teacher's expertise.

TRANSITION TO KINDERGARTEN OR FIRST GRADE

Leaving a comfortable early childhood setting to go to the *big school* is a major adjustment for young children. Though they may look forward to the idea of being "grown up" enough for this next step, the unknown is still scary. Preschool teachers can make the process less scary. The best way to help children and their families is to be familiar with the diverse settings where the children will be transferring. This happens through regularly scheduled meetings with kindergarten and primary teachers. Discussions can focus on curricula and transition plans.

Articulation of Preschool/Kindergarten Goals

Preschool programs need not change philosophy and goals in response to pressure from primary teachers, if such proposed practices from primary teachers seem developmentally inappropriate. Teachers should articulate child progress and the preschool program philosophy in developmentally appropriate language and function.

For example, instead of responding to the demand from school districts to interpret reading readiness as letter recognition, letter writing, and other specific skills, describe readiness to learn in broader terms with illustrations of child performance to support this broader response to literacy development. As interpreted by early childhood advocates, literacy activities support the development of children, including physical well-being, emotional maturity, social confidence, language richness, and general knowledge (cf. Morrow, 2009; Neuman, Copple, & Bredekamp, 2000). Literacy development is fostered through the peer collaboration that occurs naturally in the classroom that is whole-child-oriented. In one example, Kissel (2009), children are encouraged to talk to each other about their pictures and to take notes about their conversations. As teachers observed the process in action, they learned more about the children's progress in using images, letters, lines, symbols, spoken words—all aspects of early literacy. As well, you may wish to focus on school readiness more broadly when articulating with kindergarten or first-grade programs. In a comprehensive view, preschool programs prepare young children for school with foci on physical well-being and motor development, social and emotional development, children's developing approaches to learning, language development, as well as cognition and general knowledge (National Education Goals Panel, 1997; Shonkoff, 2004). Also, schools need to accept responsibility for readiness for young children. This vision is articulated by the

National Association of Elementary School Principals (NAESP), which developed six leadership standards and strategies for principals:

1. Embrace high-quality early childhood programs, principles, and practices as the foundation for education throughout the school community.
2. Work with families and community organizations to support children at home, in the community, and in pre-K and kindergarten programs.
3. Provide appropriate learning environments for young children.
4. Ensure high-quality curriculum and instructional practices that foster young children's learning and development in all areas.
5. Use multiple assessments to create experiences that strengthen student learning.
6. Advocate for universal opportunity for children to attend high-quality early child education programs. (NAESP, 2005, pp. 8–9)

With this holistic approach to early childhood programs in elementary schools, articulation should proceed smoothly. Because 81 percent of young children enroll in preschool or other child-care programs before kindergarten, articulation and collaboration is critical (West, Denton, & Germino-Hausken, 2000).

Appropriately planned preschool settings can describe child progress in terms of broad developmental categories that underlie the development of academic skills and knowledge acquisition. Summative or final/cumulative reports should describe children in terms that highlight their knowledge, skills, and attitudes as problem solvers, self-confident and independent learners, cooperative group workers, and so on. This gives schools or parents the big picture about individual children. Descriptions of children as curious learners or effective group participants are the global behaviors that will serve children well in tackling learning to read, compute, and write.

VOICES FROM THE FIELD

Public School Pre-K Teacher of 3s, 4s, and 5s

In my school, we use teacher observation and the DIBELS to identify five-year-olds who need intensive help. Those scoring at the lowest levels on the DIBELS are pulled out by a reading teacher for small group teaching. The pre-K, kindergarten, and reading teachers make the decision about who should be pulled out for this service. To assist the children, the reading teacher also uses a state-created reading skills test. She uses this measure to isolate skills for teaching intervention. This year, we are adding the Fountas and Pinnell assessment for all kindergarten children, which we hope will provide additional data for our decision-making about who should get extra attention in reading.

Even though it wasn't required by my school, I kept records for individual children on the following:

- *Letter recognition*
- *Colors*
- *Shapes*
- *Counting 1–20*
- *Writing skills*

These records helped me individualize instruction.

Preschool programs form the foundation of exploration and socialization for children to begin the discovery of the primary-school educational agenda. By describing children in this way, you have redefined readiness in service to individual children. The list of narrowly defined concepts such as knowledge of colors and numbers, ability to write one's name and the alphabet, ability to count, and so on may cast some children in a bad light if they are missing some of these concepts or skills. To the receiving teacher, it may sound as if the absence of these items is yielding a class of slow learners when quite the contrary is true. The children in your program have learned to investigate the answers to questions of concern to them, and they are expressing their thinking in words, pictures, and invented spelling. They have learned to work together, to respect diversity, to appreciate stories, to memorize favorite songs, and so on.

Rich preschool reports describing learning style and accomplishments can go a long way to bridging the transition to primary school. In addition to being advocates for children with the primary-grade teachers, you need to help parents make the transition from preschool to the primary-grade experience—arm them with the knowledge that their children are "ready" to learn to read by showing them all the ways that this has occurred.

Teachers should equip parents with information about the appropriate use and misuse of tests. In settings where school districts have adopted screening tests as placement tests, teachers can help parents lobby for a differentiated diagnosis, if necessary. This avoids the heartache experienced by someone like Sue Long of Denver City, Texas (Atkins, 1990), who discovered that one of her twin daughters was scheduled for the developmental kindergarten and the other for the regular kindergarten, based on the results of a screening test. Screening tests are inappropriately used for this purpose.

Preschool teachers who assist parents in understanding and anticipating kindergarten issues such as screening, entrance age, extra-year kindergarten programs, and readiness as a child characteristic (Pianta & Kraft-Sayre, 2003) make the process of going to school a smooth one for children and families. Preschool teachers pave the way for continuity in education. They articulate the *real* characteristics of successful students—motivated, self-confident, curious, proud of accomplishments, knowledgeable in the process of inquiry, and capable of communicating in verbal and early writing ways.

Preschool teachers can advocate that the only true criterion for admission to kindergarten is chronological age. It is not *child readiness* that should concern teachers, schools, and parents, but broad curricula that allow the acceptance of all children (Maxwell & Clifford, 2004; NAEYC, 1995; 2009). Broadly focused teacher descriptions of children address the attention to this approach. "Early childhood education research provides for preschool teachers a clear notion of child development, an awareness of the role of play in the young child's life, and an understanding of the collaborative role of parents. Early childhood educators, as the experts, must present facts, illustrations, and a firm commitment to best practices in kindergarten" (Mindes, 1990; see also Fromberg, 2002; Johnson, Christie, & Wardle, 2005). In this way, preschool teachers serve children and families as the foundation of a rewarding trip through the educational system. We must always be on our toes and advocate for young children.

SUMMARY

The preschool teacher is a busy professional. Child assessment is a vital part of the job. Teachers share the responsibility for choosing wisely when selecting informal and formal instruments. They must serve as reflective, conscientious teachers of young children. This involves knowing the children, planning, and making changes based on children's work. Responsible and responsive teaching of children involves sensitivity. Sensitive teachers report their knowledge to parents and others, based on their observations and routinely collected, fair assessments.

FIELD ACTIVITIES

1. If possible, observe a screening session at a local child-care or school setting. Are appropriate safeguards for privacy and confidentiality in place?
2. Interview a teacher about his experiences with screening procedures. Focus some of the discussion on the way the teacher uses screening results in planning instruction.
3. With permission, observe a multidisciplinary staffing. Note the diverse ways that assessment data are included. After the meeting, plan how you would instruct the children in your class.
4. Visit some first-grade classrooms in your community. Outline an articulation procedure for a preschool of your choice.

IN-CLASS ACTIVITIES

1. Bring examples of assessment systems to class. With a classmate, compare assessment systems used by Head Start, other child-care settings, and the local school district. What are the differences and similarities? Would you make any suggestions for change in any of the three settings?
2. Develop an articulation plan for a preschool program that will graduate children for the local school district. Decide what kinds of information you will share at each quarter of the year that will show what the four-year-olds are learning.
3. With a partner, develop a list of questions to use to help three-year-olds critique their work.
4. Develop a symbol system that can be used to show whether skills are emerging, accomplished, or absent in four-year-olds.

STUDY QUESTIONS

1. What role does assessment play in the enrollment of preschoolers? How are parents and children often mistreated during this process? In what ways can teachers prevent this?
2. What can the teacher do to ensure that the children in the preschool program remain intrinsically motivated to explore and learn within the classroom?

3. Why is it important for teachers to offer continually a wide range of activities and manipulatives to children within the program?
4. Teachers must establish developmentally appropriate assessment techniques. List the guidelines that will assist teachers in this endeavor. How do portfolios fit into these guidelines?
5. How can teachers introduce parents to the concept of developmentally appropriate practices in school and the home?
6. How do you integrate developmental milestones into the assessment process?
7. What steps must a teacher take in the referral process?
8. Explain the steps included in the continuum of referral for children. What role does the early childhood teacher play in this process? How can the early childhood teacher advocate for the children with special needs in the classroom?

REFLECT AND RE-READ

- I know what a comprehensive preschool assessment system looks like.
- I know how to find young children who are academically or developmentally at-risk.
- I know how to assess educational outcomes holistically.
- I have in mind the key ingredients for the successful transition from preschool to primary grades for young children and their parents.

CASE VIGNETTE

Kristal, a 5.7-year-old kindergartner, lives with her mother (her father returned to Puerto Rico when she was four months old and she never sees him) and grandmother. Although members of Kristal's family speak Spanish, the home language is English and Kristal knows only a few Spanish words. Kristal attends half-day kindergarten and an after-school child-care program. The observer notes that Kristal can run very fast and has strong fine-motor skills—her printing is "beautiful." On the Early Screening Inventory—Revised,* when asked to draw a person, she drew a girl sitting in a chair with many more details than classmates. On the Peabody Picture Vocabulary Test—III,† Kristal's scores are as follows:

Raw Score	Standard Score	Percentile Rank	Stanine	Age Equivalent
107	126	96	9	8–01

As the kindergarten teacher preparing a report for the family and the first-grade teacher, what additional assessment information might you include? What recommendations will you make to Kristal's family for summer enrichment?

*Meisels, S. et al. (2001). *Early Screening Inventory—Revised (ESI-K) for Children 4.6 to 6.0.* Pearson Early Learning. http://www.pearsonearlylearning.com.

†Dunn, L. M., & Dunn, L. M. (1997). *Peabody Picture Vocabulary Test—III Form A.* Circle Pines, MN: American Guidance Services.

Source: From T. Kennedy, 2003, submitted in partial fulfillment of T&L 411, Assessment in Early Childhood Education: DePaul University.

TECHNOLOGY LINKS

http://www.teachingstrategies.com

Teaching Strategies. Curricular and assessment materials for teaching in preschool settings.

http://www.naeyc.org

National Association for Education of Young Children. Position papers, articles on teaching.

http://www.vanderbilt.edu/csefel/preschool.html

Center on the Social Emotional Foundations for Early Learning. Research, training, and practical materials to facilitate social-emotional learning.

http://www.kindersay.com

Kindersay. Flashcards and activities for children to learn English.

SUGGESTED READINGS

Cook, R. E., Klein, M. D., & Tessier, A. (2008). *Adapting early childhood curricula for children in inclusive settings* (6th ed.). Upper Saddle River, NJ: Merrill/Prentice Hall.

Head Start Bulletin on Mental Health 80. (2009). Washington DC: author.

Hohman, M., & Weikart, D. P. (2002). *Educating young children* (2nd ed.). Ypsilanti, MI: High Scope Press.

Lewin-Benham, A. (2008). *Powerful children: Understanding how to teach and learn using the Reggio approach.* New York: Teachers College.

Stacey, S. (2009). *Emergent curriculum in early childhood settings: From theory to practice.* St Paul, MN: Red Leaf Press.

CHAPTER 11

Special Issues in Primary Grades

TERMS TO KNOW

- learner outcomes
- informal evaluation
- objectivity
- constructivist perspective
- accountability
- portfolios
- standards-based teaching
- textbook tests
- individualized academic tests

CHAPTER OVERVIEW

This chapter presents special assessment issues in the primary grades. Teachers must assess a diverse population of children in these programs. Children in the primary grades have different learning styles and developmental and educational strengths. Teachers can use many informal methods to determine the learning needs of these children. A feature of the chapter is the topic of learner outcomes and accountability. The discussion incorporates the special issues of urban and nontraditional learners. Effective ways for incorporating portfolios in an assessment system are also discussed. The implications of No Child Left Behind (NCLB) for practice in the primary grades is a focus in this chapter. Finally, there is a description of textbook and individualized academic tests.

ASSESS AS YOU READ

- What can I learn from preschool teachers?
- How can I use assessment to plan for instruction?
- If I teach in an urban area or work with nontraditional learners, what must I know?
- How do I prepare my students for achievement tests?
- Where do portfolios fit in the primary program?

PRIMARY ASSESSMENT SYSTEMS ISSUES

Primary teachers are responsible for formal assessment decisions for all the children they serve. In addition, teachers must prepare report cards, keep cumulative records, and use assessment to plan. Primary teachers must give standardized tests. These begin usually in grade 3 by federal law (P.L. 107–110) with the NCLB. The reauthorization of this act is under discussion across the nation. Most proposed versions for revision of the NCLB include accountability provisions that will include standardized assessment for all young children. To see up-to-date news about the provisions of the legislation, visit the U.S. Department of Education website: http://www.ed.gov/nclb/landing.jhtml, as well as the website for your state department of education, which will post the assessment and accountability requirements for your state. As a teacher, you are accountable for meeting learner goals or outcomes. **Learner outcomes** are expectations for children's performances as defined by professional associations, the federal government, state legislatures, and school districts. In most cases, these various government and policy bodies are not concerned with the learner outcomes for preschool children. The notable exceptions are the Head Start Outcomes Framework, with its associated assessment imperatives that began in 2000 (Head Start, 2003), although mandated testing ended in 2007, as well as the requirements for early intervention for infants, toddlers, and preschoolers with special needs that require greater alignment with NCLB (IDEA, 2004) and IDEA 2006 regulations, which include Response to Intervention (RTI) (http://idea.ed.gov/explore/home).

learner outcomes expectations for children's performances.

Finally, the Committee for Economic Development (CED) calls for universal early childhood education for children age 3 and older. The CED issued the report *Preschool for All: Investing in a Productive and Just Society* in 2002. The report "argues for a strong federal/state partnership that expands access to high-quality learning opportunities and links providers and programs into coherent state-based early education systems. To achieve this goal, CED is calling on the business community to help build public understanding about the economic and social need for early childhood education in the United States" (CED, 2002 & 2006; see also Karly & Bigelow, 2005 and pending 2009 legislation, HR 555.Universal Prekindergarten Act). Thus, the broad outcome expected by the CED is social and economic in nature. Although universal preschool education is not yet available and there is limited public concern about specific outcomes for most preschool programs, early childhood educators are eager to make a difference in the lives of young children. Recently, however, there is a federal priority on preschool reading programs, with the "Early Reading First, part of the president's (Bush's) 'Good Start, Grow Smart' initiative (2002), designed to transform existing early education programs into centers of excellence providing high-quality, early education to young children, especially those from low-income families. The overall purpose of the Early Reading First Program is to prepare young children to enter kindergarten with the necessary language, cognitive, and early reading skills to prevent reading difficulties and ensure school success" (Good Start, Grow Smart, 2002; Early Reading First, 2009 84.359A; 84.359B).

Therefore, preschool children are busy learning and have already entered the assessment system in increasing numbers with the growth of Head Start, early intervention programs, and special projects of school districts and states. Yet the formal assessment experience of young children and their teachers intensifies in the primary years. As well, too often, the stakes of assessment become higher.

TRANSITION FROM PRESCHOOL

What, then, is the experience that preschool children bring to the primary grades? According to a report on the state of America's children by the Children's Defense Fund Key Data Findings (2007), "Working Parents in 2007: About 2 out of 3 mothers of preschool-age children and 3 out of 4 mothers of school-age children are in the labor force. Six in 10 preschool-age children and 7 in 10 school-age children have all parents in the labor force." Consequently, their children are in out-of-home care. In the best situations, children have discovered how to learn, feel confident about themselves, enjoy their relationships with peers and teachers, possess basic self-help skills, and know some basic concepts—colors, numbers, letters, shapes, and so on. They are curious and ready to hit the big school running. Unfortunately, not all children have optimum preschool experiences. "In 2008 (Children's Defense Fund, 2008), the cost of center-based child care for a four-year-old is greater than tuition at a four-year public college. Income eligibility for the one million families who receive child care assistance ranges from just above the poverty line in Missouri to 275 percent of the poverty line in Maine. The Urban Institute has calculated that 2.7 million people would be lifted out of poverty if child care assistance were provided to all families with children whose incomes are below 200 percent of the federal poverty line (FPL). In 2008, 200 percent of the FPL was $35,200 for a family of three." Only about 3 percent of eligible infants and young children are enrolled in the Early Head Start program. About 900,000 children are enrolled in Head Start programs, about 800,000 in state programs,and another 100,000 in migrant and Indian tribal programs and in the territories. Only about one-half to two-thirds of children eligible for Head Start are enrolled (Children's Defense Fund, 2008). Some children are coping with risk factors in their lives. "Twenty states have no state-funded prekindergarten programs for 3-year-olds; eight states have no programs for 4-year-olds. Yet research has shown that early childhood programs significantly increase a child's chances of avoiding the prison pipeline, instead helping give him a head start and put him in the "pipeline to success" (Children's Defense Fund, 2008). As a result, you will find that not everyone is on the same developmental step in your class. Even under the best family and social conditions, development occurs in an uneven fashion. So, a big part of a teacher's job is assessment of developmental and educational progress. This assessment is essential to appropriate planning for the individuals and group in each teacher's class.

ASSESSING TEACHING LEVEL

Therefore, in September, when children transfer schools, and throughout the year, teachers must quickly find out the instructional needs and levels of their children. Besides observation, the primary mode of assessment for young children, teachers review records of children. When records are not available, not complete, or not definitive, teachers must quickly assess children as they teach.

Informal Evaluation

informal evaluation task activities used to assess the instructional needs and levels of children.

Informal evaluation is composed of techniques used in these circumstances. These techniques are task activities for the learner to solve. The activities fit into the routine of the day. They are similar to the tasks or activities that engage children in learning centers and in didactic experiences with the teacher, both solely and in small groups. These are the same tasks that you use for formative assessment—assessment for understanding as you are teaching. The tasks are often called authentic or performance-based assessment. Characteristics of authentic tasks include the following attributes:

- Children see them as purposeful.
- The tasks are real, and classroom-like.
- They embody high expectations and relate to standards.
- Complex thinking is required. (Benson & Barnett, 2005)

Formative assessment provides both the learner and you with information to adjust the learning and teaching activities. With formative assessment, you can adjust the subgoals of learner outcomes, specify clearly the required elements of learning tasks and goals, give children clear description of what they need to do to become or continue successful learning, and provide children with opportunities for self-assessment, as well as peer collaboration and assessment (McManus, 2008).

The tasks involved in authentic formative assessment specify scoring criteria or rubrics. These scoring criteria ensure **objectivity**—the same score regardless of who marks the answers. In the boxes that follow (Boxes 11.1 through 11.3), examples of performance tasks with rubrics are shown.

objectivity implies that a scoring scheme is sufficiently clear and discrete so that all those applying the criteria will obtain similar scores.

Besides teacher-conducted assessment, children can be involved in self-assessment that assures them that they are successful learners. Examples of self-assessment protocols are shown in Boxes 11.4, 11.5, and 11.6.

BOX 11.1

Math Assessment

Teachers watch children perform classroom activities to see/assess what they are learning.

Activities to observe children performing include:

- Group games involving logico-mathematical thinking (Kamii, 2000; 2004). An example is the game "Always 12," consisting of 72 round cards bearing the numbers 0 through 6. The object of play is to make a total of 12 with 4 cards. Two to four children can play. The winner is the child with the most cards (Kamii, 1989b).
- Using computers to record data; calculators to add, subtract, multiply, divide.
- Counting and using numbers as names.
- Activities involving the demonstration of number facts, properties, procedures, algorithms, and skills (Schultz, Colarusso & Strawderman, 1989).
- Geometric analysis of characteristics and properties of two- and three-dimensional geometric shapes, including recognizing, naming, building, drawing, comparing and sorting shapes, and investigating and predicting results of putting together and taking apart geometric shapes (NCTM, 2000).
- Measurement activities including recognizing attributes of length, volume, weight, area, and time, comparing and ordering objects, and using standard and nonstandard measures as tools. (NCTM, 2000).
- Incorporating writing in math helps you see the way children are thinking. Ask them to describe more than one strategy of solving problems. Involve the class in discussion of problems, as well (Burns, 2005).
- Plan to help children master basic number combinations through "three phases: counting using objects—blocks, fingers, marks; reasoning strategies—using known facts and relationships to deduce answers; mastery—fast & accurate production of answers" (Baroody, 2006, 22). Games such as Number Tic Tac Toe, Road Hog, Car Race Games with Numbers and Cars that race across the board (Baroody, 2006).

Examples of specific informal tasks that can be used include:

M&M Task for Pre-K to Second Grade

Materials

Small bags of M&Ms, napkins, paper, crayons, markers or other recording materials.

The Task

Conduct this task in small groups or with individual children. Give each child a bag of M&Ms. Ask each child to show the color distribution in the bag. Explain that each bag will have a different amount of candy of each color, so that there is not one right answer, but multiple answers to this problem.

Allow children to express their answers in diverse ways. Children may draw circles to represent the numbers of red, green, yellow, and so on. They may summarize their count—2 green, 3 red, and so on. They may prepare a graph.

The teacher's role in this task is to observe. Ask the children to give a product showing their work. When finished, children may eat the M&Ms.

Scoring the Task

0 = unable

1 = can sort by color, but cannot illustrate the solution

2 = can identify same, more, less

3 = illustrates task

4 = makes a pictorial graph

5 = makes a numerical or tabular graph

(continued)

Pizza Party for Second Grade

Materials

A large cardboard circle resembling a pizza.

The Task

Conduct this task in small groups or with individual children. Show the cardboard pizza form to the children. Tell the children to pretend that they have two pizzas that size. The two pizzas are for a party. Seven boys and five girls will attend the party. Then say, "We want to give everyone a piece the same size. How can we do that?" Ask children to illustrate the answer to this question. Explain that each child may answer this question in different ways.

Supply paper, crayons, markers, pencils, or other recording materials and scissors for children to show their work. Allow children to express their answers in diverse ways. Children may draw circles and divide the pizza; they may cut out paper to represent pieces and children; they may illustrate the answer with fractions, and so on.

The teacher's role in this task is to observe and ask the children to give a product showing their work.

Scoring of the Task

0 = no idea

1 = drawing stick children (or hatch marks) to decide the number of pieces needed

2 = cutting up paper to show the answer

3 = drawing fractional representations of circles

4 = showing the answer arithmetically with numbers

BOX 11.2

Informal Language Arts Assessment

As the children move in the room around the interest centers, observe literacy development (cf. McKenna & Stahl, 2009). Categories of observation and informal assessment include the following:

- ***Interest in books.*** Teachers can see which children are interested in books. Children and teachers can record lists of favorite books. Parents can be involved in this recording of favorites.
- ***Concept of print.*** Teachers can evaluate students ability to read environment print, own words as sight vocabulary, attempts to read predictable books, identification of letters of the alphabet, association of letters and sounds, and the use of story books (Morrow, 2009).
- ***Story concept awareness.*** Teachers observe how students attend to pictures, but not stories; attend to pictures and form oral stories; attend to a mix of pictures, reading, and storytelling; attend to pictures but form written stories, and attend to print (Sulzby, 1985). This can be evaluated by observing story retelling, attempted reading of favorite storybooks, role playing, picture sequencing, use of puppet or felt board, and questions and comments during story reading (Morrow, 2009).
- ***Reading strategies.*** This includes evidence of how the children approach reading. Where does each child fall in the continuum toward conventional reading?
- ***Using reading.*** In which ways do children use reading for pleasure, to discover information, and so on?
- ***Writing strategies.*** Developmentally, writing begins with scribbling and proceeds through a number of stages to conventional spelling and grammar (cf. Teale & Sulzby, 1986; see also Treiman & Bourassa, 2000; Ehri, 2000).

- ***Handwriting mechanics.*** This task includes use of pencils and markers and ability to form letters, stay on line, and so on.
- ***Listening strategies.*** This task includes the child's ability to grasp information in one-to-one situations, small groups, large groups, note taking, and so on.
- ***Speaking strategies as evidence of language development.*** This task includes phonology, syntax, and semantics (cf. Morrow, 2009).

Examples of informal performance tasks are described in the following sections.

Morris's Ten Words

This is a means to assess invented spelling (child's creation of a word, based on his or her understanding of the sounds involved) and potential readiness for formal reading instruction. Model phonetic spelling for children by showing them how to sound out the word *mat*. Write it on the chalkboard or on chart paper as you sound out the word. Continue this process with the words *let* and *stop*. Use these words in sentences, so the children have a context.

Give the children paper and pencils. Then dictate the following 10 words and sentences.

1. *fit:* These shoes do not fit correctly.
2. *side:* I have one hand on each side of my body.
3. *dress:* Latoya's new dress is pretty.
4. *stick:* Juan found a stick under the tree.
5. *rice:* I like to have rice with dinner.
6. *beg:* The dog likes to beg at the table.
7. *seed:* The flower grew from a tiny seed.
8. *gate:* The gate on the fence was open.
9. *drop:* If you drop the plate, it will break.
10. *lake:* Jennifer is swimming in the lake.

Scoring

0 = only unrelated letters are used

1 = first or last letter of the word

2 = part of the sounds represented

3 = initial consonant, vowel, and final consonant

4 = conventional English spelling

Composition Assessment

Assign a topic. For example, "One day, I found a magic hat." Then ask the child to dictate, write, and/or illustrate the story, as age-appropriate.

Scoring

0 = undecipherable or blank composition

1 = random words or child repeats prompts

2 = ideas have little or no relationship to the magic hat or simply repeats ideas from the story

3 = at least one new idea present, ideas lack development or are contradictory, writing may simply list ideas or wishes

4 = several new ideas present; ideas are not fully developed; sentence structure is repetitious; lacks structure

5 = ideas are fairly well-developed and expressed; writing has some structure (beginning, middle, end); development and organization could be improved

(continued)

6 = ideas are very well-developed and expressed; fully developed structure with beginning, middle, and end; logical and well-organized; good sentences, variety, and expression (Morris & Perney, 1984).

While assessing reading and spelling informally, you will need to be sure that there is "close articulation between reading and writing so that their acquisition is mutually facilitative and reciprocal" (Ehri, 2000, p. 34). With informal assessment and collection of child-work products, you can make learning visible with the systematic use of informal assessment.

Each of these informal assessment procedures can be incorporated into the day-to-day activity of the classroom. These activities are performance-based assessments. The examples are drawn from teachers in the field. In implementing these procedures, teachers think about what they need to know about the children so they can provide the activities that lead the children to academic success. Starting from learner outcomes, specified by school districts and state legislatures, teachers plan what to teach. Using the tools of books and other materials in their classroom, they carry out the required curriculum. Knowing where the children are, developmentally speaking, is the key to creating meaningful activities and successful experiences.

BOX 11.3

Social/Emotional Assessment

Teachers need to plan assessment to measure social/emotional adjustment to school. Zvetina and Guiterrez (1994) have described this adjustment as "the school self." It is the child's sense of him or herself as a learner and as a member of the community of learners that influences behavioral adjustment to academic demands of the environment. The school self can be seen in children who participate and invest in the community of learners. Zvetina and Guiterrez suggest that such students will:

- Show a sense of themselves as competent learners.
- Display increasing motivation manifested by their own curiosity, interest, and persistence toward school-related tasks and experiences.
- Initiate, participate, and connect in relationships with their peers and teachers.
- Use problem-solving skills to work through and resolve problems related to tasks and interpersonal conflicts.
- Draw upon a repertoire of internal and external coping strategies for controlling their impulses, modulating these affects, and effectively using time and space.

Through their work with teachers in urban classrooms, Zvetina and Guiterrez (1994; see also Bowman & Moore, 2006) have developed this concept of the child role in behavioral adjustment. They are developing observational criteria for assessing this adjustment.

Traditionally, teachers have used categories such as self-esteem, achievement motivation peer relationships, relationships with teachers, persistence, and attention to describe social/emotional adjustment. Today's teachers must be aware of contextual and cultural factors relating to adjustment as they develop distinct specific criteria for describing the *successful*. Henning-Stout (1994; see also Beaty, 2006; Copple, 2003) reminds us that learning is a personal process mediated by the culture of a given community as well as the community of the school. In schools where cooperative learning and child-initiated activity are valued, social/emotional assessment must include opportunities for students and teachers toward the assessment of these valued practices.

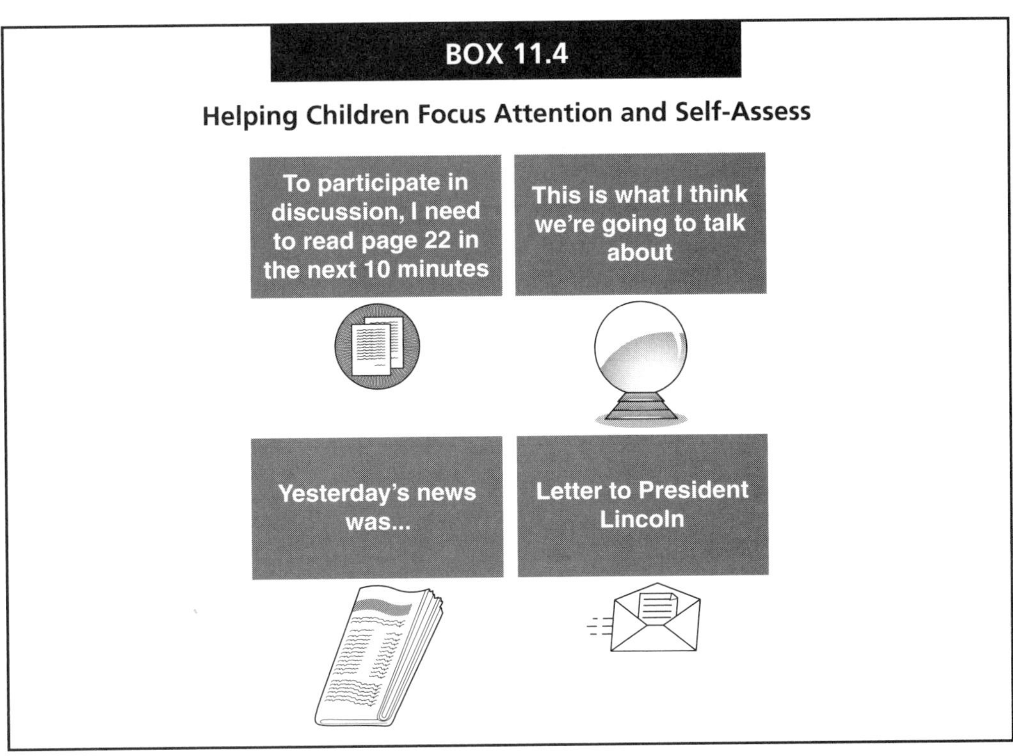
BOX 11.4
Helping Children Focus Attention and Self-Assess
To participate in discussion, I need to read page 22 in the next 10 minutes
This is what I think we're going to talk about
Yesterday's news was...
Letter to President Lincoln

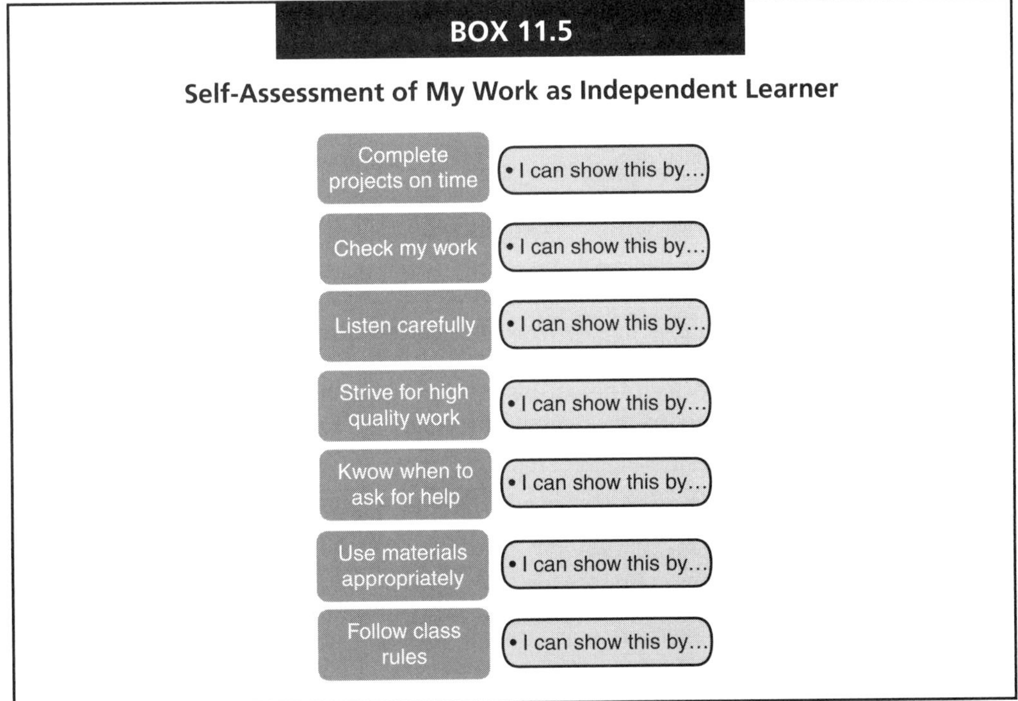
BOX 11.5
Self-Assessment of My Work as Independent Learner
Complete projects on time
• I can show this by...
Check my work
• I can show this by...
Listen carefully
• I can show this by...
Strive for high quality work
• I can show this by...
Kwow when to ask for help
• I can show this by...
Use materials appropriately
• I can show this by...
Follow class rules
• I can show this by...

BOX 11.6

Self-Assessment for Learner Who Needs Frequent Support

Today in social studies, I…

	Very well	Most of the time	Hardly ever
Remembered class rules			
Completed independent work			
Class discussion participant			

My social studies notebook is Awesome Okay Pretty messy

Student signature__________________

Teacher's signature____________________

Family member's signature__________________________

BOX 11.7

Writing a Report Using Informational Texts in Third Grade

My report on our state—Kansas

To do this report,
I read:

1. History of Kansas for Children
2. The Sunflower State
3. Booklets that I got at the Shawnee Mission Museum

I interviewed:

1. My 75-year-old neighbor
2. My grandmother who lives in Seattle now

I visited the official Kansas website: http://www.kansas.gov/index.php

To make the report, I checked the following reminder list:

1. The title explains what the report is about.
2. The first sentence tells what the report is going to be about.
3. The first sentence will grab reader interest.
4. I have used my own words in the report.
5. I used facts to support my sentences.
6. I have a good ending that sums up the message.
7. I checked for writing errors.
8. I made a three-slide PowerPoint to share with the class about Kansas.

Adapted from Kletzien, S. B., & Decker, M. J. (2004), *Informational text in K–3 classrooms: Helping children read and write*, Newark, DE: International Reading Association, pp. 134–135.

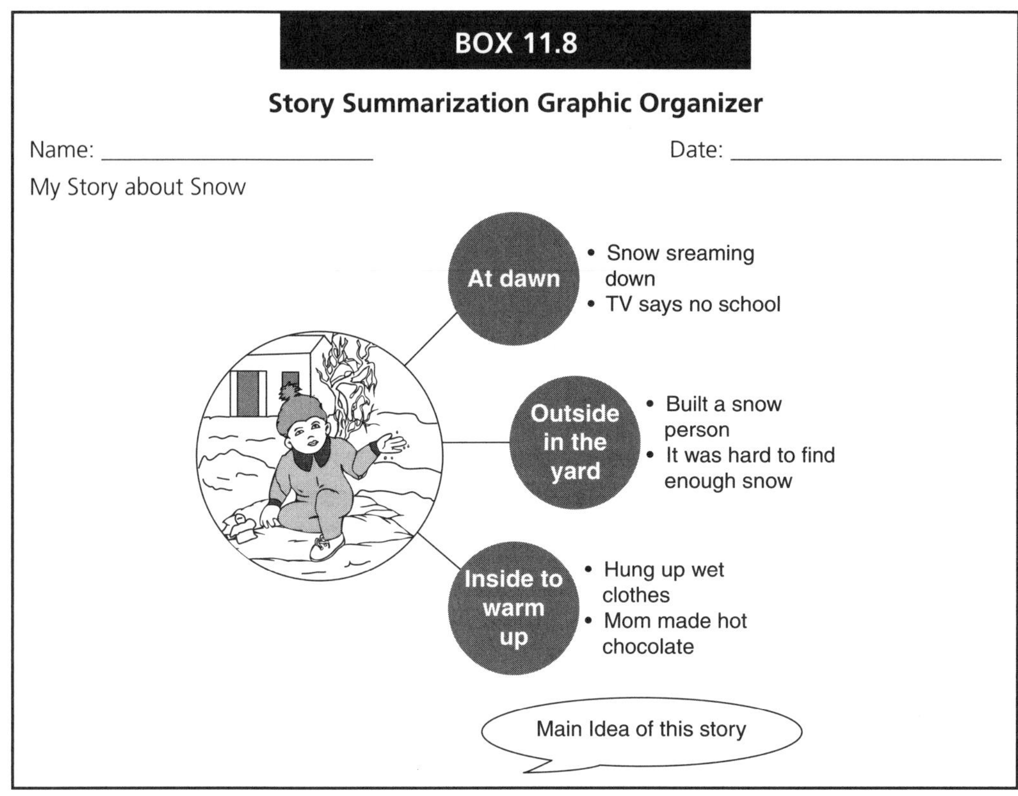

BOX 11.8
Story Summarization Graphic Organizer
Name: ______________________
Date: ______________________
My Story about Snow
At dawn
• Snow sreaming down
• TV says no school
Outside in the yard
• Built a snow person
• It was hard to find enough snow
Inside to warm up
• Hung up wet clothes
• Mom made hot chocolate
Main Idea of this story

As teachers, you also want to keep track of child progress so that you can easily plan for groups. Examples are shown in the following:

BOX 11.9

Keeping Track of Child Progress with Measuring Skills

Child	Counts with rods when measuring class objects, e.g. desk, table, books...	Can estimate length before completing task	Keeps accurate record	Can tell what he/she did
Dorothy	✓	✓	✓	✓
Sheila	✓	✓		
Jeff	✓	—	—	
Waldo	absent			
Arnetta				
Alvin	✓	—	✓	—
Tracey	✓	—	—	
Griffin	✓	✓	—	
Amelia	✓	✓	✓	✓

✓ = mastery
— = sometimes
Blank = not evident

Adapted from Meisels, S. J., Harrington, H. L., McMahon, P., Dichtelmiller, M. L., & Jablon, J. R., (2002), *Thinking like a teacher: Using observational assessment to improve teaching and learning*, Boston: Allyn & Bacon.

BOX 11.10

Assessment of Science Standard

- Describe an observed event. Uses each of the these skills and tools.
- Task: Tasting fruits: persimmon, star fruit, mango, orange

Child's Name	1	2	3	4	5	6	7	8	Comments
Kenneth	1	1	1	1	NA	1	1	0	Needs help in representing experience in chart
Skye	2	2	2	0	NA	1	0	1	Needs help in describing the fruits; vocab
Kelly	2	2	2	2	NA	2	2	2	Completed chart and made detailed pix
Derek	2	2	0	2	NA	2	2	2	Reluctant to taste "new" fruits
Karen	2	2	2	2	NA	2	2	2	
Sarah	1	2	2	2	NA	2	2	2	
Stanley	2	2	2	2	NA	2	2	2	
Tonya	2	2	2	0	NA	2	2	2	Reluctant to smell "strange" fruits
Jill	0	2	1	2	NA	1	1	1	"I don't like science!" need to explore this...
Bill	2	2	2	2	NA	2	2	2	
Hans	2	2	2	2	NA	2	2	2	

Adapted from: Anderson, K. L., Martin, D. M., & Faszewski, E. E. (2006), Unlocking the power of observation, *Science and children* 44.1: 32–35.

Scoring key:
0 = shows limited understanding
1 = developing understanding
2 = achieved understanding

1. Sight
2. Touch
3. Taste
4. Smell
5. Hearing
6. Magnifying glass
7. Talks about
8. Picture made

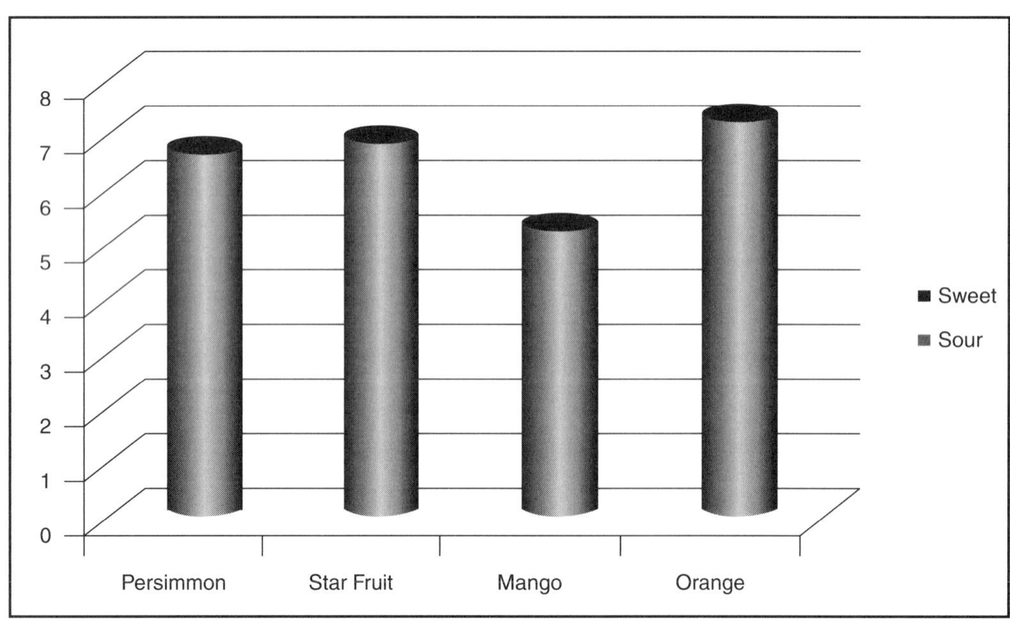

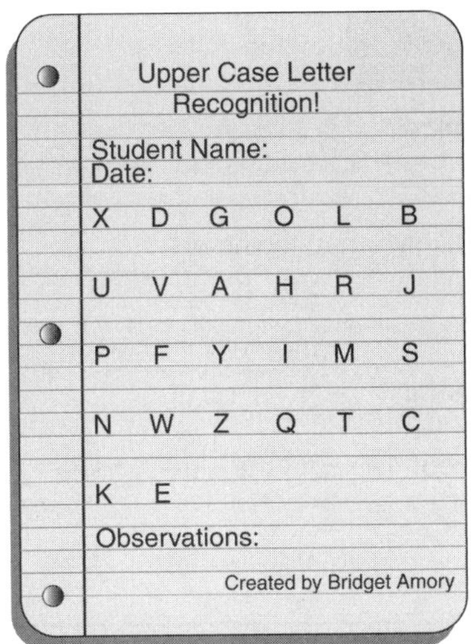

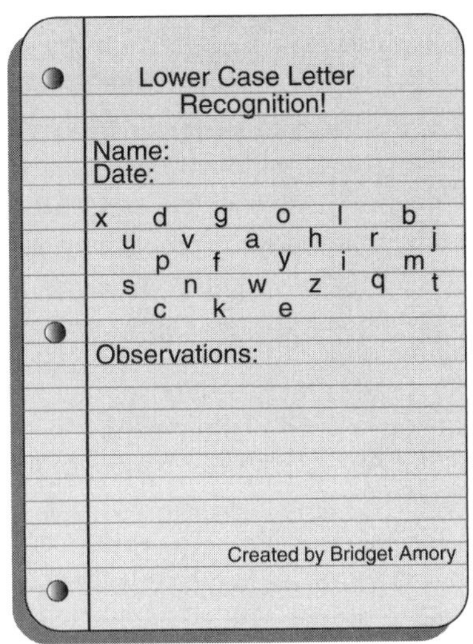

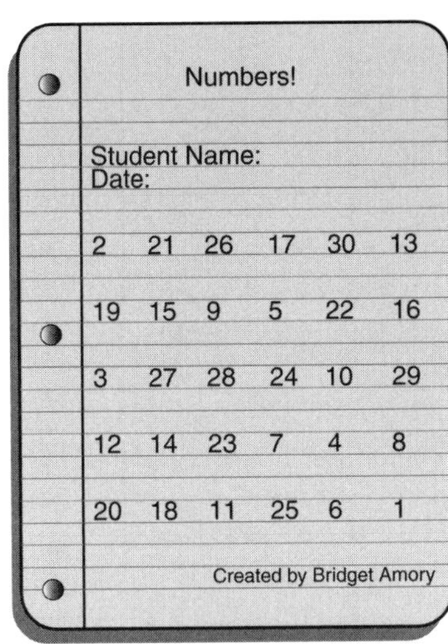

FIGURE 11.1 Example of Teacher's Notebook.

You also plan to support children with special needs. See examples of record-keeping below:

BOX 11.11

Supporting Learners with Special Needs

In my class, I provide:

	Always	Why not?
Give shorter assignments		
Reduced standards for handwriting		
Use games to heighten attention to task		
Help child with marking books and papers so material can be studied		
Teach for active listening		
Encourage doodling with paper, clay		
Provide private cues		
Tape prompts for how to do tasks inside child's folder		
Ignore minor disruptions		

Adapted from McKinley, L. A., & Stormont, M. A., (2008), The school supports checklist: Identifying support needs and barriers for children with ADHD, *Teaching Exceptional Children 41.2:* 14–19.

BOX 11.12

Supporting Reluctant Learners

Effective responses to "I can't":

- Agree with Amy that there is a problem by saying, "Hey, Amy, what's going on?"
- Give Amy time to stop whining or crying because she can't...
- Change the task to one that you know that Amy can do
- Help Amy try the difficult task another time
- Figure out how to scaffold the task so Amy can be successful
- Tell Amy that you know it's hard when...
- Gradually let the Amy do more and more of the task without help until she is ready to do it alone

Adapted from Dous, A., & Kriete, R., Getting past "I can't": Teaching children to persevere when the going gets tough, *Responsive Classroom Newsletter 20.1* (February 2008), http://www.responsiveclassroom.org.

PERFORMANCE ASSESSMENT WITH TECHNOLOGY

Besides using observation of children at learning centers, in small groups and in large groups, you will want to familiarize yourself with all the ways in which technology can facilitate assessment and individualization of instruction. Technology to explore includes Personal Response Systems, also known as Clickers (cf. http://www.iclicker.com/dnn/SolutionsFor/K12Education/tabid/185/Default.aspx)

These small electronic devices, the size of a remote control, allow you to poll everyone so that children record answers to large-group questions; for the children, the responses are anonymous. For you, you not only know quickly whether the children understand the question or problem, but you have an electronic record of the answers, which allows you to individualize instruction later.

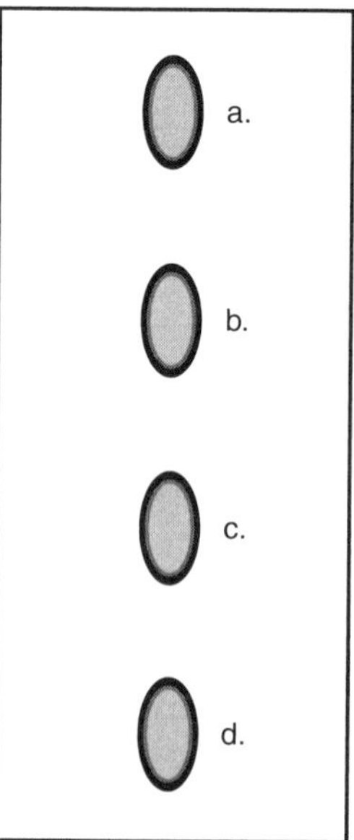

To use, the child pushes one of the buttons to record an answer to the teacher's question. All answers are collected in a receiver. The teacher can show the class the answers and additional discussion and problem solving can occur.

FIGURE 11.2 Personal Response System–Clicker

Another convenient way to collect observational and assessment data is with the use of the Personal Digital Assistant (PDA). In this case, as you assess, you record the data using special software for the assessment. For example, DIBELS (Dynamic Indicators of Basic Early Literacy Skills; https://dibels.uoregon.edu), a popular assessment system used in Reading First Programs as well as in many school districts, can be used with a PDA. For examples of this process in operation, see Early Literacy Resource Collection of Enhancing Education Through Technology Title II Part D—Corinth Partnership—New York State (http://www.wswheboces.org/modsch/ELRC.htm).

Besides these assessment-focused hardware products and specialized software for the classroom, you may wish to consider various software programs that permit you to monitor child progress. You can also try software that allows you to make your own games and quizzes for electronic use. An example is Gameshow Prep, which allows you to build video-game style materials for use in your classroom. (http://www.learningware.com/gameshowpro.html). Consult International Society for Technology in Education (http://www.iste.org) for the latest research and reviews of products as well as other classroom resources. Of course, you may wish to explore podcasting, to provide individualized assistance for English language learners and children with special needs. See Podcast Tools (http://www.podcasting-tools.com) for more help and ideas. Finally, many tools—including Rubistar, a rubric maker, and ThinkTank, a research organizer—are available at the Advanced Learning Technologies project at the University of Kansas Center for Research on Learning, "(which) utilizes the most advanced and innovative technologies available to improve teaching and learning" (http://www.altec.org) and is well worth an exploratory visit. In all of these ways, technology offers the opportunity to facilitate and individualize learning for children so that your class can successfully meet the district and state learner outcome requirements.

Learner Outcomes

From the perspective of educators, learner outcomes are a discrete expression of a philosophy of education. That is, what do you want children to know and be able to do or how do you want them to behave? Once you have decided the goals—learner outcomes—you can match the teaching method with the assessment method. For example, the Illinois State Goal 7 for Early Elementary is as follows:

- Estimate, make, and use measurements of objects, quantities, and relationships and determine acceptable levels of accuracy.
- Measure length, volume and weight/mass using rulers, scales, and other appropriate measuring instruments in the customary and metric systems.
- Measure units of time using appropriate instruments (e.g., calendars, clocks, watches—both analog and digital).
- Identify and describe the relative values and relationships among coins and solve addition and subtraction problems using currency.
- Read temperatures to the nearest degree from Celsius and Fahrenheit thermometers.

One inappropriate way to teach this curriculum is to select workbooks containing all or most of these activities. The teacher then divides the children into groups by ability or by convenience. On day 1, children look at cardboard coins, count them, and then go to their seats and circle the right pictures—identifying sums of pennies, nickels, dimes, quarters—in their workbooks. Everyone marches through the same pages of the workbook. The teacher plans extra sheets for those who don't grasp the particular concept being taught. He or she judges success by right answers on the workbook pages and the answers in small-group discussion.

In this scene, children are discussing the calendar every day. "Today is Tuesday, October 15. It is sunny and bright. We go to gym today. It is Audrey's birthday and she is 7 years old." In some classes, children would then copy this story from the chalkboard. This example shows in appropriate practice (Bredekamp & Copple, 1997; NAEYC, 2009).

Instead, you might bring in a jar of pennies and ask children to guess the number in the jar; ask children to measure the size of the shoes of the people in their families, using paperclips to graph their answers; or measure the classroom using pieces of yarn. As well, you tie the mathematics curriculum to science through an analysis of the weather trends for the month. Tie the mathematics curriculum to social studies through historical examination of money in the United States or changes in trading and currency practices around the world. And, of course, tie math to reading by using newspapers, books, and the Internet to read about data and data analysis—for example, economic trends or weather trends. These activities come from the experiences that children bring from kindergarten and first grade and coordinate with school-district goals based on state standards for learning.

Today, most states and many school districts have adopted a standards-based approach to instruction. Many of these state standards link to state-developed or other standardized tests. Most of the state and local standards are derived from the national standards of the subject areas—mathematics, reading, science, and social studies. Thus, primary-grade teachers are required to plan lessons geared toward the accomplishment of the local and state standards. A useful way to begin planning is through a process called *Understanding by Design* (Wiggins & McTighe, 2005) In this process, you start with the end goals or outcomes and work backward through the plan of action for your class and for individual students who may need specialized plans. For children with special needs, the process allows you to identify learning priorities from the IEP and the curricular expected outcomes, then design an assessment framework and finally plan the learning activities (Children, Sands, & Pope, 2009). As a check on teaching, schools use standardized tests to assess children at third grade and report results to the public. The Council of Chief State School Officers published *State Content Standards: A 50-State Resource* (2005); its website (http://www.ccsso.org) serves as a ready reference for the standards across the country. As well, state departments of education show the outcomes expected for schools in the state.

constructivist perspective views teaching and learning as a process of discovery for the learner, based on the learner's prior knowledge. Teacher facilitates knowledge, skills, and attitude learning to support individual development.

You still have the choice of teaching from a **constructivist perspective**—a child-centered, holistic, problem-solving, investigatory approach to creating curriculum experiences. This perspective is also described as inquiry-based and as emergent curriculum. A key component of this kind of teaching is asking thought-provoking questions. See examples in Box 11.13.

One example of holistic, standards-based teaching is offered by the National Council of Teachers of Mathematics (http://illuminations.nctm.org). Its website lists the standards by grade level and divides them according to content and process standards. You can see both standards with explanations and lesson plans on this site. Teachers can pick activities to meet the objectives of the curriculum. For example, an algebra activity might involve classifying the animals in Old MacDonald's Farm. A data analysis activity might involve the collection of buttons with several analyses performed subsequently. In addition, the suggested activities contain links to children's literature (http://illuminations.nctm.org/Lessons.aspx).

Using National Standards to Develop Checklists

With the enhanced focus on accountability as well as the emphasis on limited teacher time, a good source for developing teacher-friendly checklists is agreed-upon national and state-specific standards. All stakeholders use these—test publishers, curriculum writers, child-text producers, and teachers. Parents are reassured that their children are meeting the demands of more than local norms so that they will be prepared wherever they move in a highly mobile society. Finally, these measures remind us of research-identified behaviors that support learning and curricular development. An example of a checklist based on the International Reading Association reading standards is found in Harp and Brewer (2000, p. 159; see also Cohen & Cowen, 2010; Tompkins, 2010), where a reading checklist is divided into emergent reader behaviors, developing reader behaviors, and fluent reader behaviors. This developmental checklist helps focus observation and

BOX 11.13

Questions to Promote Thinking and to Document Learning

Ask:

1. How is ___________ similar to/different from ________________?
2. In what other ways might you show ____________________?
3. What is the big idea here?
4. Can you add details?
5. What is wrong with ___________?
6. What might happen if _________________?
7. What else could you do to _____________?
8. How can you say this differently?
9. Can you give an example of ____________?
10. How can you show this in action?
11. Based on what you know, what can you predict?
12. How can you be sure that your conclusion is true?
13. How would you feel if?
14. What kind of person or character do you think _________ is and why?
15. How would you tell this story differently?
16. Why is ____________ important?
17. How can you make use of ______________?
18. Can you tell why ___________ happened? How would you say it?
19. Do you agree with the end of the story? Why?
20. Can you explain why you like this one better than that one?

informal classroom assessment. Items on the emergent reader behaviors checklist may contain items such as "enjoys listening to stories, rhymes, songs, and poems," something that most teachers would think to observe and record. Another item that is indicative of reading progress is the item "uses pictures to help create meaning," a task that some may not readily associate with reading fluency. Taken together, the 15 items on the checklist provide the busy teacher with a focus for observation and record keeping, particularly when you format the checklist to comprise the categories of "not yet," "some of the time," and "most of the time." The use of these measures also assists with parent communication. You can say with confidence, "Our program uses national standards based on research as part of our record-keeping system." See Boxes 11.14 through 11.16 for examples of checklists that you might develop for yourself based on curricular outcome requirements. As well, there are prepared software programs to assist you in the systematic development of performance tasks associated with standards.

One of these programs is the Classroom Planner® (Innovative Education, 2009). The software program provides features for grading, lesson plans, seating charts, calendars, budgets, attendance, state and local objectives/standards, assessment markers, medical information, and IEPs (Individual Education Plans) from Leader Services IEP Writer http://www.iepwriter.com/home/faq.asp. PLATO® eduTest Assessment is a comprehensive online assessment solution that quickly identifies strengths and needs for students, classrooms, schools, or the entire district, guiding instructional decisions to improve student achievement over time. Teachers use "Strengths & Needs" reports to understand exactly how individual students and the class as a whole performed on each state standard (T.H.E. Journal, 2005; see also http://www.plato.com/Products/PLATO-eduTest-Assessment.aspx). In addition, many school districts use conventional productivity software to custom-build programs to manage instructional assessment. Thus, this software can be useful as you prepare to answer the stakeholder questions of your state education department who must implement the accountability plans of state legislators and those required by NCLB.

BOX 11.14

Writing Rubric for Third Grade

Name: ___________ Date: ___________

Did you write a story?

Did it have a beginning, middle, and end?

Did you stay on topic?

Did you read your story to a classmate?

Did your classmate understand the story?

Did you check for spelling and punctuation errors?

Did you revise?

Did you illustrate or use graphic organizer?

Compare this student rubric, for example, to the New Jersey Core Curriculum Standards for Language Arts at http://www.state.nj.us/education/cccs/2009/final.htm to see what information would be collected for the required outcomes. Develop modifications to this template for documenting all of the required elements.

accountability being responsible for the proper education of all children.

Outcome-based **accountability** requirements—specified learning objectives stated in broad behavioral terms, including NCLB—come from the input/output philosophy of business. The debate then becomes "What is worthwhile to know?" Currently, the definition of what is worthwhile is what is measured on standardized achievement tests. If definitions for academic success move toward more holistic definitions, then assessment must change as well. Performance on the outcomes shows success. The risks, of course, are the re-creation of another set of *high-stakes* test hurdles for children. Much of the debate about NCLB focuses not on the desire to reduce learning opportunities for children, but the current high-stakes nature of the outcomes-based assessment requirements. As states attempt to modify this

BOX 11.15

Rating Scales

Make these charts for each member of your class. Choose skills to rate that are of interest for report cards or other data collection demands.

Skill	Child's name	All of the time	Some of the time	None of the time
Uses a variety of reading strategies				
Shows oral reading fluency				
Reads fiction and nonfiction				
Interprets pictures				
Interprets charts and graphs				
Responds orally to reading				
Responds in writing to reading				

BOX 11.16

Oral Presentation Rubric

Name: ____________ Date: ____________

Attribute	Evident	Not Evident	Emerging
On topic			
Organized			
Creative			
Transitions			
Eye contact			
Loud enough			
Involved audience			
Visual aids			

requirement in the climate of the ongoing debate, performance assessment may become an added part of the process.

From an educational policy perspective, learner outcomes and performance assessment improve programs for all children. However, the weight of the assessment should not fall on the back of an individual child and thus deny access in an unfair way. That is, when judging a child based on performance tasks, educators must assure that prior educational experience included tasks similar to those requiring proficiency at specified age or grade levels. It is easy to see that a standardized achievement test requiring an in-depth knowledge of static electricity is not *fair* for children who have not studied electricity. Teachers must also keep well in mind that performance tasks have the capacity for bias, as well. If children have not participated in *hands-on* science, for example, they may not be able to handle problems that are presented by asking, "How many ways can you use a widget?"

Illinois Learning Standards "are content standards that describe 'what' students should know and be able to do . . . each . . . includes 5 benchmarks" in the K–12 span (Illinois State Board of Education (ISBE), 2001; 2009). Illinois, like other states, is developing performance standards that "will indicate 'how well' students are to perform to meet the standards" (ISBE, 2001; 2009).

BOX 11.17

Problem Solving and Reasoning

	Accomplished	Practicing	Emerging
Organizes information			
Develops strategies			
Uses different strategies			
Keeps after the problem until solved			
Draws pictures			
Uses trial & error			
Can explain solution			

An example follows from the field-test draft of science performance descriptors for the "Standard 11A: Students who meet the standard know and apply the concepts, principles, and processes of scientific inquiry" (ISBE, 2001). The performance indicators are divided into five stages for each grade level. Thus, one aspect teachers must observe and measure is whether their kindergartners can "describe an observed event by:

- Using senses to describe an event
- Observing measurements made by an event
- Listening to what might happen in an event based on previous observations
- Explaining what happened in an event
- Choosing a prediction based on observation." (ISBE, 2001)

The challenge for teachers is to take this discrete and content-free objective and turn it into part of an integrated curriculum. Because the blame for nonachievement or underachievement is usually laid at the door of the teachers and children, rather than at the door of school conditions—absence of materials, digital divide, and limited time—hundreds of discrete objectives and standards must be "taught." In addition, most often schools that do not meet state goals are beset with children who are at risk—children who are poor; who may be malnourished; who may live in violent situations; and whose schools are in disrepair, poorly equipped, and often filled with teachers who are new to the field or tired and disheartened. If you choose to dedicate your teaching career to the children in urban and nontraditional settings who need you most, you will need special skills.

Urban and Nontraditional Learner Issues

The task for the teacher in urban and nontraditional settings is to look beyond the traditional academic readiness rubric: assess the child's conformity to traditional learning settings. What bridges must you provide? Does Erica need a bit of phonics instruction because she has not heard standard English? Should you show Garth, a seven-year-old who comes to school for the first time, how to use lockers? To what extent have teachers incorporated an understanding of cultural groups in their approach to education in these urban schools?

Independence and interdependent functioning are not universally accepted values by all cultures in our society. For example, doing your own work is a traditional American value, a part of the self-actualization ethic of America. Some cultures value teamwork more than independence. Not putting yourself forward is yet another value held by many cultures (Greenfield

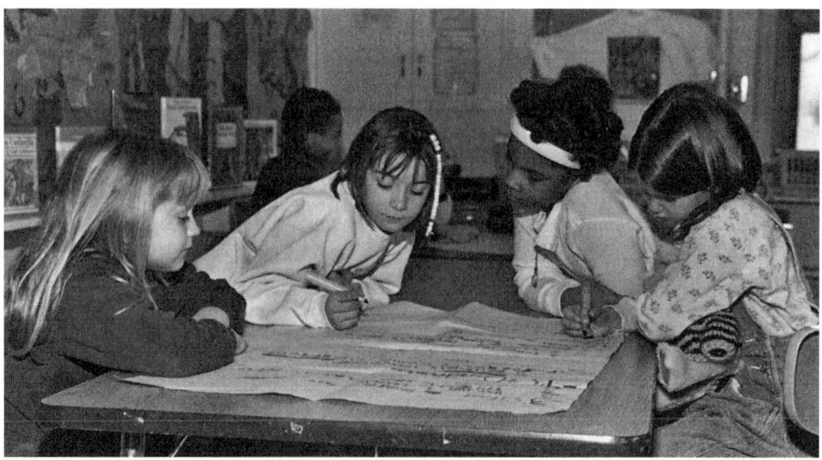

& Cocking, 2003; see also Spodek & Saracho, 2005; Genishi & Goodwin, 2008). Thus, if a teacher is measuring initiative as maturity, without consideration for the traditional values of the children taught, the teacher may misjudge the child and decide that the child is lazy or dumb or mentally assign another negative characteristic. Other threats to the validity of assessment, particularly standardized assessment, include your own attitudes, values and behaviors related to racial or ethnic groups, the child's perception of meaning associated with belonging to a racial or ethnic group, and child and family experience with discrimination and prejudice. In addition, issues concerning nonequivalent community experiences due to economic circumstances, variation in acculturation to mainstream "American" values, and variation in language use affect child performance. And, sometimes individuals adopt the "inferior" stereotypes held by the majority culture or resist perceived traditional cultural expectations because family members, or they themselves, may see the demands for conformance to "values" and the consequent behavioral expectations as being one-way—from the mainstream without reciprocity and appreciation for the special racial and ethnic differences (Armour-Thomas, 2004). For these and other reasons, cultural understanding of learners and their familial experiences profoundly influence their perceptions and attitudes toward school and learning. Teachers' knowledge and skills regarding cultural expectations and experiences of the particular learners they serve also profoundly influence educational experience and learner outcomes for each of the learners in their care. All of this required sensitivity must occur in a climate of documenting child progress on multiple variables. Constructivist teachers employ performance assessment measures for this documentation.

Collecting evidence on learner outcomes with performance tasks requires a new format for record keeping. The most common method is evidence collection in a portfolio. Portfolios are dynamic and inclusive—involving the child, teacher, and parent. (See Appendix F for a sample template for portfolios.) These dynamic documents also are useful for recording the progress of students with disabilities.

Inclusion of Students with Disabilities

The portfolio reflects the learning goals for such children in the mainstream. As teachers strive to individualize instruction for all learners, including those with disabilities, there are curricular and assessment implications. These include the following principles of integrated curriculum and assessment (Pugach & Warger, 1996, p. 229; see also Polloway, Patton, & Serna, 2008):

- Covering less material, but covering it in depth
- Focusing on meaning rather than rote learning of facts
- Teaching facilitates child learning
- Linking ideas across subject matter
- Constructing knowledge and building on prior knowledge
- Creating authentic activity where students work collaboratively in a community
- Embedding skill acquisition into meaningful learning activities
- Engaging children in problem solving and cooperative learning
- Closely aligning curriculum, instruction, and assessment

When you review these principles, compare them to the best practice guidelines for teaching in early childhood settings—they are remarkably similar. Examine and compare the multidisciplinary team and the interdisciplinary team recommendations. Box 11.18 shows a handy form to use to record instructional modifications for learners with special needs. Thus, including students with disabilities in the mainstream requires, and is supported by, good teaching practices.

BOX 11.18

Instructional Modifications Form for a Child with Special Needs

Classroom Modifications for ____________________

Date ______________

Seating

Near the teacher ___________

Away from others ___________

Near special friend ___________

Instructional Modifications

Assessment Modifications

Structural supports: calendar, assignment chart, PDA

Give directions with pictures or other clues

Special materials

PORTFOLIOS

portfolios keeping all of the information known about each child's progress and overall classroom activities.

The collection and development of **portfolios** is the most current way to link teaching and assessment. Most approaches to the collection of portfolios suggest that the process should be as important as the products stored. Teachers and students must think critically about what to include in these folders/boxes/baskets or electronic files. Parents are sometimes involved in helping teachers and children.

Portfolios serve several important purposes:

- Integrating instruction and assessment
- Providing students, teachers, parents, administrators, and other decision-makers with essential information about child progress and overall classroom activities,
- Making it possible for children to participate in assessing their own work
- Keeping track of individual child progress,
- Forming the basis for evaluating the quality of a child's total performance (Meisels & Steele, 1991; see also Eckert & Arbolino, 2005)

It is ideal to use portfolios according to an established purpose. Define goals and design activities to carry out the goals. Students and teachers determine the criteria for success. Students choose, under teacher guidance, examples of their work efforts for the year.

Examples of categories for math portfolios (Stenmark, 1991; see also NCTM, 2000) include:

- Problem comprehension
- Approaches and strategies
- Relationships
- Flexibility
- Communication
- Curiosity and hypotheses
- Equality and equity
- Solutions
- Examining results
- Mathematical learning
- Self-assessment

Work samples for math include:

- Written or dictated description of the results of investigations
- Pictures: drawings, paintings, photos of the child engaged in significant activity
- Teacher or student sketches of products made with manipulatives
- Diagrams, graphs
- Excerpts from students' math journals
- Sample solutions of problems (Charlesworth, 2005, p. 53)

For early literacy documentation, work samples that might be included in a portfolio are progress in writing—for example, from scribbling to mock letters to conventional writing. For composition, elements to include are the young child's ability to develop a story from words as labels, to single statement, simple story, complex story (McGee & Morrow, 2005).

In portfolio development, students help teachers generate criteria for effective work (Hebert, 2001; Shores & Grace, 2005; Kingore, 2008). Children form criteria for good and great work. They evolve clear models for the required assignments. Children refer to the criteria for success as they work. Children reflect upon their work. An example of a child's portfolio reflection sheet is shown in Box 11.19. The teacher's job is to provide resources for quality work.

One system of assessment that meets the highest standards is the *Work Sampling System*™ (Meisels, Jablon, Dichtelmiller, Dorfman, & Marsden, 2001). This assessment system contains developmental guidelines and checklists, covers all curricular areas, and provides for the development of summary reports. The system is standards-based, can be modified for local or state needs, and includes children with special needs in its approach. Finally, it models the involvement of young children in portfolio development. The *Work Sampling System*™ (Meisels et al., 2001) yields developmental guidelines and checklists as well as portfolios that include core items to show growth over time and individualized items that reflect original characteristics of learners. This research-based assessment system keys to state and national standards, as well as developmental guidelines. To guide planning and to summarize growth, teachers produce summary reports three times per year. The system separates developmental readiness and progress from academic knowledge and skills. Parents, students, and teachers are involved in creating the system. The system models a comprehensive approach for the assessment of young children. Materials included in the assessment system in addition to the developmental guidelines and developmental checklists are *Omnibus Guidelines* that show "how performance indicators change over time and provides examples of active learning" (http://www.pearsonassessments.com/pai/Pearson Assessments, 2009). Child work is organized in portfolios with suggestions for collecting core items—those planned—and spontaneous items that emerge as documentation for unique accomplishments of individuals. The complete system for portfolio assessment includes

BOX 11.19

Portfolio Reflection Sheet

My thoughts about the project on the Pioneers in Kansas:

	Most of the time	So-so	Not very much
I liked working on the Pony Express history.			
I chose good books, maps, charts, videos, and Internet sites for research.			
I can show my work with notes, diagrams, presentation, or other materials.			
The final product shows my best work.			

Next time I might . . .

the following elements: "portfolio item record and self-stick notes for teacher annotations, reproducible master of core item collection plan form (what you will collect to match the developmental guidelines), reproducible master of "Thoughts About My Portfolio" form, portfolio domain labels, Reproducible Master of Portfolio Tally form" (Dichtelmiller, Jablon, Dorfman, Marsden, & Meisels, 2001, 58). Report formats for standards and narrative summaries are available in print and electronically.

In all of these examples of portfolio assessment, the reader gains an appreciation for the similarity of day-to-day curriculum with the periodic assessment tasks. The assessment procedure is not a "get the learner" activity, but part of the check on learning progress. Where is the learner in relation to goals? Teachers, parents, and children collaborate to address these issues. Many examples of performance tasks and portfolio examples are available in published form today. Teachers must use good judgment in choosing published tasks or portfolios. The crucial factors are the relationships of philosophy, goals, activities, and assessment strategy. There must be a match between all of these elements.

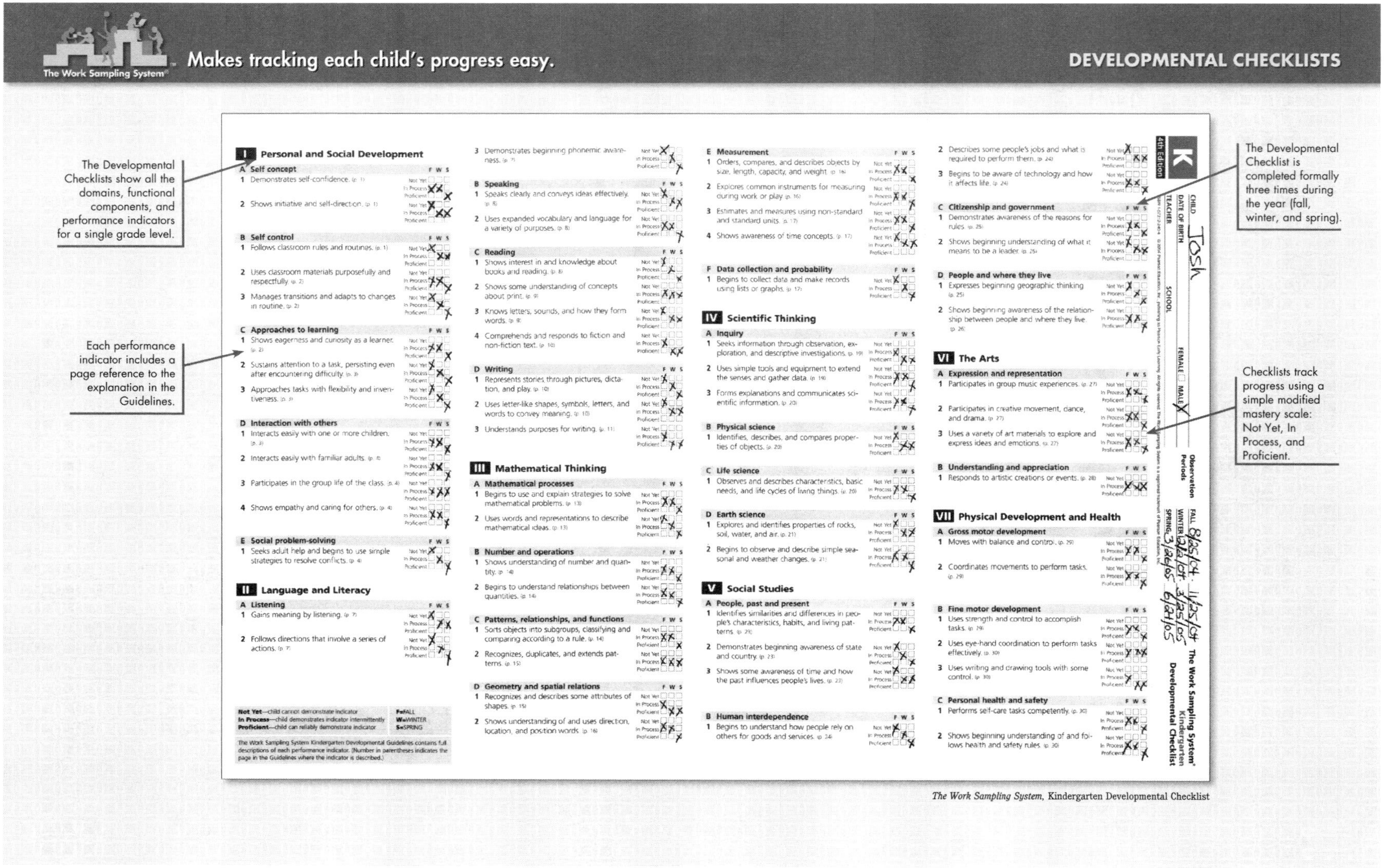

The Work Sampling System, Kindergarten Developmental Checklist

FIGURE 11.3 Example of Work Sampling Developmental Checklist.

Involving Children in Portfolio Data Collection

Young children who study in schools that appreciate their problem-solving approaches and learning styles can learn early on about the link from curriculum to assessment to reporting through the modeling that teachers provide. Questions that teachers might ask include:

1. What is your work plan?
2. What difficulties are you having in accomplishing your plan?
3. Are your goals realistic for the time period?
4. What are you especially interested in?
5. What strategies have you tried? What might you try?
6. How will you know when your work is ready to turn in? (Costa & Kallick, 2003, p. 36)
7. What did I enjoy learning most this week?
8. What have I learned about ______________?
9. What have I learned when trying to explain ______________ to my classmate? (Martin-Kniep, 2000, p. 24)
10. How do the pieces in your collection illustrate what you can do as a reader, writer, mathematician?
11. What do you notice about your work in September and now?
12. What strategies have you learned for problem solving?
13. If you picked one thing that helped you most as a learner, what would it be?
14. What have you learned about yourself as a learner as you put together your portfolio? (Martin-Kniep, 2000, p. 71)
15. What makes this your best piece of work?
16. How does this relate to what you have learned before?
17. "How are you doing now?
18. What do you need to work on to improve?
19. What strategies could you use to improve? (Benson, 2008, p. 122)
20. When did you do this? How much time did it take?
21. Why is this work in your portfolio? What does it show? (Kingore, 2008, 93)

The Work Sampling System suggests the following guidelines for children to think about as they choose work for the portfolio:

- Something that was enjoyable to do
- Something that shows how much they are learning

- Work that was difficult
- A piece of writing that shows their use of descriptive language
- Work that shows at least two strategies they used to solve a math problem
- Something they wrote that describes an important observation they made (Dichtelmiller et al., 2001, p. 103)

These advance organizers that you might post on the wall for your class help children be involved in assessing their work and shows them that evaluation is a process that involves reflection or thinking about work done.

In addition, students can construct statements such as the following:

1. I still don't understand ______________.
2. I didn't enjoy ______________ because ______________.
3. I find ______________ most challenging because . . .
4. This assignment is quality work, because . . . (Benson, 2003, p. 173)

In beginning the portfolio conference with each child, you want to focus on student-empowered learning, so you will start with inviting statements like, "Let's look at your portfolio . . . What would you like to talk about first? . . . Which of these pieces are you most proud of? . . . Do you see any patterns in this work? . . . Here's something else I see . . ." (Brookhart, 2008, pp. 52–53). Or, "What would you like to do next? Let's make a plan for your learning."

In addition to conversation geared to child's linguistic sophistication, you may consider using some paper-and-pencil methods to promote reflection. For example, teachers can develop self-evaluation forms for children to fill out. Morrow (2008) suggests one that includes items related to letters and sounds, reading, and writing. Items consist of *I know all the letters of the alphabet, the things I need to learn how to do better*, and *the things I do well*. Assessment becomes a part of the everyday classroom using these paper-and-pencil self-evaluation forms. These forms grow out of the classroom discussion with young readers and writers of kindergarten age in which teachers ask children to be involved in the planning of the evaluation of activities.

In an activity entitled *I can paint a picture*, kindergartners listen to a story and are then asked to draw a picture about the story or to draw a picture of the new ending. Before children begin the activity, they develop a rubric for successful completion of the assignment (Mindes & Donovan, 2001, pp. 34–35; see also Strickland, 2005; Hampton, Murphy, & Lowry, 2009). Rubrics can be holistic—giving a single score or rating for a work products—or analytical—dividing a product or performance into essential elements so that the performance can be studied in its component

parts. A holistic rubric is quick and easy to use, but gives less information to the learner. For example, children with identical holistic scores may have very different component skills. Children can participate in the aspects of rubric development by identifying attributes for the quality for a product or process, thinking about and drafting the weight of the attributes of the rubric, using the rubric for self-assessment, using the rubric to assess anonymous classmates' work, and using the rubric for peer assessment (Martin-Kniep, 2000, p. 54; see also Stiggins, 2008).

Another promising way to help children organize for learning and assessment is graphic organizer completion. The most familiar is the Venn diagram—two circles that overlap in the middle. This diagram is frequently used to show similarities between concepts or stories. Another familiar organizer is the web described earlier in the project approach discussion. In addition to commercially available template books (cf. Jacobson & Raymer, 1999), a popular software program called Kidspiration® (http://www.inspiration.com) provides a dynamic vehicle to organize information in all subject areas. These visual organizational cues help learners see where they are in a project or process, making it possible for them to decide how to display their knowledge and skills and what to include. Finally, some children may wish to show their learning by using Kid Pix® Deluxe 4 (published by Broderbund, http://www.broderbund.com), a presentation software package, for part of or their entire portfolio. By involving children in day-to-day assessment, testing, and reviewing, the leap to the spring achievement test program is clearly established. The classroom evaluation is a counterpoint to achievement testing.

STANDARDS-BASED TEACHING

Currently, most school districts require you to key your teaching to standards and show that you have done so on your lesson plans. More and more school districts also expect to see the link from standard to lesson to assessment. In addition to locally developed and mandated materials, technological sources of information are also helpful. Several commercial products are available now to assist busy teachers. Some products that meet the demand for comprehensive and appropriate practice that you may wish to explore include those developed by the following organizations:

- Mid-continent Research for Education and Learning, http://www.mcrel.org
- Learning Village http://hmlt.hmco.com/LV.php
- Teachmaster from PLATO®, http://www.plato.com
- K-12 Solutions http://www.scantron.com/k12/
- Homeroom.com from Princeton Review, http://www.theprincetonreviewk12.com/

standards-based teaching an approach to teaching that requires teachers to coordinate instruction to specified standards or goals.

These are but a few of the products available to support **standards-based teaching**, which connects teaching and assessment. These products are, however, among the most comprehensive and appropriate resources for use by early childhood teachers. All of the major testing companies have some products related to curriculum, standards, and assessment. No doubt, more products will explode on the Web and in software packages marketed to schools. Finally, state departments of education and school districts use conventional software to create accountability systems for particular stakeholder-driven questions.

A working example of using standards and working with accountability demands in the service of children in an urban environment is located at the DePaul University Center for Urban Education (http://teacher.depaul.edu). Under the leadership of Barbara Radner, the Center developed Teachers' Toolkit. Boxes 11.20 through 11.22 show excerpts from this Teachers Toolkit. The Toolkit links to national, state, and local standards. A working document links teaching plans to assessment strategies. Many downloadable teacher materials are available on this site. The Toolkit fosters a holistic approach to learning while being mindful of real accountability demands. This Toolkit supports teachers working in a system where achievement testing is used in a high-stakes way and is applicable to similar situations across the country.

BOX 11.20

Teachers' Toolkit—Language Arts Strategies

Focus ➡ **Get It Clear ➪** **Think More ➥** **Think It Through ➲** **Get It Together ❖** **Get It Across ➯**

LANGUAGE ARTS STRATEGY DEVELOPMENT WITH ACTIVITIES/ASSESSMENTS	
WORD KNOWLEDGE STRATEGIES *1A apply word analysis and vocabulary skills to comprehend selections* > Focus on one kind of decoding/word attack strategy each week. > Use words of the week all week. > Use structural analysis strategies. > Develop vocabulary in content areas. > Display words and pictures by phonics/structural patterns and topic.	***Activities/Assessment*** ❖ *Draw words or pictures to explain vocabulary.* ❖ *Chart word-picture-word.* ❖ *Chart or match word/synonym, word/antonym.* ❖ *Find word in newspaper, book.* ❖ *Write sentence with word(s).* ❖ *Make/complete grammar chart or glossary.* ❖ *Make/complete prefix-suffix chart/guide.* ❖ *Write with the "words of the week."*
FLUENCY STRATEGIES *Also include 4A (listen) and 4B (speak) effectively plus comprehension standards.* > Read aloud, think aloud. > Coach. > Model fluent reading of a variety of kinds of texts.	***Activities/Assessments*** ❖ *Read aloud from texts and their own writing.* ❖ *Re-read texts individually and in groups.* ❖ *Partner reading* ❖ *Poetry reading across the curriculum* ❖ *Make your own read-aloud guide.*
COMPREHENSION STRATEGIES *1B Apply reading strategies to improve understanding and fluency.* *1C Comprehend a broad range of reading materials.* *2A Understand how literary elements and techniques are used to convey meaning.* *2B Read and interpret a variety of literary works.* *5A Locate, organize, and use information from various sources to answer questions, solve problems, and communicate ideas.* *5B Analyze and evaluate information acquired from various sources.* *5C Apply acquired information, concepts, and ideas to communicate in a variety of formats.* ✓ Think out loud. ✓ Read with a partner. ✓ Use a variety of strategies. ✓ Read aloud; re-read independently.	***Activities/Assessments*** ❖ *Illustrate text.* ❖ *Construct and explain graphic organizers.* ❖ *Answer questions; justify answer choice.* ❖ *Make up questions (and provide answers).* ❖ *Sequence events in pictures or words.* ❖ *Write or match sentences that describe or explain __________.* ❖ *Infer and explain basis of inference.* ❖ *Outline text.* ❖ *Outline topic with information from two or more texts.* ❖ *Identify main idea or theme and explain its basis in text.* ❖ *Write the next part.* ❖ *Write a paragraph, poem, booklet, letter about what you read.* ❖ *Make your own "How To" reader's guide.*
WRITING STRATEGIES *3A Use correct grammar, spelling, punctuation, capitalization, and structure.* *3B Compose well-organized and coherent writing for specific purposes and audiences.* *3C Communicate ideas in writing to accomplish a variety of purposes.* ✓ Incorporate writing in all subjects ✓ Model—"write aloud." ✓ Focus on one writing element weekly. ✓ Model how to write.	***Activities/Assessments*** ❖ Write with focus, organization, support, coherence, and clarity. ❖ *Edit writing.* ❖ *Write in a variety of formats—letters, poems, diaries, fiction, nonfiction, booklets, etc.* ❖ *Make your own Writer's Guide that explains how to write.*

Source: http://teacher.depaul.edu; Polk Bros. Foundation Teacher Leadership Network, DePaul Center for Urban Education © 2003. Used by permission.

BOX 11.21

Teachers' Toolkit—Reading Outcomes and Assessments

Focus ➡ Get It Clear ⇨ Think More ➡ Think It Through ⊃ Get It Together ❖ Get It Across ⇨

Reading Outcomes and Assessments

	Standards	Performance Descriptors	Assessments
Word Knowledge	*1A Can apply word analysis and vocabulary skills to comprehend selections.*	✓ Recognize literary devices in text. ✓ Use roots and affixes to figure unfamiliar words. ✓ Infer meaning from context.	✓ Make guide to using this quarter's word analysis skills. ✓ Test on unfamiliar words requiring use of roots, affixes, inference.
Reading Comprehension	*1B Can apply reading strategies to improve understanding and fluency.* *1C Can comprehend a broad range of reading materials. 5A Locates, organizes, and uses information from various sources to answer questions, solve problems, and communicate ideas.*	✓ Apply survey strategies (e.g., use of bold print, organization of content, key words, graphics). ✓ Infer and draw conclusions about text, and explain basis. ✓ Organize and integrate information from a variety of sources.	✓ Create "my own reading strategy guide." ✓ Open-ended questions/multiple-choice questions—students justify responses. ✓ Make Venn diagram with information from different texts.
Fluency	*4B Can speak effectively using language appropriate to the situation and audience.*	✓ Read aloud fluently (with expression, accuracy, and appropriate speed).	✓ Read aloud with appropriate rate and expression. ✓ Present poem effectively. ✓ Set and reach fluency goal—rate and comprehension levels.
Writing	*3B Can compose well-organized and coherent writing for specific purposes and audiences.* *3C Can communicate ideas in writing to accomplish a variety of purposes.*	✓ Use adjectives and other elements to enhance writing. ✓ Edit and revise content.	✓ Edit, revise paragraph, letter, or poem. ✓ Write guide to writing with this quarter's elements.

Reading Outcomes and Assessments for ___________Quarter

Word Knowledge	*1A Can apply word analysis and vocabulary skills to comprehend selections.*		✓ Make glossary. ✓ Demonstrate word attack skills of the quarter in reading aloud and/or guide.
Reading Comprehension	*1B Can apply reading strategies to improve understanding and fluency.* *1C Can comprehend a range of reading materials.* *5A Locates, organizes, and uses information from various sources to answer questions, solve problems, and communicate ideas.*		✓ Answer questions. ✓ Make graphic organizer to show relationships in text. ✓ Write about a text. ✓ Illustrate a text.
Fluency	*1B Can apply reading strategies to improve understanding and fluency.*		✓ Read with appropriate expression and rate. ✓ Set and reach fluency goal.
Writing	*3A Can use correct grammar, spelling, punctuation, capitalization, and structure.* *3B Can compose well-organized and coherent writing for specific purposes and audiences.*		✓ Write a ___________. ✓ Write guide to writing with this quarter's elements.

Source: http://teacher.depaul.edu; Polk Bros. Foundation Teacher Leadership Network, DePaul Center for Urban Education © 2004. Used by permission.

BOX 11.22

Teachers' Toolkit—Math Outcomes and Assessments

Focus ➡ Get It Clear ⇨ Think More ➡ Think It Through ⊃ Get It Together ❖ Get It Across ⇨

Math Outcomes and Assessments for __________Quarter **Grade: __________**

Some elements of math may not be emphasized in a specific quarter. Include the performance descriptors for the math emphasized this quarter.

	Standards	Performance Descriptors	Assessments
Number Sense and Operations	*6A Demonstrate knowledge and use of numbers and their many representations in a broad range of theoretical and practical settings.* *6B Investigate, represent, and solve problems using number facts, operations and their properties, algorithms, and relationships.* *6C Compute and estimate using mental mathematics, paper-and-pencil methods, calculators, and computers.*		✓ Make glossary. ✓ Make guide to operations of the quarter. ✓ Solve problems. *Primary: Make number book.*
Measurement	*7A Can measure and compare quantities using appropriate units, instruments, and methods.* *7B Estimate.* *7C Solve problems.*		✓ Make glossary. ✓ Solve problems. ✓ Make measurement guide.
Math Patterns/ Algebra	*8A Describe numerical relationships using variables and patterns.*		✓ Make glossary. ✓ Make guide to algebra of the quarter.
Reading Outcomes and Assessments for __________Quarter			
	8B Describe numerical relationships using tables, graphs, and symbols. *8C Solve problems.* *8D Solve algebra problems.*		✓ Solve problems.
Geometry	*9A Demonstrate and apply geometric concepts involving points, lines, planes, and space.* *9B Identify, describe, classify, and compare relationships using points, lines, planes, and solids.* *9C Construct convincing arguments and proofs to solve problems.* *9D Solve problems.*		✓ Make glossary. ✓ Solve problems. ✓ Make geometry guide.
Data Collection and Analysis	*10A Organize, describe, and make predictions from existing data.* *10B Formulate questions, design data collection methods, gather and analyze data, and communicate findings.* *10C Determine, describe, and apply the probabilities of events.*		✓ Make glossary. ✓ Solve problems. ✓ Make data analysis guide. ✓ Organize data project.

Source: http://teacher.depaul.edu; Polk Bros. Foundation Teacher Leadership Network, DePaul Center for Urban Education © 2004. Used by permission.

ACHIEVEMENT TESTING

Across the country, achievement tests are part of the primary program. Some districts use tests to assess readiness for reading at the kindergarten level. States and school districts may require regular achievement testing at the third grade. The federal priority for annual assessment beginning in third grade (P.L. 107–110, No Child Left Behind, 2001) requires states to develop plans for the annual assessment of children and to report the results. This is a way to check the curriculum and instruction process for children who have historically been underserved or disserved by schools. Yet, this accountability emphasis must not rely on the high-stakes use of achievement tests:

- Using tests to decide which children should fail kindergarten and other grades
- Ignoring the limitations and technical aspects of tests (i.e., using instruments that are not matched to the curriculum)
- Placing inappropriate weight on the statistics of tests (e.g., ignoring stanines and percentiles, but placing great faith in grade-level equivalents)
- Using closed-answer instruments to judge the effectiveness of constructionist curriculum
- Relying on test scores to evaluate the success of students, schools, and teachers
- Accepting without question "the science" of tests. (Kamii see also Popham, 2004)

One of the potentially most devastating ways that schools misuse tests with young children is in readiness testing. Administered at the beginning of a child's career in school, children are subject to failure experiences that shape their entire lives. Relying on a readiness test to determine placement in grades is inappropriate. Such measures neglect the social/cultural context and typical individual developmental deviation found in all groups of children. The National Association for Education of Young Children (1995; 2009) disseminated a position statement on readiness that is more holistic. Recently, the concept of school readiness implies that the school is ready for the child at whatever skill and knowledge level the child brings to school (cf. Maxwell & Clifford, 2004; NAEYC, 2009). However, reading and reading readiness are a sustained federal focus, as seen with the Reading First Initiative.

The No Child Left Behind Act signed into law by President George W. Bush on January 8, 2002, established Reading First as a new, high-quality evidence-based program for the students of America. The Reading First initiative builds on the findings of years of scientific research, which, at the request of Congress, were compiled by the National Reading Panel. Ensuring that more children receive effective reading instruction in the early grades is of critical importance to the President and the nation: "Reading First is a focused nationwide effort to enable all students to become successful early readers. Funds are dedicated to help states and local school districts eliminate the reading deficit by establishing high-quality, comprehensive reading instruction in kindergarten through grade 3 . . . . Building on a solid foundation of research, the program is designed to select, implement, and provide professional development for teachers using scientifically based reading programs, and to ensure accountability through ongoing, valid and reliable screening, diagnostic, and classroom-based assessment" (U.S. Department of Education, 2005a; see also 2009).

Reading readiness can be appropriately assessed by redesigning the concept of reading to include the topics thought of as emergent writing and reading (Sulzby, 1989; see also McGee & Morrow, 2005). "Children appear to add new understandings about writing, somewhat as a repertoire of understandings in the sociolinguistic sense . . . . Their development does not follow one invariant, hierarchical order. We see several patterns of development, with a general progressive track . . . to conventional writing" (Sulzby, 1989, p. 85). Sulzby defines conventional writing as "the child's production of text that another conventionally literate person can read and that the child himself or herself reads conventionally" (Sulzby, 1989, p. 88; see also McGee & Morrow, 2005).

Children simultaneously learn to read contextually and specifically. That is, young children can read the word *stop* when it appears on a sign, but not in a book or on a chalkboard

(Teale, 1989, p. 49; see also McGee & Morrow, 2005). They have read the word in context. Through exposure to familiar words—*dog, pat, dinosaur, Barney*—in favorite stories, they learn the specifics. Gradually, they can form greater understandings from contextual situations. Teachers of young children must keep these academic developmental principles in mind, particularly at the kindergarten level.

In a position statement, the National Association of Early Childhood Specialists in State Government and the National Association for the Education of Young Children (2001) point to the continuing inappropriate use of assessment measures for the entry and placement of kindergartners. The call to action includes the following principles for kindergarten teachers:

- Guard the integrity of effective, developmentally appropriate programs for young children.
- Enroll children based on their legal right to enter (i.e., at age 5).
- Inform yourself about assessment strategies and techniques.
- Reject retention as a viable option for kindergartners.
- Use valid, reliable tests; align these with curriculum; involve all stakeholders.
- Welcome all children in kindergarten; avoid extra year or other special discriminatory programs. (p. 60)

When Teachers Do Use Achievement Tests

Teachers should involve the decision-makers in carrying out the testing practice in the classroom. A kindergarten teacher in a suburban school district, Ms. Green, was told that she must administer a reading readiness test to her group in November. The teacher, an experienced early childhood teacher of three- to five-year-olds, was hired late in August. Her assignment was to teach a group of 25 children whose parents had just registered them for school. The parents had not registered the children in the spring round-up, as many families had done. The group of children had limited experience in a formal learning situation—many were learning English. The classroom supplies given to Ms. Green were workbooks, blackline masters, crayons, and a limited number of table games. She immediately went to garage sales to find housekeeping center materials, borrowed big books from the library, and reorganized the room into interest centers. Ms. Green created a developmentally appropriate environment. She developed an assessment system based on district goals as stated on the kindergarten report card. She organized folders for each child, kept work samples, and made anecdotal notes. Ms. Green created partnerships with parents and children. They (teacher, children, and parents) all knew that they were:

- Learning how to be students
- Satisfying their curiosity
- Enjoying the group experience
- Discovering new information
- Learning English
- Writing and reading at the preliteracy level
- Solving problems
- Using numbers and equations

All of this information about achievement was available by teacher report. What would a reading readiness test add?

Ms. Green protested to the district test coordinator. She gave all the reasons about why not to test. She even referred to the National Association for the Education of Young Children Position Statement on Early Childhood Curriculum, Assessment, and Program Evaluation (2003; see also Copple & Bredekamp, 2006). The test coordinator remained firm. All kindergarten children would be tested.

The teacher asked for help to administer the test. She was working alone in the room with 25 children, except for an occasional parent volunteer. Test day arrived. The children were prepared. The test director could not get the children to cooperate! Testing was abandoned. Ms. Green served as an advocate for the young children in her program. She did so at personal risk to her career in that district. When teachers choose to resist tests, they must be prepared to show why the tests are inappropriate and how the necessary progress and accountability information can be obtained in a different way.

As teachers, we need to be aware of the research that shows that teachers do not always pay attention to the learning environment by providing work that is intellectually challenging, aligned to required standards, with clear criteria and specific feedback to students on the performance of particular tasks. Often, teachers give unclear rubrics for assignments. Finally, teachers give higher ratings to students than a standards-based assessment yields (Aschbacher, 2000, pp. 6–8).

When you plan to use an achievement test, keep the following in mind:

- Help the district be aware of the limitations of testing for young children.
- Point them in the direction of some newer standardized tests that attempt to include problem solving and multiple correct answers.
- Lobby to have testing begin—at the earliest—at third grade. Then, at least, children have some capacity for sustained attention to detail, writing, and reading skills.
- Prepare the children in advance for the experience.

There are two distinct aspects of preparation: preparation for the actual administration of the test and cluing the children in to the activity. Teachers must review the test and available samples so that they know what tasks children will be required to complete. Teachers must also be thoroughly familiar with the required testing conditions. This familiarity is not *teaching to the test*, but providing appropriate experience so that children can be successful. Once teachers have completed their homework, then they may help the children in the following ways:

- Provide opportunities to mark papers in the same way required by the test.
- Provide directions as limited by the test.
- Include opportunities to work under time pressure.
- Use separate answer sheets for assignments if children will be required to juggle these.
- Use the real machine-scorable answer sheets.
- Describe and practice appropriate test behavior: do one's own work, be quiet.
- Talk about guessing.
- Identify strategies for managing the number of items (i.e., which ones to do first).
- Help children cope with the anxiety of the task through story reading.
- Incorporate test materials in the literacy or other interest centers so children can cope through play.

To be fair to children, teachers must be thoroughly familiar with the test, its components, and procedures; follow the directions explicitly; adhere strictly to the time components; note any deviations made inadvertently; record notes about any unusual circumstances that occur with individual children; and be prepared to help children live with the stress that they feel during the test administration.

Federal law (IDEA) requires the inclusion of children with disabilities in the achievement-testing program. So that these measures are fair for students with disabilities, accommodations must be made. Elliott and Braden (2000; see also Elliott & Thurlow, 2005; Thurlow, Elliott, & Ysseldyke, 2003) list the most common testing accommodations as:

- Reading the test to the student
- Allowing extra time

- Breaking a test into shorter sessions
- Reducing the number of students in the room to minimize distractions
- Providing a quiet room for testing

The point of accommodations for child assessment is to provide the opportunity for young children to show what they know and understand without the encumbrance of using skills and dispositions that they don't have that may be irrelevant to assessing the concept at hand (cf. Salvia, Ysseldyke, & Bolt, 2010). One way to improve accessibility of assessment for all learners is to apply the principles of **universal design**—"the concept (represents the idea) of products and environments (to) be useable by all people to the greatest extent possible, without the need for adaptation or specialized design" (Center for Universal Design, 1997). The principles of universal design include:

- Equitable use—useful to people with diverse abilities
- Flexibility of use—accommodates to wide variety of individuals
- Simple and intuitive—use is easy to understand without extensive experience
- Tolerance for error—minimizes hazards

It is easy to see that with these principles in mind that assessment for children planned can make it possible for diverse learners to use the same task. This is particularly true when you use project-based assessment or make sensitive decisions about the length and format of traditional tests for all children. These principles are less likely to be applied to the current high-stakes achievement tests, when the format is preset for everyone. Then, test accommodations based on IEPs are essential.

Parents need to prepare for the achievement test experience as well. You don't want Greg's mother saying on the day of the test: "This is the most important thing you will do this year at school—don't mess it up." To prevent this anxiety-provoking experience or others that parents may create, prepare newsletter announcements about the role that this standardized experience will play in the total assessment plan for the year. Consider using commercial explanation materials from the publisher of the instrument you will be using. For example, "The main purposes of the ITBS are to provide the school with information to improve instruction and to help teachers make sound educational decisions about each student's learning. The scores allow teachers to check each student's year-to-year growth and to identify some of each student's strongest and weakest areas of achievement. The Iowa Tests of Basic Skills cover many of the fundamental skills your child is learning in school" (Hoover et al., 2001, p. 1). In addition to a statement of purpose, the testing booklet has examples of the kinds of items used on the test.

Once the test is over, skillful teachers go back to business as usual in the classroom. However, starting where children are comfortable or with favorite activities is a good way to recapture the momentum of life in the classroom. The test is just one of the cycles of student life.

Using Achievement Test Results

You gave the tests—now what? Look at the results for individual children. An example of one commonly used standardized test program—The Iowa Tests—makes it easy for districts to provide teachers and other stakeholders with essential information. Through *Interactive Results Manager* (http://www.riverpub.com/products/achievement.html), users can

- Analyze assessment results to inform instruction and ensure that students are making progress in academic achievement
- Disaggregate data by race/ethnicity, special program involvement, and gender to effectively monitor the progress of mandated reporting groups
- Investigate student performance in comprehensive content areas or in each test within a content area—providing flexibility with the level of achievement analysis desired

- Examine group achievement data using an advanced analysis tool included with the application, providing an unsurpassed level of reporting flexibility
- Control report access at three different levels—class, building, and system
- Export group level data in a variety of formats so that data may be used in other applications

Once you receive the appropriately customized report for classroom teachers, put the scores into the context of what a teacher knows about the child. Do the scores make sense? Often the answer will be "yes." For those cases where the answer is "no"—the child's performance is higher, lower, or different—gather support for the position through observation, task analysis, or individualized academic assessment. Then document the results. When it will be in the best interest of a particular child, ask that the results be set aside, considered as a minimal estimate of performance, and supply corroborating evidence.

The next major task is to interpret the test results to parents. To do this most effectively, be thoroughly familiar with the technical terms of the test, know what the scores mean, and be able to explain the results to parents in comparison to classroom functioning.

Parents will want to understand what the test means about their child. Is it a fair assessment? Does the test measure the curriculum? Can the parents help their child to improve? Will the score influence school practices? That is, will it entitle their child to special services?

Explain the meaning of *percentile, stanine, standard scores, mean, median*, and *variance* to parents. The best preparation is a thorough understanding of the terms and the limitations of testing in the early years. In addition to achievement tests, another common form of tests used by primary-grade teachers are textbook tests.

TEXTBOOK TESTS

Publishers of textbooks publish **textbook tests**. These include sample test items, chapter reviews, and other assessment materials to go with instructional materials. Examine these materials with the same intensity that you apply to the texts. Are the materials harmonious with the philosophy of education? If teaching from a process approach, use the suggested performance tasks that can be set up for children to solve. Use the record-keeping forms that are compatible with your learner outcome requirements.

textbook tests assessment materials published by textbook publishers to accompany their instructional materials.

Because these items say "test," do not assume that they are necessarily appropriate to use. Examine the materials as if they were tests. Are the materials valid? Do they match what you are teaching? Is there another way to gather the information that will be more efficient? Do the materials fit into the portfolio plan? See examples of textbook tests in Boxes 11.23, 11.24, and 11.25.

BOX 11.23

Textbook for Third-Grade Social Studies

Textbook for Third-Grade Social Studies	Teacher's Key
Pioneers	
The pioneers lived in the time period ___________	1800s
They traveled on ___________	horseback
Some of the pioneers ran out of ___________	food
Others did not bring enough ___________	warm clothes
Many lost ___________	family members

This test relies on reading and memorization. Also, it promotes one-right-answer thinking.

BOX 11.24

Pioneers in California for Third Grade

Pioneers in California for Third Grade	Teacher's Key
Tell the ways pioneers came to California.	Look for answers that show: by sea, by wagon train, by horseback.
What were these people seeking?	Answers that range from gold to a better way of life.
Draw a picture showing some important ideas about early California history.	Check to see whether the pictures represent the time period and idea (e.g., Gold Rush San Francisco fire and so on).

BOX 11.25

Graphic Organizer to Support Assessment of Prior Knowledge for Study of Pioneers (Produced w/Inspiration)

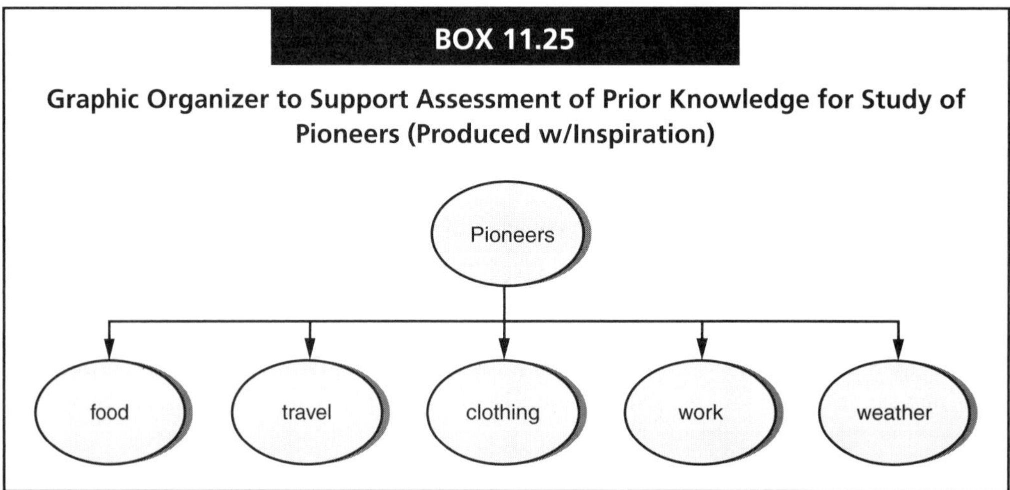

INDIVIDUALIZED ACADEMIC TESTS

individualized academic tests formal interviews of children on specific topics.

Sometimes it may be convenient to use an individualized academic test for determining reading or math instructional level. These instruments may be particularly helpful when children move to the classroom without records or when you are puzzled about how a child is learning. **Individualized academic tests** are formal interviews of children on a topic such as reading or mathematics. Through the standardized interview process, the teacher not only learns firsthand what the second or third grader knows, but also how he or she approached the task. For example, if assessing knowledge of double-digit addition, watch Marcey at work. Give her some double-digit addition problems. You can readily assess Marcey's ability with this problem, $22 + 49 = 611$, which shows that she does not understand place value.

Such information can be gathered through informal means if that is the only question. But if more information is needed about math facts, math concepts, or math vocabulary, spend 30 minutes in a structured interview with an individualized math test and Marcey to gather this information—it may take several days of observation. Used selectively, tests can be helpful efficiency tools.

TEST PREP

As the stakes for achievement testing increase, school districts and teachers have increased their use of test prep materials. Thus, the issue of teaching to the test emerges. If teaching to the test means aligning the curriculum and assessment procedures, this practice assures stakeholders—parents and the public—that students learn what they need to know; teachers, students, and administrators are accountable. If teaching to the test means *item-teaching*, teachers organize their instruction around the actual items found either on a test or around a set of look-alike items. For instance: "Gloria has 14 pears but ate 3." The test-taker must choose from four choices the number of pears that Gloria has now. Suppose the teacher revised this item slightly: "Joe has 14 bananas but ate 3." The test-taker chooses from the same four answers, ordered slightly differently (Popham, 2001b).

Such practice blows the predictive validity of test scores and in the end cheats students. As you cope with the high-stakes demands of your curriculum, avoid the use of such materials and concentrate on matching your teaching to the concepts in the best interests of your students. You will use the results of your classroom-based authentic assessments and occasional paper-and-pencil tests to assess the effectiveness of your program so that your students will be successful on the standardized achievement tests aligned with the outcome expectations of your state. You may also wish to include conversations about how to decode test questions. That is how can you help children be test-savvy about using pictures, test developer words, and time management strategies. In a discussion of what to expect regarding test format and questions, you have the chance to see what might be confusing to children while also giving them good strategies (cf. Greene & Melton, 2007). One technique to help children work together to learn about test-type problems and questions: Think-Pair-Share or Write-Pair-Share. In the first strategy, each child thinks about the question or problem; then they talk together to compare the answer, sharing the combined answer with the class. Writing first offers a way to prepare children for extended response questions.

The best test preparation is the knowledgeable teacher—one who knows program standards and plans activities that will help children accomplish the standards, one who promotes mastery of skills for all children, one who describes tests as just another part of the life in a classroom, and one who teaches general test-taking skills by using the kinds of formats that children will encounter in the formal standardized experiences (cf. Green & Johnson, 2010). This preparation is in addition to the conversations described earlier. Because third grade is often the time that standardized tests begin in the lives of children, the Center for Urban Education at DePaul University developed a list of Test Prep ideas based on IL Learning Standards. These are shown in Figure 11.4.

Next Grade Prep
Priorities for Progress: Third Grade© from the Polk Bros. Foundation Center for Urban Education website: http:/teacher.depaul.edu

What's important for 3rd Graders to complete this school year?

- Continue to write in their journals, expressing their thoughts and their feelings.
- Continue to develop their reading skills.
- Learning their times tables better so division will be easier.
- Continuing to improve in phonics, identifying letters to pronounce words.
- Basic phonetic skills, decoding abilities.
- Learn to weigh items.
- Sufficient writers.
- Critical thinking skills.
- Word problems.
- How to write a multiple-choice question.
- Language arts: creative writing of poems and stories.
- To better understand problem solving by using what's left, difference and more than for subtraction.
- Work on cubic volume activities.
- Working together on projects to present.
- Focus on writing.
- They understand inferential questions better. To read more, and to comprehend what they have read.
- Paragraph structures.
- They need to practice new vocabulary words (bilingual).
- My students need to focus on their language skills (bilingual).
- Learn how to write complete sentences.
- Learn multiplication.
- Double-digit multiplication.
- Multiplication and division beyond basic facts.
- Encourage reading of more advanced material (provide exposure to next grade level's material).
- Review of all skills since many are "forgotten" as the year progresses.
- How to think while you are reading.
- To be able to draw conclusion according to passage.
- To be able to write and respond to an essay question.
- Trading 3 and 4 digits.
- Math multiplication facts, division.
- To better understand problem solving by using altogether, total, in all, and both of them for adding.
- To be able to reason and make assumptions and recognize it. To be able to understand main idea.
- I would like for my students to learn how to do all of their multiplication tables.
- To be able to write more questions: literal, inferential, analytical and evaluative.
- Compare and contrast objects.
- To be able to organize the writing process more thoroughly.

Recommendations for Second Grade Teachers:
What's most important for students to prepare for 3rd grade success?

- Write a complete sentence that is punctuated and grammatically correct.
- Make sure students are familiar with literal questions, and how to find answers in a story.
- Teach the children to regroup at least to the tens column.
- Learn basic phonetic skills.

FIGURE 11.4 Example of Third Grade Priorities from Teachers' Viewpoint.

- At least teach the children to write a short narrative using grammatically correct sentences.
- Word attack skills.
- Regrouping.
- Sentence structure.
- Math word problems.
- Reading longer passages.
- To be able to comprehend text.
- Knowledge (mastery) of basic sight words.
- Begin to foster more independence.
- Read silently more and comprehend.
- The students could prepare a chart to tell what important things they learned in 2nd grade—save it and take it to 3rd grade teacher in August.
- Phonics decoding skills.
- Language skills: complete sentences, usage (grammar), capitalization, how/when to make a paragraph, how to write a sentence.
- Math: addition and subtraction facts.
- Test taking skills and strategies.
- To become critical thinkers.
- To be able to express themselves verbally and through writing.
- Divide words in syllables and sounds.
- How to transfer a complete thought to make a complete sentence.
- Know each alphabet's sound and how to use letters to make a word.
- Be a silent reader.
- To be able to retell what they've read in their own words.
- Addition and subtraction facts.
- Problem solving and multiplication.
- Know how to multiply.
- Phonics readiness skills.
- Complete heading.
- Knowledge of basic sight words, fostering independence, phonics readiness, transferring a complete thought to make a complete sentence.
- Organizational skills.
- Awareness—answering factual questions (all types of questions).
- Writing an essay independently.
- Become a fluent reader.
- The students of 3rd grade can prepare their own booklet—subject by subject—glossary. My Reading Glossary.

FIGURE 11.4 *(continued)*

In addition to school test-prep programs, many books are available for parents to use to assess their children against state standards. Some parents enroll their children in test-prep classes, as well. As an early childhood teacher, you will reassure parents that the best preparation for success is the holistic, outcome-based program that you create with rich opportunities for children to investigate projects, obtain skills as part of this work, and sustain learning curiosity that will last a lifetime.

VOICES FROM THE FIELD

The View from Fourth Grade: A Best Practice Example

In our private school, we use results of annual Terra Nova as one piece of information in grades 2–7. The test is given in March and results are sent to families in May, so for me it is a baseline to check against. For reading, we administer Fountas and Pinnell to group children for reading—our third year using it. I find that it gives a fairly accurate reading level and is comprehensive with assessment of fluency and comprehension—broader assessment than some other measures. We have the Fountas and Pinnell library of leveled readers, which helps.

What I expect of entering fourth graders:

- *Work independently*
- *Experience with formal testing*

What else I do to assess:

- *Give some multiple-choice tests in math, as well as using observation of the problem-solving process*
- *Some essays*
- *Observation and projects*

Our fourth year of portfolios is an evolving process—the first year was mostly show-case. Now we're working on student reflection and portfolio as assessment.

We're a school that works at articulation across the grades.

SUMMARY

At the primary level, tests and testing become a formal part of student life. Though best early childhood practice eschews the use of tests for the most part, assessment in the service of instruction is required. Sometimes tests are the most efficient way to gather information quickly. Sometimes tests are required as part of the accountability mechanism, particularly in third grade. Teachers must pick the procedure to match the philosophy of their school's program and be prepared to answer responsibly when asked to describe child progress.

FIELD ACTIVITIES

1. With a small group of children, try one or more of the informal assessment measures described. Report the results—respecting confidentiality—to your class.
2. For your state, find out about the required learning goals or learning outcomes. Make a plan for assessing children for the acquisition of these for a grade level of your choice.
3. Examine portfolios in a local school. Discuss with your classmates the similarities or differences across grades and schools.
4. Look at textbook tests and compare them to the curricular goals for a theme of your choice. How would these measures assist your efforts in assessment? What limitations did you find?
5. Review an individualized academic test. Try administering part or all of it to a volunteer child. How will you use these measures in your program of the future?

IN-CLASS ACTIVITIES

1. Review the test manual for a standardized achievement test. Try giving the test to a classmate. Analyze your efforts. Discuss ways to improve performance on subsequent administrations.
2. Bring to class a state report card for your state, or another. Review the assessment results reported statewide and one urban, one rural, and one suburban district. For each of the districts, identify curricular modifications that may be appropriate for enhanced student achievement.
3. In a small group, plan a presentation to a group of parents about portfolios. Describe how you will involve children in their own assessment and why you will do so. In addition, identify ways that parents will be involved in the process.
4. Develop a checklist for judging authentic portfolio assessment. Describe how teachers collect and store information in portfolios. Then, examine in class some commercially available systems, including the following: Grady Profile (http://www.aurbach.com/gp3/index.html); Pupil Pages (http:www.pupilpages.com); and those that may be used locally, which are part of a larger data-management system. Looking at your checklists, identify how the electronic portfolio might be useful in an early childhood program. Are there any disadvantages?

STUDY QUESTIONS

1. Define learner outcomes. Who establishes these and what is the early childhood teacher's role in the assessment of learner outcomes? What influence should learner outcomes have on curriculum or program goals? What responsibility do teachers have in accountability within their program goals?
2. How does informal assessment fit into a typical school day?
3. How do you integrate content as seen in the examples of classroom activities? How do you likewise integrate assessment?
4. Why is it important for assessments to remain dynamic and inclusive? How do portfolios accomplish this?
5. How are achievement tests often misused in schools? How can parents be encouraged to advocate for their children in schools where readiness tests form the basis for placement?
6. What are some steps teachers can take to ensure their students are treated fairly and appropriately throughout the testing process? What should teachers keep in mind while using readiness tests?
7. In which classroom situations will textbook tests be used? How can teachers ensure each child is appropriately assessed by textbook tests?

REFLECT AND RE-READ

- I understand achievement tests and their role in primary education.
- I can develop a reasonable approach toward portfolios and know the limitations of these documentation procedures.
- I can link standards to planning and assessment.

CASE VIGNETTE

Sabah, the oldest son of recent immigrant parents, is seven years old. The native language is spoken at home; Sabah seems to experience some difficulty in understanding English conversation with the observer, herself fluent in the child's language. Mrs. Shakil, his mother, reports that Sabah's grades in school since kindergarten have been Cs and Ds; she expects him to do well in school and sits him down after school to do homework. This process takes forever, more than an hour, and is accomplished with much yelling and cajoling. Often, Sabah doesn't complete homework, begging to go play; Mrs. Shakil finally relents.

What should the second-grade teacher do to assist Sabah and his family? What assessments should be planned?

Source: From S. Umar, 2004, submitted in partial fulfillment of ECE 375 Early Childhood Assessment: DePaul University. Used by permission.

RUBRIC RESOURCES

http://jonathan.mueller.faculty.noctrl.edu/toolbox/rubrics.htm; Authentic Assessment Toolbox by Jonathan Mueller

http://altec.org/index.php; University of Kansas Tech Tools for Teachers, includes Rubistar

http://www.uwstout.edu/soe/profdev/rubrics.shtml; University of Wisconsin-Stout

http://school.discoveryeducation.com/schrockguide/assess.html; Kathy Schrock

http://eduscapes.com/tap/topic69.htm; Bloom's Taxonomy verbs for critical thinking

http://www.rubrics4teachers.com/; rubrics for teachers

http://www.teach-nology.com/web_tools/rubrics/; Subscription service, some examples accessible

http://www.teachervision.fen.com/rubrics/assessment/26773.html; teacher vision

http://www.thinkfinity.org/SearchResults.aspx?subject=all&partner=all&resource_type=all&q=rubric&grade=all&WebSiteArea=educator; Thinkfinity

TECHNOLOGY LINKS

http://www.learningpt.org

Learning Point Associates. Publishes occasional papers and links to curricular and assessment materials for use in the primary years.

http://www.nctm.org

National Council of Teachers of Mathematics. Practical examples for implementation of standards in the classroom.

http://www.reading.org

International Reading Association. Position papers and publications on teaching reading.

http://www.nsta.org

National Science Teachers Association. Standards, position papers, and examples for teaching.

http://www.socialstudies.org

National Council for Social Studies. Standards, position papers, and publications on teaching the social studies.

http://www.leadandlearn.com

Center for Performance Assessment. Examples of teaching plans and position papers.

http://ies.ed.gov/ncee/wwc

What Works Clearinghouse. Presents classroom practice that shows promise for success.

SUGGESTED READINGS

Benson, B. P. (2009). *How to meet standards, motivate students, and still enjoy teaching* (2nd ed.). Thousand Oaks, CA: Corwin.

Bickart, T. S., Dodge, D. T., & Jablon, J. R. (2004). *What every parent needs to know about 1st, 2nd & 3rd graders: An essential guide to your child's education.* Washington, DC: Teaching Strategies.

Brookhart, S. M. (2008). *How to give effective feedback to your students.* Alexandria, VA: Association for Supervision and Curriculum Development.

Cohen, R. (2008). *Developing essential literacy skills: A continuum of lessons for grades K–3.* Newark, DE: International Reading Association.

Corgill, A. M. (2008). *Of primary importance: What's essential in teaching young writers.* Portland, ME: Stenhouse.

Denton, P. (2007). *Power of our words: Teacher language that helps children learn.* Turner Falls, MA: Northeast Foundation for Children.

Fisher, D. & Frey, N. (2007). *Checking for understanding: Formative assessment techniques for your classroom.* Alexandria, VA: Association for Supervision and Curriculum Development.

Kingore, B. (2008). *Developing portfolios for authentic assessment, PreK–3: Guiding potential in young learners.* Thousand Oaks, CA: Corwin.

Resnick, L. B. & Snow, C. E. (2009). *Speaking and listening for preschool through third grade. Rev. Ed.* Pittsburgh: The University of Pittsburgh and International Reading Association.

APPENDIX A

Self-Assessment Pretest Associated with Terms to Know

<table>
<tr><th colspan="2">Early Childhood Preassessment Inventory</th></tr>
<tr><td>I am familiar with methods of observation and recording of children's behavior for purposes of assessing goals, providing for individual needs, and appropriately teaching young children. I am familiar with terms such as
• observations
• observation records
• anecdotal notes
• running records
• class journals
• checklists
• frequency records
• event sampling
• time sampling
• rating scales
• portfolios
• documentation panel
• formative evaluation
• summative evaluation
• rating scales
• typical development
• atypical development
• developmental delay</td><td>I need to know more about __________.</td></tr>
<tr><td>I can create assessment plans for learning environments that address the needs of young children from culturally diverse backgrounds and including both typical and atypical children. I am knowledgeable about the related terms, such as
• intrinsically motivating
• ecological assessment
• resiliency
• authentic assessment
• task analysis
• presentation mode
• response mode
• dynamic assessment
• mediated learning experience (MLE)
• functional assessment
• techniques
• ecological
• behavior intervention plans
• inventory
• diagnostic measures
• IEP goals
• learner outcomes
• informal evaluation
• objectivity</td><td>I need to know more about __________.</td></tr>
</table>

(*continued*)

<table>
<tr><td>

- strength-based assessment
- multiple intelligences theory
- prereferral screening
- diagnostic tests
- curriculum-based measures
- criterion-referenced measures
- performance assessment
- portfolios
- Child Find team
- diagnostic evaluation
- referral question
- psychoeducational evaluation
- Individualized Family Service Plans (IFSP)
- multidisciplinary staffing
- play-based assessment
- inventory
- diagnostic measures
- IEP Goals
- learner outcomes
- informal evaluation
- objectivity

</td><td></td></tr>
<tr><td>

I am aware of value issues regarding assessment best practice and the existence of codes of ethics in professional life. I am knowledgeable of the related terms, such as

- stakeholders
- accountability
- high-stakes measure
- confidentiality
- child study
- high stakes decisions
- inclusion
- Response to Intervention (RTI)
- RTI Conference
- Initial referral conference
- Multidisciplinary staffing
- Primary responsibility
- Diagnostic evaluation
- Referral question

</td><td>I need to know more about ____________.</td></tr>
<tr><td>

I am familiar with ways to gather information through the use of library resources, the Internet, professional and organizational resources, and community resources. I know what role the following play in assessment:

- NAEYC, CEC, AERA, Buros Institute, Chicago Public Schools, ISBE

</td><td>I need to know more about ____________.</td></tr>
</table>

I am acquainted with the physical, cognitive, emotional, social, and spiritual developmental milestones of young children. I know about typical and atypical development. I am familiar with the following related terms: • case finding • screening • diagnosis • Apgar Rating Scale • prenatal testing • amniocentesis • ultrasound • chorionic villus biopsy (CVS) • gestational age • established risk • biological risk • environmental risk • drug-exposed babies • fetal alcohol syndrome (FAS) • Apgar Score • Prenatal Test • Precutaneous umbilical blood sampling (PUBS or cordocentesis)	I need to know more about ____________.
I can choose, administer, and interpret correctly various assessment techniques appropriate for the early childhood age span. I am familiar with the statistics of testing and terms such as: • mean • raw score • range • standard deviation • normal curve • standardized test • norm-referenced test • population • normative sample • norms • criterion-referenced test • derived scores • age-equivalent scores • grade-equivalent scores • interpolated score • extrapolated score • percentile ranks • deviation quotients • normal-curve equivalents • stanines • reliability • test-retest reliability • interscorer reliability • correlation coefficient • standard error of measurement (SEM) • validity • face validity • content validity • criterion-related validity • concurrent validity • predictive validity • sensitivity	I need to know more about ____________.

(*continued*)

• specificity • construct validity • objectivity • scale scores • norming • standard score • absence of bias • technical issues • construct validity • discriminant validity • social validity	
I am aware of the complex social and cultural context in which child-care and educational settings are embedded. I know how these issues apply to assessment of young children: • developmentally appropriate practice • portfolios • accountability • learner outcomes • informal evaluation • portfolios • individualized academic tests • artifacts • project-based learning • webbing • Regio Emilia • Constructivist perspective • textbook tests • standards-based teaching • achievement testing • test prep	I need to know more about ____________.
I appreciate the family role in the assessment process. I know the differences and the roles for stakeholders on the • multidisciplinary team • interdisciplinary team	I need to know more about ____________.
I know that I must commit to an assessment system that is comprehensive, multidimensional, and holistic for the diverse population of young learners and their families. I am familiar with the following terms and practices: • tests • norm-based instruments • screening tests • inventory • rubric • interrater reliability • accountability • report card • grades • student-led conferences • stakeholders • accountability • authentic assessment • intrinsically motivating • standards based • outcomes	I need to know more about ____________.

I appreciate the role of assessment processes and results in IEP and IFSP development. I know about the role that the following play in the process: • parent perspective • developmental questionnaires • parental reports • behavioral questionnaires • parental questionnaires • parent interview • family collaboration	I need to know more about ____________.
I am aware of legislation and public policy as it affects children, families, and programs for young children, particularly the issues of high-stakes testing. For example: IDEA No Child Left Behind Act Head Start Performance Standards parents rights	I need to know more about ____________.
If asked, I would define *assessment* as	
My most recent positive experience with *assessment* is	
The worst experience of my life with *assessment* is	

APPENDIX B

Child Development Chart for Typical Development

Sources: Adapted from the following: *The Carolina Curriculum for Handicapped Infants and Infants at Risk,* by N. Johnson-Martin, K. G. Jens, and S. M. Attermeier, 1986, Baltimore: Brookes; *The Carolina Curriculum for Preschoolers with Special Needs,* by N. Johnson-Martin, S. M. Attermeier, and B. Hacker. 1990, Baltimore: Brookes; *Help for Special Preschoolers Assessment Checklist,* 1987, Palo Alto. CA: VORT Corporation; *HELP Hauraii Early Learning Profile Activity Guide,* by S. Furuno. K. A. O'Reiley, C. M. Hosaka, T. T. Inatsoka, T. L. Allman, and B. Zeisloft, 1985, Palo Alto, CA: VORT Corporation; *Mainstreaming Preschoolers,* by CRC Education and Human Development, Inc. for the Administration for Children, Youth and Families, 1978, Washington, DC: U.S. Government Printing Office (1979620–182/5708); *Transdisciplinary Play-Based Assessment: A Functional Approach to Working with Young Children,* by T. W. Linder, 1990, Baltimore: Brookes.

Child Development Chart for Typical Development

	Gross-Motor Skills	Fine-Motor Skills	Language Comprehension	Expressive Communication	Cognitive Skills	Self-Help Skills	Social Skills
0–3 Months	Holds head up in prone position. Lifts head when held at shoulder. Kicks reciprocally. Rolls from side to supine position.	Moves arms symmetrically. Follows with eyes to midline. Brings hands to midline in supine position. Activates arms on sight of toy.	Responds to voice. Watches speaker's eyes and mouth. Searches with eyes for sound.	Cries when hungry or uncomfortable. Makes comfort sounds.	Inspects surroundings. Shows anticipation. Inspects own hands.	Opens mouth in response to food stimulus. Coordinates sucking, swallowing, and breathing.	Regards face. Enjoys physical contact: molds, relaxes body when held. Makes eye contact. Expresses distress.
3–6 Months	Holds head in line with body when pulled to sitting. Bears weight on hands in prone position. Sits with light support. Holds head steady in supported sitting position. Rolls from supine position to side.	Follows with eyes without moving head. Keeps hands open most of time. Uses palmar grasp. Reaches and grasps objects.	Quiets to mother's voice. Distinguishes between friendly and angry voices. Responds to own name.	Coos variety of vowel sounds. Laughs. Takes turns. Responds to speech by vocalizing. Expresses displeasure and excitement.	Begins rattle play. Repeats/continues familiar activity. Uses hands and mouth for sensory exploration of objects. Plays with own hands, fingers, toes.	Brings hand to mouth holding toy or object. Swallows strained or pureed foods. Inhibits rooting reflex.	Smiles socially. Discriminates strangers. Demands attention. Vocalizes pleasure or displeasure. Enjoys social play, e.g., "This Little Piggy." Lifts arms to mother.
6–9 Months	Exhibits body-righting reaction. Extends arms protectively. Sits independently, but may use hands. Stands holding on. Pulls to stand. Crawls backward. Gets into sitting position without assistance.	Transfers object. Manipulates toy actively with wrist movement. Reaches and grasps with extended elbow.	Looks at pictures briefly. Looks for family members or pets when named. Responds to simple requests with gesture.	Babbles to people. Produces variety of consonants in babbling. Babbles with adult inflection. Babbles reduplicated syllables. "mama." "baba." etc. Vocalizes loudly to get attention.	Works to obtain desired out-of-reach object. Finds object observed being hidden. Touches adult's hand or toy to restart an activity. Plays 2 to 3 minutes with single toy. Follows trajectory of fast-moving object. Shows interest in sounds of object.	Uses tongue to move food in mouth (4–8 months). Holds own bottle. Mouths and gums solid foods. Bites voluntarily: inhibits bite reflex. Feeds self a cracker.	Recognizes mother (4–8 months). Displays stranger anxiety. Smiles at mirror image. Shows anxiety to separation from mother.

(continued)

	Gross-Motor Skills	Fine-Motor Skills	Language Comprehension	Expressive Communication	Cognitive Skills	Self-Help Skills	Social Skills
9–12 Months	Creeps on hands and knees. Moves from sitting to prone position. Stands momentarily. Walks holding on to furniture (cruises).	Takes objects out of container. Uses both hands freely. Tries to imitate scribble. Puts object into container. Releases object voluntarily. Pokes with index finger. Uses neat pincer grasp.	Understands "no no." Listens selectively to familiar words. Enjoys looking at books.	Babbles single consonant-vowel syllables, e.g., "ba." Responds to certain words (e.g., "wave bye bye") with appropriate gesture. Uses behaviors and vocalization to express needs.	Overcomes obstacle to obtain object. Retrieves object using other material. Imitates gestures. Unwraps a toy. Enjoys looking at books.	Finger feeds variety of foods. Holds spoon. Cooperates with dressing by extending arm or leg. Chews by munching.	Enjoys turn-taking game. Resists supine position. Shows like and dislike for certain people, objects, or situations. Shows toys to others; does not release. Tests parents' reactions at feeding and bedtime by new and mischievous behavior.
12–18 Months	Stands from supine position. Walks without support. Throws ball. Creeps up stairs. Pulls toy while walking. Carries large toy while walking. Moves to music.	Uses two hands in midline, one holding, one manipulating. Scribbles spontaneously. Place pegs in pegboard. Builds two- to three-cube tower.	Responds to simple verbal requests; identifies one body part. Understand many nouns. Brings objects from another room on request.	Combines gestures and vocalizations to express a variety of communicative functions. Says "Dada" or "Mama" purposefully. Uses single words. Uses exclamations, e.g., "Oh, oh!" Says "no" meaningfully. Uses 10–15 words (by 18 months).	Understands adult's pointing. Hands toy back to adult. Matches objects. Places round and square pieces in form board. Nests two or three cans. Identifies self in mirror.	May refuse food; appetite decreases. Brings spoon to mouth. Drinks from cup with some spilling. Indicates discomfort over soiled pants. Removes socks.	Displays independent behavior; may be difficult to discipline. May display tantrum behavior. Demonstrates sense of humor. Is easily distractible; has difficulty sitting still.
18–24 Months	Moves on "ride-on" toys without pedals. Walks upstairs holding railing, both feet on step. Picks up toy from floor without falling. Runs.	Imitates circular scribble. Imitates horizontal stroke. Holds crayon with fist.	Identifies three to six body parts. Matches sounds to animals. Understands personal pronouns, some action verbs, and some adjectives. Enjoys nursery rhymes.	Uses intelligible words about 65% of the time. May use jargon (syllable strings that sound like speech). Tells experience using jargon and words. Uses two-word sentences. Names two or three pictures. Attempts to sing songs with words. Imitates three- to four-word phrase.	Finds object not observed being hidden. Activates mechanical toy. Matches objects to pictures. Sorts objects. Explores cabinets and drawers. Remembers where objects belong. Recognizes self in photo.	Scoops food, feeds self with spoon. Chews with rotary jaw movements. Plays with food. Removes shoe when laces undone. Zips/unzips large zipper. Shows awareness of need to eliminate.	Expresses affection. Expresses wide range of emotions including jealously, fear, anger, sympathy, embarrassment, anxiety, and joy. Attempts to control others; resists control: somewhat Aggressive. Engages in parallel play. Enjoys solitary play occasionally.

24–36 Months	Runs forward well. Jumps in place, two feet together. Stands on one foot, with aid. Walks on tiptoe. Kicks ball forward.	Strings four large beads. Turns pages singly. Snips with scissors. Holds crayon with thumb and fingers, not fist. Uses one hand consistently in most activities. Paints with some wrist action; makes dots, lines, circular strokes. Rolls, pounds, squeezes, and pulls clay.	Points to pictures of common objects when they are named. Can identify objects when told their use. Understands question forms *what* and *where*. Understands negative *no, not, can't,* and *don't*. Enjoys listening to simple storybooks and requests them again.	Joins vocabulary words together in two-word phrases. Gives first and last name. Asks *what* and *where* questions. Makes negative statements (e.g., "Can't open it"). Shows frustration at not being understood. Sustains conversation for two or three turns.	Selects and looks at picture books, names pictured objects, and identifies several objects within one picture. Matches and uses associated objects meaningfully (e.g., given cup, saucer, and head, puts cup and saucer together). Stacks rings on peg in order of size. Uses self and objects in pretend play.	Can talk briefly about what he or she is doing. Imitates adult actions (e.g., housekeeping play). Has limited attention span; learning is through exploration and adult direction (as in reading of picture stories). Is beginning to understand functional concepts of familiar objects (e.g., that a spoon is used for eating) and part/whole concepts (e.g., parts of the body).	Gets drink from fountain or faucet unassisted. Open door by turning handle. Takes off coat. Puts on coat with assistance. Washes and dries hands with assistance.	Watches other children; joins briefly in their play. Defends own possessions. Begins to play house. Participates in simple group activity (e.g., sings, claps, dances). Knows gender identity.
36–48 Months	Runs around obstacles. Walks on a line. Balances on one foot for 5 to 10 seconds. Hops on one foot. Pushes, pulls, steers wheeled toys. Rides (i.e., steers and pedals) tricycle. Uses slide without assistance. Jumps over 15 cm (6 in.) high object, landing on both feet together. Throws ball over head. Catches ball bounced to him or her.	Builds tower of nine small blocks. Drives nails and pegs. Copies circle, Imitates cross. Manipulates clay materials (e.g., rolls balls, snakes, cookies).	Begins to understand sentences involving time concepts (e.g., "We are going to the zoo tomorrow"). Understands size comparatives such as *big* and *bigger.* Understands relationships expressed by *if . . . then* or *because* sentences. Carries out a series of two to four related directions. Understands when told, "Let's pretend."	Talks in sentences of three or more words, which take the form agent-action-object ("I see the ball") or agent action-location ("Daddy sit on chair"). Tells about past experiences. Uses *-s* on nouns to indicate plurals. Uses *-ed* on verbs to include past tense. Refers to self using pronouns *I* or *me.* Repeats at least one nursery rhyme and can sing a song. Speech is understandable to strangers, but there are still some sound errors.	Recognizes and matches six colors. Intentionally stacks blocks or rings in order of size. Draws somewhat recognizable picture that is meaningful to child, if not to adult; names and briefly explains picture. Asks questions for information: *why* and *how* questions requiring simple answers. Knows own age. Knows own last name.	Has short attention span; learns through observing and imitating adults, and by adult instruction and explanation; is easily distracted. Has increased understanding of concepts of the functions and grouping of objects (e.g., can put doll house furniture in correct rooms); part/whole (e.g.,) can identify pictures of hand and foot as parts of body). Begins to be aware of past and present (e.g., "Yesterday we went to the park. today we go to the library.").	Pours well from small pitcher. Spreads soft butter with knife. Buttons and unbuttons large buttons. Washes hands unsassisted. Blows nose when reminded. Uses toilet independently.	Joins in play with other children: begins to interact. Shares toys; takes turns with assistance. Begins dramatic play acting out whole scenes (for example, scenes) (for example, house, pretending to be animals). Comforts peers in distress.

(*continued*)

	Gross-Motor Skills	Fine-Motor Skills	Language Comprehension	Expressive Communication	Cognitive Skills		Self-Help Skills	Social Skills
48–60 Months	Walks backward toe-heel. Jumps forward 10 times without falling. Walks up and down stairs alone, alternating feet. Turns somersault.	Cuts on line continuously. Copies cross. Copies square. Prints a few capital letters.	Follows three unrelated commands in proper order. Understands comparatives such as *pretty, prettier,* and *prettiest*. Listens to long stories, but often misinterprets the facts. Incorporates verbal directions into play activities. Understands sequencing of events when told them (e.g., "First we have to go to the store, then we can make the cake, and tomorrow we will eat it").	Asks *when, how,* and *why* questions. Uses modals such as *can, will, shall, should,* and *might*. Joins sentences together (e.g,. "I went to the store and I bought some ice cream"). Talks about causality by using *because* and *so*. Tells the content of a story but may confuse facts.	Points to and names four to six colors. Matches pictures of familiar objects (e.g., show, sock, foot, apple, orange, banana). Draws a person with two to six recognizable parts, such as head, arms, legs; can name or match drawn parts to own body. Draws, names, and describes recognizable picture. Rote counts to 5. imitating adults. Describes what will happen next. Dramatic play is closer to reality: with attention paid to detail, time, and space.	Knows own street and town. Has more extended attention span; learns through observing and listening to adults as well as through exploration; is easily distracted. Has increased understanding of concepts of function, time, part/whole relationships. Function or use of objects may be stated in addition to names of objects. Time concepts are expanding. The child can talk about yesterday or last week (a long time ago), about today, and about what will happen tomorrow.	Cuts easy foods with a knife (e.g., hamburger patty, tomato slice). Laces shoes.	Plays and interacts with other children. Plays dress-up. Shows interest in exploring gender differences.
60–72 Months	Runs lightly on toes. Walks on balance beam. Can cover 2 meters (6.5 feet) hopping. Skips on alternate feet. Jumps rope. Skates.	Cuts out simple shapes. Copies triangle. Traces diamond. Copies first name. Prints numerals 1 to 5. Colors within lines. Has adult grasp of pencil. Has handedness well established (i.e., child is left- or right-handed). Pastes and glues appropriately. Uses classroom tools appropriately.	Demonstrates preacademic skills.	There are few obvious differences between child's grammar and adult's grammar. Still needs to learn such things as subject-verb agreement and some irregular past-tense verbs. Can take appropriate turns in a conversion. Gives and receives information. Communicates well with family, friends or strangers. Retells story from picture book with accuracy.	Names some letters and numerals. Rote counts to 10. Sorts objects by single character-isitics (e.g., by color, shape, or size—if the difference is obvious). Is beginning to use accurately time concepts of *tomorrow* and *yesterday*.	Begins to relate check time to daily. schedule. Attention span increases noticeably; learns through adult instruction; when interested. can ignore distractions. Concepts of function increase as well as understanding of why things happen; time concepts are expanding into an understanding of the future in terms of major events (e.g., "Christmas will come after two weekends").	Dresses self completely. Ties shoes. Brushes teeth unassisted. Crosses street safely.	Chooses own friend(s). Plays simple table games. Plays competitive games. Engages in cooperative play with other children involving group decisions, role assignments, fair play.

APPENDIX C

Selected Early Childhood Tests to Consider for Use in Educational and Child-Care Settings

Brief descriptive information useful for teachers on a variety of tests designed for young children follows. All tests are individually administered except for those followed by an asterisk (*), which indicates that group administration is possible. The tests are grouped in 10 categories:

1. School Readiness and Screening Tests
2. Diagnostic Tests of Development, Ability, and Aptitude
3. Tests of Academic Achievement
4. Tests of Achievement in Language
5. Tests of Achievement in Reading
6. Tests of Achievement in Spelling
7. Tests of Achievement in Mathematics
8. Tests to Identify Giftedness
9. Tests of Perceptual and/or Motor Skills
10. Tests of Behavior and Conduct

1. School Readiness and Screening Tests

Name: Ages and Stages Questionnaires 3rd Edition^{TM} (ASQ-3)
Author(s): Bricker, D., et al.
Publisher: Paul H. Brookes
Copyright Date: 2007
Age Range: 4 months to 4 years
Purpose: A parent-completed questionnaire used to identify children at risk for developmental delays and to monitor the child's progress at four- to six-month intervals. Records child's abilities in five areas: gross-motor, fine-motor, communication, personal–social, and problem-solving. Also available in Spanish.
Approximate Testing Time: 10 minutes
Type(s) of Response: Rater

Name: Boehm Test of Basic Concepts–Revised (BTBC–3)*
Author(s): Boehm, A.
Publisher: Psychological Corporation
Copyright Date: 2001
Age Range: 3 to 5 and kindergarten to second grade
Purpose: Measures children's mastery of the concepts considered necessary for achievement in the first years of school. Concepts tested include those of space (location, direction, orientation, and dimension), time, and quantity (number).
Approximate Testing Time: 15–30 minutes
Type(s) of Response: Nonverbal (pencil and booklet)

Name: Bracken School Readiness Assessment: BSRA
Author(s): Bracken, B. A.
Publisher: PsychCorp
Copyright Date: 2002
Age Range: 2 to 7 years
Purpose: To help determine if a child may have an underlying language disorder that requires further evaluation.
Approximate Testing Time: 10 to 15 minutes
Type(s) of Response: Verbal

Name: Brigance Infant and Toddler Screens
Author(s): Brigance, A. H. & Glascoe, F. P.
Publisher: Curriculum Associates
Copyright Date: 2002
Age Range: birth–21 months
Purpose: Assesses infant and toddler developmental skills and observes caregivers' involvement and interactions.
Approximate Testing Time: 10–12 minutes
Type(s) of Response: Verbal and nonverbal

Name: Brigance Early Preschool Screen II
Author(s): Brigance, A. H.
Publisher: Curriculum Associates
Copyright Date: 2005
Age Range: 2–5 years and 11 months
Purpose: Assesses children's skills in developmental areas.
Approximate Testing Time: 10–15 minutes
Type(s) of Response: Verbal and nonverbal

Name: Brigance K and 1 Screen II
Author(s): Brigance, A. H.
Publisher: Curriculum Associates
Copyright Date: 2005
Age Range: 2–5 years and 11 months
Purpose: Indicates developmental problems-language, learning or cognitive delays. Identifies children who are talented or gifted. Also assists teachers with program planning.
Approximate Testing Time: 10–15 minutes
Type(s) of Response: Verbal and nonverbal

Name: Child Development Inventory (CDI)
Author(s): Ireton, H.
Publisher: American Guidance Service
Copyright Date: 2004
Age Range: 15 months–6 years
Purpose: Measures a young child's present development according to the parent's report. Includes eight scales: Social Development, Self Help, Gross Motor, Fine Motor, Expressive Language, Language Comprehension, Letters, and Numbers. Also a 30-item problems checklist. Profiles child's development, strengths, and problems.
Approximate Testing Time: 45 minutes
Type(s) of Response: Verbal, nonverbal, rater

Name: Developmental Indicators for the Assessment of Learning–Revised (DIAL–3)
Author(s): Mardell-Czudnowski, C., & Goldenberg, D.
Publisher: American Guidance Service
Copyright Date: 1998
Age Range: 2–0 to 5–11
Purpose: Designed to identify children with potential learning problems or potential giftedness. Areas measured include motor, concepts, self-help, social development, and language. Although this test is administered individually, it is designed to handle screening of large numbers of children with different examiners administering each of the three areas.
Approximate Testing Time: 20–30 minutes
Type(s) of Response: Verbal, nonverbal

Name: Early Screening Inventory–Revised (ESI-R)
Author(s): Meisels, S., & Wiske, M.
Publisher: Pearson Assessments
Copyright Date: 2008
Purpose: Identifies children who are at-risk in the areas defined by IDEA (Individuals with Disabilities Education Act). Domains include cognition, communication, and motor. An optional social-emotional scale and adaptive behavior checklist are also available.
Approximate Testing Time: 15 minutes
Type(s) of Response: Verbal, nonverbal, rater

Name: Learing Accomplishment Profile Kindergarten Screen—3rd Edition (LAP-3)
Author(s): Chapel Hill Training Outreach Project
Publisher: Kaplan School Supply
Copyright Date: 2003
Age Range: 36 months to 72 months
Purpose: Provides a measure of skills in the areas of fine motor-writing and manipulation, language comprehension and naming, gross motor, and cognitive.
Approximate Testing Time: 15 minutes
Type(s) of Response: Verbal and nonverbal

Name: Miller Assessment for Preschoolers (MAP)
Author(s): Miller L. J.
Publisher: Western Psychological
Copyright Date: 2002
Age Range: 2.9–5.8
Purpose: evaluates young children for mild to moderate developmental delays.
Approximate Testing Time: 30–40 minutes
Type(s) of Response: Verbal and nonverbal

Name: Parents' Observations of Infants and Toddlers (POINT)
Author(s): Mardell, C. D. & Goldenberg, D.
Publisher: Master Publishing Corp.
Copyright Date: 2006
Age Range: 2.0 months to 36 months
Approximate Testing Time: 15–20 minutes
Type of Response: Observation of infant/toddler by parents or caregivers

(*continued*)

Name: Pervasive Developmental Disorders Screening Test-II (PDDST-II)
Author(s): Siegel, B.
Publisher: PsychCorp
Copyright Date: 2004
Age Range: 18 months and up
Purpose: Designed to detect autism at an early age.
Approximate Testing Time: 10–20 minutes
Type(s) of Response: Verbal

Name: School Readiness Test Revised (SRT)*
Author(s): Anderhalter, O., & Perney, J.
Publisher: Scholastic Testing Service
Copyright Date: 2005
Age Range: End of kindergarten to first three weeks of first grade
Purpose: A tool for evaluating a child's readiness for first grade. The eight subtests are administered over several sessions and include vocabulary, identifying letters, visual discrimination, auditory discrimination, comprehension and interpretation, number knowledge, handwriting ability, and developmental spelling ability.
Approximate Testing Time: 90 minutes
Type(s) of Response: Nonverbal (pencil and booklet)

Name: Wide Range Achievement (Test-4)
Author(s): Robertson, G. J.
Publisher: Psychological Assessment Resources, Inc.,
Copyright Date: 2006
Age Range: 5 years and up
Purpose: Designed to comprehensively assess reading comprehension, mathematics, nonverbal reasoning.
Approximate Testing Time: 15 minutes
Type(s) of Response: Written

2. Diagnostic Tests of Development, Ability, and Aptitude

Name: Bayley Scales of Infant and Toddler Development, 3rd Edition (Bayley-III)
Author(s): Bayley, Nancy
Publisher: The Psychological Corporation
Copyright Date: 2005
Age Range: 1–42 months
Purpose: Examine all of the facets of a young child's development.
Approximate Testing Time: 30–90 minutes, depending on the age of the child
Types of Response: Rater

Name: Batelle Developmental Inventory 2nd ed. (BDI)
Author(s): Jean Newborg & Batelle Memorial Institute
Publisher: Thomson Nelson
Copyright Date: 2005
Age Range: Birth to 0–8
Purpose: A measure of basic developmental skills in five domains: personal–social, adaptive, motor, communication, and cognitive. Information is gained by means of observations of the child in a natural setting, parent interview, and a structured test format. Developed for planning and designing educational programs and for program evaluation. A 10–30 minute screening component is also available.
Approximate Testing Time: Varies
Type(s) of Response: Verbal, nonverbal, rater

Name: Bracken Basic Concept Scale—3rd Ed
Author(s): Bracken, B.
Publisher: Psychological Corporation
Copyright Date: 2006
Age Range: 2–6 to 8–0
Purpose: Measures knowledge of general concepts usually acquired during preschool and early school years. Subtests include colors, letter identification, numbers and counting, comparisons, shapes, direction/position, social/emotional, size, texture/material, quantity, and time/sequence.
Approximate Testing Time: 20–30 minutes
Type(s) of Response: Nonverbal

Name: Brigance Diagnostic Inventory of Early Development II (IED-II)
Author(s): Brigance, A.
Publisher: Curriculum Associates
Copyright Date: 2004
Age Range: Early Development, birth to 7; Basic Skills, kindergarten to sixth grade
Purpose: This easel format, criterion-referenced inventories are part of a three-part series that provides information on mastered and unmastered skills, concepts, and behavior. This information can be used to determine strengths and weaknesses and to plan instruction.
Approximate Testing Time: Not reported (test is untimed)
Type(s) of Response: Verbal and nonverbal

Name: Brigance Diagnostic Comprehensive Inventory of Basic Skills—Revised (CIBS-R)
Author: Brigance, A. H.
Publisher: Curriculum Associates
Copyright Date: 2009
Age Range: PK–9
Purpose: Identify performance levels, set instructional goals, report progress on basic skills. Norm options. Available in Spanish.
Approximate Testing Time: Varies by age and items presented
Type of Response: Written and verbal

Name: Child Observation Record Revised (COR)
Author(s): Publisher
Publisher: High/Scope Educational Research Foundation
Copyright Date: 2003
Age Range: 2½ to 6
Purpose: Measures a young child's developmental status using teacher observations throughout the year. The teacher makes note of child behavior in six domains: initiative, social relations, creative representation, music and movement, language and literacy, and logic and mathematics. The information gained from on-going administration of the COR is useful for evaluating programs, monitoring progress, and planning developmentally appropriate experiences for each child. Initial training is recommended.
Approximate Testing Time: Varies (on-going process)
Type(s) of Response: Rater

Name: Cognitive Abilities Test (CogAT)*
Author(s): Lohman, D. & Hagen, E.
Publisher: Riverside Publishing
Copyright Date: 2002
Age Range: Grades K–12
Purpose: Designed to assess students' abilities in reasoning and problem-solving using verbal, quantitative, and spatial (nonverbal) symbols.
Approximate Testing Time: 120–170 minutes
Types of Response: Written

Name: Draw-A-Person Intellectual Ability Test for Children, Adolescents, and Adults (DAP:IQ)
Author(s): Reynolds C. R., and Hickman J. A.,
Publisher: Pro-Ed
Copyright Date: 2004
Age Range: 4–0 through 89–11
Purpose: Measures cognitive ability by scoring elements representative of universal features of the human figure.
Approximate Testing Time: 10–12 minutes
Type(s) of Response: Nonverbal (drawing)

Name: Early Learning Accomplishment Profile-Revised (E-LAP)
Author(s): Glover, M., et al.
Publisher: Kaplan School Supply
Copyright Date: 2001
Age Range: Birth to 36 months
Purpose: A criterion-referenced measure of gross- and fine-motor, cognitive, language, self-help, and social/emotional development.
Approximate Testing Time: Varies
Type(s) of Response: Verbal, nonverbal, rater

(continued)

Name: Learning Accomplishment Profile Diagnostic Assessment Kit (LAP–D Screens)
Author(s): Sanford, A., et al.
Publisher: Kaplan School Supply
Copyright Date: 2007
Age Range: 2–6 to 6–0
Purpose: Originally a criterion-referenced test, the LAP–D is now norm-referenced. It provides assessment in five areas of development: motor, social, self-help, language, and cognition.
Approximate Testing Time: 45 minutes
Type(s) of Response: Verbal, nonverbal, and rater (parent)

Name: Process Assessment of the Learner: Test Battery for Reading and Writing (PAL)
Author(s): Berninger, W. W.
Publisher: Psych Corp
Copyright Date: 2001
Age Range: 4–11 years
Purpose: Provides an individual assessment of the reading and writing skills of students from kindergarten through grade 6.
Approximate Testing Time: 30–60 minutes
Type(s) of Response: Writing

Name: Partners in Play: Assessing Infant and Toddlers in Natural Contexts (PIP)
Author(s): Ensher, G., Bobish, T., Garndern, E., Reinson, C., Bryden, D., & Foertsch, D.
Publisher: Thomson Delmar Learning
Copyright Date: 2007
Age Range: 1–36 months
Purpose: Designed for the identification and follow-up of infants and toddlers who might be eligible for early intervention services.
Approximate Testing Time: Varies
Types of Response: Caregiver interviews and ratings

3. Tests of Academic Achievement

Name: Aprenda: La prueba de logros en espanol 3rd ed.*
Author(s): Publisher
Publisher: Psychological Corporation
Copyright Date: 2006
Age Range: Kindergarten to 8th grade
Purpose: A norm-referenced test of achievement for Spanish-speaking students. This is not a translation of an English language test, rather it was specifically developed for the Spanish-speaking population. Subtests include sounds and letters, word reading, sentence reading, listening to words and stories, and mathematics.
Approximate Testing Time: 2 hours 25 minutes for kindergarten, ranging to 4 hours 45 minutes at higher levels
Type(s) of Response: Nonverbal (pencil and booklet)

Name: Communication and Symbolic Behavior Scales Developmental Profile: First Normed Edition (CSBS DP)
Author(s): Wetherby. A. & Prizant, B.
Publisher: Brookes Publishing Co.
Copyright Date: 2002
Age Range: 6–24 Months
Purpose: Designed to 'evaluate communication and symbolic abilities of children whose functional communication is between 6 months and 2 years.
Approximate Testing Time: 5–30 minutes
Types of Response: Infant-Toddler Checklist, Caregiver Questionnaire, Behavior Sample

Name: California Achievement Tests—6th Edition (CAT–6)*
Author(s): Publisher
Publisher: CTB/McGraw-Hill
Copyright Date: 2002
Age Range: Kindergarten to 12th grade
Purpose: A set of norm-referenced tests that assess mastery of instructional objectives. Content areas include reading, spelling, language, mathematics, study skills, science and social studies. Braille and large print editions are available.
Approximate Testing Time: 1 hour 30 minutes for kindergarten, ranging to 5 hours 30 minutes at higher levels
Type(s) of Response: Nonverbal (pencil and booklet)

Name: Child Observation Record for Infants and Toddlers
Author(s): High Scope
Publisher: High Scope
Copyright Date: 2003
Age Range: 6 weeks to 3 years
Purpose: Assesses broad areas of child development
Approximate Testing Time: Checklist for teacher completion
Type(s) of Response: Electronic versions available

Name: Diagnostic Achievement Battery—3rd Edition (DAB–3)*
Author(s): Newcomer, P.
Publisher: Pro-Ed
Copyright Date: 2001
Age Range: 6–14
Purpose: Assesses performance in listening, speaking, reading, writing, and mathematics.
Approximate Testing Time: 40–50 minutes
Type(s) of Response: Verbal and nonverbal

Name: Diagnostic Screening Test: Achievement—3rd Edition (DSTA)*
Author(s): Gnagey, T., & Gnagey, P.
Publisher: Slosson Educational Publications
Copyright Date: 2002
Age Range: Kindergarten to 12th grade
Purpose: Provides a measure of achievement in science, social studies, literature, and the arts, plus a total achievement score and an estimated mental age.
Approximate Testing Time: 5–10 minutes
Type(s) of Response: Nonverbal (pencil & booklet)

Name: Iowa Tests of Basic Skills (ITBS)*
Author(s): Hieronymus, A., et al.
Publisher: Riverside
Copyright Date: 2003
Age Range: Kindergarten to 9th grade
Purpose: A criterion- and norm-referenced set of tests which measure overall functioning rather than specific content. The tests can provide a continuous measure of the development of fundamental skills necessary for school and life success.
Approximate Testing Time: 125–150 minutes
Type(s) of Response: Nonverbal (pencil and booklet)

Name: Kaufman Test of Educational Achievement—2nd ed. (KTEAII)
Author(s): Kaufman, A., & Kaufman, N.
Publisher: American Guidance Service
Copyright Date: 2004
Age Range: 1st to 12th grade
Purpose: A norm-referenced, easel format test of multiple skills. The KTEA contains both a Brief and Comprehensive Form. Either can be used for program planning and placement decisions. Additionally, the Brief Form is useful for screening, and the Comprehensive Form for identifying strengths and weaknesses.
Approximate Testing Time: Brief Form, 10–35 minutes; Comprehensive, 20–75 minutes
Type(s) of Response: Verbal and nonverbal

(*continued*)

Name: Monitoring Basic Skills Progress—2nd ed. (MBSP)
Author(s): Fuchs, L., et al.
Publisher: Pro-Ed
Copyright Date: 1998
Age Range: 1st to 6th grade
Purpose: A computer-assisted measurement program that both tests and monitors progress in reading, math, and spelling. Students are tested at the computer, each time with a different test form. Results are computer-plotted graphically over time so that teachers can easily monitor progress. The program also reports a performance analysis and remedial program recommendations.
Approximate Testing Time: Varies
Type(s) of Response: Nonverbal (keyboard)

Name: The Ounce Scale
Author(s): Meisels S. J., Marsden D. B., Dombro A. L., Weston D. R., & Jewkes A. M.
Publisher: Pearson Early Learning Group
Copyright Date: 2004
Age Range: birth to 3 1/2 years
Purpose: Provides information about infants' and young children's development
Approximate Testing Time: Varies
Type(s) of Response: Visual

Name: Stanford Achievement Test, 10th Ed. (SESAT)*
Author(s): Publisher
Publisher: Harcourt Assessment, Inc.
Copyright Date: 2003
Age Range: Grades K–12
Purpose: Measures student achievement in reading, language, spelling, study skills, listening, mathematics, science, and social studies.
Approximate Testing Time: 105–295 minutes
Types of Response: Written

Name: Test of Memory and Learning: Second Edition (TOMAL-2)
Author(s): Reynolds, C. R., & Bigler, E. D.
Publisher: AGS Publishing
Copyright Date: 2004
Age Range: 5–19 years
Purpose: Allows the assessment of strengths and weakness in a child's memory as well as potentially pathologic indicators of memory disturbances.
Approximate Testing Time: 45 minutes
Type(s) of Response: Verbal

Name: Wechsler Individual Achievement Test—2nd ed. (WIAT-II)
Author(s): Publisher
Publisher: Psychological Corporation
Copyright Date: 2001
Age Range: 5–19
Purpose: A comprehensive battery for measuring academic difficulties. Measures eight areas: basic reading, mathematics reasoning, spelling, reading comprehension, numerical operations, listening comprehension, oral expression, and written expression. A shorter screening battery can also be given.
Approximate Testing Time: Comprehensive Batter, 30–50 minutes for young children; Screener, 10–18 minutes
Type(s) of Response: Verbal and nonverbal

Name: Work Sampling for Head Start
Author(s): Meisels S. J., Marsden D. B., Dichtelmiller M. L., Dorfman A. B. and Jablon J. R.
Publisher: Pearson Early Learning Group
Copyright Date: 2005
Age Range: P3–P4
Purpose: Assessment that tracks progress and improves learning.
Approximate Testing Time: Varies
Type(s) of Response: Visual

Name: Work Sampling System
Author(s): Meisels, Jablon, et al.
Publisher: Author
Copyright Date: 2003
Age Range: Preschool through grade 5
Purpose: An on-going evaluation process designed as an alternative to standardized achievement tests. The System is composed of three elements: developmental checklists, portfolios, and summary reports, which are all intended to be classroom-focused and relevant to instruction.
Approximate Testing Time: Varies (on-going process)
Type(s) of Response: Verbal, nonverbal, rater

4. Tests of Achievement in Language

Name: Clinical Evaluation of Language Fundamentals, Fourth Edition: CELF-4
Author(s): Semel, E., Wiig, E. H., Secord, W.A.
Publisher: Psych Corp
Copyright Date: 2003
Age Range: 5–21 years
Purpose: Provides the bridge that helps you understand a child's need for classroom language adaptations, enhancements, or curriculum accommodations.
Approximate Testing Time: 30–60 minutes
Type(s) of Response: Verbal

Name: Clinical Evaluation of Language Fundamentals–Preschool–2 (CELF–Preschool)
Author(s): Wiig, E., et al.
Publisher: Psychological Corporation
Copyright Date: 2004
Age Range: 3–6
Purpose: Assesses a wide range of expressive and receptive language skills: basic concepts, sentence structure, word structure, formulating labels, recalling sentences in context, and linguistic concepts.
Approximate Testing Time: 30–45 minutes
Type(s) of Response: Verbal and nonverbal

Name: Comprehensive Assessment of Spoken Language: CASL
Author(s): Carrow-Woolfolk, E.
Publisher: AGS Publishing
Copyright Date: 1999
Age Range: 3 years and up
Purpose: CASL is comprised of 15 tests that measure language processing skills, comprehension, expression, retrieval, etc., in four language structure categories: lexical, syntactic, supralinguistic, and pragmatic.
Approximate Testing Time: 30–45 minutes
Type(s) of Response: Verbal

Name: Comprehensive Receptive and Expressive Vocabulary Test—2nd ed. (CREVT-2)
Author(s): Wallace, G., & Hammill, D.
Publisher: Pro-Ed
Copyright Date: 2002
Age Range: 4–17
Purpose: Used to identify students with difficulties, define strengths and weaknesses, and measure progress. The CREVT measures two skills: receptive language, for which the student points to the correct picture for the word spoken by the examiner, and expressive language, for which the student defines the word spoken.
Approximate Testing Time: 20–30 minutes
Type(s) of Response: Verbal and nonverbal

Name: Diagnostic Evaluation of Language Variation—Norm-Referenced (DELV-Norm-Referenced)
Author(s): Seymour, H. N., Roeper, T. W., & de Villiers, J.
Publisher: PsychCorp
Copyright Date: 2005
Age Range: 4–12 years
Purpose: Used to accurately diagnose child's speech and language disorder.
Approximate Testing Time: 45–50 minutes
Type(s) of Response: Written, Verbal

(continued)

Name: Expressive One-Word Picture Vocabulary Test– 2000 Edition (EOWPVT)
Author(s): Gardner, M.
Publisher: Academic Therapy Publications
Copyright Date: 2000
Age Range: 2–0 to 11–11
Purpose: Provides a measure of a child's expressive vocabulary through the presentation of picture cards. The test can be used to appraise definitional and interpretational skills, estimate fluency in English, and indicate possible speech or language difficulties.
Approximate Testing Time: 5–10 minutes
Type(s) of Response: Verbal

Name: Expressive Vocabulary Test: EVT 2nd Ed
Author(s): Williams, K. T.
Publisher: AGS Publishing
Copyright Date: 2007
Age Range: 2–6 years
Purpose: EVT is an individually administered, norm referenced test of expressive vocabulary and word retrieval.
Approximate Testing Time: 15 minutes
Type(s) of Response: Visual and Verbal

Name: Expressive One-Word Picture Vocabulary Test-Spanish Billingual Edition (EOWPVT-SBE)
Author(s): Brownell, R.
Publisher: Harcourt
Copyright Date: 2000
Age Range: 2–18 years
Purpose: Assesses how a person processes language and other elements of verbal expression.
Approximate Testing Time: 10–15 minutes
Type(s) of Response: Verbal

Name: Goldman-Fristoe-Woodcock Test of Auditory Discrimination 2 (G-F-WTAD)
Author(s): Goldman, R., Fristoe, M., & Woodcock, R.
Publisher: American Guidance Service
Copyright Date: 2007
Age Range: 3–8 to adult
Purpose: Evaluates an individual's ability to discriminate among speech sounds in both quiet and noisy backgrounds. Words are presented on cassette.
Approximate Testing Time: 15 minutes
Type(s) of Response: Nonverbal

Name: Illinois Test of Psycholinguistic Abilities—3rd ed. (ITPA-3)
Author(s): Hammill, D. Mather, N., and Roberts, R.
Publisher: Pro-Ed
Copyright Date: 2001
Age Range: 2–4 to 10–3
Purpose: Assesses both verbal and nonverbal psycholinguistic ability. The "representation level" tests skills with language symbols, and the "automatic level" assesses skills in retention and retrieval of language.
Approximate Testing Time: 1 hour
Type(s) of Response: Verbal and nonverbal

Name: Kaufman Survey of Early Academic and Language Skills (K-SEALS)
Author(s): Kaufman, A., & Kaufman, N.
Publisher: American Guidance Service
Copyright Date: 2007
Age Range: 3–6
Purpose: A norm-reference measure of children's language (expressive and receptive), articulation, and pre-academic skills with numbers, letters, and words.
Approximate Testing Time: 15–25 minutes
Type(s) of Response: Verbal and nonverbal

Name: Peabody Picture Vocabulary Test—4th ed. (PPVT4)
Author(s): Dunn, L., & Dunn, L.
Publisher: American Guidance Service
Copyright Date: 2007
Age Range: 2–6 to 40
Purpose: An easel format, receptive vocabulary test intended to measure verbal ability and scholastic aptitude. A suitable test for students with reading or writing difficulties or those who are severely physically impaired since any method of indicating "yes" or "no" is an acceptable response.
Approximate Testing Time: 10–15 minutes
Type(s) of Response: Verbal and nonverbal

Name: Pre-LAS (Language Assessment Scales)
Author(s): Duncan, S., & DeAvila, F.
Publisher: CTB/McGraw-Hill
Copyright Date: 2000
Age Range: Preschool to 1st grade
Purpose: Assesses the oral language proficiency of children in three areas: morphology, syntax, and semantics. There are two separate tests, English and Spanish. Useful for identifying limited or non-English speaking students.
Approximate Testing Time: 10 minutes
Type(s) of Response: Verbal and nonverbal

Name: Language Assessment Skills Links Benchmark Assessment (LAS)
Author(s): Publisher
Publisher: CTB/MCGraw-Hill
Copyright Date: 2005
Age Range: Grades K–12
Purpose: Designed to measure students (English language learners) skills in speaking, listening, reading, and writing.
Approximate Testing Time: Untimed
Types of Response: Verbal and nonverbal

Name: Preschool Language Scale–4 (PLS–4)
Author(s): Zimmerman, I., et al.
Publisher: Psychological Corporation
Copyright Date: 2002
Age Range: Birth–6
Purpose: A norm-referenced test of pre-language skills (attention, vocal development, social communication), and receptive and expressive skills (semantics, structure, and integrative thinking skills). Uses play-like test activities. Spanish edition available.
Approximate Testing Time: 20–30 minutes
Type(s) of Response: Verbal and nonverbal

Name: Receptive-Expressive Emergent Language Test 3rd ed. (REEL–3)
Author(s): Bzoch, K., & League, R.
Publisher: Pro-Ed
Copyright Date: 2003
Age Range: Birth–3
Purpose: Measures children's language development in the first three years of life. The test covers areas of receptive, expressive, and inner language through an interview with a parent or other caregiver. The REEL–2 is useful for developing interventions for at-risk infants and toddlers.
Approximate Testing Time: 30–40 minutes
Type(s) of Response: Rater

Name: Receptive One-Word Picture Vocabulary Test, 2000 Edition (ROWPVT)
Author(s): Brownel. R
Publisher: Academic Therapy Publications
Copyright Date: 2000
Age Range: 2–0 to 11–11
Purpose: Designed as a companion test to the EOWPVT, this test assesses receptive language skills and is especially useful for bilingual, speech-impaired, immature and withdrawn, and emotionally or physically impaired children.
Approximate Testing Time: 20 minutes
Type(s) of Response: Nonverbal

(continued)

Name: Test of Early Language Development–3rd Edition (TELD–3)
Author(s): Hresko, W., et al.
Publisher: Pro-Ed
Copyright Date: 1999
Age Range: 2–0 to 7–11
Purpose: Provides an overall score of language proficiency as well as a diagnostic profile of a child's language skills in both reception and expression.
Approximate Testing Time: 20 minutes
Type(s) of Response: Verbal and nonverbal

Name: Test of Language Development–Primary, 4th Edition (TOLD–P4 2008)
Author(s): Newcomer, P., & Hammill, D.
Publisher: Pro-Ed
Copyright Date: 1997
Age Range: 4–0 to 8–11
Purpose: Designed to identify and isolate disorders through testing the basic linguistic skills of listening, speaking, semantics, syntax, and phonology.
Approximate Testing Time: 30–60 minutes
Type(s) of Response: Verbal and nonverbal

Name: Test of Narrative Language (TNL)
Author(s): Gillam R. B. & Pearson N. A.
Publisher: Pro-Ed
Copyright Date: 2004
Age Range: 5–0 through 11–11
Purpose: Assesses how well children use their knowledge of the components of language while they engage in functional discourse
Approximate Testing Time: 15–20 minutes
Type(s) of Response: Verbal

Name: Test of Phonological Awareness, 2nd Edition Plus (TOPA)*
Author(s): Torgesen, J., & Bryant, B.
Publisher: Pro-Ed
Copyright Date: 2004
Age Range: Kindergarten to 2nd grade
Purpose: Provides a measure of a child's ability to hear individual sounds in words. Since this ability is related to ease in learning to read, this test can be used to identify children in kindergarten who may benefit from specialized instruction to prepare them for reading. One test is available for kindergarten and another for 1st and 2nd grade.
Approximate Testing Time: 20 minutes
Type(s) of Response: Nonverbal

5. Tests of Achievement in Reading

Name: The Classroom Reading Inventory—10th ed.
Author(s): Silvaroli, N., Wheelock, W.
Publisher: McGraw-Hill
Copyright Date: 2004
Purpose: An informal reading inventory test to help identify students' reading problems.
Approximate Testing Time: Varies
Type of Response: Verbal

Name: Comprehensive Test of Phonological Processing (CTOPP)
Author(s): Wagner R., Torgeson J. and Rashotte C.
Publisher: Pro-Ed
Copyright Date: 1999
Age Range: 5–0 and 24–11
Purpose: Assesses phonological awareness, phonological memory and rapid naming.
Approximate Testing Time: 30 minutes
Type(s) of Response: Nonverbal

Name: Comprehensive Assessment of Reading Strategies (CARS Series)
Author(s): Adcock, D.
Publisher: Curriculum Associates
Copyright Date: 2006
Age Range: Grades 1–8
Purpose: Diagnoses students' strength and weaknesses. Builds and reinforces reading skills.
Approximate Testing Time: Varies
Type(s) of Response: Nonverbal

Name: Dynamic Indicators of Basic Early Literacy Skills (DIBELS)
Author(s): Good, R., Kaminski, R.
Publisher: University of Oregon
Copyright Date: 2005
Age Range: 4–11 years
Purpose: DIBELS is designed to be short (one-minute) fluency measures—sound, letter naming, phoneme segmentation, nonsense word, oral reading fluency, word use—used to regularly monitor the development of pre-reading and early reading skills.
Approximate Testing Time: 5–10 minutes
Type(s) of Response: Written or verbal

Name: Early Reading Diagnostic Assessment—2nd Edition (ERDA Second Edition)
Author(s): Psych Corp
Publisher: PsychCorp
Copyright Date: 2003
Age Range: 4–8 years
Purpose: Administered to identify young children at risk for reading difficulty or failure.
Approximate Testing Time: 45–60 minutes
Type(s) of Response: Visual, Verbal

Name: Early Reading Success Indicator: ERSI
Author(s): Psych Corp
Publisher: PsychCorp
Copyright Date: 2004
Age Range: 5–10 years
Purpose: Helps to prevent reading failure and enriches the WISC-IV tests.
Approximate Testing Time: 20–25 minutes
Type(s) of Response: Verbal, reading

Name: Gray Oral Reading Test—4th ed. (GORT-4)
Author(s): Wiederholt, L., & Bryant, B.
Publisher: Harcourt
Copyright Date: 2001
Age Range: 6.0 through 18.0
Purpose: This test requires students to read passages aloud and answer literal, inferential, critical, and affective comprehension questions. The GORT–4 identifies students who may benefit from additional help, indicates strengths and weaknesses, and monitors progress.
Approximate Testing Time: 15–30 minutes
Type(s) of Response: Verbal

Name: Gray Silent Reading Tests (GSRT)
Author(s): Wiederholt J. L. and Blalock, G.
Publisher: Pro-Ed
Copyright Date: 2000
Age Range: 7–25
Purpose: Measures a person's silent reading comprehension ability
Approximate Testing Time: 20 minutes
Type(s) of Response: Written

(continued)

Name: Group Reading Assessment and Diagnostic Evaluation: GRADE
Author(s): Williams, K. T.
Publisher: AGS Publishing
Copyright Date: 2001
Age Range: 3 years and up
Purpose: To deliver reliable reading diagnostics for individual students, including intervention suggestions that profile both individual and classroom strengths and weaknesses.
Approximate Testing Time: 45–90 minutes
Type(s) of Response: Written

Name: Khan-Lewis Phonological Analysis, 2nd Edition: KLPA-2
Author(s): Khan, L., Lewis, N.
Publisher: AGS Publishing
Copyright Date: 2002
Age Range: 2 years and up
Purpose: Provides a comprehensive diagnosis of both articulation and use of the phonological process.
Approximate Testing Time: 10–30 minutes
Type(s) of Response: Verbal

Name: Reading Fluency Indicator: RFI
Author(s): Williams, K. T.
Publisher: AGS Publishing
Copyright Date: 2004
Age Range: 5–18 years
Purpose: Provides information about a student's ability both to read independently and participate in classroom activities that require reading.
Approximate Testing Time: 5–10 minutes
Type(s) of Response: Written

Name: Slosson Oral Reading Test–Revised (SORT–R)
Author(s): Slosson, R.
Publisher: Slosson Educational Publications
Copyright Date: 2002
Age Range: Preschool–adult
Purpose: A quick estimate of target-word recognition useful for identifying individuals with reading difficulties.
Approximate Testing Time: 3–5 minutes
Type(s) of Response: Verbal

Name: Sounds and Symbols Early Reading Program
Author(s): Goldman, R., Lynch, M.
Publisher: AGS Publishing
Copyright Date: 2007
Age Range: 3–8 years
Purpose: Addresses the five building blocks for early reading development outlined in the No Child Left Behind Act.
Approximate Testing Time: Varies
Type(s) of Response: Verbal

Name: Test of Early Reading Ability—Third Edition: TERA-3
Author(s): Reid, D. K., Hresko, W. P., Hammill, D. D.
Publisher: AGS Publishing
Copyright Date: 2007
Age Range: 3–6 years
Purpose: Screens children's early reading abilities through the measurement of knowledge of contextual meaning, the alphabet, and conventions such as reading from left to right.
Approximate Testing Time: 30 minutes
Type(s) of Response: Visual and verbal

Name: Test of Phonological Awareness in Spanish (TPAS)
Author(s): Riccio A. C., Imhoff B., Hasbrouck J. E., & Davis G. N.
Publisher: Pro-Ed
Copyright Date: 2004
Age Range: 4–0 through 10–11
Purpose: Measures phonological awareness ability in Spanish-speaking children.
Approximate Testing Time: 15–30 minutes
Type(s) of Response: Verbal

Name: Test of Phonological Awareness Skills (TOPAS)
Author(s): Newcomer P. and Barenbaum E.
Publisher: Pro-Ed
Copyright Date: 2003
Age Range: 5–10
Purpose: Helps identify children who have problems in phonological awareness.
Approximate Testing Time: 15–30 minutes
Type(s) of Response: Verbal

Name: Test of Word Reading Efficiency (TOWRE)
Author(s): Torgesen J., Wagner R., & Rashotte C.
Publisher: Pro-ed
Copyright Date: 1999
Age Range: 6–0 through 24–11
Purpose: Measures word reading accuracy and fluency.
Approximate Testing Time: 5–10 minutes
Type(s) of Response: Verbal

Name: Woodcock Reading Mastery Tests—1998 Normative Update (WRMT–R/NU)
Author(s): Woodcock, R.
Publisher: American Guidance Service
Copyright Date: 1998
Age Range: 5–75+
Purpose: Provides an assessment of reading skills in six areas: visual–auditory learning, letter identification, word identification, word attack, word comprehension, and passage comprehension. Computer scoring is available.
Approximate Testing Time: 10–30 minutes
Type(s) of Response: Verbal

6. Tests of Achievement in Spelling

Name: Test of Written Spelling—4th Edition (TWS–4)*
Author(s): Larsen, S., & Hammill, D.
Publisher: Pro-Ed
Copyright Date: 1999
Age Range: 1st–12th grade
Purpose: An assessment of spelling ability which includes a comparison between ability with predictable sound-letter patterns and with less predictable patterns.
Approximate Testing Time: 20 minutes
Type(s) of Response: Nonverbal

7. Tests of Achievement in Mathematics

Name: Group Mathematics Assessment and Diagnostic Evaluation (GMADE)
Author(s): Williams, K. T.
Publisher: AGS Publishing
Copyright Date: 2004
Age Range: 5 years and up
Purpose: Provides a clear, accurate account of a student's mathematics skills and a direct link to effective intervention if necessary.
Approximate Testing Time: 50–90 minutes
Type(s) of Response: Written

(continued)

Name: Test of Early Mathematics Ability—3rd Edition (TEMA–3)
Author(s): Ginsburg, H., & Baroody, A.
Publisher: Pro-Ed
Copyright Date: 2003
Age Range: 3–0 to 8–11
Purpose: Measures both formal and informal math skills and identifies specific strengths and weaknesses. Useful for assessing specific difficulties, measuring progress, designing instruction and remediation, and identifying gifted students. A book of remedial techniques and instructional activities for each area tested is also available.
Approximate Testing Time: 20–30 minutes
Type(s) of Response: Verbal and nonverbal

Name: Test of Mathematical Abilities for Gifted Students (TOMAGS)
Author(s): Ryser, G. R. & Johnsen, S. K.
Publisher: Pro-Ed
Copyright Date: 1998
Age Range: Grades K–3 and 4–6
Purpose: Identifies children gifted in mathematics through use of mathematical reasoning and mathematical problem solving.
Approximate Testing Time: 20–30 minutes
Type(s) of Response: Nonverbal (written)

8. Tests to Identify Giftedness

Name: Gifted Rating Scales (GRS; GRS-P; GRS-S)
Author(s): Pfeiffer, S., & Jarosewich, T.
Publisher: PsychCorp
Copyright Date: 2003
Age Range: 4–6 years
Purpose: Norm-referencing rating scales base don current theories of giftedness and federal and state guidelines regarding the definition of gifted and talented students.
Approximate Testing Time: 5–10 minutes
Type(s) of Response: Written

Name: Torrance Tests of Creative Thinking: Figural (TTCT:F)*
Author(s): Torrance, E.
Publisher: Scholastic Testing Service
Copyright Date: 1998
Age Range: Kindergarten–adult
Purpose: Evaluates creative potential in a wide variety of areas. The test has two sections: Figural (involves thinking creatively with pictures) and Verbal (involves thinking creatively with words). Tests of thinking creatively with actions and movement are also available for ages three to kindergarten.
Approximate Testing Time: Figural, 30 minutes; Verbal, 45 minutes
Type(s) of Response: Nonverbal

9. Tests of Perceptual and/or Motor Skills

Name: Bruininks-Oseretsky Test of Motor Proficiency, 2nd Ed. (BOT-2)
Author(s): Buininks, R.
Publisher: American Guidance Service
Copyright Date: 2005
Age Range: 4½ to 14½
Purpose: A measure of both gross- and fine-motor functioning. Skills sampled include running, speed and agility, balance, bilateral coordination, strength, upper limb coordination, response speed, visual-motor control, and upper limb speed and dexterity.
Approximate Testing Time: 45–60 minutes
Type(s) of Response: Nonverbal

Name: Beery-Buktenica Developmental Test of Visual-Motor Integration: 5th ed. (Beery VMI)*
Author(s): Beery, K., Beery, N., & Buktenica, N.
Publisher: Modern Curriculum Press
Copyright Date: 2004
Age Range: 2–15
Purpose: Designed to determine the level at which visual-motor perception and motor performance are integrated. The VMI consists of geometric figures that are copied by the student as accurately as possible.
Approximate Testing Time: 15–20 minutes
Type(s) of Response: Nonverbal

Name: Motor-Free Visual Perception Test 3 (MVPT-3)
Author(s): Colarusso, R., & Hammill, D.
Publisher: Academic Therapy Publications
Copyright Date: 2003
Age Range: 4–0 to 8–0
Purpose: Useful for screening or diagnosis with learning disabled, mentally challenged, or physically challenged children. The MVPT measures visual perception by presenting a student with a line drawing which he or she must match with an identical drawing presented in a multiple choice format.
Approximate Testing Time: 10 minutes
Type(s) of Response: Nonverbal

Name: Peabody Developmental Motor Scales 2 (PDMS-2)
Author(s): Folio, M., & Fewell, R.
Publisher: Western Psychological Services
Copyright Date: 2000
Age Range: Birth–83 months
Purpose: Assesses both gross- and fine-motor skills in children. The PDMS was developed to meet the programming needs of handicapped children in physical education. Gross-motor items are classified into five skill categories: reflexes, balance, non-locomotor, locomotor, and receipt and propulsion of objects. Fine-motor items are classified into four skill categories: grasping, hand use, eye-hand coordination, and manual dexterity.
Approximate Testing Time: 45–60 minutes
Type(s) of Response: Nonverbal

Name: Test of Auditory-Perceptual Skills 3rd ed. (TAPS-3)
Author(s): Gardner, M.
Publisher: Pro-Ed
Copyright Date: 2005
Age Range: 4–12
Purpose: Useful for identifying auditory-perceptual difficulties, imperceptions of auditory modality, and language and learning problems.
Approximate Testing Time: 10–15 minutes
Type(s) of Response: Verbal

Name: Test of Gross Motor Development 2 (TGMD-2)
Author(s): Ulrich, D.
Publisher: Pro-Ed
Copyright Date: 2000
Age Range: 3–10
Purpose: Assesses appropriate motor skills in the areas of locomotion and object control. The TGMD is useful for identifying children who are significantly behind their peers and may be eligible for special physical education services.
Approximate Testing Time: 15 minutes
Type(s) of Response: Nonverbal

10. Tests of Behavior and Conduct

Name: Adaptive Behavior Assessment System-Second Edition: ABAS-II
Author(s): Harrison, P., & Oakland, T.
Publisher: PsychCorp
Copyright Date: 2003
Age Range: 3 years and up
Purpose: Measures eligibility under the IDEA.
Approximate Testing Time: 15–20 minutes
Type(s) of Response: Verbal and Written

Name: Academic Competence Evaluation Scales: ACES
Author(s): DiPerna, J. C., & Elliott, S. N.
Publisher: PsychCorp
Copyright Date: 2000
Age Range: 4 years and up
Purpose: A standardized instrument to screen students who have difficulty learning, determine how the student functions in the classroom, and prioritize skills that may need intervention.
Approximate Testing Time: 10–15 minutes
Type(s) of Response: Written

Name: Greenspan Social-Emotional Growth Chart
Author(s): Greenspan, S.
Publisher: The Psychological Corporation
Copyright Date: 2004
Age Range: Birth–3.5 years
Purpose: Designed to help determine a child's social-emotional development and growth.
Approximate Testing Time: 5–15 minutes
Types of Response: Questionnaire

Name: Asperger Syndrome Diagnostic Scale: ASDS
Author(s): Myles, B., Bock, S., Simpson, R.
Publisher: Western Psychological Services
Copyright Date: 2001
Age Range: 5 to 18 years
Purpose: ASDS helps to quickly rule out other possible diagnoses and determine the likelihood that a child or adolescent has Asperger Syndrome.
Approximate Testing Time: 5 minutes
Type(s) of Response: Parent or therapist questionnaire

Name: Autism Diagnostic Interview Revised—ADI-R
Author(s): Rutter, M., LeCouteur, A., & Lord, C.
Publisher: Western Psychological Services
Copyright Date: 2003
Age Range: 2 years and older
Purpose: ADI-R attempts tot assess individuals suspected of having autism or other autism spectrum disorders. Useful for formal diagnosis as we as treatment and educational planning.
Approximate Testing Time: 1.5–2.5 hours
Type(s) of Response: Verbal

Name: Behavior Assessment System for Children, 2nd ed. (BASC-2)
Author(s): Reynolds, C., & Kamphaus, R.
Publisher: American Guidance Service
Copyright Date: 2004
Age Range: 4–18
Purpose: A set of rating scales for describing an individual's behavior and emotions. Contains teacher, parent, and self-reports plus directly observed classroom behavior and a structured developmental history. Computer scoring is available.
Approximate Testing Time: Varies
Type(s) of Response: Nonverbal (pencil and booklet), rater

Name: Comprehensive Test of Adaptive Behavior Revised (CTAB-R)
Author(s): Adams, G.
Publisher: Psychological Corporation
Copyright Date: 2000
Age Range: Birth–60
Purpose: Assesses level of independent behavior in individuals with mental and/or physical disabilities. Includes both a student test and a parent/guardian survey.
Approximate Testing Time: Varies
Type(s) of Response: Rater

Name: Conners' Rating Scales—3rd Ed.
Author(s): Conners, C.
Publisher: Western Psychological Services
Copyright Date: 2008
Age Range: 3–17
Purpose: A standard scale for identifying attention deficit disorder and other problem behaviors. The test can also be used for charting progress and evaluating intervention programs. A Hyperactivity Index is included or can be administered separately as Connors' Abbreviated Symptom Questionnaire (CASQ). Long and short forms of the CRS are available for both teachers and parents.
Approximate Testing Time: Varies
Type(s) of Response: Rater

Name: Culture-Free Self-Esteem Inventories—3rd Ed. (CFSEI–3)
Author(s): Battle, J.
Publisher: Pro-Ed
Copyright Date: 2002
Age Range: 5–0 to adult
Purpose: A series of self-report scales which measure an individual's self-esteem in a variety of contexts: general, peers, school, and parents. A "lie" (defensiveness) scale is also included.
Approximate Testing Time: 15–20 minutes
Type(s) of Response: Verbal and nonverbal

Name: Krug Aspergers Disorder Index (KADI)
Author(s): Krug, D., Arick, J.
Publisher: Western Psychological Services
Copyright Date: 2003
Age Range: 6–22 years
Purpose: Helps clinicians distinguish individuals with Asperger's disorder from those who have other forms of high-functioning autism.
Approximate Testing Time: 15–20 minutes
Type(s) of Response: Parent or therapist questionnaire

Name: Outcomes: Planning, Monitoring, Evaluating (PME)
Author(s): Stoiber, K. C., & Kratochwill, T. R.
Publisher: PsychCorp
Copyright Date: 2002
Age Range: 5 years and up
Purpose: To evaluate a student's progress toward identified behavior improvement goals.
Approximate Testing Time: Varies
Type(s) of Response: Written and Verbal

Name: Autism Diagnostic Observation Schedule (ADOS)
Author(s): Lord, C., Rutter, M., DiLavore, P. C., & Risi, S.
Publisher: Western Psychological Services
Copyright Date: 2001
Age Range: 2 years or older
Purpose: ADOS is used to evaluate almost anyone suspected of having autism, from toddlers to adults, children with no speech to adults who are fluent.
Approximate Testing Time: 160 minutes
Type(s) of Response: Verbal

(*continued*)

Name: Beck Youth Inventories of Emotional & Social Impairment (BDI-Y; BAI-Y; BANY-Y; BDBI-Y; BSCI-Y)
Author(s): Beck, J. S., Beck, A. T., & Jolly, J.
Publisher: PychCorp
Copyright Date: 2001
Age Range: 7–14 years
Purpose: Assesses symptoms of depression, anxiety, anger, disruptive behavior, and self-concept in children and adolescents.
Approximate Testing Time: 5–10 minutes
Type(s) of Response: Written

Name: Behavior Assessment System for Children, 2nd Edition (BASC-2)
Author(s): Reynolds, C. R., Kamphaus, R. W.
Publisher: AGS Publishing
Copyright Date: 2004
Age Range: 2–21 years
Purpose: Examines adaptive and maladaptive behavior in reference to IDEA.
Approximate Testing Time: 10–30 minutes
Type(s) of Response: Written

Name: Behavior Rating Inventory of Executive Function (BRIEF)
Author(s): Gioia, G. A., Espy, K. A., & Isquith, P. K.
Publisher: PsychCorp
Copyright Date: 2002
Age Range: 2–5 years
Purpose: To assess impairment of executive function in children and young people from preschool age through adolescents.
Approximate Testing Time: 10–15 minutes
Type(s) of Response: Verbal

Name: Brown Attention-Deficit Disorder Scales (Brown ADD Scales)
Author(s): Brown, T. E.
Publisher: PsychCorp
Copyright Date: 2001
Age Range: 3–7 years
Purpose: Identifies ADHD in primary grade students.
Approximate Testing Time: 10–20 minutes
Type(s) of Response: Verbal

Name: Caregiver-Teacher's Report Form (C-TRF)
Author(s): Achenbach, T., & Edelbrock, C.
Publisher: Author
Copyright Date: 2000
Age Range: 6–11 and 12–16
Purpose: Provides a profile of problem-behavior syndromes, adaptive behavior, and school performance. Eight scales are included: anxious, social withdrawal, unpopular, self-destructive, obsessive-compulsive, inattentive, nervous-overactive, and aggressive.
Approximate Testing Time: Varies
Type(s) of Response: Rater

Name: Carey Temperament Scales (CTS)
Author(s): Carey, W. B., McDevitt, S. C
Publisher: PsychCorp
Copyright Date: 1998
Age Range: 1 month to 12 years
Purpose: To quickly and accurately gain a deeper understanding of a children's temperament or behavioral style.
Approximate Testing Time: 20 minutes
Type(s) of Response: Written

Name: Piers-Harris Children's Self-Concept Scale, Second Edition (Piers-Harris 2)
Author(s): Piers, E. Harris, D., & Herzberg, D.
Publisher: Western Psychological Services
Copyright Date: 2002
Age Range: 7–18
Purpose: To quickly identify youngsters who need further testing or treatment, based on self-concept in ages 7–18.
Approximate Testing Time: 10–15 minutes
Type(s) of Response: Written

Name: Social-Emotional Dimension Scale, 2nd Edition (SEDS-2)
Author(s): Hudson, J., & Roberts, T.
Publisher: Pro-Ed
Copyright Date: 2004
Age Range: 5½ to 18½
Purpose: A rating scale to screen for students at risk for conduct disorders, behavior problems, or emotional disturbance.
Approximate Testing Time: Not reported
Type(s) of Response: Rater

Name: Social Communication Questionnaire: SCQ
Author(s): Rutter, M., Bailey, A., & Lord, C.
Publisher: Western Psychological Services
Copyright Date: 2003
Age Range: 4 years and older
Purpose: This instrument helps evaluate communication skills and social functioning in children who may have autism or autism spectrum disorders.
Approximate Testing Time: 10 minutes
Type(s) of Response: Written, by parent

Name: Temperament and Atypical Behavior Scale (TABS)
Author(s): Neisworth, J., Bagnato, S., Salvia, J., & Hunt, F.
Publisher: Brookes Publishing Co.
Copyright Date: 1999
Age Range: 11–71 months
Purpose: Designed to measure temperament and dysfunctional behavior.
Approximate Testing Time: 5 minutes for screener, 15 minutes for assessment tool
Types of Response: Ratings by parents, surrogates, or other professionals

Name: Vineland Social-Emotional Early Childhood Scales: Vineland SEEC
Author(s): Sparrow, S. S., Balla, D. A., Cicchetti, D. V.
Publisher: Pearson
Copyright Date: 1998
Age Range: Birth through 6 years
Purpose: Measures early childhood social-emotional development, including interpersonal relationships, play and leisure time, and coping skills.
Approximate Testing Time: 15–25 minutes
Type(s) of Response: Verbal

APPENDIX D

Test Evaluation Guidelines*

When reviewing tests, first be clear about your purpose for choosing the test. Then, to learn more about how the test typically is used by professionals, consult the publisher's catalog or website, whatever technical and administration manuals the publisher includes with the test, the test technical manual, and any available professional reviews of the test. Also reread Chapters 4 and 5 of this book to help you answer the following questions. As well, consult the *Standards for Educational and Psychological Testing*[1] for guidance on ethical and technical questions as applied to your assessment purpose. Some questions to consider as you review.

What behavior or knowledge is sampled in the test?

Whom is the test designed to assess?

If there are subtests, how do these relate to each other?

How clear are the directions?

Is extra equipment required?

How easy is it to administer?

What kinds of space and room conditions are necessary in order to administer the test?

What special training is needed to administer?

Can it be administered by paraprofessionals?

What kinds of scores does the test yield?

Is there software available for calculating scores?

Can you export scores to planning instruments?

Does it have suggestions for communicating results to parents?

Do the projected results contribute to parents' understanding of their child as a learner?

Does the information obtained yield useful information for planning intervention or instruction?

What information is given about the technical qualities, if it is a standardized instrument?

- Norms (Do these match the population you are teaching?)
- Reliability
- Validity

If this is a high-stakes test, are the technical qualities appropriate for this use? (The available technical information convinces you research is solid and in keeping with the *Standards for Educational and Psychological Testing*.)

Summary of strengths:

- Technical adequacy
- Efficiency
- Matches purpose planned

---

*Permission is granted by the publisher to reproduce this appendix for record-keeping or classroom use. From Gayle Mindes, *Assessing Young Children* (4th ed.).

[1]AERA, APA, & NCME. (1999). *Standards for educational and psychological testing*. Washington, DC: American Educational Research Association.

DESCRIPTIVE INFORMATION

<table>
<tr><td colspan="2">Title</td></tr>
<tr><td colspan="2">Author</td></tr>
<tr><td colspan="2">Copyright date/edition</td></tr>
<tr><td colspan="2">Publisher</td></tr>
<tr><td colspan="2">Stated purpose of test</td></tr>
<tr><td>Are there subtests?</td><td>Separate scores for these?</td></tr>
<tr><td>Standardized</td><td>Criterion-referenced</td></tr>
<tr><td></td><td>Portfolio</td></tr>
<tr><td colspan="2">Multipurpose (screening, monitoring, etc.)</td></tr>
<tr><td colspan="2">Appropriate number of items for age range?</td></tr>
<tr><td colspan="2">Qualifications for administrator</td></tr>
<tr><td colspan="2">Components in the kit (manual, equipment)</td></tr>
<tr><td>Individual</td><td>Group</td></tr>
<tr><td colspan="2">Total time required to administer</td></tr>
<tr><td>Age range</td><td>Available in other languages?</td></tr>
<tr><td colspan="2">Cost</td></tr>
</table>

ANALYSIS AND CONCLUSION

Do the claims or interpretations made about the test's performance match the evidence you have available?

Is the evidence clear, credible, easily located, and easily understood?

Does the test have suggestions for collection, use, and interpretation of appropriate collateral information?

Does this measure provide the most efficient manner for gathering the needed information?

Will the gathered data facilitate or enhance your work with the child?

Does it match your purpose?

APPENDIX E

Choosing Technology and Software to Support Assessment*

When you choose software to support your assessment program, you will find a wide variety of available programs. Choices include the following:

- Links to state and national association goals and benchmarks, Head Start Outcomes, NCLB
- Record-keeping capacity
- Lesson plan suggestions
- Specially formulated "tests" for students
- Report-generation capacity
- Web-based format with access by multiple stakeholders

The programs are available on CD-ROM and on the Internet, specially formulated for your program, and are released commercially every day. So you will need to keep in mind several principles when evaluating programs that might meet your needs. The evaluation process will call upon your knowledge of child development, instructional methodology, and assessment. You are in effect choosing an electronic tool to facilitate your work with young children. Some of the relevant issues and questions to think about follow.

The first step in the process of decision-making is the *evaluation of your hardware.* Most sophisticated assessment systems utilizing CD-ROM technology will require not only storage for the electronic files but also a good amount of memory for on-screen viewing and processing of your data collection. The electronic files may be stored on CD-ROMs, on a school network server, or on your hard drive. If you use external storage of student records, lesson plans, or whatever, you will want to have enough storage on your hard drive so that you can effectively sort data and use it in planning for your students. If stored elsewhere, you will want to know about the developer's reputation for security of data, including backup systems. If you are using a Personal Digital Assistant (PDA) with software, you will need to think about the ease of syncing the information with a data storage system.

More and more, assessment systems utilize the Web. For these programs, you will want to have high-speed cable or DSL access to the Internet for ease of use. Once you have evaluated your hardware, you will want to think about the content of the *software programs* themselves. You will need to think about the program from the perspective of each of the stakeholders in the system: child, family, administrator, community, and of course, you—the teacher. These perspectives overlap, but the primary interests of the various stakeholders follow.

Child and family perspective

- Does the program provide appropriate safeguards for confidentiality?
- Is the material free from obvious cultural bias?
- Can the materials be used in multiple languages?
- Are there options for children and family members with disabilities?
- Who has access to stored data on individual children?
- Where will the data be stored?

---

*Permission is granted by the publisher to reproduce this appendix for record-keeping or classroom use. From Gayle Mindes, *Assessing Young Children* (4th ed.).

- What is the deletion policy for stored data, both formative and summative?
- Can the family access the stored information? Under what conditions?

Child perspective

- If children will be using the program to assess themselves, is it simple enough for them to use independently?
- Does the program provide options for cooperative use, if this is part of your assessment program?
- Is the program design intuitive? Familiar?
- Does the program provide sufficient branching to assess in depth?
- Is the program enticing for children? Similar to classroom curriculum?
- Can a child review answers or process? Change answers if necessary?
- Does the material provide a challenge?
- Are the items in keeping with best developmentally appropriate practice?
- Are there links to support additional learning or assessment opportunities?
- Does the program support diverse levels of computer literacy for the spectrum of learners?
- How much adult help is required? Initially? On-going?

Administrator perspective

- Does the technology match program goals?
- Does the program add efficiency?
- Does the program provide maintenance support and regular updates? Is the fee for this service reasonable?
- Does the program combine many instructional and assessment decisions in a usable format with appropriate confidentiality safeguards?
- Does the program support all the accountability demands? Link appropriately to existing databases?

Community

- Do the reports support accountability goals?
- Are the prepared reports nontechnical, jargon-free, and easily understood?
- Do the reports model best practice in accountability reporting?
- Does the program answer the questions of Head Start and NCLB?

Teacher

- Does the program provide appropriate, but not cumbersome, password protection to guard the privacy of individual children?
- Is the scope and sequence of the program appropriate for the children you are teaching?
- Does the program help individualize instruction?
- Does the program provide easy ways to navigate through it—table of contents, easy access to help?
- Does the program include the capacity to sort the standards and goals that you must achieve with your students?
- Is the technology user-friendly? Can you point and click your way through the program? Is it intuitive? Does it contain effective and efficient search capacities?
- Does the program accomplish what you want it to do?
  - Provide class summaries?
  - Link to standards?
  - Link to lesson planning?
  - Provide suggestions for curriculum integration?

  - Generate accountability reports?
  - Generate parent reports?

- Are the technical manuals or online support well organized and clearly written in teacher-friendly language?
- Does the promotional material show examples that are compatible to your classroom situation? Are they believable?

Note: Technology resource to consult: International Society for Technology in Education at http://www.iste.org. See also ISTE (2000), *National Educational Technology Standards for Students Connecting Curriculum and Technology* Eugene, OR: ISTE.

APPENDIX F

Portfolio Template*

Name	School

Teacher's name ______________________________ Grade _____________

A picture of me in school.

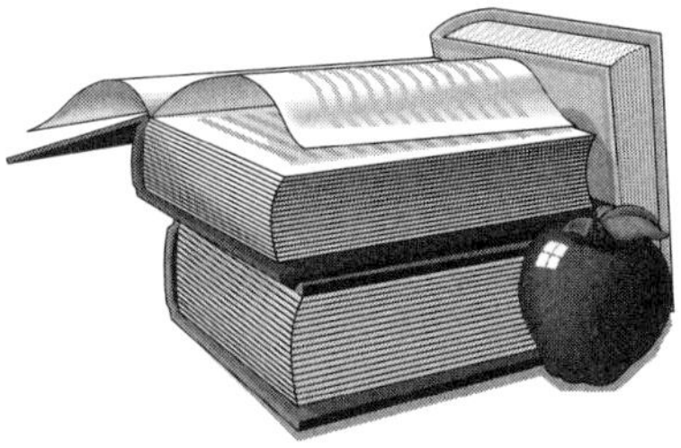

*Permission is granted by the publisher to reproduce this appendix for record-keeping or classroom use. From Gayle Mindes, *Assessing Young Children* (4th ed.). Copyright © 2011 by Pearson Education, Inc. All rights reserved.

Table of Contents

Date Added	Portfolio Artifact[1]	How I Feel About My Work
	Reading/Writing Artifacts	☺ 😐 ☹
	Math/Science Artifacts	☺ 😐 ☹
	Social Studies Artifacts	☺ 😐 ☹
	Cooperative Project Artifacts	☺ 😐 ☹
	Art/Music/Drama Artifacts	☺ 😐 ☹
	School Social Skills	☺ 😐 ☹
	Self-Efficacy Development	☺ 😐 ☹
	Other	☺ 😐 ☹

[1]Insert spaces as needed for the year.

Note: Artifacts may be drawings, writings, interviews, graphic organizers, peer evaluations, self-assessments—narrative or in response to rubric or checklist, teacher-completed checklists, log or journal, record of performance recorded by rubric, photos, video, graphic organizer, or any other demonstration/documentation of academic progress.

Did you think about the following artifacts? (Teacher: Select those appropriate for age/grade and ask child to reflect upon choices.)

1. Poems written
2. Songs composed
3. Handwriting samples
4. Stories written or narrated
5. Math problems solved
6. PowerPoint presentations created
7. Audiotapes or videos made
8. Photos of projects
9. Dioramas
10. Science lab notes

Selection process includes:

1. All subject areas or learning domains
2. Reference to all required standards or outcomes
3. Student reflection
4. Teacher guidance in selection
5. Parent review

Artifacts included for the fall quarter:

Drawings that show [in this space each child can show reflections about work completed or can dictate to the teacher the reasons why the material is in the portfolio]

____

____

____

____

Samples of work showing that I can solve problems [again include the reflections about why each is included]

____

____

____

____

____

My strengths as a learner include

1. ____
2. ____
3. ____

I am working on

____

____

____

____

My learning challenges are

____

____

____

____

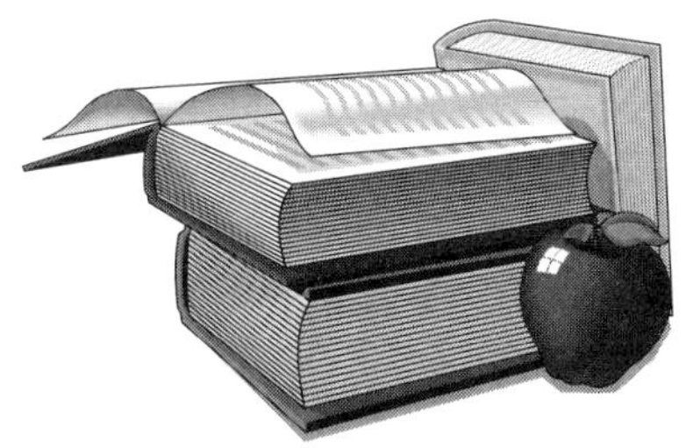

Standards for my grade (you will need the teacher's assistance with the next section)

In this space, list all that you will evaluate for the quarter in each subject area.

Standard 1:[2] Students will use mathematical analysis, scientific inquiry [etc.] as appropriate, to pose questions, seek answers, and develop solutions.

[2]New York State Mathematics and Science Partnership Program.

Evidence for progress toward this standard

1. ______
2. ______
3. ______
4. ______
5. ______

[continue with all the required standards]

Bull's eye![3] I hit the target on this standard!

Standard: [insert learning standard here]

Achieving this standard was

Easy

Hard for me

Okay for me

To achieve this standard, I include the following artifacts

______

______

______

Parent Review

1. I appreciated seeing

______

______

______

______

______

[3]Developed by Bridget Amory, Ph.D., Principal, Lake Forest South Elementary School Harrington, Delaware.

2. How this compares to what I see at home

3. Next quarter, I hope to see

APPENDIX G

Child Interview Protocols*

Interview or Questionnaire for the Beginning of the Year or for New Student

Name ______________________________ Date ______________________________

1. What were your favorite things to do in school last year?
2. What did you like to do in your free time? Who did you do these things with?
3. Were there things you liked to do by yourself?
4. What did you like to do on the playground? Were there games? Which ones? Did children organize these?
5. If you could change something about last year [old school], what would you change?

Interview of Child to Determine Academic Interests

Name ______________________________ Date ______________________________

1. I have time to play before school and like to . . .
2. After school, I go to . . . We usually . . . [have a snack—your favorite?], then . . .
3. I do my homework . . . [e.g., right after school, after dinner, right before bed]
4. On weekends, I like to . . .
5. My favorite books that my mom/dad/babysitter read to me are . . .
6. My favorite game is . . .
7. I like to learn . . .
8. My favorite field trip of all time was . . .

Reading Questions

Name ______________________________ Date ______________________________

1. Do you like to read? Why? Why not?
2. Do you like to have others read to you?
3. What do you look at when someone reads to you?
4. Does everyone read to you in English?
5. What are your favorite things to read?
6. If we added books to our library, what should we get?
7. When you get a book that is too hard to read, what do you do?

APPENDIX H

Example Forms for Collecting Assessment Information*

Name ______________________________ Date ____________________

MOTOR SKILLS FOR 5/6-YEAR-OLD

Skill	Evident	Emerging
Zips		
Buttons		
Ties shoes		
Strings beads		
Uses scissors with accuracy		
Controls writing tools		
Throws large ball		
Catches large ball		

EVENT CHECKLIST FOR WHOLE CLASS

	Color Concepts[1]			
Names of Children in the Class	Matches Basic Colors	Points to When Named	Names Basic Colors	Names Many Other Colors
1.				
2.				
3.				
4.				
[. . .]				
17.				
18.				
19.				
20.				

[1]Insert date of observation or of assessment conducted. For example, 3/15/11: 8/8 colors or 3/15/11: attempted, emerging, not observed/completed.

EXAMPLE FORMS FOR COLLECTING ASSESMENT INFORMATION

CHECKLISTS

Name ______________________________ Date ____________________

Skill of Interest (e.g., Using Ruler Can Measure to the Nearest Inch)	Child's Name (for Ease, Preprint all the Children's Names in a Group or in Your Class)	Yes	No
	1.		
	2.		
	3.		
	4.		
	5.		
	[. . .]		
	25.		
	26.		
	27.		

Teacher's Name ______________________ Week of ________________

EVENT TO RECORD (e.g., GETS FOLDER OUT PROMPTLY; PUTS BOOKS AWAY QUIETLY)

Name	Mon	Tues	Wed	Thur	Fri	Mon	Tues	Wed

RATING SCALES[2]

Skill	Child's name	All of the time	Some of the time	None of the time
Uses a variety of reading strategies				
Shows oral reading fluency				
Reads fiction and nonfiction				
Interprets pictures				
Interprets charts and graphs				
Responds orally to reading				
Responds in writing to reading				

[2]Make these charts for each member of your class. Choose skills to rate that are of interest for report cards or other data collection demands.

End-of-Day Summative and Formative Evaluation

Date ________

As you think about the day, what worked well?

List three or four main ideas that you will ponder during the week.

What additional information do you need from the instructor that will clarify the experience of today?

Teacher's Name: ________________

APPENDIX I

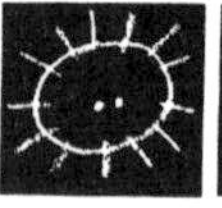

CHICAGO EARLY DEVELOPMENT SCREENING INVENTORY FOR TEACHERS II

By: Evelyn Baumann, Jack Kavanagh, and Gayle Mindes

CEDSIT II: Version of Screening Inventory for Teachers of 4 and 5 Year Olds

IDENTIFYING INFORMATION

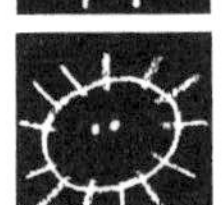

Date: ______________

Child's Name: ______________________________ **Sex:** __________
first middle last

Parent or Guardian: ______________________________

Date of Birth: ______________________________ **Age:** __________
year month day

Preschool Center: ______________________ **Teacher:** ______________________

BACKGROUND INFORMATION

- This checklist has been designed as a screening instrument to identify those children who are "at high risk". It is developed to quickly find those children who may require referral and special services. It has been standardized on Head Start children and is designed to reflect each child's strengths and special needs.

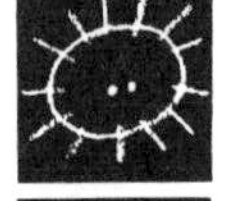

- For greater accuracy in using this checklist, it is recommended that it be completed after the child has been in the program for a period of four weeks. Also, it is recommended that teachers or other program staff complete a parent interview, as the child enters the program. The **CEDSI II,** the parent interview instrument has been specifically designed for this purpose and has been standardized on Head Start children.

- Following the scoring of the **CEDSIT II**, if the child is found to be at risk for special needs, an appropriate referral for professional diagnosis should be made. The **CEDSI II** Interview Form and the **CEDSIT II** Form can be of help to the diagnostians and should be utilized for periodic review.

DIRECTIONS

- Please read over the entire checklist before planning to complete the **CEDSIT II**. You will then be familiar with the kinds of skills that you must plan to observe.

- Plan to complete the **CEDSIT II** on individual children when you can observe the child. Answer each item carefully with a firm decision that the child does or does not possess the particular skill on the checklist.

- It will ordinarily take 30 to 40 minutes to complete this observation on each child.

KBM DEVELOPMENTAL ASSESSMENT, INC. • 507 N. Elmhurst Road • Prospect Heights, Illinois 60070

Chicago Early Development Screening Inventory for Teachers II (CEDSIT II)

Motor / Communication / Cognitive Skills

This child:	*YES*	*NO*
1. Often bumps into things	______	______
2. Seems unusually clumsy	______	______
3. Has trouble using buttons	______	______
4. Has trouble using zippers	______	______
5. Has trouble putting on coat	______	______
6. Has trouble tying shoes	______	______
7. Has trouble washing self when told to do so	______	______
8. Has trouble hopping on one foot	______	______
9. Has trouble catching a ball	______	______
10. Has trouble copying a square	______	______
11. Has trouble copying a circle	______	______
12. Tends to scribble rather than draw shapes or pictures of things	______	______
13. Has trouble using scissors	______	______
14. Has trouble assembling puzzles	______	______
15. Has trouble naming the primary colors (red, blue, yellow)	______	______
16. Has trouble counting beyond three	______	______
17. Has trouble naming the letters of the alphabet	______	______
18. Has trouble telling how old he/she is (or showing the correct number of fingers)	______	______
19. Has trouble stating correctly whether he/she is a boy or girl	______	______
20. Has trouble naming more than one or two body parts of his/her body	______	______
21. Has trouble stating his/her full name	______	______

Social / Emotional Skills

This child:	*YES*	*NO*
1. Has difficulty sitting still seems to be in continual motion	______	______
2. Frequently has temper tantrums	______	______
3. Often provokes other children (starts fights, hits, and throws things)	______	______
4. Has trouble accepting limits	______	______
5. Shows considerable frustration when his/her activities are interferred with	______	______
6. Is excessively demanding of the teacher	______	______
7. Very seldom shares with others	______	______
8. Seems more restless and fidgety than other children	______	______
9. Is easily distracted from his activities	______	______
10. Often asks for food other than at snack or mealtimes	______	______
11. Tends to cry easily or frequently	______	______
12. Mostly whines and complains when asked to do or get something	______	______
13. Often pouts and is sullen when he/she doesn't get what he/she wants	______	______
14. Tends to react to strange adults by clinging to that person	______	______
15. Tends to react to strange adults by showing fear and withdrawal	______	______
16. Tends to give up easily when things are not going his/her way	______	______
17. Seems mostly shy and withdrawn	______	______
18. Tends to interact more with adults than with other children	______	______
19. Seems to prefer toys or activities more appropriate for younger children (pull toys, stack blocks or rings)	______	______

(*continued on next page*)

22. Has trouble describing items in a picture ______ ______
23. Has trouble repeating a sentence spoken to him/her ______ ______
24. Has trouble singing songs or nursery rhymes ______ ______
25. Has trouble telling a story about a picture shown to him/her ______ ______
26. Has trouble repeating (in his/her own words) a simple story ______ ______
27. Has trouble when required to do two things, one right after the other ("Put the book on the table and close the door.") ______ ______
28. Has trouble following directions ______ ______
29. Does not seem to like to look at books ______ ______
30. Often says "huh?" or "what?" or asks for repetition of what is said ______ ______
31. Very seldom copies actions he/she has seen others perform ______ ______
32. Very seldom uses two or more sentences to tell me something ______ ______
33. Very seldom asks questions ______ ______
34. Very seldom asks questions about how things work ______ ______
35. Very seldom asks questions about why ______ ______
36. Has trouble understanding and responding when I talk to him/her ______ ______
37. Seems to have trouble hearing from across the room ______ ______
38. Seems to have trouble hearing when spoken to in a whisper ______ ______
39. May have a speech problem
40. Tends to stutter ______ ______
41. Speech seems unclear and hard to understand ______ ______
42. Seems afraid to talk ______ ______
43. Tends to use "me" rather than "I" when speaking ______ ______

20. Seems to prefer repetitious involvement with records, puzzles or other toys ______ ______
21. In general does not seem to be liked by other children ______ ______
22. In general does not find eating pleasurable ______ ______
23. Tends to wet his/her pants more than other children ______ ______
24. Seems to often indulge in body-play (rocking, finger-twiddling, or masturbation) ______ ______

Teacher notes: ______________________________

CEDSIT II SCORING

DIRECTIONS

1. Give one point for each **YES** answer on the **Motor** / **Communication** / **Cognitive Skills Scale**. Add the points together to make a total.
2. Give one point for each **YES** answer on the **Social** / **Emotional Skills Scale**. Add the points together to make a total.
3. Record the scores in the space provided below and interpret the scales according to the directions.

INTERPRETATION

TOTALS: ________________ **Motor** / **Communication** / **Cognitive**

________________ **Social** / **Emotional**

Refer for evaluation:

12 – 20* on **Motor** / **Communication** / **Cognitive Scale**

7 – 11* on **Social** / **Emotional Scale**

Observe further:

4 – 11 on **Motor** / **Communication** / **Cognitive Scale**

2 – 6 on **Social** / **Emotional Scale**

Not likely to require referral:

0 – 3 on **Motor** / **Comminication** / **Cognitive Scale**

0 – 1 on **Social** / **Emotional Scale**

***or scores above**

PLEASE NOTE **A high score on either scale indicates a need to refer the child for an in-depth diagnostic assessment.**

Teacher's Comments ____

____

____

____

____ Teacher's Signature

APPENDIX J

Websites that Address Assessment for Teachers of Young Children

General Assessment / Teaching resources

http://www.aap.org. American Academy of Pediatrics (AAP) has information for educators as well as parents, and covers everything from health topics to advocacy.

http://www.aera.net. American Educational Research Association (AERA), includes position papers and books about assessment.

http://aft.org. The American Federation of Teachers (AFT)

- **http://aft.org/earlychildhood/professional-growth.htm.** For information for early childhood teachers

http://www.altec.org. The Advanced Learning Technologies (ALTEC) project at the University of Kansas Center for Research on Learning utilizes the most advanced and innovative technologies available to improve teaching and learning.

http://apa.org. The American Psychological Association: Website includes position papers and books about assessment.

http://www.annenberginstitute.org. Annenberg Institute As part of Brown University, Website includes position papers on standardized testing.

http://www.ascd.org. The Association for Supervision and Curriculum Development: Website includes searchable database on topics such as report cards and other instructional issues. See also:

- **http://www.ascd.org/programs/The_Whole_Child/The_Whole_Child.aspx.** Information on their Whole Child campaign (Advocacy Action Example).
- **http://ascd.typepad.com/blog/.** ASCD Community Blog, topics for practicing teachers.

http://www.BankStreet.edu. Bank Street College of Education Website includes occasional papers and links to current in early childhood.

http://ceee.gwu.edu/. George Washington University Center for Equity and Excellence in Education (GW-CEEE)'s mission is to advance education reform so that all students achieve high standards.

http://www.childrensdefense.org. The Children's Defense Fund (CDF) is the foremost national proponent of policies and programs that provide children with the resources they need to succeed. Website includes child research data and publications.

http://www.cfw.tufts.edu. Tufts University Child and Family Site. The Child & Family WebGuide describes trustworthy websites on topics of interest to parents and professionals.

http://www.cse.ucla.edu. The UCLA Center for the Study of Evaluation (CSE) and, more recently, the National Center for Research on Evaluation, Standards, and Student Testing (CRESST) contributed to the development of scientifically based evaluation and testing techniques, vigorously encouraged the development, validation and use of sound data for improved accountability and decision making, and aggressively explored technological applications to improve assessment and evaluation practice.

http://dibels.uoregon.edu. DIBELS (Dynamic Indicators of Basic Early Literacy Skills) are a set of procedures and measures for assessing the acquisition of early literacy skills from kindergarten through sixth grade. They are designed to be short (one minute) fluency measures used to regularly monitor the development of early literacy and early reading skills. Website includes information about instruments and research.

http://www.ed.gov. U.S. Department of Education website. Website posts highlights of legislation so that you can read first-hand about assessment legislation and regulations. Subheadings of note include:

- **http://www.dww.ed.gov/priority_area/priority_landing.cfm?PA_ID=7#.** Includes information about early childhood education
- **http://www.whatworks.ed.gov.** A clearinghouse of best practices in education.
- **http://www.osepideasthatwork.org/toolkit/index.asp.** Online toolkit for assessing students with special needs, through the U.S. department of education.

- **http://www.ed.gov/about/inits/ed/lep-partnership/index.html.** Specifically addresses how the U.S. Department of Education is improving assessments of English Language proficiency, reading, and mathematics of LEP students.
- **http://www.free.ed.gov/displaydate.cfm.** Listing of free resources for educators.

http://www.edexcellence.net/template/index.cfm. The Thomas B. Fordham Institute is nonprofit think tank dedicated to advancing educational excellence in America's K–12 schools.

http://www.eduhound.com. EduHound organizes topics by site sets, which are topic-based online education resources—great for general information on topics from Aaron Burr to Zoos.

http://www.edutopia.org. Edutopia.org is the George Lucas Foundation website, which features holistic assessment and project-based learning.

http://www.edweek.org. *Edweek,* a newspaper for teachers, cover local, state, and national news and issues from preschool through the twelfth grade.

http://www.fairtest.org. The National Center for Fair & Open Testing (FairTest). This website has position papers on tests and assessment, newsletter, and other activities.

http://www.fcrr.org. The mission of the Florida Center for Reading Research. This website contains research and best practice information on reading assessment.

http://www.google.com/educators/index.html. Google for Educators Offers discussion groups as well as activities for class, classroom posters, and general educational tools.

http://www.highscope.org. HighScope Educational Research Foundation website includes assessment and instructional materials for teaching in preschool settings.

http://ies.ed.gov/ncee/wwc/reports/dropout/ams/. U.S. Department of Education Institute of Education Sciences' "what works" clearinghouse.

http://www.kidsource.com. KidSource OnLine site covers a broad spectrum of issues related to assessment, observation, and teaching.

http://www.leadandlearn.com. Website includes examples of teaching plans and position papers.

http://www.lessonplanz.com. Lesson Planz contains worksheets and many other suggestions for assessment and teaching in all grades and subjects.

http://www.nationalpirc.org/index.html. National PIRC (Parental Information and Resource Center) Coordination Center Website. PIRCs help implement successful and effective parental involvement policies, programs.

http://pzweb.harvard.edu. Project Zero at Harvard University. The site is a source of research and information about applied multiple intelligences applications.

http://www.researchconnections.org. Research Connections is a resource that promotes high-quality research and the use of that research in policymaking. The website includes a Child Care & Early Education Research Source for research on urban issues affecting children and families.

http://www.responsiveclassroom.org. The Responsive Classroom is an approach to elementary teaching that emphasizes social, emotional, and academic growth in a strong and safe school community.

http://www.rethinkingschools.org. Rethinking Schools is a not-for-profit educational reform organization with educational materials and opinion newsletters.

http://rubistar.4teachers.org/index.php. A quick program for creating rubrics for project-based assignments.

http://www.serve.org. Part of the University of North Carolina at Greensborough, SERVE. Includes information on their Assessment, Accountability, and Standards Program.

http://school.discoveryeducation.com/schrockguide/Kathy. Schrock's Guide for Educators is a categorized list of sites useful for enhancing curriculum and professional growth.

http://www.schoolmatters.com. School Matters is run by Standard and Poor's School Evaluation Services, and provides parents and taxpayers with an objective analysis of school and school district data via this publicly accessible site.

http://www.teach-nology.com/web_tools/rubrics/. A website that focuses on building rubrics—part of the teach-nology website.

http://teacher.depaul.edu. DePaul University's Center for Urban Education. Includes many examples of assistance to urban schools.

http://www.teachermagazine.org/tm/index.html. A division of *Education Week*, this website has email subscription status and many interesting articles.

http://unl.edu/buros/. The Buros Institute of Mental Measurements (BIMM). This site is the online link to the series of Mental Measurements Yearbooks and is the place to find reviews of published tests.

http://www.webenglishteacher.com. Web English Teacher contains lesson plans and teaching ideas from kindergarten through twelfth grade.

Early Childhood

http://nnell.org. The National Network for Early Language Learning is an educational community providing leadership in support of successful early language learning and teaching.

http://thechp.syr.edu/Behavioral_Observation_Checklist.pdf. An early childhood behavioral checklist created by the Early Childhood Direction Center (ECHP), Syracuse University.

http://www.fpg.unc.edu. University of North Carolina Chapel Hill Early Childhood Center: issues related to best practice in preschool.

http://www.naeyc.org. The National Association for the Education of Young Children (NAEYC). The website regularly presents position statements and links to policy related to the assessment of young children.

http://www.nhsa.org. The National Head Start Association. This is the advocacy organization for families and children in Head Start. There are links to family-friendly information.

http://www.srcd.org. Society for Research on Child Development (SRCD): The purposes of the society are to promote multidisciplinary research in the field of human development, to foster the exchange of information among scientists and other professionals of various disciplines, and to encourage applications of research findings.

http://www.thinkfinity.org. Thinkfinity.org is the cornerstone of Verizon Foundation's literacy, education and technology initiatives. Their goal is to improve student achievement in traditional classroom settings and beyond by providing high-quality content and extensive professional development training.

http://www.vanderbilt.edu/csefel. The Center on the Social and Emotional Foundations for Early Learning (CSEFEL) is a national resource center for disseminating research and evidence-based practices to early childhood programs across the country.

http://www.zerotothree.org. Zero to Three is a national nonprofit, multidisciplinary organization that supports the healthy development and well-being of infants, toddlers and their families.

STANDARDIZED TESTS AND NCLB-SPECIFIC INFORMATION

http://www.edutopia.org/. Edutopia, the George Lucas Foundation. Source for latest holistic ideas on incorporation of technology into classroom practice from a constructivist perspective.

http://www.ed.gov/nclb. NCLB section of U.S. Department of Education website, includes information about the law, the status of your specific state, and the contact information for your state.

http://www.aft.org/topics/nclb/funding.htm. Information about NCLB, specifically related to funding, provided by the American Federation of Teachers.

http://www.elladvocates.org/nclb/funding.html. Issue brief by the Institute for Language and Education Policy, focusing on the funding issues of NCLB and how they affect English language learners.

http://www.aasa.org/policy/content.cfm?ItemNumber=2001&snItemNumber=1971. Website of the American Association of School Administrators, specifically addressing funding issues of the NCLB.

http://www.law.berkeley.edu/centers/ewi-old/research/k12equity/Hawley.html. This website offers a concise review of some of the issues in an article by Willis D. Hawley, Professor Emeritus of Education and Public Policy at the University of Maryland.

http://www.civilrightsproject.ucla.edu/news/pressreleases/pressrelease20080109-book.html. Press release for *Holding NCLB Accountable: Achieving Accountability, Equity, and Social Reform* (Corwin Press, 2008), edited by the Civil Rights Project/Protecto Derechos Civiles (through UCLA's Graduate School of Education and Information) senior researcher Gail L. Sunderman.

http://www.fairtest.org/realitytesting-nclb. August 2007 article by FairTest (The National Center for Fair and Open Testing) about the claims and realities that proponents of NCLB make about school progress.

http://www.heritage.org/Research/Education/ednotes62.cfm. An article on the education website of the Heritage Foundation, addressing whether NCLB should be reauthorized.

http://www.nclr.org/. The National Council of La Raza is the largest national Latino civil rights and advocacy organization in the U.S. and works to improve opportunities for Hispanic Americans.

http://www2.scholastic.com/browse/article.jsp?id=3748845. Article on Scholastic Books website that addresses the top 10 terms students should know to be successful on standardized tests.

TEACHING/ASSESSING ENGLISH LANGUAGE LEARNERS AND STUDENTS WITH SPECIAL NEEDS

http://www.cal.org. The Center for Applied Linguistics (CAL) carries out a wide range of activities to accomplish its mission of improving communication through better understanding of language and culture. CAL is a source for research and applied information on teaching children who are English Language Learners. (CAL's historical archive can be found at http://www.cal.org/crede/.)

http://www.circleofinclusion.org. The Circle of Inclusion website for early childhood service providers and families of young children offers demonstrations of and information about the effective practices of inclusive educational programs for children from birth through age 8. Resources are available in several languages, including Spanish.

http://clas.uiuc.edu. The Early Childhood Research Institute on Culturally and Linguistically Appropriate Services (CLAS) is a federally funded collaborative effort of the University of Illinois at Urbana-Champaign, the Council for Exceptional Children, the University of Wisconsin–Milwaukee, the ERIC Clearinghouse on Elementary and Early Childhood Education, and the ERIC Clearinghouse on Disabilities and Gifted Education. The CLAS Institute identifies, evaluates, and promotes effective and appropriate early intervention practices and preschool practices that are sensitive and respectful to children and families from culturally and linguistically diverse backgrounds.

http://www.clmer.csulb.edu/. Research-based approaches to relevant human, organizational and educational change. CLMER places priority on creative use of technology to promote equity.

http://www.colorinColorado.org. Focus of this site for families and teachers is on English Language Learners.

http://www.ed.gov/offices/OELA. The website for the Office of English Language Learners for the federal government posts federal laws and informational materials related to English language learners.

http://www.english-the-easy-way.com. English Grammar: The Easy Way, an excellent site to learn English grammar. This site explains English so that everyone can understand.

http://www.ed.gov/about/offices/list/ocr/ell/index.html. The Department of Education's web page regarding programs for English language learners.

http://idea.ed.gov/explore/home. This site was created to provide a "one-stop shop" for resources related to IDEA and its implementing regulations.

http://www.ldonline.org. A site with information for teachers, parents, and other professionals about learning disabilities.

http://www.migrationpolicy.org. The Migration Policy Institute is an independent, nonpartisan, nonprofit think tank. It aims to meet the rising demand for pragmatic and thoughtful responses to the challenges and opportunities that large-scale migration, whether voluntary or forced, presents to communities and institutions in an increasingly integrated world.

http://nabe.org. National Association for Bilingual Education (NABE). Source for publications, information, and professional development related to bilingual education.

http://www.ncela.gwu.edu. The National Clearinghouse for English Language Acquisition (NCELA) collects, coordinates, and conveys a broad range of research and resources in support of an inclusive approach to high quality education for ELLs.

http://www.specialconnections.ku.edu/cgi-bin/cgiwrap/specconn/index.php. Online resources for teachers of students with special needs, including information on assessment, instruction, and behavior plans.

http://www.teachers.net/mentors/esl_language/. ESL and Language Teachers' Chatboard: use this function to chat with other teachers.

http://www.tesol.org/s_tesol/index.asp. Teachers of English to Speakers of Other Languages.
Website promotes effective teaching techniques and position statements on the topic.

http://www.wida.us/. The World-Class Instructional Design and Assessment (WIDA) Consortium site. Research and professional development activities importantly complement the WIDA standards and assessment products.

TECHNOLOGY/CORPORATE SOURCES FOR ASSESSMENT

http://www.ael.org/dbdm/overview.cfm. Provides guidance through the steps of data-based decision-making processes and access to useful examples, real school stories, and the best available tools and resources to help schools build effective data-based decision making systems.

http://www.altec.org. The Advanced Learning Technologies (ALTEC) project at the University of Kansas Center for Research on Learning utilizes the most advanced and innovative technologies available to improve teaching and learning. This website includes instructional resources that utilize technology.

http://www.ati-online.com. Assessment Technology Incorporated (ATI) is a company that develops online assessment materials for ECE.

http://www.ctb.com. CTB/McGraw-Hill is the leading provider of high-quality educational assessment products and services for the early learner, K–12, and adult education markets, helping learners of all ages meet their potential. Includes glossary, position papers, and test descriptions.

http://www.easyworksheet.com. Easy Worksheet is an online system that generates math tests and worksheets.

http://www.eduplace.com/rdg/index.jsp. Houghton-Mifflin Publisher's site, which includes reading tests.

http://www.ets.org. Educational Testing Service (ETS) advances quality and equity in education for people worldwide by creating assessments based on rigorous research. Includes test descriptions, as well as position papers and research related to tests and testing.

http://www.grownetwork.com. Grow Network. A commercial provider of standardized test score analyses for individual children to be used by teachers in planning instruction. Part of McGraw-Hill publishers.

http://www2.scholastic.com/browse/home.jsp. Website for Teacher Scholastic, it contains resources for planning, developing lesson plans and assessment.

http://www.schoolnet.com. A system for schools to manage assessment and standards data. Their Instructional Management Suite (IMS) helps districts improve efficiency and increase student achievement by providing users with the data, reports and tools they need to align curriculum, assess performance, analyze results, individualize instruction, and communicate with parents.

http://www.teachingstrategies.com. Teaching Strategies, Inc. is an educational publishing company that specializes in early childhood curriculum development, related technology and assessment products, and related staff development services.

http://www.tlc2.uh.edu/times. The Texas Institute for Measurement, Evaluation, and Statistics (TIMES). The mission of TIMES is to advance scientific discovery through the development and application of measurement, evaluation, and statistical research methods.

http://www.thejournal.com. *T.H.E. Journal* is dedicated to informing and educating K–12 senior-level district and school administrators, technologists, and tech-savvy educators within districts, schools, and classrooms to improve and advance the learning process through the use of technology.

http://www.thinklinklearning.com. Think Link Learning is a commercial assessment system offered through Discovery Education Assessment, which uses a scientific-research-based Continuous Improvement Model and diagnostic assessments that mirror each state's high-stakes test, including performance indicators. The website contains samples of the approach.

http://www.pearsondigital.com. Pearson Digital Learning includes technology-driven curriculum solutions and delivers implementation models that build foundations, foster achievement, promote graduation, and provide path for your school's continuous improvement. Also see:

- **http://www.pearsonschoolsystems.com.** Pearson School Systems products to analyze student and school district performance.

http://www.kaplank12.com/us/home. Kaplan K–12 Learning Services' system for linking student achievement to teaching to assessment.

ALTERNATIVES TO TRADITIONAL ASSESSMENTS

http://www.ncrel.org/sdrs/areas/issues/students/earlycld/ea5lk14.htm. Chart of the purposes and types of assessments (as a continuum between informal and formal assessment) on the website for the North Central Regional Educational Laboratory.

http://artswork.asu.edu/arts/teachers/assessment/performance2.htm. Assessment materials for art lessons, created by Arizona State University.

http://fcit.usf.edu/assessment/classroom/Behavior%20Observation%20Checklist.pdf. Assessment of student behavior created by the Florida Center for Instructional Technology.

http://www.readingrockets.org/teaching/reading101/assessment. Information on informal class-based assessment, as well as articles and resources to get started.

Portfolios

http://www.aurbach.com/gp3/index.html. Grady Profile is software that helps classroom teachers (preK–college) manage the assessment models for performance assessment, authentic assessment, project-based, standards-based assessment, collaborative and cooperative learning and portfolios.

SUBJECT-SPECIFIC ASSESSMENT

Social Studies/Social Studies Assessment

http://www.socialstudies.org. National Council for Social Studies (NCSS). The mission of NCSS is to provide leadership, service, and support for all social studies educators. Standards, position papers and publications on teaching the social studies.

Mathematics/Mathematics Assessment

http://www.freemathtest.com. Online resource that generates free online math tests and worksheets for students in grades K–3.

http://www.moneyinstructor.com. Online resource for educators and parents to teach students about money, business skills, and jobs and career skills.

http://www.nctm.org. National Council for Teachers of Mathematics (NCTM). NCTM Website includes practical examples for implementation of standards in the classroom.

http://www.thatquiz.org. Online resource for teachers that creates math test activities for students of all grade levels.

Reading/Reading Assessment

http://www.reading.org. International Reading Association (IRA) Position papers and publications on teaching reading.

http://grammar.ccc.commnet.edu/grammar/. The Guide to Grammar and Writing, which is sponsored by the Capital Community College Foundation, a nonprofit 501 c-3 organization that supports scholarships, faculty development, and curriculum innovation.

Websites compiled and organized by Rebecca Manuel, DePaul University graduate student.

APPENDIX K

Assessment Bibliography for Kindergarten and Primary Teachers[1]

Boaler, J. (2008). *What's math got to do with it?: Helping children learn to love their least favorite subject—and why it's important for America*. London: Viking Adult.

Written in a narrative form, emphasizes assessment "for learning (and) aims . . . to create self-regulating learners—learners who have the knowledge and power to monitor their own learning." Provides ways to make math more interesting for parents and teachers.

Curtis, D., & Carter, M. (2004). *The art of awareness: How observation can transform your teaching*. St. Paul, MN: Redleaf Press.

Takes a look at how observation can aid in teaching and can be useful in assessment. Explains how to observe children using their senses, exploring, seeking power, forming relationships. Examples are provided along with additional references.

Fisher, D., & Frey, N. (2007). *Checking for understanding: Formative assessment techniques for your classroom*. Alexandria, VA: ASCD.

Provides simple descriptions that are easy to understand on assessment terminology. Gives examples. There are many activities included in this book that will help children build understanding.

Fogarty, R., Burke, K., & Belgrad, S. (2008). *The portfolio connection: Student work linked to standards*. Thousand Oaks, CA: Corwin Press.

Explains how to build portfolios for each student in your classroom. Provides a list of topics that need to be covered in each portfolio and suggests dates to use to meet the criteria needed in the portfolio.

Gober, S. Y. (2002). *Six simple ways to assess young children*. Albany, NY: Delmar Learning.

Focuses on six sections of assessment: developmental check lists; parent interviews; self-portraits; scribbling, drawing, and writing samples; audio tapes; and anecdotal records. Explains how to pull it all together and which assessments you should use for your students.

McConaughy, S. H. (2005). *Clinical interviews for children and adolescents: assessment to intervention (The Guilford Practical Intervention in Schools Series)*. New York: The Guilford Press.

Discusses the use of clinical child interviews and the interpretation of them as they are used in assessment, for intervention planning. Several cases are provided as examples sample questions to ask during the interviews. Provides characteristics of children that might be referred to school-based risk assessments, because they might be of harm to others, themselves, or cause violence.

Nilsen, B. A. (2004). *Week by week: Documenting the development of young children*. Albany, NY: Delmar Learning.

Explains how to use class list logs for separation and school adjustment, anecdotal recordings to look at self-care, checklists for physical development, running records for social development, frequency counts for emotional development, conversations for speech and language, time samples for attention span, rating scales for literacy, work samples for creativity, using technology for socio-dramatic play.

Veigut, D., & Ainsworth, L. (2006). *Common formative assessments: How to connect standards-based instruction and assessment*. Thousand Oaks, CA: Corwin Press.

Gives explanations for when parents are wondering how their children are doing in school. Explains how the use of formative assessments can actually help your students' achievement in the classroom. Explains how to align these formative assessments with the standards and how to refine.

---

[1]This bibliography was prepared by Holly Ortiz, in partial fulfillment of early childhood education coursework at DePaul University School of Education.

GLOSSARY

accountability being responsible for the proper education of all children.

age-equivalent score derived score giving a child's performance as that which is normal for a certain age.

amniocentesis a prenatal test in which amniotic fluid is withdrawn from the embryonic sac of a fetus.

anecdotal notes brief notes of significant events or critical incidents in a particular child's day.

Apgar Rating Scale screening test given to newborn infants 1 minute and 5 minutes after birth.

artifacts the materials that children produce to demonstrate knowledge, skills, or dispositions.

assessment process for gathering information to make decisions.

atypical development unusual developmental pattern of children.

authentic assessment *see* performance assessment.

behavioral intervention plans plans made based on assessment of young children who present troubling behavior. Modifications to the regular program are made and monitored.

behavior questionnaires questionnaires designed to give parents an opportunity to report any behavior problems of their children.

biological risk risk to infant because of prenatal, perinatal, or neonatal difficulty.

checklists forms for recording the skills or attributes of the children in a class.

Child Find federal requirement for teachers (and others working with young children) to identify young children with disabilities so they may receive appropriate services and interventions to ameliorate such disabilities.

Child Find team group of professionals whose responsibility it is to determine children with special needs.

child study in-depth look at a particular child at a specific point in time.

chorionic villus biopsy a prenatal test in which chorionic tissue is removed from the developing placenta.

class journals diaries that teachers keep about a group's progress toward meeting educational goals.

concurrent validity relationship between a test and another criterion when both are obtained at about the same time.

confidentiality allowing a child's assessment and other records to be available only to school personnel, agency officials, and parents.

content validity extent of how well a test tests the subject matter it is supposed to test.

construct validity the extent to which a test measures a theoretical characteristic or trait.

constructivist perspective views teaching and learning as a process of discovery for the learner, based on the learner's prior knowledge. Teacher facilitates knowledge, skills, and attitude learning to support individual development.

convergent validity is demonstrated when similar instruments measuring similar constructs yield comparable results.

correlation coefficient degree of relationship between two variables.

criterion-based instruments are those based on a learning goal or standard. Finite steps in the learning of particular concepts are measured.

criterion-referenced measures tests that compare performance in certain skills to accepted levels.

criterion-referenced test a standardized test that compares a child's performance to his or her own progress in a certain skill or behavior.

criterion-related validity relationship between the scores on a test and another criterion.

curriculum-based language assessment a process for determining a child's functional language skills and vocabulary related to the subject matter being studied.

curriculum-based measures diagnostic tests for specific subjects.

derived score score obtained by comparing the raw score with the performance of children of known characteristics on a standardized test.

developmentally appropriate practice planning instruction for preschool children around topics rooted in the children's social world.

deviation quotients standard scores with a mean of 100 and a standard deviation of usually 15.

diagnostic evaluation *see* diagnostic tests.

diagnostic measures are those used by psychologists and others who receive special training, and often certification for using these specialized instruments, that become a key determinant to entitle young children for special educational intervention and service.

diagnostic tests tests used to identify a child's specific areas of strength and weakness, determine the nature of the problems, and suggest the cause of the problems and possible remediation strategies.

documentation collection of artifacts to support record keeping of child's progress in learning.

documentation panel is the part of the Reggio Emilia process that shows, publicly, the learning accomplishments of young children.

dynamic assessment one-to-one interview approach between teacher and student using available assessment information for teaching a specific skill.

ecological assessment an approach that includes the classroom environment, personal interactions, and the learning tasks as variables in the collection of evidence for the measure of learning for individuals.

event sampling record of skills or behaviors a teacher wants the children to know or to do.

extrapolated score derived score estimated from norm scores because the raw score is either less than or greater than anyone in the normative sample.

face validity whether a test looks as if it is testing what it is supposed to be testing.

family collaboration involving the family reciprocally in all phases of the assessment of a child with a developmental problem.

formative assessment data is gathered while teaching or program implementation is occurring; changes to instruction and programs are made while they are in process.

formative evaluation assessment an approach to examining young children that holds that assessment is an ongoing process. It is similar to the scientific approach, in which a query is generated, validated or not, and then another query is formed.

frequency records checklists for recording the presence or absence of, frequency of, or quality of selected behaviors.

functional assessment focused observational method that links individual assessment to curricular intervention for one student.

grade-equivalent score derived score giving a child's performance as that which is normal for a certain grade.

grades letters or numbers ascribed to child performance, based on a summative judgment by the teacher regarding child accomplishment of a task, a course, or a marking period—quarter, semester, year.

high-stakes decision any test applied to make life-affecting decisions for the educational futures of young children.

IDEA federal law that governs the practices for delivery of educational services to all children with disabilities.

IEP goals the specified learning goals for children with disabilities. These are established by a multidisciplinary team that includes the child's parents.

individualized academic tests formal interviews of children on specific topics.

Individualized Educational Plan (IEP) the formal document that governs the contract for educational intervention for a young child with disabilities.

Individualized Educational Plan conference (IEP conference) the multidisciplinary meeting where parents and those involved in intervention with a young child with disabilities meet to assess progress, or review initial assessment results, and plan educational interventions to support the child's learning.

Individualized Family Service Plan (IFSP) specific plan for the assessing of needs and for the services needed for a child with a developmental problem.

informal evaluation task activities used to assess the instructional needs and levels of children.

initial referral conference the meeting where teachers and parents meet to share concerns about a child's progress in the learning situation.

interpolated score derived score estimated from norm scores because no one with that particular score was actually part of the normative sample.

interrater reliability *see* interscorer reliability.

interscorer reliability ability of a test to produce the same results regardless of who administers it.

intrinsically motivating causing a child to do something or continue doing something because of the nature of the thing or activity itself.

inventory test to assess overall ability in a given area.

learner outcomes expectations for children's performances.

mastery learning the philosophy that promotes the idea that everyone should learn particular concepts or skills and that teachers are responsible for teaching toward this level of accomplishment for all children.

mean the arithmetic average of a group of scores.

mediated learning experience (MLE) teaching approach in which the teacher uses questions, suggestions, and cues to prompt the child to think more consciously about the task and to expand learner expertise.

multidisciplinary staffing group of professionals involved in the assessment of children with special needs, the teaching of these children, and the evaluation of their progress.

multiple intelligence theory theory that children have seven areas of intellectual competence that are relatively independent of each other.

normal curve bell-shaped curve representing the usual distribution of human attributes.

normal-curve equivalents standard scores for group tests; scale has 100 equal parts, mean is usually 50, and standard deviation is usually 21.06.

normative sample subset of a population that is tested for a standardized test.

norm-based instruments tests that compare children to others of similar age, grade level, or other important characteristics.

norm-referenced test *see* standardized test.

norms scores obtained from the testing of a normative sample for a standardized test.

objectivity implies that a scoring scheme is sufficiently clear and discrete so that all those applying the criteria will obtain similar scores.

observation records written records of the observations of a child including anecdotes, daily logs, and in-depth running records.

observations systematic means of gathering information about children by watching them.

outcomes are the specifications used by school districts, states, and professional associations to describe measurable educational goals.

parent interview an interview of a child-care professional with a parent for determining how well a child is doing.

parent perspective a parent's perception of a child's development, learning, and education.

parent questionnaires questionnaires given by child-care professionals to parents for obtaining information about a child.

parental reports information from a parent concerning a child.

parents' rights as specified in state and federal law, parents are assured that schools and agencies will fully involve and inform parents in the care and education of their children.

percentile ranks derived scores indicating the percentage of individuals in the normative group whose test scores fall at or below a given raw score.

performance refers to actions on the part of learners that can be assessed through observation, review of child-produced documents, or other learning products.

performance assessment determining developmental progress of children through a variety of means, including observations and special problems or situations.

performance-based assessment is based on child-action related to an educational activity. That is, the child does the task and the teacher watches and scores the results.

P.L. 99–457 Education of the Handicapped Act Amendments, 1986.

play-based assessment relies on the teacher's knowledge of child's play to judge the social/emotional, language, cognitive, and physical development of a young child. This can be conducted in a natural situation or by interview.

population group of individuals on which a standardized test is normed.

portfolios places, such as folders, boxes, or baskets, for keeping all the information known about the children in a class.

precutaneous umbilical blood sampling a specialized prenatal test performed during pregnancy. The test predicts the potential for biological disability.

predictive validity how accurately a test score can be used to estimate performance on some variable or criterion in the future.

prenatal testing testing done prior to the birth of a baby.

prereferral screening refers to the evidence that you gather to substantiate a developmental concern regarding child progress.

presentation mode way a task or learning situation is presented to a child as part of instruction.

primary responsibility the person expected to perform a certain task.

project-based learning curricula organized on the basis of child-generated curiosities.

psychological evaluation assessment that incorporates developmental psychological and educational tasks.

range the spread of the scores or the difference between the top score and the bottom score on a test.

rating scales methods of recording whether children possess certain skills or attributes and to what extent.

raw score the number of items that a child answered correctly on a test.

referral questions questions posed in a child study to aid in the determination of the specific problems and needs of a child and the assessing of the developmental progress of the child.

Reggio Emilia approach holistic community way to develop early childhood programs that includes all stakeholders—child, parents, teachers, school leaders, and the community at large.

reliability consistency, dependability, or stability of test results.

report card formal, written documents that form a legal academic history for a child.

reporting ways that teachers generate their knowledge about children's accomplishments.

resiliency capacity of children and families to overcome odds in spite of obstacles that developmental and environmental factors may place in the way of individuals.

response mode how a child responds to a direction or instruction.

RTI conference the conference with one or more specialists to discuss Tier 1 (modified tasks in the typical classroom), Tier 2 (specialized intervention), Tier 3 (intensive intervention).

rubrics scoring criteria for performance tasks.

running records notes made of routine functioning of an individual child or a small group of children.

scaled score statistically determined scores that are used to derive total scores or that refer to results on subtests of an instrument.

screening results documentation of broad-based, quick overview of child's developmental or educational progress on a set of objectives/milestones.

screening test test used to identify children who may be in need of special services, as a first step in identifying children in need of further diagnosis; focuses on the child's ability to acquire skills.

social validity describes the usefulness of assessment information for the teacher in the educational setting.

specificity percentage of children without developmental problems who are correctly identified by a developmental screening test.

stakeholders people important in the lives of children, especially regarding the assessment of children.

standard deviation the distance scores depart from the mean.

standard error of measurement (SEM) estimate of the amount of variation that can be expected in test scores as a result of reliability correlations.

standard score is created statistically. This process converts raw scores to numbers that can be used to compare child progress on a particular dimension.

standardized test test that interprets a child's performance in comparison to the performance of other children with similar characteristics.

standards-based teaching an approach to teaching that requires teachers to coordinate instruction to specified standards or goals.

stanines standard scores with nine unequal bands; bands four, five, and six represent average performance.

strength-based assessment requires the assessor to focus on a child's capacities to plan intervention.

student-led conferences are those meetings between teacher and child where the learner holds the responsibility for reviewing and judging self-progress in relationship to class standards and teacher judgment. May include parents.

summative evaluation reports the final results of a given assessment. For teachers, this often means the end-of-the-year-summary of child progress.

task analysis process in which large goals are broken down into smaller objectives or parts and sequenced for instruction.

technical issues variables of task, learner, and context that can cause problems with performance assessment.

techniques methods, whether formal or informal, for gathering assessment information.

test instrument for measuring skills, knowledge, development, aptitudes, and so on.

test-retest reliability ability to get the same results from a test taken twice within two weeks.

textbook tests assessment materials published by textbook publishers to accompany their instructional materials.

time sampling checklist for determining what is happening at a particular time with one or more children.

treatment validity the usefulness of test results for planning intervention.

typical development the usual or expected developmental pattern of children.

ultrasound a prenatal test in which sound waves are used to determine a fetus's development.

validity the extent to which a test measures what it is supposed to measure.

REFERENCES

Abel, E. L. (1998). *Fetal alcohol abuse syndrome.* New York: Plenum.

Ahola, D., & Kovacik, A. (2007). *Observing and understanding child development: A child study manual.* Belmont, CA: Cengage/Delmar.

Airasian, P. W. (2008). *Classroom assessment: Concepts and applications* (6th ed.). New York: McGraw-Hill.

Almy, M., & Genishi, C. (1979). *Ways of studying children* (rev. ed.). New York: Teachers College Press.

American Academy of Pediatrics Committee on Children with Disabilities. (2001). Developmental surveillance and screening of infants and young children. *Pediatrics, 108*(1), 192–196.

American Cancer Society. (2009). Women and smoking: An epidemic. Available online at http://amc.org.

American College of Obstetricians and Gynecologists. (2007). *Screening tests for birth defects.* Washington, DC: Author.

American Educational Research Association, American Psychological Association, & National Council on Measurement in Education. (1999). *Standards for educational and psychological testing.* Washington, DC: American Psychological Association.

American Educational Research Association. (2000). *AERA position statement concerning high-stakes testing in Pre-K–12 education.* Washington, DC: Author.

American Speech and Hearing Association. (2005). Cultural differences in communication and learning styles. Available online at http://asha.org.

Apfel, N. H. (2001). The birth of a new instrument: The Infant-Toddler and Family Instrument (ITFI). *Zero to Three, 21*(4), 29–35.

Apgar, V. (1953). Proposal for a new method of evaluating the newborn infant. *Anesthesia and Analgesia, 32*, 260–267.

Armour-Thomas, E. (2004). What is the nature of evaluation and assessment in an urban context? In S. R. Steinberg & J. L. Kincheloe (Eds.), *19 Urban questions: Teaching in the city.* New York: Peter Lang.

Arter, J., & Chappuis, J. (2007). *Creating and recognizing quality rubrics.* Upper Saddle River, NJ: Pearson/Merrill/Prentice Hall.

ASCD. (2005). NCLB update: Measuring student learning. *EdPolicy Update, 4*(6), 1. Available online at http://www.ascd.org.

Aschbacher, P. R. (2000). Developing indicators of classroom practice to monitor and support school reform. *The CRESST Line*, Winter 2000, 6–8.

Atkins, A. (1990). Do kindergarten tests fail our kids? Don't let a misused test direct your child to the wrong classroom. *Better Homes and Gardens, 68*, 22–24.

Austin, T. (1994). *Changing the view: Student-led parent conferences.* Portsmouth, NH: Heinemann.

Baca, L. M., & Cervantes, H. T. (2004). *The bilingual special education interface* (4th ed.). Upper Saddle River, NJ: Merrill/Prentice Hall.

Bagnato, S. J. (2007). *Authentic assessment for early childhood intervention: Best practices.* New York: Guilford.

Bagnato, S. J., Neisworth, J. T., & Munson, S. M. (1997). *Linking assessment and early intervention: An authentic curriculum-based approach.* Baltimore: P. H. Brookes Pub.

Bailey, J. M., & Guskey, T. R. (2001). *Implementing student-led conferences.* Thousand Oaks, CA: Corwin.

Banks, R. A., Santos, R. M., & Roof, V. (2009). Discovering family concerns, priorities, and resources: Sensitive family information gathering. *Young Exceptional Children, 6*(2), 11–19.

Barnett, D., Macmann, G., & Carey, K. (1992). Early intervention and the assessment of developmental skills: Challenges and directions. *Topics in Early Childhood Special Education, 12*(1), 21–43.

Baroody, A. J. (2006). Why children have difficulties mastering the basic number combinations and how to help them. *Teaching children mathematics, 13*(1), 22–31.

Barton, P. E. & Coley, R. J. (2008). *Windows on achievement and inequality.* Princeton, NJ: Educational Testing Services.

Baum, S., Viens, J., & Slatin, B. (2005). *Multiple intelligences in the elementary classroom: A teacher's toolkit.* New York: Teachers College.

Baumann, E., McDonough, S., & Mindes, G. (1974). *Classroom observation guide for Head Start teachers.* Chicago: City of Chicago, Department of Human Services.

Bayat, M. (2011). *Teaching exceptional children.* New York: McGraw Hill.

Beaty, J. J. (2006). *50 early childhood guidance strategies.* Upper Saddle River, NJ: Merrill/Prentice Hall/Pearson.

Beaty, J. J. (2010). *Observing the development of the young child* (7th ed.). Upper Saddle River, NJ: Merrill/Prentice Hall.

Bell, G. E. (1989). Making the most of parent–teacher conferences: Tips for teachers. *Focus on Early Childhood, 2*(2), 1–11.

Benson, B. (2008). *How to meet standards, motivate students, and still enjoy teaching.* Thousand Oaks, CA: Corwin.

Benson, B. & Barnett, S. P. (2005). *Student-led conferencing: Using showcase portfolios.* Thousand Oaks, CA: Corwin.

Bergen, D., Reid, R., & Torelli, L. (2009). *Educating and caring for very young children: The infant/toddler curriculum* (2nd ed.). New York: Teachers College.

Berger, E. H. (2008). *Parents as partners in education: The school and home working together* (7th ed.). Upper Saddle River, NJ: Merrill/Prentice Hall.

Berk, L. E. (2008). *Infants and children* (6th ed.). Boston: Allyn & Bacon.

Berlin, L. J., Brooks-Gunn, J., McCarton, C., & McCormick, M. C. (2004). The effectiveness of early intervention: Examining risk factors and pathways to enhanced development. In M. Batshaw (Ed.), *Children with disabilities* (5th ed.). Baltimore: Paul H. Brookes.

Berns, R. A. (2010). *Child, family, community: Socialization and support* (8th ed.). Belmont, CA: Wadsworth.

Berry, C. F., & Mindes, G. (1993). *Planning a theme-based curriculum: Goals, themes, and planning guides for 4s and 5s.* Glenview, IL: Good Year Books.

Bielenberg, B., & Fillmore, L. W. (2005). The English they need for the test. *Educational Leadership, 62*(4), 45–49.

Bodrova, E., & Leong, D. J. (1996). *Tools of the mind: The Vygotskian approach to early childhood education.* Upper Saddle River, NJ: Merrill/Prentice Hall.

Borich, G. D., & Tombari, M. L. (2004). *Educational assessment for the elementary and middle school classroom* (2nd ed.). Upper Saddle River, NJ: Merrill/Prentice Hall.

Bowman, B. & Moore, E. K. (Eds.). (2006). *School readiness and social-emotional development: Perspectives on cultural diversity.* Washington DC: National Black Child Development Institute.

Bracey, G. W. (2004). *Setting the record straight: Responses to misconceptions about public education in the U.S.* (2nd ed.). Portsmouth, NH: Heinemann.

Braun, H. I., & Mislevy, R. (2005). Intuitive test theory. *Phi Delta Kappan, 86*(7), 489–497.

Brazelton, T. B., & Nugent, J. K. (1995). *Brazelton Neonatal Assessment Scale* (3rd ed.). London: McKeith Press.

Bredekamp, S., & Copple, C. (Eds.). (1997). *Developmentally appropriate practice in early childhood programs serving children from birth through age 8* (rev. ed.). Washington, DC: National Association for the Education of Young Children.

Bredekamp, S., & Rosegrant, T. (1992). *Reaching potentials: Appropriate curriculum and assessment for young children* (Vol. 1). Washington, DC: National Association for the Education of Young Children.

Bricker, D. (1989). *Early intervention for at-risk and handicapped infants, toddlers and children* (2nd ed.). Baltimore: Paul H. Brookes.

Bricker, D. (2009). *Assessment, Evaluation, and Programming System (AEPS®) for Infants and Children* (3rd ed.). Baltimore: Paul H. Brookes.

Bricker, D., & Squires, J. (2009). *Ages and stages questionnaires: A parent-completed child monitoring system* (3rd ed.). Baltimore: Paul H. Brookes.

Brigance, A. (2004). *BRIGANCE® Inventory of Early Development–II (IED–II).* North Billerica, MA: Curriculum Associates.

Bronfenbrenner, U. (1979). *The ecology of human development.* Cambridge, MA: Harvard University Press.

Brookhart, S. M. (2008). *Grading* (2nd ed.). Upper Saddle River, NJ: Merrill/Prentice Hall.

Brookhart, S. M. (2008). *How to give effective feedback to your students.* Alexandria, VA: Association for Supervision and Curriculum Development.

Brookhart, S. M. (2007/2008). Feedback that fits. *Educational Leadership, 65*(4), 54–59.

Brookhart, S. M. & Nitko, A. J. (2008). *Assessment and grading in classrooms.* Upper Saddle River NJ: Pearson/Merrill/Prentice Hall.

Brown, H. D. (2007). *Teaching by principles: An interactive approach to language pedagogy* (3rd ed.). Boston: Allyn & Bacon.

Brown, W. (2008). Young children assess their learning: The power of the quick check strategy. *Young Children, 63*(6), 14–20.

Brown-Chidsey, R. (Ed.). (2005). *Assessment for intervention.* Baltimore: Guilford.

Burke, K. (2009). *How to assess authentic learning* (5th ed.). Thousand Oaks, CA: Corwin.

Burns, M. (2005). Looking at how students reason. *Educational Leadership, 63*(3), 26–31.

Bushouse, B. K. (2009). *Universal preschool: Policy change, stability and the Pew Charitable Trusts.* Albany, NY: State University of New York Press.

Busse, R. T. (2005). Rating scale applications within the problem-solving model. In R. Brown-Chidney (Ed.), *Assessment for intervention.* New York: Guilford.

Carr, J. F., & Harris, D. E. (2001). *Succeeding with standards: Linking curriculum, assessment and action planning.* Alexandria, VA: Association for Supervision and Curriculum Development.

Cegelka, P. T., & Berdine, W. H. (1995). *Effective instruction for students with learning problems.* Boston: Allyn & Bacon.

Center on Education Policy. (2007). Answering the question that matters most: Has student achievement increased since No Child Left Behind? Washington, DC: Author.

Center for Universal Design. (1997). About universal design. Raleigh NC: Author. Retrieved from http://design.ncsu.edu/cud/about_ud/udprinciples.htm.

Chalufour, I., & Worth, K. (2004). *Building structures with young children.* St. Paul, MN: Redleaf Press.

Chandler, L. K., & Dahlquist, C. M. (2010). *Functional assessment: Strategies to prevent and remediate challenging behavior in school settings* (3rd ed.). Upper Saddle River, NJ: Merrill/Prentice Hall.

Chappuis, S. & Chappuis, J. (2007/2008). The best value in formative assessment. *Educational leadership, 65*(4), 14–19.

Charlesworth, R. (2005). *Experiences in math for young children* (5th ed.). Clifton Park, NY: Delmar/Thomson.

Children, A. Sands, J. R. & Pope, S. T. (2009). Backward design: Targeting depth of understanding for all learners. *Teaching exceptional children, 41*(5), 6–14.

Children's Defense Fund. (2007). *Key data findings.* Washington, DC: Author.

Children's Defense Fund. (2008). *The state of America's children.* Washington, DC: Author.

Clark, D. A. (2009). Pregnancy, labor, and delivery. In G. L. Ensher, D. A. Clark, N. S. Songer, (Eds.), *Families, infants, and young children at risk: Pathways to best practice.* Baltimore: Paul Brookes.

Clay, M. (2006). *An observational survey of early literacy achievement* (2nd ed.). Portsmouth, NH: Heinemann.

Clements, D. H. & Sarama, J. A. (2009). *Learning and teaching early math: The learning trajectrory approach.* New York: Routledge.

Cochran-Smith, M. (2005). No Child Left Behind: Three years and counting. *Journal of Teacher Education, 56*(2), 99–103.

Cohen, V. L., & Cowen, J. E. (2010). *Literacy for children in an information age: Teaching reading, writing, and thinking* (2nd ed.). Belmont, CA: Wadsworth.

Cohen, R., Stern, V., Balaban, N., & Gropper, N. (2008). *Observing and recording the behavior of young children* (5th ed.). New York: Teachers College Press.

Committee for Economic Development. (2002). *Preschool for all: Investing in a productive and just society.* Washington, DC: Author. Retrieved from http://www.ced.org.

Committee for Economic Development. (2006). *The economic promise of investing in high-quality preschool: Using early education to improve economic growth and the fiscal sustainability of states and the nation.* Washington, DC: Author.

Connolly, A. J. (1998). *Key Math Revised: A diagnostic inventory of essential mathematics.* Circle Pines, MN: American Guidance.

Cook, R. E., Klein, M. D., & Tessier, A. (2008). *Adapting early childhood curricula for children in inclusive settings* (7th ed.). Upper Saddle River, NJ: Merrill/Prentice Hall.

Connor, C. M., Morrison, F. J., Fishman, B. J., Ponitz, C. C., Glasney, S., Underwood, P. S., Piasta, S. B., Crowe, E. C., & Schatschneider, C. (2009). *Educational Researcher, 38*(2), 85–99.

Copple, C. (Ed.). (2003). *A world of difference: Readings on teaching young children in a diverse society.* Washington, DC: National Association for the Education of Young Children.

Copple, C., & Bredekamp, S. (Eds.). (2009). *Developmentally appropriate practice in early childhood programs: Serving children birth through age 8.* Washington, DC: National Association for the Education of Young Children.

Cook, R. E., Tessier, A., & Klein, M. D. (2004). *Adapting early childhood curriculum for children with special needs* (6th ed.). Upper Saddle River, NJ: Merrill/Prentice Hall.

Costa, A. L., & Kallick, B. (2003). *Assessment strategies for self-directed learning.* Thousand Oaks, CA: Corwin.

Council of Chief State School Officers (2005). *State content standards: A 50 state resource.* Washington, DC: Author. Retrieved from http://www.ccsso.org.

Council for Exceptional Children. (2008). CEC's position on response to intervention (RTI): The unique role of special education and special educators. *Teaching Exceptional Children, 40*(3), 74–75.

Cromwell, E. S. (2000). *Nurturing readiness in early childhood education* (2nd ed.). Needham Heights, MA: Allyn & Bacon.

Curtis, D., & Carter, M. (2008). *Learning together with young children: A curriculum framework for reflective teachers.* St. Paul, MN: Red Leaf Press.

Developmentally Appropriate Practice in 2005: Updates from the Field (2005). *Young Children, 60*(4).

Davidson, P. W., & Myers, G. J. (2007). Environmental toxins. In M. L. Batshaw, L. Pellegrino, & N. J. Rosen (Eds.). *Children with disabilities* (6th ed.). Baltimore: Paul H. Brookes.

Day, C. B. (2006). Leveraging diversity to benefit children's social-emotional development and school readiness. In B. Bowman & E. K. Moore (Eds.). (2006). *School readiness and social-emotional development: Perspectives on cultural diversity.* Washington, DC: National Black Child Development Institute.

de Bettencourt, L. U. (1987). How to develop parent partnerships. *Teaching Exceptional Children, 19*, 26–27.

Delandshere, G. (2002). Assessment as inquiry. *Teachers College Record, 104*(7), 1461–1484.

Deno, S. (1985). Curriculum-based measurement: The emerging alternative. *Exceptional Children, 52*, 219–232.

Deno, S. (1990). Individual differences and individual difference: The essential difference in special education. *Journal of Special Education, 24*, 160–173.

Denton, P. (2007). *The power of our words.* Turner Falls, MA: Northeast Foundation for Children, Inc.

Denton, P. (2008). The power of our words. *Educational Leadership, 66*(1), 28–31.

Dewey, D., Crawford, S. G., & Kaplan, B. J. (2003). Clinical importance of parent ratings of everyday cognitive abilities in children with learning and attention problems. *Journal of Learning Disabilities, 36*(1), 87–95.

Dewey, D., Crawford, S. G., Creighton, D. E., & Sauve, R. S. (2000). Parents' ratings of everyday cognitive abilities in very low birth weight children. *Journal of Developmental and Behavioural Pediatrics, 21*, 37–43.

Dietel, R. (2001). How is my child doing in school? Ten research-based ways to find out. *National PTA: Our Children.* Retrieved from http://www.pta.org.

Diffily, D., & Sassman, C. (2002). *Project-based learning with young children.* Portsmouth, NH: Heinemann.

Dichtelmiller, M. L., Jablon, J. R., Dorfman, A. B., Marsden, D. B., & Meisels, S. J. (2001). *Work sampling in the classroom. A teacher's manual* (3rd ed.) *for use with the 4th ed. Work Sampling materials.* Minneapolis, MN: Pearson Assessments.

Division for Early Childhood, Council for Exceptional Children. (1998). *Position statement on services for children birth to age eight with special needs.* Denver: Author.

Division for Early Childhood, Council for Exceptional Children. (2000). *DEC-recommended practices in early intervention/early childhood special education.* Denver: Author.

Division for Early Childhood, Council for Exceptional Children. (2002). DEC position statement on responsiveness to family cultures, values, and languages. Missoula, MT: Author.

Division for Early Childhood. (2007). Promoting positive outcomes for children with disabilities: Recommendations for curriculum, assessment, and program evaluation. Missoula, MT: Author.

Division for Early Childhood, Council for Exceptional Children/National Association for the Education of Young Children. (2009). *Early childhood inclusion: A joint position statement of the Division for Early Childhood (DEC) and the National Association for the Education of Young Children (NAEYC).* Missoula, MT: DEC; Washington, DC: NAEYC.

Doctoroff, G., & Arnold, D. H. (2004). Parent-rated externalizing behavior in preschoolers: The predictive utility of structured interviews, teacher reports, and classroom observations. *Journal of Clinical Child & Adolescent Psychology, 33*(4), 813–818.

Dodge, D. T., & Colker, L. J. (2002). *The creative curriculum for preschool.* Washington, DC: Teaching Strategies.

Dombro, A. L., Colker, L. J., Dodge, D. T. (2006). *The creative curriculum for infants & toddlers* (2nd ed.). Washington, DC: Teaching Strategies.

Donovan, M. (1995). *Parent response form for Chicago Public Schools Project.* Chicago: Erikson Institute on Early Education.

Duckworth, E. (1987). *The having of wonderful ideas and other essays on teaching and learning.* New York: Teachers College Press.

Dunst, C. J., & Trivette, C. M. (2009). Capacity-building family-systems intervention practices. *Journal of Family Social Work, 12*(2), 119–143.

Dyson, A. & Genishi, C. (2005). *On the case: Approaches to language and literature research.* New York: Teachers College.

Eckert, T. L., & Arbolino, L. A. (2005). The role of teacher perspectives in diagnostic and program evaluation decision making. In R. Brown-Chidsey (Ed.), *Assessment for intervention: A problem-solving approach.* New York: Guilford.

Edwards, C., Gandini, L., & Forman, G. E. (1998). *The hundred languages of children: The Reggio Emilia approach* (advanced edition). New York: Greenwood.

Educational Testing Service. (1990). Testing in the schools. *ETS Policy Notes, 2*(3).

Educational Testing Service. (1993). Learning by doing: A manual for teaching and assessing higher-order thinking in science and mathematics. In *Performance assessment sampler: A workbook.* Princeton: Author.

Eggers-Pierola, C. (2005). *Connections and commitments: Reflecting Latino values in early childhood programs.* Portsmouth, NH: Heinemann.

Ehri, L. C. (2000). Learning to read and learning to spell: Two sides of a coin. *Topics in Learning Disabilities, 20*(3), 19–36.

Eisner, E. (2002). *The educational imagination: On the design and evaluation of educational programs* (3rd ed.). New York: Macmillan.

Elliott, S. N. (1993). *Creating meaningful performance assessments: Fundamental concepts.* Reston, VA: Council for Exceptional Children.

Elliott, J. L., & Thurlow, M. L. (2005). *Improving test performance of students with disabilities . . . on district and state assessments* (2nd ed.). Thousand Oaks, CA: Corwin.

Elliott, S., & Braden, J. (2000). *Educational assessment and accountability for all students: Facilitating the meaningful participation of students with disabilities in district and statewide assessment programs.* Madison: Wisconsin Department of Public Instruction.

Ensher, G. L. (2009). Performance assessment. In G. L. Ensher, D. A. Clark, & N. S. Songer (Eds.). *Families, infants & young children at risk: Pathways to best practice.* Baltimore: Paul Brookes Publishing Co,.

Ensher, G. L., Clark, D. A. & Songer, N. S. (2009). *Families, infants & young children at risk: Pathways to best practice.* Baltimore: Paul Brookes Publishing Co,.

Epps, S., & Jackson, B. J. (2000). *Empowered families, successful children: Early intervention programs that work.* Washington, DC: American Psychological Association.

Epstein, A. (2008). Planning and reflection: Two ways children learn to think. *Teaching young children, 1*(3), 18–19.

Epstein, M. H. (1998). Using strength-based assessment in programs for children with emotional and behavioral disorders. *Beyond Behavior, 9*(2), 25–27.

Erera, P. I. (2002). Family diversity: Continuity and change in the contemporary family. Thousand Oaks, CA: Sage.

Escamilla, K., Chavez, L., & Vigil, P. (2005). Rethinking the gap: High stakes testing and Spanish-speaking students in Colorado. *Journal of Teacher Education, 56*(2), 132–144.

Eyer, D. W., & Gonzalez-Mena, J. (2009). *Infants, toddlers, and caregivers* (8th ed.). New York: McGraw-Hill.

Fair Test: The National Center for Fair & Open Testing. (2007, August 27). The value of formative assessment. Retrieved June 22, 2009, from http://www.fairtest.org/value-formative-assessment-pdf.

Fair Test: The National Center for Fair & Open Testing. (2009). *Empowering schools and improving learning: A joint organizational statement on the federal role in public schooling vision of public education.* Retrieved June 21, 2009, from http://www.fairtest.org.

Family Educational Rights and Privacy Act. (1974). 20 U.S.C.A. Section 123g, with accompanying regulations set forth in 45 C.F.R. part 99.

Farr, R., & Tone, B. (1998). *Portfolio and performance assessment: Helping students evaluate their progress as readers and writers* (2nd ed.). Fort Worth: Harcourt.

Feeney, S., & Kipnis, K. (1989). The National Association for the Education of Young Children code of ethical conduct and statement of commitment. *Young Children, 45*, 24–29.

Feeney, S., Moravcik, E., Nolte, S., & Christensen, D. (2010). *Who am I in the lives of children?* (8th ed.). Upper Saddle River, NJ: Merrill/Prentice Hall.

Feldman, R. S. (2010). *Child development* (5th ed.). Upper Saddle River, NJ: Pearson/Merrill/Prentice Hall.

Feuer, M. J., & Fulton, K. (1993). The many faces of performance assessment. *Phi Delta Kappan, 74*, 478.

Feuerstein, R. (1979). *The dynamic assessment of retarded performers: The learning potential assessment device, theory, instruments, and techniques.* Baltimore: University Park Press.

Fewell, R., & Glick, M. (1998). The role of play in assessment. In D. P. Fromberg & D. Bergen (Eds.), *Play from birth to twelve and beyond: Contexts, perspectives, and meanings.* New York: Garland.

Fields-Smith, C. & Neuharth-Pritchett, S. (2009). Families as decision-makers: When researchers and advocates work together. *Childhood Education, 85*(4), 237–242.

Fisher, D., & Frey, N. (2007). *Checking for understanding: Formative assessment techniques for your classroom.* Alexandria, VA: Association for Supervision and Curriculum Development.

Flesch, R. (1955). *Why Johnny can't read.* New York: Harper.

Fogarty, R., Burke, K., & Belgrad, S. (2008). *The portfolio connection: student work linked to standards.* Thousand Oaks, CA: Corwin.

Fountas, I. & Pinnell, G. S. (2008). *Fountas and Pinnell benchmark assessment system.* Portsmouth, NH: Heinemann.

Fredericks, A. D., & Rasinski, T. V. (1990). Involving parents in the assessment process. *The Reading Teacher, 44*, 346–349.

Fromberg, D. P. (2002). *Play and meaning in early childhood education.* Boston: Allyn & Bacon.

Fromberg, D. P., & Bergen, D. (2006). *Play from birth to twelve and beyond: Contexts, perspectives, and meanings* (2nd ed.). New York: Routledge.

Frost, J. L., Wortham, S. C., & Reifel, S. (2008). *Play and child development* (3rd ed.). Upper Saddle River, NJ: Pearson/Merrill/Prentice Hall.

Fuchs, L. S. (1993). *Connecting performance assessment to instruction.* Reston, VA: Council for Exceptional Children.

Garcia, E. E. (2005). *Teaching and learning in two languages: Bilingualism & schooling in the United States.* New York: Teachers College

Garcia, E. E., & Jensen, B. T. (2009). Early educational opportunities for children of Hispanic origins. *Social policy report, 23*(2), 1–19.

Garcia, E. E., Jensen, B. T., & Scribner, K. P. (2009). The demographic imperative. *Educational Leadership, 66*(7), 8–13.

Gardner, H. (1999). *The disciplined mind: What all students should understand.* New York: Simon & Schuster.

Gardner, H. (2004). *Frames of mind: The theory of multiple intelligences.* New York: Basic Books.

Gardner, H. (2006). *Multiple intelligences: New horizons in theory and practice.* New York: Basic.

Gardner, H. (2009). *Five minds for the future.* Cambridge MA: Harvard Business.

Garfinkle, A. N. (2004). *Assessing play skills.* In M. McLean, M. Worley, & D. B. Bailey (Eds.), *Assessing infants and preschoolers with special needs* (3rd ed.). Upper Saddle River, NJ: Merrill/Prentice Hall.

Garvey, C. (1993). Special topic: New directions in studying pretend play. *Human Development, 35*(4), 235–240.

Geisinger, K. F., Spies, R. A., Carlson, J. F., Plake, B. S., & Impara, J. C. (Eds.). (2007). *The seventeenth mental measurements yearbook.* Lincoln: Buros Institute.

Gelfer, J. I., & Perkins, P. G. (1992). Constructing student portfolios: A process and product that fosters communication with families. *Day Care and Early Education, 20*, 9–13.

Genishi, C. & Goodwin, A. L. (2008). *Diversities in early childhood education: Rethinking and doing.* New York: Routledge.

Gesell, A. L., & Amatruda, C. S. (1954). *Developmental diagnosis* (3rd ed.). New York: Hoeber.

Gestwicki, C. (2010). *Home, school and community relations* (7th ed.). Albany, NY: Delmar.

Gil, E., & Drewes, J. C. (Eds.). (2005). *Cultural issues in play therapy.* New York: Guilford.

Ginsburg, H. P., & Baroody, A. J. (2003). *Test of early mathematics ability* (3rd ed.). Austin, TX: Pro-Ed.

Gitlin-Weiner, K., Sandgrund, A., & Schaefer, C., eds. (2000). *Play diagnosis and assessment.* New York: Wiley.

Glascoe, F. P. (1998). *Collaborating with parents: Using parents' evaluation of developmental status to detect and address developmental and behavioral problems.* Nashville, TN: Ellsworth & Vanderneer Press.

Glascoe, F. P. (1999). Communicating with parents. *Young Exceptional Children, 2*(4), 17–25.

Glascoe, F. P., MacLean, W. E., & Stone, W. L. (1991). The importance of parents' concerns about their child's behavior. *Clinical Pediatrics, 30*, 8–11.

Goffin, S. G., & Wilson, C. (2001). *Curriculum models and early childhood education: Appraising the relationship* (2nd ed.). Upper Saddle River, NJ: Merrill/Prentice Hall.

Gonzalez-Mena, J. (2009). *The child in the family and the community* (5th ed.). Upper Saddle River, NJ: Merrill/Prentice Hall.

Goodenough, F. L. (1949). *Mental testing: Its history, principles, and applications.* New York: Rinehart.

Goodwin, W. L., & Goodwin, L. D. (1997). Using standardized measures for evaluating young children's learning. In B. Spodek & O. N. Saracho (Eds.), *Issues in early childhood education assessment and evaluation.* New York: Teachers College Press.

Gosso, Y. (2010). Play in different cultures. In P. K. Smith, *Children and play: Understanding children's worlds.* New York: Wiley.

Gould, P. & Sullivan, J. (2005). *The inclusive early childhood classroom: Easy ways to adapt learning centers for all children.* Upper Saddle River, NJ: Merrill/Prentice Hall.

Grant, K. B., & Ray, J. A. (2010). *Home, school & community collaboration.* Thousand Oaks, CA: Sage.

Gredler, G. R. (1992). *School readiness: Assessment and educational issues.* Brandon, VT: Clinical Psychology Publishing.

Green, S. K., & Johnson, R. L. (2010). *Assessment is essential.* New York: McGraw Hill.

Greene, A. H., & Melton, G. D. (2007). *Test talk: Integrating test preparation into reading workshop.* Portland ME: Stenhouse.

Greenfield, P. M., & Cocking, P. R. (2003). *Crosscultural roots of minority child development.* Hillsdale, NJ: Laurence Erlbaum Associates.

Greenspan, S. I. (2003). *The clinical interview of the child* (3rd ed.). Washington, DC: American Psychiatric Association.

Greenspan, S. I. (2004). *Greenspan social-emotional growth chart: A screening questionnaire for infants and young children.* San Antonio TX: Psychcorp/Pearson.

Greenspan, S. I., & Wieder, S. (1997). An integrated developmental approach to interventions for young children with severe difficulties in relating and communicating. In S. I. Greenspan, B. Kalmanson, R. Shahmoon-Shanok, S. Wieder, G. G. Williamson, & M. Anzalone (Eds.), *Assessing and treating infants and young children with severe difficulties in relating and communicating*. Washington, DC: National Center for Infants, Toddlers, and Families.

Greenspan, S. I., & Wieder, S. (1998). *The child with special needs: Encouraging intellectual and emotional growth*. Reading, MA: Perseus.

Greenspan, S. I., & Wieder, S. (2006a). *Engaging autism: The Floortime^{TM} approach to helping children relate, communicate and think.* New York: Perseus Books.

Greenspan, S. I., & Wieder, S. (2006b). *Infant and early childhood mental health: A comprehensive, developmental approach to assessment and intervention.* Washington, DC: American Psychiatric Association.

Grigorenko, E. L. (Ed.). (2009). *Multicultural psychoeducational assessment.* New York: Springer Publishing Co.

Gronlund, G., & Engel, B. (2001). *Focused portfolios(tm): A comprehensive assessment for the young child.* St. Paul, MN: Redleaf Press.

Guerin, G. R., & Maier, A. S. (1983). *Informal assessment in education.* Palo Alto: Mayfield.

Guidry, J., & van den Pol, R. (1996). Augmenting traditional assessment and information: The videoshare model. *Topics in Early Childhood Special Education, 16*(1), 51–65.

Gullo, D. F. (2005). *Understanding assessment and evaluation in early childhood education* (2nd ed.). New York: Teachers College.

Gunning, T. J. (2008). *Creating literacy instruction for all children* (6th ed.). Needham Heights, MA: Allyn & Bacon.

Guralnick, M. J. (Ed.). (2000). *Interdisciplinary clinical assessment of young children with developmental disabilities*. Baltimore: Paul H. Brookes.

Guralnick, M. J. (Ed.). (2005). *The developmental systems approach to early intervention.* Baltimore: Paul H. Brookes.

Guralnick, M. J., & Conlon, C. J. (2007). Early intervention. In M. Batshaw, L. Pelligrino, & N. Roizen (Eds.), Children with Disabilities (6th ed.), pp. 511–521. Baltimore: Paul H. Brookes.

Guskey, T. R. (2001). *Implementing mastery learning* (2nd ed.). Belmont, CA: Wadsworth.

Guskey, T. R. (Ed.). (1994). *High-stakes performance assessment: Perspectives on Kentucky's educational reform.* Thousand Oaks, CA: Corwin.

Guskey, T. R., & Bailey, J. M. (2001). *Developing grading and reporting systems for student learning.* Thousand Oaks, CA: Corwin.

Guskey, T. R., & Bailey, J. M. (2009). *Developing standards-based report cards.* Thousand Oaks, CA: Corwin.

Halverson, A. T., & Neary, T. (2009). *Building inclusive schools: Tools and strategies for success.* Upper Saddle River, NJ: Pearson/Merrill/Prentice Hall.

Hampton, S., Murphy, S., & Lowry, M. (2009). *Using rubrics to improve student writing: K.* (rev. ed.). Pittsburgh: University of Pittsburgh and the International Reading Association.

Hannon, J. H. (2000). Learning to like Matthew. *Young Children, 55*, 24–28.

Hanson, M. J. (2004). Ethnic, cultural, and language diversity in intervention settings. In E. W. Lynch, & M. J. Hanson (Eds.), *Developing cross-cultural competence: A guide for working with children and their families* (3rd ed.). Baltimore: Paul H. Brookes.

Harlan, J. D., & Rivkin, M. S. (2008). *Science experiences for the early childhood years: An integrated affective approach* (9th ed.). Upper Saddle River, NJ: Pearson/Merrill/Prentice Hall.

Harp, B., & Brewer, J. (2000). Assessing reading and writing in the early years. In D. S. Stickland & L. M. Morrow (Eds.), *Beginning reading and writing* (Chap. 13). New York: Teachers College Press.

Haynes, J. (2007). *Getting started with English language learners: How educators can meet the challenge.* Alexandria, VA: Association for Supervision and Curriculum Development.

Haynes, S. N., Hersen, M., & Heiby, E. M. (2003). *Comprehensive handbook of psychological assessment, behavioral assessment.* Thousand Oaks: Sage.

Haywood, H. C., & Lidz, C. (2007). *Dynamic assessment in practice: Clinical and educational applications.* New York: Cambridge University Press.

Hauser-Cram, P., & Shonkoff, J. (1988). Rethinking the assessment of child-focused outcomes. In H. Weiss & F. Jacobs (Eds.), *Evaluating family programs* (pp. 73–94). Hawthorne, NY: Aldine.

Head Start. (2002). Technical Assistance Paper No. 4. Developmental Screening, Assessment, and Evaluation: Key Elements for Individualizing Curricula in Early Head Start Programs. Washington, DC: Author. Retrieved from http://www.headstartinfo.org.

Head Start. (2003 July). Head Start Child Outcomes—Setting the Context for the National Reporting System. *Head Start Bulletin No. 76.*

Head Start. (1993). Performance Standards §1308.6 Assessment of Children http://eclkc.ohs.acf.hhs.gov/ Accessed June 29, 2009.

Hebert, E. A. (2001). *The power of portfolios: What children can teach us about learning and assessment.* San Francisco: Jossey Bass.

Helm, J. H. (2008). Got standards? Don't give up on engaged learning! *Young Children, 63*(4), 14–21.

Helm J. H., & Beneke, S. (Eds.). (2003). *The power of projects: Meeting contemporary challenges in early childhood classrooms—strategies & solutions.* New York: Teachers College.

Helm, J. H., Beneke, S., & Steinheimer, K. (2007). *Windows on learning: Documenting young children's work* (2nd ed.). New York: Teachers College Press.

Hemmeter, M. L., Ostrosky, M. M., Artman, K. M., & Kinder, K. A. (2008). Moving right along…Planning transitions to prevent challenging behavior. *Young Children, 63*(3), 18–25.

Henning-Stout, M. (1994). *Responsive assessment: A new way of thinking about learning*. San Francisco: Jossey-Bass.

Herman, J., Aschbacher, P., & Winters, L. (1992). *A practical guide to alternative assessment*. Alexandria, VA: Association for the Supervision of Curriculum Development.

Heward, W. L. (2009). *Exceptional children: An introduction to special education* (9th ed.). Upper Saddle River, NJ: Merrill/Prentice Hall.

Higginbotham, M. L. O., & Pretzello, L. (n.d.). *Observation: Implications for appropriate early childhood assessment.* Unpublished manuscript. Louisiana State University Medical Center, New Orleans.

Hill, B. C., Kamber, P., & Norwick, L. (1994). Six ways to make student portfolios more meaningful and manageable: Involving students, peers, and parents in portfolio assessment. *Instructor, 104*, 118–120.

Hilliard, A. G. (2000). Excellence in education versus high-stakes standardized testing. *Journal of Teacher Education, 51*(4), 293–304.

Hills, T. W. (1987). *Screening for school entry, ERIC Digest.* Champaign, IL: ERIC Clearinghouse on Elementary and Early Childhood Education.

Hills, T. W. (1992). Reaching potentials through appropriate assessment. In S. Bredekamp & T. Rosegrant (Eds.), *Reaching potentials: Appropriate curriculum and assessment for young children* (Vol. 1). Washington, DC: National Association for the Education of Young Children.

Hirsch, E. S. (Ed.). (1984). *The block book* (rev. ed.). Washington, DC: National Association for the Education of Young Children.

Hirshberg, L. (1996). History-making, not history-taking: Clinical interviews with infants and their families. In S. J. Meisels & E. Genichel (Eds.), *New visions for the developmental assessment of infants and young children.* Washington, DC: Zero to Three: National Center for Infants, Toddlers, and Families.

Hohmann, M., & Weikart, D. P. (2008). *Educating young children: Active learning practices for preschool and child care programs* (2nd ed.). Ypsilanti, MI: High Scope.

Hooper, S. R., & Umansky, W. (2009). *Young children with special needs* (5th ed.). Upper Saddle River, NJ: Merrill/Prentice Hall.

Hoover, H. D., Hieronymous, A. N., Frisbie, D. A., & Dunbar, S. B. (1996). *Iowa Tests of Basic Skills.* Chicago: Riverside Publishing Company.

Hoover, H. D., Dunbar, S. B., Frisbie, D. A., Oberley, K. R., Ordman, V. L., Naylor, R. J., Bray, G. B., Lewis, J. C., & Qualls, A. L. (2005). *Message to parents: Iowa Test of Basic Skills.* Itasca, IL: Riverside Publishing.

Horn, M., & Giacobbe, E. (2007). *Talking, drawing, writing: Lessons for our youngest writers.* Portland, ME: Stenhouse.

Hosp, M. K., Hosp, J. L., & Howell, K. W. (2007). *The ABCs of CBM: A practical guide to curriculum-based measurement.* New York: Guilford.

Howard, V. F., Lepper, C., & Williams, B. F. (2010). *Very young children with special needs: A formative approach for today's children* (4th ed.). Upper Saddle River, NJ: Merrill/Prentice Hall.

Hoy, C., & Gregg, N. (1994). *Assessment: The special educator's role.* Pacific Grove, CA: Brooks/Cole.

Individuals with Disabilities Education Act (IDEA) PL 108-446 (2004). Regulations update: U.S. Department of Education, Office of Special Education Programs 10.04.06.

Illinois State Board of Education. (2001). Illinois learning standards. Retrieved from http://www.isbe.net/ils/standards.html.

Illinois State Board of Education. (2005). English language learning proficiency standards. Retrieved from http://www.isbe.net/bilingual/htmls/elp_standards.htm.

Innovative Education. (2009). Retrieved from http://www.innovativeeducation.com.

Interdisciplinary Council on Developmental and Learning Disorders. (2000). *ICDL clinical practice guidelines for infants, children, and families with special needs.* Bethesda, MD: Author.

Ireton, H. R. (1994). *The child development review manual.* Minneapolis: Behavior Science Systems.

Ireton, H. R. (1997). *Child development inventories in education and health care.* Minneapolis: Behavior Science Systems.

Jacobs, G. & Crowley, K. (2006). *Play, projects, and preschool standards: Nurturing children's sense of wonder and joy in learning.* Thousand Oaks, CA: Corwin.

Jablon, J. R., Dombro, A. L., & Dichtelmiller, M. L. (2007). *The power of observation* (2nd ed.). Washington, DC: Teaching Strategies

Jacobson, J., & Raymer, A. (1999). *The big book of reproducible graphic organizers: 50 great templates to help kids get more out of reading, writing, social studies & more.* New York: Scholastic.

Javier, R. A. (2007). *The bilingual mind: Thinking, feeling, and speaking in two languages.* New York: Springer.

Johnson, J. E., Christie, J. F., & Wardle, F. (2005). *Play, development and early education.* Needham Heights, MA: Allyn & Bacon.

Johnston, P. (2005). Literacy assessment and the future. *The reading teacher, 58*(7), 684–686.

Jones, E., & Reynolds, G. (1992). *The play's the thing: Teachers' roles in children's play.* New York: Teachers College Press.

Jordan, L., Reyes-Blanes, M. E., Peel, B. B., Peel, H. A., & Lane, H. B. (1998). Developing teacher–parent partnerships across cultures: Effective parent conferences. *Intervention in School and Clinic, 33*(3), 141–147.

Jung, L. A. (2007). Writing Individualized Family Service Plan strategies that fit into the ROUTINE. *Young Exceptional Children, 10*(3), 2–8.

Kaiser, A. P., Xinsheng, C., Hancock, T. B., & Foster, E. M. (2002). Teacher-reported behavior problems and language delays in boys and girls enrolled in Head Start. *Behavioral Disorders, 28*(1), 23–39.

Kaiser, A. P., Hancock, T. B., Xinsheng, C., Foster, E. M., & Hester, P. P. (2000). Parent-reported behavioral problems and language delays in boys and girls enrolled in Head Start classrooms. *Behavioral Disorders, 26*(1), 26–41.

Kamii, C. (1990). *Achievement testing in the early grades: The games grown-ups play.* Washington, DC: National Association for the Education of Young Children.

Kamii, C. (2000). *Young children reinvent arithmetic: Implications of Piaget's theory* (2nd ed.). New York: Teachers College.

Kamii, C. (2004). *Young children continue to reinvent arthimetic, 2nd grade: Implications of Piaget's theory* (2nd ed.). New York: Teachers College.

Kamii, C., & Rosenblum, V. (1990). An approach to assessment in mathematics. In C. Kamii (Ed.), *Achievement testing in the early grades: The games grown-ups play.* Washington, DC: National Association for the Education of Young Children.

Karly, L. A. & Bigelow, J. H. (2005). *The economics of investing in universal preschool education in California.* Santa Monica, CA: Rand Corp. Retrieved July 1, 2009, from http://www.rand.org/pubs/monographs/MG349/.

Katz, L., & Chard, S. (2000). *Engaging children's minds: The project approach.* Norwood, NJ: Ablex.

Kentucky State Department of Education. (2005). What's new. Retrieved from http://www.education.ky.gov.

Kerr, M. M., & Nelson, C. M. (2010). *Strategies for addressing behavior problems in the classroom* (6th ed.). Upper Saddle River, NJ: Merrill/Prentice Hall.

Kingore, B. (2008). *Developing portfolios for authentic assessment, prek–3: Guiding potential in young learners.* Thousand Oaks, CA: Corwin.

Kissel, B. T. (2009). Beyond the page: Peers influence pre-kindergarten writing through image, movement, and talk. *Childhood Education, 85*(3), 160–166.

Klinger, J. K., Hoover, J. H., & Baca, L. M. (Eds.). (2008). *Why do English language learners struggle with reading? Distinguishing language acquisition from learning disabilities.* Thousand Oaks, CA : Corwin Press.

Knobloch, H., Steven, F., Malone, A., Ellison, P., & Risemberg, H. (1979). The validity of parental reporting of infant development. *Pediatrics, 63*, 873–878.

Kochhar-Bryant, C. A., & Shaw, S. (2009). What every teacher should know about: Transition and IDEA 2004. Upper Saddle River, NJ: Pearson.

Kohn, A. (2004). *What does it mean to be well educated? And more essays on standards, grading, and other follies.* Boston: Beacon.

Kostelnik, M. J., Stein, L. C., Whiren, A. P., Soderman, A. K., & Gregory, K. (2009). *Guiding children's social development* (6th ed.) Clifton Park, NY: Delmar.

Kostelnik, M. J., Soderman, A. K., & Whiren, A. P. (2007). *Developmentally appropriate curriculum: Best practices in early childhood education* (4th ed.). Upper Saddle River, NJ: Merrill/Prentice Hall.

Kovas, M. A. (1993). Making your grading motivating: Keys to performance-based evaluation. *Quill and Scroll, 68*, 10–11.

Krechevsky, M., ed. (2003). *Making teaching visible: Documenting individual and group learning as professional development.* Cambridge, MA: Harvard Project Zero.

Krogh, S. & Morehouse, P. J. (2008). *The early childhood curriculum: Inquiry learning through integration.* New York: McGraw Hill.

Kroth, R. L., & Edge, D. (1997). *Strategies for communicating with parents and families of exceptional children.* Denver: Love.

Kubiszyn, T., & Borich, G. (2009). *Educational testing and measurement: Classroom application and practice* (9th ed.). New York: Wiley.

Kuhs, T. M., Johnson, R. L., Agruso, S. A., & Monrad, D. M. (2001). *Put to the test: Tools and techniques for classroom assessment.* Portsmouth, NH: Heinemann.

Landgraf, K. (2008). Addressing achievement gaps: The language acquisition and educational achievement of English-language learners. *Policy Notes: News from the ETS Policy Information Center. 16.2*, 1-16.

Lally, J. R. (2008). Teacher research as the base for curriculum planning. San Francisco: WestEd.

Lantz, H. B. (2004). *Rubrics for assessing student achievement in science, grades K–12.* Thousand Oaks, CA: Corwin.

Lee-Katz, L., Ellis, M., & Jewett, J. (1993). *There's math in deviled eggs: Strategies for teaching young children.* Bloomington, IN: Agency for Instructional Technology.

Lee, J. M., & McDougal, O. (2000). Guidelines for writing notes to families of young children. *Focus on Pre-K and K, 13*(2), 4–6.

Lerner, J., Lowenthal, B., & Egan, R. (2002). *Preschoolers with special needs: Children-at-risk or who have disabilities.* 2nd ed. Needham Heights, MA: Allyn & Bacon.

Lewin-Benham, A. (2008). Powerful children: Understanding how to teach and learn using the Reggio approach. New York: Teachers College.

Lewis, R. B., & Doorlag, D. H. (2006). *Teaching special students in general education classrooms* (7th ed.). Upper Saddle River, NJ: Merrill/Prentice Hall.

Lichtenstein, R., & Ireton, H. R. (1984). *Preschool screening: Early identification of school problems.* New York: Grune & Stratton.

Lidz, C. (2003). *Early childhood assessment.* New York: Wiley.

Lieber, J., Schwartz, I., Sandall, S., Horn, E., & Wolery, R. A. (1999). Curricular considerations for young children in inclusive settings. In C. Seefeldt (Ed.), *The early childhood curriculum: Current findings in theory and practice* (3rd ed.). New York: Teachers College Press.

Linder, T. (2008a). *Administration guide for TPBA2 & TPBI2.* Baltimore: Paul H. Brookes.

Linder, T. (2008b). *Transdisciplinary play-based assessment: A functional approach to working with young children* (2nd ed.). Baltimore: Paul H. Brookes.

Linn, R. (2003). Accountability, responsibility and reasonable expectations. *Educational Researcher, 32*(7), 3–13.

Linn, R. L., Miller, D. M., & Gronlund, N. E. (2009). *Measurement and assessment in teaching* (10th ed.). Upper Saddle River, NJ: Merrill/Prentice Hall.

Losardo, A., & Notari-Syverson, A. (2001). *Alternative approaches to assessing young children.* Baltimore: Paul H. Brookes.

Lynch, E. W., & Hanson, M. J. (2004). *Developing cross-cultural competence: A guide for working with children and their families* (3rd ed.). Baltimore: Paul H. Brookes.

MacDonald, S. (2001). *Block play: The complete guide to learning and playing with blocks.* Beltsville, MD: Gryphon House.

Macy, M., & Hoyt-Gonzales, K. (2007). A linked system approach to early childhood special education assessment. *Teaching exceptional children, 39*(3), 40–44.

Maeroff, G. I. (2006). *Building blocks: Making children successful in the early years of school.* New York: Palgrove.

Mah, R. (2007). *Difficult behavior in early childhood: Positive discipline for pre-k classrooms and beyond.* Thousand Oaks: Corwin.

Maldonado-Duran, J. M. (Ed.). (2002). *Infant and toddler mental health: Models of clinical intervention with infants and their families.* Washington, DC: American Psychiatric Association.

Mapp, K., & Henderson, A. (2005). *A new wave of evidence: The impact of school, family, and community connections on student achievement.* Reported in *Education Update*, March 2005. Alexandria, VA: Association for Supervision and Curriculum Development.

Mardell-Czudnowski, C., and Goldenberg, D. (1998). *DIAL-3 (Developmental Indicators for the Assessment of Learning-Revised) Manual.* Austin, TX: Pearson.

Mardell Czudnowski, C., & Goldenberg, D. Parents' Observation of Infants and Toddlers (POINT) 2006.

Marsili, A., & Hughes, M. (2009). Finding Kirk's words: An infant mental health approach to preschool intervention. *Young Exceptional Children, 12*(2), 2–14.

Martin-Kniep, G. O. (1998). *Why am I doing this? Purposeful teaching through portfolio assessment.* Portsmouth, NH: Heinemann.

Martin-Kniep, G. O. (2000). *Becoming a better teacher: Eight innovations that work.* Alexandria, VA: Association for Supervision and Curriculum Development.

Marzano, R. J. (2007). *Art and science of teaching: A comprehensive framework for effective instruction.* Alexandria, VA: Association for Supervision and Curriculum Development.

Marzano, R. J., Pickering, D., & McTighe, J. (1993). *Assessing student outcomes: Performance assessment using the dimensions of learning model.* Alexandria, VA: Association for the Supervision of Curriculum Development.

Marzano, R. J., Norford, J. S., Paynter, D. E., Pickering, D. J., & Geddy, B. B. (2001). *Handbook for Classroom Instruction That Works.* Alexandria, VA: Association for Supervision and Curriculum Development.

Maslow, A. (1943). A theory of human motivation. *Psychological Review, 50*, 370–396.

Maxwell, K. L., & Clifford, R. M. (2004). School readiness assessment. *Young Children, 59*(1), 42–49.

McAfee, O., & Leong, D. J. (2007). *Assessing and guiding young children's development and learning* (4th ed.). Boston: Allyn & Bacon.

McCollum, J., Azar-Mathis, R., Henderson, K., & Kusmierek, A. (1989). Assessment of infants and toddlers: Supporting developmentally and ecologically relevant intervention. *Illinois technical assistance project.* Springfield, IL: Illinois State Board of Education.

McCormick, K. M., Stricklin, S., Nowak, T. M., & Rous, B. (2008). Using eco-mapping to understand family strengths and resources. *Young Exceptional Children, 11*(2), 17–28.

McDonnell, L. M. (2008). The politics of educational accountability: Can the clock be turned back? In K. E. Ryan & L. A. Shepard, L. A. (Eds.), *The future of test-based educational accountability.* New York: Routledge.

McGee, L. M., & Morrow, L. M. (2005). *Teaching literacy in kindergarten.* Baltimore: Paul H. Brookes.

McGonigel, M. J., Woodruff, G., & Roszmann-Millican, M. (1994). Parents in the infant-toddler assessment process. *Zero to Three, 14*, 59–65.

McGuire, J. M. Scott, S. S. & Shaw. S. F. (2006). Universal Design and Its Applications in Educational Environments. *Remedial and Special Education, 27*(3), 166–175.

McKenna, M. C., & Stahl, K. A. (2009). *Assessment for reading instruction* (2nd ed.). New York: Guilford.

McLaughlin, M. J., & Warren, S. H. (1994). *Performance assessment and students with disabilities: Usage in outcomes-based accountability systems.* Reston, VA: Council for Exceptional Children.

McLean, M., Wolery, M., & Bailey, D. B. (2004). *Assessing infants and preschoolers with special needs* (3rd ed.). Upper Saddle River, NJ: Merrill/Prentice Hall.

McLoughlin, J. A., & Lewis, R. B. (2008). *Assessing special students* (7th ed.). Upper Saddle River, NJ: Merrill/Prentice Hall.

McManus, S. (2008). Attributes of effective formative assessment. Washington, DC: Council of Chief State School Officers (CCSSO).

McTighe, J., & Wiggins, G. (2006). *The understanding by design handbook* (2nd ed.). Alexandria, VA: Association for the Supervision of Curriculum Development.

McWilliam, R. A., & Casey, A. M. (2008). *Engagement of every child in the preschool classroom.* Baltimore: Paul H. Brookes.

McWilliam, R. A., Wolery, M., & Odom, S. L. (2001). Instructional perspectives in inclusive preschool classrooms. In M. J. Guralnick (Ed.), *Early childhood inclusion: Focus on change.* Baltimore: Paul H. Brookes.

Meisels, S. J. (2000). On the side of the child: Personal reflections on testing, teaching, and early childhood education. *Young Children, 55*(6), 16–19.

Meisels, S. J. (2001). Fusing assessment and intervention: Changing parents' and providers' views of young children. *Zero to Three, 21*(4), 4–10.

Meisels, S. J. (2007). Accountability in early childhood. In R. Pianta, M. J. Cox, & K. L. Snow (eds.). *School readiness, early learning, and the transition to kindergarten.* Baltimore: Brookes Publishing.

Meisels, S. J., & Atkins-Burnett, S. (2005). *Developmental screening in early childhood: A guide* (5th ed.). Washington, DC: NAEYC.

Meisels, S. J., Harrington, H. L., McMahon, P., Dichtelmiller, M. L., & Jablon, J. R. (2001). *Thinking like a teacher: Using observational assessment to improve teaching and learning.* Needham Heights, MA: Allyn & Bacon.

Meisels, S. J., & Provence, S. (1989). *Screening and assessment: Guidelines for identifying young disabled and developmentally vulnerable children and their families.* Washington, DC: National Center for Clinical Infant Programs.

Meisels, S. J., & Steele, D. M. (1991). *The early childhood portfolio collection process.* Ann Arbor: Center for Human Growth and Development, University of Michigan.

Meisels, S. J., Marsden, D. B., Dombro A. L., Weston, D. R., Jewkes, A. M. (2003). *Ounce Scale*™. Rebus Inc., a Pearson Education Inc., Company.

Meisels, S. J., Jablon, J. R., Dichtelmiller, M. L., Dorfman, A. B., & Marsden, D. B. (2001). *The Work Sampling System*™ (4th ed.). Rebus, Inc., a Pearson Education Inc., Company.

Mercer, C. D., & Mercer, A. R. (2005). *Teaching students with learning problems* (7th ed). Upper Saddle River, NJ: Merrill/Prentice Hall.

Mertler, C.A. (2007). *Interpreting standardized test scores.* Thousand Oaks, CA: Sage Publications.

Million, J. (2005). Getting teachers set for parent conferences. *Communicator, 28* (February), 5–6.

Mindes, G. (1982). Social and cognitive aspects of play in young handicapped children. *Topics of Early Childhood Special Education, 2*, 14.

Mindes, G. (1990). Kindergarten in our nation. In C. Seefeldt (Ed.), *Continuing issues in early childhood education.* Upper Saddle River, NJ: Merrill/Prentice Hall.

Mindes, G., & Donovan, M. A. (2001). *Building character: Five enduring themes for a stronger early childhood curriculum.* Boston: Allyn & Bacon.

Morris, D., & Perney, J. (1984). Developmental spelling as a predictor of first grade reading achievement. *Elementary School Journal, 84*, 441–457.

Morrow, L. M. (2009). *Literacy development in the early years: Helping children read and write* (6th ed.). Boston: Allyn & Bacon.

Morse, B. A., & Weiner, L. (2005). Fetal alcohol syndrome. In S. Parker, B. Zuckerman, & M. Augustyn (Eds.). *Developmental and behavioral pediatrics: A handbook for primary care* (2nd ed.). Philadelphia: Lippincott Williams & Wilkins.

Mowder, B. A., Rubinson, F., & Yasik, A.E. (Eds.). (2009). *Evidence-based practice in infant and early childhood psychology.* New York: Wiley.

Musial, D., Nieminen, G., Thomas, J., & Burke, K. (2009). *Foundations of meaningful educational assessment.* New York: McGraw-Hill.

National Association for the Education of Young Children. (1995). Position statement on school readiness. *Young Children, 46*, 21–23.

National Association for Education of Young Children. (1996). NAEYC position statement: Responding to linguistic and cultural diversity—recommendations for effective early childhood education. *Young Children, 51*(2), 4–12.

National Association for Education of Young Children. (2002). Early learning standards: Creating the conditions for success. A joint position statement of the National Association for the Education of Young Children (NAEYC) and the National Association of Early childhood Specialists in State Departments of Education (NAECS/SDE). Washington, DC: Author.

National Association for the Education of Young Children. (2005). *NAEYC code of ethical conduct and statement of commitment.* Washington, DC: Author. Retrieved from http://www.naeyc.org.

National Association for the Education of Young Children. (2009). *Developmentally appropriate practice in early childhood programs serving children from birth through age 8.* Retrieved from http://www.naeyc.org.

National Association for the Education of Young Children & National Association of Early Childhood Specialists in State Departments of Education. (2003a). *Position statement on early childhood curriculum, assessment, and program evaluation.* Washington, DC: Author. Available online at http://www.naeyc.org.

National Association for the Education of Young Children and National Association of Early Childhood Specialists in State Departments of Education. (2003b). *Early childhood curriculum, assessment, and program evaluation: Building an effective, accountable system in programs for children birth through age 8.* Washington, DC: Author. Retrieved from http://www.naeyc.org and http://naecs.crc.uiuc.edu.

National Association of Early Childhood Specialists in State Departments of Education & National Association for the Education of Young Children. (2001). Still unacceptable trends in kindergarten entry and placement. *Young Children, 56*(5), 59–62.

National Association for Elementary School Principals (2006). *Leading early childhood communities: What principals should know & be able to do.* Alexandria, VA: Author.

National Association for School Psychologists. (2005). Position statement on early childhood assessment. Bethesda, MD: Author.

National Center for Learning Disabilities. (2009). Roadmap to Pre-K RTI: Applying response to intervention in preschool settings. New York: Author.

National Coalition for Parent Involvement in Education. Building family-school partnerships that work. Retrieved June 15, 2009, from http://www.ncpie.org.

National Commission on Excellence in Education. (1983). *A nation at risk: The imperative for school reform.* Washington, DC: U.S. Government Printing Office.

National Council of Teachers of Mathematics. (2000). *Principles and standards for school mathematics.* Reston, VA: National Council for Teachers of Mathematics.

National Council of Teachers of Mathematics. (2000). *Principles and standards: Setting higher standards for our students, higher standards for ourselves.* Washington, DC: Author.

National Council for Teachers of Mathematics. (2005). *Illuminations.* Retrieved from http://illuminations.nctm.org.

National Early Childhood Technical Assistance Center. (2009). Minimum Components Under IDEA for Statewide, Comprehensive Services to Infants and Toddlers with Special Needs. Adapted from 20 U.S.C. §1435(a). Retrieved July 5, 2009, from http://www.nectac.org/partc/componen.asp.

National Education Goals Panel. (1997). *Getting a good start in school.* Washington, DC: US Government Printing Office.

Neisworth, J. T., & Bagnato, S. J. (2000). Recommended practices in assessment. In S. Sandall, M. E. McLean, & B. J. Smith (Eds.), *DEC recommend practices in early intervention/early childhood special education.* Denver: Division for Early Childhood.

Neuman, S. B., Copple, C., & Bredekamp, S. (2000). *Learning to read and write: Developmentally appropriate practices for children.* Washington, DC: National Association for the Education of Young Children.

Nilsen, B. A. (2007). *Week by week: Plans for documenting children's development* (4th ed.). Clifton Park, NJ: Delmar/Cengage.

Nitko, A. J. & Brookhart, S. M. (2007). *Educational assessment of students* (5th ed.). Upper Saddle River, NJ: Pearson Merrill Prentice Hall.

No Child Left Behind Act of 2001. U.S. Public Law 107–110. 107th Congress, January 8, 2002.

Noonan, M. J., & McCormick, L. (2006). *Young children with disabilities in natural environments: Methods and procedures.* Baltimore: Paul Brookes.

Odom, S. L., Horner, R. H., Snell, M.E., Blacher, J. (2007). *Handbook of developmental disorders.* New York: Guilford Press.

Ofstedal, K. (1993). Parent-teacher conferences using the child development review-parent questionnaire. (Personal communication.)

Ohio Department of Education. (1990a). *Study skills begin at home: Book 1: Preschool.* Columbus, OH: Ohio Department of Education.

Ohio Department of Education. (1990b). *Study skills begin at home: Book 2: Kindergarten–Grade 3.* Columbus, OH: Ohio Department of Education.

Otto, B. (2008). *Literacy development in early childhood: Reflective teaching for birth to age eight.* Upper Saddle River, NJ: Pearson Merrill/Prentice Hall.

Otto, B. (2010). *Language development in early childhood* (3rd ed.). Upper Saddle River, NJ: Merrill/Prentice Hall.

Owens, R. E. (2010). *Language disorders: A functional approach to assessment and intervention.* Upper Saddle River, NJ: Merrill Prentice Hall.

Paley, V. G. (2004). *A child's work: The importance of fantasy play.* Chicago: University of Chicago.

Pavri, S. (2001). Developmental delay or cultural difference? *Young Exceptional Children, 4*(4), 2–9.

Payan, R. M., & Nettles, M. T. (2007). *Current state of English-language-learners in the U.S. K–12 student population.* Princeton, NJ: Educational Testing Services.

Pellegrini, A. D. (2004). *Observing children in their natural worlds: A methodological primer* (2nd ed.). Mahwah, NJ: Lawrence Erlbaum.

Perrin, E. C. (1995). Behavioral screening. In S. Parker & B. Zukerman (Eds.), *Behavioral and developmental pediatrics: A handbook for primary care*, pp. 22–23. Boston: Little, Brown & Company.

Petersen, S., & Wittmer, D. (2008). Relationship-based infant care: Responsive, on demand, and predictable. *Young Children, 63*(3), 40–42.

Pianta, R. C., LaParo, K. M., & Hamre, B. K. (2008). *Classroom assessment scoring system™ Manual K–3.* Baltimore: Paul H. Brookes.

Pianta, R. C., LaParo, K. M., & Hamre, B. K. (2008). *Classroom assessment scoring system™ Manual PK–K.* Baltimore: Paul H. Brookes.

Pianta, R. C., & Kraft-Sayre, M. (2003). *Successful kindergarten transition: Your guide to connecting children, families & schools.* Baltimore: Paul H. Brookes.

Pierangelo, R. & Giuliani, G. A. (2009). *Assessment in special education: A practical approach.* (3rd ed.). Boston: Allyn & Bacon.

Poehner, M. E. (2008). *Dynamic assessment: A Vygotskian approach to understanding and promoting L2 development.* New York: Springer.

Polloway, E. A., Patton, J. R., &. Serna, S. (2008). *Strategies for teaching learners with special needs.* Upper Saddle River, NJ: Merrill/Prentice Hall/Pearson.

Popham, W. J. (2000). *Testing! Testing! What every parent should know about school tests.* Boston: Allyn & Bacon.

Popham, W. J. (2001a). *The truth about testing: An educator's call to action.* Alexandria, VA: Association for Supervision and Curriculum Development.

Popham, W. J. (2001b). Teaching to the test? *Educational Leadership, 58*(6), 16–21.

Popham, W. J. (2003). *Test better, teach better: The instructional role of assessment.* Alexandria, VA: Association for Supervision and Curriculum Development.

Popham, W. J. (2004). *America's "failing" schools.* New York: Routledge/Falmer.

Popham, W. J. (2008a). *Transformative assessment.* Alexandria, VA: Association for Supervision and Curriculum Development.

Popham, W. J. (2008b). *Classroom assessment: What teachers need to know* (5th ed.). Boston: Allyn & Bacon.

Popp, R. J. (1992). *Family portfolios: Documenting change in parent–child relationships.* Louisville, KY: National Center for Family Literacy, occasional paper.

Potter, L., & Bulach, C. (2001). Do's and don'ts of parent–teacher conferences. *Here's How, 19* (Spring), 1–4.

Pretti-Frontczak, K., & Bricker, D. (2004). *An activity-based approach to early intervention* (3rd ed.). Baltimore: Paul H. Brookes.

Project Zero. (2009). Project Zero at the Harvard Graduate School of Education. Retrieved from http://www.pz.harvard.edu/index.htm.

Provence, S., & Apfel, N. H. (2001). *Infant-Toddler and Family Instrument (ITFI).* Baltimore: Paul H. Brookes.

Pugach, M. C., & Warger, C. L. (Eds.). (1996). Challenges for the special education-curriculum reform partnership. *In curriculum trends, special education and reform: Refocusing the conversation.* New York: Teachers College Press.

Quinn, K. (2005). *Ivy chronicles.* New York: Penguin.

Raab, M. M., Whaley, K. T., & Cisar, C. L. (1993). Looking beyond instructional interactions: An ecological perspective of classroom programming. Presentation made at the 20th International Early Childhood Conference on Children with Special Needs, San Diego, CA, December.

Ramsey, P. G. (2004). *Teaching and learning in a diverse world: Multicultural education for young children* (3rd ed.). New York: Teachers College.

Raver, S. A. (2009). *Early childhood special education—0 to 8 years.* Upper Saddle River, NJ: Merrill.

Reed, V. A. (2005). *Introduction to children with language disorders* (3rd ed.). Needham Heights, MA: Allyn & Bacon.

Reeves, D. B. (2004). *Accountability in action: A blueprint for learning organizations* (2nd ed.). Denver: Center for Performance Assessment.

Renzulli, P. (2005). Philadelphia Public Schools On-line Report Cards. Retrieved from http://www.phila.k12.pa.us.

Rhodes, R. L., Ochoa, S. H., & Ortiz, S. O. (2005). *Assessing culturally and linguistically diverse students: A practical guide.* New York: Guilford.

Ritchhart, R., & Perkins, D. (2008). Making thinking visible, *Educational leadership, 65*(5), 57–61.

Robinson, J. (1988). *The baby boards: A parents' guide to preschool & primary school entrance tests.* New York: Arco.

Romero, I. (1999). Individual assessment procedures with preschool children. In E. V. Nuttall, I. Romero, & J. Kalesnik (Eds.), *Assessing and screening preschoolers: Psychological and education dimensions* (2nd ed.). Needham Heights, MA: Allyn & Bacon.

Rosenkoetter, S. E., & Squires, S. (2000). Writing outcomes that make a difference for children and families. *Young Exceptional Children, 4*(1), 2–8.

Roswell, F. G., Chall, J. S. Curtis, M. E. & Kerns, G. (2005). *Diagnostic assessments of reading* (DAR) (2nd ed.). Rolling Meadows, IL: Riverside Publishing.

Rothstein, R. (2000). Toward a composite index of school performance. *The Elementary School Journal, 100*(5), 409–442.

Rothstein, R. (2009). The myopia of testing basic skills alone. *School Administrator. 66*(2): 1.

Sacks, P. (1999). *Standardized minds: The high price of America's testing culture and what we can do to change it.* Cambridge, MA: Perseus Books.

Sadowski, M. (Ed.). (2004). Teaching the new generation of U.S. students. *Teaching immigrant and second-language students: Strategies for success.* Cambridge, MA: Harvard University Press.

Sagor, R. (2008). Cultivating optimism in the classroom. *Educational leadership, 65*(6), 26–31.

Salend, S. J. (2008). Determining appropriate testing accommodations: Complying with NCLB and IDEA. *Teaching Exceptional Children, 40*(4), 14–22.

Salvia, J., Ysseldyke, J., & Bolt, S. (2010). *Assessment* (11th ed.). Belmont, CA: Wadsworth/Cengage.

Sapon-Shevin, M. (2008). Learning in an inclusive community. *Educational leadership, 66*(1), 49–53.

Sandall, S. R., & Schwartz, I. S. (2008). *Building blocks for teaching preschoolers with special needs* (2nd ed.). Baltimore, MD: Paul H. Brookes.

Sandall, S. McLean, M. E. & Smith, B. J. (2005). *Division for Early Childhood, Recommended Practices in early intervention/early childhood special education.* Denver: Division for Early Childhood.

Sandall, S., McLean, M. E., & Smith, B. J. (2000). *DEC recommended practices in early intervention/early childhood special education.* Longmont, CO: Sopris West.

Sanford, A. R., & Zelman, J. G. (2004). *Learning Accomplishment Profile–Third Edition.* Lewisville, NC: Kaplan.

Scheinfeld, D., Haigh, K., & Scheinfeld, S. (2008). *We are all explorers: Learning and teaching with reggio principles in urban settings.* New York: Teachers College.

Santos, R. M., & Ostrosky, M. M. (2005). Understanding the impact of language difference on classroom behavior. *What works briefs.* Champaign, IL: Center on the Social and Emotional Foundations for Early Education. Retrieved from http://csefel.uiuc.edu.

Schmid, R. E. (1999). An elementary school application of pre-referral assessment and intervention. *Diagnostique, 25*(1), 59–70.

Schonberg, R. L., & Tifft, C. J. (2007). Birth defects, prenatal diagnosis, and fetal therapy. In M. Batshaw (Ed.), *Children with disabilities* (6th ed.) Baltimore: Paul H. Brookes.

Schroeder, F. C., & Pryor, S. (2001). Multiple measures: Beginning with ends. *The School Administrator, 58*(11), 22–25.

Schultz, K. A., Colarusso, R. P., & Strawderman, V. W. (1989). *Mathematics for every young child.* Columbus, OH: Merrill/Prentice Hall.

Seefeldt, C., & Barbour, N. (1998). *Early Childhood education: An introduction* (4th ed.). Columbus, OH: Merrill/Prentice Hall.

Seitz, H. (2008). The power of documentation in the early childhood classroom. *Young Children, 63*(2), 88–93.

Seligman, M. (2000). *Conducting effective conferences with parents of children with disabilities: A guide for teachers.* New York: Guilford.

Seligman, M. & Darling, R. B. (2007). *Ordinary families, special children: A systems to childhood disability* (3rd ed.). New York: Guilford Press.

Seplocha, H. (2004). Partnerships for learning: Conferencing with families. *Beyond the Journal, Young Children on the Web,* September. Retrieved from http://naeyc.org.

Serafini, F. (2001). Three paradigms of assessment: Measurement, procedure, and inquiry. *Reading Teacher 54*(4), 384–393.

Serna, L. A., Nielsen, E. Mattern, N., & Forness, S. (2003). Primary prevention in mental health for Head Start classrooms: Partial replication with teachers as interveners. *Behavioral Disorders, 28*(2), 124–129.

Shackelford, J. (2009). State and jurisdictional eligibility definitions for infants and toddlers with disabilities under IDEA. *NECTAS notes.* Issue No: 5, revised. Retrieved from http://www.nectas.unc.edu.

Shepard, L. A. (2000). The role of assessment in a learning culture. *Educational Researcher, 29*(7), 4–14.

Shepard, L. A. (2005). Linking formative assessment to scaffolding. *Educational Leadership, 63*(5), 70–75.

Shepard, L. A., Hammerness, K., Darling-Hammond, L., & Rust, F. (2005). Assessment. In L. Darling-Hammond & J. Bransford (Eds.), *Preparing teachers for a changing world: What teachers should learn and be able to do.* San Francisco: Jossey-Bass.

Sheridan, S. M., & McCurdy, M. (2005). Ecological variables in school-based assessment and intervention planning. In R. Brown-Chidsey (Ed.), *Assessment for intervention: A problem-solving approach,* pp. 43–64. New York: Guilford.

Shonkoff, J. P. (2004). *Science, policy and the young developing child: Closing the gap between what we know and what we do.* Chicago: Ounce of Prevention.

Shonkoff, J. P., & Meisels, S. J. (Eds.). (2000). *Handbook of early intervention* (2nd ed.). New York: Cambridge.

Shores, E. F., & Grace, C. (2005). *The portfolio book: A step-by-step guide for teachers.* Upper Saddle River, NJ: Merrill/Prentice Hall.

Smith, A. F. (2000). Reflective portfolios: Preschool possibilities. *Childhood Education, 76*(4), 204–208.

Smith, D., & Goldhaber, J. (2004). *Poking, pinching & pretending: Documenting toddlers' explorations with clay.* St Paul: Redleaf Press.

Smith, T., Pretzel, R., & Landry, K. (2001). Infant assessment. In R. J. Simeonsson & S. Rosenthal (Eds.), *Psychological and developmental assessment: Children with disabilities and chronic conditions.* New York: Guilford.

Southall, M. (2007). *Differentiated literacy centers.* New York: Scholastic.

Spieker, S. J., Solchany, J., McKenna, M., DeKlyen, M., & Barnard, K. E. (2000). The story of mothers who are difficult to engage in prevention programs. In J. D. Osofsky & H. E. Fitzgerald (Eds.), *WAIMH handbook of infant mental health. Vol. 3: Parenting and child care.* New York: John Wiley.

Spinelli, C. G. (2006). *Classroom assessment for students in special and general education. 2nd ed.* Upper Saddle River, NJ: Pearson Merrill Prentice Hall.

Spodek, B., & Saracho, O. N. (Eds.). (2005). *Handbook of research on the education of young children.* Hillsdale, NJ: Lawrence Erlbaum.

Squires, J. & Bricker, D., (2009). *An activity-based approach to developing young children's social emotional competence.* Baltimore: Paul H. Brookes.

Stacey, S. (2009). *Emergent curriculum in early childhood settings: From theory to practice.* St. Paul, MN: Red Leaf Press.

Stefanakis, E. H. (1998). *Whose judgment counts? Assessing bilingual children, K–3.* Portsmouth, NH: Heinemann.

Stenmark, J. K. (1991). Math portfolios: A new form of assessment. *Teaching K–8, 21,* 62–68.

Stenmark, J. K. (Ed.). (1991). *Mathematics assessment: Myths, models, good questions, and practical suggestions.* Reston, VA: National Council of Teachers of Mathematics.

Sternberg, R. J., & Grigorenko, E. L. (2002). *Dynamic testing: The nature and measurement of learning potential.* New York: Cambridge.

Stiggins, R. J. (2008a). Correcting "errors of measurement" that sabotage student learning. In Dwyer, C. A. ed. *The future of assessment: Shaping teaching and learning.* New York: Lawrence Erlbaum Associates.

Stiggins, R. J. (2008b). *Student-involved assessment for learning* (4th ed.). Upper Saddle River, NJ: Merrill/Prentice Hall.

Stiggins, R. J., & DuFour, R. (2009). Maximizing the power of formative assessments. *Phi Delta Kappan, 90*(9), 640–644.

Stiggins, R., Arter, J., Chappuis, J., & Chappuis, S. (2006). *Classroom assessment for student learning: Doing it right—using it well.* Portland, OR: Educational Testing Service.

Strickland, K. (2005). *What's after assessment? Follow-up instruction for phonics, fluency, and comprehension.* Portsmouth, NH: Heinemann.

Strickland, K., & Strickland, J. (2000). *Making assessment elementary.* Portsmouth, NH: Heinemann.

Stoneman, Z., Rugg, M. E. & Gregg, K. (2009). Partnerships with families. In S. R. Hooper & W. Umansky. *Young children with special needs* (5th ed.). Upper Saddle River, NJ: Merrill.

Stormont, M. (2007). Fostering resilience in young children at risk for failure: Strategies for grades K–3. Upper Saddle River, NJ: Pearson/Prentice Hall.

Suarez, S. C. & Daniels, K. J. (2009). Listening for competence through documentation: Assessing children with language delays using digital video. *Remedial & Special Education. 30*(3), 14, 177–190.

Sulzby, E. (1985). Children's emergent reading of favorite storybooks. *Reading Research Quarterly, 20,* 458–481.

Sulzby, E. (1989). Assessment of writing and children's language while writing. In L. M. Morrow & J. K. Smith (Eds.), *Assessment of instruction in early literacy.* Upper Saddle River, NJ: Prentice Hall.

Suzuki, L. A., & Ponteroto, J. G. (2007). *Handbook of multicultural assessment: Clinical, psychological, and educational applications* (3rd ed.). Thousand Oaks, CA: Jossey-Bass.

T.H.E. Journal. (2005). http://www.edtechinfocenter.com.

Takushi, R., & Uomoto, J. M. (2001). The clinical interview from a multicultural perspective. In L. A. Suzuki, J. G. Ponterotto, & P. J. Meller (Eds.), *Handbook of multicultural assessment* (2nd ed.). San Francisco: Jossey-Bass.

Taylor, C. S., & Nolen, S. B. (2005). *Classroom assessment: Supporting teaching and learning in real classrooms.* Upper Saddle River, NJ: Merrill/Prentice Hall.

Taylor, R. (1998). Check your cultural competence. *Nursing Management, 29*(8), 30–32.

Teale, W. H. (1989). The promise and challeng of informal assessment in early literacy. In L. M. Morrow & J. K. Smith (Eds.), *Assessment for instruction in early literacy.* Upper Saddle River, NJ: Prentice Hall.

Teale, W. H. (1990). The promise and challenge of informal assessment in early literacy. In L. M. Morrow & J. K. Smith (Eds.), *Assessment for instruction in early literacy.* Upper Saddle River, NJ: Prentice Hall.

Teale, W. H., & Sulzby, E. (Eds.). (1986). *Emergent literacy: Writing and reading.* Norwood Park, NJ: Ablex.

Tervo, R. C., & Asis, M. (2009). Parents' reports predict abnormal investigations in global developmental delay. *Clinical Pediatrics, 48*(5), 513–521.

Thomas, R. M. (2005). *High stakes testing: Coping with collateral damage.* Mahwah, NJ: Lawrence Erlbaum.

Thompson, S. J., & Quenemoen, R. F. (2001). Eight steps to effective implementation of alternate assessments. *Assessment for Effective Intervention, 26*(2), 67–74.

Thurlow, M. L. (2001). Special issue: Students with disabilities and high stakes testing. *Assessment for Effective Intervention, 26*(2).

Thurlow, M. L., Elliott, J. L., & Ysseldyke, J. E. (2003). *Testing students with disabilities: Practical strategies for complying with district and state requirements* (2nd ed.). Thousand Oaks, CA: Corwin.

Tompkins, G. E. (2010). *Literacy for the 21st century: A balanced approach* (5th ed.). Upper Saddle River, NJ: Merrill/Prentice Hall.

Tomlinson, C. & McTighe, J. (2006). *Integrating differentiated instruction & understanding by design: Connecting content and kids.* Alexandria, VA: Association for Supervision and Curriculum Development.

Treiman, R. & Bourassa, D. C. (2000). The development of spelling skill. *Topics in Learning Disabilities, 20*(3), 1–18.

Tuckman, B. W. (1988). *Testing for teachers* (2nd ed.). NewYork: Harcourt, Brace, Jovanovich.

Turnbull, A. Turnbull, R., Erwin, E., & Soodak, L. (2006). *Families, professionals & exceptionality: positive outcomes through partnership and trust* (5th ed.). Upper Saddle River, NJ: Merrill/Prentice Hall.

Turnbull, A. P., Turnbull, R., & Wehmeyer, M. L. (2010). *Exceptional lives: Special education in today's schools* (6th ed.). Upper Saddle River, NJ: Merrill/Prentice Hall.

Turnbull, R., Huerta, N., & Stowe, M. (2006). *The Individuals with Disabilities Act as amended in 2004.* Upper Saddle River, NJ: Merrill/Prentice Hall.

Twombly, E., & Fink, G. (2004). *Ages & stages learning activities.* Baltimore: Paul H. Brookes.

U.S. Department of Education. (1991a). *America 2000: An educational strategy sourcebook.* Washington, DC: Author.

U.S. Department of Education. (1991b). *Individuals with Disabilities Education Act (IDEA).* Washington, DC: Author.

U.S. Department of Education. (1997). *Individuals with Disabilities Education Act (IDEA).* Washington, DC: Author.

U.S. Department of Education. (2004). *Individuals with Disabilities Education Act (IDEA).* Washington, DC: Author.

U.S. Department of Education. (2006). *Individuals with Disabilities Education Act (IDEA).* Washington, DC: Author.

U.S. Department of Education. (2005a). CFDA Number: 84.357 Reading First. http://ed.gov.

U.S. Department of Education. (2005b). CFDA Number: 84.359 Early Reading First. http://ed.gov.

U.S. Department of Health and Human Services (2002). President Bush's Plan to Strengthen Early Learning: Good Start, Grow Smart. USDOE Early Reading First 2009 84.359A; 84.359B.

Urbina, S. (2004). *Essentials of psychological testing.* New York: Wiley.

Uribe, M., & Nathenson-Mejia, S. (2008). *Literacy essentials for English language learners: Successful transitions.* New York: Teachers College Press.

Van Hoorn, J., Nourot, P., Scales, B., & Alward, K. (2007). *Play at the center of the curriculum* (4th ed.). Upper Saddle River, NJ: Merrill/Prentice Hall.

Vermont Department of Education. (2009). Programs and services: Assessment. Retrieved June 20, 2009, from http://www.education.vermont.gov/new/html/pgm_assessment.html.

Vygotsky, L. (1978). *Mind in society: The development of higher psychological processes* (M. Cole, V. John Steiner, S.Scribner, & E. Souberman, Eds.). Cambridge, MA: Harvard University Press.

Vygotsky, L. (1986). *Thought and language* (A. Kozulin, Trans.). Cambridge, MA: MIT Press.

Wagner, R., Torgesen, J., & Rashotte, C. (1998). *Comprehensive Test of Phonological Processing (CTOPP).* Austin, TX: Pro-Ed.

Walker, D. K., & Wiske, M. S. (1981). *A guide to developmental assessments for young children* (2nd ed.). Boston: Massachusetts Department of Education, Early Childhood Project.

Weber, C., Behl, D., & Summers, M. (1994). Watch them play; watch them learn. *Teaching Exceptional Children,* Fall, 30–35.

Weinstein, R. S. (2004). *Reaching higher: The power of expectations in schooling.* Cambridge, MA: Harvard University Press.

Young Children. (2005). Special issue: DAP in 2005, *60*(4).

Weis, H., Caspe, M., & Lopez, M. E. (2008). Family involvement promotes success for young children: A review of recent research. In

M. M. Cornish (Ed.). *Promising practices for partnering with families in the early years.* Charlotte, NC: Information Age Publishing.

WestEd. (2009). *Infant and toddler spaces design for a quality classroom.* San Francisco: Author.

West, J., Denton, K., & Germino-Hausken, E. (2000). *America's kindergarteners: Findings from the Early Childhood Longitudinal Study, Kindergarten Class of 1998–99, Fall 1998.* Washington, DC: U.S. Department of Education, National Center for Educational Statistics.

Wherry, J. H. (2009). Shattering barriers to parent participation. *Principal, 88*(5), 7.

Widerstrom, A. H. (2005). *Achieving learning goals through play: Teaching young children with special needs* (2nd ed.). Baltimore, MD: Paul H. Brookes.

Wieder, S., & Greenspan, S. (2001). The DIR (developmental, individual-difference, relationship-based) approach to assessment and intervention planning. *Zero to Three, 21*(4), 11–19.

Wiggins, G. (1994). Toward better report cards. *Educational Leadership, 52*, 28–37.

Wiggins, G. & McTighe, J. (2005). *Understanding by Design, Expanded 2nd Edition.* Alexandria, VA: Association for Supervision and Curriculum Development.

Wilford, S. (2009). *Nurturing young children's disposition to learn.* St. Paul, MN: Red Leaf Press.

Williams, D. (2003). The complexities of learning in a small group. In R. Kantor & D. Fernie (Eds.), *Early childhood classroom processes.* Cresskill, NJ: Hampton Press.

Williams, K. (2007). *Expressive Vocabulary Test* (2nd ed.). San Antonio: Pearson.

Winsch, M. J., Conlon, C. J., & Scheidt, P. C. (2002). Substance abuse: A preventable threat to development. In M. Batshaw (Ed.), *Children with disabilities* (5th ed.). Baltimore: Paul H. Brookes.

Winton, P. J., Brotherson, M. J., & Summers, J. A. (2008). Learning from the field of early intervention about partnering with families. In M. M. Cornish (Ed.), *Promising practices for partnering with families in the early years.* Charlotte, NC: Information Age Publishing.

Wood, J. W. (2009). *Pathways to teaching series: Practical strategies for the inclusive classroom.* Upper Saddle River, NJ: Merrill/Prentice Hall.

Wortham, S. C. (2010). *Early childhood curriculum: Developmental bases for learning and teaching* (5th ed.). Upper Saddle River, NJ: Merrill/Prentice Hall.

Wurm, J. P. (2005). *Working in the Reggio way: A beginner's guide for American teachers.* St. Paul, MN: Redleaf Press.

Xu, Y. (2008). Developing meaningful IFSP outcomes through a family-centered approach using the double ABCX model. *Young Exceptional Children, 12*(1), 2–19.

Yelland, N. J. (Ed.). (2000). *Promoting meaningful learning: Innovations in educating early childhood professionals.* Washington DC: National Association for the Education of Young Children.

Zero to Three Work Group. (1994). Toward a new vision for the developmental assessment of infants and young children. *Zero to Three, 14*, 1–8.

Zero to Three. (1995). *Diagnostic classification: 0–3.* Arlington, VA: National Center for Clinical Infant Programs.

Zero to Three. (2003). Infant and early childhood mental health: Promoting healthy social and emotional development. Washington, DC: Author. Retrieved from http://www.zerotothree.org.

Zero to Three. (2005). Diagnostic Classification of Mental Health and Developmental Disorders of Infancy and Early Childhood, Revised (DC:0-3R) Washington DC: Author.

Zero to Three. (2005). Laying the foundation for successful prekindergarteners by building bridges to infants and toddlers. Washington, DC: Author. Retrieved from http://www.zerotothree.org.

Zigler, E., Gilliam, W. S., & Jones, S. M. (2006). *A vision for universal preschool education.* Cambridge, MA: Harvard University Press.

Zimmerman, I. L., Steiner, V. G., & Pond, R. E. (2002). *Preschool Language Scale, 4th Ed.* (PLS-4) San Antonio, TX: Harcourt/Pearson.

Zvetina, D., & Guiterrez, J. (1994). *Social emotional observation criteria.* Chicago: Erikson Institute.

NAME INDEX

SUBJECT INDEX